FOURTH EDITION

Hadoop: The Definitive Guide

Tom White

Beijing · Cambridge · Farnham · Köln · Sebastopol · Tokyo

Hadoop: The Definitive Guide, Fourth Edition

by Tom White

Copyright © 2015 Tom White. All rights reserved.

Printed in the United States of America.

Published by O'Reilly Media, Inc., 1005 Gravenstein Highway North, Sebastopol, CA 95472.

O'Reilly books may be purchased for educational, business, or sales promotional use. Online editions are also available for most titles (*http://safaribooksonline.com*). For more information, contact our corporate/institutional sales department: 800-998-9938 or *corporate@oreilly.com*.

Editors: Mike Loukides and Meghan Blanchette	**Indexer:** Lucie Haskins
Production Editor: Matthew Hacker	**Cover Designer:** Ellie Volckhausen
Copyeditor: Jasmine Kwityn	**Interior Designer:** David Futato
Proofreader: Rachel Head	**Illustrator:** Rebecca Demarest

June 2009:	First Edition
October 2010:	Second Edition
May 2012:	Third Edition
April 2015:	Fourth Edition

Revision History for the Fourth Edition:

2015-03-19: First release

See *http://oreilly.com/catalog/errata.csp?isbn=9781491901632* for release details.

ISBN: 978-1-491-90163-2

[M]

For Eliane, Emilia, and Lottie

Table of Contents

Part IV. Related Projects

Part V. Case Studies

Foreword

Hadoop got its start in Nutch. A few of us were attempting to build an open source web search engine and having trouble managing computations running on even a handful of computers. Once Google published its GFS and MapReduce papers, the route became clear. They'd devised systems to solve precisely the problems we were having with Nutch. So we started, two of us, half-time, to try to re-create these systems as a part of Nutch.

We managed to get Nutch limping along on 20 machines, but it soon became clear that to handle the Web's massive scale, we'd need to run it on thousands of machines, and moreover, that the job was bigger than two half-time developers could handle.

Around that time, Yahoo! got interested, and quickly put together a team that I joined. We split off the distributed computing part of Nutch, naming it Hadoop. With the help of Yahoo!, Hadoop soon grew into a technology that could truly scale to the Web.

In 2006, Tom White started contributing to Hadoop. I already knew Tom through an excellent article he'd written about Nutch, so I knew he could present complex ideas in clear prose. I soon learned that he could also develop software that was as pleasant to read as his prose.

From the beginning, Tom's contributions to Hadoop showed his concern for users and for the project. Unlike most open source contributors, Tom is not primarily interested in tweaking the system to better meet his own needs, but rather in making it easier for anyone to use.

Initially, Tom specialized in making Hadoop run well on Amazon's EC2 and S3 services. Then he moved on to tackle a wide variety of problems, including improving the Map-Reduce APIs, enhancing the website, and devising an object serialization framework. In all cases, Tom presented his ideas precisely. In short order, Tom earned the role of Hadoop committer and soon thereafter became a member of the Hadoop Project Management Committee.

Tom is now a respected senior member of the Hadoop developer community. Though he's an expert in many technical corners of the project, his specialty is making Hadoop easier to use and understand.

Given this, I was very pleased when I learned that Tom intended to write a book about Hadoop. Who could be better qualified? Now you have the opportunity to learn about Hadoop from a master—not only of the technology, but also of common sense and plain talk.

—Doug Cutting, April 2009
Shed in the Yard, California

Preface

Martin Gardner, the mathematics and science writer, once said in an interview:

> Beyond calculus, I am lost. That was the secret of my column's success. It took me so long to understand what I was writing about that I knew how to write in a way most readers would understand.[1]

In many ways, this is how I feel about Hadoop. Its inner workings are complex, resting as they do on a mixture of distributed systems theory, practical engineering, and common sense. And to the uninitiated, Hadoop can appear alien.

But it doesn't need to be like this. Stripped to its core, the tools that Hadoop provides for working with big data are simple. If there's a common theme, it is about raising the level of abstraction—to create building blocks for programmers who have lots of data to store and analyze, and who don't have the time, the skill, or the inclination to become distributed systems experts to build the infrastructure to handle it.

With such a simple and generally applicable feature set, it seemed obvious to me when I started using it that Hadoop deserved to be widely used. However, at the time (in early 2006), setting up, configuring, and writing programs to use Hadoop was an art. Things have certainly improved since then: there is more documentation, there are more examples, and there are thriving mailing lists to go to when you have questions. And yet the biggest hurdle for newcomers is understanding what this technology is capable of, where it excels, and how to use it. That is why I wrote this book.

The Apache Hadoop community has come a long way. Since the publication of the first edition of this book, the Hadoop project has blossomed. "Big data" has become a household term.[2] In this time, the software has made great leaps in adoption, performance, reliability, scalability, and manageability. The number of things being built and run on the Hadoop platform has grown enormously. In fact, it's difficult for one person to keep

---

1. Alex Bellos, "The science of fun," (*http://bit.ly/science_of_fun*) *The Guardian*, May 31, 2008.
2. It was added to the *Oxford English Dictionary (http://bit.ly/6_13_oed_update)* in 2013.

track. To gain even wider adoption, I believe we need to make Hadoop even easier to use. This will involve writing more tools; integrating with even more systems; and writing new, improved APIs. I'm looking forward to being a part of this, and I hope this book will encourage and enable others to do so, too.

Administrative Notes

During discussion of a particular Java class in the text, I often omit its package name to reduce clutter. If you need to know which package a class is in, you can easily look it up in the Java API documentation for Hadoop (linked to from the Apache Hadoop home page (*http://hadoop.apache.org/*)), or the relevant project. Or if you're using an integrated development environment (IDE), its auto-complete mechanism can help find what you're looking for.

Similarly, although it deviates from usual style guidelines, program listings that import multiple classes from the same package may use the asterisk wildcard character to save space (for example, `import org.apache.hadoop.io.*`).

The sample programs in this book are available for download from the book's website (*http://www.hadoopbook.com/*). You will also find instructions there for obtaining the datasets that are used in examples throughout the book, as well as further notes for running the programs in the book and links to updates, additional resources, and my blog.

What's New in the Fourth Edition?

The fourth edition covers Hadoop 2 exclusively. The Hadoop 2 release series is the current active release series and contains the most stable versions of Hadoop.

There are new chapters covering YARN (Chapter 4), Parquet (Chapter 13), Flume (Chapter 14), Crunch (Chapter 18), and Spark (Chapter 19). There's also a new section to help readers navigate different pathways through the book ("What's in This Book?" on page 15).

This edition includes two new case studies (Chapters 22 and 23): one on how Hadoop is used in healthcare systems, and another on using Hadoop technologies for genomics data processing. Case studies from the previous editions can now be found online (*http://bit.ly/hadoop_tdg_prev*).

Many corrections, updates, and improvements have been made to existing chapters to bring them up to date with the latest releases of Hadoop and its related projects.

What's New in the Third Edition?

The third edition covers the 1.x (formerly 0.20) release series of Apache Hadoop, as well as the newer 0.22 and 2.x (formerly 0.23) series. With a few exceptions, which are noted in the text, all the examples in this book run against these versions.

This edition uses the new MapReduce API for most of the examples. Because the old API is still in widespread use, it continues to be discussed in the text alongside the new API, and the equivalent code using the old API can be found on the book's website.

The major change in Hadoop 2.0 is the new MapReduce runtime, MapReduce 2, which is built on a new distributed resource management system called YARN. This edition includes new sections covering MapReduce on YARN: how it works (Chapter 7) and how to run it (Chapter 10).

There is more MapReduce material, too, including development practices such as packaging MapReduce jobs with Maven, setting the user's Java classpath, and writing tests with MRUnit (all in Chapter 6). In addition, there is more depth on features such as output committers and the distributed cache (both in Chapter 9), as well as task memory monitoring (Chapter 10). There is a new section on writing MapReduce jobs to process Avro data (Chapter 12), and one on running a simple MapReduce workflow in Oozie (Chapter 6).

The chapter on HDFS (Chapter 3) now has introductions to high availability, federation, and the new WebHDFS and HttpFS filesystems.

The chapters on Pig, Hive, Sqoop, and ZooKeeper have all been expanded to cover the new features and changes in their latest releases.

In addition, numerous corrections and improvements have been made throughout the book.

What's New in the Second Edition?

The second edition has two new chapters on Sqoop and Hive (Chapters 15 and 17, respectively), a new section covering Avro (in Chapter 12), an introduction to the new security features in Hadoop (in Chapter 10), and a new case study on analyzing massive network graphs using Hadoop.

This edition continues to describe the 0.20 release series of Apache Hadoop, because this was the latest stable release at the time of writing. New features from later releases are occasionally mentioned in the text, however, with reference to the version that they were introduced in.

Conventions Used in This Book

The following typographical conventions are used in this book:

Italic

> Indicates new terms, URLs, email addresses, filenames, and file extensions.

`Constant width`

> Used for program listings, as well as within paragraphs to refer to commands and command-line options and to program elements such as variable or function names, databases, data types, environment variables, statements, and keywords.

`Constant width bold`

> Shows commands or other text that should be typed literally by the user.

`Constant width italic`

> Shows text that should be replaced with user-supplied values or by values determined by context.

 This icon signifies a general note.

 This icon signifies a tip or suggestion.

 This icon indicates a warning or caution.

Using Code Examples

Supplemental material (code, examples, exercise, etc.) is available for download at this book's website (*http://hadoopbook.com*) and on GitHub (*https://github.com/tomwhite/hadoop-book/*).

This book is here to help you get your job done. In general, you may use the code in this book in your programs and documentation. You do not need to contact us for permission unless you're reproducing a significant portion of the code. For example, writing a program that uses several chunks of code from this book does not require permission. Selling or distributing a CD-ROM of examples from O'Reilly books does require permission. Answering a question by citing this book and quoting example code does not require permission. Incorporating a significant amount of example code from this book into your product's documentation does require permission.

We appreciate, but do not require, attribution. An attribution usually includes the title, author, publisher, and ISBN. For example: "*Hadoop: The Definitive Guide*, Fourth Edition, by Tom White (O'Reilly). Copyright 2015 Tom White, 978-1-491-90163-2."

If you feel your use of code examples falls outside fair use or the permission given here, feel free to contact us at *permissions@oreilly.com*.

Safari® Books Online

 *Safari Books Online* is an on-demand digital library that delivers expert content in both book and video form from the world's leading authors in technology and business.

Technology professionals, software developers, web designers, and business and creative professionals use Safari Books Online as their primary resource for research, problem solving, learning, and certification training.

Safari Books Online offers a range of plans and pricing for enterprise, government, education, and individuals.

Members have access to thousands of books, training videos, and prepublication manuscripts in one fully searchable database from publishers like O'Reilly Media, Prentice Hall Professional, Addison-Wesley Professional, Microsoft Press, Sams, Que, Peachpit Press, Focal Press, Cisco Press, John Wiley & Sons, Syngress, Morgan Kaufmann, IBM Redbooks, Packt, Adobe Press, FT Press, Apress, Manning, New Riders, McGraw-Hill, Jones & Bartlett, Course Technology, and hundreds more. For more information about Safari Books Online, please visit us online.

How to Contact Us

Please address comments and questions concerning this book to the publisher:

O'Reilly Media, Inc.
1005 Gravenstein Highway North
Sebastopol, CA 95472
800-998-9938 (in the United States or Canada)
707-829-0515 (international or local)
707-829-0104 (fax)

We have a web page for this book, where we list errata, examples, and any additional information. You can access this page at *http://bit.ly/hadoop_tdg_4e*.

To comment or ask technical questions about this book, send email to *bookquestions@oreilly.com*.

For more information about our books, courses, conferences, and news, see our website at *http://www.oreilly.com*.

Find us on Facebook: *http://facebook.com/oreilly*

Follow us on Twitter: *http://twitter.com/oreillymedia*

Watch us on YouTube: *http://www.youtube.com/oreillymedia*

Acknowledgments

I have relied on many people, both directly and indirectly, in writing this book. I would like to thank the Hadoop community, from whom I have learned, and continue to learn, a great deal.

In particular, I would like to thank Michael Stack and Jonathan Gray for writing the chapter on HBase. Thanks also go to Adrian Woodhead, Marc de Palol, Joydeep Sen Sarma, Ashish Thusoo, Andrzej Białecki, Stu Hood, Chris K. Wensel, and Owen O'Malley for contributing case studies.

I would like to thank the following reviewers who contributed many helpful suggestions and improvements to my drafts: Raghu Angadi, Matt Biddulph, Christophe Bisciglia, Ryan Cox, Devaraj Das, Alex Dorman, Chris Douglas, Alan Gates, Lars George, Patrick Hunt, Aaron Kimball, Peter Krey, Hairong Kuang, Simon Maxen, Olga Natkovich, Benjamin Reed, Konstantin Shvachko, Allen Wittenauer, Matei Zaharia, and Philip Zeyliger. Ajay Anand kept the review process flowing smoothly. Philip ("flip") Kromer kindly helped me with the NCDC weather dataset featured in the examples in this book. Special thanks to Owen O'Malley and Arun C. Murthy for explaining the intricacies of the MapReduce shuffle to me. Any errors that remain are, of course, to be laid at my door.

For the second edition, I owe a debt of gratitude for the detailed reviews and feedback from Jeff Bean, Doug Cutting, Glynn Durham, Alan Gates, Jeff Hammerbacher, Alex Kozlov, Ken Krugler, Jimmy Lin, Todd Lipcon, Sarah Sproehnle, Vinithra Varadharajan, and Ian Wrigley, as well as all the readers who submitted errata for the first edition. I would also like to thank Aaron Kimball for contributing the chapter on Sqoop, and Philip ("flip") Kromer for the case study on graph processing.

For the third edition, thanks go to Alejandro Abdelnur, Eva Andreasson, Eli Collins, Doug Cutting, Patrick Hunt, Aaron Kimball, Aaron T. Myers, Brock Noland, Arvind Prabhakar, Ahmed Radwan, and Tom Wheeler for their feedback and suggestions. Rob

Weltman kindly gave very detailed feedback for the whole book, which greatly improved the final manuscript. Thanks also go to all the readers who submitted errata for the second edition.

For the fourth edition, I would like to thank Jodok Batlogg, Meghan Blanchette, Ryan Blue, Jarek Jarcec Cecho, Jules Damji, Dennis Dawson, Matthew Gast, Karthik Kambatla, Julien Le Dem, Brock Noland, Sandy Ryza, Akshai Sarma, Ben Spivey, Michael Stack, Kate Ting, Josh Walter, Josh Wills, and Adrian Woodhead for all of their invaluable review feedback. Ryan Brush, Micah Whitacre, and Matt Massie kindly contributed new case studies for this edition. Thanks again to all the readers who submitted errata.

I am particularly grateful to Doug Cutting for his encouragement, support, and friendship, and for contributing the Foreword.

Thanks also go to the many others with whom I have had conversations or email discussions over the course of writing the book.

Halfway through writing the first edition of this book, I joined Cloudera, and I want to thank my colleagues for being incredibly supportive in allowing me the time to write and to get it finished promptly.

I am grateful to my editors, Mike Loukides and Meghan Blanchette, and their colleagues at O'Reilly for their help in the preparation of this book. Mike and Meghan have been there throughout to answer my questions, to read my first drafts, and to keep me on schedule.

Finally, the writing of this book has been a great deal of work, and I couldn't have done it without the constant support of my family. My wife, Eliane, not only kept the home going, but also stepped in to help review, edit, and chase case studies. My daughters, Emilia and Lottie, have been very understanding, and I'm looking forward to spending lots more time with all of them.

PART I

Hadoop Fundamentals

Meet Hadoop

In pioneer days they used oxen for heavy pulling, and when one ox couldn't budge a log, they didn't try to grow a larger ox. We shouldn't be trying for bigger computers, but for more systems of computers.

—Grace Hopper

Data!

We live in the data age. It's not easy to measure the total volume of data stored electronically, but an IDC estimate put the size of the "digital universe" at 4.4 zettabytes in 2013 and is forecasting a tenfold growth by 2020 to 44 zettabytes.[1] A zettabyte is 10^{21} bytes, or equivalently one thousand exabytes, one million petabytes, or one billion terabytes. That's more than one disk drive for every person in the world.

This flood of data is coming from many sources. Consider the following:[2]

- The New York Stock Exchange generates about 4–5 terabytes of data per day.
- Facebook hosts more than 240 billion photos, growing at 7 petabytes per month.
- Ancestry.com, the genealogy site, stores around 10 petabytes of data.
- The Internet Archive stores around 18.5 petabytes of data.

---

1. These statistics were reported in a study entitled "The Digital Universe of Opportunities: Rich Data and the Increasing Value of the Internet of Things." (*http://bit.ly/digital_universe*)

2. All figures are from 2013 or 2014. For more information, see Tom Groenfeldt, "At NYSE, The Data Deluge Overwhelms Traditional Databases" (*http://bit.ly/nyse_data_deluge*); Rich Miller, "Facebook Builds Exabyte Data Centers for Cold Storage" (*http://bit.ly/facebook_exabyte*); Ancestry.com's "Company Facts" (*http://corporate.ancestry.com/press/company-facts/*); Archive.org's "Petabox" (*https://archive.org/web/petabox.php*); and the Worldwide LHC Computing Grid project's welcome page (*http://wlcg.web.cern.ch/*).

- The Large Hadron Collider near Geneva, Switzerland, produces about 30 petabytes of data per year.

So there's a lot of data out there. But you are probably wondering how it affects you. Most of the data is locked up in the largest web properties (like search engines) or in scientific or financial institutions, isn't it? Does the advent of big data affect smaller organizations or individuals?

I argue that it does. Take photos, for example. My wife's grandfather was an avid photographer and took photographs throughout his adult life. His entire corpus of medium-format, slide, and 35mm film, when scanned in at high resolution, occupies around 10 gigabytes. Compare this to the digital photos my family took in 2008, which take up about 5 gigabytes of space. My family is producing photographic data at 35 times the rate my wife's grandfather's did, and the rate is increasing every year as it becomes easier to take more and more photos.

More generally, the digital streams that individuals are producing are growing apace. Microsoft Research's MyLifeBits project (*http://bit.ly/ms_mylifebits*) gives a glimpse of the archiving of personal information that may become commonplace in the near future. MyLifeBits was an experiment where an individual's interactions—phone calls, emails, documents—were captured electronically and stored for later access. The data gathered included a photo taken every minute, which resulted in an overall data volume of 1 gigabyte per month. When storage costs come down enough to make it feasible to store continuous audio and video, the data volume for a future MyLifeBits service will be many times that.

The trend is for every individual's data footprint to grow, but perhaps more significantly, the amount of data generated by machines as a part of the Internet of Things will be even greater than that generated by people. Machine logs, RFID readers, sensor networks, vehicle GPS traces, retail transactions—all of these contribute to the growing mountain of data.

The volume of data being made publicly available increases every year, too. Organizations no longer have to merely manage their own data; success in the future will be dictated to a large extent by their ability to extract value from other organizations' data.

Initiatives such as Public Data Sets on Amazon Web Services (*http://aws.amazon.com/public-data-sets/*) and Infochimps.org (*http://infochimps.org/*) exist to foster the "information commons," where data can be freely (or for a modest price) shared for anyone to download and analyze. Mashups between different information sources make for unexpected and hitherto unimaginable applications.

Take, for example, the Astrometry.net project (*http://astrometry.net/*), which watches the Astrometry group on Flickr for new photos of the night sky. It analyzes each image and identifies which part of the sky it is from, as well as any interesting celestial bodies, such as stars or galaxies. This project shows the kinds of things that are possible when data (in this case, tagged photographic images) is made available and used for something (image analysis) that was not anticipated by the creator.

It has been said that "more data usually beats better algorithms," which is to say that for some problems (such as recommending movies or music based on past preferences), however fiendish your algorithms, often they can be beaten simply by having more data (and a less sophisticated algorithm).[3]

The good news is that big data is here. The bad news is that we are struggling to store and analyze it.

Data Storage and Analysis

The problem is simple: although the storage capacities of hard drives have increased massively over the years, access speeds—the rate at which data can be read from drives— have not kept up. One typical drive from 1990 could store 1,370 MB of data and had a transfer speed of 4.4 MB/s,[4] so you could read all the data from a full drive in around five minutes. Over 20 years later, 1-terabyte drives are the norm, but the transfer speed is around 100 MB/s, so it takes more than two and a half hours to read all the data off the disk.

This is a long time to read all data on a single drive—and writing is even slower. The obvious way to reduce the time is to read from multiple disks at once. Imagine if we had 100 drives, each holding one hundredth of the data. Working in parallel, we could read the data in under two minutes.

Using only one hundredth of a disk may seem wasteful. But we can store 100 datasets, each of which is 1 terabyte, and provide shared access to them. We can imagine that the users of such a system would be happy to share access in return for shorter analysis times, and statistically, that their analysis jobs would be likely to be spread over time, so they wouldn't interfere with each other too much.

There's more to being able to read and write data in parallel to or from multiple disks, though.

The first problem to solve is hardware failure: as soon as you start using many pieces of hardware, the chance that one will fail is fairly high. A common way of avoiding data loss is through replication: redundant copies of the data are kept by the system so that in the event of failure, there is another copy available. This is how RAID works, for

---

3. The quote is from Anand Rajaraman's blog post "More data usually beats better algorithms," (*http://bit.ly/ more_data*) in which he writes about the Netflix Challenge. Alon Halevy, Peter Norvig, and Fernando Pereira make the same point in "The Unreasonable Effectiveness of Data," (*http://bit.ly/unreasonable_effect*) *IEEE Intelligent Systems*, March/April 2009.

4. These specifications are for the Seagate ST-41600n.

instance, although Hadoop's filesystem, the Hadoop Distributed Filesystem (HDFS), takes a slightly different approach, as you shall see later.

The second problem is that most analysis tasks need to be able to combine the data in some way, and data read from one disk may need to be combined with data from any of the other 99 disks. Various distributed systems allow data to be combined from multiple sources, but doing this correctly is notoriously challenging. MapReduce provides a programming model that abstracts the problem from disk reads and writes, transforming it into a computation over sets of keys and values. We look at the details of this model in later chapters, but the important point for the present discussion is that there are two parts to the computation—the map and the reduce—and it's the interface between the two where the "mixing" occurs. Like HDFS, MapReduce has built-in reliability.

In a nutshell, this is what Hadoop provides: a reliable, scalable platform for storage and analysis. What's more, because it runs on commodity hardware and is open source, Hadoop is affordable.

Querying All Your Data

The approach taken by MapReduce may seem like a brute-force approach. The premise is that the entire dataset—or at least a good portion of it—can be processed for each query. But this is its power. MapReduce is a *batch* query processor, and the ability to run an ad hoc query against your whole dataset and get the results in a reasonable time is transformative. It changes the way you think about data and unlocks data that was previously archived on tape or disk. It gives people the opportunity to innovate with data. Questions that took too long to get answered before can now be answered, which in turn leads to new questions and new insights.

For example, Mailtrust, Rackspace's mail division, used Hadoop for processing email logs. One ad hoc query they wrote was to find the geographic distribution of their users. In their words:

> This data was so useful that we've scheduled the MapReduce job to run monthly and we will be using this data to help us decide which Rackspace data centers to place new mail servers in as we grow.

By bringing several hundred gigabytes of data together and having the tools to analyze it, the Rackspace engineers were able to gain an understanding of the data that they otherwise would never have had, and furthermore, they were able to use what they had learned to improve the service for their customers.

Beyond Batch

For all its strengths, MapReduce is fundamentally a batch processing system, and is not suitable for interactive analysis. You can't run a query and get results back in a few seconds or less. Queries typically take minutes or more, so it's best for offline use, where there isn't a human sitting in the processing loop waiting for results.

However, since its original incarnation, Hadoop has evolved beyond batch processing. Indeed, the term "Hadoop" is sometimes used to refer to a larger ecosystem of projects, not just HDFS and MapReduce, that fall under the umbrella of infrastructure for distributed computing and large-scale data processing. Many of these are hosted by the Apache Software Foundation (*http://www.apache.org/*), which provides support for a community of open source software projects, including the original HTTP Server from which it gets its name.

The first component to provide online access was HBase, a key-value store that uses HDFS for its underlying storage. HBase provides both online read/write access of individual rows and batch operations for reading and writing data in bulk, making it a good solution for building applications on.

The real enabler for new processing models in Hadoop was the introduction of YARN (which stands for *Yet Another Resource Negotiator*) in Hadoop 2. YARN is a cluster resource management system, which allows any distributed program (not just MapReduce) to run on data in a Hadoop cluster.

In the last few years, there has been a flowering of different processing patterns that work with Hadoop. Here is a sample:

Interactive SQL
By dispensing with MapReduce and using a distributed query engine that uses dedicated "always on" daemons (like Impala) or container reuse (like Hive on Tez), it's possible to achieve low-latency responses for SQL queries on Hadoop while still scaling up to large dataset sizes.

Iterative processing
Many algorithms—such as those in machine learning—are iterative in nature, so it's much more efficient to hold each intermediate working set in memory, compared to loading from disk on each iteration. The architecture of MapReduce does not allow this, but it's straightforward with Spark, for example, and it enables a highly exploratory style of working with datasets.

Stream processing
Streaming systems like Storm, Spark Streaming, or Samza make it possible to run real-time, distributed computations on unbounded streams of data and emit results to Hadoop storage or external systems.

Search

The Solr search platform can run on a Hadoop cluster, indexing documents as they are added to HDFS, and serving search queries from indexes stored in HDFS.

Despite the emergence of different processing frameworks on Hadoop, MapReduce still has a place for batch processing, and it is useful to understand how it works since it introduces several concepts that apply more generally (like the idea of input formats, or how a dataset is split into pieces).

Comparison with Other Systems

Hadoop isn't the first distributed system for data storage and analysis, but it has some unique properties that set it apart from other systems that may seem similar. Here we look at some of them.

Relational Database Management Systems

Why can't we use databases with lots of disks to do large-scale analysis? Why is Hadoop needed?

The answer to these questions comes from another trend in disk drives: seek time is improving more slowly than transfer rate. Seeking is the process of moving the disk's head to a particular place on the disk to read or write data. It characterizes the latency of a disk operation, whereas the transfer rate corresponds to a disk's bandwidth.

If the data access pattern is dominated by seeks, it will take longer to read or write large portions of the dataset than streaming through it, which operates at the transfer rate. On the other hand, for updating a small proportion of records in a database, a traditional B-Tree (the data structure used in relational databases, which is limited by the rate at which it can perform seeks) works well. For updating the majority of a database, a B-Tree is less efficient than MapReduce, which uses Sort/Merge to rebuild the database.

In many ways, MapReduce can be seen as a complement to a Relational Database Management System (RDBMS). (The differences between the two systems are shown in Table 1-1.) MapReduce is a good fit for problems that need to analyze the whole dataset in a batch fashion, particularly for ad hoc analysis. An RDBMS is good for point queries or updates, where the dataset has been indexed to deliver low-latency retrieval and update times of a relatively small amount of data. MapReduce suits applications where the data is written once and read many times, whereas a relational database is good for datasets that are continually updated.[5]

Table 1-1. RDBMS compared to MapReduce

	Traditional RDBMS	MapReduce
Data size	Gigabytes	Petabytes
Access	Interactive and batch	Batch
Updates	Read and write many times	Write once, read many times
Transactions	ACID	None
Structure	Schema-on-write	Schema-on-read
Integrity	High	Low
Scaling	Nonlinear	Linear

However, the differences between relational databases and Hadoop systems are blurring. Relational databases have started incorporating some of the ideas from Hadoop, and from the other direction, Hadoop systems such as Hive are becoming more interactive (by moving away from MapReduce) and adding features like indexes and transactions that make them look more and more like traditional RDBMSs.

Another difference between Hadoop and an RDBMS is the amount of structure in the datasets on which they operate. *Structured data* is organized into entities that have a defined format, such as XML documents or database tables that conform to a particular predefined schema. This is the realm of the RDBMS. *Semi-structured data*, on the other hand, is looser, and though there may be a schema, it is often ignored, so it may be used only as a guide to the structure of the data: for example, a spreadsheet, in which the structure is the grid of cells, although the cells themselves may hold any form of data. *Unstructured data* does not have any particular internal structure: for example, plain text or image data. Hadoop works well on unstructured or semi-structured data because it is designed to interpret the data at processing time (so called *schema-on-read*). This provides flexibility and avoids the costly data loading phase of an RDBMS, since in Hadoop it is just a file copy.

Relational data is often *normalized* to retain its integrity and remove redundancy. Normalization poses problems for Hadoop processing because it makes reading a record a nonlocal operation, and one of the central assumptions that Hadoop makes is that it is possible to perform (high-speed) streaming reads and writes.

---

5. In January 2007, David J. DeWitt and Michael Stonebraker caused a stir by publishing "MapReduce: A major step backwards," (*http://bit.ly/step_backwards*) in which they criticized MapReduce for being a poor substitute for relational databases. Many commentators argued that it was a false comparison (see, for example, Mark C. Chu-Carroll's "Databases are hammers; MapReduce is a screwdriver" (*http://bit.ly/dbs_are_hammers*)), and DeWitt and Stonebraker followed up with "MapReduce II," where they addressed the main topics brought up by others.

A web server log is a good example of a set of records that is *not* normalized (for example, the client hostnames are specified in full each time, even though the same client may appear many times), and this is one reason that logfiles of all kinds are particularly well suited to analysis with Hadoop. Note that Hadoop can perform joins; it's just that they are not used as much as in the relational world.

MapReduce—and the other processing models in Hadoop—scales linearly with the size of the data. Data is partitioned, and the functional primitives (like map and reduce) can work in parallel on separate partitions. This means that if you double the size of the input data, a job will run twice as slowly. But if you also double the size of the cluster, a job will run as fast as the original one. This is not generally true of SQL queries.

Grid Computing

The high-performance computing (HPC) and grid computing communities have been doing large-scale data processing for years, using such application program interfaces (APIs) as the Message Passing Interface (MPI). Broadly, the approach in HPC is to distribute the work across a cluster of machines, which access a shared filesystem, hosted by a storage area network (SAN). This works well for predominantly compute-intensive jobs, but it becomes a problem when nodes need to access larger data volumes (hundreds of gigabytes, the point at which Hadoop really starts to shine), since the network bandwidth is the bottleneck and compute nodes become idle.

Hadoop tries to co-locate the data with the compute nodes, so data access is fast because it is local.[6] This feature, known as *data locality*, is at the heart of data processing in Hadoop and is the reason for its good performance. Recognizing that network bandwidth is the most precious resource in a data center environment (it is easy to saturate network links by copying data around), Hadoop goes to great lengths to conserve it by explicitly modeling network topology. Notice that this arrangement does not preclude high-CPU analyses in Hadoop.

MPI gives great control to programmers, but it requires that they explicitly handle the mechanics of the data flow, exposed via low-level C routines and constructs such as sockets, as well as the higher-level algorithms for the analyses. Processing in Hadoop operates only at the higher level: the programmer thinks in terms of the data model (such as key-value pairs for MapReduce), while the data flow remains implicit.

Coordinating the processes in a large-scale distributed computation is a challenge. The hardest aspect is gracefully handling partial failure—when you don't know whether or not a remote process has failed—and still making progress with the overall computation. Distributed processing frameworks like MapReduce spare the programmer from having

---

6. Jim Gray was an early advocate of putting the computation near the data. See "Distributed Computing Economics," (*http://bit.ly/dist_comp_econ*) March 2003.

to think about failure, since the implementation detects failed tasks and reschedules replacements on machines that are healthy. MapReduce is able to do this because it is a *shared-nothing* architecture, meaning that tasks have no dependence on one other. (This is a slight oversimplification, since the output from mappers is fed to the reducers, but this is under the control of the MapReduce system; in this case, it needs to take more care rerunning a failed reducer than rerunning a failed map, because it has to make sure it can retrieve the necessary map outputs and, if not, regenerate them by running the relevant maps again.) So from the programmer's point of view, the order in which the tasks run doesn't matter. By contrast, MPI programs have to explicitly manage their own checkpointing and recovery, which gives more control to the programmer but makes them more difficult to write.

Volunteer Computing

When people first hear about Hadoop and MapReduce they often ask, "How is it different from SETI@home?" SETI, the Search for Extra-Terrestrial Intelligence, runs a project called SETI@home (*http://setiathome.berkeley.edu/*) in which volunteers donate CPU time from their otherwise idle computers to analyze radio telescope data for signs of intelligent life outside Earth. SETI@home is the most well known of many *volunteer computing* projects; others include the Great Internet Mersenne Prime Search (to search for large prime numbers) and Folding@home (to understand protein folding and how it relates to disease).

Volunteer computing projects work by breaking the problems they are trying to solve into chunks called *work units*, which are sent to computers around the world to be analyzed. For example, a SETI@home work unit is about 0.35 MB of radio telescope data, and takes hours or days to analyze on a typical home computer. When the analysis is completed, the results are sent back to the server, and the client gets another work unit. As a precaution to combat cheating, each work unit is sent to three different machines and needs at least two results to agree to be accepted.

Although SETI@home may be superficially similar to MapReduce (breaking a problem into independent pieces to be worked on in parallel), there are some significant differences. The SETI@home problem is very CPU-intensive, which makes it suitable for running on hundreds of thousands of computers across the world[7] because the time to transfer the work unit is dwarfed by the time to run the computation on it. Volunteers are donating CPU cycles, not bandwidth.

---

7. In January 2008, SETI@home was reported (*http://bit.ly/new_seti_at_home_data*) to be processing 300 gigabytes a day, using 320,000 computers (most of which are not dedicated to SETI@home; they are used for other things, too).

MapReduce is designed to run jobs that last minutes or hours on trusted, dedicated hardware running in a single data center with very high aggregate bandwidth interconnects. By contrast, SETI@home runs a perpetual computation on untrusted machines on the Internet with highly variable connection speeds and no data locality.

A Brief History of Apache Hadoop

Hadoop was created by Doug Cutting, the creator of Apache Lucene, the widely used text search library. Hadoop has its origins in Apache Nutch, an open source web search engine, itself a part of the Lucene project.

The Origin of the Name "Hadoop"

The name Hadoop is not an acronym; it's a made-up name. The project's creator, Doug Cutting, explains how the name came about:

> The name my kid gave a stuffed yellow elephant. Short, relatively easy to spell and pronounce, meaningless, and not used elsewhere: those are my naming criteria. Kids are good at generating such. Googol is a kid's term.

Projects in the Hadoop ecosystem also tend to have names that are unrelated to their function, often with an elephant or other animal theme ("Pig," for example). Smaller components are given more descriptive (and therefore more mundane) names. This is a good principle, as it means you can generally work out what something does from its name. For example, the namenode[8] manages the filesystem namespace.

Building a web search engine from scratch was an ambitious goal, for not only is the software required to crawl and index websites complex to write, but it is also a challenge to run without a dedicated operations team, since there are so many moving parts. It's expensive, too: Mike Cafarella and Doug Cutting estimated a system supporting a one-billion-page index would cost around $500,000 in hardware, with a monthly running cost of $30,000.[9] Nevertheless, they believed it was a worthy goal, as it would open up and ultimately democratize search engine algorithms.

Nutch was started in 2002, and a working crawler and search system quickly emerged. However, its creators realized that their architecture wouldn't scale to the billions of pages on the Web. Help was at hand with the publication of a paper in 2003 that described the architecture of Google's distributed filesystem, called GFS, which was being used in

---

8. In this book, we use the lowercase form, "namenode," to denote the entity when it's being referred to generally, and the CamelCase form NameNode to denote the Java class that implements it.

9. See Mike Cafarella and Doug Cutting, "Building Nutch: Open Source Search," (*http://bit.ly/build ing_nutch*) *ACM Queue*, April 2004.

production at Google.[10] GFS, or something like it, would solve their storage needs for the very large files generated as a part of the web crawl and indexing process. In particular, GFS would free up time being spent on administrative tasks such as managing storage nodes. In 2004, Nutch's developers set about writing an open source implementation, the Nutch Distributed Filesystem (NDFS).

In 2004, Google published the paper that introduced MapReduce to the world.[11] Early in 2005, the Nutch developers had a working MapReduce implementation in Nutch, and by the middle of that year all the major Nutch algorithms had been ported to run using MapReduce and NDFS.

NDFS and the MapReduce implementation in Nutch were applicable beyond the realm of search, and in February 2006 they moved out of Nutch to form an independent subproject of Lucene called Hadoop. At around the same time, Doug Cutting joined Yahoo!, which provided a dedicated team and the resources to turn Hadoop into a system that ran at web scale (see the following sidebar). This was demonstrated in February 2008 when Yahoo! announced that its production search index was being generated by a 10,000-core Hadoop cluster.[12]

Hadoop at Yahoo!

Building Internet-scale search engines requires huge amounts of data and therefore large numbers of machines to process it. Yahoo! Search consists of four primary components: the *Crawler*, which downloads pages from web servers; the *WebMap*, which builds a graph of the known Web; the *Indexer*, which builds a reverse index to the best pages; and the *Runtime*, which answers users' queries. The WebMap is a graph that consists of roughly 1 trillion (10^{12}) edges, each representing a web link, and 100 billion (10^{11}) nodes, each representing distinct URLs. Creating and analyzing such a large graph requires a large number of computers running for many days. In early 2005, the infrastructure for the WebMap, named *Dreadnaught*, needed to be redesigned to scale up to more nodes. Dreadnaught had successfully scaled from 20 to 600 nodes, but required a complete redesign to scale out further. Dreadnaught is similar to MapReduce in many ways, but provides more flexibility and less structure. In particular, each fragment in a Dreadnaught job could send output to each of the fragments in the next stage of the job, but the sort was all done in library code. In practice, most of the WebMap phases were pairs

---

10. Sanjay Ghemawat, Howard Gobioff, and Shun-Tak Leung, "The Google File System," (*http:// research.google.com/archive/gfs.html*) October 2003.

11. Jeffrey Dean and Sanjay Ghemawat, "MapReduce: Simplified Data Processing on Large Clusters," (*http:// research.google.com/archive/mapreduce.html*) December 2004.

12. "Yahoo! Launches World's Largest Hadoop Production Application," (*http://bit.ly/yahoo_hadoop*) February 19, 2008.

that corresponded to MapReduce. Therefore, the WebMap applications would not require extensive refactoring to fit into MapReduce.

Eric Baldeschwieler (aka Eric14) created a small team, and we started designing and prototyping a new framework, written in C++ modeled and after GFS and MapReduce, to replace Dreadnaught. Although the immediate need was for a new framework for WebMap, it was clear that standardization of the batch platform across Yahoo! Search was critical and that by making the framework general enough to support other users, we could better leverage investment in the new platform.

At the same time, we were watching Hadoop, which was part of Nutch, and its progress. In January 2006, Yahoo! hired Doug Cutting, and a month later we decided to abandon our prototype and adopt Hadoop. The advantage of Hadoop over our prototype and design was that it was already working with a real application (Nutch) on 20 nodes. That allowed us to bring up a research cluster two months later and start helping real customers use the new framework much sooner than we could have otherwise. Another advantage, of course, was that since Hadoop was already open source, it was easier (although far from easy!) to get permission from Yahoo!'s legal department to work in open source. So, we set up a 200-node cluster for the researchers in early 2006 and put the WebMap conversion plans on hold while we supported and improved Hadoop for the research users.

—Owen O'Malley, 2009

In January 2008, Hadoop was made its own top-level project at Apache, confirming its success and its diverse, active community. By this time, Hadoop was being used by many other companies besides Yahoo!, such as Last.fm, Facebook, and the *New York Times*.

In one well-publicized feat, the *New York Times* used Amazon's EC2 compute cloud to crunch through 4 terabytes of scanned archives from the paper, converting them to PDFs for the Web.[13] The processing took less than 24 hours to run using 100 machines, and the project probably wouldn't have been embarked upon without the combination of Amazon's pay-by-the-hour model (which allowed the *NYT* to access a large number of machines for a short period) and Hadoop's easy-to-use parallel programming model.

In April 2008, Hadoop broke a world record to become the fastest system to sort an entire terabyte of data. Running on a 910-node cluster, Hadoop sorted 1 terabyte in 209 seconds (just under 3.5 minutes), beating the previous year's winner of 297 seconds.[14] In November of the same year, Google reported that its MapReduce implementation

---

13. Derek Gottfrid, "Self-Service, Prorated Super Computing Fun!" (*http://bit.ly/supercomputing_fun*) November 1, 2007.

14. Owen O'Malley, "TeraByte Sort on Apache Hadoop," (*http://sortbenchmark.org/YahooHadoop.pdf*) May 2008.

sorted 1 terabyte in 68 seconds.[15] Then, in April 2009, it was announced that a team at Yahoo! had used Hadoop to sort 1 terabyte in 62 seconds.[16]

The trend since then has been to sort even larger volumes of data at ever faster rates. In the 2014 competition, a team from Databricks were joint winners of the Gray Sort benchmark. They used a 207-node Spark cluster to sort 100 terabytes of data in 1,406 seconds, a rate of 4.27 terabytes per minute.[17]

Today, Hadoop is widely used in mainstream enterprises. Hadoop's role as a general-purpose storage and analysis platform for big data has been recognized by the industry, and this fact is reflected in the number of products that use or incorporate Hadoop in some way. Commercial Hadoop support is available from large, established enterprise vendors, including EMC, IBM, Microsoft, and Oracle, as well as from specialist Hadoop companies such as Cloudera, Hortonworks, and MapR.

What's in This Book?

The book is divided into five main parts: Parts I to III are about core Hadoop, Part IV covers related projects in the Hadoop ecosystem, and Part V contains Hadoop case studies. You can read the book from cover to cover, but there are alternative pathways through the book that allow you to skip chapters that aren't needed to read later ones. See Figure 1-1.

Part I is made up of five chapters that cover the fundamental components in Hadoop and should be read before tackling later chapters. Chapter 1 (this chapter) is a high-level introduction to Hadoop. Chapter 2 provides an introduction to MapReduce. Chapter 3 looks at Hadoop filesystems, and in particular HDFS, in depth. Chapter 4 discusses YARN, Hadoop's cluster resource management system. Chapter 5 covers the I/O building blocks in Hadoop: data integrity, compression, serialization, and file-based data structures.

Part II has four chapters that cover MapReduce in depth. They provide useful understanding for later chapters (such as the data processing chapters in Part IV), but could be skipped on a first reading. Chapter 6 goes through the practical steps needed to develop a MapReduce application. Chapter 7 looks at how MapReduce is implemented in Hadoop, from the point of view of a user. Chapter 8 is about the MapReduce programming model and the various data formats that MapReduce can work with. Chapter 9 is on advanced MapReduce topics, including sorting and joining data.

---

15. Grzegorz Czajkowski, "Sorting 1PB with MapReduce," (*http://bit.ly/sorting_1pb*) November 21, 2008.

16. Owen O'Malley and Arun C. Murthy, "Winning a 60 Second Dash with a Yellow Elephant," (*http://sortbench mark.org/Yahoo2009.pdf*) April 2009.

17. Reynold Xin et al., "GraySort on Apache Spark by Databricks," (*http://sortbenchmark.org/ApacheS park2014.pdf*) November 2014.

Part III concerns the administration of Hadoop: Chapters 10 and 11 describe how to set up and maintain a Hadoop cluster running HDFS and MapReduce on YARN.

Part IV of the book is dedicated to projects that build on Hadoop or are closely related to it. Each chapter covers one project and is largely independent of the other chapters in this part, so they can be read in any order.

The first two chapters in this part are about data formats. Chapter 12 looks at Avro, a cross-language data serialization library for Hadoop, and Chapter 13 covers Parquet, an efficient columnar storage format for nested data.

The next two chapters look at data ingestion, or how to get your data into Hadoop. Chapter 14 is about Flume, for high-volume ingestion of streaming data. Chapter 15 is about Sqoop, for efficient bulk transfer of data between structured data stores (like relational databases) and HDFS.

The common theme of the next four chapters is data processing, and in particular using higher-level abstractions than MapReduce. Pig (Chapter 16) is a data flow language for exploring very large datasets. Hive (Chapter 17) is a data warehouse for managing data stored in HDFS and provides a query language based on SQL. Crunch (Chapter 18) is a high-level Java API for writing data processing pipelines that can run on MapReduce or Spark. Spark (Chapter 19) is a cluster computing framework for large-scale data processing; it provides a *directed acyclic graph* (DAG) engine, and APIs in Scala, Java, and Python.

Chapter 20 is an introduction to HBase, a distributed column-oriented real-time database that uses HDFS for its underlying storage. And Chapter 21 is about ZooKeeper, a distributed, highly available coordination service that provides useful primitives for building distributed applications.

Finally, Part V is a collection of case studies contributed by people using Hadoop in interesting ways.

Supplementary information about Hadoop, such as how to install it on your machine, can be found in the appendixes.

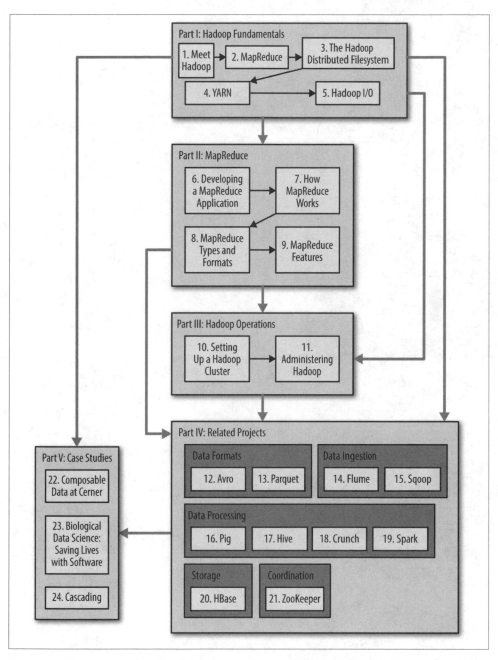

Figure 1-1. Structure of the book: there are various pathways through the content

MapReduce

MapReduce is a programming model for data processing. The model is simple, yet not too simple to express useful programs in. Hadoop can run MapReduce programs written in various languages; in this chapter, we look at the same program expressed in Java, Ruby, and Python. Most importantly, MapReduce programs are inherently parallel, thus putting very large-scale data analysis into the hands of anyone with enough machines at their disposal. MapReduce comes into its own for large datasets, so let's start by looking at one.

A Weather Dataset

For our example, we will write a program that mines weather data. Weather sensors collect data every hour at many locations across the globe and gather a large volume of log data, which is a good candidate for analysis with MapReduce because we want to process all the data, and the data is semi-structured and record-oriented.

Data Format

The data we will use is from the National Climatic Data Center (*http://www.ncdc.noaa.gov/*), or NCDC. The data is stored using a line-oriented ASCII format, in which each line is a record. The format supports a rich set of meteorological elements, many of which are optional or with variable data lengths. For simplicity, we focus on the basic elements, such as temperature, which are always present and are of fixed width.

Example 2-1 shows a sample line with some of the salient fields annotated. The line has been split into multiple lines to show each field; in the real file, fields are packed into one line with no delimiters.

Example 2-1. Format of a National Climatic Data Center record

```
0057
332130   # USAF weather station identifier
99999    # WBAN weather station identifier
19500101 # observation date
0300     # observation time
4
+51317   # latitude (degrees x 1000)
+028783  # longitude (degrees x 1000)
FM-12
+0171    # elevation (meters)
99999
V020
320      # wind direction (degrees)
1        # quality code
N
0072
1
00450    # sky ceiling height (meters)
1        # quality code
C
N
010000   # visibility distance (meters)
1        # quality code
N
9
-0128    # air temperature (degrees Celsius x 10)
1        # quality code
-0139    # dew point temperature (degrees Celsius x 10)
1        # quality code
10268    # atmospheric pressure (hectopascals x 10)
1        # quality code
```

Datafiles are organized by date and weather station. There is a directory for each year from 1901 to 2001, each containing a gzipped file for each weather station with its readings for that year. For example, here are the first entries for 1990:

```
% ls raw/1990 | head
010010-99999-1990.gz
010014-99999-1990.gz
010015-99999-1990.gz
010016-99999-1990.gz
010017-99999-1990.gz
010030-99999-1990.gz
010040-99999-1990.gz
010080-99999-1990.gz
010100-99999-1990.gz
010150-99999-1990.gz
```

There are tens of thousands of weather stations, so the whole dataset is made up of a large number of relatively small files. It's generally easier and more efficient to process a smaller number of relatively large files, so the data was preprocessed so that each year's readings were concatenated into a single file. (The means by which this was carried out is described in Appendix C.)

Analyzing the Data with Unix Tools

What's the highest recorded global temperature for each year in the dataset? We will answer this first without using Hadoop, as this information will provide a performance baseline and a useful means to check our results.

The classic tool for processing line-oriented data is *awk*. Example 2-2 is a small script to calculate the maximum temperature for each year.

Example 2-2. A program for finding the maximum recorded temperature by year from NCDC weather records

```
#!/usr/bin/env bash
for year in all/*
do
  echo -ne `basename $year .gz`"\t"
  gunzip -c $year | \
    awk '{ temp = substr($0, 88, 5) + 0;
           q = substr($0, 93, 1);
           if (temp !=9999 && q ~ /[01459]/ && temp > max) max = temp }
         END { print max }'
done
```

The script loops through the compressed year files, first printing the year, and then processing each file using *awk*. The *awk* script extracts two fields from the data: the air temperature and the quality code. The air temperature value is turned into an integer by adding 0. Next, a test is applied to see whether the temperature is valid (the value 9999 signifies a missing value in the NCDC dataset) and whether the quality code indicates that the reading is not suspect or erroneous. If the reading is OK, the value is compared with the maximum value seen so far, which is updated if a new maximum is found. The END block is executed after all the lines in the file have been processed, and it prints the maximum value.

Here is the beginning of a run:

```
% ./max_temperature.sh
1901 317
1902 244
1903 289
1904 256
1905 283
...
```

The temperature values in the source file are scaled by a factor of 10, so this works out as a maximum temperature of 31.7°C for 1901 (there were very few readings at the beginning of the century, so this is plausible). The complete run for the century took 42 minutes in one run on a single EC2 High-CPU Extra Large instance.

To speed up the processing, we need to run parts of the program in parallel. In theory, this is straightforward: we could process different years in different processes, using all the available hardware threads on a machine. There are a few problems with this, however.

First, dividing the work into equal-size pieces isn't always easy or obvious. In this case, the file size for different years varies widely, so some processes will finish much earlier than others. Even if they pick up further work, the whole run is dominated by the longest file. A better approach, although one that requires more work, is to split the input into fixed-size chunks and assign each chunk to a process.

Second, combining the results from independent processes may require further processing. In this case, the result for each year is independent of other years, and they may be combined by concatenating all the results and sorting by year. If using the fixed-size chunk approach, the combination is more delicate. For this example, data for a particular year will typically be split into several chunks, each processed independently. We'll end up with the maximum temperature for each chunk, so the final step is to look for the highest of these maximums for each year.

Third, you are still limited by the processing capacity of a single machine. If the best time you can achieve is 20 minutes with the number of processors you have, then that's it. You can't make it go faster. Also, some datasets grow beyond the capacity of a single machine. When we start using multiple machines, a whole host of other factors come into play, mainly falling into the categories of coordination and reliability. Who runs the overall job? How do we deal with failed processes?

So, although it's feasible to parallelize the processing, in practice it's messy. Using a framework like Hadoop to take care of these issues is a great help.

Analyzing the Data with Hadoop

To take advantage of the parallel processing that Hadoop provides, we need to express our query as a MapReduce job. After some local, small-scale testing, we will be able to run it on a cluster of machines.

Map and Reduce

MapReduce works by breaking the processing into two phases: the map phase and the reduce phase. Each phase has key-value pairs as input and output, the types of which may be chosen by the programmer. The programmer also specifies two functions: the map function and the reduce function.

The input to our map phase is the raw NCDC data. We choose a text input format that gives us each line in the dataset as a text value. The key is the offset of the beginning of the line from the beginning of the file, but as we have no need for this, we ignore it.

Our map function is simple. We pull out the year and the air temperature, because these are the only fields we are interested in. In this case, the map function is just a data preparation phase, setting up the data in such a way that the reduce function can do its work on it: finding the maximum temperature for each year. The map function is also a good place to drop bad records: here we filter out temperatures that are missing, suspect, or erroneous.

To visualize the way the map works, consider the following sample lines of input data (some unused columns have been dropped to fit the page, indicated by ellipses):

```
0067011990999991950051507004...9999999N9+00001+99999999999...
0043011990999991950051512004...9999999N9+00221+99999999999...
0043011990999991950051518004...9999999N9-00111+99999999999...
0043012650999991949032412004...0500001N9+01111+99999999999...
0043012650999991949032418004...0500001N9+00781+99999999999...
```

These lines are presented to the map function as the key-value pairs:

```
(0, 0067011990999991950051507004...9999999N9+00001+99999999999...)
(106, 0043011990999991950051512004...9999999N9+00221+99999999999...)
(212, 0043011990999991950051518004...9999999N9-00111+99999999999...)
(318, 0043012650999991949032412004...0500001N9+01111+99999999999...)
(424, 0043012650999991949032418004...0500001N9+00781+99999999999...)
```

The keys are the line offsets within the file, which we ignore in our map function. The map function merely extracts the year and the air temperature (indicated in bold text), and emits them as its output (the temperature values have been interpreted as integers):

```
(1950, 0)
(1950, 22)
(1950, -11)
(1949, 111)
(1949, 78)
```

The output from the map function is processed by the MapReduce framework before being sent to the reduce function. This processing sorts and groups the key-value pairs by key. So, continuing the example, our reduce function sees the following input:

```
(1949, [111, 78])
(1950, [0, 22, -11])
```

Each year appears with a list of all its air temperature readings. All the reduce function has to do now is iterate through the list and pick up the maximum reading:

```
(1949, 111)
(1950, 22)
```

This is the final output: the maximum global temperature recorded in each year.

The whole data flow is illustrated in Figure 2-1. At the bottom of the diagram is a Unix pipeline, which mimics the whole MapReduce flow and which we will see again later in this chapter when we look at Hadoop Streaming.

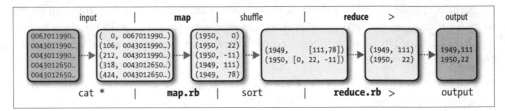

Figure 2-1. MapReduce logical data flow

Java MapReduce

Having run through how the MapReduce program works, the next step is to express it in code. We need three things: a map function, a reduce function, and some code to run the job. The map function is represented by the Mapper class, which declares an abstract map() method. Example 2-3 shows the implementation of our map function.

Example 2-3. Mapper for the maximum temperature example

```java
import java.io.IOException;

import org.apache.hadoop.io.IntWritable;
import org.apache.hadoop.io.LongWritable;
import org.apache.hadoop.io.Text;
import org.apache.hadoop.mapreduce.Mapper;

public class MaxTemperatureMapper
    extends Mapper<LongWritable, Text, Text, IntWritable> {

  private static final int MISSING = 9999;

  @Override
  public void map(LongWritable key, Text value, Context context)
      throws IOException, InterruptedException {

    String line = value.toString();
    String year = line.substring(15, 19);
    int airTemperature;
    if (line.charAt(87) == '+') { // parseInt doesn't like leading plus signs
      airTemperature = Integer.parseInt(line.substring(88, 92));
    } else {
      airTemperature = Integer.parseInt(line.substring(87, 92));
    }
    String quality = line.substring(92, 93);
```

```
    if (airTemperature != MISSING && quality.matches("[01459]")) {
      context.write(new Text(year), new IntWritable(airTemperature));
    }
  }
}
```

The Mapper class is a generic type, with four formal type parameters that specify the input key, input value, output key, and output value types of the map function. For the present example, the input key is a long integer offset, the input value is a line of text, the output key is a year, and the output value is an air temperature (an integer). Rather than using built-in Java types, Hadoop provides its own set of basic types that are optimized for network serialization. These are found in the org.apache.hadoop.io package. Here we use LongWritable, which corresponds to a Java Long, Text (like Java String), and IntWritable (like Java Integer).

The map() method is passed a key and a value. We convert the Text value containing the line of input into a Java String, then use its substring() method to extract the columns we are interested in.

The map() method also provides an instance of Context to write the output to. In this case, we write the year as a Text object (since we are just using it as a key), and the temperature is wrapped in an IntWritable. We write an output record only if the temperature is present and the quality code indicates the temperature reading is OK.

The reduce function is similarly defined using a Reducer, as illustrated in Example 2-4.

Example 2-4. Reducer for the maximum temperature example

```java
import java.io.IOException;

import org.apache.hadoop.io.IntWritable;
import org.apache.hadoop.io.Text;
import org.apache.hadoop.mapreduce.Reducer;

public class MaxTemperatureReducer
    extends Reducer<Text, IntWritable, Text, IntWritable> {

  @Override
  public void reduce(Text key, Iterable<IntWritable> values, Context context)
      throws IOException, InterruptedException {

    int maxValue = Integer.MIN_VALUE;
    for (IntWritable value : values) {
      maxValue = Math.max(maxValue, value.get());
    }
    context.write(key, new IntWritable(maxValue));
  }
}
```

Again, four formal type parameters are used to specify the input and output types, this time for the reduce function. The input types of the reduce function must match the output types of the map function: Text and IntWritable. And in this case, the output types of the reduce function are Text and IntWritable, for a year and its maximum temperature, which we find by iterating through the temperatures and comparing each with a record of the highest found so far.

The third piece of code runs the MapReduce job (see Example 2-5).

Example 2-5. Application to find the maximum temperature in the weather dataset

```java
import org.apache.hadoop.fs.Path;
import org.apache.hadoop.io.IntWritable;
import org.apache.hadoop.io.Text;
import org.apache.hadoop.mapreduce.Job;
import org.apache.hadoop.mapreduce.lib.input.FileInputFormat;
import org.apache.hadoop.mapreduce.lib.output.FileOutputFormat;

public class MaxTemperature {

  public static void main(String[] args) throws Exception {
    if (args.length != 2) {
      System.err.println("Usage: MaxTemperature <input path> <output path>");
      System.exit(-1);
    }

    Job job = new Job();
    job.setJarByClass(MaxTemperature.class);
    job.setJobName("Max temperature");

    FileInputFormat.addInputPath(job, new Path(args[0]));
    FileOutputFormat.setOutputPath(job, new Path(args[1]));

    job.setMapperClass(MaxTemperatureMapper.class);
    job.setReducerClass(MaxTemperatureReducer.class);

    job.setOutputKeyClass(Text.class);
    job.setOutputValueClass(IntWritable.class);

    System.exit(job.waitForCompletion(true) ? 0 : 1);
  }
}
```

A Job object forms the specification of the job and gives you control over how the job is run. When we run this job on a Hadoop cluster, we will package the code into a JAR file (which Hadoop will distribute around the cluster). Rather than explicitly specifying the name of the JAR file, we can pass a class in the Job's setJarByClass() method, which Hadoop will use to locate the relevant JAR file by looking for the JAR file containing this class.

Having constructed a `Job` object, we specify the input and output paths. An input path is specified by calling the static `addInputPath()` method on `FileInputFormat`, and it can be a single file, a directory (in which case, the input forms all the files in that directory), or a file pattern. As the name suggests, `addInputPath()` can be called more than once to use input from multiple paths.

The output path (of which there is only one) is specified by the static `setOutput Path()` method on `FileOutputFormat`. It specifies a directory where the output files from the reduce function are written. The directory shouldn't exist before running the job because Hadoop will complain and not run the job. This precaution is to prevent data loss (it can be very annoying to accidentally overwrite the output of a long job with that of another).

Next, we specify the map and reduce types to use via the `setMapperClass()` and `setReducerClass()` methods.

The `setOutputKeyClass()` and `setOutputValueClass()` methods control the output types for the reduce function, and must match what the `Reduce` class produces. The map output types default to the same types, so they do not need to be set if the mapper produces the same types as the reducer (as it does in our case). However, if they are different, the map output types must be set using the `setMapOutputKeyClass()` and `setMapOutputValueClass()` methods.

The input types are controlled via the input format, which we have not explicitly set because we are using the default `TextInputFormat`.

After setting the classes that define the map and reduce functions, we are ready to run the job. The `waitForCompletion()` method on `Job` submits the job and waits for it to finish. The single argument to the method is a flag indicating whether verbose output is generated. When `true`, the job writes information about its progress to the console.

The return value of the `waitForCompletion()` method is a Boolean indicating success (`true`) or failure (`false`), which we translate into the program's exit code of `0` or `1`.

> The Java MapReduce API used in this section, and throughout the book, is called the "new API"; it replaces the older, functionally equivalent API. The differences between the two APIs are explained in Appendix D, along with tips on how to convert between the two APIs. You can also find the old API equivalent of the maximum temperature application there.

A test run

After writing a MapReduce job, it's normal to try it out on a small dataset to flush out any immediate problems with the code. First, install Hadoop in standalone mode (there are instructions for how to do this in Appendix A). This is the mode in which Hadoop runs using the local filesystem with a local job runner. Then, install and compile the examples using the instructions on the book's website.

Let's test it on the five-line sample discussed earlier (the output has been slightly reformatted to fit the page, and some lines have been removed):

```
% export HADOOP_CLASSPATH=hadoop-examples.jar
% hadoop MaxTemperature input/ncdc/sample.txt output
14/09/16 09:48:39 WARN util.NativeCodeLoader: Unable to load native-hadoop
library for your platform... using builtin-java classes where applicable
14/09/16 09:48:40 WARN mapreduce.JobSubmitter: Hadoop command-line option
parsing not performed. Implement the Tool interface and execute your application
with ToolRunner to remedy this.
14/09/16 09:48:40 INFO input.FileInputFormat: Total input paths to process : 1
14/09/16 09:48:40 INFO mapreduce.JobSubmitter: number of splits:1
14/09/16 09:48:40 INFO mapreduce.JobSubmitter: Submitting tokens for job:
job_local26392882_0001
14/09/16 09:48:40 INFO mapreduce.Job: The url to track the job:
http://localhost:8080/
14/09/16 09:48:40 INFO mapreduce.Job: Running job: job_local26392882_0001
14/09/16 09:48:40 INFO mapred.LocalJobRunner: OutputCommitter set in config null
14/09/16 09:48:40 INFO mapred.LocalJobRunner: OutputCommitter is
org.apache.hadoop.mapreduce.lib.output.FileOutputCommitter
14/09/16 09:48:40 INFO mapred.LocalJobRunner: Waiting for map tasks
14/09/16 09:48:40 INFO mapred.LocalJobRunner: Starting task:
attempt_local26392882_0001_m_000000_0
14/09/16 09:48:40 INFO mapred.Task:  Using ResourceCalculatorProcessTree : null
14/09/16 09:48:40 INFO mapred.LocalJobRunner:
14/09/16 09:48:40 INFO mapred.Task: Task:attempt_local26392882_0001_m_000000_0
is done. And is in the process of committing
14/09/16 09:48:40 INFO mapred.LocalJobRunner: map
14/09/16 09:48:40 INFO mapred.Task: Task 'attempt_local26392882_0001_m_000000_0'
 done.
14/09/16 09:48:40 INFO mapred.LocalJobRunner: Finishing task:
attempt_local26392882_0001_m_000000_0
14/09/16 09:48:40 INFO mapred.LocalJobRunner: map task executor complete.
14/09/16 09:48:40 INFO mapred.LocalJobRunner: Waiting for reduce tasks
14/09/16 09:48:40 INFO mapred.LocalJobRunner: Starting task:
attempt_local26392882_0001_r_000000_0
14/09/16 09:48:40 INFO mapred.Task:  Using ResourceCalculatorProcessTree : null
14/09/16 09:48:40 INFO mapred.LocalJobRunner: 1 / 1 copied.
14/09/16 09:48:40 INFO mapred.Merger: Merging 1 sorted segments
14/09/16 09:48:40 INFO mapred.Merger: Down to the last merge-pass, with 1
segments left of total size: 50 bytes
14/09/16 09:48:40 INFO mapred.Merger: Merging 1 sorted segments
14/09/16 09:48:40 INFO mapred.Merger: Down to the last merge-pass, with 1
segments left of total size: 50 bytes
14/09/16 09:48:40 INFO mapred.LocalJobRunner: 1 / 1 copied.
14/09/16 09:48:40 INFO mapred.Task: Task:attempt_local26392882_0001_r_000000_0
is done. And is in the process of committing
14/09/16 09:48:40 INFO mapred.LocalJobRunner: 1 / 1 copied.
14/09/16 09:48:40 INFO mapred.Task: Task attempt_local26392882_0001_r_000000_0
```

```
is allowed to commit now
14/09/16 09:48:40 INFO output.FileOutputCommitter: Saved output of task
'attempt...local26392882_0001_r_000000_0' to file:/Users/tom/book-workspace/
hadoop-book/output/_temporary/0/task_local26392882_0001_r_000000
14/09/16 09:48:40 INFO mapred.LocalJobRunner: reduce > reduce
14/09/16 09:48:40 INFO mapred.Task: Task 'attempt_local26392882_0001_r_000000_0'
done.
14/09/16 09:48:40 INFO mapred.LocalJobRunner: Finishing task:
attempt_local26392882_0001_r_000000_0
14/09/16 09:48:40 INFO mapred.LocalJobRunner: reduce task executor complete.
14/09/16 09:48:41 INFO mapreduce.Job: Job job_local26392882_0001 running in uber
mode : false
14/09/16 09:48:41 INFO mapreduce.Job:  map 100% reduce 100%
14/09/16 09:48:41 INFO mapreduce.Job: Job job_local26392882_0001 completed
successfully
14/09/16 09:48:41 INFO mapreduce.Job: Counters: 30
    File System Counters
        FILE: Number of bytes read=377168
        FILE: Number of bytes written=828464
        FILE: Number of read operations=0
        FILE: Number of large read operations=0
        FILE: Number of write operations=0
    Map-Reduce Framework
        Map input records=5
        Map output records=5
        Map output bytes=45
        Map output materialized bytes=61
        Input split bytes=129
        Combine input records=0
        Combine output records=0
        Reduce input groups=2
        Reduce shuffle bytes=61
        Reduce input records=5
        Reduce output records=2
        Spilled Records=10
        Shuffled Maps =1
        Failed Shuffles=0
        Merged Map outputs=1
        GC time elapsed (ms)=39
        Total committed heap usage (bytes)=226754560
    File Input Format Counters
        Bytes Read=529
    File Output Format Counters
        Bytes Written=29
```

When the hadoop command is invoked with a classname as the first argument, it
launches a Java virtual machine (JVM) to run the class. The hadoop command adds the
Hadoop libraries (and their dependencies) to the classpath and picks up the Hadoop
configuration, too. To add the application classes to the classpath, we've defined an
environment variable called HADOOP_CLASSPATH, which the *hadoop* script picks up.

When running in local (standalone) mode, the programs in this book all assume that you have set the HADOOP_CLASSPATH in this way. The commands should be run from the directory that the example code is installed in.

The output from running the job provides some useful information. For example, we can see that the job was given an ID of job_local26392882_0001, and it ran one map task and one reduce task (with the following IDs: attempt_lo cal26392882_0001_m_000000_0 and attempt_local26392882_0001_r_000000_0). Knowing the job and task IDs can be very useful when debugging MapReduce jobs.

The last section of the output, titled "Counters," shows the statistics that Hadoop generates for each job it runs. These are very useful for checking whether the amount of data processed is what you expected. For example, we can follow the number of records that went through the system: five map input records produced five map output records (since the mapper emitted one output record for each valid input record), then five reduce input records in two groups (one for each unique key) produced two reduce output records.

The output was written to the *output* directory, which contains one output file per reducer. The job had a single reducer, so we find a single file, named *part-r-00000*:

```
% cat output/part-r-00000
1949 111
1950 22
```

This result is the same as when we went through it by hand earlier. We interpret this as saying that the maximum temperature recorded in 1949 was 11.1°C, and in 1950 it was 2.2°C.

Scaling Out

You've seen how MapReduce works for small inputs; now it's time to take a bird's-eye view of the system and look at the data flow for large inputs. For simplicity, the examples so far have used files on the local filesystem. However, to scale out, we need to store the data in a distributed filesystem (typically HDFS, which you'll learn about in the next chapter). This allows Hadoop to move the MapReduce computation to each machine hosting a part of the data, using Hadoop's resource management system, called YARN (see Chapter 4). Let's see how this works.

Data Flow

First, some terminology. A MapReduce *job* is a unit of work that the client wants to be performed: it consists of the input data, the MapReduce program, and configuration information. Hadoop runs the job by dividing it into *tasks*, of which there are two types: *map tasks* and *reduce tasks*. The tasks are scheduled using YARN and run on nodes in the cluster. If a task fails, it will be automatically rescheduled to run on a different node.

Hadoop divides the input to a MapReduce job into fixed-size pieces called *input splits*, or just *splits*. Hadoop creates one map task for each split, which runs the user-defined map function for each *record* in the split.

Having many splits means the time taken to process each split is small compared to the time to process the whole input. So if we are processing the splits in parallel, the processing is better load balanced when the splits are small, since a faster machine will be able to process proportionally more splits over the course of the job than a slower machine. Even if the machines are identical, failed processes or other jobs running concurrently make load balancing desirable, and the quality of the load balancing increases as the splits become more fine grained.

On the other hand, if splits are too small, the overhead of managing the splits and map task creation begins to dominate the total job execution time. For most jobs, a good split size tends to be the size of an HDFS block, which is 128 MB by default, although this can be changed for the cluster (for all newly created files) or specified when each file is created.

Hadoop does its best to run the map task on a node where the input data resides in HDFS, because it doesn't use valuable cluster bandwidth. This is called the *data locality optimization*. Sometimes, however, all the nodes hosting the HDFS block replicas for a map task's input split are running other map tasks, so the job scheduler will look for a free map slot on a node in the same rack as one of the blocks. Very occasionally even this is not possible, so an off-rack node is used, which results in an inter-rack network transfer. The three possibilities are illustrated in Figure 2-2.

It should now be clear why the optimal split size is the same as the block size: it is the largest size of input that can be guaranteed to be stored on a single node. If the split spanned two blocks, it would be unlikely that any HDFS node stored both blocks, so some of the split would have to be transferred across the network to the node running the map task, which is clearly less efficient than running the whole map task using local data.

Map tasks write their output to the local disk, not to HDFS. Why is this? Map output is intermediate output: it's processed by reduce tasks to produce the final output, and once the job is complete, the map output can be thrown away. So, storing it in HDFS with replication would be overkill. If the node running the map task fails before the map output has been consumed by the reduce task, then Hadoop will automatically rerun the map task on another node to re-create the map output.

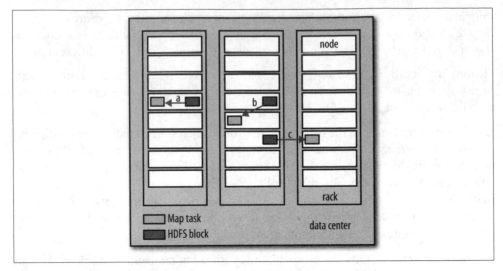

Figure 2-2. Data-local (a), rack-local (b), and off-rack (c) map tasks

Reduce tasks don't have the advantage of data locality; the input to a single reduce task is normally the output from all mappers. In the present example, we have a single reduce task that is fed by all of the map tasks. Therefore, the sorted map outputs have to be transferred across the network to the node where the reduce task is running, where they are merged and then passed to the user-defined reduce function. The output of the reduce is normally stored in HDFS for reliability. As explained in Chapter 3, for each HDFS block of the reduce output, the first replica is stored on the local node, with other replicas being stored on off-rack nodes for reliability. Thus, writing the reduce output does consume network bandwidth, but only as much as a normal HDFS write pipeline consumes.

The whole data flow with a single reduce task is illustrated in Figure 2-3. The dotted boxes indicate nodes, the dotted arrows show data transfers on a node, and the solid arrows show data transfers between nodes.

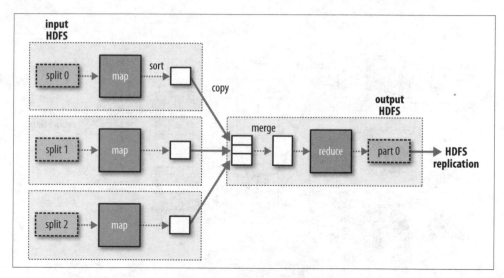

Figure 2-3. MapReduce data flow with a single reduce task

The number of reduce tasks is not governed by the size of the input, but instead is specified independently. In "The Default MapReduce Job" on page 214, you will see how to choose the number of reduce tasks for a given job.

When there are multiple reducers, the map tasks *partition* their output, each creating one partition for each reduce task. There can be many keys (and their associated values) in each partition, but the records for any given key are all in a single partition. The partitioning can be controlled by a user-defined partitioning function, but normally the default partitioner—which buckets keys using a hash function—works very well.

The data flow for the general case of multiple reduce tasks is illustrated in Figure 2-4. This diagram makes it clear why the data flow between map and reduce tasks is collo-quially known as "the shuffle," as each reduce task is fed by many map tasks. The shuffle is more complicated than this diagram suggests, and tuning it can have a big impact on job execution time, as you will see in "Shuffle and Sort" on page 197.

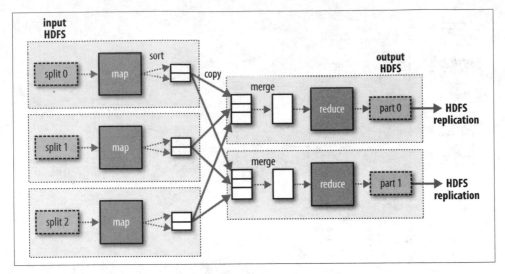

Figure 2-4. MapReduce data flow with multiple reduce tasks

Finally, it's also possible to have zero reduce tasks. This can be appropriate when you don't need the shuffle because the processing can be carried out entirely in parallel (a few examples are discussed in "NLineInputFormat" on page 234). In this case, the only off-node data transfer is when the map tasks write to HDFS (see Figure 2-5).

Combiner Functions

Many MapReduce jobs are limited by the bandwidth available on the cluster, so it pays to minimize the data transferred between map and reduce tasks. Hadoop allows the user to specify a *combiner function* to be run on the map output, and the combiner function's output forms the input to the reduce function. Because the combiner function is an optimization, Hadoop does not provide a guarantee of how many times it will call it for a particular map output record, if at all. In other words, calling the combiner function zero, one, or many times should produce the same output from the reducer.

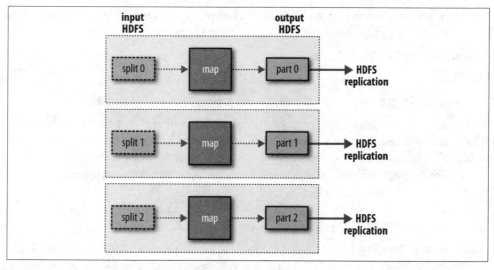

Figure 2-5. MapReduce data flow with no reduce tasks

The contract for the combiner function constrains the type of function that may be used. This is best illustrated with an example. Suppose that for the maximum temperature example, readings for the year 1950 were processed by two maps (because they were in different splits). Imagine the first map produced the output:

```
(1950, 0)
(1950, 20)
(1950, 10)
```

and the second produced:

```
(1950, 25)
(1950, 15)
```

The reduce function would be called with a list of all the values:

```
(1950, [0, 20, 10, 25, 15])
```

with output:

```
(1950, 25)
```

since 25 is the maximum value in the list. We could use a combiner function that, just like the reduce function, finds the maximum temperature for each map output. The reduce function would then be called with:

```
(1950, [20, 25])
```

and would produce the same output as before. More succinctly, we may express the function calls on the temperature values in this case as follows:

max(0, 20, 10, 25, 15) = max(max(0, 20, 10), max(25, 15)) = max(20, 25) = 25

Not all functions possess this property.[1] For example, if we were calculating mean temperatures, we couldn't use the mean as our combiner function, because:

```
mean(0, 20, 10, 25, 15) = 14
```

but:

```
mean(mean(0, 20, 10), mean(25, 15)) = mean(10, 20) = 15
```

The combiner function doesn't replace the reduce function. (How could it? The reduce function is still needed to process records with the same key from different maps.) But it can help cut down the amount of data shuffled between the mappers and the reducers, and for this reason alone it is always worth considering whether you can use a combiner function in your MapReduce job.

Specifying a combiner function

Going back to the Java MapReduce program, the combiner function is defined using the Reducer class, and for this application, it is the same implementation as the reduce function in MaxTemperatureReducer. The only change we need to make is to set the combiner class on the Job (see Example 2-6).

Example 2-6. Application to find the maximum temperature, using a combiner function for efficiency

```java
public class MaxTemperatureWithCombiner {

  public static void main(String[] args) throws Exception {
    if (args.length != 2) {
      System.err.println("Usage: MaxTemperatureWithCombiner <input path> " +
          "<output path>");
      System.exit(-1);
    }

    Job job = new Job();
    job.setJarByClass(MaxTemperatureWithCombiner.class);
    job.setJobName("Max temperature");

    FileInputFormat.addInputPath(job, new Path(args[0]));
    FileOutputFormat.setOutputPath(job, new Path(args[1]));

    job.setMapperClass(MaxTemperatureMapper.class);
    job.setCombinerClass(MaxTemperatureReducer.class);
    job.setReducerClass(MaxTemperatureReducer.class);

    job.setOutputKeyClass(Text.class);
```

---

1. Functions with this property are called *commutative* and *associative*. They are also sometimes referred to as *distributive*, such as by Jim Gray et al.'s "Data Cube: A Relational Aggregation Operator Generalizing Group-By, Cross-Tab, and Sub-Totals," (*http://bit.ly/data_cube*) February1995.

```
    job.setOutputValueClass(IntWritable.class);

    System.exit(job.waitForCompletion(true) ? 0 : 1);
  }
}
```

Running a Distributed MapReduce Job

The same program will run, without alteration, on a full dataset. This is the point of
MapReduce: it scales to the size of your data and the size of your hardware. Here's one
data point: on a 10-node EC2 cluster running High-CPU Extra Large instances, the
program took six minutes to run.[2]

We'll go through the mechanics of running programs on a cluster in Chapter 6.

Hadoop Streaming

Hadoop provides an API to MapReduce that allows you to write your map and reduce
functions in languages other than Java. *Hadoop Streaming* uses Unix standard streams
as the interface between Hadoop and your program, so you can use any language that
can read standard input and write to standard output to write your MapReduce
program.[3]

Streaming is naturally suited for text processing. Map input data is passed over standard
input to your map function, which processes it line by line and writes lines to standard
output. A map output key-value pair is written as a single tab-delimited line. Input to
the reduce function is in the same format—a tab-separated key-value pair—passed over
standard input. The reduce function reads lines from standard input, which the framework guarantees are sorted by key, and writes its results to standard output.

Let's illustrate this by rewriting our MapReduce program for finding maximum temperatures by year in Streaming.

Ruby

The map function can be expressed in Ruby as shown in Example 2-7.

---

2. This is a factor of seven faster than the serial run on one machine using *awk*. The main reason it wasn't
   proportionately faster is because the input data wasn't evenly partitioned. For convenience, the input files
   were gzipped by year, resulting in large files for later years in the dataset, when the number of weather records
   was much higher.

3. Hadoop Pipes is an alternative to Streaming for C++ programmers. It uses sockets to communicate with the
   process running the C++ map or reduce function.

Example 2-7. Map function for maximum temperature in Ruby

```ruby
#!/usr/bin/env ruby

STDIN.each_line do |line|
  val = line
  year, temp, q = val[15,4], val[87,5], val[92,1]
  puts "#{year}\t#{temp}" if (temp != "+9999" && q =~ /[01459]/)
end
```

The program iterates over lines from standard input by executing a block for each line from STDIN (a global constant of type IO). The block pulls out the relevant fields from each input line and, if the temperature is valid, writes the year and the temperature separated by a tab character, \t, to standard output (using puts).

> It's worth drawing out a design difference between Streaming and the Java MapReduce API. The Java API is geared toward processing your map function one record at a time. The framework calls the map() method on your Mapper for each record in the input, whereas with Streaming the map program can decide how to process the input— for example, it could easily read and process multiple lines at a time since it's in control of the reading. The user's Java map implementation is "pushed" records, but it's still possible to consider multiple lines at a time by accumulating previous lines in an instance variable in the Mapper.[4] In this case, you need to implement the close() method so that you know when the last record has been read, so you can finish processing the last group of lines.

Because the script just operates on standard input and output, it's trivial to test the script without using Hadoop, simply by using Unix pipes:

```
% cat input/ncdc/sample.txt | ch02-mr-intro/src/main/ruby/max_temperature_map.rb
1950    +0000
1950    +0022
1950    -0011
1949    +0111
1949    +0078
```

The reduce function shown in Example 2-8 is a little more complex.

Example 2-8. Reduce function for maximum temperature in Ruby

```ruby
#!/usr/bin/env ruby

last_key, max_val = nil, -1000000
STDIN.each_line do |line|
  key, val = line.split("\t")
```

---

4. Alternatively, you could use "pull"-style processing in the new MapReduce API; see Appendix D.

```
    if last_key && last_key != key
      puts "#{last_key}\t#{max_val}"
      last_key, max_val = key, val.to_i
    else
      last_key, max_val = key, [max_val, val.to_i].max
    end
end
puts "#{last_key}\t#{max_val}" if last_key
```

Again, the program iterates over lines from standard input, but this time we have to store some state as we process each key group. In this case, the keys are the years, and we store the last key seen and the maximum temperature seen so far for that key. The MapReduce framework ensures that the keys are ordered, so we know that if a key is different from the previous one, we have moved into a new key group. In contrast to the Java API, where you are provided an iterator over each key group, in Streaming you have to find key group boundaries in your program.

For each line, we pull out the key and value. Then, if we've just finished a group (last_key && last_key != key), we write the key and the maximum temperature for that group, separated by a tab character, before resetting the maximum temperature for the new key. If we haven't just finished a group, we just update the maximum temperature for the current key.

The last line of the program ensures that a line is written for the last key group in the input.

We can now simulate the whole MapReduce pipeline with a Unix pipeline (which is equivalent to the Unix pipeline shown in Figure 2-1):

```
% cat input/ncdc/sample.txt | \
  ch02-mr-intro/src/main/ruby/max_temperature_map.rb | \
  sort | ch02-mr-intro/src/main/ruby/max_temperature_reduce.rb
1949 111
1950 22
```

The output is the same as that of the Java program, so the next step is to run it using Hadoop itself.

The hadoop command doesn't support a Streaming option; instead, you specify the Streaming JAR file along with the jar option. Options to the Streaming program specify the input and output paths and the map and reduce scripts. This is what it looks like:

```
% hadoop jar $HADOOP_HOME/share/hadoop/tools/lib/hadoop-streaming-*.jar \
  -input input/ncdc/sample.txt \
  -output output \
  -mapper ch02-mr-intro/src/main/ruby/max_temperature_map.rb \
  -reducer ch02-mr-intro/src/main/ruby/max_temperature_reduce.rb
```

When running on a large dataset on a cluster, we should use the -combiner option to set the combiner:

```
% hadoop jar $HADOOP_HOME/share/hadoop/tools/lib/hadoop-streaming-*.jar \
  -files ch02-mr-intro/src/main/ruby/max_temperature_map.rb,\
ch02-mr-intro/src/main/ruby/max_temperature_reduce.rb \
  -input input/ncdc/all \
  -output output \
  -mapper ch02-mr-intro/src/main/ruby/max_temperature_map.rb \
  -combiner ch02-mr-intro/src/main/ruby/max_temperature_reduce.rb \
  -reducer ch02-mr-intro/src/main/ruby/max_temperature_reduce.rb
```

Note also the use of `-files`, which we use when running Streaming programs on the cluster to ship the scripts to the cluster.

Python

Streaming supports any programming language that can read from standard input and write to standard output, so for readers more familiar with Python, here's the same example again.[5] The map script is in Example 2-9, and the reduce script is in Example 2-10.

Example 2-9. Map function for maximum temperature in Python

```python
#!/usr/bin/env python

import re
import sys

for line in sys.stdin:
  val = line.strip()
  (year, temp, q) = (val[15:19], val[87:92], val[92:93])
  if (temp != "+9999" and re.match("[01459]", q)):
    print "%s\t%s" % (year, temp)
```

Example 2-10. Reduce function for maximum temperature in Python

```python
#!/usr/bin/env python

import sys

(last_key, max_val) = (None, -sys.maxint)
for line in sys.stdin:
  (key, val) = line.strip().split("\t")
  if last_key and last_key != key:
    print "%s\t%s" % (last_key, max_val)
    (last_key, max_val) = (key, int(val))
  else:
    (last_key, max_val) = (key, max(max_val, int(val)))
```

---

5. As an alternative to Streaming, Python programmers should consider Dumbo (*http://klbostee.github.io/dumbo/*), which makes the Streaming MapReduce interface more Pythonic and easier to use.

```
if last_key:
  print "%s\t%s" % (last_key, max_val)
```

We can test the programs and run the job in the same way we did in Ruby. For example, to run a test:

```
% cat input/ncdc/sample.txt | \
  ch02-mr-intro/src/main/python/max_temperature_map.py | \
  sort | ch02-mr-intro/src/main/python/max_temperature_reduce.py
1949    111
1950    22
```

## CHAPTER 3

The Hadoop Distributed Filesystem

When a dataset outgrows the storage capacity of a single physical machine, it becomes necessary to partition it across a number of separate machines. Filesystems that manage the storage across a network of machines are called *distributed filesystems*. Since they are network based, all the complications of network programming kick in, thus making distributed filesystems more complex than regular disk filesystems. For example, one of the biggest challenges is making the filesystem tolerate node failure without suffering data loss.

Hadoop comes with a distributed filesystem called HDFS, which stands for *Hadoop Distributed Filesystem*. (You may sometimes see references to "DFS"—informally or in older documentation or configurations—which is the same thing.) HDFS is Hadoop's flagship filesystem and is the focus of this chapter, but Hadoop actually has a general-purpose filesystem abstraction, so we'll see along the way how Hadoop integrates with other storage systems (such as the local filesystem and Amazon S3).

The Design of HDFS

HDFS is a filesystem designed for storing very large files with streaming data access patterns, running on clusters of commodity hardware.[1] Let's examine this statement in more detail:

---

1. The architecture of HDFS is described in Robert Chansler et al.'s, "The Hadoop Distributed File System," (*http://www.aosabook.org/en/hdfs.html*) which appeared in *The Architecture of Open Source Applications: Elegance, Evolution, and a Few Fearless Hacks* by Amy Brown and Greg Wilson (eds.).

Very large files

"Very large" in this context means files that are hundreds of megabytes, gigabytes, or terabytes in size. There are Hadoop clusters running today that store petabytes of data.[2]

Streaming data access

HDFS is built around the idea that the most efficient data processing pattern is a write-once, read-many-times pattern. A dataset is typically generated or copied from source, and then various analyses are performed on that dataset over time. Each analysis will involve a large proportion, if not all, of the dataset, so the time to read the whole dataset is more important than the latency in reading the first record.

Commodity hardware

Hadoop doesn't require expensive, highly reliable hardware. It's designed to run on clusters of commodity hardware (commonly available hardware that can be obtained from multiple vendors)[3] for which the chance of node failure across the cluster is high, at least for large clusters. HDFS is designed to carry on working without a noticeable interruption to the user in the face of such failure.

It is also worth examining the applications for which using HDFS does not work so well. Although this may change in the future, these are areas where HDFS is not a good fit today:

Low-latency data access

Applications that require low-latency access to data, in the tens of milliseconds range, will not work well with HDFS. Remember, HDFS is optimized for delivering a high throughput of data, and this may be at the expense of latency. HBase (see Chapter 20) is currently a better choice for low-latency access.

Lots of small files

Because the namenode holds filesystem metadata in memory, the limit to the number of files in a filesystem is governed by the amount of memory on the namenode. As a rule of thumb, each file, directory, and block takes about 150 bytes. So, for example, if you had one million files, each taking one block, you would need at least 300 MB of memory. Although storing millions of files is feasible, billions is beyond the capability of current hardware.[4]

---

2. See Konstantin V. Shvachko and Arun C. Murthy, "Scaling Hadoop to 4000 nodes at Yahoo!" (*http://bit.ly/scaling_hadoop*), September 30, 2008.

3. See Chapter 10 for a typical machine specification.

4. For an exposition of the scalability limits of HDFS, see Konstantin V. Shvachko, "HDFS Scalability: The Limits to Growth" (*http://bit.ly/limits_to_growth*), April 2010.

Multiple writers, arbitrary file modifications

Files in HDFS may be written to by a single writer. Writes are always made at the end of the file, in append-only fashion. There is no support for multiple writers or for modifications at arbitrary offsets in the file. (These might be supported in the future, but they are likely to be relatively inefficient.)

HDFS Concepts

Blocks

A disk has a block size, which is the minimum amount of data that it can read or write. Filesystems for a single disk build on this by dealing with data in blocks, which are an integral multiple of the disk block size. Filesystem blocks are typically a few kilobytes in size, whereas disk blocks are normally 512 bytes. This is generally transparent to the filesystem user who is simply reading or writing a file of whatever length. However, there are tools to perform filesystem maintenance, such as *df* and *fsck*, that operate on the filesystem block level.

HDFS, too, has the concept of a block, but it is a much larger unit—128 MB by default. Like in a filesystem for a single disk, files in HDFS are broken into block-sized chunks, which are stored as independent units. Unlike a filesystem for a single disk, a file in HDFS that is smaller than a single block does not occupy a full block's worth of underlying storage. (For example, a 1 MB file stored with a block size of 128 MB uses 1 MB of disk space, not 128 MB.) When unqualified, the term "block" in this book refers to a block in HDFS.

Why Is a Block in HDFS So Large?

HDFS blocks are large compared to disk blocks, and the reason is to minimize the cost of seeks. If the block is large enough, the time it takes to transfer the data from the disk can be significantly longer than the time to seek to the start of the block. Thus, transferring a large file made of multiple blocks operates at the disk transfer rate.

A quick calculation shows that if the seek time is around 10 ms and the transfer rate is 100 MB/s, to make the seek time 1% of the transfer time, we need to make the block size around 100 MB. The default is actually 128 MB, although many HDFS installations use larger block sizes. This figure will continue to be revised upward as transfer speeds grow with new generations of disk drives.

This argument shouldn't be taken too far, however. Map tasks in MapReduce normally operate on one block at a time, so if you have too few tasks (fewer than nodes in the cluster), your jobs will run slower than they could otherwise.

Having a block abstraction for a distributed filesystem brings several benefits. The first benefit is the most obvious: a file can be larger than any single disk in the network. There's nothing that requires the blocks from a file to be stored on the same disk, so they can take advantage of any of the disks in the cluster. In fact, it would be possible, if unusual, to store a single file on an HDFS cluster whose blocks filled all the disks in the cluster.

Second, making the unit of abstraction a block rather than a file simplifies the storage subsystem. Simplicity is something to strive for in all systems, but it is especially important for a distributed system in which the failure modes are so varied. The storage subsystem deals with blocks, simplifying storage management (because blocks are a fixed size, it is easy to calculate how many can be stored on a given disk) and eliminating metadata concerns (because blocks are just chunks of data to be stored, file metadata such as permissions information does not need to be stored with the blocks, so another system can handle metadata separately).

Furthermore, blocks fit well with replication for providing fault tolerance and availability. To insure against corrupted blocks and disk and machine failure, each block is replicated to a small number of physically separate machines (typically three). If a block becomes unavailable, a copy can be read from another location in a way that is transparent to the client. A block that is no longer available due to corruption or machine failure can be replicated from its alternative locations to other live machines to bring the replication factor back to the normal level. (See "Data Integrity" on page 97 for more on guarding against corrupt data.) Similarly, some applications may choose to set a high replication factor for the blocks in a popular file to spread the read load on the cluster.

Like its disk filesystem cousin, HDFS's `fsck` command understands blocks. For example, running:

```
% hdfs fsck / -files -blocks
```

will list the blocks that make up each file in the filesystem. (See also "Filesystem check (fsck)" on page 326.)

Namenodes and Datanodes

An HDFS cluster has two types of nodes operating in a master–worker pattern: a *namenode* (the master) and a number of *datanodes* (workers). The namenode manages the filesystem namespace. It maintains the filesystem tree and the metadata for all the files and directories in the tree. This information is stored persistently on the local disk in the form of two files: the namespace image and the edit log. The namenode also knows the datanodes on which all the blocks for a given file are located; however, it does not store block locations persistently, because this information is reconstructed from datanodes when the system starts.

A *client* accesses the filesystem on behalf of the user by communicating with the name-node and datanodes. The client presents a filesystem interface similar to a Portable Operating System Interface (POSIX), so the user code does not need to know about the namenode and datanodes to function.

Datanodes are the workhorses of the filesystem. They store and retrieve blocks when they are told to (by clients or the namenode), and they report back to the namenode periodically with lists of blocks that they are storing.

Without the namenode, the filesystem cannot be used. In fact, if the machine running the namenode were obliterated, all the files on the filesystem would be lost since there would be no way of knowing how to reconstruct the files from the blocks on the datanodes. For this reason, it is important to make the namenode resilient to failure, and Hadoop provides two mechanisms for this.

The first way is to back up the files that make up the persistent state of the filesystem metadata. Hadoop can be configured so that the namenode writes its persistent state to multiple filesystems. These writes are synchronous and atomic. The usual configuration choice is to write to local disk as well as a remote NFS mount.

It is also possible to run a *secondary namenode*, which despite its name does not act as a namenode. Its main role is to periodically merge the namespace image with the edit log to prevent the edit log from becoming too large. The secondary namenode usually runs on a separate physical machine because it requires plenty of CPU and as much memory as the namenode to perform the merge. It keeps a copy of the merged name-space image, which can be used in the event of the namenode failing. However, the state of the secondary namenode lags that of the primary, so in the event of total failure of the primary, data loss is almost certain. The usual course of action in this case is to copy the namenode's metadata files that are on NFS to the secondary and run it as the new primary. (Note that it is possible to run a hot standby namenode instead of a secondary, as discussed in "HDFS High Availability" on page 48.)

See "The filesystem image and edit log" on page 318 for more details.

Block Caching

Normally a datanode reads blocks from disk, but for frequently accessed files the blocks may be explicitly cached in the datanode's memory, in an off-heap *block cache*. By default, a block is cached in only one datanode's memory, although the number is con-figurable on a per-file basis. Job schedulers (for MapReduce, Spark, and other frame-works) can take advantage of cached blocks by running tasks on the datanode where a block is cached, for increased read performance. A small lookup table used in a join is a good candidate for caching, for example.

Users or applications instruct the namenode which files to cache (and for how long) by adding a *cache directive* to a *cache pool*. Cache pools are an administrative grouping for managing cache permissions and resource usage.

HDFS Federation

The namenode keeps a reference to every file and block in the filesystem in memory, which means that on very large clusters with many files, memory becomes the limiting factor for scaling (see "How Much Memory Does a Namenode Need?" on page 294). HDFS federation, introduced in the 2.x release series, allows a cluster to scale by adding namenodes, each of which manages a portion of the filesystem namespace. For example, one namenode might manage all the files rooted under */user*, say, and a second namenode might handle files under */share*.

Under federation, each namenode manages a *namespace volume*, which is made up of the metadata for the namespace, and a *block pool* containing all the blocks for the files in the namespace. Namespace volumes are independent of each other, which means namenodes do not communicate with one another, and furthermore the failure of one namenode does not affect the availability of the namespaces managed by other namenodes. Block pool storage is *not* partitioned, however, so datanodes register with each namenode in the cluster and store blocks from multiple block pools.

To access a federated HDFS cluster, clients use client-side mount tables to map file paths to namenodes. This is managed in configuration using `ViewFileSystem` and the `viewfs://` URIs.

HDFS High Availability

The combination of replicating namenode metadata on multiple filesystems and using the secondary namenode to create checkpoints protects against data loss, but it does not provide high availability of the filesystem. The namenode is still a *single point of failure* (SPOF). If it did fail, all clients—including MapReduce jobs—would be unable to read, write, or list files, because the namenode is the sole repository of the metadata and the file-to-block mapping. In such an event, the whole Hadoop system would effectively be out of service until a new namenode could be brought online.

To recover from a failed namenode in this situation, an administrator starts a new primary namenode with one of the filesystem metadata replicas and configures datanodes and clients to use this new namenode. The new namenode is not able to serve requests until it has (i) loaded its namespace image into memory, (ii) replayed its edit log, and (iii) received enough block reports from the datanodes to leave safe mode. On large clusters with many files and blocks, the time it takes for a namenode to start from cold can be 30 minutes or more.

The long recovery time is a problem for routine maintenance, too. In fact, because unexpected failure of the namenode is so rare, the case for planned downtime is actually more important in practice.

Hadoop 2 remedied this situation by adding support for HDFS high availability (HA). In this implementation, there are a pair of namenodes in an active-standby configuration. In the event of the failure of the active namenode, the standby takes over its duties to continue servicing client requests without a significant interruption. A few architectural changes are needed to allow this to happen:

- The namenodes must use highly available shared storage to share the edit log. When a standby namenode comes up, it reads up to the end of the shared edit log to synchronize its state with the active namenode, and then continues to read new entries as they are written by the active namenode.

- Datanodes must send block reports to both namenodes because the block mappings are stored in a namenode's memory, and not on disk.

- Clients must be configured to handle namenode failover, using a mechanism that is transparent to users.

- The secondary namenode's role is subsumed by the standby, which takes periodic checkpoints of the active namenode's namespace.

There are two choices for the highly available shared storage: an NFS filer, or a *quorum journal manager* (QJM). The QJM is a dedicated HDFS implementation, designed for the sole purpose of providing a highly available edit log, and is the recommended choice for most HDFS installations. The QJM runs as a group of *journal nodes*, and each edit must be written to a majority of the journal nodes. Typically, there are three journal nodes, so the system can tolerate the loss of one of them. This arrangement is similar to the way ZooKeeper works, although it is important to realize that the QJM implementation does not use ZooKeeper. (Note, however, that HDFS HA *does* use ZooKeeper for electing the active namenode, as explained in the next section.)

If the active namenode fails, the standby can take over very quickly (in a few tens of seconds) because it has the latest state available in memory: both the latest edit log entries and an up-to-date block mapping. The actual observed failover time will be longer in practice (around a minute or so), because the system needs to be conservative in deciding that the active namenode has failed.

In the unlikely event of the standby being down when the active fails, the administrator can still start the standby from cold. This is no worse than the non-HA case, and from an operational point of view it's an improvement, because the process is a standard operational procedure built into Hadoop.

Failover and fencing

The transition from the active namenode to the standby is managed by a new entity in the system called the *failover controller*. There are various failover controllers, but the default implementation uses ZooKeeper to ensure that only one namenode is active. Each namenode runs a lightweight failover controller process whose job it is to monitor its namenode for failures (using a simple heartbeating mechanism) and trigger a failover should a namenode fail.

Failover may also be initiated manually by an administrator, for example, in the case of routine maintenance. This is known as a *graceful failover*, since the failover controller arranges an orderly transition for both namenodes to switch roles.

In the case of an ungraceful failover, however, it is impossible to be sure that the failed namenode has stopped running. For example, a slow network or a network partition can trigger a failover transition, even though the previously active namenode is still running and thinks it is still the active namenode. The HA implementation goes to great lengths to ensure that the previously active namenode is prevented from doing any damage and causing corruption—a method known as *fencing*.

The QJM only allows one namenode to write to the edit log at one time; however, it is still possible for the previously active namenode to serve stale read requests to clients, so setting up an SSH fencing command that will kill the namenode's process is a good idea. Stronger fencing methods are required when using an NFS filer for the shared edit log, since it is not possible to only allow one namenode to write at a time (this is why QJM is recommended). The range of fencing mechanisms includes revoking the namenode's access to the shared storage directory (typically by using a vendor-specific NFS command), and disabling its network port via a remote management command. As a last resort, the previously active namenode can be fenced with a technique rather graphically known as *STONITH*, or "shoot the other node in the head," which uses a specialized power distribution unit to forcibly power down the host machine.

Client failover is handled transparently by the client library. The simplest implementation uses client-side configuration to control failover. The HDFS URI uses a logical hostname that is mapped to a pair of namenode addresses (in the configuration file), and the client library tries each namenode address until the operation succeeds.

The Command-Line Interface

We're going to have a look at HDFS by interacting with it from the command line. There are many other interfaces to HDFS, but the command line is one of the simplest and, to many developers, the most familiar.

We are going to run HDFS on one machine, so first follow the instructions for setting up Hadoop in pseudodistributed mode in Appendix A. Later we'll see how to run HDFS on a cluster of machines to give us scalability and fault tolerance.

There are two properties that we set in the pseudodistributed configuration that deserve further explanation. The first is `fs.defaultFS`, set to `hdfs://localhost/`, which is used to set a default filesystem for Hadoop.[5] Filesystems are specified by a URI, and here we have used an `hdfs` URI to configure Hadoop to use HDFS by default. The HDFS daemons will use this property to determine the host and port for the HDFS namenode. We'll be running it on localhost, on the default HDFS port, 8020. And HDFS clients will use this property to work out where the namenode is running so they can connect to it.

We set the second property, `dfs.replication`, to 1 so that HDFS doesn't replicate filesystem blocks by the default factor of three. When running with a single datanode, HDFS can't replicate blocks to three datanodes, so it would perpetually warn about blocks being under-replicated. This setting solves that problem.

Basic Filesystem Operations

The filesystem is ready to be used, and we can do all of the usual filesystem operations, such as reading files, creating directories, moving files, deleting data, and listing directories. You can type `hadoop fs -help` to get detailed help on every command.

Start by copying a file from the local filesystem to HDFS:

```
% hadoop fs -copyFromLocal input/docs/quangle.txt \
  hdfs://localhost/user/tom/quangle.txt
```

This command invokes Hadoop's filesystem shell command `fs`, which supports a number of subcommands—in this case, we are running `-copyFromLocal`. The local file *quangle.txt* is copied to the file */user/tom/quangle.txt* on the HDFS instance running on localhost. In fact, we could have omitted the scheme and host of the URI and picked up the default, `hdfs://localhost`, as specified in *core-site.xml*:

```
% hadoop fs -copyFromLocal input/docs/quangle.txt /user/tom/quangle.txt
```

We also could have used a relative path and copied the file to our home directory in HDFS, which in this case is */user/tom*:

```
% hadoop fs -copyFromLocal input/docs/quangle.txt quangle.txt
```

Let's copy the file back to the local filesystem and check whether it's the same:

```
% hadoop fs -copyToLocal quangle.txt quangle.copy.txt
% md5 input/docs/quangle.txt quangle.copy.txt
MD5 (input/docs/quangle.txt) = e7891a2627cf263a079fb0f18256ffb2
MD5 (quangle.copy.txt) = e7891a2627cf263a079fb0f18256ffb2
```

---

5. In Hadoop 1, the name for this property was `fs.default.name`. Hadoop 2 introduced many new property names, and deprecated the old ones (see "Which Properties Can I Set?" on page 150). This book uses the new property names.

The MD5 digests are the same, showing that the file survived its trip to HDFS and is back intact.

Finally, let's look at an HDFS file listing. We create a directory first just to see how it is displayed in the listing:

```
% hadoop fs -mkdir books
% hadoop fs -ls .
Found 2 items
drwxr-xr-x   - tom supergroup          0 2014-10-04 13:22 books
-rw-r--r--   1 tom supergroup        119 2014-10-04 13:21 quangle.txt
```

The information returned is very similar to that returned by the Unix command ls -l, with a few minor differences. The first column shows the file mode. The second column is the replication factor of the file (something a traditional Unix filesystem does not have). Remember we set the default replication factor in the site-wide configuration to be 1, which is why we see the same value here. The entry in this column is empty for directories because the concept of replication does not apply to them—directories are treated as metadata and stored by the namenode, not the datanodes. The third and fourth columns show the file owner and group. The fifth column is the size of the file in bytes, or zero for directories. The sixth and seventh columns are the last modified date and time. Finally, the eighth column is the name of the file or directory.

File Permissions in HDFS

HDFS has a permissions model for files and directories that is much like the POSIX model. There are three types of permission: the read permission (r), the write permission (w), and the execute permission (x). The read permission is required to read files or list the contents of a directory. The write permission is required to write a file or, for a directory, to create or delete files or directories in it. The execute permission is ignored for a file because you can't execute a file on HDFS (unlike POSIX), and for a directory this permission is required to access its children.

Each file and directory has an *owner*, a *group*, and a *mode*. The mode is made up of the permissions for the user who is the owner, the permissions for the users who are members of the group, and the permissions for users who are neither the owners nor members of the group.

By default, Hadoop runs with security disabled, which means that a client's identity is not authenticated. Because clients are remote, it is possible for a client to become an arbitrary user simply by creating an account of that name on the remote system. This is not possible if security is turned on; see "Security" on page 309. Either way, it is worthwhile having permissions enabled (as they are by default; see the dfs.permis sions.enabled property) to avoid accidental modification or deletion of substantial parts of the filesystem, either by users or by automated tools or programs.

When permissions checking is enabled, the owner permissions are checked if the client's username matches the owner, and the group permissions are checked if the client is a member of the group; otherwise, the other permissions are checked.

There is a concept of a superuser, which is the identity of the namenode process. Permissions checks are not performed for the superuser.

Hadoop Filesystems

Hadoop has an abstract notion of filesystems, of which HDFS is just one implementation. The Java abstract class `org.apache.hadoop.fs.FileSystem` represents the client interface to a filesystem in Hadoop, and there are several concrete implementations. The main ones that ship with Hadoop are described in Table 3-1.

Table 3-1. Hadoop filesystems

Filesystem	URI scheme	Java implementation (all under org.apache.hadoop)	Description
Local	file	`fs.LocalFileSystem`	A filesystem for a locally connected disk with client-side checksums. Use `RawLocal FileSystem` for a local filesystem with no checksums. See "LocalFileSystem" on page 99.
HDFS	hdfs	`hdfs.DistributedFileSystem`	Hadoop's distributed filesystem. HDFS is designed to work efficiently in conjunction with MapReduce.
WebHDFS	webhdfs	`hdfs.web.WebHdfsFileSystem`	A filesystem providing authenticated read/write access to HDFS over HTTP. See "HTTP" on page 54.
Secure WebHDFS	swebhdfs	`hdfs.web.SWebHdfsFileSystem`	The HTTPS version of WebHDFS.
HAR	har	`fs.HarFileSystem`	A filesystem layered on another filesystem for archiving files. Hadoop Archives are used for packing lots of files in HDFS into a single archive file to reduce the namenode's memory usage. Use the `hadoop archive` command to create HAR files.
View	viewfs	`viewfs.ViewFileSystem`	A client-side mount table for other Hadoop filesystems. Commonly used to create mount points for federated namenodes (see "HDFS Federation" on page 48).
FTP	ftp	`fs.ftp.FTPFileSystem`	A filesystem backed by an FTP server.
S3	s3a	`fs.s3a.S3AFileSystem`	A filesystem backed by Amazon S3. Replaces the older `s3n` (S3 native) implementation.

Filesystem	URI scheme	Java implementation (all under org.apache.hadoop)	Description
Azure	wasb	`fs.azure.NativeAzureFileSystem`	A filesystem backed by Microsoft Azure.
Swift	swift	`fs.swift.snative.SwiftNativeFileSystem`	A filesystem backed by OpenStack Swift.

Hadoop provides many interfaces to its filesystems, and it generally uses the URI scheme to pick the correct filesystem instance to communicate with. For example, the filesystem shell that we met in the previous section operates with all Hadoop filesystems. To list the files in the root directory of the local filesystem, type:

```
% hadoop fs -ls file:///
```

Although it is possible (and sometimes very convenient) to run MapReduce programs that access any of these filesystems, when you are processing large volumes of data you should choose a distributed filesystem that has the data locality optimization, notably HDFS (see "Scaling Out" on page 30).

Interfaces

Hadoop is written in Java, so most Hadoop filesystem interactions are mediated through the Java API. The filesystem shell, for example, is a Java application that uses the Java `FileSystem` class to provide filesystem operations. The other filesystem interfaces are discussed briefly in this section. These interfaces are most commonly used with HDFS, since the other filesystems in Hadoop typically have existing tools to access the underlying filesystem (FTP clients for FTP, S3 tools for S3, etc.), but many of them will work with any Hadoop filesystem.

HTTP

By exposing its filesystem interface as a Java API, Hadoop makes it awkward for non-Java applications to access HDFS. The HTTP REST API exposed by the WebHDFS protocol makes it easier for other languages to interact with HDFS. Note that the HTTP interface is slower than the native Java client, so should be avoided for very large data transfers if possible.

There are two ways of accessing HDFS over HTTP: directly, where the HDFS daemons serve HTTP requests to clients; and via a proxy (or proxies), which accesses HDFS on the client's behalf using the usual `DistributedFileSystem` API. The two ways are illustrated in Figure 3-1. Both use the WebHDFS protocol.

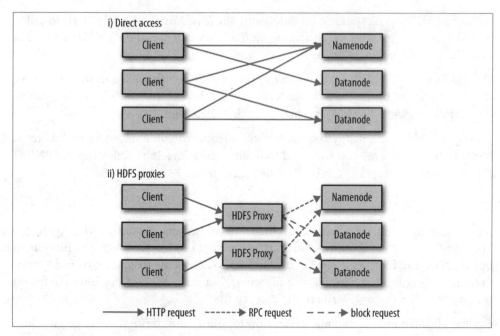

Figure 3-1. Accessing HDFS over HTTP directly and via a bank of HDFS proxies

In the first case, the embedded web servers in the namenode and datanodes act as WebHDFS endpoints. (WebHDFS is enabled by default, since dfs.webhdfs.enabled is set to true.) File metadata operations are handled by the namenode, while file read (and write) operations are sent first to the namenode, which sends an HTTP redirect to the client indicating the datanode to stream file data from (or to).

The second way of accessing HDFS over HTTP relies on one or more standalone proxy servers. (The proxies are stateless, so they can run behind a standard load balancer.) All traffic to the cluster passes through the proxy, so the client never accesses the namenode or datanode directly. This allows for stricter firewall and bandwidth-limiting policies to be put in place. It's common to use a proxy for transfers between Hadoop clusters located in different data centers, or when accessing a Hadoop cluster running in the cloud from an external network.

The HttpFS proxy exposes the same HTTP (and HTTPS) interface as WebHDFS, so clients can access both using webhdfs (or swebhdfs) URIs. The HttpFS proxy is started independently of the namenode and datanode daemons, using the *httpfs.sh* script, and by default listens on a different port number (14000).

C

Hadoop provides a C library called *libhdfs* that mirrors the Java FileSystem interface (it was written as a C library for accessing HDFS, but despite its name it can be used to access any Hadoop filesystem). It works using the *Java Native Interface* (JNI) to call a Java filesystem client. There is also a *libwebhdfs* library that uses the WebHDFS interface described in the previous section.

The C API is very similar to the Java one, but it typically lags the Java one, so some newer features may not be supported. You can find the header file, *hdfs.h*, in the *include* directory of the Apache Hadoop binary tarball distribution.

The Apache Hadoop binary tarball comes with prebuilt *libhdfs* binaries for 64-bit Linux, but for other platforms you will need to build them yourself by following the *BUILD ING.txt* instructions at the top level of the source tree.

NFS

It is possible to mount HDFS on a local client's filesystem using Hadoop's NFSv3 gateway. You can then use Unix utilities (such as `ls` and `cat`) to interact with the filesystem, upload files, and in general use POSIX libraries to access the filesystem from any programming language. Appending to a file works, but random modifications of a file do not, since HDFS can only write to the end of a file.

Consult the Hadoop documentation for how to configure and run the NFS gateway and connect to it from a client.

FUSE

Filesystem in Userspace (FUSE) allows filesystems that are implemented in user space to be integrated as Unix filesystems. Hadoop's Fuse-DFS contrib module allows HDFS (or any Hadoop filesystem) to be mounted as a standard local filesystem. Fuse-DFS is implemented in C using *libhdfs* as the interface to HDFS. At the time of writing, the Hadoop NFS gateway is the more robust solution to mounting HDFS, so should be preferred over Fuse-DFS.

The Java Interface

In this section, we dig into the Hadoop `FileSystem` class: the API for interacting with one of Hadoop's filesystems.[6] Although we focus mainly on the HDFS implementation, `DistributedFileSystem`, in general you should strive to write your code against the `FileSystem` abstract class, to retain portability across filesystems. This is very useful when testing your program, for example, because you can rapidly run tests using data stored on the local filesystem.

---

6. In Hadoop 2 and later, there is a new filesystem interface called `FileContext` with better handling of multiple filesystems (so a single `FileContext` can resolve multiple filesystem schemes, for example) and a cleaner, more consistent interface. `FileSystem` is still more widely used, however.

Reading Data from a Hadoop URL

One of the simplest ways to read a file from a Hadoop filesystem is by using a `java.net.URL` object to open a stream to read the data from. The general idiom is:

```
InputStream in = null;
try {
  in = new URL("hdfs://host/path").openStream();
  // process in
} finally {
  IOUtils.closeStream(in);
}
```

There's a little bit more work required to make Java recognize Hadoop's `hdfs` URL scheme. This is achieved by calling the `setURLStreamHandlerFactory()` method on URL with an instance of `FsUrlStreamHandlerFactory`. This method can be called only once per JVM, so it is typically executed in a static block. This limitation means that if some other part of your program—perhaps a third-party component outside your control—sets a `URLStreamHandlerFactory`, you won't be able to use this approach for reading data from Hadoop. The next section discusses an alternative.

Example 3-1 shows a program for displaying files from Hadoop filesystems on standard output, like the Unix `cat` command.

Example 3-1. Displaying files from a Hadoop filesystem on standard output using a URLStreamHandler

```
public class URLCat {

  static {
    URL.setURLStreamHandlerFactory(new FsUrlStreamHandlerFactory());
  }

  public static void main(String[] args) throws Exception {
    InputStream in = null;
    try {
      in = new URL(args[0]).openStream();
      IOUtils.copyBytes(in, System.out, 4096, false);
    } finally {
      IOUtils.closeStream(in);
    }
  }
}
```

We make use of the handy `IOUtils` class that comes with Hadoop for closing the stream in the `finally` clause, and also for copying bytes between the input stream and the output stream (`System.out`, in this case). The last two arguments to the `copyBytes()` method are the buffer size used for copying and whether to close the streams when the copy is complete. We close the input stream ourselves, and `System.out` doesn't need to be closed.

Here's a sample run:[7]

```
% export HADOOP_CLASSPATH=hadoop-examples.jar
% hadoop URLCat hdfs://localhost/user/tom/quangle.txt
On the top of the Crumpetty Tree
The Quangle Wangle sat,
But his face you could not see,
On account of his Beaver Hat.
```

Reading Data Using the FileSystem API

As the previous section explained, sometimes it is impossible to set a URLStreamHand
lerFactory for your application. In this case, you will need to use the FileSystem API
to open an input stream for a file.

A file in a Hadoop filesystem is represented by a Hadoop Path object (and not
a java.io.File object, since its semantics are too closely tied to the local filesystem).
You can think of a Path as a Hadoop filesystem URI, such as hdfs://localhost/user/
tom/quangle.txt.

FileSystem is a general filesystem API, so the first step is to retrieve an instance for the
filesystem we want to use—HDFS, in this case. There are several static factory methods
for getting a FileSystem instance:

```
public static FileSystem get(Configuration conf) throws IOException
public static FileSystem get(URI uri, Configuration conf) throws IOException
public static FileSystem get(URI uri, Configuration conf, String user)
    throws IOException
```

A Configuration object encapsulates a client or server's configuration, which is set
using configuration files read from the classpath, such as *etc/hadoop/core-site.xml*. The
first method returns the default filesystem (as specified in *core-site.xml*, or the default
local filesystem if not specified there). The second uses the given URI's scheme and
authority to determine the filesystem to use, falling back to the default filesystem if no
scheme is specified in the given URI. The third retrieves the filesystem as the given user,
which is important in the context of security (see "Security" on page 309).

In some cases, you may want to retrieve a local filesystem instance. For this, you can
use the convenience method getLocal():

```
public static LocalFileSystem getLocal(Configuration conf) throws IOException
```

With a FileSystem instance in hand, we invoke an open() method to get the input
stream for a file:

```
public FSDataInputStream open(Path f) throws IOException
public abstract FSDataInputStream open(Path f, int bufferSize) throws IOException
```

---

7. The text is from *The Quangle Wangle's Hat* by Edward Lear.

The first method uses a default buffer size of 4 KB.

Putting this together, we can rewrite Example 3-1 as shown in Example 3-2.

Example 3-2. Displaying files from a Hadoop filesystem on standard output by using the FileSystem directly

```java
public class FileSystemCat {

  public static void main(String[] args) throws Exception {
    String uri = args[0];
    Configuration conf = new Configuration();
    FileSystem fs = FileSystem.get(URI.create(uri), conf);
    InputStream in = null;
    try {
      in = fs.open(new Path(uri));
      IOUtils.copyBytes(in, System.out, 4096, false);
    } finally {
      IOUtils.closeStream(in);
    }
  }
}
```

The program runs as follows:

```
% hadoop FileSystemCat hdfs://localhost/user/tom/quangle.txt
On the top of the Crumpetty Tree
The Quangle Wangle sat,
But his face you could not see,
On account of his Beaver Hat.
```

FSDataInputStream

The open() method on FileSystem actually returns an FSDataInputStream rather than a standard java.io class. This class is a specialization of java.io.DataInputStream with support for random access, so you can read from any part of the stream:

```java
package org.apache.hadoop.fs;

public class FSDataInputStream extends DataInputStream
    implements Seekable, PositionedReadable {
  // implementation elided
}
```

The Seekable interface permits seeking to a position in the file and provides a query method for the current offset from the start of the file (getPos()):

```java
public interface Seekable {
  void seek(long pos) throws IOException;
  long getPos() throws IOException;
}
```

Calling seek() with a position that is greater than the length of the file will result in an IOException. Unlike the skip() method of java.io.InputStream, which positions the stream at a point later than the current position, seek() can move to an arbitrary, absolute position in the file.

A simple extension of Example 3-2 is shown in Example 3-3, which writes a file to standard output twice: after writing it once, it seeks to the start of the file and streams through it once again.

Example 3-3. Displaying files from a Hadoop filesystem on standard output twice, by using seek()

```
public class FileSystemDoubleCat {

  public static void main(String[] args) throws Exception {
    String uri = args[0];
    Configuration conf = new Configuration();
    FileSystem fs = FileSystem.get(URI.create(uri), conf);
    FSDataInputStream in = null;
    try {
      in = fs.open(new Path(uri));
      IOUtils.copyBytes(in, System.out, 4096, false);
      in.seek(0); // go back to the start of the file
      IOUtils.copyBytes(in, System.out, 4096, false);
    } finally {
      IOUtils.closeStream(in);
    }
  }
}
```

Here's the result of running it on a small file:

```
% hadoop FileSystemDoubleCat hdfs://localhost/user/tom/quangle.txt
On the top of the Crumpetty Tree
The Quangle Wangle sat,
But his face you could not see,
On account of his Beaver Hat.
On the top of the Crumpetty Tree
The Quangle Wangle sat,
But his face you could not see,
On account of his Beaver Hat.
```

FSDataInputStream also implements the PositionedReadable interface for reading parts of a file at a given offset:

```
public interface PositionedReadable {

  public int read(long position, byte[] buffer, int offset, int length)
      throws IOException;

  public void readFully(long position, byte[] buffer, int offset, int length)
      throws IOException;
```

```
    public void readFully(long position, byte[] buffer) throws IOException;
}
```

The read() method reads up to length bytes from the given position in the file into the buffer at the given offset in the buffer. The return value is the number of bytes actually read; callers should check this value, as it may be less than length. The read Fully() methods will read length bytes into the buffer (or buffer.length bytes for the version that just takes a byte array buffer), unless the end of the file is reached, in which case an EOFException is thrown.

All of these methods preserve the current offset in the file and are thread safe (although FSDataInputStream is not designed for concurrent access; therefore, it's better to create multiple instances), so they provide a convenient way to access another part of the file—metadata, perhaps—while reading the main body of the file.

Finally, bear in mind that calling seek() is a relatively expensive operation and should be done sparingly. You should structure your application access patterns to rely on streaming data (by using MapReduce, for example) rather than performing a large number of seeks.

Writing Data

The FileSystem class has a number of methods for creating a file. The simplest is the method that takes a Path object for the file to be created and returns an output stream to write to:

```
    public FSDataOutputStream create(Path f) throws IOException
```

There are overloaded versions of this method that allow you to specify whether to forcibly overwrite existing files, the replication factor of the file, the buffer size to use when writing the file, the block size for the file, and file permissions.

The create() methods create any parent directories of the file to be written that don't already exist. Though convenient, this behavior may be unexpected. If you want the write to fail when the parent directory doesn't exist, you should check for the existence of the parent directory first by calling the exists() method. Alternatively, use FileContext, which allows you to control whether parent directories are created or not.

There's also an overloaded method for passing a callback interface, Progressable, so your application can be notified of the progress of the data being written to the datanodes:

```
package org.apache.hadoop.util;

public interface Progressable {
  public void progress();
}
```

As an alternative to creating a new file, you can append to an existing file using the append() method (there are also some other overloaded versions):

```
public FSDataOutputStream append(Path f) throws IOException
```

The append operation allows a single writer to modify an already written file by opening it and writing data from the final offset in the file. With this API, applications that produce unbounded files, such as logfiles, can write to an existing file after having closed it. The append operation is optional and not implemented by all Hadoop filesystems. For example, HDFS supports append, but S3 filesystems don't.

Example 3-4 shows how to copy a local file to a Hadoop filesystem. We illustrate progress by printing a period every time the progress() method is called by Hadoop, which is after each 64 KB packet of data is written to the datanode pipeline. (Note that this particular behavior is not specified by the API, so it is subject to change in later versions of Hadoop. The API merely allows you to infer that "something is happening.")

Example 3-4. Copying a local file to a Hadoop filesystem

```
public class FileCopyWithProgress {
  public static void main(String[] args) throws Exception {
    String localSrc = args[0];
    String dst = args[1];

    InputStream in = new BufferedInputStream(new FileInputStream(localSrc));

    Configuration conf = new Configuration();
    FileSystem fs = FileSystem.get(URI.create(dst), conf);
    OutputStream out = fs.create(new Path(dst), new Progressable() {
      public void progress() {
        System.out.print(".");
      }
    });

    IOUtils.copyBytes(in, out, 4096, true);
  }
}
```

Typical usage:

```
% hadoop FileCopyWithProgress input/docs/1400-8.txt
hdfs://localhost/user/tom/1400-8.txt
.................
```

Currently, none of the other Hadoop filesystems call progress() during writes. Progress is important in MapReduce applications, as you will see in later chapters.

FSDataOutputStream

The `create()` method on `FileSystem` returns an `FSDataOutputStream`, which, like `FSDataInputStream`, has a method for querying the current position in the file:

```
package org.apache.hadoop.fs;

public class FSDataOutputStream extends DataOutputStream implements Syncable {

  public long getPos() throws IOException {
    // implementation elided
  }

  // implementation elided

}
```

However, unlike `FSDataInputStream`, `FSDataOutputStream` does not permit seeking. This is because HDFS allows only sequential writes to an open file or appends to an already written file. In other words, there is no support for writing to anywhere other than the end of the file, so there is no value in being able to seek while writing.

Directories

`FileSystem` provides a method to create a directory:

```
public boolean mkdirs(Path f) throws IOException
```

This method creates all of the necessary parent directories if they don't already exist, just like the `java.io.File`'s `mkdirs()` method. It returns `true` if the directory (and all parent directories) was (were) successfully created.

Often, you don't need to explicitly create a directory, because writing a file by calling `create()` will automatically create any parent directories.

Querying the Filesystem

File metadata: FileStatus

An important feature of any filesystem is the ability to navigate its directory structure and retrieve information about the files and directories that it stores. The `FileStatus` class encapsulates filesystem metadata for files and directories, including file length, block size, replication, modification time, ownership, and permission information.

The method `getFileStatus()` on `FileSystem` provides a way of getting a `FileStatus` object for a single file or directory. Example 3-5 shows an example of its use.

Example 3-5. Demonstrating file status information

```java
public class ShowFileStatusTest {

  private MiniDFSCluster cluster; // use an in-process HDFS cluster for testing
  private FileSystem fs;

  @Before
  public void setUp() throws IOException {
    Configuration conf = new Configuration();
    if (System.getProperty("test.build.data") == null) {
      System.setProperty("test.build.data", "/tmp");
    }
    cluster = new MiniDFSCluster.Builder(conf).build();
    fs = cluster.getFileSystem();
    OutputStream out = fs.create(new Path("/dir/file"));
    out.write("content".getBytes("UTF-8"));
    out.close();
  }

  @After
  public void tearDown() throws IOException {
    if (fs != null) { fs.close(); }
    if (cluster != null) { cluster.shutdown(); }
  }

  @Test(expected = FileNotFoundException.class)
  public void throwsFileNotFoundForNonExistentFile() throws IOException {
    fs.getFileStatus(new Path("no-such-file"));
  }

  @Test
  public void fileStatusForFile() throws IOException {
    Path file = new Path("/dir/file");
    FileStatus stat = fs.getFileStatus(file);
    assertThat(stat.getPath().toUri().getPath(), is("/dir/file"));
    assertThat(stat.isDirectory(), is(false));
    assertThat(stat.getLen(), is(7L));
    assertThat(stat.getModificationTime(),
        is(lessThanOrEqualTo(System.currentTimeMillis())));
    assertThat(stat.getReplication(), is((short) 1));
    assertThat(stat.getBlockSize(), is(128 * 1024 * 1024L));
    assertThat(stat.getOwner(), is(System.getProperty("user.name")));
    assertThat(stat.getGroup(), is("supergroup"));
    assertThat(stat.getPermission().toString(), is("rw-r--r--"));
  }

  @Test
  public void fileStatusForDirectory() throws IOException {
    Path dir = new Path("/dir");
    FileStatus stat = fs.getFileStatus(dir);
    assertThat(stat.getPath().toUri().getPath(), is("/dir"));
    assertThat(stat.isDirectory(), is(true));
```

```
    assertThat(stat.getLen(), is(0L));
    assertThat(stat.getModificationTime(),
        is(lessThanOrEqualTo(System.currentTimeMillis())));
    assertThat(stat.getReplication(), is((short) 0));
    assertThat(stat.getBlockSize(), is(0L));
    assertThat(stat.getOwner(), is(System.getProperty("user.name")));
    assertThat(stat.getGroup(), is("supergroup"));
    assertThat(stat.getPermission().toString(), is("rwxr-xr-x"));
  }

}
```

If no file or directory exists, a FileNotFoundException is thrown. However, if you are interested only in the existence of a file or directory, the exists() method on FileSystem is more convenient:

```
public boolean exists(Path f) throws IOException
```

Listing files

Finding information on a single file or directory is useful, but you also often need to be able to list the contents of a directory. That's what FileSystem's listStatus() methods are for:

```
public FileStatus[] listStatus(Path f) throws IOException
public FileStatus[] listStatus(Path f, PathFilter filter) throws IOException
public FileStatus[] listStatus(Path[] files) throws IOException
public FileStatus[] listStatus(Path[] files, PathFilter filter)
        throws IOException
```

When the argument is a file, the simplest variant returns an array of FileStatus objects of length 1. When the argument is a directory, it returns zero or more FileStatus objects representing the files and directories contained in the directory.

Overloaded variants allow a PathFilter to be supplied to restrict the files and directories to match. You will see an example of this in the section "PathFilter" on page 67. Finally, if you specify an array of paths, the result is a shortcut for calling the equivalent single-path listStatus() method for each path in turn and accumulating the FileStatus object arrays in a single array. This can be useful for building up lists of input files to process from distinct parts of the filesystem tree. Example 3-6 is a simple demonstration of this idea. Note the use of stat2Paths() in Hadoop's FileUtil for turning an array of FileStatus objects into an array of Path objects.

Example 3-6. Showing the file statuses for a collection of paths in a Hadoop filesystem

```
public class ListStatus {

  public static void main(String[] args) throws Exception {
    String uri = args[0];
    Configuration conf = new Configuration();
    FileSystem fs = FileSystem.get(URI.create(uri), conf);
```

```
    Path[] paths = new Path[args.length];
    for (int i = 0; i < paths.length; i++) {
      paths[i] = new Path(args[i]);
    }

    FileStatus[] status = fs.listStatus(paths);
    Path[] listedPaths = FileUtil.stat2Paths(status);
    for (Path p : listedPaths) {
      System.out.println(p);
    }
  }
}
```

We can use this program to find the union of directory listings for a collection of paths:

```
% hadoop ListStatus hdfs://localhost/ hdfs://localhost/user/tom
hdfs://localhost/user
hdfs://localhost/user/tom/books
hdfs://localhost/user/tom/quangle.txt
```

File patterns

It is a common requirement to process sets of files in a single operation. For example, a MapReduce job for log processing might analyze a month's worth of files contained in a number of directories. Rather than having to enumerate each file and directory to specify the input, it is convenient to use wildcard characters to match multiple files with a single expression, an operation that is known as *globbing*. Hadoop provides two FileSystem methods for processing globs:

```
public FileStatus[] globStatus(Path pathPattern) throws IOException
public FileStatus[] globStatus(Path pathPattern, PathFilter filter)
    throws IOException
```

The globStatus() methods return an array of FileStatus objects whose paths match the supplied pattern, sorted by path. An optional PathFilter can be specified to restrict the matches further.

Hadoop supports the same set of glob characters as the Unix bash shell (see Table 3-2).

Table 3-2. Glob characters and their meanings

Glob	Name	Matches
*	asterisk	Matches zero or more characters
?	question mark	Matches a single character
[ab]	character class	Matches a single character in the set {a, b}
[^ab]	negated character class	Matches a single character that is not in the set {a, b}
[a-b]	character range	Matches a single character in the (closed) range [a, b], where a is lexicographically less than or equal to b

Glob	Name	Matches
[^a-b]	*negated character range*	Matches a single character that is not in the (closed) range [a, b], where a is lexicographically less than or equal to b
{a,b}	*alternation*	Matches either expression a or b
\c	*escaped character*	Matches character c when it is a metacharacter

Imagine that logfiles are stored in a directory structure organized hierarchically by date. So, logfiles for the last day of 2007 would go in a directory named */2007/12/31*, for example. Suppose that the full file listing is:

```
/
├── 2007/
│   └── 12/
│       ├── 30/
│       └── 31/
└── 2008/
    └── 01/
        ├── 01/
        └── 02/
```

Here are some file globs and their expansions:

Glob	Expansion
/*	*/2007 /2008*
/*/*	*/2007/12 /2008/01*
/*/12/*	*/2007/12/30 /2007/12/31*
/200?	*/2007 /2008*
/200[78]	*/2007 /2008*
/200[7-8]	*/2007 /2008*
/200[^01234569]	*/2007 /2008*
/*/*/{31,01}	*/2007/12/31 /2008/01/01*
/*/*/3{0,1}	*/2007/12/30 /2007/12/31*
/*/{12/31,01/01}	*/2007/12/31 /2008/01/01*

PathFilter

Glob patterns are not always powerful enough to describe a set of files you want to access. For example, it is not generally possible to exclude a particular file using a glob pattern. The listStatus() and globStatus() methods of FileSystem take an optional PathFilter, which allows programmatic control over matching:

```
package org.apache.hadoop.fs;

public interface PathFilter {
  boolean accept(Path path);
}
```

`PathFilter` is the equivalent of `java.io.FileFilter` for `Path` objects rather than `File` objects.

Example 3-7 shows a `PathFilter` for excluding paths that match a regular expression.

Example 3-7. A PathFilter for excluding paths that match a regular expression

```
public class RegexExcludePathFilter implements PathFilter {

  private final String regex;

  public RegexExcludePathFilter(String regex) {
    this.regex = regex;
  }

  public boolean accept(Path path) {
    return !path.toString().matches(regex);
  }
}
```

The filter passes only those files that *don't* match the regular expression. After the glob picks out an initial set of files to include, the filter is used to refine the results. For example:

```
fs.globStatus(new Path("/2007/*/*"), new RegexExcludeFilter("^.*/2007/12/31$"))
```

will expand to */2007/12/30*.

Filters can act only on a file's name, as represented by a `Path`. They can't use a file's properties, such as creation time, as their basis. Nevertheless, they can perform matching that neither glob patterns nor regular expressions can achieve. For example, if you store files in a directory structure that is laid out by date (like in the previous section), you can write a `PathFilter` to pick out files that fall in a given date range.

Deleting Data

Use the `delete()` method on `FileSystem` to permanently remove files or directories:

```
public boolean delete(Path f, boolean recursive) throws IOException
```

If `f` is a file or an empty directory, the value of `recursive` is ignored. A nonempty directory is deleted, along with its contents, only if `recursive` is `true` (otherwise, an `IOException` is thrown).

Data Flow

Anatomy of a File Read

To get an idea of how data flows between the client interacting with HDFS, the name-node, and the datanodes, consider Figure 3-2, which shows the main sequence of events when reading a file.

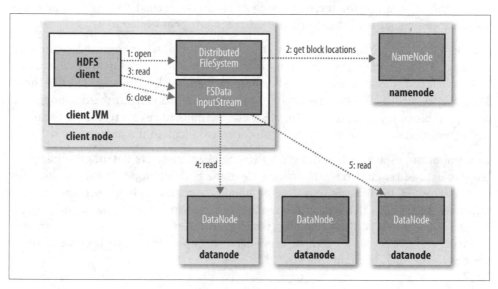

Figure 3-2. A client reading data from HDFS

The client opens the file it wishes to read by calling open() on the FileSystem object, which for HDFS is an instance of DistributedFileSystem (step 1 in Figure 3-2). DistributedFileSystem calls the namenode, using remote procedure calls (RPCs), to determine the locations of the first few blocks in the file (step 2). For each block, the namenode returns the addresses of the datanodes that have a copy of that block. Furthermore, the datanodes are sorted according to their proximity to the client (according to the topology of the cluster's network; see "Network Topology and Hadoop" on page 70). If the client is itself a datanode (in the case of a MapReduce task, for instance), the client will read from the local datanode if that datanode hosts a copy of the block (see also Figure 2-2 and "Short-circuit local reads" on page 308).

The DistributedFileSystem returns an FSDataInputStream (an input stream that supports file seeks) to the client for it to read data from. FSDataInputStream in turn wraps a DFSInputStream, which manages the datanode and namenode I/O.

The client then calls read() on the stream (step 3). DFSInputStream, which has stored the datanode addresses for the first few blocks in the file, then connects to the first (closest) datanode for the first block in the file. Data is streamed from the datanode back to the client, which calls `read()` repeatedly on the stream (step 4). When the end of the block is reached, DFSInputStream will close the connection to the datanode, then find the best datanode for the next block (step 5). This happens transparently to the client, which from its point of view is just reading a continuous stream.

Blocks are read in order, with the DFSInputStream opening new connections to datanodes as the client reads through the stream. It will also call the namenode to retrieve the datanode locations for the next batch of blocks as needed. When the client has finished reading, it calls `close()` on the FSDataInputStream (step 6).

During reading, if the DFSInputStream encounters an error while communicating with a datanode, it will try the next closest one for that block. It will also remember datanodes that have failed so that it doesn't needlessly retry them for later blocks. The DFSInput Stream also verifies checksums for the data transferred to it from the datanode. If a corrupted block is found, the DFSInputStream attempts to read a replica of the block from another datanode; it also reports the corrupted block to the namenode.

One important aspect of this design is that the client contacts datanodes directly to retrieve data and is guided by the namenode to the best datanode for each block. This design allows HDFS to scale to a large number of concurrent clients because the data traffic is spread across all the datanodes in the cluster. Meanwhile, the namenode merely has to service block location requests (which it stores in memory, making them very efficient) and does not, for example, serve data, which would quickly become a bottleneck as the number of clients grew.

Network Topology and Hadoop

What does it mean for two nodes in a local network to be "close" to each other? In the context of high-volume data processing, the limiting factor is the rate at which we can transfer data between nodes—bandwidth is a scarce commodity. The idea is to use the bandwidth between two nodes as a measure of distance.

Rather than measuring bandwidth between nodes, which can be difficult to do in practice (it requires a quiet cluster, and the number of pairs of nodes in a cluster grows as the square of the number of nodes), Hadoop takes a simple approach in which the network is represented as a tree and the distance between two nodes is the sum of their distances to their closest common ancestor. Levels in the tree are not predefined, but it is common to have levels that correspond to the data center, the rack, and the node that a process is running on. The idea is that the bandwidth available for each of the following scenarios becomes progressively less:

- Processes on the same node
- Different nodes on the same rack

- Nodes on different racks in the same data center
- Nodes in different data centers[8]

For example, imagine a node *n1* on rack *r1* in data center *d1*. This can be represented as */d1/r1/n1*. Using this notation, here are the distances for the four scenarios:

- *distance(/d1/r1/n1, /d1/r1/n1)* = 0 (processes on the same node)
- *distance(/d1/r1/n1, /d1/r1/n2)* = 2 (different nodes on the same rack)
- *distance(/d1/r1/n1, /d1/r2/n3)* = 4 (nodes on different racks in the same data center)
- *distance(/d1/r1/n1, /d2/r3/n4)* = 6 (nodes in different data centers)

This is illustrated schematically in Figure 3-3. (Mathematically inclined readers will notice that this is an example of a distance metric.)

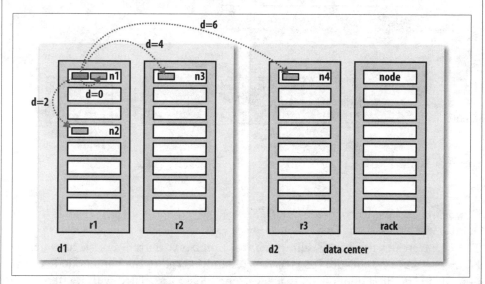

Figure 3-3. Network distance in Hadoop

Finally, it is important to realize that Hadoop cannot magically discover your network topology for you; it needs some help (we'll cover how to configure topology in "Network Topology" on page 286). By default, though, it assumes that the network is flat—a single-level hierarchy—or in other words, that all nodes are on a single rack in a single data center. For small clusters, this may actually be the case, and no further configuration is required.

---

8. At the time of this writing, Hadoop is not suited for running across data centers.

Anatomy of a File Write

Next we'll look at how files are written to HDFS. Although quite detailed, it is instructive to understand the data flow because it clarifies HDFS's coherency model.

We're going to consider the case of creating a new file, writing data to it, then closing the file. This is illustrated in Figure 3-4.

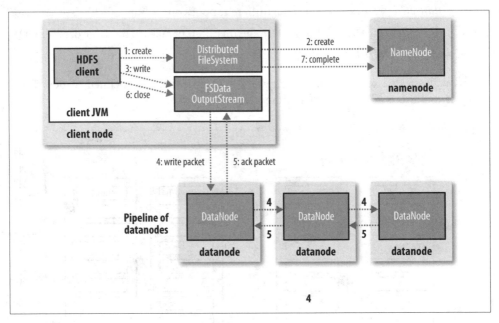

Figure 3-4. A client writing data to HDFS

The client creates the file by calling `create()` on `DistributedFileSystem` (step 1 in Figure 3-4). `DistributedFileSystem` makes an RPC call to the namenode to create a new file in the filesystem's namespace, with no blocks associated with it (step 2). The namenode performs various checks to make sure the file doesn't already exist and that the client has the right permissions to create the file. If these checks pass, the namenode makes a record of the new file; otherwise, file creation fails and the client is thrown an `IOException`. The `DistributedFileSystem` returns an `FSDataOutputStream` for the client to start writing data to. Just as in the read case, `FSDataOutputStream` wraps a `DFSOutputStream`, which handles communication with the datanodes and namenode.

As the client writes data (step 3), the `DFSOutputStream` splits it into packets, which it writes to an internal queue called the *data queue*. The data queue is consumed by the `DataStreamer`, which is responsible for asking the namenode to allocate new blocks by picking a list of suitable datanodes to store the replicas. The list of datanodes forms a pipeline, and here we'll assume the replication level is three, so there are three nodes in the pipeline. The DataStreamer streams the packets to the first datanode in the pipeline, which stores each packet and forwards it to the second datanode in the pipeline. Similarly, the second datanode stores the packet and forwards it to the third (and last) datanode in the pipeline (step 4).

The DFSOutputStream also maintains an internal queue of packets that are waiting to be acknowledged by datanodes, called the *ack queue*. A packet is removed from the ack queue only when it has been acknowledged by all the datanodes in the pipeline (step 5).

If any datanode fails while data is being written to it, then the following actions are taken, which are transparent to the client writing the data. First, the pipeline is closed, and any packets in the ack queue are added to the front of the data queue so that datanodes that are downstream from the failed node will not miss any packets. The current block on the good datanodes is given a new identity, which is communicated to the namenode, so that the partial block on the failed datanode will be deleted if the failed datanode recovers later on. The failed datanode is removed from the pipeline, and a new pipeline is constructed from the two good datanodes. The remainder of the block's data is written to the good datanodes in the pipeline. The namenode notices that the block is under-replicated, and it arranges for a further replica to be created on another node. Subsequent blocks are then treated as normal.

It's possible, but unlikely, for multiple datanodes to fail while a block is being written. As long as dfs.namenode.replication.min replicas (which defaults to 1) are written, the write will succeed, and the block will be asynchronously replicated across the cluster until its target replication factor is reached (dfs.replication, which defaults to 3).

When the client has finished writing data, it calls close() on the stream (step 6). This action flushes all the remaining packets to the datanode pipeline and waits for acknowledgments before contacting the namenode to signal that the file is complete (step 7). The namenode already knows which blocks the file is made up of (because Data Streamer asks for block allocations), so it only has to wait for blocks to be minimally replicated before returning successfully.

Replica Placement

How does the namenode choose which datanodes to store replicas on? There's a trade-off between reliability and write bandwidth and read bandwidth here. For example, placing all replicas on a single node incurs the lowest write bandwidth penalty (since the replication pipeline runs on a single node), but this offers no real redundancy (if the node fails, the data for that block is lost). Also, the read bandwidth is high for off-rack reads. At the other extreme, placing replicas in different data centers may maximize redundancy, but at the cost of bandwidth. Even in the same data center (which is what all Hadoop clusters to date have run in), there are a variety of possible placement strategies.

Hadoop's default strategy is to place the first replica on the same node as the client (for clients running outside the cluster, a node is chosen at random, although the system tries not to pick nodes that are too full or too busy). The second replica is placed on a different rack from the first (*off-rack*), chosen at random. The third replica is placed on the same rack as the second, but on a different node chosen at random. Further replicas are placed on random nodes in the cluster, although the system tries to avoid placing too many replicas on the same rack.

Once the replica locations have been chosen, a pipeline is built, taking network topology into account. For a replication factor of 3, the pipeline might look like Figure 3-5.

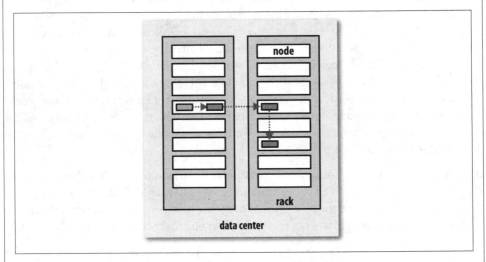

Figure 3-5. A typical replica pipeline

Overall, this strategy gives a good balance among reliability (blocks are stored on two racks), write bandwidth (writes only have to traverse a single network switch), read performance (there's a choice of two racks to read from), and block distribution across the cluster (clients only write a single block on the local rack).

Coherency Model

A coherency model for a filesystem describes the data visibility of reads and writes for a file. HDFS trades off some POSIX requirements for performance, so some operations may behave differently than you expect them to.

After creating a file, it is visible in the filesystem namespace, as expected:

```
Path p = new Path("p");
fs.create(p);
assertThat(fs.exists(p), is(true));
```

However, any content written to the file is not guaranteed to be visible, even if the stream is flushed. So, the file appears to have a length of zero:

```
Path p = new Path("p");
OutputStream out = fs.create(p);
out.write("content".getBytes("UTF-8"));
out.flush();
assertThat(fs.getFileStatus(p).getLen(), is(0L));
```

Once more than a block's worth of data has been written, the first block will be visible to new readers. This is true of subsequent blocks, too: it is always the current block being written that is not visible to other readers.

HDFS provides a way to force all buffers to be flushed to the datanodes via the hflush() method on FSDataOutputStream. After a successful return from hflush(), HDFS guarantees that the data written up to that point in the file has reached all the datanodes in the write pipeline and is visible to all new readers:

```
Path p = new Path("p");
FSDataOutputStream out = fs.create(p);
out.write("content".getBytes("UTF-8"));
out.hflush();
assertThat(fs.getFileStatus(p).getLen(), is(((long) "content".length())));
```

Note that hflush() does not guarantee that the datanodes have written the data to disk, only that it's in the datanodes' memory (so in the event of a data center power outage, for example, data could be lost). For this stronger guarantee, use hsync() instead.[9]

The behavior of hsync() is similar to that of the fsync() system call in POSIX that commits buffered data for a file descriptor. For example, using the standard Java API to write a local file, we are guaranteed to see the content after flushing the stream and synchronizing:

```
FileOutputStream out = new FileOutputStream(localFile);
out.write("content".getBytes("UTF-8"));
out.flush(); // flush to operating system
out.getFD().sync(); // sync to disk
assertThat(localFile.length(), is(((long) "content".length())));
```

Closing a file in HDFS performs an implicit hflush(), too:

```
Path p = new Path("p");
OutputStream out = fs.create(p);
out.write("content".getBytes("UTF-8"));
out.close();
assertThat(fs.getFileStatus(p).getLen(), is(((long) "content".length())));
```

---

9. In Hadoop 1.x, hflush() was called sync(), and hsync() did not exist.

Consequences for application design

This coherency model has implications for the way you design applications. With no calls to hflush() or hsync(), you should be prepared to lose up to a block of data in the event of client or system failure. For many applications, this is unacceptable, so you should call hflush() at suitable points, such as after writing a certain number of records or number of bytes. Though the hflush() operation is designed to not unduly tax HDFS, it does have some overhead (and hsync() has more), so there is a trade-off between data robustness and throughput. What constitutes an acceptable trade-off is application dependent, and suitable values can be selected after measuring your application's performance with different hflush() (or hsync()) frequencies.

Parallel Copying with distcp

The HDFS access patterns that we have seen so far focus on single-threaded access. It's possible to act on a collection of files—by specifying file globs, for example—but for efficient parallel processing of these files, you would have to write a program yourself. Hadoop comes with a useful program called *distcp* for copying data to and from Hadoop filesystems in parallel.

One use for *distcp* is as an efficient replacement for hadoop fs -cp. For example, you can copy one file to another with:[10]

```
% hadoop distcp file1 file2
```

You can also copy directories:

```
% hadoop distcp dir1 dir2
```

If *dir2* does not exist, it will be created, and the contents of the *dir1* directory will be copied there. You can specify multiple source paths, and all will be copied to the destination.

If *dir2* already exists, then *dir1* will be copied under it, creating the directory structure *dir2/dir1*. If this isn't what you want, you can supply the -overwrite option to keep the same directory structure and force files to be overwritten. You can also update only the files that have changed using the -update option. This is best shown with an example. If we changed a file in the *dir1* subtree, we could synchronize the change with *dir2* by running:

```
% hadoop distcp -update dir1 dir2
```

---

10. Even for a single file copy, the *distcp* variant is preferred for large files since hadoop fs -cp copies the file via the client running the command.

If you are unsure of the effect of a *distcp* operation, it is a good idea to try it out on a small test directory tree first.

distcp is implemented as a MapReduce job where the work of copying is done by the maps that run in parallel across the cluster. There are no reducers. Each file is copied by a single map, and *distcp* tries to give each map approximately the same amount of data by bucketing files into roughly equal allocations. By default, up to 20 maps are used, but this can be changed by specifying the `-m` argument to *distcp*.

A very common use case for *distcp* is for transferring data between two HDFS clusters. For example, the following creates a backup of the first cluster's */foo* directory on the second:

```
% hadoop distcp -update -delete -p hdfs://namenode1/foo hdfs://namenode2/foo
```

The `-delete` flag causes *distcp* to delete any files or directories from the destination that are not present in the source, and `-p` means that file status attributes like permissions, block size, and replication are preserved. You can run *distcp* with no arguments to see precise usage instructions.

If the two clusters are running incompatible versions of HDFS, then you can use the `webhdfs` protocol to *distcp* between them:

```
% hadoop distcp webhdfs://namenode1:50070/foo webhdfs://namenode2:50070/foo
```

Another variant is to use an HttpFs proxy as the *distcp* source or destination (again using the `webhdfs` protocol), which has the advantage of being able to set firewall and bandwidth controls (see "HTTP" on page 54).

Keeping an HDFS Cluster Balanced

When copying data into HDFS, it's important to consider cluster balance. HDFS works best when the file blocks are evenly spread across the cluster, so you want to ensure that *distcp* doesn't disrupt this. For example, if you specified `-m 1`, a single map would do the copy, which—apart from being slow and not using the cluster resources efficiently— would mean that the first replica of each block would reside on the node running the map (until the disk filled up). The second and third replicas would be spread across the cluster, but this one node would be unbalanced. By having more maps than nodes in the cluster, this problem is avoided. For this reason, it's best to start by running *distcp* with the default of 20 maps per node.

However, it's not always possible to prevent a cluster from becoming unbalanced. Perhaps you want to limit the number of maps so that some of the nodes can be used by other jobs. In this case, you can use the *balancer* tool (see "Balancer" on page 329) to subsequently even out the block distribution across the cluster.

YARN

Apache YARN (Yet Another Resource Negotiator) is Hadoop's cluster resource management system. YARN was introduced in Hadoop 2 to improve the MapReduce implementation, but it is general enough to support other distributed computing paradigms as well.

YARN provides APIs for requesting and working with cluster resources, but these APIs are not typically used directly by user code. Instead, users write to higher-level APIs provided by distributed computing frameworks, which themselves are built on YARN and hide the resource management details from the user. The situation is illustrated in Figure 4-1, which shows some distributed computing frameworks (MapReduce, Spark, and so on) running as *YARN applications* on the cluster compute layer (YARN) and the cluster storage layer (HDFS and HBase).

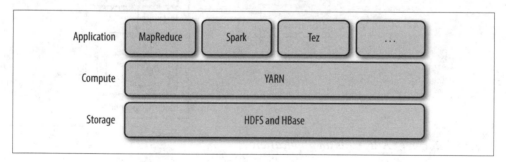

Figure 4-1. YARN applications

There is also a layer of applications that build on the frameworks shown in Figure 4-1. Pig, Hive, and Crunch are all examples of processing frameworks that run on MapReduce, Spark, or Tez (or on all three), and don't interact with YARN directly.

This chapter walks through the features in YARN and provides a basis for understanding later chapters in Part IV that cover Hadoop's distributed processing frameworks.

Anatomy of a YARN Application Run

YARN provides its core services via two types of long-running daemon: a *resource manager* (one per cluster) to manage the use of resources across the cluster, and *node managers* running on all the nodes in the cluster to launch and monitor *containers*. A container executes an application-specific process with a constrained set of resources (memory, CPU, and so on). Depending on how YARN is configured (see "YARN" on page 300), a container may be a Unix process or a Linux cgroup. Figure 4-2 illustrates how YARN runs an application.

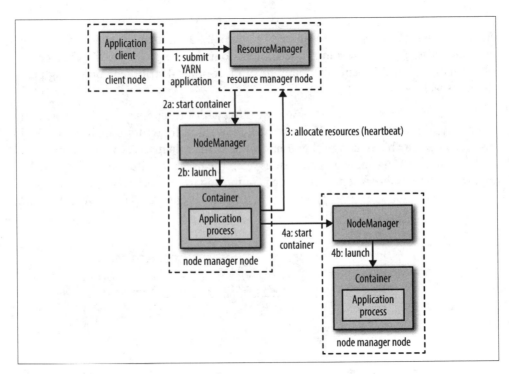

Figure 4-2. How YARN runs an application

To run an application on YARN, a client contacts the resource manager and asks it to run an *application master* process (step 1 in Figure 4-2). The resource manager then finds a node manager that can launch the application master in a container (steps 2a and 2b).[1] Precisely what the application master does once it is running depends on the application. It could simply run a computation in the container it is running in and return the result to the client. Or it could request more containers from the resource managers (step 3), and use them to run a distributed computation (steps 4a and 4b). The latter is what the MapReduce YARN application does, which we'll look at in more detail in "Anatomy of a MapReduce Job Run" on page 185.

Notice from Figure 4-2 that YARN itself does not provide any way for the parts of the application (client, master, process) to communicate with one another. Most nontrivial YARN applications use some form of remote communication (such as Hadoop's RPC layer) to pass status updates and results back to the client, but these are specific to the application.

Resource Requests

YARN has a flexible model for making resource requests. A request for a set of containers can express the amount of computer resources required for each container (memory and CPU), as well as locality constraints for the containers in that request.

Locality is critical in ensuring that distributed data processing algorithms use the cluster bandwidth efficiently,[2] so YARN allows an application to specify locality constraints for the containers it is requesting. Locality constraints can be used to request a container on a specific node or rack, or anywhere on the cluster (off-rack).

Sometimes the locality constraint cannot be met, in which case either no allocation is made or, optionally, the constraint can be loosened. For example, if a specific node was requested but it is not possible to start a container on it (because other containers are running on it), then YARN will try to start a container on a node in the same rack, or, if that's not possible, on any node in the cluster.

In the common case of launching a container to process an HDFS block (to run a map task in MapReduce, say), the application will request a container on one of the nodes hosting the block's three replicas, or on a node in one of the racks hosting the replicas, or, failing that, on any node in the cluster.

A YARN application can make resource requests at any time while it is running. For example, an application can make all of its requests up front, or it can take a more dynamic approach whereby it requests more resources dynamically to meet the changing needs of the application.

---

1. It's also possible for the client to start the application master, possibly outside the cluster, or in the same JVM as the client. This is called an *unmanaged application master*.

2. For more on this topic see "Scaling Out" on page 30 and "Network Topology and Hadoop" on page 70.

Spark takes the first approach, starting a fixed number of executors on the cluster (see "Spark on YARN" on page 571). MapReduce, on the other hand, has two phases: the map task containers are requested up front, but the reduce task containers are not started until later. Also, if any tasks fail, additional containers will be requested so the failed tasks can be rerun.

Application Lifespan

The lifespan of a YARN application can vary dramatically: from a short-lived application of a few seconds to a long-running application that runs for days or even months. Rather than look at how long the application runs for, it's useful to categorize applications in terms of how they map to the jobs that users run. The simplest case is one application per user job, which is the approach that MapReduce takes.

The second model is to run one application per workflow or user session of (possibly unrelated) jobs. This approach can be more efficient than the first, since containers can be reused between jobs, and there is also the potential to cache intermediate data between jobs. Spark is an example that uses this model.

The third model is a long-running application that is shared by different users. Such an application often acts in some kind of coordination role. For example, Apache Slider (*http://slider.incubator.apache.org/*) has a long-running application master for launching other applications on the cluster. This approach is also used by Impala (see "SQL-on-Hadoop Alternatives" on page 484) to provide a proxy application that the Impala daemons communicate with to request cluster resources. The "always on" application master means that users have very low-latency responses to their queries since the overhead of starting a new application master is avoided.[3]

Building YARN Applications

Writing a YARN application from scratch is fairly involved, but in many cases is not necessary, as it is often possible to use an existing application that fits the bill. For example, if you are interested in running a directed acyclic graph (DAG) of jobs, then Spark or Tez is appropriate; or for stream processing, Spark, Samza, or Storm works.[4]

There are a couple of projects that simplify the process of building a YARN application. Apache Slider, mentioned earlier, makes it possible to run existing distributed applications on YARN. Users can run their own instances of an application (such as HBase) on a cluster, independently of other users, which means that different users can run different versions of the same application. Slider provides controls to change the number

---

3. The low-latency application master code lives in the Llama project (*http://cloudera.github.io/llama/*).

4. All of these projects are Apache Software Foundation projects.

of nodes an application is running on, and to suspend then resume a running application.

Apache Twill (*http://twill.incubator.apache.org/*) is similar to Slider, but in addition provides a simple programming model for developing distributed applications on YARN. Twill allows you to define cluster processes as an extension of a Java Runnable, then runs them in YARN containers on the cluster. Twill also provides support for, among other things, real-time logging (log events from runnables are streamed back to the client) and command messages (sent from the client to runnables).

In cases where none of these options are sufficient—such as an application that has complex scheduling requirements—then the *distributed shell* application that is a part of the YARN project itself serves as an example of how to write a YARN application. It demonstrates how to use YARN's client APIs to handle communication between the client or application master and the YARN daemons.

YARN Compared to MapReduce 1

The distributed implementation of MapReduce in the original version of Hadoop (version 1 and earlier) is sometimes referred to as "MapReduce 1" to distinguish it from MapReduce 2, the implementation that uses YARN (in Hadoop 2 and later).

It's important to realize that the old and new MapReduce APIs are not the same thing as the MapReduce 1 and MapReduce 2 implementations. The APIs are user-facing client-side features and determine how you write MapReduce programs (see Appendix D), whereas the implementations are just different ways of running MapReduce programs. All four combinations are supported: both the old and new MapReduce APIs run on both MapReduce 1 and 2.

In MapReduce 1, there are two types of daemon that control the job execution process: a *jobtracker* and one or more *tasktrackers*. The jobtracker coordinates all the jobs run on the system by scheduling tasks to run on tasktrackers. Tasktrackers run tasks and send progress reports to the jobtracker, which keeps a record of the overall progress of each job. If a task fails, the jobtracker can reschedule it on a different tasktracker.

In MapReduce 1, the jobtracker takes care of both job scheduling (matching tasks with tasktrackers) and task progress monitoring (keeping track of tasks, restarting failed or slow tasks, and doing task bookkeeping, such as maintaining counter totals). By contrast, in YARN these responsibilities are handled by separate entities: the resource manager and an application master (one for each MapReduce job). The jobtracker is also responsible for storing job history for completed jobs, although it is possible to run a job history server as a separate daemon to take the load off the jobtracker. In YARN, the equivalent role is the timeline server, which stores application history.[5]

The YARN equivalent of a tasktracker is a node manager. The mapping is summarized in Table 4-1.

Table 4-1. A comparison of MapReduce 1 and YARN components

MapReduce 1	YARN
Jobtracker	Resource manager, application master, timeline server
Tasktracker	Node manager
Slot	Container

YARN was designed to address many of the limitations in MapReduce 1. The benefits to using YARN include the following:

Scalability

YARN can run on larger clusters than MapReduce 1. MapReduce 1 hits scalability bottlenecks in the region of 4,000 nodes and 40,000 tasks,[6] stemming from the fact that the jobtracker has to manage both jobs *and* tasks. YARN overcomes these limitations by virtue of its split resource manager/application master architecture: it is designed to scale up to 10,000 nodes and 100,000 tasks.

In contrast to the jobtracker, each instance of an application—here, a MapReduce job—has a dedicated application master, which runs for the duration of the application. This model is actually closer to the original Google MapReduce paper, which describes how a master process is started to coordinate map and reduce tasks running on a set of workers.

Availability

High availability (HA) is usually achieved by replicating the state needed for another daemon to take over the work needed to provide the service, in the event of the service daemon failing. However, the large amount of rapidly changing complex state in the jobtracker's memory (each task status is updated every few seconds, for example) makes it very difficult to retrofit HA into the jobtracker service.

With the jobtracker's responsibilities split between the resource manager and application master in YARN, making the service highly available became a divide-and-conquer problem: provide HA for the resource manager, then for YARN applications (on a per-application basis). And indeed, Hadoop 2 supports HA both

---

5. As of Hadoop 2.5.1, the YARN timeline server does not yet store MapReduce job history, so a MapReduce job history server daemon is still needed (see "Cluster Setup and Installation" on page 288).

6. Arun C. Murthy, "The Next Generation of Apache Hadoop MapReduce," (*http://bit.ly/next_gen_mapre duce*) February 14, 2011.

for the resource manager and for the application master for MapReduce jobs. Failure recovery in YARN is discussed in more detail in "Failures" on page 193.

Utilization

In MapReduce 1, each tasktracker is configured with a static allocation of fixed-size "slots," which are divided into map slots and reduce slots at configuration time. A map slot can only be used to run a map task, and a reduce slot can only be used for a reduce task.

In YARN, a node manager manages a pool of resources, rather than a fixed number of designated slots. MapReduce running on YARN will not hit the situation where a reduce task has to wait because only map slots are available on the cluster, which can happen in MapReduce 1. If the resources to run the task are available, then the application will be eligible for them.

Furthermore, resources in YARN are fine grained, so an application can make a request for what it needs, rather than for an indivisible slot, which may be too big (which is wasteful of resources) or too small (which may cause a failure) for the particular task.

Multitenancy

In some ways, the biggest benefit of YARN is that it opens up Hadoop to other types of distributed application beyond MapReduce. MapReduce is just one YARN application among many.

It is even possible for users to run different versions of MapReduce on the same YARN cluster, which makes the process of upgrading MapReduce more manageable. (Note, however, that some parts of MapReduce, such as the job history server and the shuffle handler, as well as YARN itself, still need to be upgraded across the cluster.)

Since Hadoop 2 is widely used and is the latest stable version, in the rest of this book the term "MapReduce" refers to MapReduce 2 unless otherwise stated. Chapter 7 looks in detail at how MapReduce running on YARN works.

Scheduling in YARN

In an ideal world, the requests that a YARN application makes would be granted immediately. In the real world, however, resources are limited, and on a busy cluster, an application will often need to wait to have some of its requests fulfilled. It is the job of the YARN scheduler to allocate resources to applications according to some defined policy. Scheduling in general is a difficult problem and there is no one "best" policy, which is why YARN provides a choice of schedulers and configurable policies. We look at these next.

Scheduler Options

Three schedulers are available in YARN: the FIFO, Capacity, and Fair Schedulers. The FIFO Scheduler places applications in a queue and runs them in the order of submission (first in, first out). Requests for the first application in the queue are allocated first; once its requests have been satisfied, the next application in the queue is served, and so on.

The FIFO Scheduler has the merit of being simple to understand and not needing any configuration, but it's not suitable for shared clusters. Large applications will use all the resources in a cluster, so each application has to wait its turn. On a shared cluster it is better to use the Capacity Scheduler or the Fair Scheduler. Both of these allow long-running jobs to complete in a timely manner, while still allowing users who are running concurrent smaller ad hoc queries to get results back in a reasonable time.

The difference between schedulers is illustrated in Figure 4-3, which shows that under the FIFO Scheduler (i) the small job is blocked until the large job completes.

With the Capacity Scheduler (ii in Figure 4-3), a separate dedicated queue allows the small job to start as soon as it is submitted, although this is at the cost of overall cluster utilization since the queue capacity is reserved for jobs in that queue. This means that the large job finishes later than when using the FIFO Scheduler.

With the Fair Scheduler (iii in Figure 4-3), there is no need to reserve a set amount of capacity, since it will dynamically balance resources between all running jobs. Just after the first (large) job starts, it is the only job running, so it gets all the resources in the cluster. When the second (small) job starts, it is allocated half of the cluster resources so that each job is using its fair share of resources.

Note that there is a lag between the time the second job starts and when it receives its fair share, since it has to wait for resources to free up as containers used by the first job complete. After the small job completes and no longer requires resources, the large job goes back to using the full cluster capacity again. The overall effect is both high cluster utilization and timely small job completion.

Figure 4-3 contrasts the basic operation of the three schedulers. In the next two sections, we examine some of the more advanced configuration options for the Capacity and Fair Schedulers.

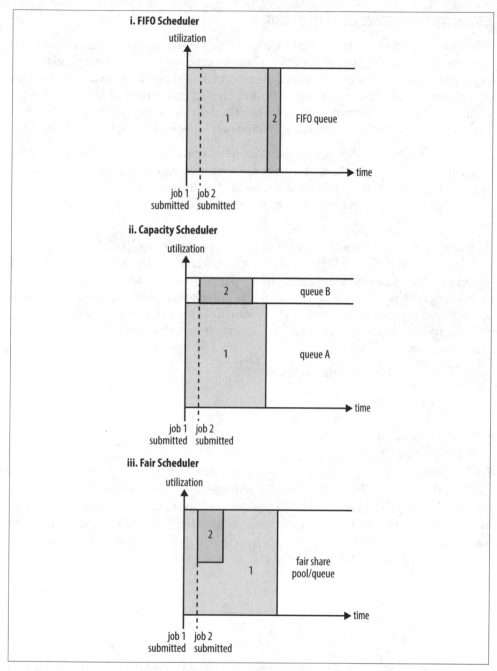

Figure 4-3. Cluster utilization over time when running a large job and a small job under the FIFO Scheduler (i), Capacity Scheduler (ii), and Fair Scheduler (iii)

Capacity Scheduler Configuration

The Capacity Scheduler allows sharing of a Hadoop cluster along organizational lines, whereby each organization is allocated a certain capacity of the overall cluster. Each organization is set up with a dedicated queue that is configured to use a given fraction of the cluster capacity. Queues may be further divided in hierarchical fashion, allowing each organization to share its cluster allowance between different groups of users within the organization. Within a queue, applications are scheduled using FIFO scheduling.

As we saw in Figure 4-3, a single job does not use more resources than its queue's capacity. However, if there is more than one job in the queue and there are idle resources available, then the Capacity Scheduler may allocate the spare resources to jobs in the queue, even if that causes the queue's capacity to be exceeded.[7] This behavior is known as *queue elasticity*.

In normal operation, the Capacity Scheduler does not preempt containers by forcibly killing them,[8] so if a queue is under capacity due to lack of demand, and then demand increases, the queue will only return to capacity as resources are released from other queues as containers complete. It is possible to mitigate this by configuring queues with a maximum capacity so that they don't eat into other queues' capacities too much. This is at the cost of queue elasticity, of course, so a reasonable trade-off should be found by trial and error.

Imagine a queue hierarchy that looks like this:

```
root
├── prod
└── dev
    ├── eng
    └── science
```

The listing in Example 4-1 shows a sample Capacity Scheduler configuration file, called *capacity-scheduler.xml*, for this hierarchy. It defines two queues under the root queue, prod and dev, which have 40% and 60% of the capacity, respectively. Notice that a particular queue is configured by setting configuration properties of the form yarn.scheduler.capacity.*<queue-path>*.*<sub-property>*, where *<queue-path>* is the hierarchical (dotted) path of the queue, such as root.prod.

---

7. If the property yarn.scheduler.capacity.*<queue-path>*.user-limit-factor is set to a value larger than 1 (the default), then a single job is allowed to use more than its queue's capacity.

8. However, the Capacity Scheduler can perform work-preserving preemption, where the resource manager asks applications to return containers to balance capacity.

Example 4-1. A basic configuration file for the Capacity Scheduler

```xml
<?xml version="1.0"?>
<configuration>
  <property>
    <name>yarn.scheduler.capacity.root.queues</name>
    <value>prod,dev</value>
  </property>
  <property>
    <name>yarn.scheduler.capacity.root.dev.queues</name>
    <value>eng,science</value>
  </property>
  <property>
    <name>yarn.scheduler.capacity.root.prod.capacity</name>
    <value>40</value>
  </property>
  <property>
    <name>yarn.scheduler.capacity.root.dev.capacity</name>
    <value>60</value>
  </property>
  <property>
    <name>yarn.scheduler.capacity.root.dev.maximum-capacity</name>
    <value>75</value>
  </property>
  <property>
    <name>yarn.scheduler.capacity.root.dev.eng.capacity</name>
    <value>50</value>
  </property>
  <property>
    <name>yarn.scheduler.capacity.root.dev.science.capacity</name>
    <value>50</value>
  </property>
</configuration>
```

As you can see, the dev queue is further divided into eng and science queues of equal capacity. So that the dev queue does not use up all the cluster resources when the prod queue is idle, it has its maximum capacity set to 75%. In other words, the prod queue always has 25% of the cluster available for immediate use. Since no maximum capacities have been set for other queues, it's possible for jobs in the eng or science queues to use all of the dev queue's capacity (up to 75% of the cluster), or indeed for the prod queue to use the entire cluster.

Beyond configuring queue hierarchies and capacities, there are settings to control the maximum number of resources a single user or application can be allocated, how many applications can be running at any one time, and ACLs on queues. See the reference page (*http://bit.ly/capacity_scheduler*) for details.

Queue placement

The way that you specify which queue an application is placed in is specific to the application. For example, in MapReduce, you set the property `mapreduce.job.queue name` to the name of the queue you want to use. If the queue does not exist, then you'll get an error at submission time. If no queue is specified, applications will be placed in a queue called `default`.

> For the Capacity Scheduler, the queue name should be the last part of the hierarchical name since the full hierarchical name is not recognized. So, for the preceding example configuration, `prod` and `eng` are OK, but `root.dev.eng` and `dev.eng` do not work.

Fair Scheduler Configuration

The Fair Scheduler attempts to allocate resources so that all running applications get the same share of resources. Figure 4-3 showed how fair sharing works for applications in the same queue; however, fair sharing actually works *between* queues, too, as we'll see next.

> The terms *queue* and *pool* are used interchangeably in the context of the Fair Scheduler.

To understand how resources are shared between queues, imagine two users *A* and *B*, each with their own queue (Figure 4-4). *A* starts a job, and it is allocated all the resources available since there is no demand from *B*. Then *B* starts a job while *A*'s job is still running, and after a while each job is using half of the resources, in the way we saw earlier. Now if *B* starts a second job while the other jobs are still running, it will share its resources with *B*'s other job, so each of *B*'s jobs will have one-fourth of the resources, while *A*'s will continue to have half. The result is that resources are shared fairly between users.

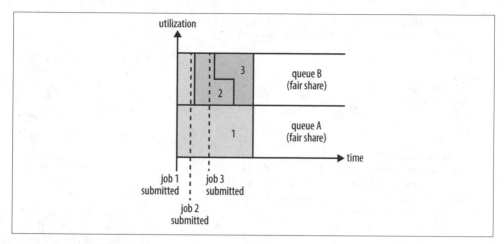

Figure 4-4. Fair sharing between user queues

Enabling the Fair Scheduler

The scheduler in use is determined by the setting of `yarn.resourcemanager.schedu ler.class`. The Capacity Scheduler is used by default (although the Fair Scheduler is the default in some Hadoop distributions, such as CDH), but this can be changed by setting `yarn.resourcemanager.scheduler.class` in *yarn-site.xml* to the fully qualified classname of the scheduler, `org.apache.hadoop.yarn.server.resourcemanag er.scheduler.fair.FairScheduler`.

Queue configuration

The Fair Scheduler is configured using an allocation file named *fair-scheduler.xml* that is loaded from the classpath. (The name can be changed by setting the property `yarn.scheduler.fair.allocation.file`.) In the absence of an allocation file, the Fair Scheduler operates as described earlier: each application is placed in a queue named after the user and queues are created dynamically when users submit their first applications.

Per-queue configuration is specified in the allocation file. This allows configuration of hierarchical queues like those supported by the Capacity Scheduler. For example, we can define `prod` and `dev` queues like we did for the Capacity Scheduler using the allocation file in Example 4-2.

Example 4-2. An allocation file for the Fair Scheduler

```
<?xml version="1.0"?>
<allocations>
  <defaultQueueSchedulingPolicy>fair</defaultQueueSchedulingPolicy>

  <queue name="prod">
```

```
    <weight>40</weight>
    <schedulingPolicy>fifo</schedulingPolicy>
  </queue>

  <queue name="dev">
    <weight>60</weight>
    <queue name="eng" />
    <queue name="science" />
  </queue>

  <queuePlacementPolicy>
    <rule name="specified" create="false" />
    <rule name="primaryGroup" create="false" />
    <rule name="default" queue="dev.eng" />
  </queuePlacementPolicy>
</allocations>
```

The queue hierarchy is defined using nested queue elements. All queues are children of the root queue, even if not actually nested in a root queue element. Here we subdivide the dev queue into a queue called eng and another called science.

Queues can have weights, which are used in the fair share calculation. In this example, the cluster allocation is considered fair when it is divided into a 40:60 proportion between prod and dev. The eng and science queues do not have weights specified, so they are divided evenly. Weights are not quite the same as percentages, even though the example uses numbers that add up to 100 for the sake of simplicity. We could have specified weights of 2 and 3 for the prod and dev queues to achieve the same queue weighting.

When setting weights, remember to consider the default queue and dynamically created queues (such as queues named after users). These are not specified in the allocation file, but still have weight 1.

Queues can have different scheduling policies. The default policy for queues can be set in the top-level defaultQueueSchedulingPolicy element; if it is omitted, fair scheduling is used. Despite its name, the Fair Scheduler also supports a FIFO (fifo) policy on queues, as well as Dominant Resource Fairness (drf), described later in the chapter.

The policy for a particular queue can be overridden using the schedulingPolicy element for that queue. In this case, the prod queue uses FIFO scheduling since we want each production job to run serially and complete in the shortest possible amount of time. Note that fair sharing is still used to divide resources between the prod and dev queues, as well as between (and within) the eng and science queues.

Although not shown in this allocation file, queues can be configured with minimum and maximum resources, and a maximum number of running applications. (See the reference page (*http://bit.ly/fair_scheduler*) for details.) The minimum resources setting is not a hard limit, but rather is used by the scheduler to prioritize resource allocations. If two queues are below their fair share, then the one that is furthest below its minimum is allocated resources first. The minimum resource setting is also used for preemption, discussed momentarily.

Queue placement

The Fair Scheduler uses a rules-based system to determine which queue an application is placed in. In Example 4-2, the queuePlacementPolicy element contains a list of rules, each of which is tried in turn until a match occurs. The first rule, specified, places an application in the queue it specified; if none is specified, or if the specified queue doesn't exist, then the rule doesn't match and the next rule is tried. The primaryGroup rule tries to place an application in a queue with the name of the user's primary Unix group; if there is no such queue, rather than creating it, the next rule is tried. The default rule is a catch-all and always places the application in the dev.eng queue.

The queuePlacementPolicy can be omitted entirely, in which case the default behavior is as if it had been specified with the following:

```
<queuePlacementPolicy>
  <rule name="specified" />
  <rule name="user" />
</queuePlacementPolicy>
```

In other words, unless the queue is explicitly specified, the user's name is used for the queue, creating it if necessary.

Another simple queue placement policy is one where all applications are placed in the same (default) queue. This allows resources to be shared fairly between applications, rather than users. The definition is equivalent to this:

```
<queuePlacementPolicy>
  <rule name="default" />
</queuePlacementPolicy>
```

It's also possible to set this policy without using an allocation file, by setting yarn.scheduler.fair.user-as-default-queue to false so that applications will be placed in the default queue rather than a per-user queue. In addition, yarn.scheduler.fair.allow-undeclared-pools should be set to false so that users can't create queues on the fly.

Preemption

When a job is submitted to an empty queue on a busy cluster, the job cannot start until resources free up from jobs that are already running on the cluster. To make the time taken for a job to start more predictable, the Fair Scheduler supports *preemption*.

Preemption allows the scheduler to kill containers for queues that are running with more than their fair share of resources so that the resources can be allocated to a queue that is under its fair share. Note that preemption reduces overall cluster efficiency, since the terminated containers need to be reexecuted.

Preemption is enabled globally by setting `yarn.scheduler.fair.preemption` to `true`. There are two relevant preemption timeout settings: one for minimum share and one for fair share, both specified in seconds. By default, the timeouts are not set, so you need to set at least one to allow containers to be preempted.

If a queue waits for as long as its *minimum share preemption timeout* without receiving its minimum guaranteed share, then the scheduler may preempt other containers. The default timeout is set for all queues via the `defaultMinSharePreemptionTimeout` top-level element in the allocation file, and on a per-queue basis by setting the `minShare PreemptionTimeout` element for a queue.

Likewise, if a queue remains below *half* of its fair share for as long as the *fair share preemption timeout*, then the scheduler may preempt other containers. The default timeout is set for all queues via the `defaultFairSharePreemptionTimeout` top-level element in the allocation file, and on a per-queue basis by setting `fairSharePreemp tionTimeout` on a queue. The threshold may also be changed from its default of 0.5 by setting `defaultFairSharePreemptionThreshold` and `fairSharePreemptionThres hold` (per-queue).

Delay Scheduling

All the YARN schedulers try to honor locality requests. On a busy cluster, if an application requests a particular node, there is a good chance that other containers are running on it at the time of the request. The obvious course of action is to immediately loosen the locality requirement and allocate a container on the same rack. However, it has been observed in practice that waiting a short time (no more than a few seconds) can dramatically increase the chances of being allocated a container on the requested node, and therefore increase the efficiency of the cluster. This feature is called *delay scheduling*, and it is supported by both the Capacity Scheduler and the Fair Scheduler.

Every node manager in a YARN cluster periodically sends a heartbeat request to the resource manager—by default, one per second. Heartbeats carry information about the node manager's running containers and the resources available for new containers, so each heartbeat is a potential *scheduling opportunity* for an application to run a container.

When using delay scheduling, the scheduler doesn't simply use the first scheduling opportunity it receives, but waits for up to a given maximum number of scheduling opportunities to occur before loosening the locality constraint and taking the next scheduling opportunity.

For the Capacity Scheduler, delay scheduling is configured by setting `yarn.scheduler.capacity.node-locality-delay` to a positive integer representing the number of scheduling opportunities that it is prepared to miss before loosening the node constraint to match any node in the same rack.

The Fair Scheduler also uses the number of scheduling opportunities to determine the delay, although it is expressed as a proportion of the cluster size. For example, setting `yarn.scheduler.fair.locality.threshold.node` to 0.5 means that the scheduler should wait until half of the nodes in the cluster have presented scheduling opportunities before accepting another node in the same rack. There is a corresponding property, `yarn.scheduler.fair.locality.threshold.rack`, for setting the threshold before another rack is accepted instead of the one requested.

Dominant Resource Fairness

When there is only a single resource type being scheduled, such as memory, then the concept of capacity or fairness is easy to determine. If two users are running applications, you can measure the amount of memory that each is using to compare the two applications. However, when there are multiple resource types in play, things get more complicated. If one user's application requires lots of CPU but little memory and the other's requires little CPU and lots of memory, how are these two applications compared?

The way that the schedulers in YARN address this problem is to look at each user's dominant resource and use it as a measure of the cluster usage. This approach is called *Dominant Resource Fairness*, or DRF for short.[9] The idea is best illustrated with a simple example.

Imagine a cluster with a total of 100 CPUs and 10 TB of memory. Application *A* requests containers of (2 CPUs, 300 GB), and application *B* requests containers of (6 CPUs, 100 GB). *A*'s request is (2%, 3%) of the cluster, so memory is dominant since its proportion (3%) is larger than CPU's (2%). *B*'s request is (6%, 1%), so CPU is dominant. Since *B*'s container requests are twice as big in the dominant resource (6% versus 3%), it will be allocated half as many containers under fair sharing.

By default DRF is not used, so during resource calculations, only memory is considered and CPU is ignored. The Capacity Scheduler can be configured to use DRF by setting

---

9. DRF was introduced in Ghodsi et al.'s "Dominant Resource Fairness: Fair Allocation of Multiple Resource Types," (*http://bit.ly/fair_allocation*) March 2011.

`yarn.scheduler.capacity.resource-calculator` to `org.apache.hadoop.yarn` `.util.resource.DominantResourceCalculator` in *capacity-scheduler.xml*.

For the Fair Scheduler, DRF can be enabled by setting the top-level element `default QueueSchedulingPolicy` in the allocation file to `drf`.

Further Reading

This chapter has given a short overview of YARN. For more detail, see *Apache Hadoop YARN (http://yarn-book.com/)* by Arun C. Murthy et al. (Addison-Wesley, 2014).

Hadoop I/O

Hadoop comes with a set of primitives for data I/O. Some of these are techniques that are more general than Hadoop, such as data integrity and compression, but deserve special consideration when dealing with multiterabyte datasets. Others are Hadoop tools or APIs that form the building blocks for developing distributed systems, such as serialization frameworks and on-disk data structures.

Data Integrity

Users of Hadoop rightly expect that no data will be lost or corrupted during storage or processing. However, because every I/O operation on the disk or network carries with it a small chance of introducing errors into the data that it is reading or writing, when the volumes of data flowing through the system are as large as the ones Hadoop is capable of handling, the chance of data corruption occurring is high.

The usual way of detecting corrupted data is by computing a *checksum* for the data when it first enters the system, and again whenever it is transmitted across a channel that is unreliable and hence capable of corrupting the data. The data is deemed to be corrupt if the newly generated checksum doesn't exactly match the original. This technique doesn't offer any way to fix the data—it is merely error detection. (And this is a reason for not using low-end hardware; in particular, be sure to use ECC memory.) Note that it is possible that it's the checksum that is corrupt, not the data, but this is very unlikely, because the checksum is much smaller than the data.

A commonly used error-detecting code is CRC-32 (32-bit cyclic redundancy check), which computes a 32-bit integer checksum for input of any size. CRC-32 is used for checksumming in Hadoop's ChecksumFileSystem, while HDFS uses a more efficient variant called CRC-32C.

Data Integrity in HDFS

HDFS transparently checksums all data written to it and by default verifies checksums when reading data. A separate checksum is created for every `dfs.bytes-per-checksum` bytes of data. The default is 512 bytes, and because a CRC-32C checksum is 4 bytes long, the storage overhead is less than 1%.

Datanodes are responsible for verifying the data they receive before storing the data and its checksum. This applies to data that they receive from clients and from other datanodes during replication. A client writing data sends it to a pipeline of datanodes (as explained in Chapter 3), and the last datanode in the pipeline verifies the checksum. If the datanode detects an error, the client receives a subclass of `IOException`, which it should handle in an application-specific manner (for example, by retrying the operation).

When clients read data from datanodes, they verify checksums as well, comparing them with the ones stored at the datanodes. Each datanode keeps a persistent log of checksum verifications, so it knows the last time each of its blocks was verified. When a client successfully verifies a block, it tells the datanode, which updates its log. Keeping statistics such as these is valuable in detecting bad disks.

In addition to block verification on client reads, each datanode runs a `DataBlockScanner` in a background thread that periodically verifies all the blocks stored on the datanode. This is to guard against corruption due to "bit rot" in the physical storage media. See "Datanode block scanner" on page 328 for details on how to access the scanner reports.

Because HDFS stores replicas of blocks, it can "heal" corrupted blocks by copying one of the good replicas to produce a new, uncorrupt replica. The way this works is that if a client detects an error when reading a block, it reports the bad block and the datanode it was trying to read from to the namenode before throwing a `ChecksumException`. The namenode marks the block replica as corrupt so it doesn't direct any more clients to it or try to copy this replica to another datanode. It then schedules a copy of the block to be replicated on another datanode, so its replication factor is back at the expected level. Once this has happened, the corrupt replica is deleted.

It is possible to disable verification of checksums by passing `false` to the `setVerify Checksum()` method on `FileSystem` before using the `open()` method to read a file. The same effect is possible from the shell by using the `-ignoreCrc` option with the `-get` or the equivalent `-copyToLocal` command. This feature is useful if you have a corrupt file that you want to inspect so you can decide what to do with it. For example, you might want to see whether it can be salvaged before you delete it.

You can find a file's checksum with `hadoop fs -checksum`. This is useful to check whether two files in HDFS have the same contents—something that *distcp* does, for example (see "Parallel Copying with distcp" on page 76).

LocalFileSystem

The Hadoop `LocalFileSystem` performs client-side checksumming. This means that when you write a file called *filename*, the filesystem client transparently creates a hidden file, *.filename.crc*, in the same directory containing the checksums for each chunk of the file. The chunk size is controlled by the `file.bytes-per-checksum` property, which defaults to 512 bytes. The chunk size is stored as metadata in the *.crc* file, so the file can be read back correctly even if the setting for the chunk size has changed. Checksums are verified when the file is read, and if an error is detected, `LocalFileSystem` throws a `ChecksumException`.

Checksums are fairly cheap to compute (in Java, they are implemented in native code), typically adding a few percent overhead to the time to read or write a file. For most applications, this is an acceptable price to pay for data integrity. It is, however, possible to disable checksums, which is typically done when the underlying filesystem supports checksums natively. This is accomplished by using `RawLocalFileSystem` in place of `LocalFileSystem`. To do this globally in an application, it suffices to remap the implementation for `file` URIs by setting the property `fs.file.impl` to the value `org.apache.hadoop.fs.RawLocalFileSystem`. Alternatively, you can directly create a `RawLocalFileSystem` instance, which may be useful if you want to disable checksum verification for only some reads, for example:

```
Configuration conf = ...
FileSystem fs = new RawLocalFileSystem();
fs.initialize(null, conf);
```

ChecksumFileSystem

`LocalFileSystem` uses `ChecksumFileSystem` to do its work, and this class makes it easy to add checksumming to other (nonchecksummed) filesystems, as `ChecksumFileSystem` is just a wrapper around `FileSystem`. The general idiom is as follows:

```
FileSystem rawFs = ...
FileSystem checksummedFs = new ChecksumFileSystem(rawFs);
```

The underlying filesystem is called the *raw* filesystem, and may be retrieved using the `getRawFileSystem()` method on `ChecksumFileSystem`. `ChecksumFileSystem` has a few more useful methods for working with checksums, such as `getChecksumFile()` for getting the path of a checksum file for any file. Check the documentation for the others.

If an error is detected by `ChecksumFileSystem` when reading a file, it will call its `reportChecksumFailure()` method. The default implementation does nothing, but `LocalFileSystem` moves the offending file and its checksum to a side directory on the same device called *bad_files*. Administrators should periodically check for these bad files and take action on them.

Compression

File compression brings two major benefits: it reduces the space needed to store files, and it speeds up data transfer across the network or to or from disk. When dealing with large volumes of data, both of these savings can be significant, so it pays to carefully consider how to use compression in Hadoop.

There are many different compression formats, tools, and algorithms, each with different characteristics. Table 5-1 lists some of the more common ones that can be used with Hadoop.

Table 5-1. A summary of compression formats

Compression format	Tool	Algorithm	Filename extension	Splittable?
DEFLATE[a]	N/A	DEFLATE	*.deflate*	No
gzip	*gzip*	DEFLATE	*.gz*	No
bzip2	*bzip2*	bzip2	*.bz2*	Yes
LZO	*lzop*	LZO	*.lzo*	No[b]
LZ4	N/A	LZ4	*.lz4*	No
Snappy	N/A	Snappy	*.snappy*	No

[a] DEFLATE is a compression algorithm whose standard implementation is zlib. There is no commonly available command-line tool for producing files in DEFLATE format, as gzip is normally used. (Note that the gzip file format is DEFLATE with extra headers and a footer.) The *.deflate* filename extension is a Hadoop convention.

[b] However, LZO files are splittable if they have been indexed in a preprocessing step. See "Compression and Input Splits" on page 105.

All compression algorithms exhibit a space/time trade-off: faster compression and decompression speeds usually come at the expense of smaller space savings. The tools listed in Table 5-1 typically give some control over this trade-off at compression time by offering nine different options: –1 means optimize for speed, and -9 means optimize for space. For example, the following command creates a compressed file *file.gz* using the fastest compression method:

```
% gzip -1 file
```

The different tools have very different compression characteristics. gzip is a general-purpose compressor and sits in the middle of the space/time trade-off. bzip2 compresses more effectively than gzip, but is slower. bzip2's decompression speed is faster than its compression speed, but it is still slower than the other formats. LZO, LZ4, and Snappy, on the other hand, all optimize for speed and are around an order of magnitude faster than gzip, but compress less effectively. Snappy and LZ4 are also significantly faster than LZO for decompression.[1]

The "Splittable" column in Table 5-1 indicates whether the compression format supports splitting (that is, whether you can seek to any point in the stream and start reading from some point further on). Splittable compression formats are especially suitable for Map-Reduce; see "Compression and Input Splits" on page 105 for further discussion.

Codecs

A *codec* is the implementation of a compression-decompression algorithm. In Hadoop, a codec is represented by an implementation of the CompressionCodec interface. So, for example, GzipCodec encapsulates the compression and decompression algorithm for gzip. Table 5-2 lists the codecs that are available for Hadoop.

Table 5-2. Hadoop compression codecs

Compression format	Hadoop CompressionCodec
DEFLATE	org.apache.hadoop.io.compress.DefaultCodec
gzip	org.apache.hadoop.io.compress.GzipCodec
bzip2	org.apache.hadoop.io.compress.BZip2Codec
LZO	com.hadoop.compression.lzo.LzopCodec
LZ4	org.apache.hadoop.io.compress.Lz4Codec
Snappy	org.apache.hadoop.io.compress.SnappyCodec

The LZO libraries are GPL licensed and may not be included in Apache distributions, so for this reason the Hadoop codecs must be downloaded separately from Google (*http://code.google.com/p/hadoop-gpl-compression/*) (or GitHub (*http://github.com/kevinweil/hadoop-lzo*), which includes bug fixes and more tools). The LzopCodec, which is compatible with the *lzop* tool, is essentially the LZO format with extra headers, and is the one you normally want. There is also an LzoCodec for the pure LZO format, which uses the *.lzo_deflate* filename extension (by analogy with DEFLATE, which is gzip without the headers).

Compressing and decompressing streams with CompressionCodec

CompressionCodec has two methods that allow you to easily compress or decompress data. To compress data being written to an output stream, use the createOutput Stream(OutputStream out) method to create a CompressionOutputStream to which you write your uncompressed data to have it written in compressed form to the

---

1. For a comprehensive set of compression benchmarks, *jvm-compressor-benchmark* (*https://github.com/ning/jvm-compressor-benchmark*) is a good reference for JVM-compatible libraries (including some native libraries).

underlying stream. Conversely, to decompress data being read from an input stream, call `createInputStream(InputStream in)` to obtain a `CompressionInputStream`, which allows you to read uncompressed data from the underlying stream.

`CompressionOutputStream` and `CompressionInputStream` are similar to `java.util.zip.DeflaterOutputStream` and `java.util.zip.DeflaterInputStream`, except that both of the former provide the ability to reset their underlying compressor or decompressor. This is important for applications that compress sections of the data stream as separate blocks, such as in a `SequenceFile`, described in "SequenceFile" on page 127.

Example 5-1 illustrates how to use the API to compress data read from standard input and write it to standard output.

Example 5-1. A program to compress data read from standard input and write it to standard output

```
public class StreamCompressor {

  public static void main(String[] args) throws Exception {
    String codecClassname = args[0];
    Class<?> codecClass = Class.forName(codecClassname);
    Configuration conf = new Configuration();
    CompressionCodec codec = (CompressionCodec)
      ReflectionUtils.newInstance(codecClass, conf);

    CompressionOutputStream out = codec.createOutputStream(System.out);
    IOUtils.copyBytes(System.in, out, 4096, false);
    out.finish();
  }
}
```

The application expects the fully qualified name of the `CompressionCodec` implementation as the first command-line argument. We use `ReflectionUtils` to construct a new instance of the codec, then obtain a compression wrapper around `System.out`. Then we call the utility method `copyBytes()` on `IOUtils` to copy the input to the output, which is compressed by the `CompressionOutputStream`. Finally, we call `finish()` on `CompressionOutputStream`, which tells the compressor to finish writing to the compressed stream, but doesn't close the stream. We can try it out with the following command line, which compresses the string "Text" using the `StreamCompressor` program with the `GzipCodec`, then decompresses it from standard input using *gunzip*:

```
% echo "Text" | hadoop StreamCompressor org.apache.hadoop.io.compress.GzipCodec \
  | gunzip -
Text
```

Inferring CompressionCodecs using CompressionCodecFactory

If you are reading a compressed file, normally you can infer which codec to use by looking at its filename extension. A file ending in *.gz* can be read with `GzipCodec`, and so on. The extensions for each compression format are listed in Table 5-1.

`CompressionCodecFactory` provides a way of mapping a filename extension to a `CompressionCodec` using its `getCodec()` method, which takes a `Path` object for the file in question. Example 5-2 shows an application that uses this feature to decompress files.

Example 5-2. A program to decompress a compressed file using a codec inferred from the file's extension

```
public class FileDecompressor {

  public static void main(String[] args) throws Exception {
    String uri = args[0];
    Configuration conf = new Configuration();
    FileSystem fs = FileSystem.get(URI.create(uri), conf);

    Path inputPath = new Path(uri);
    CompressionCodecFactory factory = new CompressionCodecFactory(conf);
    CompressionCodec codec = factory.getCodec(inputPath);
    if (codec == null) {
      System.err.println("No codec found for " + uri);
      System.exit(1);
    }

    String outputUri =
        CompressionCodecFactory.removeSuffix(uri, codec.getDefaultExtension());

    InputStream in = null;
    OutputStream out = null;
    try {
      in = codec.createInputStream(fs.open(inputPath));
      out = fs.create(new Path(outputUri));
      IOUtils.copyBytes(in, out, conf);
    } finally {
      IOUtils.closeStream(in);
      IOUtils.closeStream(out);
    }
  }
}
```

Once the codec has been found, it is used to strip off the file suffix to form the output filename (via the `removeSuffix()` static method of `CompressionCodecFactory`). In this way, a file named *file.gz* is decompressed to *file* by invoking the program as follows:

```
% hadoop FileDecompressor file.gz
```

`CompressionCodecFactory` loads all the codecs in Table 5-2, except LZO, as well as any listed in the `io.compression.codecs` configuration property (Table 5-3). By default, the property is empty; you would need to alter it only if you have a custom codec that you wish to register (such as the externally hosted LZO codecs). Each codec knows its default filename extension, thus permitting `CompressionCodecFactory` to search through the registered codecs to find a match for the given extension (if any).

Table 5-3. Compression codec properties

Property name	Type	Default value	Description
`io.compression.codecs`	Comma-separated `Class` names		A list of additional `CompressionCodec` classes for compression/decompression

Native libraries

For performance, it is preferable to use a native library for compression and decompression. For example, in one test, using the native gzip libraries reduced decompression times by up to 50% and compression times by around 10% (compared to the built-in Java implementation). Table 5-4 shows the availability of Java and native implementations for each compression format. All formats have native implementations, but not all have a Java implementation (LZO, for example).

Table 5-4. Compression library implementations

Compression format	Java implementation?	Native implementation?
DEFLATE	Yes	Yes
gzip	Yes	Yes
bzip2	Yes	Yes
LZO	No	Yes
LZ4	No	Yes
Snappy	No	Yes

The Apache Hadoop binary tarball comes with prebuilt native compression binaries for 64-bit Linux, called *libhadoop.so*. For other platforms, you will need to compile the libraries yourself, following the *BUILDING.txt* instructions at the top level of the source tree.

The native libraries are picked up using the Java system property `java.library.path`. The *hadoop* script in the *etc/hadoop* directory sets this property for you, but if you don't use this script, you will need to set the property in your application.

By default, Hadoop looks for native libraries for the platform it is running on, and loads them automatically if they are found. This means you don't have to change any configuration settings to use the native libraries. In some circumstances, however, you may wish to disable use of native libraries, such as when you are debugging a compression-related problem. You can do this by setting the property io.native.lib.available to false, which ensures that the built-in Java equivalents will be used (if they are available).

CodecPool. If you are using a native library and you are doing a lot of compression or decompression in your application, consider using CodecPool, which allows you to reuse compressors and decompressors, thereby amortizing the cost of creating these objects.

The code in Example 5-3 shows the API, although in this program, which creates only a single Compressor, there is really no need to use a pool.

Example 5-3. A program to compress data read from standard input and write it to standard output using a pooled compressor

```
public class PooledStreamCompressor {

  public static void main(String[] args) throws Exception {
    String codecClassname = args[0];
    Class<?> codecClass = Class.forName(codecClassname);
    Configuration conf = new Configuration();
    CompressionCodec codec = (CompressionCodec)
        ReflectionUtils.newInstance(codecClass, conf);
    Compressor compressor = null;
    try {
      compressor = CodecPool.getCompressor(codec);
      CompressionOutputStream out =
          codec.createOutputStream(System.out, compressor);
      IOUtils.copyBytes(System.in, out, 4096, false);
      out.finish();
    } finally {
      CodecPool.returnCompressor(compressor);
    }
  }
}
```

We retrieve a Compressor instance from the pool for a given CompressionCodec, which we use in the codec's overloaded createOutputStream() method. By using a finally block, we ensure that the compressor is returned to the pool even if there is an IOException while copying the bytes between the streams.

Compression and Input Splits

When considering how to compress data that will be processed by MapReduce, it is important to understand whether the compression format supports splitting. Consider an uncompressed file stored in HDFS whose size is 1 GB. With an HDFS block size of 128 MB, the file will be stored as eight blocks, and a MapReduce job using this file as input will create eight input splits, each processed independently as input to a separate map task.

Imagine now that the file is a gzip-compressed file whose compressed size is 1 GB. As before, HDFS will store the file as eight blocks. However, creating a split for each block won't work, because it is impossible to start reading at an arbitrary point in the gzip stream and therefore impossible for a map task to read its split independently of the others. The gzip format uses DEFLATE to store the compressed data, and DEFLATE stores data as a series of compressed blocks. The problem is that the start of each block is not distinguished in any way that would allow a reader positioned at an arbitrary point in the stream to advance to the beginning of the next block, thereby synchronizing itself with the stream. For this reason, gzip does not support splitting.

In this case, MapReduce will do the right thing and not try to split the gzipped file, since it knows that the input is gzip-compressed (by looking at the filename extension) and that gzip does not support splitting. This will work, but at the expense of locality: a single map will process the eight HDFS blocks, most of which will not be local to the map. Also, with fewer maps, the job is less granular and so may take longer to run.

If the file in our hypothetical example were an LZO file, we would have the same problem because the underlying compression format does not provide a way for a reader to synchronize itself with the stream. However, it is possible to preprocess LZO files using an indexer tool that comes with the Hadoop LZO libraries, which you can obtain from the Google and GitHub sites listed in "Codecs" on page 101. The tool builds an index of split points, effectively making them splittable when the appropriate MapReduce input format is used.

A bzip2 file, on the other hand, does provide a synchronization marker between blocks (a 48-bit approximation of pi), so it does support splitting. (Table 5-1 lists whether each compression format supports splitting.)

Which Compression Format Should I Use?

Hadoop applications process large datasets, so you should strive to take advantage of compression. Which compression format you use depends on such considerations as file size, format, and the tools you are using for processing. Here are some suggestions, arranged roughly in order of most to least effective:

- Use a container file format such as sequence files (see the section on page 127), Avro datafiles (see the section on page 352), ORCFiles (see the section on page 136), or Parquet files (see the section on page 370), all of which support both compression and splitting. A fast compressor such as LZO, LZ4, or Snappy is generally a good choice.

- Use a compression format that supports splitting, such as bzip2 (although bzip2 is fairly slow), or one that can be indexed to support splitting, such as LZO.

- Split the file into chunks in the application, and compress each chunk separately using any supported compression format (it doesn't matter whether it is splittable). In this case, you should choose the chunk size so that the compressed chunks are approximately the size of an HDFS block.

- Store the files uncompressed.

For large files, you should *not* use a compression format that does not support splitting on the whole file, because you lose locality and make MapReduce applications very inefficient.

Using Compression in MapReduce

As described in "Inferring CompressionCodecs using CompressionCodecFactory" on page 103, if your input files are compressed, they will be decompressed automatically as they are read by MapReduce, using the filename extension to determine which codec to use.

In order to compress the output of a MapReduce job, in the job configuration, set the `mapreduce.output.fileoutputformat.compress` property to `true` and set the `mapreduce.output.fileoutputformat.compress.codec` property to the classname of the compression codec you want to use. Alternatively, you can use the static convenience methods on `FileOutputFormat` to set these properties, as shown in Example 5-4.

Example 5-4. Application to run the maximum temperature job producing compressed output

```
public class MaxTemperatureWithCompression {

  public static void main(String[] args) throws Exception {
    if (args.length != 2) {
      System.err.println("Usage: MaxTemperatureWithCompression <input path> " +
          "<output path>");
      System.exit(-1);
    }

    Job job = new Job();
    job.setJarByClass(MaxTemperature.class);

    FileInputFormat.addInputPath(job, new Path(args[0]));
    FileOutputFormat.setOutputPath(job, new Path(args[1]));

    job.setOutputKeyClass(Text.class);
    job.setOutputValueClass(IntWritable.class);

    FileOutputFormat.setCompressOutput(job, true);
```

```
    FileOutputFormat.setOutputCompressorClass(job, GzipCodec.class);

    job.setMapperClass(MaxTemperatureMapper.class);
    job.setCombinerClass(MaxTemperatureReducer.class);
    job.setReducerClass(MaxTemperatureReducer.class);

    System.exit(job.waitForCompletion(true) ? 0 : 1);
  }
}
```

We run the program over compressed input (which doesn't have to use the same compression format as the output, although it does in this example) as follows:

```
% hadoop MaxTemperatureWithCompression input/ncdc/sample.txt.gz output
```

Each part of the final output is compressed; in this case, there is a single part:

```
% gunzip -c output/part-r-00000.gz
1949    111
1950    22
```

If you are emitting sequence files for your output, you can set the mapreduce.out
put.fileoutputformat.compress.type property to control the type of compression
to use. The default is RECORD, which compresses individual records. Changing this to
BLOCK, which compresses groups of records, is recommended because it compresses
better (see "The SequenceFile format" on page 133).

There is also a static convenience method on SequenceFileOutputFormat called
setOutputCompressionType() to set this property.

The configuration properties to set compression for MapReduce job outputs are summarized in Table 5-5. If your MapReduce driver uses the Tool interface (described in "GenericOptionsParser, Tool, and ToolRunner" on page 148), you can pass any of these properties to the program on the command line, which may be more convenient than modifying your program to hardcode the compression properties.

Table 5-5. MapReduce compression properties

Property name	Type	Default value	Description
mapreduce.output.fileoutput format.compress	boolean	false	Whether to compress outputs
mapreduce.output.fileoutput format.compress.codec	Class name	org.apache.hadoop.io.com press.DefaultCodec	The compression codec to use for outputs
mapreduce.output.fileoutput format.compress.type	String	RECORD	The type of compression to use for sequence file outputs: NONE, RECORD, or BLOCK

Compressing map output

Even if your MapReduce application reads and writes uncompressed data, it may benefit from compressing the intermediate output of the map phase. The map output is written to disk and transferred across the network to the reducer nodes, so by using a fast compressor such as LZO, LZ4, or Snappy, you can get performance gains simply because the volume of data to transfer is reduced. The configuration properties to enable compression for map outputs and to set the compression format are shown in Table 5-6.

Table 5-6. Map output compression properties

Property name	Type	Default value	Description
mapreduce.map.output.compress	boolean	false	Whether to compress map outputs
mapreduce.map.output.compress.codec	Class	org.apache.hadoop.io.compress.DefaultCodec	The compression codec to use for map outputs

Here are the lines to add to enable gzip map output compression in your job (using the new API):

```
Configuration conf = new Configuration();
conf.setBoolean(Job.MAP_OUTPUT_COMPRESS, true);
conf.setClass(Job.MAP_OUTPUT_COMPRESS_CODEC, GzipCodec.class,
    CompressionCodec.class);
Job job = new Job(conf);
```

In the old API (see Appendix D), there are convenience methods on the `JobConf` object for doing the same thing:

```
conf.setCompressMapOutput(true);
conf.setMapOutputCompressorClass(GzipCodec.class);
```

Serialization

Serialization is the process of turning structured objects into a byte stream for transmission over a network or for writing to persistent storage. *Deserialization* is the reverse process of turning a byte stream back into a series of structured objects.

Serialization is used in two quite distinct areas of distributed data processing: for interprocess communication and for persistent storage.

In Hadoop, interprocess communication between nodes in the system is implemented using *remote procedure calls* (RPCs). The RPC protocol uses serialization to render the message into a binary stream to be sent to the remote node, which then deserializes the binary stream into the original message. In general, it is desirable that an RPC serialization format is:

Compact

> A compact format makes the best use of network bandwidth, which is the most scarce resource in a data center.

Fast

> Interprocess communication forms the backbone for a distributed system, so it is essential that there is as little performance overhead as possible for the serialization and deserialization process.

Extensible

> Protocols change over time to meet new requirements, so it should be straightforward to evolve the protocol in a controlled manner for clients and servers. For example, it should be possible to add a new argument to a method call and have the new servers accept messages in the old format (without the new argument) from old clients.

Interoperable

> For some systems, it is desirable to be able to support clients that are written in different languages to the server, so the format needs to be designed to make this possible.

On the face of it, the data format chosen for persistent storage would have different requirements from a serialization framework. After all, the lifespan of an RPC is less than a second, whereas persistent data may be read years after it was written. But it turns out, the four desirable properties of an RPC's serialization format are also crucial for a persistent storage format. We want the storage format to be compact (to make efficient use of storage space), fast (so the overhead in reading or writing terabytes of data is minimal), extensible (so we can transparently read data written in an older format), and interoperable (so we can read or write persistent data using different languages).

Hadoop uses its own serialization format, Writables, which is certainly compact and fast, but not so easy to extend or use from languages other than Java. Because Writables are central to Hadoop (most MapReduce programs use them for their key and value types), we look at them in some depth in the next three sections, before looking at some of the other serialization frameworks supported in Hadoop. Avro (a serialization system that was designed to overcome some of the limitations of Writables) is covered in Chapter 12.

The Writable Interface

The `Writable` interface defines two methods—one for writing its state to a `DataOutput` binary stream and one for reading its state from a `DataInput` binary stream:

```
package org.apache.hadoop.io;

import java.io.DataOutput;
```

```
import java.io.DataInput;
import java.io.IOException;

public interface Writable {
  void write(DataOutput out) throws IOException;
  void readFields(DataInput in) throws IOException;
}
```

Let's look at a particular `Writable` to see what we can do with it. We will use `IntWritable`, a wrapper for a Java `int`. We can create one and set its value using the `set()` method:

```
IntWritable writable = new IntWritable();
writable.set(163);
```

Equivalently, we can use the constructor that takes the integer value:

```
IntWritable writable = new IntWritable(163);
```

To examine the serialized form of the `IntWritable`, we write a small helper method that wraps a `java.io.ByteArrayOutputStream` in a `java.io.DataOutputStream` (an implementation of `java.io.DataOutput`) to capture the bytes in the serialized stream:

```
public static byte[] serialize(Writable writable) throws IOException {
  ByteArrayOutputStream out = new ByteArrayOutputStream();
  DataOutputStream dataOut = new DataOutputStream(out);
  writable.write(dataOut);
  dataOut.close();
  return out.toByteArray();
}
```

An integer is written using four bytes (as we see using JUnit 4 assertions):

```
byte[] bytes = serialize(writable);
assertThat(bytes.length, is(4));
```

The bytes are written in big-endian order (so the most significant byte is written to the stream first, which is dictated by the `java.io.DataOutput` interface), and we can see their hexadecimal representation by using a method on Hadoop's `StringUtils`:

```
assertThat(StringUtils.byteToHexString(bytes), is("000000a3"));
```

Let's try deserialization. Again, we create a helper method to read a `Writable` object from a byte array:

```
public static byte[] deserialize(Writable writable, byte[] bytes)
    throws IOException {
  ByteArrayInputStream in = new ByteArrayInputStream(bytes);
  DataInputStream dataIn = new DataInputStream(in);
  writable.readFields(dataIn);
  dataIn.close();
  return bytes;
}
```

We construct a new, value-less IntWritable, and then call deserialize() to read from the output data that we just wrote. Then we check that its value, retrieved using the get() method, is the original value, 163:

```
IntWritable newWritable = new IntWritable();
deserialize(newWritable, bytes);
assertThat(newWritable.get(), is(163));
```

WritableComparable and comparators

IntWritable implements the WritableComparable interface, which is just a subinterface of the Writable and java.lang.Comparable interfaces:

```
package org.apache.hadoop.io;

public interface WritableComparable<T> extends Writable, Comparable<T> {
}
```

Comparison of types is crucial for MapReduce, where there is a sorting phase during which keys are compared with one another. One optimization that Hadoop provides is the RawComparator extension of Java's Comparator:

```
package org.apache.hadoop.io;

import java.util.Comparator;

public interface RawComparator<T> extends Comparator<T> {

  public int compare(byte[] b1, int s1, int l1, byte[] b2, int s2, int l2);

}
```

This interface permits implementors to compare records read from a stream without deserializing them into objects, thereby avoiding any overhead of object creation. For example, the comparator for IntWritables implements the raw compare() method by reading an integer from each of the byte arrays b1 and b2 and comparing them directly from the given start positions (s1 and s2) and lengths (l1 and l2).

WritableComparator is a general-purpose implementation of RawComparator for WritableComparable classes. It provides two main functions. First, it provides a default implementation of the raw compare() method that deserializes the objects to be compared from the stream and invokes the object compare() method. Second, it acts as a factory for RawComparator instances (that Writable implementations have registered). For example, to obtain a comparator for IntWritable, we just use:

```
RawComparator<IntWritable> comparator =
    WritableComparator.get(IntWritable.class);
```

The comparator can be used to compare two IntWritable objects:

```
IntWritable w1 = new IntWritable(163);
IntWritable w2 = new IntWritable(67);
assertThat(comparator.compare(w1, w2), greaterThan(0));
```

or their serialized representations:

```
byte[] b1 = serialize(w1);
byte[] b2 = serialize(w2);
assertThat(comparator.compare(b1, 0, b1.length, b2, 0, b2.length),
    greaterThan(0));
```

Writable Classes

Hadoop comes with a large selection of Writable classes, which are available in the org.apache.hadoop.io package. They form the class hierarchy shown in Figure 5-1.

Writable wrappers for Java primitives

There are Writable wrappers for all the Java primitive types (see Table 5-7) except char (which can be stored in an IntWritable). All have a get() and set() method for retrieving and storing the wrapped value.

Table 5-7. Writable wrapper classes for Java primitives

Java primitive	Writable implementation	Serialized size (bytes)
boolean	BooleanWritable	1
byte	ByteWritable	1
short	ShortWritable	2
int	IntWritable	4
	VIntWritable	1–5
float	FloatWritable	4
long	LongWritable	8
	VLongWritable	1–9
double	DoubleWritable	8

When it comes to encoding integers, there is a choice between the fixed-length formats (IntWritable and LongWritable) and the variable-length formats (VIntWritable and VLongWritable). The variable-length formats use only a single byte to encode the value if it is small enough (between –112 and 127, inclusive); otherwise, they use the first byte to indicate whether the value is positive or negative, and how many bytes follow. For example, 163 requires two bytes:

```
byte[] data = serialize(new VIntWritable(163));
assertThat(StringUtils.byteToHexString(data), is("8fa3"));
```

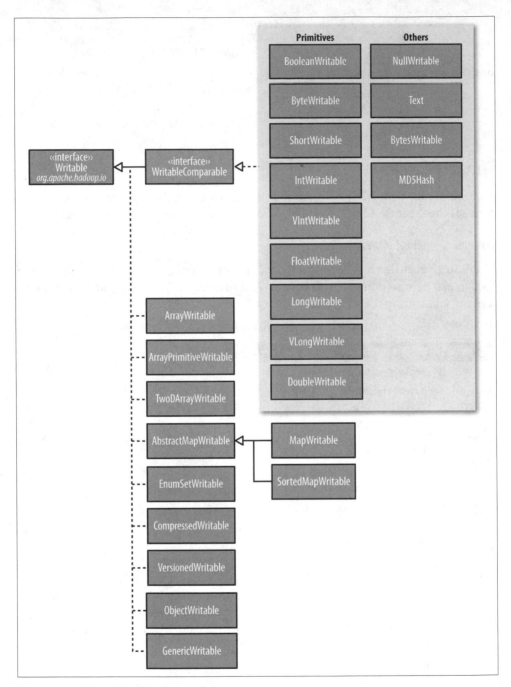

Figure 5-1. Writable class hierarchy

How do you choose between a fixed-length and a variable-length encoding? Fixed-length encodings are good when the distribution of values is fairly uniform across the whole value space, such as when using a (well-designed) hash function. Most numeric variables tend to have nonuniform distributions, though, and on average, the variable-length encoding will save space. Another advantage of variable-length encodings is that you can switch from VIntWritable to VLongWritable, because their encodings are actually the same. So, by choosing a variable-length representation, you have room to grow without committing to an 8-byte long representation from the beginning.

Text

Text is a Writable for UTF-8 sequences. It can be thought of as the Writable equivalent of java.lang.String.

The Text class uses an int (with a variable-length encoding) to store the number of bytes in the string encoding, so the maximum value is 2 GB. Furthermore, Text uses standard UTF-8, which makes it potentially easier to interoperate with other tools that understand UTF-8.

Indexing. Because of its emphasis on using standard UTF-8, there are some differences between Text and the Java String class. Indexing for the Text class is in terms of position in the encoded byte sequence, not the Unicode character in the string or the Java char code unit (as it is for String). For ASCII strings, these three concepts of index position coincide. Here is an example to demonstrate the use of the charAt() method:

```
Text t = new Text("hadoop");
assertThat(t.getLength(), is(6));
assertThat(t.getBytes().length, is(6));

assertThat(t.charAt(2), is((int) 'd'));
assertThat("Out of bounds", t.charAt(100), is(-1));
```

Notice that charAt() returns an int representing a Unicode code point, unlike the String variant that returns a char. Text also has a find() method, which is analogous to String's indexOf():

```
Text t = new Text("hadoop");
assertThat("Find a substring", t.find("do"), is(2));
assertThat("Finds first 'o'", t.find("o"), is(3));
assertThat("Finds 'o' from position 4 or later", t.find("o", 4), is(4));
assertThat("No match", t.find("pig"), is(-1));
```

Unicode. When we start using characters that are encoded with more than a single byte, the differences between `Text` and `String` become clear. Consider the Unicode characters shown in Table 5-8.[2]

Table 5-8. Unicode characters

Unicode code point	U+0041	U+00DF	U+6771	U+10400
Name	LATIN CAPITAL LETTER A	LATIN SMALL LETTER SHARP S	N/A (a unified Han ideograph)	DESERET CAPITAL LETTER LONG I
UTF-8 code units	41	c3 9f	e6 9d b1	f0 90 90 80
Java representation	\u0041	\u00DF	\u6771	\uD801\uDC00

All but the last character in the table, U+10400, can be expressed using a single Java char. U+10400 is a supplementary character and is represented by two Java chars, known as a *surrogate pair*. The tests in Example 5-5 show the differences between `String` and `Text` when processing a string of the four characters from Table 5-8.

Example 5-5. Tests showing the differences between the String and Text classes

```
public class StringTextComparisonTest {

  @Test
  public void string() throws UnsupportedEncodingException {

    String s = "\u0041\u00DF\u6771\uD801\uDC00";
    assertThat(s.length(), is(5));
    assertThat(s.getBytes("UTF-8").length, is(10));

    assertThat(s.indexOf("\u0041"), is(0));
    assertThat(s.indexOf("\u00DF"), is(1));
    assertThat(s.indexOf("\u6771"), is(2));
    assertThat(s.indexOf("\uD801\uDC00"), is(3));

    assertThat(s.charAt(0), is('\u0041'));
    assertThat(s.charAt(1), is('\u00DF'));
    assertThat(s.charAt(2), is('\u6771'));
    assertThat(s.charAt(3), is('\uD801'));
    assertThat(s.charAt(4), is('\uDC00'));

    assertThat(s.codePointAt(0), is(0x0041));
    assertThat(s.codePointAt(1), is(0x00DF));
    assertThat(s.codePointAt(2), is(0x6771));
    assertThat(s.codePointAt(3), is(0x10400));
  }
```

---

2. This example is based on one from Norbert Lindenberg and Masayoshi Okutsu's "Supplementary Characters in the Java Platform," (*http://bit.ly/java_supp_characters*) May 2004.

```
@Test
public void text() {

    Text t = new Text("\u0041\u00DF\u6771\uD801\uDC00");
    assertThat(t.getLength(), is(10));

    assertThat(t.find("\u0041"), is(0));
    assertThat(t.find("\u00DF"), is(1));
    assertThat(t.find("\u6771"), is(3));
    assertThat(t.find("\uD801\uDC00"), is(6));

    assertThat(t.charAt(0), is(0x0041));
    assertThat(t.charAt(1), is(0x00DF));
    assertThat(t.charAt(3), is(0x6771));
    assertThat(t.charAt(6), is(0x10400));
  }
}
```

The test confirms that the length of a String is the number of char code units it contains (five, made up of one from each of the first three characters in the string and a surrogate pair from the last), whereas the length of a Text object is the number of bytes in its UTF-8 encoding (10 = 1+2+3+4). Similarly, the indexOf() method in String returns an index in char code units, and find() for Text returns a byte offset.

The charAt() method in String returns the char code unit for the given index, which in the case of a surrogate pair will not represent a whole Unicode character. The code PointAt() method, indexed by char code unit, is needed to retrieve a single Unicode character represented as an int. In fact, the charAt() method in Text is more like the codePointAt() method than its namesake in String. The only difference is that it is indexed by byte offset.

Iteration. Iterating over the Unicode characters in Text is complicated by the use of byte offsets for indexing, since you can't just increment the index. The idiom for iteration is a little obscure (see Example 5-6): turn the Text object into a java.nio.ByteBuffer, then repeatedly call the bytesToCodePoint() static method on Text with the buffer. This method extracts the next code point as an int and updates the position in the buffer. The end of the string is detected when bytesToCodePoint() returns –1.

Example 5-6. Iterating over the characters in a Text object

```
public class TextIterator {

  public static void main(String[] args) {
    Text t = new Text("\u0041\u00DF\u6771\uD801\uDC00");

    ByteBuffer buf = ByteBuffer.wrap(t.getBytes(), 0, t.getLength());
    int cp;
    while (buf.hasRemaining() && (cp = Text.bytesToCodePoint(buf)) != -1) {
```

```
        System.out.println(Integer.toHexString(cp));
    }
  }
}
```

Running the program prints the code points for the four characters in the string:

```
% hadoop TextIterator
41
df
6771
10400
```

Mutability. Another difference from `String` is that `Text` is mutable (like all `Writable` implementations in Hadoop, except `NullWritable`, which is a singleton). You can reuse a `Text` instance by calling one of the `set()` methods on it. For example:

```
Text t = new Text("hadoop");
t.set("pig");
assertThat(t.getLength(), is(3));
assertThat(t.getBytes().length, is(3));
```

> In some situations, the byte array returned by the `getBytes()` meth-
> od may be longer than the length returned by `getLength()`:
>
> ```
> Text t = new Text("hadoop");
> t.set(new Text("pig"));
> assertThat(t.getLength(), is(3));
> assertThat("Byte length not shortened", t.getBytes().length,
>     is(6));
> ```
>
> This shows why it is imperative that you always call `getLength()`
> when calling `getBytes()`, so you know how much of the byte array
> is valid data.

Resorting to String. `Text` doesn't have as rich an API for manipulating strings as `java.lang.String`, so in many cases, you need to convert the `Text` object to a `String`. This is done in the usual way, using the `toString()` method:

```
assertThat(new Text("hadoop").toString(), is("hadoop"));
```

BytesWritable

`BytesWritable` is a wrapper for an array of binary data. Its serialized format is a 4-byte integer field that specifies the number of bytes to follow, followed by the bytes themselves. For example, the byte array of length 2 with values 3 and 5 is serialized as a 4-byte integer (`00000002`) followed by the two bytes from the array (`03` and `05`):

```
BytesWritable b = new BytesWritable(new byte[] { 3, 5 });
byte[] bytes = serialize(b);
assertThat(StringUtils.byteToHexString(bytes), is("000000020305"));
```

BytesWritable is mutable, and its value may be changed by calling its set() method. As with Text, the size of the byte array returned from the getBytes() method for BytesWritable—the capacity—may not reflect the actual size of the data stored in the BytesWritable. You can determine the size of the BytesWritable by calling get Length(). To demonstrate:

```
b.setCapacity(11);
assertThat(b.getLength(), is(2));
assertThat(b.getBytes().length, is(11));
```

NullWritable

NullWritable is a special type of Writable, as it has a zero-length serialization. No bytes are written to or read from the stream. It is used as a placeholder; for example, in Map-Reduce, a key or a value can be declared as a NullWritable when you don't need to use that position, effectively storing a constant empty value. NullWritable can also be useful as a key in a SequenceFile when you want to store a list of values, as opposed to key-value pairs. It is an immutable singleton, and the instance can be retrieved by calling NullWritable.get().

ObjectWritable and GenericWritable

ObjectWritable is a general-purpose wrapper for the following: Java primitives, String, enum, Writable, null, or arrays of any of these types. It is used in Hadoop RPC to marshal and unmarshal method arguments and return types.

ObjectWritable is useful when a field can be of more than one type. For example, if the values in a SequenceFile have multiple types, you can declare the value type as an ObjectWritable and wrap each type in an ObjectWritable. Being a general-purpose mechanism, it wastes a fair amount of space because it writes the classname of the wrapped type every time it is serialized. In cases where the number of types is small and known ahead of time, this can be improved by having a static array of types and using the index into the array as the serialized reference to the type. This is the approach that GenericWritable takes, and you have to subclass it to specify which types to support.

Writable collections

The org.apache.hadoop.io package includes six Writable collection types: Array Writable, ArrayPrimitiveWritable, TwoDArrayWritable, MapWritable, SortedMapWritable, and EnumSetWritable.

ArrayWritable and TwoDArrayWritable are Writable implementations for arrays and two-dimensional arrays (array of arrays) of Writable instances. All the elements of an

`ArrayWritable` or a `TwoDArrayWritable` must be instances of the same class, which is specified at construction as follows:

```
ArrayWritable writable = new ArrayWritable(Text.class);
```

In contexts where the `Writable` is defined by type, such as in `SequenceFile` keys or values or as input to MapReduce in general, you need to subclass `ArrayWritable` (or `TwoDArrayWritable`, as appropriate) to set the type statically. For example:

```
public class TextArrayWritable extends ArrayWritable {
  public TextArrayWritable() {
    super(Text.class);
  }
}
```

`ArrayWritable` and `TwoDArrayWritable` both have `get()` and `set()` methods, as well as a `toArray()` method, which creates a shallow copy of the array (or 2D array).

`ArrayPrimitiveWritable` is a wrapper for arrays of Java primitives. The component type is detected when you call `set()`, so there is no need to subclass to set the type.

`MapWritable` is an implementation of `java.util.Map<Writable, Writable>`, and `SortedMapWritable` is an implementation of `java.util.SortedMap<WritableComparable, Writable>`. The type of each key and value field is a part of the serialization format for that field. The type is stored as a single byte that acts as an index into an array of types. The array is populated with the standard types in the `org.apache.hadoop.io` package, but custom `Writable` types are accommodated, too, by writing a header that encodes the type array for nonstandard types. As they are implemented, `MapWritable` and `SortedMapWritable` use positive `byte` values for custom types, so a maximum of 127 distinct nonstandard `Writable` classes can be used in any particular `MapWritable` or `SortedMapWritable` instance. Here's a demonstration of using a `MapWritable` with different types for keys and values:

```
MapWritable src = new MapWritable();
src.put(new IntWritable(1), new Text("cat"));
src.put(new VIntWritable(2), new LongWritable(163));

MapWritable dest = new MapWritable();
WritableUtils.cloneInto(dest, src);
assertThat((Text) dest.get(new IntWritable(1)), is(new Text("cat")));
assertThat((LongWritable) dest.get(new VIntWritable(2)),
    is(new LongWritable(163)));
```

Conspicuous by their absence are `Writable` collection implementations for sets and lists. A general set can be emulated by using a `MapWritable` (or a `SortedMapWritable` for a sorted set) with `NullWritable` values. There is also `EnumSetWritable` for sets of enum types. For lists of a single type of `Writable`, `ArrayWritable` is adequate, but to store different types of `Writable` in a single list, you can use `GenericWritable` to wrap the elements in an `ArrayWritable`. Alternatively, you could write a general `ListWrita` `ble` using the ideas from `MapWritable`.

Implementing a Custom Writable

Hadoop comes with a useful set of `Writable` implementations that serve most purposes; however, on occasion, you may need to write your own custom implementation. With a custom `Writable`, you have full control over the binary representation and the sort order. Because `Writables` are at the heart of the MapReduce data path, tuning the binary representation can have a significant effect on performance. The stock `Writable` implementations that come with Hadoop are well tuned, but for more elaborate structures, it is often better to create a new `Writable` type rather than composing the stock types.

 If you are considering writing a custom `Writable`, it may be worth trying another serialization framework, like Avro, that allows you to define custom types declaratively. See "Serialization Frameworks" on page 126 and Chapter 12.

To demonstrate how to create a custom `Writable`, we shall write an implementation that represents a pair of strings, called `TextPair`. The basic implementation is shown in Example 5-7.

Example 5-7. A Writable implementation that stores a pair of Text objects

```java
import java.io.*;

import org.apache.hadoop.io.*;

public class TextPair implements WritableComparable<TextPair> {

  private Text first;
  private Text second;

  public TextPair() {
    set(new Text(), new Text());
  }

  public TextPair(String first, String second) {
    set(new Text(first), new Text(second));
  }

  public TextPair(Text first, Text second) {
    set(first, second);
  }

  public void set(Text first, Text second) {
```

```java
    this.first = first;
    this.second = second;
  }

  public Text getFirst() {
    return first;
  }

  public Text getSecond() {
    return second;
  }

  @Override
  public void write(DataOutput out) throws IOException {
    first.write(out);
    second.write(out);
  }

  @Override
  public void readFields(DataInput in) throws IOException {
    first.readFields(in);
    second.readFields(in);
  }

  @Override
  public int hashCode() {
    return first.hashCode() * 163 + second.hashCode();
  }

  @Override
  public boolean equals(Object o) {
    if (o instanceof TextPair) {
      TextPair tp = (TextPair) o;
      return first.equals(tp.first) && second.equals(tp.second);
    }
    return false;
  }

  @Override
  public String toString() {
    return first + "\t" + second;
  }

  @Override
  public int compareTo(TextPair tp) {
    int cmp = first.compareTo(tp.first);
    if (cmp != 0) {
      return cmp;
    }
    return second.compareTo(tp.second);
  }
}
```

The first part of the implementation is straightforward: there are two Text instance variables, first and second, and associated constructors, getters, and setters. All Writable implementations must have a default constructor so that the MapReduce framework can instantiate them, then populate their fields by calling readFields(). Writable instances are mutable and often reused, so you should take care to avoid allocating objects in the write() or readFields() methods.

TextPair's write() method serializes each Text object in turn to the output stream by delegating to the Text objects themselves. Similarly, readFields() deserializes the bytes from the input stream by delegating to each Text object. The DataOutput and DataInput interfaces have a rich set of methods for serializing and deserializing Java primitives, so, in general, you have complete control over the wire format of your Writable object.

Just as you would for any value object you write in Java, you should override the hashCode(), equals(), and toString() methods from java.lang.Object. The hash Code() method is used by the HashPartitioner (the default partitioner in MapReduce) to choose a reduce partition, so you should make sure that you write a good hash function that mixes well to ensure reduce partitions are of a similar size.

If you plan to use your custom Writable with TextOutputFormat, you must implement its toString() method. TextOutputFormat calls toString() on keys and values for their output representation. For TextPair, we write the underlying Text objects as strings separated by a tab character.

TextPair is an implementation of WritableComparable, so it provides an implementation of the compareTo() method that imposes the ordering you would expect: it sorts by the first string followed by the second. Notice that, apart from the number of Text objects it can store, TextPair differs from TextArrayWritable (which we discussed in the previous section), since TextArrayWritable is only a Writable, not a Writable Comparable.

Implementing a RawComparator for speed

The code for TextPair in Example 5-7 will work as it stands; however, there is a further optimization we can make. As explained in "WritableComparable and comparators" on page 112, when TextPair is being used as a key in MapReduce, it will have to be deserialized into an object for the compareTo() method to be invoked. What if it were possible to compare two TextPair objects just by looking at their serialized representations?

It turns out that we can do this because TextPair is the concatenation of two Text objects, and the binary representation of a Text object is a variable-length integer containing the number of bytes in the UTF-8 representation of the string, followed by the

UTF-8 bytes themselves. The trick is to read the initial length so we know how long the first Text object's byte representation is; then we can delegate to Text's RawCompara tor and invoke it with the appropriate offsets for the first or second string. Example 5-8 gives the details (note that this code is nested in the TextPair class).

Example 5-8. A RawComparator for comparing TextPair byte representations

```java
public static class Comparator extends WritableComparator {

  private static final Text.Comparator TEXT_COMPARATOR = new Text.Comparator();

  public Comparator() {
    super(TextPair.class);
  }

  @Override
  public int compare(byte[] b1, int s1, int l1,
                     byte[] b2, int s2, int l2) {

    try {
      int firstL1 = WritableUtils.decodeVIntSize(b1[s1]) + readVInt(b1, s1);
      int firstL2 = WritableUtils.decodeVIntSize(b2[s2]) + readVInt(b2, s2);
      int cmp = TEXT_COMPARATOR.compare(b1, s1, firstL1, b2, s2, firstL2);
      if (cmp != 0) {
        return cmp;
      }
      return TEXT_COMPARATOR.compare(b1, s1 + firstL1, l1 - firstL1,
                                     b2, s2 + firstL2, l2 - firstL2);
    } catch (IOException e) {
      throw new IllegalArgumentException(e);
    }
  }
}

static {
  WritableComparator.define(TextPair.class, new Comparator());
}
```

We actually subclass WritableComparator rather than implementing RawComparator directly, since it provides some convenience methods and default implementations. The subtle part of this code is calculating firstL1 and firstL2, the lengths of the first Text field in each byte stream. Each is made up of the length of the variable-length integer (returned by decodeVIntSize() on WritableUtils) and the value it is encoding (returned by readVInt()).

The static block registers the raw comparator so that whenever MapReduce sees the TextPair class, it knows to use the raw comparator as its default comparator.

Custom comparators

As you can see with `TextPair`, writing raw comparators takes some care because you have to deal with details at the byte level. It is worth looking at some of the implementations of `Writable` in the `org.apache.hadoop.io` package for further ideas if you need to write your own. The utility methods on `WritableUtils` are very handy, too.

Custom comparators should also be written to be `RawComparators`, if possible. These are comparators that implement a different sort order from the natural sort order defined by the default comparator. Example 5-9 shows a comparator for `TextPair`, called `FirstComparator`, that considers only the first string of the pair. Note that we override the `compare()` method that takes objects so both `compare()` methods have the same semantics.

We will make use of this comparator in Chapter 9, when we look at joins and secondary sorting in MapReduce (see "Joins" on page 268).

Example 5-9. A custom RawComparator for comparing the first field of TextPair byte representations

```java
public static class FirstComparator extends WritableComparator {

  private static final Text.Comparator TEXT_COMPARATOR = new Text.Comparator();

  public FirstComparator() {
    super(TextPair.class);
  }

  @Override
  public int compare(byte[] b1, int s1, int l1,
                     byte[] b2, int s2, int l2) {

    try {
      int firstL1 = WritableUtils.decodeVIntSize(b1[s1]) + readVInt(b1, s1);
      int firstL2 = WritableUtils.decodeVIntSize(b2[s2]) + readVInt(b2, s2);
      return TEXT_COMPARATOR.compare(b1, s1, firstL1, b2, s2, firstL2);
    } catch (IOException e) {
      throw new IllegalArgumentException(e);
    }
  }

  @Override
  public int compare(WritableComparable a, WritableComparable b) {
    if (a instanceof TextPair && b instanceof TextPair) {
      return ((TextPair) a).first.compareTo(((TextPair) b).first);
    }
    return super.compare(a, b);
  }
}
```

Serialization Frameworks

Although most MapReduce programs use Writable key and value types, this isn't mandated by the MapReduce API. In fact, any type can be used; the only requirement is a mechanism that translates to and from a binary representation of each type.

To support this, Hadoop has an API for pluggable serialization frameworks. A serialization framework is represented by an implementation of Serialization (in the org.apache.hadoop.io.serializer package). WritableSerialization, for example, is the implementation of Serialization for Writable types.

A Serialization defines a mapping from types to Serializer instances (for turning an object into a byte stream) and Deserializer instances (for turning a byte stream into an object).

Set the io.serializations property to a comma-separated list of classnames in order to register Serialization implementations. Its default value includes org.apache.hadoop.io.serializer.WritableSerialization and the Avro Specific and Reflect serializations (see "Avro Data Types and Schemas" on page 346), which means that only Writable or Avro objects can be serialized or deserialized out of the box.

Hadoop includes a class called JavaSerialization that uses Java Object Serialization. Although it makes it convenient to be able to use standard Java types such as Integer or String in MapReduce programs, Java Object Serialization is not as efficient as Writables, so it's not worth making this trade-off (see the following sidebar).

Why Not Use Java Object Serialization?

Java comes with its own serialization mechanism, called Java Object Serialization (often referred to simply as "Java Serialization"), that is tightly integrated with the language, so it's natural to ask why this wasn't used in Hadoop. Here's what Doug Cutting said in response to that question:

> Why didn't I use Serialization when we first started Hadoop? Because it looked big and hairy and I thought we needed something lean and mean, where we had precise control over exactly how objects are written and read, since that is central to Hadoop. With Serialization you can get some control, but you have to fight for it.
>
> The logic for not using RMI [Remote Method Invocation] was similar. Effective, high-performance inter-process communications are critical to Hadoop. I felt like we'd need to precisely control how things like connections, timeouts and buffers are handled, and RMI gives you little control over those.

The problem is that Java Serialization doesn't meet the criteria for a serialization format listed earlier: compact, fast, extensible, and interoperable.

Serialization IDL

There are a number of other serialization frameworks that approach the problem in a different way: rather than defining types through code, you define them in a language-neutral, declarative fashion, using an *interface description language* (IDL). The system can then generate types for different languages, which is good for interoperability. They also typically define versioning schemes that make type evolution straightforward.

Apache Thrift (*http://thrift.apache.org/*) and Google Protocol Buffers (*http://code.google.com/p/protobuf/*) are both popular serialization frameworks, and both are commonly used as a format for persistent binary data. There is limited support for these as MapReduce formats;[3] however, they are used internally in parts of Hadoop for RPC and data exchange.

Avro is an IDL-based serialization framework designed to work well with large-scale data processing in Hadoop. It is covered in Chapter 12.

File-Based Data Structures

For some applications, you need a specialized data structure to hold your data. For doing MapReduce-based processing, putting each blob of binary data into its own file doesn't scale, so Hadoop developed a number of higher-level containers for these situations.

SequenceFile

Imagine a logfile where each log record is a new line of text. If you want to log binary types, plain text isn't a suitable format. Hadoop's SequenceFile class fits the bill in this situation, providing a persistent data structure for binary key-value pairs. To use it as a logfile format, you would choose a key, such as timestamp represented by a LongWritable, and the value would be a Writable that represents the quantity being logged.

SequenceFiles also work well as containers for smaller files. HDFS and MapReduce are optimized for large files, so packing files into a SequenceFile makes storing and processing the smaller files more efficient ("Processing a whole file as a record" on page 228 contains a program to pack files into a SequenceFile).[4]

---

3. Twitter's Elephant Bird project (*http://github.com/kevinweil/elephant-bird*) includes tools for working with Thrift and Protocol Buffers in Hadoop.

4. In a similar vein, the blog post "A Million Little Files" (*http://stuartsierra.com/2008/04/24/a-million-little-files*) by Stuart Sierra includes code for converting a tar file into a SequenceFile.

Writing a SequenceFile

To create a SequenceFile, use one of its createWriter() static methods, which return a SequenceFile.Writer instance. There are several overloaded versions, but they all require you to specify a stream to write to (either an FSDataOutputStream or a FileSystem and Path pairing), a Configuration object, and the key and value types. Optional arguments include the compression type and codec, a Progressable callback to be informed of write progress, and a Metadata instance to be stored in the SequenceFile header.

The keys and values stored in a SequenceFile do not necessarily need to be Writables. Any types that can be serialized and deserialized by a Serialization may be used.

Once you have a SequenceFile.Writer, you then write key-value pairs using the append() method. When you've finished, you call the close() method (SequenceFile.Writer implements java.io.Closeable).

Example 5-10 shows a short program to write some key-value pairs to a SequenceFile using the API just described.

Example 5-10. Writing a SequenceFile

```
public class SequenceFileWriteDemo {

  private static final String[] DATA = {
    "One, two, buckle my shoe",
    "Three, four, shut the door",
    "Five, six, pick up sticks",
    "Seven, eight, lay them straight",
    "Nine, ten, a big fat hen"
  };

  public static void main(String[] args) throws IOException {
    String uri = args[0];
    Configuration conf = new Configuration();
    FileSystem fs = FileSystem.get(URI.create(uri), conf);
    Path path = new Path(uri);

    IntWritable key = new IntWritable();
    Text value = new Text();
    SequenceFile.Writer writer = null;
    try {
      writer = SequenceFile.createWriter(fs, conf, path,
          key.getClass(), value.getClass());

      for (int i = 0; i < 100; i++) {
        key.set(100 - i);
        value.set(DATA[i % DATA.length]);
        System.out.printf("[%s]\t%s\t%s\n", writer.getLength(), key, value);
        writer.append(key, value);
      }
```

```
    } finally {
      IOUtils.closeStream(writer);
    }
  }
}
```

The keys in the sequence file are integers counting down from 100 to 1, represented as IntWritable objects. The values are Text objects. Before each record is appended to the SequenceFile.Writer, we call the getLength() method to discover the current position in the file. (We will use this information about record boundaries in the next section, when we read the file nonsequentially.) We write the position out to the console, along with the key and value pairs. The result of running it is shown here:

```
% hadoop SequenceFileWriteDemo numbers.seq
[128]   100   One, two, buckle my shoe
[173]   99    Three, four, shut the door
[220]   98    Five, six, pick up sticks
[264]   97    Seven, eight, lay them straight
[314]   96    Nine, ten, a big fat hen
[359]   95    One, two, buckle my shoe
[404]   94    Three, four, shut the door
[451]   93    Five, six, pick up sticks
[495]   92    Seven, eight, lay them straight
[545]   91    Nine, ten, a big fat hen
...
[1976]  60    One, two, buckle my shoe
[2021]  59    Three, four, shut the door
[2088]  58    Five, six, pick up sticks
[2132]  57    Seven, eight, lay them straight
[2182]  56    Nine, ten, a big fat hen
...
[4557]  5     One, two, buckle my shoe
[4602]  4     Three, four, shut the door
[4649]  3     Five, six, pick up sticks
[4693]  2     Seven, eight, lay them straight
[4743]  1     Nine, ten, a big fat hen
```

Reading a SequenceFile

Reading sequence files from beginning to end is a matter of creating an instance of SequenceFile.Reader and iterating over records by repeatedly invoking one of the next() methods. Which one you use depends on the serialization framework you are using. If you are using Writable types, you can use the next() method that takes a key and a value argument and reads the next key and value in the stream into these variables:

```
public boolean next(Writable key, Writable val)
```

The return value is true if a key-value pair was read and false if the end of the file has been reached.

For other, non-Writable serialization frameworks (such as Apache Thrift), you should use these two methods:

```
public Object next(Object key) throws IOException
public Object getCurrentValue(Object val) throws IOException
```

In this case, you need to make sure that the serialization you want to use has been set in the io.serializations property; see "Serialization Frameworks" on page 126.

If the next() method returns a non-null object, a key-value pair was read from the stream, and the value can be retrieved using the getCurrentValue() method. Otherwise, if next() returns null, the end of the file has been reached.

The program in Example 5-11 demonstrates how to read a sequence file that has Writable keys and values. Note how the types are discovered from the Sequence File.Reader via calls to getKeyClass() and getValueClass(), and then Reflectio nUtils is used to create an instance for the key and an instance for the value. This technique allows the program to be used with any sequence file that has Writable keys and values.

Example 5-11. Reading a SequenceFile

```
public class SequenceFileReadDemo {

  public static void main(String[] args) throws IOException {
    String uri = args[0];
    Configuration conf = new Configuration();
    FileSystem fs = FileSystem.get(URI.create(uri), conf);
    Path path = new Path(uri);

    SequenceFile.Reader reader = null;
    try {
      reader = new SequenceFile.Reader(fs, path, conf);
      Writable key = (Writable)
          ReflectionUtils.newInstance(reader.getKeyClass(), conf);
      Writable value = (Writable)
          ReflectionUtils.newInstance(reader.getValueClass(), conf);
      long position = reader.getPosition();
      while (reader.next(key, value)) {
        String syncSeen = reader.syncSeen() ? "*" : "";
        System.out.printf("[%s%s]\t%s\t%s\n", position, syncSeen, key, value);
        position = reader.getPosition(); // beginning of next record
      }
    } finally {
      IOUtils.closeStream(reader);
    }
  }
}
```

Another feature of the program is that it displays the positions of the *sync points* in the sequence file. A sync point is a point in the stream that can be used to resynchronize with a record boundary if the reader is "lost"—for example, after seeking to an arbitrary position in the stream. Sync points are recorded by SequenceFile.Writer, which inserts a special entry to mark the sync point every few records as a sequence file is being written. Such entries are small enough to incur only a modest storage overhead—less than 1%. Sync points always align with record boundaries.

Running the program in Example 5-11 shows the sync points in the sequence file as asterisks. The first one occurs at position 2021 (the second one occurs at position 4075, but is not shown in the output):

```
% hadoop SequenceFileReadDemo numbers.seq
[128]    100    One, two, buckle my shoe
[173]    99     Three, four, shut the door
[220]    98     Five, six, pick up sticks
[264]    97     Seven, eight, lay them straight
[314]    96     Nine, ten, a big fat hen
[359]    95     One, two, buckle my shoe
[404]    94     Three, four, shut the door
[451]    93     Five, six, pick up sticks
[495]    92     Seven, eight, lay them straight
[545]    91     Nine, ten, a big fat hen
[590]    90     One, two, buckle my shoe
...
[1976]   60     One, two, buckle my shoe
[2021*]  59     Three, four, shut the door
[2088]   58     Five, six, pick up sticks
[2132]   57     Seven, eight, lay them straight
[2182]   56     Nine, ten, a big fat hen
...
[4557]   5      One, two, buckle my shoe
[4602]   4      Three, four, shut the door
[4649]   3      Five, six, pick up sticks
[4693]   2      Seven, eight, lay them straight
[4743]   1      Nine, ten, a big fat hen
```

There are two ways to seek to a given position in a sequence file. The first is the seek() method, which positions the reader at the given point in the file. For example, seeking to a record boundary works as expected:

```
reader.seek(359);
assertThat(reader.next(key, value), is(true));
assertThat(((IntWritable) key).get(), is(95));
```

But if the position in the file is not at a record boundary, the reader fails when the next() method is called:

```
reader.seek(360);
reader.next(key, value); // fails with IOException
```

The second way to find a record boundary makes use of sync points. The sync(long position) method on SequenceFile.Reader positions the reader at the next sync point after position. (If there are no sync points in the file after this position, then the reader will be positioned at the end of the file.) Thus, we can call sync() with any position in the stream—not necessarily a record boundary—and the reader will reestablish itself at the next sync point so reading can continue:

```
reader.sync(360);
assertThat(reader.getPosition(), is(2021L));
assertThat(reader.next(key, value), is(true));
assertThat(((IntWritable) key).get(), is(59));
```

 SequenceFile.Writer has a method called sync() for inserting a sync point at the current position in the stream. This is not to be confused with the hsync() method defined by the Syncable interface for synchronizing buffers to the underlying device (see "Coherency Model" on page 74).

Sync points come into their own when using sequence files as input to MapReduce, since they permit the files to be split and different portions to be processed independently by separate map tasks (see "SequenceFileInputFormat" on page 236).

Displaying a SequenceFile with the command-line interface

The hadoop fs command has a -text option to display sequence files in textual form. It looks at a file's magic number so that it can attempt to detect the type of the file and appropriately convert it to text. It can recognize gzipped files, sequence files, and Avro datafiles; otherwise, it assumes the input is plain text.

For sequence files, this command is really useful only if the keys and values have meaningful string representations (as defined by the toString() method). Also, if you have your own key or value classes, you will need to make sure they are on Hadoop's classpath.

Running it on the sequence file we created in the previous section gives the following output:

```
% hadoop fs -text numbers.seq | head
100    One, two, buckle my shoe
99     Three, four, shut the door
98     Five, six, pick up sticks
97     Seven, eight, lay them straight
96     Nine, ten, a big fat hen
95     One, two, buckle my shoe
94     Three, four, shut the door
93     Five, six, pick up sticks
92     Seven, eight, lay them straight
91     Nine, ten, a big fat hen
```

Sorting and merging SequenceFiles

The most powerful way of sorting (and merging) one or more sequence files is to use MapReduce. MapReduce is inherently parallel and will let you specify the number of reducers to use, which determines the number of output partitions. For example, by specifying one reducer, you get a single output file. We can use the sort example that comes with Hadoop by specifying that the input and output are sequence files and by setting the key and value types:

```
% hadoop jar \
  $HADOOP_HOME/share/hadoop/mapreduce/hadoop-mapreduce-examples-*.jar \
  sort -r 1 \
  -inFormat org.apache.hadoop.mapreduce.lib.input.SequenceFileInputFormat \
  -outFormat org.apache.hadoop.mapreduce.lib.output.SequenceFileOutputFormat \
  -outKey org.apache.hadoop.io.IntWritable \
  -outValue org.apache.hadoop.io.Text \
  numbers.seq sorted
% hadoop fs -text sorted/part-r-00000 | head
1       Nine, ten, a big fat hen
2       Seven, eight, lay them straight
3       Five, six, pick up sticks
4       Three, four, shut the door
5       One, two, buckle my shoe
6       Nine, ten, a big fat hen
7       Seven, eight, lay them straight
8       Five, six, pick up sticks
9       Three, four, shut the door
10      One, two, buckle my shoe
```

Sorting is covered in more detail in "Sorting" on page 255.

An alternative to using MapReduce for sort/merge is the SequenceFile.Sorter class, which has a number of sort() and merge() methods. These functions predate Map-Reduce and are lower-level functions than MapReduce (for example, to get parallelism, you need to partition your data manually), so in general MapReduce is the preferred approach to sort and merge sequence files.

The SequenceFile format

A sequence file consists of a header followed by one or more records (see Figure 5-2). The first three bytes of a sequence file are the bytes SEQ, which act as a magic number; these are followed by a single byte representing the version number. The header contains other fields, including the names of the key and value classes, compression details, user-defined metadata, and the sync marker.[5] Recall that the sync marker is used to allow a reader to synchronize to a record boundary from any position in the file. Each file has

---

5. Full details of the format of these fields may be found in SequenceFile's documentation (*http://bit.ly/ sequence_file_docs*) and source code.

a randomly generated sync marker, whose value is stored in the header. Sync markers appear between records in the sequence file. They are designed to incur less than a 1% storage overhead, so they don't necessarily appear between every pair of records (such is the case for short records).

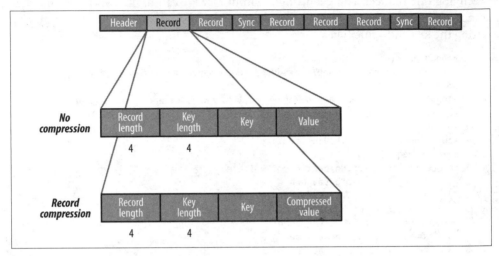

Figure 5-2. The internal structure of a sequence file with no compression and with re-cord compression

The internal format of the records depends on whether compression is enabled, and if it is, whether it is record compression or block compression.

If no compression is enabled (the default), each record is made up of the record length (in bytes), the key length, the key, and then the value. The length fields are written as 4-byte integers adhering to the contract of the `writeInt()` method of `java.io.DataOut put`. Keys and values are serialized using the `Serialization` defined for the class being written to the sequence file.

The format for record compression is almost identical to that for no compression, except the value bytes are compressed using the codec defined in the header. Note that keys are not compressed.

Block compression (Figure 5-3) compresses multiple records at once; it is therefore more compact than and should generally be preferred over record compression because it has the opportunity to take advantage of similarities between records. Records are added to a block until it reaches a minimum size in bytes, defined by the `io.seqfile.compress.blocksize` property; the default is one million bytes. A sync marker is written before the start of every block. The format of a block is a field indicating the number of records in the block, followed by four compressed fields: the key lengths, the keys, the value lengths, and the values.

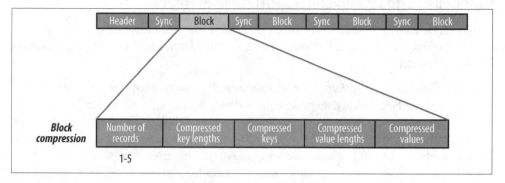

Figure 5-3. The internal structure of a sequence file with block compression

MapFile

A MapFile is a sorted SequenceFile with an index to permit lookups by key. The index is itself a SequenceFile that contains a fraction of the keys in the map (every 128th key, by default). The idea is that the index can be loaded into memory to provide fast lookups from the main data file, which is another SequenceFile containing all the map entries in sorted key order.

MapFile offers a very similar interface to SequenceFile for reading and writing—the main thing to be aware of is that when writing using MapFile.Writer, map entries must be added in order, otherwise an IOException will be thrown.

MapFile variants

Hadoop comes with a few variants on the general key-value MapFile interface:

- SetFile is a specialization of MapFile for storing a set of Writable keys. The keys must be added in sorted order.

- ArrayFile is a MapFile where the key is an integer representing the index of the element in the array and the value is a Writable value.

- BloomMapFile is a MapFile that offers a fast version of the get() method, especially for sparsely populated files. The implementation uses a dynamic Bloom filter for testing whether a given key is in the map. The test is very fast because it is in-memory, and it has a nonzero probability of false positives. Only if the test passes (the key is present) is the regular get() method called.

Other File Formats and Column-Oriented Formats

While sequence files and map files are the oldest binary file formats in Hadoop, they are not the only ones, and in fact there are better alternatives that should be considered for new projects.

Avro datafiles (covered in "Avro Datafiles" on page 352) are like sequence files in that they are designed for large-scale data processing—they are compact and splittable—but they are portable across different programming languages. Objects stored in Avro datafiles are described by a schema, rather than in the Java code of the implementation of a Writable object (as is the case for sequence files), making them very Java-centric. Avro datafiles are widely supported across components in the Hadoop ecosystem, so they are a good default choice for a binary format.

Sequence files, map files, and Avro datafiles are all row-oriented file formats, which means that the values for each row are stored contiguously in the file. In a column-oriented format, the rows in a file (or, equivalently, a table in Hive) are broken up into row splits, then each split is stored in column-oriented fashion: the values for each row in the first column are stored first, followed by the values for each row in the second column, and so on. This is shown diagrammatically in Figure 5-4.

A column-oriented layout permits columns that are not accessed in a query to be skipped. Consider a query of the table in Figure 5-4 that processes only column 2. With row-oriented storage, like a sequence file, the whole row (stored in a sequence file record) is loaded into memory, even though only the second column is actually read. Lazy deserialization saves some processing cycles by deserializing only the column fields that are accessed, but it can't avoid the cost of reading each row's bytes from disk.

With column-oriented storage, only the column 2 parts of the file (highlighted in the figure) need to be read into memory. In general, column-oriented formats work well when queries access only a small number of columns in the table. Conversely, row-oriented formats are appropriate when a large number of columns of a single row are needed for processing at the same time.

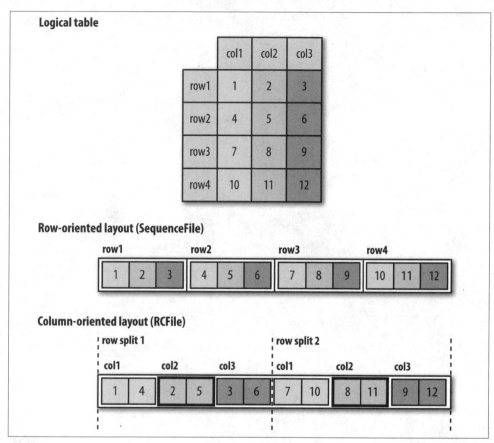

Figure 5-4. Row-oriented versus column-oriented storage

Column-oriented formats need more memory for reading and writing, since they have to buffer a row split in memory, rather than just a single row. Also, it's not usually possible to control when writes occur (via flush or sync operations), so column-oriented formats are not suited to streaming writes, as the current file cannot be recovered if the writer process fails. On the other hand, row-oriented formats like sequence files and Avro datafiles can be read up to the last sync point after a writer failure. It is for this reason that Flume (see Chapter 14) uses row-oriented formats.

The first column-oriented file format in Hadoop was Hive's *RCFile*, short for *Record Columnar File*. It has since been superseded by Hive's *ORCFile* (*Optimized Record Columnar File*), and *Parquet* (covered in Chapter 13). Parquet is a general-purpose column-oriented file format based on Google's Dremel, and has wide support across Hadoop components. Avro also has a column-oriented format called *Trevni*.

## PART II

MapReduce

Developing a MapReduce Application

In Chapter 2, we introduced the MapReduce model. In this chapter, we look at the practical aspects of developing a MapReduce application in Hadoop.

Writing a program in MapReduce follows a certain pattern. You start by writing your map and reduce functions, ideally with unit tests to make sure they do what you expect. Then you write a driver program to run a job, which can run from your IDE using a small subset of the data to check that it is working. If it fails, you can use your IDE's debugger to find the source of the problem. With this information, you can expand your unit tests to cover this case and improve your mapper or reducer as appropriate to handle such input correctly.

When the program runs as expected against the small dataset, you are ready to unleash it on a cluster. Running against the full dataset is likely to expose some more issues, which you can fix as before, by expanding your tests and altering your mapper or reducer to handle the new cases. Debugging failing programs in the cluster is a challenge, so we'll look at some common techniques to make it easier.

After the program is working, you may wish to do some tuning, first by running through some standard checks for making MapReduce programs faster and then by doing task profiling. Profiling distributed programs is not easy, but Hadoop has hooks to aid in the process.

Before we start writing a MapReduce program, however, we need to set up and configure the development environment. And to do that, we need to learn a bit about how Hadoop does configuration.

The Configuration API

Components in Hadoop are configured using Hadoop's own configuration API. An instance of the Configuration class (found in the org.apache.hadoop.conf package) represents a collection of configuration *properties* and their values. Each property is named by a String, and the type of a value may be one of several, including Java primitives such as boolean, int, long, and float; other useful types such as String, Class, and java.io.File; and collections of Strings.

Configurations read their properties from *resources*—XML files with a simple structure for defining name-value pairs. See Example 6-1.

Example 6-1. A simple configuration file, configuration-1.xml

```xml
<?xml version="1.0"?>
<configuration>
  <property>
    <name>color</name>
    <value>yellow</value>
    <description>Color</description>
  </property>

  <property>
    <name>size</name>
    <value>10</value>
    <description>Size</description>
  </property>

  <property>
    <name>weight</name>
    <value>heavy</value>
    <final>true</final>
    <description>Weight</description>
  </property>

  <property>
    <name>size-weight</name>
    <value>${size},${weight}</value>
    <description>Size and weight</description>
  </property>
</configuration>
```

Assuming this Configuration is in a file called *configuration-1.xml*, we can access its properties using a piece of code like this:

```
Configuration conf = new Configuration();
conf.addResource("configuration-1.xml");
assertThat(conf.get("color"), is("yellow"));
assertThat(conf.getInt("size", 0), is(10));
assertThat(conf.get("breadth", "wide"), is("wide"));
```

There are a couple of things to note: type information is not stored in the XML file; instead, properties can be interpreted as a given type when they are read. Also, the get() methods allow you to specify a default value, which is used if the property is not defined in the XML file, as in the case of breadth here.

Combining Resources

Things get interesting when more than one resource is used to define a `Configuration`. This is used in Hadoop to separate out the default properties for the system, defined internally in a file called *core-default.xml*, from the site-specific overrides in *core-site.xml*. The file in Example 6-2 defines the `size` and `weight` properties.

Example 6-2. A second configuration file, configuration-2.xml

```xml
<?xml version="1.0"?>
<configuration>
  <property>
    <name>size</name>
    <value>12</value>
  </property>

  <property>
    <name>weight</name>
    <value>light</value>
  </property>
</configuration>
```

Resources are added to a `Configuration` in order:

```
Configuration conf = new Configuration();
conf.addResource("configuration-1.xml");
conf.addResource("configuration-2.xml");
```

Properties defined in resources that are added later override the earlier definitions. So the `size` property takes its value from the second configuration file, *configuration-2.xml*:

```
assertThat(conf.getInt("size", 0), is(12));
```

However, properties that are marked as `final` cannot be overridden in later definitions. The `weight` property is `final` in the first configuration file, so the attempt to override it in the second fails, and it takes the value from the first:

```
assertThat(conf.get("weight"), is("heavy"));
```

Attempting to override `final` properties usually indicates a configuration error, so this results in a warning message being logged to aid diagnosis. Administrators mark properties as `final` in the daemon's site files that they don't want users to change in their client-side configuration files or job submission parameters.

Variable Expansion

Configuration properties can be defined in terms of other properties, or system properties. For example, the property `size-weight` in the first configuration file is defined as `${size},${weight}`, and these properties are expanded using the values found in the configuration:

```
assertThat(conf.get("size-weight"), is("12,heavy"));
```

System properties take priority over properties defined in resource files:

```
System.setProperty("size", "14");
assertThat(conf.get("size-weight"), is("14,heavy"));
```

This feature is useful for overriding properties on the command line by using -D*property*=*value* JVM arguments.

Note that although configuration properties can be defined in terms of system proper-ties, unless system properties are redefined using configuration properties, they are *not* accessible through the configuration API. Hence:

```
System.setProperty("length", "2");
assertThat(conf.get("length"), is((String) null));
```

Setting Up the Development Environment

The first step is to create a project so you can build MapReduce programs and run them in local (standalone) mode from the command line or within your IDE. The Maven Project Object Model (POM) in Example 6-3 shows the dependencies needed for build-ing and testing MapReduce programs.

Example 6-3. A Maven POM for building and testing a MapReduce application

```
<project>
  <modelVersion>4.0.0</modelVersion>
  <groupId>com.hadoopbook</groupId>
  <artifactId>hadoop-book-mr-dev</artifactId>
  <version>4.0</version>
  <properties>
    <project.build.sourceEncoding>UTF-8</project.build.sourceEncoding>
    <hadoop.version>2.5.1</hadoop.version>
  </properties>
  <dependencies>
    <!-- Hadoop main client artifact -->
    <dependency>
      <groupId>org.apache.hadoop</groupId>
      <artifactId>hadoop-client</artifactId>
      <version>${hadoop.version}</version>
    </dependency>
    <!-- Unit test artifacts -->
    <dependency>
      <groupId>junit</groupId>
      <artifactId>junit</artifactId>
      <version>4.11</version>
      <scope>test</scope>
    </dependency>
    <dependency>
      <groupId>org.apache.mrunit</groupId>
      <artifactId>mrunit</artifactId>
```

```
        <version>1.1.0</version>
        <classifier>hadoop2</classifier>
        <scope>test</scope>
    </dependency>
    <!-- Hadoop test artifact for running mini clusters -->
    <dependency>
        <groupId>org.apache.hadoop</groupId>
        <artifactId>hadoop-minicluster</artifactId>
        <version>${hadoop.version}</version>
        <scope>test</scope>
    </dependency>
  </dependencies>
  <build>
    <finalName>hadoop-examples</finalName>
    <plugins>
      <plugin>
        <groupId>org.apache.maven.plugins</groupId>
        <artifactId>maven-compiler-plugin</artifactId>
        <version>3.1</version>
        <configuration>
          <source>1.6</source>
          <target>1.6</target>
        </configuration>
      </plugin>
      <plugin>
        <groupId>org.apache.maven.plugins</groupId>
        <artifactId>maven-jar-plugin</artifactId>
        <version>2.5</version>
        <configuration>
          <outputDirectory>${basedir}</outputDirectory>
        </configuration>
      </plugin>
    </plugins>
  </build>
</project>
```

The dependencies section is the interesting part of the POM. (It is straightforward to use another build tool, such as Gradle or Ant with Ivy, as long as you use the same set of dependencies defined here.) For building MapReduce jobs, you only need to have the `hadoop-client` dependency, which contains all the Hadoop client-side classes needed to interact with HDFS and MapReduce. For running unit tests, we use `junit`, and for writing MapReduce tests, we use `mrunit`. The `hadoop-minicluster` library contains the "mini-" clusters that are useful for testing with Hadoop clusters running in a single JVM.

Many IDEs can read Maven POMs directly, so you can just point them at the directory containing the *pom.xml* file and start writing code. Alternatively, you can use Maven to generate configuration files for your IDE. For example, the following creates Eclipse configuration files so you can import the project into Eclipse:

```
% mvn eclipse:eclipse -DdownloadSources=true -DdownloadJavadocs=true
```

Managing Configuration

When developing Hadoop applications, it is common to switch between running the application locally and running it on a cluster. In fact, you may have several clusters you work with, or you may have a local "pseudodistributed" cluster that you like to test on (a pseudodistributed cluster is one whose daemons all run on the local machine; setting up this mode is covered in Appendix A).

One way to accommodate these variations is to have Hadoop configuration files containing the connection settings for each cluster you run against and specify which one you are using when you run Hadoop applications or tools. As a matter of best practice, it's recommended to keep these files outside Hadoop's installation directory tree, as this makes it easy to switch between Hadoop versions without duplicating or losing settings.

For the purposes of this book, we assume the existence of a directory called *conf* that contains three configuration files: *hadoop-local.xml*, *hadoop-localhost.xml*, and *hadoop-cluster.xml* (these are available in the example code for this book). Note that there is nothing special about the names of these files; they are just convenient ways to package up some configuration settings. (Compare this to Table A-1 in Appendix A, which sets out the equivalent server-side configurations.)

The *hadoop-local.xml* file contains the default Hadoop configuration for the default filesystem and the local (in-JVM) framework for running MapReduce jobs:

```
<?xml version="1.0"?>
<configuration>

  <property>
    <name>fs.defaultFS</name>
    <value>file:///</value>
  </property>

  <property>
    <name>mapreduce.framework.name</name>
    <value>local</value>
  </property>

</configuration>
```

The settings in *hadoop-localhost.xml* point to a namenode and a YARN resource manager both running on localhost:

```
<?xml version="1.0"?>
<configuration>

  <property>
    <name>fs.defaultFS</name>
    <value>hdfs://localhost/</value>
```

```
    </property>

    <property>
      <name>mapreduce.framework.name</name>
      <value>yarn</value>
    </property>

    <property>
      <name>yarn.resourcemanager.address</name>
      <value>localhost:8032</value>
    </property>

</configuration>
```

Finally, *hadoop-cluster.xml* contains details of the cluster's namenode and YARN resource manager addresses (in practice, you would name the file after the name of the cluster, rather than "cluster" as we have here):

```
<?xml version="1.0"?>
<configuration>

    <property>
      <name>fs.defaultFS</name>
      <value>hdfs://namenode/</value>
    </property>

    <property>
      <name>mapreduce.framework.name</name>
      <value>yarn</value>
    </property>

    <property>
      <name>yarn.resourcemanager.address</name>
      <value>resourcemanager:8032</value>
    </property>

</configuration>
```

You can add other configuration properties to these files as needed.

Setting User Identity

The user identity that Hadoop uses for permissions in HDFS is determined by running the whoami command on the client system. Similarly, the group names are derived from the output of running groups.

If, however, your Hadoop user identity is different from the name of your user account on your client machine, you can explicitly set your Hadoop username by setting the HADOOP_USER_NAME environment variable. You can also override user group mappings by means of the hadoop.user.group.static.mapping.overrides configuration property. For example, `dr.who=;preston=directors,inventors` means that the `dr.who` user is in no groups, but `preston` is in the `directors` and `inventors` groups.

You can set the user identity that the Hadoop web interfaces run as by setting the `hadoop.http.staticuser.user` property. By default, it is `dr.who`, which is not a superuser, so system files are not accessible through the web interface.

Notice that, by default, there is no authentication with this system. See "Security" on page 309 for how to use Kerberos authentication with Hadoop.

With this setup, it is easy to use any configuration with the `-conf` command-line switch. For example, the following command shows a directory listing on the HDFS server running in pseudodistributed mode on localhost:

```
% hadoop fs -conf conf/hadoop-localhost.xml -ls .
Found 2 items
drwxr-xr-x   - tom supergroup          0 2014-09-08 10:19 input
drwxr-xr-x   - tom supergroup          0 2014-09-08 10:19 output
```

If you omit the `-conf` option, you pick up the Hadoop configuration in the *etc/hadoop* subdirectory under `$HADOOP_HOME`. Or, if `HADOOP_CONF_DIR` is set, Hadoop configuration files will be read from that location.

 Here's an alternative way of managing configuration settings. Copy the *etc/hadoop* directory from your Hadoop installation to another location, place the **-site.xml* configuration files there (with appropriate settings), and set the `HADOOP_CONF_DIR` environment variable to the alternative location. The main advantage of this approach is that you don't need to specify `-conf` for every command. It also allows you to isolate changes to files other than the Hadoop XML configuration files (e.g., *log4j.properties*) since the `HADOOP_CONF_DIR` directory has a copy of all the configuration files (see "Hadoop Configuration" on page 292).

Tools that come with Hadoop support the `-conf` option, but it's straightforward to make your programs (such as programs that run MapReduce jobs) support it, too, using the `Tool` interface.

GenericOptionsParser, Tool, and ToolRunner

Hadoop comes with a few helper classes for making it easier to run jobs from the command line. `GenericOptionsParser` is a class that interprets common Hadoop command-line options and sets them on a `Configuration` object for your application to use as desired. You don't usually use `GenericOptionsParser` directly, as it's more convenient to implement the Tool interface and run your application with the ToolRunner, which uses GenericOptionsParser internally:

```
public interface Tool extends Configurable {
    int run(String [] args) throws Exception;
}
```

Example 6-4 shows a very simple implementation of Tool that prints the keys and values of all the properties in the Tool's Configuration object.

Example 6-4. An example Tool implementation for printing the properties in a Configuration

```
public class ConfigurationPrinter extends Configured implements Tool {

  static {
    Configuration.addDefaultResource("hdfs-default.xml");
    Configuration.addDefaultResource("hdfs-site.xml");
    Configuration.addDefaultResource("yarn-default.xml");
    Configuration.addDefaultResource("yarn-site.xml");
    Configuration.addDefaultResource("mapred-default.xml");
    Configuration.addDefaultResource("mapred-site.xml");
  }

  @Override
  public int run(String[] args) throws Exception {
    Configuration conf = getConf();
    for (Entry<String, String> entry: conf) {
      System.out.printf("%s=%s\n", entry.getKey(), entry.getValue());
    }
    return 0;
  }

  public static void main(String[] args) throws Exception {
    int exitCode = ToolRunner.run(new ConfigurationPrinter(), args);
    System.exit(exitCode);
  }
}
```

We make ConfigurationPrinter a subclass of Configured, which is an implementation of the Configurable interface. All implementations of Tool need to implement Configurable (since Tool extends it), and subclassing Configured is often the easiest way to achieve this. The run() method obtains the Configuration using Configurable's getConf() method and then iterates over it, printing each property to standard output.

The static block makes sure that the HDFS, YARN, and MapReduce configurations are picked up, in addition to the core ones (which Configuration knows about already).

ConfigurationPrinter's main() method does not invoke its own run() method directly. Instead, we call ToolRunner's static run() method, which takes care of creating a `Configuration` object for the `Tool` before calling its `run()` method. `ToolRunner` also uses a `GenericOptionsParser` to pick up any standard options specified on the command line and to set them on the `Configuration` instance. We can see the effect of picking up the properties specified in *conf/hadoop-localhost.xml* by running the following commands:

```
% mvn compile
% export HADOOP_CLASSPATH=target/classes/
% hadoop ConfigurationPrinter -conf conf/hadoop-localhost.xml \
  | grep yarn.resourcemanager.address=
yarn.resourcemanager.address=localhost:8032
```

Which Properties Can I Set?

`ConfigurationPrinter` is a useful tool for discovering what a property is set to in your environment. For a running daemon, like the namenode, you can see its configuration by viewing the */conf* page on its web server. (See Table 10-6 to find port numbers.)

You can also see the default settings for all the public properties in Hadoop by looking in the *share/doc* directory of your Hadoop installation for files called *core-default.xml*, *hdfs-default.xml*, *yarn-default.xml*, and *mapred-default.xml*. Each property has a description that explains what it is for and what values it can be set to.

The default settings files' documentation can be found online at pages linked from *http://hadoop.apache.org/docs/current/* (look for the "Configuration" heading in the navigation). You can find the defaults for a particular Hadoop release by replacing *current* in the preceding URL with *r<version>*—for example, *http://hadoop.apache.org/docs/r2.5.0/*.

Be aware that some properties have no effect when set in the client configuration. For example, if you set `yarn.nodemanager.resource.memory-mb` in your job submission with the expectation that it would change the amount of memory available to the node managers running your job, you would be disappointed, because this property is honored only if set in the node manager's *yarn-site.xml* file. In general, you can tell the component where a property should be set by its name, so the fact that `yarn.nodemanager.resource.memory-mb` starts with `yarn.nodemanager` gives you a clue that it can be set only for the node manager daemon. This is not a hard and fast rule, however, so in some cases you may need to resort to trial and error, or even to reading the source.

Configuration property names have changed in Hadoop 2 onward, in order to give them a more regular naming structure. For example, the HDFS properties pertaining to the namenode have been changed to have a `dfs.namenode` prefix, so `dfs.name.dir` is now `dfs.namenode.name.dir`. Similarly, MapReduce properties have the `mapreduce` prefix rather than the older `mapred` prefix, so `mapred.job.name` is now `mapreduce.job.name`.

> This book uses the new property names to avoid deprecation warnings. The old property names still work, however, and they are often referred to in older documentation. You can find a table listing the deprecated property names and their replacements on the Hadoop website (*http://bit.ly/deprecated_props*).
>
> We discuss many of Hadoop's most important configuration properties throughout this book.

`GenericOptionsParser` also allows you to set individual properties. For example:

```
% hadoop ConfigurationPrinter -D color=yellow | grep color
color=yellow
```

Here, the `-D` option is used to set the configuration property with key `color` to the value `yellow`. Options specified with `-D` take priority over properties from the configuration files. This is very useful because you can put defaults into configuration files and then override them with the `-D` option as needed. A common example of this is setting the number of reducers for a MapReduce job via `-D mapreduce.job.reduces=`*n*. This will override the number of reducers set on the cluster or set in any client-side configuration files.

The other options that `GenericOptionsParser` and `ToolRunner` support are listed in Table 6-1. You can find more on Hadoop's configuration API in "The Configuration API" on page 141.

> Do not confuse setting Hadoop properties using the `-D` *property=value* option to `GenericOptionsParser` (and Tool Runner) with setting JVM system properties using the `-D`*proper ty=value* option to the `java` command. The syntax for JVM system properties does not allow any whitespace between the `D` and the property name, whereas `GenericOptionsParser` does allow whitespace.
>
> JVM system properties are retrieved from the `java.lang.System` class, but Hadoop properties are accessible only from a `Configura tion` object. So, the following command will print nothing, even though the `color` system property has been set (via `HADOOP_OPTS`), because the `System` class is not used by `ConfigurationPrinter`:
>
> ```
> % HADOOP_OPTS='-Dcolor=yellow' \
>   hadoop ConfigurationPrinter | grep color
> ```
>
> If you want to be able to set configuration through system properties, you need to mirror the system properties of interest in the configuration file. See "Variable Expansion" on page 143 for further discussion.

Table 6-1. GenericOptionsParser and ToolRunner options

Option	Description
-D *property=value*	Sets the given Hadoop configuration property to the given value. Overrides any default or site properties in the configuration and any properties set via the -conf option.
-conf *filename* ...	Adds the given files to the list of resources in the configuration. This is a convenient way to set site properties or to set a number of properties at once.
-fs *uri*	Sets the default filesystem to the given URI. Shortcut for -D fs.defaultFS=*uri*.
-jt *host:port*	Sets the YARN resource manager to the given host and port. (In Hadoop 1, it sets the jobtracker address, hence the option name.) Shortcut for -D yarn.resource manager.address=*host:port*.
-files *file1,file2,...*	Copies the specified files from the local filesystem (or any filesystem if a scheme is specified) to the shared filesystem used by MapReduce (usually HDFS) and makes them available to MapReduce programs in the task's working directory. (See "Distributed Cache" on page 274 for more on the distributed cache mechanism for copying files to machines in the cluster.)
-archives *archive1,archive2,...*	Copies the specified archives from the local filesystem (or any filesystem if a scheme is specified) to the shared filesystem used by MapReduce (usually HDFS), unarchives them, and makes them available to MapReduce programs in the task's working directory.
-libjars *jar1,jar2,...*	Copies the specified JAR files from the local filesystem (or any filesystem if a scheme is specified) to the shared filesystem used by MapReduce (usually HDFS) and adds them to the MapReduce task's classpath. This option is a useful way of shipping JAR files that a job is dependent on.

Writing a Unit Test with MRUnit

The map and reduce functions in MapReduce are easy to test in isolation, which is a consequence of their functional style. MRUnit (*https://mrunit.apache.org/*) is a testing library that makes it easy to pass known inputs to a mapper or a reducer and check that the outputs are as expected. MRUnit is used in conjunction with a standard test execution framework, such as JUnit, so you can run the tests for MapReduce jobs in your normal development environment. For example, all of the tests described here can be run from within an IDE by following the instructions in "Setting Up the Development Environment" on page 144.

Mapper

The test for the mapper is shown in Example 6-5.

Example 6-5. Unit test for MaxTemperatureMapper

```java
import java.io.IOException;
import org.apache.hadoop.io.*;
import org.apache.hadoop.mrunit.mapreduce.MapDriver;
import org.junit.*;

public class MaxTemperatureMapperTest {

  @Test
  public void processesValidRecord() throws IOException, InterruptedException {
    Text value = new Text("0043011990099999919500515180004+68750+023550FM-12+0382" +
                                    // Year ^^^^
        "99999V0203201N00261220001CN9999999N9-00111+99999999999");
                          // Temperature ^^^^^
    new MapDriver<LongWritable, Text, Text, IntWritable>()
      .withMapper(new MaxTemperatureMapper())
      .withInput(new LongWritable(0), value)
      .withOutput(new Text("1950"), new IntWritable(-11))
      .runTest();
  }
}
```

The idea of the test is very simple: pass a weather record as input to the mapper, and check that the output is the year and temperature reading.

Since we are testing the mapper, we use MRUnit's `MapDriver`, which we configure with the mapper under test (`MaxTemperatureMapper`), the input key and value, and the expected output key (a `Text` object representing the year, 1950) and expected output value (an `IntWritable` representing the temperature, −1.1°C), before finally calling the `runTest()` method to execute the test. If the expected output values are not emitted by the mapper, MRUnit will fail the test. Notice that the input key could be set to any value because our mapper ignores it.

Proceeding in a test-driven fashion, we create a `Mapper` implementation that passes the test (see Example 6-6). Because we will be evolving the classes in this chapter, each is put in a different package indicating its version for ease of exposition. For example, `v1.MaxTemperatureMapper` is version 1 of `MaxTemperatureMapper`. In reality, of course, you would evolve classes without repackaging them.

Example 6-6. First version of a Mapper that passes MaxTemperatureMapperTest

```java
public class MaxTemperatureMapper
    extends Mapper<LongWritable, Text, Text, IntWritable> {

  @Override
```

```
  public void map(LongWritable key, Text value, Context context)
      throws IOException, InterruptedException {

    String line = value.toString();
    String year = line.substring(15, 19);
    int airTemperature = Integer.parseInt(line.substring(87, 92));
    context.write(new Text(year), new IntWritable(airTemperature));
  }
}
```

This is a very simple implementation that pulls the year and temperature fields from the line and writes them to the Context. Let's add a test for missing values, which in the raw data are represented by a temperature of +9999:

```
    @Test
    public void ignoresMissingTemperatureRecord() throws IOException,
        InterruptedException {
      Text value = new Text("0043011990999991950051518004+68750+023550FM-12+0382" +
                                  // Year ^^^^
          "99999V0203201N00261220001CN9999999N9+99991+99999999999");
                                  // Temperature ^^^^^
      new MapDriver<LongWritable, Text, Text, IntWritable>()
        .withMapper(new MaxTemperatureMapper())
        .withInput(new LongWritable(0), value)
        .runTest();
    }
```

A `MapDriver` can be used to check for zero, one, or more output records, according to the number of times that `withOutput()` is called. In our application, since records with missing temperatures should be filtered out, this test asserts that no output is produced for this particular input value.

The new test fails since +9999 is not treated as a special case. Rather than putting more logic into the mapper, it makes sense to factor out a parser class to encapsulate the parsing logic; see Example 6-7.

Example 6-7. A class for parsing weather records in NCDC format

```
public class NcdcRecordParser {

  private static final int MISSING_TEMPERATURE = 9999;

  private String year;
  private int airTemperature;
  private String quality;

  public void parse(String record) {
    year = record.substring(15, 19);
    String airTemperatureString;
    // Remove leading plus sign as parseInt doesn't like them (pre-Java 7)
    if (record.charAt(87) == '+') {
      airTemperatureString = record.substring(88, 92);
```

```
  } else {
    airTemperatureString = record.substring(87, 92);
  }
  airTemperature = Integer.parseInt(airTemperatureString);
  quality = record.substring(92, 93);
}

public void parse(Text record) {
  parse(record.toString());
}

public boolean isValidTemperature() {
  return airTemperature != MISSING_TEMPERATURE && quality.matches("[01459]");
}

public String getYear() {
  return year;
}

public int getAirTemperature() {
  return airTemperature;
}
}
```

The resulting mapper (version 2) is much simpler (see Example 6-8). It just calls the parser's parse() method, which parses the fields of interest from a line of input, checks whether a valid temperature was found using the isValidTemperature() query method, and, if it was, retrieves the year and the temperature using the getter methods on the parser. Notice that we check the quality status field as well as checking for missing temperatures in isValidTemperature(), to filter out poor temperature readings.

 Another benefit of creating a parser class is that it makes it easy to write related mappers for similar jobs without duplicating code. It also gives us the opportunity to write unit tests directly against the parser, for more targeted testing.

Example 6-8. A Mapper that uses a utility class to parse records

```
public class MaxTemperatureMapper
    extends Mapper<LongWritable, Text, Text, IntWritable> {

  private NcdcRecordParser parser = new NcdcRecordParser();

  @Override
  public void map(LongWritable key, Text value, Context context)
      throws IOException, InterruptedException {

    parser.parse(value);
    if (parser.isValidTemperature()) {
```

```
        context.write(new Text(parser.getYear()),
            new IntWritable(parser.getAirTemperature())));
    }
  }
}
```

With the tests for the mapper now passing, we move on to writing the reducer.

Reducer

The reducer has to find the maximum value for a given key. Here's a simple test for this feature, which uses a ReduceDriver:

```
@Test
public void returnsMaximumIntegerInValues() throws IOException,
    InterruptedException {
  new ReduceDriver<Text, IntWritable, Text, IntWritable>()
    .withReducer(new MaxTemperatureReducer())
    .withInput(new Text("1950"),
        Arrays.asList(new IntWritable(10), new IntWritable(5)))
    .withOutput(new Text("1950"), new IntWritable(10))
    .runTest();
}
```

We construct a list of some IntWritable values and then verify that MaxTemperatureReducer picks the largest. The code in Example 6-9 is for an implementation of MaxTemperatureReducer that passes the test.

Example 6-9. Reducer for the maximum temperature example

```
public class MaxTemperatureReducer
    extends Reducer<Text, IntWritable, Text, IntWritable> {

  @Override
  public void reduce(Text key, Iterable<IntWritable> values, Context context)
      throws IOException, InterruptedException {

    int maxValue = Integer.MIN_VALUE;
    for (IntWritable value : values) {
      maxValue = Math.max(maxValue, value.get());
    }
    context.write(key, new IntWritable(maxValue));
  }
}
```

Running Locally on Test Data

Now that we have the mapper and reducer working on controlled inputs, the next step is to write a job driver and run it on some test data on a development machine.

Running a Job in a Local Job Runner

Using the Tool interface introduced earlier in the chapter, it's easy to write a driver to run our MapReduce job for finding the maximum temperature by year (see MaxTemperatureDriver in Example 6-10).

Example 6-10. Application to find the maximum temperature

```
public class MaxTemperatureDriver extends Configured implements Tool {

  @Override
  public int run(String[] args) throws Exception {
    if (args.length != 2) {
      System.err.printf("Usage: %s [generic options] <input> <output>\n",
          getClass().getSimpleName());
      ToolRunner.printGenericCommandUsage(System.err);
      return -1;
    }

    Job job = new Job(getConf(), "Max temperature");
    job.setJarByClass(getClass());

    FileInputFormat.addInputPath(job, new Path(args[0]));
    FileOutputFormat.setOutputPath(job, new Path(args[1]));

    job.setMapperClass(MaxTemperatureMapper.class);
    job.setCombinerClass(MaxTemperatureReducer.class);
    job.setReducerClass(MaxTemperatureReducer.class);

    job.setOutputKeyClass(Text.class);
    job.setOutputValueClass(IntWritable.class);

    return job.waitForCompletion(true) ? 0 : 1;
  }

  public static void main(String[] args) throws Exception {
    int exitCode = ToolRunner.run(new MaxTemperatureDriver(), args);
    System.exit(exitCode);
  }
}
```

MaxTemperatureDriver implements the Tool interface, so we get the benefit of being able to set the options that GenericOptionsParser supports. The run() method constructs a Job object based on the tool's configuration, which it uses to launch a job. Among the possible job configuration parameters, we set the input and output file paths; the mapper, reducer, and combiner classes; and the output types (the input types are determined by the input format, which defaults to TextInputFormat and has LongWrit able keys and Text values). It's also a good idea to set a name for the job (Max temper ature) so that you can pick it out in the job list during execution and after it has completed. By default, the name is the name of the JAR file, which normally is not particularly descriptive.

Now we can run this application against some local files. Hadoop comes with a local job runner, a cut-down version of the MapReduce execution engine for running Map-Reduce jobs in a single JVM. It's designed for testing and is very convenient for use in an IDE, since you can run it in a debugger to step through the code in your mapper and reducer.

The local job runner is used if `mapreduce.framework.name` is set to `local`, which is the default.[1]

From the command line, we can run the driver by typing:

```
% mvn compile
% export HADOOP_CLASSPATH=target/classes/
% hadoop v2.MaxTemperatureDriver -conf conf/hadoop-local.xml \
  input/ncdc/micro output
```

Equivalently, we could use the `-fs` and `-jt` options provided by `GenericOptionsParser`:

```
% hadoop v2.MaxTemperatureDriver -fs file:/// -jt local input/ncdc/micro output
```

This command executes `MaxTemperatureDriver` using input from the local *input/ncdc/micro* directory, producing output in the local *output* directory. Note that although we've set `-fs` so we use the local filesystem (`file:///`), the local job runner will actually work fine against any filesystem, including HDFS (and it can be handy to do this if you have a few files that are on HDFS).

We can examine the output on the local filesystem:

```
% cat output/part-r-00000
1949    111
1950    22
```

Testing the Driver

Apart from the flexible configuration options offered by making your application implement `Tool`, you also make it more testable because it allows you to inject an arbitrary `Configuration`. You can take advantage of this to write a test that uses a local job runner to run a job against known input data, which checks that the output is as expected.

There are two approaches to doing this. The first is to use the local job runner and run the job against a test file on the local filesystem. The code in Example 6-11 gives an idea of how to do this.

---

1. In Hadoop 1, `mapred.job.tracker` determines the means of execution: `local` for the local job runner, or a colon-separated host and port pair for a jobtracker address.

Example 6-11. A test for MaxTemperatureDriver that uses a local, in-process job runner

```
@Test
public void test() throws Exception {
  Configuration conf = new Configuration();
  conf.set("fs.defaultFS", "file:///");
  conf.set("mapreduce.framework.name", "local");
  conf.setInt("mapreduce.task.io.sort.mb", 1);

  Path input = new Path("input/ncdc/micro");
  Path output = new Path("output");

  FileSystem fs = FileSystem.getLocal(conf);
  fs.delete(output, true); // delete old output

  MaxTemperatureDriver driver = new MaxTemperatureDriver();
  driver.setConf(conf);

  int exitCode = driver.run(new String[] {
      input.toString(), output.toString() });
  assertThat(exitCode, is(0));

  checkOutput(conf, output);
}
```

The test explicitly sets `fs.defaultFS` and `mapreduce.framework.name` so it uses the local filesystem and the local job runner. It then runs the `MaxTemperatureDriver` via its `Tool` interface against a small amount of known data. At the end of the test, the `check Output()` method is called to compare the actual output with the expected output, line by line.

The second way of testing the driver is to run it using a "mini-" cluster. Hadoop has a set of testing classes, called `MiniDFSCluster`, `MiniMRCluster`, and `MiniYARNCluster`, that provide a programmatic way of creating in-process clusters. Unlike the local job runner, these allow testing against the full HDFS, MapReduce, and YARN machinery. Bear in mind, too, that node managers in a mini-cluster launch separate JVMs to run tasks in, which can make debugging more difficult.

 You can run a mini-cluster from the command line too, with the following:

```
% hadoop jar \
  $HADOOP_HOME/share/hadoop/mapreduce/hadoop-mapreduce-*-tests.jar \
  minicluster
```

Mini-clusters are used extensively in Hadoop's own automated test suite, but they can be used for testing user code, too. Hadoop's `ClusterMapReduceTestCase` abstract class provides a useful base for writing such a test, handles the details of starting and stopping the in-process HDFS and YARN clusters in its `setUp()` and `tearDown()` methods, and generates a suitable `Configuration` object that is set up to work with them. Subclasses need only populate data in HDFS (perhaps by copying from a local file), run a MapReduce job, and confirm the output is as expected. Refer to the `MaxTemperatureDriver MiniTest` class in the example code that comes with this book for the listing.

Tests like this serve as regression tests, and are a useful repository of input edge cases and their expected results. As you encounter more test cases, you can simply add them to the input file and update the file of expected output accordingly.

Running on a Cluster

Now that we are happy with the program running on a small test dataset, we are ready to try it on the full dataset on a Hadoop cluster. Chapter 10 covers how to set up a fully distributed cluster, although you can also work through this section on a pseudo-distributed cluster.

Packaging a Job

The local job runner uses a single JVM to run a job, so as long as all the classes that your job needs are on its classpath, then things will just work.

In a distributed setting, things are a little more complex. For a start, a job's classes must be packaged into a *job JAR file* to send to the cluster. Hadoop will find the job JAR automatically by searching for the JAR on the driver's classpath that contains the class set in the `setJarByClass()` method (on `JobConf` or `Job`). Alternatively, if you want to set an explicit JAR file by its file path, you can use the `setJar()` method. (The JAR file path may be local or an HDFS file path.)

Creating a job JAR file is conveniently achieved using a build tool such as Ant or Maven. Given the POM in Example 6-3, the following Maven command will create a JAR file called *hadoop-examples.jar* in the project directory containing all of the compiled classes:

```
% mvn package -DskipTests
```

If you have a single job per JAR, you can specify the main class to run in the JAR file's manifest. If the main class is not in the manifest, it must be specified on the command line (as we will see shortly when we run the job).

Any dependent JAR files can be packaged in a *lib* subdirectory in the job JAR file, although there are other ways to include dependencies, discussed later. Similarly, resource files can be packaged in a *classes* subdirectory. (This is analogous to a Java *Web application archive*, or WAR, file, except in that case the JAR files go in a *WEB-INF/lib* subdirectory and classes go in a *WEB-INF/classes* subdirectory in the WAR file.)

The client classpath

The user's client-side classpath set by `hadoop jar <jar>` is made up of:

- The job JAR file
- Any JAR files in the *lib* directory of the job JAR file, and the *classes* directory (if present)
- The classpath defined by `HADOOP_CLASSPATH`, if set

Incidentally, this explains why you have to set `HADOOP_CLASSPATH` to point to dependent classes and libraries if you are running using the local job runner without a job JAR (`hadoop CLASSNAME`).

The task classpath

On a cluster (and this includes pseudodistributed mode), map and reduce tasks run in separate JVMs, and their classpaths are *not* controlled by `HADOOP_CLASSPATH`. `HADOOP_CLASSPATH` is a client-side setting and only sets the classpath for the driver JVM, which submits the job.

Instead, the user's task classpath is comprised of the following:

- The job JAR file
- Any JAR files contained in the *lib* directory of the job JAR file, and the *classes* directory (if present)
- Any files added to the distributed cache using the `-libjars` option (see Table 6-1), or the `addFileToClassPath()` method on `DistributedCache` (old API), or `Job` (new API)

Packaging dependencies

Given these different ways of controlling what is on the client and task classpaths, there are corresponding options for including library dependencies for a job:

- Unpack the libraries and repackage them in the job JAR.
- Package the libraries in the *lib* directory of the job JAR.
- Keep the libraries separate from the job JAR, and add them to the client classpath via `HADOOP_CLASSPATH` and to the task classpath via `-libjars`.

The last option, using the distributed cache, is simplest from a build point of view because dependencies don't need rebundling in the job JAR. Also, using the distributed cache can mean fewer transfers of JAR files around the cluster, since files may be cached on a node between tasks. (You can read more about the distributed cache on page 274.)

Task classpath precedence

User JAR files are added to the end of both the client classpath and the task classpath, which in some cases can cause a dependency conflict with Hadoop's built-in libraries if Hadoop uses a different, incompatible version of a library that your code uses. Sometimes you need to be able to control the task classpath order so that your classes are picked up first. On the client side, you can force Hadoop to put the user classpath first in the search order by setting the HADOOP_USER_CLASSPATH_FIRST environment variable to true. For the task classpath, you can set mapreduce.job.user.classpath.first to true. Note that by setting these options you change the class loading for Hadoop framework dependencies (but only in your job), which could potentially cause the job submission or task to fail, so use these options with caution.

Launching a Job

To launch the job, we need to run the driver, specifying the cluster that we want to run the job on with the -conf option (we equally could have used the -fs and -jt options):

```
% unset HADOOP_CLASSPATH
% hadoop jar hadoop-examples.jar v2.MaxTemperatureDriver \
  -conf conf/hadoop-cluster.xml input/ncdc/all max-temp
```

 We unset the HADOOP_CLASSPATH environment variable because we don't have any third-party dependencies for this job. If it were left set to target/classes/ (from earlier in the chapter), Hadoop wouldn't be able to find the job JAR; it would load the MaxTempera tureDriver class from *target/classes* rather than the JAR, and the job would fail.

The waitForCompletion() method on Job launches the job and polls for progress, writing a line summarizing the map and reduce's progress whenever either changes. Here's the output (some lines have been removed for clarity):

```
14/09/12 06:38:11 INFO input.FileInputFormat: Total input paths to process : 101
14/09/12 06:38:11 INFO impl.YarnClientImpl: Submitted application
application_1410450250506_0003
14/09/12 06:38:12 INFO mapreduce.Job: Running job: job_1410450250506_0003
14/09/12 06:38:26 INFO mapreduce.Job:  map 0% reduce 0%
...
14/09/12 06:45:24 INFO mapreduce.Job:  map 100% reduce 100%
14/09/12 06:45:24 INFO mapreduce.Job: Job job_1410450250506_0003 completed
successfully
14/09/12 06:45:24 INFO mapreduce.Job: Counters: 49
    File System Counters
        FILE: Number of bytes read=93995
        FILE: Number of bytes written=10273563
        FILE: Number of read operations=0
        FILE: Number of large read operations=0
```

```
        FILE: Number of write operations=0
        HDFS: Number of bytes read=33485855415
        HDFS: Number of bytes written=904
        HDFS: Number of read operations=327
        HDFS: Number of large read operations=0
        HDFS: Number of write operations=16
    Job Counters
        Launched map tasks=101
        Launched reduce tasks=8
        Data-local map tasks=101
        Total time spent by all maps in occupied slots (ms)=5954495
        Total time spent by all reduces in occupied slots (ms)=74934
        Total time spent by all map tasks (ms)=5954495
        Total time spent by all reduce tasks (ms)=74934
        Total vcore-seconds taken by all map tasks=5954495
        Total vcore-seconds taken by all reduce tasks=74934
        Total megabyte-seconds taken by all map tasks=6097402880
        Total megabyte-seconds taken by all reduce tasks=76732416
    Map-Reduce Framework
        Map input records=1209901509
        Map output records=1143764653
        Map output bytes=10293881877
        Map output materialized bytes=14193
        Input split bytes=14140
        Combine input records=1143764772
        Combine output records=234
        Reduce input groups=100
        Reduce shuffle bytes=14193
        Reduce input records=115
        Reduce output records=100
        Spilled Records=379
        Shuffled Maps =808
        Failed Shuffles=0
        Merged Map outputs=808
        GC time elapsed (ms)=101080
        CPU time spent (ms)=5113180
        Physical memory (bytes) snapshot=60509106176
        Virtual memory (bytes) snapshot=167657209856
        Total committed heap usage (bytes)=68220878848
    Shuffle Errors
        BAD_ID=0
        CONNECTION=0
        IO_ERROR=0
        WRONG_LENGTH=0
        WRONG_MAP=0
        WRONG_REDUCE=0
    File Input Format Counters
        Bytes Read=33485841275
    File Output Format Counters
        Bytes Written=90
```

The output includes more useful information. Before the job starts, its ID is printed; this is needed whenever you want to refer to the job—in logfiles, for example—or when interrogating it via the `mapred job` command. When the job is complete, its statistics (known as counters) are printed out. These are very useful for confirming that the job did what you expected. For example, for this job, we can see that 1.2 billion records were analyzed ("Map input records"), read from around 34 GB of compressed files on HDFS ("HDFS: Number of bytes read"). The input was broken into 101 gzipped files of reasonable size, so there was no problem with not being able to split them.

You can find out more about what the counters mean in "Built-in Counters" on page 247.

Job, Task, and Task Attempt IDs

In Hadoop 2, MapReduce job IDs are generated from YARN application IDs that are created by the YARN resource manager. The format of an application ID is composed of the time that the resource manager (not the application) started and an incrementing counter maintained by the resource manager to uniquely identify the application to that instance of the resource manager. So the application with this ID:

```
application_1410450250506_0003
```

is the third (`0003`; application IDs are 1-based) application run by the resource manager, which started at the time represented by the timestamp `1410450250506`. The counter is formatted with leading zeros to make IDs sort nicely—in directory listings, for example. However, when the counter reaches `10000`, it is *not* reset, resulting in longer application IDs (which don't sort so well).

The corresponding job ID is created simply by replacing the `application` prefix of an application ID with a `job` prefix:

```
job_1410450250506_0003
```

Tasks belong to a job, and their IDs are formed by replacing the `job` prefix of a job ID with a `task` prefix and adding a suffix to identify the task within the job. For example:

```
task_1410450250506_0003_m_000003
```

is the fourth (`000003`; task IDs are 0-based) map (`m`) task of the job with ID `job_1410450250506_0003`. The task IDs are created for a job when it is initialized, so they do not necessarily dictate the order in which the tasks will be executed.

Tasks may be executed more than once, due to failure (see "Task Failure" on page 193) or speculative execution (see "Speculative Execution" on page 204), so to identify different instances of a task execution, task attempts are given unique IDs. For example:

```
attempt_1410450250506_0003_m_000003_0
```

---

is the first (0; attempt IDs are 0-based) attempt at running task
task_1410450250506_0003_m_000003. Task attempts are allocated during the job run
as needed, so their ordering represents the order in which they were created to run.

The MapReduce Web UI

Hadoop comes with a web UI for viewing information about your jobs. It is useful for
following a job's progress while it is running, as well as finding job statistics and logs
after the job has completed. You can find the UI at *http://resource-manager-host:
8088/*.

The resource manager page

A screenshot of the home page is shown in Figure 6-1. The "Cluster Metrics" section
gives a summary of the cluster. This includes the number of applications currently running on the cluster (and in various other states), the number of resources available on
the cluster ("Memory Total"), and information about node managers.

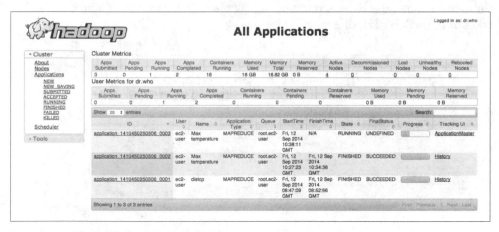

Figure 6-1. Screenshot of the resource manager page

The main table shows all the applications that have run or are currently running on the
cluster. There is a search box that is useful for filtering the applications to find the ones
you are interested in. The main view can show up to 100 entries per page, and the
resource manager will keep up to 10,000 completed applications in memory at a time
(set by yarn.resourcemanager.max-completed-applications), before they are only
available from the job history page. Note also that the job history is persistent, so you
can find jobs there from previous runs of the resource manager, too.

The MapReduce job page

Clicking on the link for the "Tracking UI" takes us to the application master's web UI (or to the history page if the application has completed). In the case of MapReduce, this takes us to the job page, illustrated in Figure 6-2.

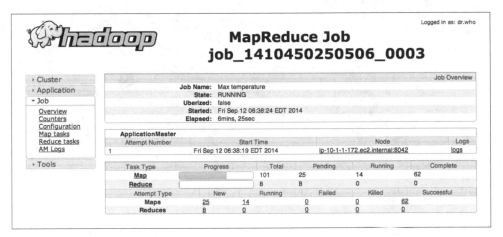

Figure 6-2. Screenshot of the job page

While the job is running, you can monitor its progress on this page. The table at the bottom shows the map progress and the reduce progress. "Total" shows the total number of map and reduce tasks for this job (a row for each). The other columns then show the state of these tasks: "Pending" (waiting to run), "Running," or "Complete" (successfully run).

The lower part of the table shows the total number of failed and killed task attempts for the map or reduce tasks. Task attempts may be marked as killed if they are speculative execution duplicates, if the node they are running on dies, or if they are killed by a user. See "Task Failure" on page 193 for background on task failure.

There also are a number of useful links in the navigation. For example, the "Configuration" link is to the consolidated configuration file for the job, containing all the properties and their values that were in effect during the job run. If you are unsure of what a particular property was set to, you can click through to inspect the file.

Retrieving the Results

Once the job is finished, there are various ways to retrieve the results. Each reducer produces one output file, so there are 30 part files named *part-r-00000* to *part-r-00029* in the *max-temp* directory.

> As their names suggest, a good way to think of these "part" files is as parts of the *max-temp* "file."
>
> If the output is large (which it isn't in this case), it is important to have multiple parts so that more than one reducer can work in parallel. Usually, if a file is in this partitioned form, it can still be used easily enough—as the input to another MapReduce job, for example. In some cases, you can exploit the structure of multiple partitions to do a map-side join, for example (see "Map-Side Joins" on page 269).

This job produces a very small amount of output, so it is convenient to copy it from HDFS to our development machine. The -getmerge option to the hadoop fs command is useful here, as it gets all the files in the directory specified in the source pattern and merges them into a single file on the local filesystem:

```
% hadoop fs -getmerge max-temp max-temp-local
% sort max-temp-local | tail
1991    607
1992    605
1993    567
1994    568
1995    567
1996    561
1997    565
1998    568
1999    568
2000    558
```

We sorted the output, as the reduce output partitions are unordered (owing to the hash partition function). Doing a bit of postprocessing of data from MapReduce is very common, as is feeding it into analysis tools such as R, a spreadsheet, or even a relational database.

Another way of retrieving the output if it is small is to use the -cat option to print the output files to the console:

```
% hadoop fs -cat max-temp/*
```

On closer inspection, we see that some of the results don't look plausible. For instance, the maximum temperature for 1951 (not shown here) is 590°C! How do we find out what's causing this? Is it corrupt input data or a bug in the program?

Debugging a Job

The time-honored way of debugging programs is via print statements, and this is certainly possible in Hadoop. However, there are complications to consider: with programs running on tens, hundreds, or thousands of nodes, how do we find and examine the output of the debug statements, which may be scattered across these nodes? For this particular case, where we are looking for (what we think is) an unusual case, we can use a debug statement to log to standard error, in conjunction with updating the task's status message to prompt us to look in the error log. The web UI makes this easy, as we pass: [will see].

We also create a custom counter to count the total number of records with implausible temperatures in the whole dataset. This gives us valuable information about how to deal with the condition. If it turns out to be a common occurrence, we might need to learn more about the condition and how to extract the temperature in these cases, rather than simply dropping the records. In fact, when trying to debug a job, you should always ask yourself if you can use a counter to get the information you need to find out what's happening. Even if you need to use logging or a status message, it may be useful to use a counter to gauge the extent of the problem. (There is more on counters in "Counters" on page 247.)

If the amount of log data you produce in the course of debugging is large, you have a couple of options. One is to write the information to the map's output, rather than to standard error, for analysis and aggregation by the reduce task. This approach usually necessitates structural changes to your program, so start with the other technique first. The alternative is to write a program (in MapReduce, of course) to analyze the logs produced by your job.

We add our debugging to the mapper (version 3), as opposed to the reducer, as we want to find out what the source data causing the anomalous output looks like:

```
public class MaxTemperatureMapper
    extends Mapper<LongWritable, Text, Text, IntWritable> {

    enum Temperature {
```

```
      OVER_100
  }

  private NcdcRecordParser parser = new NcdcRecordParser();

  @Override
  public void map(LongWritable key, Text value, Context context)
      throws IOException, InterruptedException {

    parser.parse(value);
    if (parser.isValidTemperature()) {
      int airTemperature = parser.getAirTemperature();
      if (airTemperature > 1000) {
        System.err.println("Temperature over 100 degrees for input: " + value);
        context.setStatus("Detected possibly corrupt record: see logs.");
        context.getCounter(Temperature.OVER_100).increment(1);
      }
      context.write(new Text(parser.getYear()), new IntWritable(airTemperature));
    }
  }
}
```

If the temperature is over 100°C (represented by 1000, because temperatures are in tenths of a degree), we print a line to standard error with the suspect line, as well as updating the map's status message using the setStatus() method on Context, directing us to look in the log. We also increment a counter, which in Java is represented by a field of an enum type. In this program, we have defined a single field, OVER_100, as a way to count the number of records with a temperature of over 100°C.

With this modification, we recompile the code, re-create the JAR file, then rerun the job and, while it's running, go to the tasks page.

The tasks and task attempts pages

The job page has a number of links for viewing the tasks in a job in more detail. For example, clicking on the "Map" link brings us to a page that lists information for all of the map tasks. The screenshot in Figure 6-3 shows this page for the job run with our debugging statements in the "Status" column for the task.

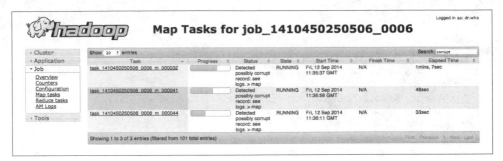

Figure 6-3. Screenshot of the tasks page

Clicking on the task link takes us to the task attempts page, which shows each task attempt for the task. Each task attempt page has links to the logfiles and counters. If we follow one of the links to the logfiles for the successful task attempt, we can find the suspect input record that we logged (the line is wrapped and truncated to fit on the page):

```
Temperature over 100 degrees for input:
0335999994331819570423022005+37950+139117SAO  +0004RJSN V0201135900315007035 6999
9994332019570101000005+35317+139650SAO +000899999V02002359002650076249N0040005...
```

This record seems to be in a different format from the others. For one thing, there are spaces in the line, which are not described in the specification.

When the job has finished, we can look at the value of the counter we defined to see how many records over 100°C there are in the whole dataset. Counters are accessible via the web UI or the command line:

```
% mapred job -counter job_1410450250506_0006 \
  'v3.MaxTemperatureMapper$Temperature' OVER_100
3
```

The -counter option takes the job ID, counter group name (which is the fully qualified classname here), and counter name (the enum name). There are only three malformed records in the entire dataset of over a billion records. Throwing out bad records is standard for many big data problems, although we need to be careful in this case because we are looking for an extreme value—the maximum temperature rather than an aggregate measure. Still, throwing away three records is probably not going to change the result.

Handling malformed data

Capturing input data that causes a problem is valuable, as we can use it in a test to check that the mapper does the right thing. In this MRUnit test, we check that the counter is updated for the malformed input:

```
@Test
public void parsesMalformedTemperature() throws IOException,
    InterruptedException {
  Text value = new Text("0335999999433181957042302005+37950+139117SAO  +0004" +
                        // Year ^^^^
       "RJSN V02011359003150070356999999433201957010100005+353");
                        // Temperature ^^^^^
  Counters counters = new Counters();
  new MapDriver<LongWritable, Text, Text, IntWritable>()
    .withMapper(new MaxTemperatureMapper())
    .withInput(new LongWritable(0), value)
    .withCounters(counters)
    .runTest();
  Counter c = counters.findCounter(MaxTemperatureMapper.Temperature.MALFORMED);
  assertThat(c.getValue(), is(1L));
}
```

The record that was causing the problem is of a different format than the other lines
we've seen. Example 6-12 shows a modified program (version 4) using a parser that
ignores each line with a temperature field that does not have a leading sign (plus or
minus). We've also introduced a counter to measure the number of records that we are
ignoring for this reason.

Example 6-12. Mapper for the maximum temperature example

```java
public class MaxTemperatureMapper
    extends Mapper<LongWritable, Text, Text, IntWritable> {

  enum Temperature {
    MALFORMED
  }

  private NcdcRecordParser parser = new NcdcRecordParser();

  @Override
  public void map(LongWritable key, Text value, Context context)
      throws IOException, InterruptedException {

    parser.parse(value);
    if (parser.isValidTemperature()) {
      int airTemperature = parser.getAirTemperature();
      context.write(new Text(parser.getYear()), new IntWritable(airTemperature));
    } else if (parser.isMalformedTemperature()) {
      System.err.println("Ignoring possibly corrupt input: " + value);
      context.getCounter(Temperature.MALFORMED).increment(1);
    }
  }
}
```

Hadoop Logs

Hadoop produces logs in various places, and for various audiences. These are summarized in Table 6-2.

Table 6-2. Types of Hadoop logs

Logs	Primary audience	Description	Further information
System daemon logs	Administrators	Each Hadoop daemon produces a logfile (using log4j) and another file that combines standard out and error. Written in the directory defined by the HADOOP_LOG_DIR environment variable.	"System logfiles" on page 295 and "Logging" on page 330
HDFS audit logs	Administrators	A log of all HDFS requests, turned off by default. Written to the namenode's log, although this is configurable.	"Audit Logging" on page 324
MapReduce job history logs	Users	A log of the events (such as task completion) that occur in the course of running a job. Saved centrally in HDFS.	"Job History" on page 166
MapReduce task logs	Users	Each task child process produces a logfile using log4j (called *syslog*), a file for data sent to standard out (*stdout*), and a file for standard error (*stderr*). Written in the *userlogs* subdirectory of the directory defined by the YARN_LOG_DIR environment variable.	This section

YARN has a service for *log aggregation* that takes the task logs for completed applications and moves them to HDFS, where they are stored in a container file for archival purposes. If this service is enabled (by setting yarn.log-aggregation-enable to true on the cluster), then task logs can be viewed by clicking on the *logs* link in the task attempt web UI, or by using the mapred job -logs command.

By default, log aggregation is not enabled. In this case, task logs can be retrieved by visiting the node manager's web UI at *http://node-manager-host:8042/logs/userlogs*.

It is straightforward to write to these logfiles. Anything written to standard output or standard error is directed to the relevant logfile. (Of course, in Streaming, standard output is used for the map or reduce output, so it will not show up in the standard output log.)

In Java, you can write to the task's *syslog* file if you wish by using the Apache Commons Logging API (or indeed any logging API that can write to log4j). This is shown in Example 6-13.

Example 6-13. An identity mapper that writes to standard output and also uses the Apache Commons Logging API

```
import org.apache.commons.logging.Log;
import org.apache.commons.logging.LogFactory;
import org.apache.hadoop.mapreduce.Mapper;

public class LoggingIdentityMapper<KEYIN, VALUEIN, KEYOUT, VALUEOUT>
    extends Mapper<KEYIN, VALUEIN, KEYOUT, VALUEOUT> {

  private static final Log LOG = LogFactory.getLog(LoggingIdentityMapper.class);

  @Override
  @SuppressWarnings("unchecked")
  public void map(KEYIN key, VALUEIN value, Context context)
      throws IOException, InterruptedException {
    // Log to stdout file
    System.out.println("Map key: " + key);

    // Log to syslog file
    LOG.info("Map key: " + key);
    if (LOG.isDebugEnabled()) {
      LOG.debug("Map value: " + value);
    }
    context.write((KEYOUT) key, (VALUEOUT) value);
  }
}
```

The default log level is INFO, so DEBUG-level messages do not appear in the *syslog* task logfile. However, sometimes you want to see these messages. To enable this, set mapre duce.map.log.level or mapreduce.reduce.log.level, as appropriate. For example, in this case, we could set it for the mapper to see the map values in the log as follows:

```
% hadoop jar hadoop-examples.jar LoggingDriver -conf conf/hadoop-cluster.xml \
  -D mapreduce.map.log.level=DEBUG input/ncdc/sample.txt logging-out
```

There are some controls for managing the retention and size of task logs. By default, logs are deleted after a minimum of three hours (you can set this using the yarn.nodemanager.log.retain-seconds property, although this is ignored if log aggregation is enabled). You can also set a cap on the maximum size of each logfile using the mapreduce.task.userlog.limit.kb property, which is 0 by default, meaning there is no cap.

 Sometimes you may need to debug a problem that you suspect is occurring in the JVM running a Hadoop command, rather than on the cluster. You can send DEBUG-level logs to the console by using an invocation like this:

```
% HADOOP_ROOT_LOGGER=DEBUG,console hadoop fs -text /foo/bar
```

Remote Debugging

When a task fails and there is not enough information logged to diagnose the error, you may want to resort to running a debugger for that task. This is hard to arrange when running the job on a cluster, as you don't know which node is going to process which part of the input, so you can't set up your debugger ahead of the failure. However, there are a few other options available:

Reproduce the failure locally

Often the failing task fails consistently on a particular input. You can try to reproduce the problem locally by downloading the file that the task is failing on and running the job locally, possibly using a debugger such as Java's VisualVM.

Use JVM debugging options

A common cause of failure is a Java out of memory error in the task JVM. You can set `mapred.child.java.opts` to include `-XX:-HeapDumpOnOutOfMemoryError -XX:HeapDumpPath=`*/path/to/dumps*. This setting produces a heap dump that can be examined afterward with tools such as *jhat* or the Eclipse Memory Analyzer. Note that the JVM options should be added to the existing memory settings specified by `mapred.child.java.opts`. These are explained in more detail in "Memory settings in YARN and MapReduce" on page 301.

Use task profiling

Java profilers give a lot of insight into the JVM, and Hadoop provides a mechanism to profile a subset of the tasks in a job. See "Profiling Tasks" on page 175.

In some cases, it's useful to keep the intermediate files for a failed task attempt for later inspection, particularly if supplementary dump or profile files are created in the task's working directory. You can set `mapreduce.task.files.preserve.failedtasks` to `true` to keep a failed task's files.

You can keep the intermediate files for successful tasks, too, which may be handy if you want to examine a task that isn't failing. In this case, set the property `mapre duce.task.files.preserve.filepattern` to a regular expression that matches the IDs of the tasks whose files you want to keep.

Another useful property for debugging is `yarn.nodemanager.delete.debug-delay-sec`, which is the number of seconds to wait to delete localized task attempt files, such as the script used to launch the task container JVM. If this is set on the cluster to a reasonably large value (e.g., `600` for 10 minutes), then you have enough time to look at the files before they are deleted.

To examine task attempt files, log into the node that the task failed on and look for the directory for that task attempt. It will be under one of the local MapReduce directories, as set by the `mapreduce.cluster.local.dir` property (covered in more detail in "Important Hadoop Daemon Properties" on page 296). If this property is a comma-separated list of directories (to spread load across the physical disks on a machine), you may need to look in all of the directories before you find the directory for that particular task attempt. The task attempt directory is in the following location:

```
mapreduce.cluster.local.dir/usercache/user/appcache/application-ID/output
    /task-attempt-ID
```

Tuning a Job

After a job is working, the question many developers ask is, "Can I make it run faster?"

There are a few Hadoop-specific "usual suspects" that are worth checking to see whether they are responsible for a performance problem. You should run through the checklist in Table 6-3 before you start trying to profile or optimize at the task level.

Table 6-3. Tuning checklist

Area	Best practice	Further information
Number of mappers	How long are your mappers running for? If they are only running for a few seconds on average, you should see whether there's a way to have fewer mappers and make them all run longer—a minute or so, as a rule of thumb. The extent to which this is possible depends on the input format you are using.	"Small files and CombineFileInputFormat" on page 226
Number of reducers	Check that you are using more than a single reducer. Reduce tasks should run for five minutes or so and produce at least a block's worth of data, as a rule of thumb.	"Choosing the Number of Reducers" on page 217
Combiners	Check whether your job can take advantage of a combiner to reduce the amount of data passing through the shuffle.	"Combiner Functions" on page 34
Intermediate compression	Job execution time can almost always benefit from enabling map output compression.	"Compressing map output" on page 109
Custom serialization	If you are using your own custom `Writable` objects or custom comparators, make sure you have implemented `RawComparator`.	"Implementing a RawComparator for speed" on page 123
Shuffle tweaks	The MapReduce shuffle exposes around a dozen tuning parameters for memory management, which may help you wring out the last bit of performance.	"Configuration Tuning" on page 201

Profiling Tasks

Like debugging, profiling a job running on a distributed system such as MapReduce presents some challenges. Hadoop allows you to profile a fraction of the tasks in a job and, as each task completes, pulls down the profile information to your machine for later analysis with standard profiling tools.

Of course, it's possible, and somewhat easier, to profile a job running in the local job runner. And provided you can run with enough input data to exercise the map and reduce tasks, this can be a valuable way of improving the performance of your mappers and reducers. There are a couple of caveats, however. The local job runner is a very different environment from a cluster, and the data flow patterns are very different. Optimizing the CPU performance of your code may be pointless if your MapReduce job is I/O-bound (as many jobs are). To be sure that any tuning is effective, you should compare the new execution time with the old one running on a real cluster. Even this is easier said than done, since job execution times can vary due to resource contention with other jobs and the decisions the scheduler makes regarding task placement. To get a good idea of job execution time under these circumstances, perform a series of runs (with and without the change) and check whether any improvement is statistically significant.

It's unfortunately true that some problems (such as excessive memory use) can be reproduced only on the cluster, and in these cases the ability to profile in situ is indispensable.

The HPROF profiler

There are a number of configuration properties to control profiling, which are also exposed via convenience methods on JobConf. Enabling profiling is as simple as setting the property mapreduce.task.profile to true:

```
% hadoop jar hadoop-examples.jar v4.MaxTemperatureDriver \
  -conf conf/hadoop-cluster.xml \
  -D mapreduce.task.profile=true \
  input/ncdc/all max-temp
```

This runs the job as normal, but adds an -agentlib parameter to the Java command used to launch the task containers on the node managers. You can control the precise parameter that is added by setting the mapreduce.task.profile.params property. The default uses HPROF, a profiling tool that comes with the JDK that, although basic, can give valuable information about a program's CPU and heap usage.

It doesn't usually make sense to profile all tasks in the job, so by default only those with IDs 0, 1, and 2 are profiled (for both maps and reduces). You can change this by setting mapreduce.task.profile.maps and mapreduce.task.profile.reduces to specify the range of task IDs to profile.

The profile output for each task is saved with the task logs in the *userlogs* subdirectory of the node manager's local log directory (alongside the *syslog*, *stdout*, and *stderr* files), and can be retrieved in the way described in "Hadoop Logs" on page 172, according to whether log aggregation is enabled or not.

MapReduce Workflows

So far in this chapter, you have seen the mechanics of writing a program using Map-Reduce. We haven't yet considered how to turn a data processing problem into the MapReduce model.

The data processing you have seen so far in this book is to solve a fairly simple problem: finding the maximum recorded temperature for given years. When the processing gets more complex, this complexity is generally manifested by having more MapReduce jobs, rather than having more complex map and reduce functions. In other words, as a rule of thumb, think about adding *more* jobs, rather than adding complexity *to* jobs.

For more complex problems, it is worth considering a higher-level language than Map-Reduce, such as Pig, Hive, Cascading, Crunch, or Spark. One immediate benefit is that it frees you from having to do the translation into MapReduce jobs, allowing you to concentrate on the analysis you are performing.

Finally, the book *Data-Intensive Text Processing with MapReduce* (*http://mapre duce.me*) by Jimmy Lin and Chris Dyer (Morgan & Claypool Publishers, 2010) is a great resource for learning more about MapReduce algorithm design and is highly recommended.

Decomposing a Problem into MapReduce Jobs

Let's look at an example of a more complex problem that we want to translate into a MapReduce workflow.

Imagine that we want to find the mean maximum recorded temperature for every day of the year and every weather station. In concrete terms, to calculate the mean maximum daily temperature recorded by station 029070-99999, say, on January 1, we take the mean of the maximum daily temperatures for this station for January 1, 1901; January 1, 1902; and so on, up to January 1, 2000.

How can we compute this using MapReduce? The computation decomposes most naturally into two stages:

1. *Compute the maximum daily temperature for every station-date pair.*

    The MapReduce program in this case is a variant of the maximum temperature program, except that the keys in this case are a composite station-date pair, rather than just the year.

2. *Compute the mean of the maximum daily temperatures for every station-day-month key.*

    The mapper takes the output from the previous job (station-date, maximum temperature) records and projects it into (station-day-month, maximum temperature) records by dropping the year component. The reduce function then takes the mean of the maximum temperatures for each station-day-month key.

The output from the first stage looks like this for the station we are interested in (the *mean_max_daily_temp.sh* script in the examples provides an implementation in Hadoop Streaming):

```
029070-99999 19010101 0
029070-99999 19020101 -94
...
```

The first two fields form the key, and the final column is the maximum temperature from all the readings for the given station and date. The second stage averages these daily maxima over years to yield:

```
029070-99999 0101 -68
```

which is interpreted as saying the mean maximum daily temperature on January 1 for station 029070-99999 over the century is −6.8°C.

It's possible to do this computation in one MapReduce stage, but it takes more work on the part of the programmer.[2]

The arguments for having more (but simpler) MapReduce stages are that doing so leads to more composable and more maintainable mappers and reducers. Some of the case studies referred to in Part V cover real-world problems that were solved using MapReduce, and in each case, the data processing task is implemented using two or more MapReduce jobs. The details in that chapter are invaluable for getting a better idea of how to decompose a processing problem into a MapReduce workflow.

It's possible to make map and reduce functions even more composable than we have done. A mapper commonly performs input format parsing, projection (selecting the relevant fields), and filtering (removing records that are not of interest). In the mappers you have seen so far, we have implemented all of these functions in a single mapper. However, there is a case for splitting these into distinct mappers and chaining them into a single mapper using the ChainMapper library class that comes with Hadoop. Combined with a ChainReducer, you can run a chain of mappers, followed by a reducer and another chain of mappers, in a single MapReduce job.

JobControl

When there is more than one job in a MapReduce workflow, the question arises: how do you manage the jobs so they are executed in order? There are several approaches, and the main consideration is whether you have a linear chain of jobs or a more complex directed acyclic graph (DAG) of jobs.

---

2. It's an interesting exercise to do this. Hint: use "Secondary Sort" on page 262.

For a linear chain, the simplest approach is to run each job one after another, waiting until a job completes successfully before running the next:

```
JobClient.runJob(conf1);
JobClient.runJob(conf2);
```

If a job fails, the `runJob()` method will throw an `IOException`, so later jobs in the pipeline don't get executed. Depending on your application, you might want to catch the exception and clean up any intermediate data that was produced by any previous jobs.

The approach is similar with the new MapReduce API, except you need to examine the Boolean return value of the `waitForCompletion()` method on `Job`: `true` means the job succeeded, and `false` means it failed.

For anything more complex than a linear chain, there are libraries that can help orchestrate your workflow (although they are also suited to linear chains, or even one-off jobs). The simplest is in the `org.apache.hadoop.mapreduce.jobcontrol` package: the `JobControl` class. (There is an equivalent class in the `org.apache.hadoop.mapred.job control` package, too.) An instance of `JobControl` represents a graph of jobs to be run. You add the job configurations, then tell the `JobControl` instance the dependencies between jobs. You run the `JobControl` in a thread, and it runs the jobs in dependency order. You can poll for progress, and when the jobs have finished, you can query for all the jobs' statuses and the associated errors for any failures. If a job fails, `JobControl` won't run its dependencies.

Apache Oozie

Apache Oozie is a system for running workflows of dependent jobs. It is composed of two main parts: a *workflow engine* that stores and runs workflows composed of different types of Hadoop jobs (MapReduce, Pig, Hive, and so on), and a *coordinator engine* that runs workflow jobs based on predefined schedules and data availability. Oozie has been designed to scale, and it can manage the timely execution of thousands of workflows in a Hadoop cluster, each composed of possibly dozens of constituent jobs.

Oozie makes rerunning failed workflows more tractable, since no time is wasted running successful parts of a workflow. Anyone who has managed a complex batch system knows how difficult it can be to catch up from jobs missed due to downtime or failure, and will appreciate this feature. (Furthermore, coordinator applications representing a single data pipeline may be packaged into a *bundle* and run together as a unit.)

Unlike `JobControl`, which runs on the client machine submitting the jobs, Oozie runs as a service in the cluster, and clients submit workflow definitions for immediate or later execution. In Oozie parlance, a workflow is a DAG of *action nodes* and *control-flow nodes*.

An action node performs a workflow task, such as moving files in HDFS; running a MapReduce, Streaming, Pig, or Hive job; performing a Sqoop import; or running an arbitrary shell script or Java program. A control-flow node governs the workflow execution between actions by allowing such constructs as conditional logic (so different execution branches may be followed depending on the result of an earlier action node) or parallel execution. When the workflow completes, Oozie can make an HTTP callback to the client to inform it of the workflow status. It is also possible to receive callbacks every time the workflow enters or exits an action node.

Defining an Oozie workflow

Workflow definitions are written in XML using the Hadoop Process Definition Language, the specification for which can be found on the Oozie website (*http://oozie.apache.org/*). Example 6-14 shows a simple Oozie workflow definition for running a single MapReduce job.

Example 6-14. Oozie workflow definition to run the maximum temperature MapReduce job

```
<workflow-app xmlns="uri:oozie:workflow:0.1" name="max-temp-workflow">
  <start to="max-temp-mr"/>
  <action name="max-temp-mr">
    <map-reduce>
      <job-tracker>${resourceManager}</job-tracker>
      <name-node>${nameNode}</name-node>
      <prepare>
        <delete path="${nameNode}/user/${wf:user()}/output"/>
      </prepare>
      <configuration>
        <property>
          <name>mapred.mapper.new-api</name>
          <value>true</value>
        </property>
        <property>
          <name>mapred.reducer.new-api</name>
          <value>true</value>
        </property>
        <property>
          <name>mapreduce.job.map.class</name>
          <value>MaxTemperatureMapper</value>
        </property>
        <property>
          <name>mapreduce.job.combine.class</name>
          <value>MaxTemperatureReducer</value>
        </property>
        <property>
          <name>mapreduce.job.reduce.class</name>
          <value>MaxTemperatureReducer</value>
        </property>
        <property>
```

```
    <name>mapreduce.job.output.key.class</name>
    <value>org.apache.hadoop.io.Text</value>
  </property>
  <property>
    <name>mapreduce.job.output.value.class</name>
    <value>org.apache.hadoop.io.IntWritable</value>
  </property>
  <property>
    <name>mapreduce.input.fileinputformat.inputdir</name>
    <value>/user/${wf:user()}/input/ncdc/micro</value>
  </property>
  <property>
    <name>mapreduce.output.fileoutputformat.outputdir</name>
    <value>/user/${wf:user()}/output</value>
  </property>
      </configuration>
    </map-reduce>
    <ok to="end"/>
    <error to="fail"/>
  </action>
  <kill name="fail">
    <message>MapReduce failed, error message[${wf:errorMessage(wf:lastErrorNode())}]
    </message>
  </kill>
  <end name="end"/>
</workflow-app>
```

This workflow has three control-flow nodes and one action node: a start control node, a map-reduce action node, a kill control node, and an end control node. The nodes and allowed transitions between them are shown in Figure 6-4.

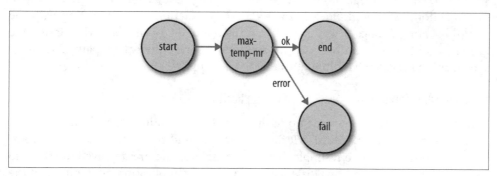

Figure 6-4. Transition diagram of an Oozie workflow

All workflows must have one start and one end node. When the workflow job starts, it transitions to the node specified by the start node (the max-temp-mr action in this example). A workflow job succeeds when it transitions to the end node. However, if the workflow job transitions to a kill node, it is considered to have failed and reports the appropriate error message specified by the message element in the workflow definition.

The bulk of this workflow definition file specifies the map-reduce action. The first two elements, job-tracker and name-node, are used to specify the YARN resource manager (or jobtracker in Hadoop 1) to submit the job to and the namenode (actually a Hadoop filesystem URI) for input and output data. Both are parameterized so that the workflow definition is not tied to a particular cluster (which makes it easy to test). The parameters are specified as workflow job properties at submission time, as we shall see later.

 Despite its name, the job-tracker element is used to specify a YARN resource manager address and port.

The optional prepare element runs before the MapReduce job and is used for directory deletion (and creation, too, if needed, although that is not shown here). By ensuring that the output directory is in a consistent state before running a job, Oozie can safely rerun the action if the job fails.

The MapReduce job to run is specified in the configuration element using nested elements for specifying the Hadoop configuration name-value pairs. You can view the MapReduce configuration section as a declarative replacement for the driver classes that we have used elsewhere in this book for running MapReduce programs (such as Example 2-5).

We have taken advantage of JSP Expression Language (EL) syntax in several places in the workflow definition. Oozie provides a set of functions for interacting with the workflow. For example, ${wf:user()} returns the name of the user who started the current workflow job, and we use it to specify the correct filesystem path. The Oozie specification lists all the EL functions that Oozie supports.

Packaging and deploying an Oozie workflow application

A workflow application is made up of the workflow definition plus all the associated resources (such as MapReduce JAR files, Pig scripts, and so on) needed to run it. Applications must adhere to a simple directory structure, and are deployed to HDFS so that they can be accessed by Oozie. For this workflow application, we'll put all of the files in a base directory called *max-temp-workflow*, as shown diagrammatically here:

```
max-temp-workflow/
├── lib/
|   └── hadoop-examples.jar
└── workflow.xml
```

The workflow definition file *workflow.xml* must appear in the top level of this directory. JAR files containing the application's MapReduce classes are placed in the *lib* directory.

Workflow applications that conform to this layout can be built with any suitable build tool, such as Ant or Maven; you can find an example in the code that accompanies this book. Once an application has been built, it should be copied to HDFS using regular Hadoop tools. Here is the appropriate command for this application:

```
% hadoop fs -put hadoop-examples/target/max-temp-workflow max-temp-workflow
```

Running an Oozie workflow job

Next, let's see how to run a workflow job for the application we just uploaded. For this we use the *oozie* command-line tool, a client program for communicating with an Oozie server. For convenience, we export the `OOZIE_URL` environment variable to tell the `oozie` command which Oozie server to use (here we're using one running locally):

```
% export OOZIE_URL="http://localhost:11000/oozie"
```

There are lots of subcommands for the *oozie* tool (type `oozie help` to get a list), but we're going to call the `job` subcommand with the `-run` option to run the workflow job:

```
% oozie job -config ch06-mr-dev/src/main/resources/max-temp-workflow.properties \
  -run
job: 0000001-140911033236814-oozie-oozi-W
```

The `-config` option specifies a local Java properties file containing definitions for the parameters in the workflow XML file (in this case, `nameNode` and `resourceManager`), as well as `oozie.wf.application.path`, which tells Oozie the location of the workflow application in HDFS. Here are the contents of the properties file:

```
nameNode=hdfs://localhost:8020
resourceManager=localhost:8032
oozie.wf.application.path=${nameNode}/user/${user.name}/max-temp-workflow
```

To get information about the status of the workflow job, we use the `-info` option, specifying the job ID that was printed by the run command earlier (type `oozie job` to get a list of all jobs):

```
% oozie job -info 0000001-140911033236814-oozie-oozi-W
```

The output shows the status: RUNNING, KILLED, or SUCCEEDED. You can also find all this information via Oozie's web UI (*http://localhost:11000/oozie*).

When the job has succeeded, we can inspect the results in the usual way:

```
% hadoop fs -cat output/part-*
1949 111
1950 22
```

This example only scratched the surface of writing Oozie workflows. The documentation on Oozie's website has information about creating more complex workflows, as well as writing and running coordinator jobs.

How MapReduce Works

In this chapter, we look at how MapReduce in Hadoop works in detail. This knowledge provides a good foundation for writing more advanced MapReduce programs, which we will cover in the following two chapters.

Anatomy of a MapReduce Job Run

You can run a MapReduce job with a single method call: `submit()` on a `Job` object (you can also call `waitForCompletion()`, which submits the job if it hasn't been submitted already, then waits for it to finish).[1] This method call conceals a great deal of processing behind the scenes. This section uncovers the steps Hadoop takes to run a job.

The whole process is illustrated in Figure 7-1. At the highest level, there are five independent entities:[2]

- The client, which submits the MapReduce job.
- The YARN resource manager, which coordinates the allocation of compute resources on the cluster.
- The YARN node managers, which launch and monitor the compute containers on machines in the cluster.
- The MapReduce application master, which coordinates the tasks running the MapReduce job. The application master and the MapReduce tasks run in containers that are scheduled by the resource manager and managed by the node managers.

---

1. In the old MapReduce API, you can call `JobClient.submitJob(conf)` or `JobClient.runJob(conf)`.

2. Not discussed in this section are the job history server daemon (for retaining job history data) and the shuffle handler auxiliary service (for serving map outputs to reduce tasks).

- The distributed filesystem (normally HDFS, covered in Chapter 3), which is used for sharing job files between the other entities.

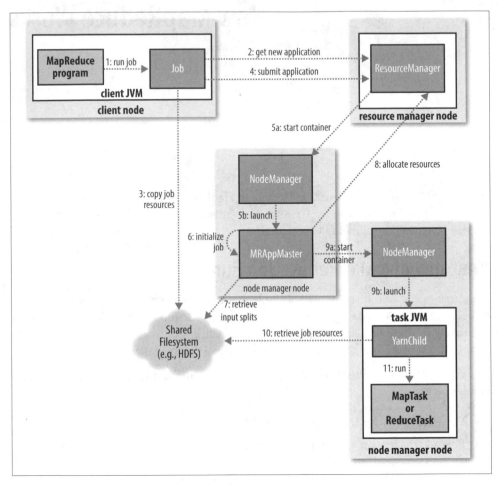

Figure 7-1. How Hadoop runs a MapReduce job

Job Submission

The submit() method on Job creates an internal JobSubmitter instance and calls submitJobInternal() on it (step 1 in Figure 7-1). Having submitted the job, waitFor Completion() polls the job's progress once per second and reports the progress to the console if it has changed since the last report. When the job completes successfully, the job counters are displayed. Otherwise, the error that caused the job to fail is logged to the console.

The job submission process implemented by JobSubmitter does the following:

- Asks the resource manager for a new application ID, used for the MapReduce job ID (step 2).

- Checks the output specification of the job. For example, if the output directory has not been specified or it already exists, the job is not submitted and an error is thrown to the MapReduce program.

- Computes the input splits for the job. If the splits cannot be computed (because the input paths don't exist, for example), the job is not submitted and an error is thrown to the MapReduce program.

- Copies the resources needed to run the job, including the job JAR file, the configuration file, and the computed input splits, to the shared filesystem in a directory named after the job ID (step 3). The job JAR is copied with a high replication factor (controlled by the `mapreduce.client.submit.file.replication` property, which defaults to 10) so that there are lots of copies across the cluster for the node managers to access when they run tasks for the job.

- Submits the job by calling `submitApplication()` on the resource manager (step 4).

Job Initialization

When the resource manager receives a call to its `submitApplication()` method, it hands off the request to the YARN scheduler. The scheduler allocates a container, and the resource manager then launches the application master's process there, under the node manager's management (steps 5a and 5b).

The application master for MapReduce jobs is a Java application whose main class is `MRAppMaster`. It initializes the job by creating a number of bookkeeping objects to keep track of the job's progress, as it will receive progress and completion reports from the tasks (step 6). Next, it retrieves the input splits computed in the client from the shared filesystem (step 7). It then creates a map task object for each split, as well as a number of reduce task objects determined by the `mapreduce.job.reduces` property (set by the `setNumReduceTasks()` method on `Job`). Tasks are given IDs at this point.

The application master must decide how to run the tasks that make up the MapReduce job. If the job is small, the application master may choose to run the tasks in the same JVM as itself. This happens when it judges that the overhead of allocating and running tasks in new containers outweighs the gain to be had in running them in parallel, compared to running them sequentially on one node. Such a job is said to be *uberized*, or run as an *uber task*.

What qualifies as a small job? By default, a small job is one that has less than 10 mappers, only one reducer, and an input size that is less than the size of one HDFS block. (Note that these values may be changed for a job by setting `mapreduce.job.ubertask.maxmaps`, `mapreduce.job.ubertask.maxreduces`, and `map reduce.job.ubertask.maxbytes`.) Uber tasks must be enabled explicitly (for an individual job, or across the cluster) by setting `mapreduce.job.ubertask.enable` to `true`.

Finally, before any tasks can be run, the application master calls the `setupJob()` method on the `OutputCommitter`. For `FileOutputCommitter`, which is the default, it will create the final output directory for the job and the temporary working space for the task output. The commit protocol is described in more detail in "Output Committers" on page 206.

Task Assignment

If the job does not qualify for running as an uber task, then the application master requests containers for all the map and reduce tasks in the job from the resource manager (step 8). Requests for map tasks are made first and with a higher priority than those for reduce tasks, since all the map tasks must complete before the sort phase of the reduce can start (see "Shuffle and Sort" on page 197). Requests for reduce tasks are not made until 5% of map tasks have completed (see "Reduce slow start" on page 308).

Reduce tasks can run anywhere in the cluster, but requests for map tasks have data locality constraints that the scheduler tries to honor (see "Resource Requests" on page 81). In the optimal case, the task is *data local*—that is, running on the same node that the split resides on. Alternatively, the task may be *rack local*: on the same rack, but not the same node, as the split. Some tasks are neither data local nor rack local and retrieve their data from a different rack than the one they are running on. For a particular job run, you can determine the number of tasks that ran at each locality level by looking at the job's counters (see Table 9-6).

Requests also specify memory requirements and CPUs for tasks. By default, each map and reduce task is allocated 1,024 MB of memory and one virtual core. The values are configurable on a per-job basis (subject to minimum and maximum values described in "Memory settings in YARN and MapReduce" on page 301) via the following properties: `mapreduce.map.memory.mb`, `mapreduce.reduce.memory.mb`, `mapreduce.map.cpu.vcores` and `mapreduce.reduce.cpu.vcores`.

Task Execution

Once a task has been assigned resources for a container on a particular node by the resource manager's scheduler, the application master starts the container by contacting the node manager (steps 9a and 9b). The task is executed by a Java application whose main class is YarnChild. Before it can run the task, it localizes the resources that the task needs, including the job configuration and JAR file, and any files from the distributed cache (step 10; see "Distributed Cache" on page 274). Finally, it runs the map or reduce task (step 11).

The YarnChild runs in a dedicated JVM, so that any bugs in the user-defined map and reduce functions (or even in YarnChild) don't affect the node manager—by causing it to crash or hang, for example.

Each task can perform setup and commit actions, which are run in the same JVM as the task itself and are determined by the OutputCommitter for the job (see "Output Committers" on page 206). For file-based jobs, the commit action moves the task output from a temporary location to its final location. The commit protocol ensures that when speculative execution is enabled (see "Speculative Execution" on page 204), only one of the duplicate tasks is committed and the other is aborted.

Streaming

Streaming runs special map and reduce tasks for the purpose of launching the user-supplied executable and communicating with it (Figure 7-2).

The Streaming task communicates with the process (which may be written in any language) using standard input and output streams. During execution of the task, the Java process passes input key-value pairs to the external process, which runs it through the user-defined map or reduce function and passes the output key-value pairs back to the Java process. From the node manager's point of view, it is as if the child process ran the map or reduce code itself.

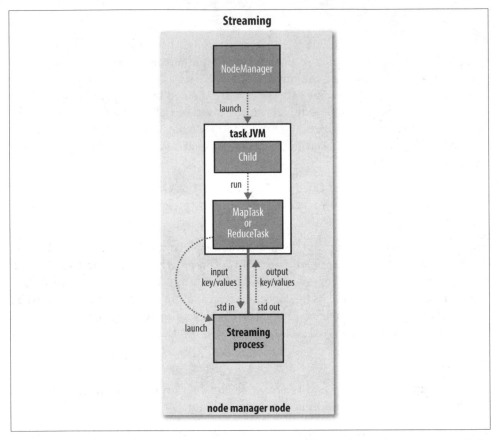

Figure 7-2. The relationship of the Streaming executable to the node manager and the task container

Progress and Status Updates

MapReduce jobs are long-running batch jobs, taking anything from tens of seconds to hours to run. Because this can be a significant length of time, it's important for the user to get feedback on how the job is progressing. A job and each of its tasks have a *status*, which includes such things as the state of the job or task (e.g., running, successfully completed, failed), the progress of maps and reduces, the values of the job's counters, and a status message or description (which may be set by user code). These statuses change over the course of the job, so how do they get communicated back to the client?

When a task is running, it keeps track of its *progress* (i.e., the proportion of the task completed). For map tasks, this is the proportion of the input that has been processed. For reduce tasks, it's a little more complex, but the system can still estimate the proportion of the reduce input processed. It does this by dividing the total progress into three parts, corresponding to the three phases of the shuffle (see "Shuffle and Sort" on page 197). For example, if the task has run the reducer on half its input, the task's progress is 5/6, since it has completed the copy and sort phases (1/3 each) and is halfway through the reduce phase (1/6).

What Constitutes Progress in MapReduce?

Progress is not always measurable, but nevertheless, it tells Hadoop that a task is doing something. For example, a task writing output records is making progress, even when it cannot be expressed as a percentage of the total number that will be written (because the latter figure may not be known, even by the task producing the output).

Progress reporting is important, as Hadoop will not fail a task that's making progress. All of the following operations constitute progress:

- Reading an input record (in a mapper or reducer)
- Writing an output record (in a mapper or reducer)
- Setting the status description (via Reporter's or TaskAttemptContext's setStatus() method)
- Incrementing a counter (using Reporter's incrCounter() method or Counter's increment() method)
- Calling Reporter's or TaskAttemptContext's progress() method

---

Tasks also have a set of counters that count various events as the task runs (we saw an example in "A test run" on page 27), which are either built into the framework, such as the number of map output records written, or defined by users.

As the map or reduce task runs, the child process communicates with its parent application master through the *umbilical* interface. The task reports its progress and status (including counters) back to its application master, which has an aggregate view of the job, every three seconds over the umbilical interface.

The resource manager web UI displays all the running applications with links to the web UIs of their respective application masters, each of which displays further details on the MapReduce job, including its progress.

During the course of the job, the client receives the latest status by polling the application master every second (the interval is set via mapreduce.client.progressmonitor.pollinterval). Clients can also use Job's getStatus() method to obtain a JobStatus instance, which contains all of the status information for the job.

The process is illustrated in Figure 7-3.

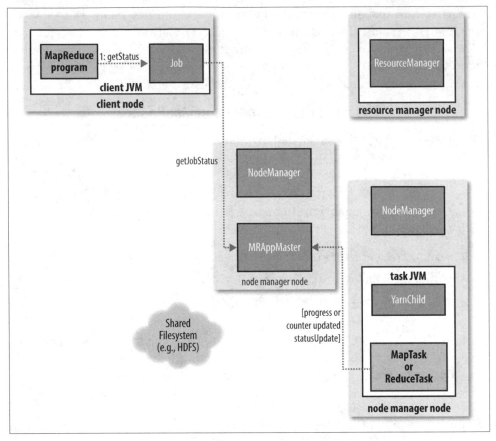

Figure 7-3. How status updates are propagated through the MapReduce system

Job Completion

When the application master receives a notification that the last task for a job is complete, it changes the status for the job to "successful." Then, when the Job polls for status, it learns that the job has completed successfully, so it prints a message to tell the user and then returns from the `waitForCompletion()` method. Job statistics and counters are printed to the console at this point.

The application master also sends an HTTP job notification if it is configured to do so. This can be configured by clients wishing to receive callbacks, via the `mapreduce.job.end-notification.url` property.

Finally, on job completion, the application master and the task containers clean up their working state (so intermediate output is deleted), and the `OutputCommitter`'s `commit Job()` method is called. Job information is archived by the job history server to enable later interrogation by users if desired.

Failures

In the real world, user code is buggy, processes crash, and machines fail. One of the major benefits of using Hadoop is its ability to handle such failures and allow your job to complete successfully. We need to consider the failure of any of the following entities: the task, the application master, the node manager, and the resource manager.

Task Failure

Consider first the case of the task failing. The most common occurrence of this failure is when user code in the map or reduce task throws a runtime exception. If this happens, the task JVM reports the error back to its parent application master before it exits. The error ultimately makes it into the user logs. The application master marks the task attempt as *failed*, and frees up the container so its resources are available for another task.

For Streaming tasks, if the Streaming process exits with a nonzero exit code, it is marked as failed. This behavior is governed by the `stream.non.zero.exit.is.failure` property (the default is `true`).

Another failure mode is the sudden exit of the task JVM—perhaps there is a JVM bug that causes the JVM to exit for a particular set of circumstances exposed by the MapReduce user code. In this case, the node manager notices that the process has exited and informs the application master so it can mark the attempt as failed.

Hanging tasks are dealt with differently. The application master notices that it hasn't received a progress update for a while and proceeds to mark the task as failed. The task JVM process will be killed automatically after this period.[3] The timeout period after which tasks are considered failed is normally 10 minutes and can be configured on a per-job basis (or a cluster basis) by setting the `mapreduce.task.timeout` property to a value in milliseconds.

Setting the timeout to a value of zero disables the timeout, so long-running tasks are never marked as failed. In this case, a hanging task will never free up its container, and over time there may be cluster slowdown as a result. This approach should therefore be avoided, and making sure that a task is reporting progress periodically should suffice (see "What Constitutes Progress in MapReduce?" on page 191).

---

3. If a Streaming process hangs, the node manager will kill it (along with the JVM that launched it) only in the following circumstances: either `yarn.nodemanager.container-executor.class` is set to `org.apache.ha doop.yarn.server.nodemanager.LinuxContainerExecutor`, or the default container executor is being used and the `setsid` command is available on the system (so that the task JVM and any processes it launches are in the same process group). In any other case, orphaned Streaming processes will accumulate on the system, which will impact utilization over time.

When the application master is notified of a task attempt that has failed, it will reschedule execution of the task. The application master will try to avoid rescheduling the task on a node manager where it has previously failed. Furthermore, if a task fails four times, it will not be retried again. This value is configurable. The maximum number of attempts to run a task is controlled by the `mapreduce.map.maxattempts` property for map tasks and `mapreduce.reduce.maxattempts` for reduce tasks. By default, if any task fails four times (or whatever the maximum number of attempts is configured to), the whole job fails.

For some applications, it is undesirable to abort the job if a few tasks fail, as it may be possible to use the results of the job despite some failures. In this case, the maximum percentage of tasks that are allowed to fail without triggering job failure can be set for the job. Map tasks and reduce tasks are controlled independently, using the `mapreduce.map.failures.maxpercent` and `mapreduce.reduce.failures.maxpercent` properties.

A task attempt may also be *killed*, which is different from it failing. A task attempt may be killed because it is a speculative duplicate (for more information on this topic, see "Speculative Execution" on page 204), or because the node manager it was running on failed and the application master marked all the task attempts running on it as killed. Killed task attempts do not count against the number of attempts to run the task (as set by `mapreduce.map.maxattempts` and `mapreduce.reduce.maxattempts`), because it wasn't the task's fault that an attempt was killed.

Users may also kill or fail task attempts using the web UI or the command line (type `mapred job` to see the options). Jobs may be killed by the same mechanisms.

Application Master Failure

Just like MapReduce tasks are given several attempts to succeed (in the face of hardware or network failures), applications in YARN are retried in the event of failure. The maximum number of attempts to run a MapReduce application master is controlled by the `mapreduce.am.max-attempts` property. The default value is 2, so if a MapReduce application master fails twice it will not be tried again and the job will fail.

YARN imposes a limit for the maximum number of attempts for any YARN application master running on the cluster, and individual applications may not exceed this limit. The limit is set by `yarn.resourcemanager.am.max-attempts` and defaults to 2, so if you want to increase the number of MapReduce application master attempts, you will have to increase the YARN setting on the cluster, too.

The way recovery works is as follows. An application master sends periodic heartbeats to the resource manager, and in the event of application master failure, the resource manager will detect the failure and start a new instance of the master running in a new container (managed by a node manager). In the case of the MapReduce application master, it will use the job history to recover the state of the tasks that were already run by the (failed) application so they don't have to be rerun. Recovery is enabled by default, but can be disabled by setting `yarn.app.mapreduce.am.job.recovery.enable` to `false`.

The MapReduce client polls the application master for progress reports, but if its application master fails, the client needs to locate the new instance. During job initialization, the client asks the resource manager for the application master's address, and then caches it so it doesn't overload the resource manager with a request every time it needs to poll the application master. If the application master fails, however, the client will experience a timeout when it issues a status update, at which point the client will go back to the resource manager to ask for the new application master's address. This process is transparent to the user.

Node Manager Failure

If a node manager fails by crashing or running very slowly, it will stop sending heartbeats to the resource manager (or send them very infrequently). The resource manager will notice a node manager that has stopped sending heartbeats if it hasn't received one for 10 minutes (this is configured, in milliseconds, via the `yarn.resourcemanager.nm.liveness-monitor.expiry-interval-ms` property) and remove it from its pool of nodes to schedule containers on.

Any task or application master running on the failed node manager will be recovered using the mechanisms described in the previous two sections. In addition, the application master arranges for map tasks that were run and completed successfully on the failed node manager to be rerun if they belong to incomplete jobs, since their intermediate output residing on the failed node manager's local filesystem may not be accessible to the reduce task.

Node managers may be *blacklisted* if the number of failures for the application is high, even if the node manager itself has not failed. Blacklisting is done by the application master, and for MapReduce the application master will try to reschedule tasks on different nodes if more than three tasks fail on a node manager. The user may set the threshold with the `mapreduce.job.maxtaskfailures.per.tracker` job property.

 Note that the resource manager does not do blacklisting across applications (at the time of writing), so tasks from new jobs may be scheduled on bad nodes even if they have been blacklisted by an application master running an earlier job.

Resource Manager Failure

Failure of the resource manager is serious, because without it, neither jobs nor task containers can be launched. In the default configuration, the resource manager is a single point of failure, since in the (unlikely) event of machine failure, all running jobs fail—and can't be recovered.

To achieve high availability (HA), it is necessary to run a pair of resource managers in an active-standby configuration. If the active resource manager fails, then the standby can take over without a significant interruption to the client.

Information about all the running applications is stored in a highly available state store (backed by ZooKeeper or HDFS), so that the standby can recover the core state of the failed active resource manager. Node manager information is not stored in the state store since it can be reconstructed relatively quickly by the new resource manager as the node managers send their first heartbeats. (Note also that tasks are not part of the resource manager's state, since they are managed by the application master. Thus, the amount of state to be stored is therefore much more manageable than that of the job-tracker in MapReduce 1.)

When the new resource manager starts, it reads the application information from the state store, then restarts the application masters for all the applications running on the cluster. This does not count as a failed application attempt (so it does not count against `yarn.resourcemanager.am.max-attempts`), since the application did not fail due to an error in the application code, but was forcibly killed by the system. In practice, the application master restart is not an issue for MapReduce applications since they recover the work done by completed tasks (as we saw in "Application Master Failure" on page 194).

The transition of a resource manager from standby to active is handled by a failover controller. The default failover controller is an automatic one, which uses ZooKeeper leader election to ensure that there is only a single active resource manager at one time. Unlike in HDFS HA (see "HDFS High Availability" on page 48), the failover controller does not have to be a standalone process, and is embedded in the resource manager by default for ease of configuration. It is also possible to configure manual failover, but this is not recommended.

Clients and node managers must be configured to handle resource manager failover, since there are now two possible resource managers to communicate with. They try connecting to each resource manager in a round-robin fashion until they find the active one. If the active fails, then they will retry until the standby becomes active.

Shuffle and Sort

MapReduce makes the guarantee that the input to every reducer is sorted by key. The process by which the system performs the sort—and transfers the map outputs to the reducers as inputs—is known as the *shuffle*.[4] In this section, we look at how the shuffle works, as a basic understanding will be helpful should you need to optimize a MapReduce program. The shuffle is an area of the codebase where refinements and improvements are continually being made, so the following description necessarily conceals many details. In many ways, the shuffle is the heart of MapReduce and is where the "magic" happens.

The Map Side

When the map function starts producing output, it is not simply written to disk. The process is more involved, and takes advantage of buffering writes in memory and doing some presorting for efficiency reasons. Figure 7-4 shows what happens.

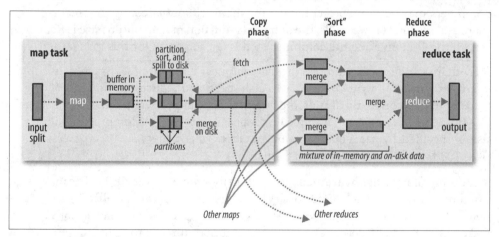

Figure 7-4. Shuffle and sort in MapReduce

Each map task has a circular memory buffer that it writes the output to. The buffer is 100 MB by default (the size can be tuned by changing the `mapreduce.task.io.sort.mb` property). When the contents of the buffer reach a certain threshold size (`mapreduce.map.sort.spill.percent`, which has the default value 0.80, or 80%), a background thread will start to *spill* the contents to disk. Map outputs will continue to be written to the buffer while the spill takes place, but if the buffer fills up during this time,

---

4. The term *shuffle* is actually imprecise, since in some contexts it refers to only the part of the process where map outputs are fetched by reduce tasks. In this section, we take it to mean the whole process, from the point where a map produces output to where a reduce consumes input.

the map will block until the spill is complete. Spills are written in round-robin fashion to the directories specified by the `mapreduce.cluster.local.dir` property, in a job specific subdirectory.

Before it writes to disk, the thread first divides the data into partitions corresponding to the reducers that they will ultimately be sent to. Within each partition, the background thread performs an in-memory sort by key, and if there is a combiner function, it is run on the output of the sort. Running the combiner function makes for a more compact map output, so there is less data to write to local disk and to transfer to the reducer.

Each time the memory buffer reaches the spill threshold, a new spill file is created, so after the map task has written its last output record, there could be several spill files. Before the task is finished, the spill files are merged into a single partitioned and sorted output file. The configuration property `mapreduce.task.io.sort.factor` controls the maximum number of streams to merge at once; the default is 10.

If there are at least three spill files (set by the `mapreduce.map.combine.minspills` property), the combiner is run again before the output file is written. Recall that combiners may be run repeatedly over the input without affecting the final result. If there are only one or two spills, the potential reduction in map output size is not worth the overhead in invoking the combiner, so it is not run again for this map output.

It is often a good idea to compress the map output as it is written to disk, because doing so makes it faster to write to disk, saves disk space, and reduces the amount of data to transfer to the reducer. By default, the output is not compressed, but it is easy to enable this by setting `mapreduce.map.output.compress` to `true`. The compression library to use is specified by `mapreduce.map.output.compress.codec`; see "Compression" on page 100 for more on compression formats.

The output file's partitions are made available to the reducers over HTTP. The maximum number of worker threads used to serve the file partitions is controlled by the `mapreduce.shuffle.max.threads` property; this setting is per node manager, not per map task. The default of 0 sets the maximum number of threads to twice the number of processors on the machine.

The Reduce Side

Let's turn now to the reduce part of the process. The map output file is sitting on the local disk of the machine that ran the map task (note that although map outputs always get written to local disk, reduce outputs may not be), but now it is needed by the machine that is about to run the reduce task for the partition. Moreover, the reduce task needs the map output for its particular partition from several map tasks across the cluster. The map tasks may finish at different times, so the reduce task starts copying their outputs as soon as each completes. This is known as the *copy phase* of the reduce task. The reduce task has a small number of copier threads so that it can fetch map outputs in parallel.

The default is five threads, but this number can be changed by setting the `mapreduce.re`
`duce.shuffle.parallelcopies` property.

How do reducers know which machines to fetch map output from?

As map tasks complete successfully, they notify their application
master using the heartbeat mechanism. Therefore, for a given job, the
application master knows the mapping between map outputs and
hosts. A thread in the reducer periodically asks the master for map
output hosts until it has retrieved them all.

Hosts do not delete map outputs from disk as soon as the first reducer has retrieved them, as the reducer may subsequently fail. Instead, they wait until they are told to delete them by the application
master, which is after the job has completed.

Map outputs are copied to the reduce task JVM's memory if they are small enough (the
buffer's size is controlled by `mapreduce.reduce.shuffle.input.buffer.percent`,
which specifies the proportion of the heap to use for this purpose); otherwise, they are
copied to disk. When the in-memory buffer reaches a threshold size (controlled by
`mapreduce.reduce.shuffle.merge.percent`) or reaches a threshold number of map
outputs (`mapreduce.reduce.merge.inmem.threshold`), it is merged and spilled to disk.
If a combiner is specified, it will be run during the merge to reduce the amount of data
written to disk.

As the copies accumulate on disk, a background thread merges them into larger, sorted
files. This saves some time merging later on. Note that any map outputs that were compressed (by the map task) have to be decompressed in memory in order to perform a
merge on them.

When all the map outputs have been copied, the reduce task moves into the *sort
phase* (which should properly be called the *merge* phase, as the sorting was carried out
on the map side), which merges the map outputs, maintaining their sort ordering. This
is done in rounds. For example, if there were 50 map outputs and the *merge factor* was
10 (the default, controlled by the `mapreduce.task.io.sort.factor` property, just like
in the map's merge), there would be five rounds. Each round would merge 10 files into
1, so at the end there would be 5 intermediate files.

Rather than have a final round that merges these five files into a single sorted file, the
merge saves a trip to disk by directly feeding the reduce function in what is the last
phase: the *reduce phase*. This final merge can come from a mixture of in-memory and
on-disk segments.

The number of files merged in each round is actually more subtle than this example suggests. The goal is to merge the minimum number of files to get to the merge factor for the final round. So if there were 40 files, the merge would not merge 10 files in each of the four rounds to get 4 files. Instead, the first round would merge only 4 files, and the subsequent three rounds would merge the full 10 files. The 4 merged files and the 6 (as yet unmerged) files make a total of 10 files for the final round. The process is illustrated in Figure 7-5.

Note that this does not change the number of rounds; it's just an optimization to minimize the amount of data that is written to disk, since the final round always merges directly into the reduce.

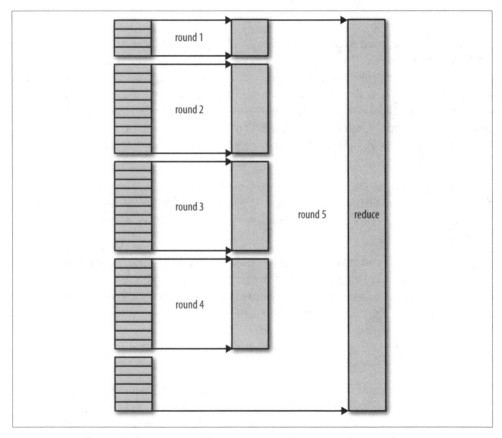

Figure 7-5. Efficiently merging 40 file segments with a merge factor of 10

During the reduce phase, the reduce function is invoked for each key in the sorted output. The output of this phase is written directly to the output filesystem, typically

HDFS. In the case of HDFS, because the node manager is also running a datanode, the first block replica will be written to the local disk.

Configuration Tuning

We are now in a better position to understand how to tune the shuffle to improve MapReduce performance. The relevant settings, which can be used on a per-job basis (except where noted), are summarized in Tables 7-1 and 7-2, along with the defaults, which are good for general-purpose jobs.

The general principle is to give the shuffle as much memory as possible. However, there is a trade-off, in that you need to make sure that your map and reduce functions get enough memory to operate. This is why it is best to write your map and reduce functions to use as little memory as possible—certainly they should not use an unbounded amount of memory (avoid accumulating values in a map, for example).

The amount of memory given to the JVMs in which the map and reduce tasks run is set by the `mapred.child.java.opts` property. You should try to make this as large as possible for the amount of memory on your task nodes; the discussion in "Memory settings in YARN and MapReduce" on page 301 goes through the constraints to consider.

On the map side, the best performance can be obtained by avoiding multiple spills to disk; one is optimal. If you can estimate the size of your map outputs, you can set the `mapreduce.task.io.sort.*` properties appropriately to minimize the number of spills. In particular, you should increase `mapreduce.task.io.sort.mb` if you can. There is a MapReduce counter (`SPILLED_RECORDS`; see "Counters" on page 247) that counts the total number of records that were spilled to disk over the course of a job, which can be useful for tuning. Note that the counter includes both map- and reduce-side spills.

On the reduce side, the best performance is obtained when the intermediate data can reside entirely in memory. This does not happen by default, since for the general case all the memory is reserved for the reduce function. But if your reduce function has light memory requirements, setting `mapreduce.reduce.merge.inmem.threshold` to 0 and `mapreduce.reduce.input.buffer.percent` to 1.0 (or a lower value; see Table 7-2) may bring a performance boost.

In April 2008, Hadoop won the general-purpose terabyte sort benchmark (as discussed in "A Brief History of Apache Hadoop" on page 12), and one of the optimizations used was keeping the intermediate data in memory on the reduce side.

More generally, Hadoop uses a buffer size of 4 KB by default, which is low, so you should increase this across the cluster (by setting `io.file.buffer.size`; see also "Other Hadoop Properties" on page 307).

Table 7-1. Map-side tuning properties

Property name	Type	Default value	Description
mapreduce.task.io.sort.mb	int	100	The size, in megabytes, of the memory buffer to use while sorting map output.
mapreduce.map.sort.spill.percent	float	0.80	The threshold usage proportion for both the map output memory buffer and the record boundaries index to start the process of spilling to disk.
mapreduce.task.io.sort.factor	int	10	The maximum number of streams to merge at once when sorting files. This property is also used in the reduce. It's fairly common to increase this to 100.
mapreduce.map.combine.minspills	int	3	The minimum number of spill files needed for the combiner to run (if a combiner is specified).
mapreduce.map.output.compress	boolean	false	Whether to compress map outputs.
mapreduce.map.output.compress.codec	Class name	org.apache.hadoop.io.compress.DefaultCodec	The compression codec to use for map outputs.
mapreduce.shuffle.max.threads	int	0	The number of worker threads per node manager for serving the map outputs to reducers. This is a cluster-wide setting and cannot be set by individual jobs. 0 means use the Netty default of twice the number of available processors.

Table 7-2. Reduce-side tuning properties

Property name	Type	Default value	Description
mapreduce.reduce.shuffle.parallelcopies	int	5	The number of threads used to copy map outputs to the reducer.
mapreduce.reduce.shuffle.maxfetchfailures	int	10	The number of times a reducer tries to fetch a map output before reporting the error.
mapreduce.task.io.sort.factor	int	10	The maximum number of streams to merge at once when sorting files. This property is also used in the map.
mapreduce.reduce.shuffle.input.buffer.percent	float	0.70	The proportion of total heap size to be allocated to the map outputs buffer during the copy phase of the shuffle.
mapreduce.reduce.shuffle.merge.percent	float	0.66	The threshold usage proportion for the map outputs buffer (defined by mapred.job.shuffle.input.buffer.percent) for starting the process of merging the outputs and spilling to disk.

Property name	Type	Default value	Description
mapreduce.reduce.merge.in mem.threshold	int	1000	The threshold number of map outputs for starting the process of merging the outputs and spilling to disk. A value of 0 or less means there is no threshold, and the spill behavior is governed solely by `mapre duce.reduce.shuffle.merge.percent`.
mapreduce.reduce.in put.buffer.percent	float	0.0	The proportion of total heap size to be used for retaining map outputs in memory during the reduce. For the reduce phase to begin, the size of map outputs in memory must be no more than this size. By default, all map outputs are merged to disk before the reduce begins, to give the reducers as much memory as possible. However, if your reducers require less memory, this value may be increased to minimize the number of trips to disk.

Task Execution

We saw how the MapReduce system executes tasks in the context of the overall job at the beginning of this chapter, in "Anatomy of a MapReduce Job Run" on page 185. In this section, we'll look at some more controls that MapReduce users have over task execution.

The Task Execution Environment

Hadoop provides information to a map or reduce task about the environment in which it is running. For example, a map task can discover the name of the file it is processing (see "File information in the mapper" on page 227), and a map or reduce task can find out the attempt number of the task. The properties in Table 7-3 can be accessed from the job's configuration, obtained in the old MapReduce API by providing an implementation of the `configure()` method for `Mapper` or `Reducer`, where the configuration is passed in as an argument. In the new API, these properties can be accessed from the context object passed to all methods of the `Mapper` or `Reducer`.

Table 7-3. Task environment properties

Property name	Type	Description	Example
mapreduce.job.id	String	The job ID (see "Job, Task, and Task Attempt IDs" on page 164 for a description of the format)	job_200811201130_0004
mapreduce.task.id	String	The task ID	task_200811201130_0004_m_000003
mapreduce.task.at tempt.id	String	The task attempt ID	attempt_200811201130_0004_m_000003_0

Property name	Type	Description	Example
mapre duce.task.parti tion	int	The index of the task within the job	3
mapreduce.task.is map	boolean	Whether this task is a map task	true

Streaming environment variables

Hadoop sets job configuration parameters as environment variables for Streaming programs. However, it replaces nonalphanumeric characters with underscores to make sure they are valid names. The following Python expression illustrates how you can retrieve the value of the `mapreduce.job.id` property from within a Python Streaming script:

```
os.environ["mapreduce_job_id"]
```

You can also set environment variables for the Streaming processes launched by MapReduce by supplying the `-cmdenv` option to the Streaming launcher program (once for each variable you wish to set). For example, the following sets the `MAGIC_PARAMETER` environment variable:

```
-cmdenv MAGIC_PARAMETER=abracadabra
```

Speculative Execution

The MapReduce model is to break jobs into tasks and run the tasks in parallel to make the overall job execution time smaller than it would be if the tasks ran sequentially. This makes the job execution time sensitive to slow-running tasks, as it takes only one slow task to make the whole job take significantly longer than it would have done otherwise. When a job consists of hundreds or thousands of tasks, the possibility of a few straggling tasks is very real.

Tasks may be slow for various reasons, including hardware degradation or software misconfiguration, but the causes may be hard to detect because the tasks still complete successfully, albeit after a longer time than expected. Hadoop doesn't try to diagnose and fix slow-running tasks; instead, it tries to detect when a task is running slower than expected and launches another equivalent task as a backup. This is termed *speculative execution* of tasks.

It's important to understand that speculative execution does not work by launching two duplicate tasks at about the same time so they can race each other. This would be wasteful of cluster resources. Rather, the scheduler tracks the progress of all tasks of the same type (map and reduce) in a job, and only launches speculative duplicates for the small proportion that are running significantly slower than the average. When a task completes successfully, any duplicate tasks that are running are killed since they are no longer needed. So, if the original task completes before the speculative task, the speculative task is killed; on the other hand, if the speculative task finishes first, the original is killed.

Speculative execution is an optimization, and not a feature to make jobs run more reliably. If there are bugs that sometimes cause a task to hang or slow down, relying on speculative execution to avoid these problems is unwise and won't work reliably, since the same bugs are likely to affect the speculative task. You should fix the bug so that the task doesn't hang or slow down.

Speculative execution is turned on by default. It can be enabled or disabled independently for map tasks and reduce tasks, on a cluster-wide basis, or on a per-job basis. The relevant properties are shown in Table 7-4.

Table 7-4. Speculative execution properties

Property name	Type	Default value	Description
`mapreduce.map.specula tive`	`boolean`	`true`	Whether extra instances of map tasks may be launched if a task is making slow progress
`mapreduce.reduce.specu lative`	`boolean`	`true`	Whether extra instances of reduce tasks may be launched if a task is making slow progress
`yarn.app.mapre duce.am.job.specula tor.class`	`Class`	`org.apache.hadoop.map reduce.v2.app.specu late.DefaultSpecula tor`	The `Speculator` class implementing the speculative execution policy (MapReduce 2 only)
`yarn.app.mapre duce.am.job.task.estima tor.class`	`Class`	`org.apache.hadoop.map reduce.v2.app.specu late.LegacyTaskRunti meEstimator`	An implementation of `TaskRunti meEstimator` used by `Specula tor` instances that provides estimates for task runtimes (MapReduce 2 only)

Why would you ever want to turn speculative execution off? The goal of speculative execution is to reduce job execution time, but this comes at the cost of cluster efficiency. On a busy cluster, speculative execution can reduce overall throughput, since redundant tasks are being executed in an attempt to bring down the execution time for a single job. For this reason, some cluster administrators prefer to turn it off on the cluster and have users explicitly turn it on for individual jobs. This was especially relevant for older versions of Hadoop, when speculative execution could be overly aggressive in scheduling speculative tasks.

There is a good case for turning off speculative execution for reduce tasks, since any duplicate reduce tasks have to fetch the same map outputs as the original task, and this can significantly increase network traffic on the cluster.

Another reason for turning off speculative execution is for nonidempotent tasks. However, in many cases it is possible to write tasks to be idempotent and use an

OutputCommitter to promote the output to its final location when the task succeeds. This technique is explained in more detail in the next section.

Output Committers

Hadoop MapReduce uses a commit protocol to ensure that jobs and tasks either succeed or fail cleanly. The behavior is implemented by the OutputCommitter in use for the job, which is set in the old MapReduce API by calling the setOutputCommitter() on Job Conf or by setting mapred.output.committer.class in the configuration. In the new MapReduce API, the OutputCommitter is determined by the OutputFormat, via its getOutputCommitter() method. The default is FileOutputCommitter, which is appropriate for file-based MapReduce. You can customize an existing OutputCommitter or even write a new implementation if you need to do special setup or cleanup for jobs or tasks.

The OutputCommitter API is as follows (in both the old and new MapReduce APIs):

```
public abstract class OutputCommitter {

    public abstract void setupJob(JobContext jobContext) throws IOException;
    public void commitJob(JobContext jobContext) throws IOException { }
    public void abortJob(JobContext jobContext, JobStatus.State state)
        throws IOException { }

    public abstract void setupTask(TaskAttemptContext taskContext)
        throws IOException;
    public abstract boolean needsTaskCommit(TaskAttemptContext taskContext)
        throws IOException;
    public abstract void commitTask(TaskAttemptContext taskContext)
        throws IOException;
    public abstract void abortTask(TaskAttemptContext taskContext)
        throws IOException;

    }
}
```

The setupJob() method is called before the job is run, and is typically used to perform initialization. For FileOutputCommitter, the method creates the final output directory, ${mapreduce.output.fileoutputformat.outputdir}, and a temporary working space for task output, _temporary, as a subdirectory underneath it.

If the job succeeds, the commitJob() method is called, which in the default file-based implementation deletes the temporary working space and creates a hidden empty marker file in the output directory called _SUCCESS to indicate to filesystem clients that the job completed successfully. If the job did not succeed, abortJob() is called with a state object indicating whether the job failed or was killed (by a user, for example). In the default implementation, this will delete the job's temporary working space.

The operations are similar at the task level. The `setupTask()` method is called before the task is run, and the default implementation doesn't do anything, because temporary directories named for task outputs are created when the task outputs are written.

The commit phase for tasks is optional and may be disabled by returning `false` from `needsTaskCommit()`. This saves the framework from having to run the distributed commit protocol for the task, and neither `commitTask()` nor `abortTask()` is called. `FileOutputCommitter` will skip the commit phase when no output has been written by a task.

If a task succeeds, `commitTask()` is called, which in the default implementation moves the temporary task output directory (which has the task attempt ID in its name to avoid conflicts between task attempts) to the final output path, `${mapreduce.output.fil eoutputformat.outputdir}`. Otherwise, the framework calls `abortTask()`, which deletes the temporary task output directory.

The framework ensures that in the event of multiple task attempts for a particular task, only one will be committed; the others will be aborted. This situation may arise because the first attempt failed for some reason—in which case, it would be aborted, and a later, successful attempt would be committed. It can also occur if two task attempts were running concurrently as speculative duplicates; in this instance, the one that finished first would be committed, and the other would be aborted.

Task side-effect files

The usual way of writing output from map and reduce tasks is by using `OutputCollec tor` to collect key-value pairs. Some applications need more flexibility than a single key-value pair model, so these applications write output files directly from the map or reduce task to a distributed filesystem, such as HDFS. (There are other ways to produce multiple outputs, too, as described in "Multiple Outputs" on page 240.)

Care needs to be taken to ensure that multiple instances of the same task don't try to write to the same file. As we saw in the previous section, the `OutputCommitter` protocol solves this problem. If applications write side files in their tasks' working directories, the side files for tasks that successfully complete will be promoted to the output directory automatically, whereas failed tasks will have their side files deleted.

A task may find its working directory by retrieving the value of the `mapreduce.task.out put.dir` property from the job configuration. Alternatively, a MapReduce program using the Java API may call the `getWorkOutputPath()` static method on `FileOutputFor mat` to get the `Path` object representing the working directory. The framework creates the working directory before executing the task, so you don't need to create it.

To take a simple example, imagine a program for converting image files from one format to another. One way to do this is to have a map-only job, where each map is given a set of images to convert (perhaps using `NLineInputFormat`; see "NLineInputFormat" on page 234). If a map task writes the converted images into its working directory, they will be promoted to the output directory when the task successfully finishes.

## CHAPTER 8

MapReduce Types and Formats

MapReduce has a simple model of data processing: inputs and outputs for the map and reduce functions are key-value pairs. This chapter looks at the MapReduce model in detail, and in particular at how data in various formats, from simple text to structured binary objects, can be used with this model.

MapReduce Types

The map and reduce functions in Hadoop MapReduce have the following general form:

```
map:    (K1, V1)        → list(K2, V2)
reduce: (K2, list(V2))  → list(K3, V3)
```

In general, the map input key and value types (K1 and V1) are different from the map output types (K2 and V2). However, the reduce input must have the same types as the map output, although the reduce output types may be different again (K3 and V3). The Java API mirrors this general form:

```java
public class Mapper<KEYIN, VALUEIN, KEYOUT, VALUEOUT> {
  public class Context extends MapContext<KEYIN, VALUEIN, KEYOUT, VALUEOUT> {
    // ...
  }
  protected void map(KEYIN key, VALUEIN value,
      Context context) throws IOException, InterruptedException {
    // ...
  }
}

public class Reducer<KEYIN, VALUEIN, KEYOUT, VALUEOUT> {
  public class Context extends ReducerContext<KEYIN, VALUEIN, KEYOUT, VALUEOUT> {
    // ...
  }
  protected void reduce(KEYIN key, Iterable<VALUEIN> values,
      Context context) throws IOException, InterruptedException {
```

```
    // ...
  }
}
```

The context objects are used for emitting key-value pairs, and they are parameterized by the output types so that the signature of the `write()` method is:

```
public void write(KEYOUT key, VALUEOUT value)
    throws IOException, InterruptedException
```

Since `Mapper` and `Reducer` are separate classes, the type parameters have different scopes, and the actual type argument of `KEYIN` (say) in the `Mapper` may be different from the type of the type parameter of the same name (`KEYIN`) in the `Reducer`. For instance, in the maximum temperature example from earlier chapters, `KEYIN` is replaced by `Long Writable` for the `Mapper` and by `Text` for the `Reducer`.

Similarly, even though the map output types and the reduce input types must match, this is not enforced by the Java compiler.

The type parameters are named differently from the abstract types (`KEYIN` versus `K1`, and so on), but the form is the same.

If a combiner function is used, then it has the same form as the reduce function (and is an implementation of `Reducer`), except its output types are the intermediate key and value types (`K2` and `V2`), so they can feed the reduce function:

```
map:      (K1, V1) → list(K2, V2)
combiner: (K2, list(V2)) → list(K2, V2)
reduce:   (K2, list(V2)) → list(K3, V3)
```

Often the combiner and reduce functions are the same, in which case K3 is the same as K2, and V3 is the same as V2.

The partition function operates on the intermediate key and value types (K2 and V2) and returns the partition index. In practice, the partition is determined solely by the key (the value is ignored):

```
partition: (K2, V2) → integer
```

Or in Java:

```
public abstract class Partitioner<KEY, VALUE> {
  public abstract int getPartition(KEY key, VALUE value, int numPartitions);
}
```

So much for the theory. How does this help you configure MapReduce jobs? Table 8-1 summarizes the configuration options for the new API (and Table 8-2 does the same for the old API). It is divided into the properties that determine the types and those that have to be compatible with the configured types.

Input types are set by the input format. So, for instance, a TextInputFormat generates keys of type LongWritable and values of type Text. The other types are set explicitly by calling the methods on the Job (or JobConf in the old API). If not set explicitly, the intermediate types default to the (final) output types, which default to LongWritable and Text. So, if K2 and K3 are the same, you don't need to call setMapOutputKey Class(), because it falls back to the type set by calling setOutputKeyClass(). Similarly, if V2 and V3 are the same, you only need to use setOutputValueClass().

It may seem strange that these methods for setting the intermediate and final output types exist at all. After all, why can't the types be determined from a combination of the mapper and the reducer? The answer has to do with a limitation in Java generics: type erasure means that the type information isn't always present at runtime, so Hadoop has to be given it explicitly. This also means that it's possible to configure a MapReduce job with incompatible types, because the configuration isn't checked at compile time. The settings that have to be compatible with the MapReduce types are listed in the lower part of Table 8-1. Type conflicts are detected at runtime during job execution, and for this reason, it is wise to run a test job using a small amount of data to flush out and fix any type incompatibilities.

Table 8-1. Configuration of MapReduce types in the new API

Property	Job setter method	Input types		Intermediate types		Output types	
		K1	V1	K2	V2	K3	V3
Properties for configuring types:							
mapreduce.job.inputformat.class	setInputFormatClass()	•	•				
mapreduce.map.output.key.class	setMapOutputKeyClass()			•			
mapreduce.map.output.value.class	setMapOutputValueClass()				•		
mapreduce.job.output.key.class	setOutputKeyClass()					•	
mapreduce.job.output.value.class	setOutputValueClass()						•
Properties that must be consistent with the types:							
mapreduce.job.map.class	setMapperClass()	•	•	•	•		
mapreduce.job.combine.class	setCombinerClass()			•	•		
mapreduce.job.partitioner.class	setPartitionerClass()			•	•		
mapreduce.job.output.key.comparator.class	setSortComparatorClass()			•			
mapreduce.job.output.group.comparator.class	setGroupingComparatorClass()			•			
mapreduce.job.reduce.class	setReducerClass()			•	•	•	•
mapreduce.job.outputformat.class	setOutputFormatClass()					•	•

Table 8-2. Configuration of MapReduce types in the old API

Property	JobConf setter method	Input types		Intermediate types		Output types	
		K1	V1	K2	V2	K3	V3
Properties for configuring types:							
mapred.input.format.class	setInputFormat()	•	•				
mapred.mapoutput.key.class	setMapOutputKeyClass()			•			
mapred.mapoutput.value.class	setMapOutputValueClass()				•		
mapred.output.key.class	setOutputKeyClass()					•	
mapred.output.value.class	setOutputValueClass()						•
Properties that must be consistent with the types:							
mapred.mapper.class	setMapperClass()	•	•	•	•		
mapred.map.runner.class	setMapRunnerClass()	•	•	•	•		
mapred.combiner.class	setCombinerClass()			•	•		
mapred.partitioner.class	setPartitionerClass()			•	•		
mapred.output.key.comparator.class	setOutputKeyComparatorClass()			•			
mapred.output.value.groupfn.class	setOutputValueGroupingComparator()			•			
mapred.reducer.class	setReducerClass()			•	•	•	
mapred.output.format.class	setOutputFormat()					•	•

The Default MapReduce Job

What happens when you run MapReduce without setting a mapper or a reducer? Let's try it by running this minimal MapReduce program:

```java
public class MinimalMapReduce extends Configured implements Tool {

  @Override
  public int run(String[] args) throws Exception {
    if (args.length != 2) {
      System.err.printf("Usage: %s [generic options] <input> <output>\n",
          getClass().getSimpleName());
      ToolRunner.printGenericCommandUsage(System.err);
      return -1;
    }

    Job job = new Job(getConf());
    job.setJarByClass(getClass());
    FileInputFormat.addInputPath(job, new Path(args[0]));
    FileOutputFormat.setOutputPath(job, new Path(args[1]));
    return job.waitForCompletion(true) ? 0 : 1;
  }

  public static void main(String[] args) throws Exception {
    int exitCode = ToolRunner.run(new MinimalMapReduce(), args);
    System.exit(exitCode);
  }
}
```

The only configuration that we set is an input path and an output path. We run it over a subset of our weather data with the following:

```
% hadoop MinimalMapReduce "input/ncdc/all/190{1,2}.gz" output
```

We do get some output: one file named *part-r-00000* in the output directory. Here's what the first few lines look like (truncated to fit the page):

```
0→0029029070999991901010106004+64333+023450FM-12+000599999V0202701N01591...
0→0035029070999991902010106004+64333+023450FM-12+000599999V0201401N01181...
135→0029029070999991901010113004+64333+023450FM-12+000599999V0202901N00821...
141→0035029070999991902010113004+64333+023450FM-12+000599999V0201401N01181...
270→0029029070999991901010120004+64333+023450FM-12+000599999V0209991C00001...
282→0035029070999991902010120004+64333+023450FM-12+000599999V0201401N01391...
```

Each line is an integer followed by a tab character, followed by the original weather data record. Admittedly, it's not a very useful program, but understanding how it produces its output does provide some insight into the defaults that Hadoop uses when running MapReduce jobs. Example 8-1 shows a program that has exactly the same effect as MinimalMapReduce, but explicitly sets the job settings to their defaults.

Example 8-1. A minimal MapReduce driver, with the defaults explicitly set

```java
public class MinimalMapReduceWithDefaults extends Configured implements Tool {

  @Override
  public int run(String[] args) throws Exception {
    Job job = JobBuilder.parseInputAndOutput(this, getConf(), args);
    if (job == null) {
      return -1;
    }

    job.setInputFormatClass(TextInputFormat.class);

    job.setMapperClass(Mapper.class);

    job.setMapOutputKeyClass(LongWritable.class);
    job.setMapOutputValueClass(Text.class);

    job.setPartitionerClass(HashPartitioner.class);

    job.setNumReduceTasks(1);
    job.setReducerClass(Reducer.class);

    job.setOutputKeyClass(LongWritable.class);
    job.setOutputValueClass(Text.class);

    job.setOutputFormatClass(TextOutputFormat.class);

    return job.waitForCompletion(true) ? 0 : 1;
  }

  public static void main(String[] args) throws Exception {
    int exitCode = ToolRunner.run(new MinimalMapReduceWithDefaults(), args);
    System.exit(exitCode);
  }
}
```

We've simplified the first few lines of the run() method by extracting the logic for printing usage and setting the input and output paths into a helper method. Almost all MapReduce drivers take these two arguments (input and output), so reducing the boilerplate code here is a good thing. Here are the relevant methods in the JobBuilder class for reference:

```java
public static Job parseInputAndOutput(Tool tool, Configuration conf,
    String[] args) throws IOException {

  if (args.length != 2) {
    printUsage(tool, "<input> <output>");
    return null;
  }
  Job job = new Job(conf);
  job.setJarByClass(tool.getClass());
```

```
    FileInputFormat.addInputPath(job, new Path(args[0]));
    FileOutputFormat.setOutputPath(job, new Path(args[1]));
    return job;
  }

  public static void printUsage(Tool tool, String extraArgsUsage) {
    System.err.printf("Usage: %s [genericOptions] %s\n\n",
        tool.getClass().getSimpleName(), extraArgsUsage);
    GenericOptionsParser.printGenericCommandUsage(System.err);
  }
```

Going back to `MinimalMapReduceWithDefaults` in Example 8-1, although there are many other default job settings, the ones bolded are those most central to running a job. Let's go through them in turn.

The default input format is `TextInputFormat`, which produces keys of type `LongWrita ble` (the offset of the beginning of the line in the file) and values of type `Text` (the line of text). This explains where the integers in the final output come from: they are the line offsets.

The default mapper is just the `Mapper` class, which writes the input key and value unchanged to the output:

```
public class Mapper<KEYIN, VALUEIN, KEYOUT, VALUEOUT> {

  protected void map(KEYIN key, VALUEIN value,
      Context context) throws IOException, InterruptedException {
    context.write((KEYOUT) key, (VALUEOUT) value);
  }
}
```

`Mapper` is a generic type, which allows it to work with any key or value types. In this case, the map input and output key is of type `LongWritable`, and the map input and output value is of type `Text`.

The default partitioner is `HashPartitioner`, which hashes a record's key to determine which partition the record belongs in. Each partition is processed by a reduce task, so the number of partitions is equal to the number of reduce tasks for the job:

```
public class HashPartitioner<K, V> extends Partitioner<K, V> {

  public int getPartition(K key, V value,
      int numReduceTasks) {
    return (key.hashCode() & Integer.MAX_VALUE) % numReduceTasks;
  }
}
```

The key's hash code is turned into a nonnegative integer by bitwise ANDing it with the largest integer value. It is then reduced modulo the number of partitions to find the index of the partition that the record belongs in.

By default, there is a single reducer, and therefore a single partition; the action of the partitioner is irrelevant in this case since everything goes into one partition. However, it is important to understand the behavior of HashPartitioner when you have more than one reduce task. Assuming the key's hash function is a good one, the records will be allocated evenly across reduce tasks, with all records that share the same key being processed by the same reduce task.

You may have noticed that we didn't set the number of map tasks. The reason for this is that the number is equal to the number of splits that the input is turned into, which is driven by the size of the input and the file's block size (if the file is in HDFS). The options for controlling split size are discussed in "FileInputFormat input splits" on page 224.

Choosing the Number of Reducers

The single reducer default is something of a gotcha for new users to Hadoop. Almost all real-world jobs should set this to a larger number; otherwise, the job will be very slow since all the intermediate data flows through a single reduce task.

Choosing the number of reducers for a job is more of an art than a science. Increasing the number of reducers makes the reduce phase shorter, since you get more parallelism. However, if you take this too far, you can have lots of small files, which is suboptimal. One rule of thumb is to aim for reducers that each run for five minutes or so, and which produce at least one HDFS block's worth of output.

The default reducer is Reducer, again a generic type, which simply writes all its input to its output:

```
public class Reducer<KEYIN, VALUEIN, KEYOUT, VALUEOUT> {

  protected void reduce(KEYIN key, Iterable<VALUEIN> values, Context context
      Context context) throws IOException, InterruptedException {
    for (VALUEIN value: values) {
      context.write((KEYOUT) key, (VALUEOUT) value);
    }
  }
}
```

For this job, the output key is LongWritable and the output value is Text. In fact, all the keys for this MapReduce program are LongWritable and all the values are Text, since these are the input keys and values, and the map and reduce functions are both identity functions, which by definition preserve type. Most MapReduce programs, however, don't use the same key or value types throughout, so you need to configure the job to declare the types you are using, as described in the previous section.

Records are sorted by the MapReduce system before being presented to the reducer. In this case, the keys are sorted numerically, which has the effect of interleaving the lines from the input files into one combined output file.

The default output format is `TextOutputFormat`, which writes out records, one per line, by converting keys and values to strings and separating them with a tab character. This is why the output is tab-separated: it is a feature of `TextOutputFormat`.

The default Streaming job

In Streaming, the default job is similar, but not identical, to the Java equivalent. The basic form is:

```
% hadoop jar $HADOOP_HOME/share/hadoop/tools/lib/hadoop-streaming-*.jar \
  -input input/ncdc/sample.txt \
  -output output \
  -mapper /bin/cat
```

When we specify a non-Java mapper and the default text mode is in effect (`-io text`), Streaming does something special. It doesn't pass the key to the mapper process; it just passes the value. (For other input formats, the same effect can be achieved by setting `stream.map.input.ignoreKey` to `true`.) This is actually very useful because the key is just the line offset in the file and the value is the line, which is all most applications are interested in. The overall effect of this job is to perform a sort of the input.

With more of the defaults spelled out, the command looks like this (notice that Streaming uses the old MapReduce API classes):

```
% hadoop jar $HADOOP_HOME/share/hadoop/tools/lib/hadoop-streaming-*.jar \
  -input input/ncdc/sample.txt \
  -output output \
  -inputformat org.apache.hadoop.mapred.TextInputFormat \
  -mapper /bin/cat \
  -partitioner org.apache.hadoop.mapred.lib.HashPartitioner \
  -numReduceTasks 1 \
  -reducer org.apache.hadoop.mapred.lib.IdentityReducer \
  -outputformat org.apache.hadoop.mapred.TextOutputFormat
  -io text
```

The `-mapper` and `-reducer` arguments take a command or a Java class. A combiner may optionally be specified using the `-combiner` argument.

Keys and values in Streaming

A Streaming application can control the separator that is used when a key-value pair is turned into a series of bytes and sent to the map or reduce process over standard input. The default is a tab character, but it is useful to be able to change it in the case that the keys or values themselves contain tab characters.

Similarly, when the map or reduce writes out key-value pairs, they may be separated by a configurable separator. Furthermore, the key from the output can be composed of more than the first field: it can be made up of the first n fields (defined by stream.num.map.output.key.fields or stream.num.reduce.output.key.fields), with the value being the remaining fields. For example, if the output from a Streaming process was a,b,c (with a comma as the separator), and n was 2, the key would be parsed as a,b and the value as c.

Separators may be configured independently for maps and reduces. The properties are listed in Table 8-3 and shown in a diagram of the data flow path in Figure 8-1.

These settings do not have any bearing on the input and output formats. For example, if stream.reduce.output.field.separator were set to be a colon, say, and the reduce stream process wrote the line a:b to standard out, the Streaming reducer would know to extract the key as a and the value as b. With the standard TextOutputFormat, this record would be written to the output file with a tab separating a and b. You can change the separator that TextOutputFormat uses by setting mapreduce.output.textoutput format.separator.

Table 8-3. Streaming separator properties

Property name	Type	Default value	Description
stream.map.in put.field.separator	String	\t	The separator to use when passing the input key and value strings to the stream map process as a stream of bytes
stream.map.out put.field.separator	String	\t	The separator to use when splitting the output from the stream map process into key and value strings for the map output
stream.num.map.out put.key.fields	int	1	The number of fields separated by stream.map.output.field.separator to treat as the map output key
stream.reduce.in put.field.separator	String	\t	The separator to use when passing the input key and value strings to the stream reduce process as a stream of bytes
stream.reduce.out put.field.separator	String	\t	The separator to use when splitting the output from the stream reduce process into key and value strings for the final reduce output
stream.num.re duce.out put.key.fields	int	1	The number of fields separated by stream.reduce.output.field.separator to treat as the reduce output key

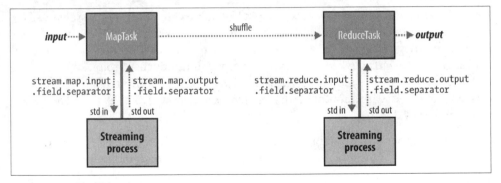

Figure 8-1. Where separators are used in a Streaming MapReduce job

Input Formats

Hadoop can process many different types of data formats, from flat text files to databases. In this section, we explore the different formats available.

Input Splits and Records

As we saw in Chapter 2, an input split is a chunk of the input that is processed by a single map. Each map processes a single split. Each split is divided into records, and the map processes each record—a key-value pair—in turn. Splits and records are logical: there is nothing that requires them to be tied to files, for example, although in their most common incarnations, they are. In a database context, a split might correspond to a range of rows from a table and a record to a row in that range (this is precisely the case with DBInputFormat, which is an input format for reading data from a relational database).

Input splits are represented by the Java class InputSplit (which, like all of the classes mentioned in this section, is in the org.apache.hadoop.mapreduce package):[1]

```
public abstract class InputSplit {
  public abstract long getLength() throws IOException, InterruptedException;
  public abstract String[] getLocations() throws IOException,
      InterruptedException;
}
```

An InputSplit has a length in bytes and a set of storage locations, which are just hostname strings. Notice that a split doesn't contain the input data; it is just a reference to the data. The storage locations are used by the MapReduce system to place map tasks as close to the split's data as possible, and the size is used to order the splits so that the

---

1. But see the classes in org.apache.hadoop.mapred for the old MapReduce API counterparts.

largest get processed first, in an attempt to minimize the job runtime (this is an instance of a greedy approximation algorithm).

As a MapReduce application writer, you don't need to deal with InputSplits directly, as they are created by an InputFormat (an InputFormat is responsible for creating the input splits and dividing them into records). Before we see some concrete examples of InputFormats, let's briefly examine how it is used in MapReduce. Here's the interface:

```
public abstract class InputFormat<K, V> {
    public abstract List<InputSplit> getSplits(JobContext context)
        throws IOException, InterruptedException;

    public abstract RecordReader<K, V>
        createRecordReader(InputSplit split, TaskAttemptContext context)
            throws IOException, InterruptedException;
}
```

The client running the job calculates the splits for the job by calling getSplits(), then sends them to the application master, which uses their storage locations to schedule map tasks that will process them on the cluster. The map task passes the split to the createRecordReader() method on InputFormat to obtain a RecordReader for that split. A RecordReader is little more than an iterator over records, and the map task uses one to generate record key-value pairs, which it passes to the map function. We can see this by looking at the Mapper's run() method:

```
public void run(Context context) throws IOException, InterruptedException {
    setup(context);
    while (context.nextKeyValue()) {
        map(context.getCurrentKey(), context.getCurrentValue(), context);
    }
    cleanup(context);
}
```

After running setup(), the nextKeyValue() is called repeatedly on the Context (which delegates to the identically named method on the RecordReader) to populate the key and value objects for the mapper. The key and value are retrieved from the RecordReader by way of the Context and are passed to the map() method for it to do its work. When the reader gets to the end of the stream, the nextKeyValue() method returns false, and the map task runs its cleanup() method and then completes.

Although it's not shown in the code snippet, for reasons of efficiency, RecordReader implementations will return the *same* key and value objects on each call to getCurrentKey() and getCurrentValue(). Only the contents of these objects are changed by the reader's nextKeyValue() method. This can be a surprise to users, who might expect keys and values to be immutable and not to be reused. This causes problems when a reference to a key or value object is retained outside the map() method, as its value can change without warning. If you need to do this, make a copy of the object you want to hold on to. For example, for a Text object, you can use its copy constructor: new Text(value).

The situation is similar with reducers. In this case, the value objects in the reducer's iterator are reused, so you need to copy any that you need to retain between calls to the iterator (see Example 9-11).

Finally, note that the Mapper's run() method is public and may be customized by users. MultithreadedMapper is an implementation that runs mappers concurrently in a configurable number of threads (set by mapreduce.mapper.multithreadedmapper.threads). For most data processing tasks, it confers no advantage over the default implementation. However, for mappers that spend a long time processing each record —because they contact external servers, for example—it allows multiple mappers to run in one JVM with little contention.

FileInputFormat

FileInputFormat is the base class for all implementations of InputFormat that use files as their data source (see Figure 8-2). It provides two things: a place to define which files are included as the input to a job, and an implementation for generating splits for the input files. The job of dividing splits into records is performed by subclasses.

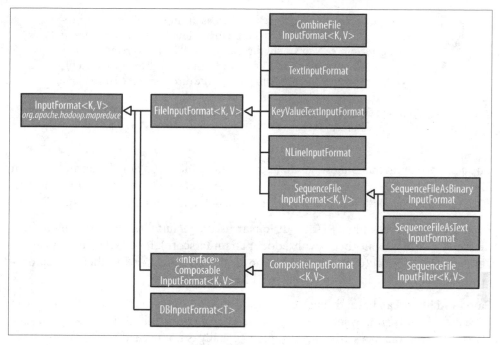

Figure 8-2. InputFormat class hierarchy

FileInputFormat input paths

The input to a job is specified as a collection of paths, which offers great flexibility in constraining the input. FileInputFormat offers four static convenience methods for setting a Job's input paths:

```
public static void addInputPath(Job job, Path path)
public static void addInputPaths(Job job, String commaSeparatedPaths)
public static void setInputPaths(Job job, Path... inputPaths)
public static void setInputPaths(Job job, String commaSeparatedPaths)
```

The addInputPath() and addInputPaths() methods add a path or paths to the list of inputs. You can call these methods repeatedly to build the list of paths. The setInput Paths() methods set the entire list of paths in one go (replacing any paths set on the Job in previous calls).

A path may represent a file, a directory, or, by using a glob, a collection of files and directories. A path representing a directory includes all the files in the directory as input to the job. See "File patterns" on page 66 for more on using globs.

The contents of a directory specified as an input path are not processed recursively. In fact, the directory should only contain files. If the directory contains a subdirectory, it will be interpreted as a file, which will cause an error. The way to handle this case is to use a file glob or a filter to select only the files in the directory based on a name pattern. Alternatively, `mapreduce.input.fileinputformat.input.dir.recursive` can be set to `true` to force the input directory to be read recursively.

The add and set methods allow files to be specified by inclusion only. To exclude certain files from the input, you can set a filter using the `setInputPathFilter()` method on `FileInputFormat`. Filters are discussed in more detail in "PathFilter" on page 67.

Even if you don't set a filter, `FileInputFormat` uses a default filter that excludes hidden files (those whose names begin with a dot or an underscore). If you set a filter by calling `setInputPathFilter()`, it acts in addition to the default filter. In other words, only nonhidden files that are accepted by your filter get through.

Paths and filters can be set through configuration properties, too (Table 8-4), which can be handy for Streaming jobs. Setting paths is done with the `-input` option for the Streaming interface, so setting paths directly usually is not needed.

Table 8-4. Input path and filter properties

Property name	Type	Default value	Description
`mapreduce.input.fileinputformat.input dir`	Comma-separated paths	None	The input files for a job. Paths that contain commas should have those commas escaped by a backslash character. For example, the glob `{a,b}` would be escaped as `{a\,b}`.
`mapreduce.input.pathFilter.class`	PathFilter classname	None	The filter to apply to the input files for a job.

FileInputFormat input splits

Given a set of files, how does `FileInputFormat` turn them into splits? `FileInputFormat` splits only large files—here, "large" means larger than an HDFS block. The split size is normally the size of an HDFS block, which is appropriate for most applications; however, it is possible to control this value by setting various Hadoop properties, as shown in Table 8-5.

Table 8-5. Properties for controlling split size

Property name	Type	Default value	Description
`mapreduce.input.fileinputformat.split.minsize`	`int`	1	The smallest valid size in bytes for a file split
`mapreduce.input.fileinputformat.split.maxsize`[a]	`long`	`Long.MAX_VALUE` (i.e., 9223372036854775807)	The largest valid size in bytes for a file split
`dfs.blocksize`	`long`	128 MB (i.e., 134217728)	The size of a block in HDFS in bytes

[a] This property is not present in the old MapReduce API (with the exception of `CombineFileInputFormat`). Instead, it is calculated indirectly as the size of the total input for the job, divided by the guide number of map tasks specified by `mapreduce.job.maps` (or the `setNumMapTasks()` method on JobConf). Because the number of map tasks defaults to 1, this makes the maximum split size the size of the input.

The minimum split size is usually 1 byte, although some formats have a lower bound on the split size. (For example, sequence files insert sync entries every so often in the stream, so the minimum split size has to be large enough to ensure that every split has a sync point to allow the reader to resynchronize with a record boundary. See "Reading a SequenceFile" on page 129.)

Applications may impose a minimum split size. By setting this to a value larger than the block size, they can force splits to be larger than a block. There is no good reason for doing this when using HDFS, because doing so will increase the number of blocks that are not local to a map task.

The maximum split size defaults to the maximum value that can be represented by a Java `long` type. It has an effect only when it is less than the block size, forcing splits to be smaller than a block.

The split size is calculated by the following formula (see the `computeSplitSize()` method in `FileInputFormat`):

```
max(minimumSize, min(maximumSize, blockSize))
```

and by default:

```
minimumSize < blockSize < maximumSize
```

so the split size is `blockSize`. Various settings for these parameters and how they affect the final split size are illustrated in Table 8-6.

Table 8-6. Examples of how to control the split size

Minimum split size	Maximum split size	Block size	Split size	Comment
1 (default)	Long.MAX_VALUE (default)	128 MB (default)	128 MB	By default, the split size is the same as the default block size.
1 (default)	Long.MAX_VALUE (default)	256 MB	256 MB	The most natural way to increase the split size is to have larger blocks in HDFS, either by setting dfs.blocksize or by configuring this on a per-file basis at file construction time.
256 MB	Long.MAX_VALUE (default)	128 MB (default)	256 MB	Making the minimum split size greater than the block size increases the split size, but at the cost of locality.
1 (default)	64 MB	128 MB (default)	64 MB	Making the maximum split size less than the block size decreases the split size.

Small files and CombineFileInputFormat

Hadoop works better with a small number of large files than a large number of small files. One reason for this is that FileInputFormat generates splits in such a way that each split is all or part of a single file. If the file is very small ("small" means significantly smaller than an HDFS block) and there are a lot of them, each map task will process very little input, and there will be a lot of them (one per file), each of which imposes extra bookkeeping overhead. Compare a 1 GB file broken into eight 128 MB blocks with 10,000 or so 100 KB files. The 10,000 files use one map each, and the job time can be tens or hundreds of times slower than the equivalent one with a single input file and eight map tasks.

The situation is alleviated somewhat by CombineFileInputFormat, which was designed to work well with small files. Where FileInputFormat creates a split per file, CombineFileInputFormat packs many files into each split so that each mapper has more to process. Crucially, CombineFileInputFormat takes node and rack locality into account when deciding which blocks to place in the same split, so it does not compromise the speed at which it can process the input in a typical MapReduce job.

Of course, if possible, it is still a good idea to avoid the many small files case, because MapReduce works best when it can operate at the transfer rate of the disks in the cluster, and processing many small files increases the number of seeks that are needed to run a job. Also, storing large numbers of small files in HDFS is wasteful of the namenode's memory. One technique for avoiding the many small files case is to merge small files into larger files by using a sequence file, as in Example 8-4; with this approach, the keys can act as filenames (or a constant such as NullWritable, if not needed) and the values as file contents. But if you already have a large number of small files in HDFS, then CombineFileInputFormat is worth trying.

CombineFileInputFormat isn't just good for small files. It can bring benefits when processing large files, too, since it will generate one split per node, which may be made up of multiple blocks. Essentially, CombineFileInputFormat decouples the amount of data that a mapper consumes from the block size of the files in HDFS.

Preventing splitting

Some applications don't want files to be split, as this allows a single mapper to process each input file in its entirety. For example, a simple way to check if all the records in a file are sorted is to go through the records in order, checking whether each record is not less than the preceding one. Implemented as a map task, this algorithm will work only if one map processes the whole file.[2]

There are a couple of ways to ensure that an existing file is not split. The first (quick-and-dirty) way is to increase the minimum split size to be larger than the largest file in your system. Setting it to its maximum value, Long.MAX_VALUE, has this effect. The second is to subclass the concrete subclass of FileInputFormat that you want to use, to override the isSplitable() method[3] to return false. For example, here's a nonsplittable TextInputFormat:

```
import org.apache.hadoop.fs.Path;
import org.apache.hadoop.mapreduce.JobContext;
import org.apache.hadoop.mapreduce.lib.input.TextInputFormat;

public class NonSplittableTextInputFormat extends TextInputFormat {
  @Override
  protected boolean isSplitable(JobContext context, Path file) {
    return false;
  }
}
```

File information in the mapper

A mapper processing a file input split can find information about the split by calling the getInputSplit() method on the Mapper's Context object. When the input format derives from FileInputFormat, the InputSplit returned by this method can be cast to a FileSplit to access the file information listed in Table 8-7.

In the old MapReduce API, and the Streaming interface, the same file split information is made available through properties that can be read from the mapper's configuration.

---

2. This is how the mapper in SortValidator.RecordStatsChecker is implemented.

3. In the method name isSplitable(), "splitable" has a single "t." It is usually spelled "splittable," which is the spelling I have used in this book.

(In the old MapReduce API this is achieved by implementing `configure()` in your `Mapper` implementation to get access to the `JobConf` object.)

In addition to the properties in Table 8-7, all mappers and reducers have access to the properties listed in "The Task Execution Environment" on page 203.

Table 8-7. File split properties

FileSplit method	Property name	Type	Description
getPath()	mapreduce.map.input.file	Path/ String	The path of the input file being processed
getStart()	mapreduce.map.input.start	long	The byte offset of the start of the split from the beginning of the file
getLength()	mapreduce.map.input.length	long	The length of the split in bytes

In the next section, we'll see how to use a `FileSplit` when we need to access the split's filename.

Processing a whole file as a record

A related requirement that sometimes crops up is for mappers to have access to the full contents of a file. Not splitting the file gets you part of the way there, but you also need to have a `RecordReader` that delivers the file contents as the value of the record. The listing for `WholeFileInputFormat` in Example 8-2 shows a way of doing this.

Example 8-2. An InputFormat for reading a whole file as a record

```
public class WholeFileInputFormat
    extends FileInputFormat<NullWritable, BytesWritable> {

  @Override
  protected boolean isSplitable(JobContext context, Path file) {
    return false;
  }

  @Override
  public RecordReader<NullWritable, BytesWritable> createRecordReader(
      InputSplit split, TaskAttemptContext context) throws IOException,
      InterruptedException {
    WholeFileRecordReader reader = new WholeFileRecordReader();
    reader.initialize(split, context);
    return reader;
  }
}
```

`WholeFileInputFormat` defines a format where the keys are not used, represented by `NullWritable`, and the values are the file contents, represented by `BytesWritable` instances. It defines two methods. First, the format is careful to specify that input files should never be split, by overriding `isSplitable()` to return `false`. Second, we implement `createRecordReader()` to return a custom implementation of RecordReader, which appears in Example 8-3.

Example 8-3. The RecordReader used by WholeFileInputFormat for reading a whole file as a record

```java
class WholeFileRecordReader extends RecordReader<NullWritable, BytesWritable> {

  private FileSplit fileSplit;
  private Configuration conf;
  private BytesWritable value = new BytesWritable();
  private boolean processed = false;

  @Override
  public void initialize(InputSplit split, TaskAttemptContext context)
      throws IOException, InterruptedException {
    this.fileSplit = (FileSplit) split;
    this.conf = context.getConfiguration();
  }

  @Override
  public boolean nextKeyValue() throws IOException, InterruptedException {
    if (!processed) {
      byte[] contents = new byte[(int) fileSplit.getLength()];
      Path file = fileSplit.getPath();
      FileSystem fs = file.getFileSystem(conf);
      FSDataInputStream in = null;
      try {
        in = fs.open(file);
        IOUtils.readFully(in, contents, 0, contents.length);
        value.set(contents, 0, contents.length);
      } finally {
        IOUtils.closeStream(in);
      }
      processed = true;
      return true;
    }
    return false;
  }

  @Override
  public NullWritable getCurrentKey() throws IOException, InterruptedException {
    return NullWritable.get();
  }

  @Override
  public BytesWritable getCurrentValue() throws IOException,
      InterruptedException {
    return value;
  }

  @Override
```

```
  public float getProgress() throws IOException {
    return processed ? 1.0f : 0.0f;
  }

  @Override
  public void close() throws IOException {
    // do nothing
  }
}
```

WholeFileRecordReader is responsible for taking a `FileSplit` and converting it into a single record, with a `null` key and a value containing the bytes of the file. Because there is only a single record, `WholeFileRecordReader` has either processed it or not, so it maintains a Boolean called `processed`. If the file has not been processed when the `nextKeyValue()` method is called, then we open the file, create a byte array whose length is the length of the file, and use the Hadoop `IOUtils` class to slurp the file into the byte array. Then we set the array on the `BytesWritable` instance that was passed into the `next()` method, and return `true` to signal that a record has been read.

The other methods are straightforward bookkeeping methods for accessing the current key and value types and getting the progress of the reader, and a `close()` method, which is invoked by the MapReduce framework when the reader is done.

To demonstrate how `WholeFileInputFormat` can be used, consider a MapReduce job for packaging small files into sequence files, where the key is the original filename and the value is the content of the file. The listing is in Example 8-4.

Example 8-4. A MapReduce program for packaging a collection of small files as a single SequenceFile

```
public class SmallFilesToSequenceFileConverter extends Configured
    implements Tool {

  static class SequenceFileMapper
      extends Mapper<NullWritable, BytesWritable, Text, BytesWritable> {

    private Text filenameKey;

    @Override
    protected void setup(Context context) throws IOException,
        InterruptedException {
      InputSplit split = context.getInputSplit();
      Path path = ((FileSplit) split).getPath();
      filenameKey = new Text(path.toString());
    }

    @Override
    protected void map(NullWritable key, BytesWritable value, Context context)
        throws IOException, InterruptedException {
      context.write(filenameKey, value);
```

```
    }
  }

  @Override
  public int run(String[] args) throws Exception {
    Job job = JobBuilder.parseInputAndOutput(this, getConf(), args);
    if (job == null) {
      return -1;
    }

    job.setInputFormatClass(WholeFileInputFormat.class);
    job.setOutputFormatClass(SequenceFileOutputFormat.class);

    job.setOutputKeyClass(Text.class);
    job.setOutputValueClass(BytesWritable.class);

    job.setMapperClass(SequenceFileMapper.class);

    return job.waitForCompletion(true) ? 0 : 1;
  }

  public static void main(String[] args) throws Exception {
    int exitCode = ToolRunner.run(new SmallFilesToSequenceFileConverter(), args);
    System.exit(exitCode);
  }
}
```

Because the input format is a `WholeFileInputFormat`, the mapper only has to find the filename for the input file split. It does this by casting the `InputSplit` from the context to a `FileSplit`, which has a method to retrieve the file path. The path is stored in a `Text` object for the key. The reducer is the identity (not explicitly set), and the output format is a `SequenceFileOutputFormat`.

Here's a run on a few small files. We've chosen to use two reducers, so we get two output sequence files:

```
% hadoop jar hadoop-examples.jar SmallFilesToSequenceFileConverter \
  -conf conf/hadoop-localhost.xml -D mapreduce.job.reduces=2 \
  input/smallfiles output
```

Two part files are created, each of which is a sequence file. We can inspect these with the `-text` option to the filesystem shell:

```
% hadoop fs -conf conf/hadoop-localhost.xml -text output/part-r-00000
hdfs://localhost/user/tom/input/smallfiles/a 61 61 61 61 61 61 61 61 61 61
hdfs://localhost/user/tom/input/smallfiles/c 63 63 63 63 63 63 63 63 63 63
hdfs://localhost/user/tom/input/smallfiles/e
% hadoop fs -conf conf/hadoop-localhost.xml -text output/part-r-00001
hdfs://localhost/user/tom/input/smallfiles/b 62 62 62 62 62 62 62 62 62 62
hdfs://localhost/user/tom/input/smallfiles/d 64 64 64 64 64 64 64 64 64 64
hdfs://localhost/user/tom/input/smallfiles/f 66 66 66 66 66 66 66 66 66 66
```

The input files were named *a*, *b*, *c*, *d*, *e*, and *f*, and each contained 10 characters of the corresponding letter (so, for example, *a* contained 10 "a" characters), except *e*, which was empty. We can see this in the textual rendering of the sequence files, which prints the filename followed by the hex representation of the file.

 There's at least one way we could improve this program. As mentioned earlier, having one mapper per file is inefficient, so subclassing `CombineFileInputFormat` instead of `FileInputFormat` would be a better approach.

Text Input

Hadoop excels at processing unstructured text. In this section, we discuss the different `InputFormats` that Hadoop provides to process text.

TextInputFormat

`TextInputFormat` is the default `InputFormat`. Each record is a line of input. The key, a `LongWritable`, is the byte offset within the file of the beginning of the line. The value is the contents of the line, excluding any line terminators (e.g., newline or carriage return), and is packaged as a `Text` object. So, a file containing the following text:

```
On the top of the Crumpetty Tree
The Quangle Wangle sat,
But his face you could not see,
On account of his Beaver Hat.
```

is divided into one split of four records. The records are interpreted as the following key-value pairs:

```
(0, On the top of the Crumpetty Tree)
(33, The Quangle Wangle sat,)
(57, But his face you could not see,)
(89, On account of his Beaver Hat.)
```

Clearly, the keys are *not* line numbers. This would be impossible to implement in general, in that a file is broken into splits at byte, not line, boundaries. Splits are processed independently. Line numbers are really a sequential notion. You have to keep a count of lines as you consume them, so knowing the line number within a split would be possible, but not within the file.

However, the offset within the file of each line is known by each split independently of the other splits, since each split knows the size of the preceding splits and just adds this onto the offsets within the split to produce a global file offset. The offset is usually sufficient for applications that need a unique identifier for each line. Combined with the file's name, it is unique within the filesystem. Of course, if all the lines are a fixed width, calculating the line number is simply a matter of dividing the offset by the width.

The Relationship Between Input Splits and HDFS Blocks

The logical records that `FileInputFormats` define usually do not fit neatly into HDFS blocks. For example, a `TextInputFormat`'s logical records are lines, which will cross HDFS boundaries more often than not. This has no bearing on the functioning of your program—lines are not missed or broken, for example—but it's worth knowing about because it does mean that data-local maps (that is, maps that are running on the same host as their input data) will perform some remote reads. The slight overhead this causes is not normally significant.

Figure 8-3 shows an example. A single file is broken into lines, and the line boundaries do not correspond with the HDFS block boundaries. Splits honor logical record boundaries (in this case, lines), so we see that the first split contains line 5, even though it spans the first and second block. The second split starts at line 6.

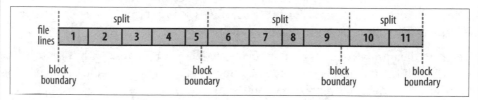

Figure 8-3. Logical records and HDFS blocks for TextInputFormat

Controlling the maximum line length. If you are using one of the text input formats discussed here, you can set a maximum expected line length to safeguard against corrupted files. Corruption in a file can manifest itself as a very long line, which can cause out-of-memory errors and then task failure. By setting `mapreduce.input.linerecordread er.line.maxlength` to a value in bytes that fits in memory (and is comfortably greater than the length of lines in your input data), you ensure that the record reader will skip the (long) corrupt lines without the task failing.

KeyValueTextInputFormat

`TextInputFormat`'s keys, being simply the offsets within the file, are not normally very useful. It is common for each line in a file to be a key-value pair, separated by a delimiter such as a tab character. For example, this is the kind of output produced by `TextOut putFormat`, Hadoop's default `OutputFormat`. To interpret such files correctly, `KeyValue TextInputFormat` is appropriate.

You can specify the separator via the `mapreduce.input.keyvaluelinere cordreader.key.value.separator` property. It is a tab character by default. Consider the following input file, where → represents a (horizontal) tab character:

```
line1→On the top of the Crumpetty Tree
line2→The Quangle Wangle sat,
line3→But his face you could not see,
line4→On account of his Beaver Hat.
```

Like in the `TextInputFormat` case, the input is in a single split comprising four records, although this time the keys are the `Text` sequences before the tab in each line:

```
(line1, On the top of the Crumpetty Tree)
(line2, The Quangle Wangle sat,)
(line3, But his face you could not see,)
(line4, On account of his Beaver Hat.)
```

NLineInputFormat

With `TextInputFormat` and `KeyValueTextInputFormat`, each mapper receives a variable number of lines of input. The number depends on the size of the split and the length of the lines. If you want your mappers to receive a fixed number of lines of input, then `NLineInputFormat` is the `InputFormat` to use. Like with `TextInputFormat`, the keys are the byte offsets within the file and the values are the lines themselves.

N refers to the number of lines of input that each mapper receives. With N set to 1 (the default), each mapper receives exactly one line of input. The `mapreduce.input.line inputformat.linespermap` property controls the value of N. By way of example, consider these four lines again:

```
On the top of the Crumpetty Tree
The Quangle Wangle sat,
But his face you could not see,
On account of his Beaver Hat.
```

If, for example, N is 2, then each split contains two lines. One mapper will receive the first two key-value pairs:

```
(0, On the top of the Crumpetty Tree)
(33, The Quangle Wangle sat,)
```

And another mapper will receive the second two key-value pairs:

```
(57, But his face you could not see,)
(89, On account of his Beaver Hat.)
```

The keys and values are the same as those that `TextInputFormat` produces. The difference is in the way the splits are constructed.

Usually, having a map task for a small number of lines of input is inefficient (due to the overhead in task setup), but there are applications that take a small amount of input data and run an extensive (i.e., CPU-intensive) computation for it, then emit their output. Simulations are a good example. By creating an input file that specifies input parameters, one per line, you can perform a *parameter sweep*: run a set of simulations in parallel to find how a model varies as the parameter changes.

If you have long-running simulations, you may fall afoul of task timeouts. When a task doesn't report progress for more than 10 minutes, the application master assumes it has failed and aborts the process (see "Task Failure" on page 193).

The best way to guard against this is to report progress periodically, by writing a status message or incrementing a counter, for example. See "What Constitutes Progress in MapReduce?" on page 191.

Another example is using Hadoop to bootstrap data loading from multiple data sources, such as databases. You create a "seed" input file that lists the data sources, one per line. Then each mapper is allocated a single data source, and it loads the data from that source into HDFS. The job doesn't need the reduce phase, so the number of reducers should be set to zero (by calling setNumReduceTasks() on Job). Furthermore, MapReduce jobs can be run to process the data loaded into HDFS. See Appendix C for an example.

XML

Most XML parsers operate on whole XML documents, so if a large XML document is made up of multiple input splits, it is a challenge to parse these individually. Of course, you can process the entire XML document in one mapper (if it is not too large) using the technique in "Processing a whole file as a record" on page 228.

Large XML documents that are composed of a series of "records" (XML document fragments) can be broken into these records using simple string or regular-expression matching to find the start and end tags of records. This alleviates the problem when the document is split by the framework because the next start tag of a record is easy to find by simply scanning from the start of the split, just like TextInputFormat finds newline boundaries.

Hadoop comes with a class for this purpose called StreamXmlRecordReader (which is in the org.apache.hadoop.streaming.mapreduce package, although it can be used outside of Streaming). You can use it by setting your input format to StreamInputFormat and setting the stream.recordreader.class property to org.apache.hadoop.streaming.mapreduce.StreamXmlRecordReader. The reader is configured by setting job configuration properties to tell it the patterns for the start and end tags (see the class documentation for details).[4]

To take an example, Wikipedia provides dumps of its content in XML form, which are appropriate for processing in parallel with MapReduce using this approach. The data is contained in one large XML wrapper document, which contains a series of elements,

---

4. See Mahout's XmlInputFormat (http://mahout.apache.org/) for an improved XML input format.

such as page elements that contain a page's content and associated metadata. Using StreamXmlRecordReader, the page elements can be interpreted as records for processing by a mapper.

Binary Input

Hadoop MapReduce is not restricted to processing textual data. It has support for binary formats, too.

SequenceFileInputFormat

Hadoop's sequence file format stores sequences of binary key-value pairs. Sequence files are well suited as a format for MapReduce data because they are splittable (they have sync points so that readers can synchronize with record boundaries from an arbitrary point in the file, such as the start of a split), they support compression as a part of the format, and they can store arbitrary types using a variety of serialization frameworks. (These topics are covered in "SequenceFile" on page 127.)

To use data from sequence files as the input to MapReduce, you can use SequenceFileInputFormat. The keys and values are determined by the sequence file, and you need to make sure that your map input types correspond. For example, if your sequence file has IntWritable keys and Text values, like the one created in Chapter 5, then the map signature would be Mapper<IntWritable, Text, K, V>, where K and V are the types of the map's output keys and values.

> Although its name doesn't give it away, SequenceFileInputFormat can read map files as well as sequence files. If it finds a directory where it was expecting a sequence file, SequenceFileInputFormat assumes that it is reading a map file and uses its datafile. This is why there is no MapFileInputFormat class.

SequenceFileAsTextInputFormat

SequenceFileAsTextInputFormat is a variant of SequenceFileInputFormat that converts the sequence file's keys and values to Text objects. The conversion is performed by calling toString() on the keys and values. This format makes sequence files suitable input for Streaming.

SequenceFileAsBinaryInputFormat

SequenceFileAsBinaryInputFormat is a variant of SequenceFileInputFormat that retrieves the sequence file's keys and values as opaque binary objects. They are encapsulated as BytesWritable objects, and the application is free to interpret the underlying byte array as it pleases. In combination with a process that creates sequence files with SequenceFile.Writer's appendRaw() method or

`SequenceFileAsBinaryOutputFormat`, this provides a way to use any binary data types with MapReduce (packaged as a sequence file), although plugging into Hadoop's serialization mechanism is normally a cleaner alternative (see "Serialization Frameworks" on page 126).

FixedLengthInputFormat

`FixedLengthInputFormat` is for reading fixed-width binary records from a file, when the records are not separated by delimiters. The record size must be set via `fixed lengthinputformat.record.length`.

Multiple Inputs

Although the input to a MapReduce job may consist of multiple input files (constructed by a combination of file globs, filters, and plain paths), all of the input is interpreted by a single `InputFormat` and a single `Mapper`. What often happens, however, is that the data format evolves over time, so you have to write your mapper to cope with all of your legacy formats. Or you may have data sources that provide the same type of data but in different formats. This arises in the case of performing joins of different datasets; see "Reduce-Side Joins" on page 270. For instance, one might be tab-separated plain text, and the other a binary sequence file. Even if they are in the same format, they may have different representations, and therefore need to be parsed differently.

These cases are handled elegantly by using the `MultipleInputs` class, which allows you to specify which `InputFormat` and `Mapper` to use on a per-path basis. For example, if we had weather data from the UK Met Office[5] that we wanted to combine with the NCDC data for our maximum temperature analysis, we might set up the input as follows:

```
MultipleInputs.addInputPath(job, ncdcInputPath,
    TextInputFormat.class, MaxTemperatureMapper.class);
MultipleInputs.addInputPath(job, metOfficeInputPath,
    TextInputFormat.class, MetOfficeMaxTemperatureMapper.class);
```

This code replaces the usual calls to `FileInputFormat.addInputPath()` and `job.set MapperClass()`. Both the Met Office and NCDC data are text based, so we use `TextInputFormat` for each. But the line format of the two data sources is different, so we use two different mappers. The `MaxTemperatureMapper` reads NCDC input data and extracts the year and temperature fields. The `MetOfficeMaxTemperatureMapper` reads Met Office input data and extracts the year and temperature fields. The important thing is that the map outputs have the same types, since the reducers (which are all of the same type) see the aggregated map outputs and are not aware of the different mappers used to produce them.

---

5. Met Office data is generally available only to the research and academic community. However, there is a small amount of monthly weather station data available at *http://www.metoffice.gov.uk/climate/uk/stationdata/*.

The `MultipleInputs` class has an overloaded version of `addInputPath()` that doesn't take a mapper:

```
public static void addInputPath(Job job, Path path,
                                Class<? extends InputFormat> inputFormatClass)
```

This is useful when you only have one mapper (set using the `Job`'s `setMapperClass()` method) but multiple input formats.

Database Input (and Output)

`DBInputFormat` is an input format for reading data from a relational database, using JDBC. Because it doesn't have any sharding capabilities, you need to be careful not to overwhelm the database from which you are reading by running too many mappers. For this reason, it is best used for loading relatively small datasets, perhaps for joining with larger datasets from HDFS using `MultipleInputs`. The corresponding output format is `DBOutputFormat`, which is useful for dumping job outputs (of modest size) into a database.

For an alternative way of moving data between relational databases and HDFS, consider using Sqoop, which is described in Chapter 15.

HBase's `TableInputFormat` is designed to allow a MapReduce program to operate on data stored in an HBase table. `TableOutputFormat` is for writing MapReduce outputs into an HBase table.

Output Formats

Hadoop has output data formats that correspond to the input formats covered in the previous section. The `OutputFormat` class hierarchy appears in Figure 8-4.

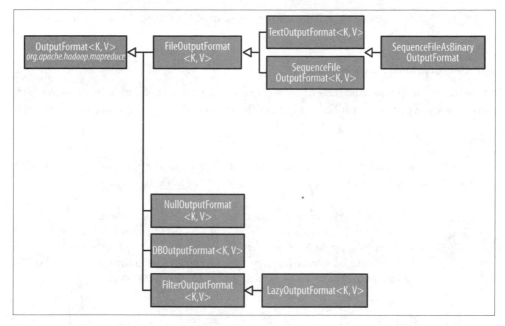

Figure 8-4. OutputFormat class hierarchy

Text Output

The default output format, `TextOutputFormat`, writes records as lines of text. Its keys and values may be of any type, since `TextOutputFormat` turns them to strings by calling `toString()` on them. Each key-value pair is separated by a tab character, although that may be changed using the `mapreduce.output.textoutputformat.separator` property. The counterpart to `TextOutputFormat` for reading in this case is `KeyValue TextInputFormat`, since it breaks lines into key-value pairs based on a configurable separator (see "KeyValueTextInputFormat" on page 233).

You can suppress the key or the value from the output (or both, making this output format equivalent to `NullOutputFormat`, which emits nothing) using a `NullWritable` type. This also causes no separator to be written, which makes the output suitable for reading in using `TextInputFormat`.

Binary Output

SequenceFileOutputFormat

As the name indicates, `SequenceFileOutputFormat` writes sequence files for its output. This is a good choice of output if it forms the input to a further MapReduce job, since it is compact and is readily compressed. Compression is controlled via the static methods on `SequenceFileOutputFormat`, as described in "Using Compression in MapReduce" on page 107. For an example of how to use `SequenceFileOutputFormat`, see "Sorting" on page 255.

SequenceFileAsBinaryOutputFormat

`SequenceFileAsBinaryOutputFormat`—the counterpart to `SequenceFileAsBinaryInputFormat`—writes keys and values in raw binary format into a sequence file container.

MapFileOutputFormat

`MapFileOutputFormat` writes map files as output. The keys in a MapFile must be added in order, so you need to ensure that your reducers emit keys in sorted order.

> The reduce *input* keys are guaranteed to be sorted, but the output keys are under the control of the reduce function, and there is nothing in the general MapReduce contract that states that the reduce *output* keys have to be ordered in any way. The extra constraint of sorted reduce output keys is just needed for `MapFileOutputFormat`.

Multiple Outputs

`FileOutputFormat` and its subclasses generate a set of files in the output directory. There is one file per reducer, and files are named by the partition number: *part-r-00000*, *part-r-00001*, and so on. Sometimes there is a need to have more control over the naming of the files or to produce multiple files per reducer. MapReduce comes with the `MultipleOutputs` class to help you do this.[6]

An example: Partitioning data

Consider the problem of partitioning the weather dataset by weather station. We would like to run a job whose output is one file per station, with each file containing all the records for that station.

One way of doing this is to have a reducer for each weather station. To arrange this, we need to do two things. First, write a partitioner that puts records from the same weather station into the same partition. Second, set the number of reducers on the job to be the number of weather stations. The partitioner would look like this:

---

6. The old MapReduce API includes two classes for producing multiple outputs: `MultipleOutputFormat` and `MultipleOutputs`. In a nutshell, `MultipleOutputs` is more fully featured, but `MultipleOutputFormat` has more control over the output directory structure and file naming. `MultipleOutputs` in the new API combines the best features of the two multiple output classes in the old API. The code on this book's website includes old API equivalents of the examples in this section using both `MultipleOutputs` and `MultipleOutputFormat`.

```
public class StationPartitioner extends Partitioner<LongWritable, Text> {

  private NcdcRecordParser parser = new NcdcRecordParser();

  @Override
  public int getPartition(LongWritable key, Text value, int numPartitions) {
    parser.parse(value);
    return getPartition(parser.getStationId());
  }

  private int getPartition(String stationId) {
    ...
  }

}
```

The getPartition(String) method, whose implementation is not shown, turns the station ID into a partition index. To do this, it needs a list of all the station IDs; it then just returns the index of the station ID in the list.

There are two drawbacks to this approach. The first is that since the number of partitions needs to be known before the job is run, so does the number of weather stations. Although the NCDC provides metadata about its stations, there is no guarantee that the IDs encountered in the data will match those in the metadata. A station that appears in the metadata but not in the data wastes a reduce task. Worse, a station that appears in the data but not in the metadata doesn't get a reduce task; it has to be thrown away. One way of mitigating this problem would be to write a job to extract the unique station IDs, but it's a shame that we need an extra job to do this.

The second drawback is more subtle. It is generally a bad idea to allow the number of partitions to be rigidly fixed by the application, since this can lead to small or uneven-sized partitions. Having many reducers doing a small amount of work isn't an efficient way of organizing a job; it's much better to get reducers to do more work and have fewer of them, as the overhead in running a task is then reduced. Uneven-sized partitions can be difficult to avoid, too. Different weather stations will have gathered a widely varying amount of data; for example, compare a station that opened one year ago to one that has been gathering data for a century. If a few reduce tasks take significantly longer than the others, they will dominate the job execution time and cause it to be longer than it needs to be.

There are two special cases when it does make sense to allow the application to set the number of partitions (or equivalently, the number of reducers):

Zero reducers

This is a vacuous case: there are no partitions, as the application needs to run only map tasks.

One reducer

It can be convenient to run small jobs to combine the output of previous jobs into a single file. This should be attempted only when the amount of data is small enough to be processed comfortably by one reducer.

It is much better to let the cluster drive the number of partitions for a job, the idea being that the more cluster resources there are available, the faster the job can complete. This is why the default `HashPartitioner` works so well: it works with any number of partitions and ensures each partition has a good mix of keys, leading to more evenly sized partitions.

If we go back to using `HashPartitioner`, each partition will contain multiple stations, so to create a file per station, we need to arrange for each reducer to write multiple files. This is where `MultipleOutputs` comes in.

MultipleOutputs

`MultipleOutputs` allows you to write data to files whose names are derived from the output keys and values, or in fact from an arbitrary string. This allows each reducer (or mapper in a map-only job) to create more than a single file. Filenames are of the form *name-m-nnnnn* for map outputs and *name-r-nnnnn* for reduce outputs, where *name* is an arbitrary name that is set by the program and *nnnnn* is an integer designating the part number, starting from *00000*. The part number ensures that outputs written from different partitions (mappers or reducers) do not collide in the case of the same name.

The program in Example 8-5 shows how to use `MultipleOutputs` to partition the dataset by station.

Example 8-5. Partitioning whole dataset into files named by the station ID using MultipleOutputs

```
public class PartitionByStationUsingMultipleOutputs extends Configured
    implements Tool {

  static class StationMapper
      extends Mapper<LongWritable, Text, Text, Text> {

    private NcdcRecordParser parser = new NcdcRecordParser();
```

```
    @Override
    protected void map(LongWritable key, Text value, Context context)
        throws IOException, InterruptedException {
      parser.parse(value);
      context.write(new Text(parser.getStationId()), value);
    }
  }

  static class MultipleOutputsReducer
      extends Reducer<Text, Text, NullWritable, Text> {

    private MultipleOutputs<NullWritable, Text> multipleOutputs;

    @Override
    protected void setup(Context context)
        throws IOException, InterruptedException {
      multipleOutputs = new MultipleOutputs<NullWritable, Text>(context);
    }

    @Override
    protected void reduce(Text key, Iterable<Text> values, Context context)
        throws IOException, InterruptedException {
      for (Text value : values) {
        multipleOutputs.write(NullWritable.get(), value, key.toString());
      }
    }

    @Override
    protected void cleanup(Context context)
        throws IOException, InterruptedException {
      multipleOutputs.close();
    }
  }

  @Override
  public int run(String[] args) throws Exception {
    Job job = JobBuilder.parseInputAndOutput(this, getConf(), args);
    if (job == null) {
      return -1;
    }

    job.setMapperClass(StationMapper.class);
    job.setMapOutputKeyClass(Text.class);
    job.setReducerClass(MultipleOutputsReducer.class);
    job.setOutputKeyClass(NullWritable.class);

    return job.waitForCompletion(true) ? 0 : 1;
  }
  public static void main(String[] args) throws Exception {
    int exitCode = ToolRunner.run(new PartitionByStationUsingMultipleOutputs(),
        args);
    System.exit(exitCode);
```

```
    }
}
```

In the reducer, which is where we generate the output, we construct an instance of MultipleOutputs in the setup() method and assign it to an instance variable. We then use the MultipleOutputs instance in the reduce() method to write to the output, in place of the context. The write() method takes the key and value, as well as a name. We use the station identifier for the name, so the overall effect is to produce output files with the naming scheme *station_identifier-r-nnnnn*.

In one run, the first few output files were named as follows:

```
output/010010-99999-r-00027
output/010050-99999-r-00013
output/010100-99999-r-00015
output/010280-99999-r-00014
output/010550-99999-r-00000
output/010980-99999-r-00011
output/011060-99999-r-00025
output/012030-99999-r-00029
output/012350-99999-r-00018
output/012620-99999-r-00004
```

The base path specified in the write() method of MultipleOutputs is interpreted relative to the output directory, and because it may contain file path separator characters (/), it's possible to create subdirectories of arbitrary depth. For example, the following modification partitions the data by station and year so that each year's data is contained in a directory named by the station ID (such as *029070-99999/1901/part-r-00000*):

```
@Override
protected void reduce(Text key, Iterable<Text> values, Context context)
    throws IOException, InterruptedException {
  for (Text value : values) {
    parser.parse(value);
    String basePath = String.format("%s/%s/part",
        parser.getStationId(), parser.getYear());
    multipleOutputs.write(NullWritable.get(), value, basePath);
  }
}
```

MultipleOutputs delegates to the mapper's OutputFormat. In this example it's a TextOutputFormat, but more complex setups are possible. For example, you can create named outputs, each with its own OutputFormat and key and value types (which may differ from the output types of the mapper or reducer). Furthermore, the mapper or reducer (or both) may write to multiple output files for each record processed. Consult the Java documentation for more information.

Lazy Output

FileOutputFormat subclasses will create output (*part-r-nnnnn*) files, even if they are empty. Some applications prefer that empty files not be created, which is where Lazy OutputFormat helps. It is a wrapper output format that ensures that the output file is created only when the first record is emitted for a given partition. To use it, call its setOutputFormatClass() method with the JobConf and the underlying output format.

Streaming supports a -lazyOutput option to enable LazyOutputFormat.

Database Output

The output formats for writing to relational databases and to HBase are mentioned in "Database Input (and Output)" on page 238.

MapReduce Features

This chapter looks at some of the more advanced features of MapReduce, including counters and sorting and joining datasets.

Counters

There are often things that you would like to know about the data you are analyzing but that are peripheral to the analysis you are performing. For example, if you were counting invalid records and discovered that the proportion of invalid records in the whole dataset was very high, you might be prompted to check why so many records were being marked as invalid—perhaps there is a bug in the part of the program that detects invalid records? Or if the data was of poor quality and genuinely did have very many invalid records, after discovering this, you might decide to increase the size of the dataset so that the number of good records was large enough for meaningful analysis.

Counters are a useful channel for gathering statistics about the job: for quality control or for application-level statistics. They are also useful for problem diagnosis. If you are tempted to put a log message into your map or reduce task, it is often better to see whether you can use a counter instead to record that a particular condition occurred. In addition to counter values being much easier to retrieve than log output for large distributed jobs, you get a record of the number of times that condition occurred, which is more work to obtain from a set of logfiles.

Built-in Counters

Hadoop maintains some built-in counters for every job, and these report various metrics. For example, there are counters for the number of bytes and records processed, which allow you to confirm that the expected amount of input was consumed and the expected amount of output was produced.

Counters are divided into groups, and there are several groups for the built-in counters, listed in Table 9-1.

Table 9-1. Built-in counter groups

Group	Name/Enum	Reference
MapReduce task counters	`org.apache.hadoop.mapreduce.TaskCounter`	Table 9-2
Filesystem counters	`org.apache.hadoop.mapreduce.FileSystemCounter`	Table 9-3
FileInputFormat counters	`org.apache.hadoop.mapreduce.lib.input.FileInputFormatCounter`	Table 9-4
FileOutputFormat counters	`org.apache.hadoop.mapreduce.lib.output.FileOutputFormatCounter`	Table 9-5
Job counters	`org.apache.hadoop.mapreduce.JobCounter`	Table 9-6

Each group either contains *task counters* (which are updated as a task progresses) or *job counters* (which are updated as a job progresses). We look at both types in the following sections.

Task counters

Task counters gather information about tasks over the course of their execution, and the results are aggregated over all the tasks in a job. The MAP_INPUT_RECORDS counter, for example, counts the input records read by each map task and aggregates over all map tasks in a job, so that the final figure is the total number of input records for the whole job.

Task counters are maintained by each task attempt, and periodically sent to the application master so they can be globally aggregated. (This is described in "Progress and Status Updates" on page 190.) Task counters are sent in full every time, rather than sending the counts since the last transmission, since this guards against errors due to lost messages. Furthermore, during a job run, counters may go down if a task fails.

Counter values are definitive only once a job has successfully completed. However, some counters provide useful diagnostic information as a task is progressing, and it can be useful to monitor them with the web UI. For example, PHYSICAL_MEMORY_BYTES, VIRTUAL_MEMORY_BYTES, and COMMITTED_HEAP_BYTES provide an indication of how memory usage varies over the course of a particular task attempt.

The built-in task counters include those in the MapReduce task counters group (Table 9-2) and those in the file-related counters groups (Tables 9-3, 9-4, and 9-5).

Table 9-2. Built-in MapReduce task counters

Counter	Description
Map input records (MAP_INPUT_RECORDS)	The number of input records consumed by all the maps in the job. Incremented every time a record is read from a RecordReader and passed to the map's map() method by the framework.
Split raw bytes (SPLIT_RAW_BYTES)	The number of bytes of input-split objects read by maps. These objects represent the split metadata (that is, the offset and length within a file) rather than the split data itself, so the total size should be small.
Map output records (MAP_OUTPUT_RECORDS)	The number of map output records produced by all the maps in the job. Incremented every time the collect() method is called on a map's OutputCollector.
Map output bytes (MAP_OUTPUT_BYTES)	The number of bytes of uncompressed output produced by all the maps in the job. Incremented every time the collect() method is called on a map's OutputCollector.
Map output materialized bytes (MAP_OUTPUT_MATERIALIZED_BYTES)	The number of bytes of map output actually written to disk. If map output compression is enabled, this is reflected in the counter value.
Combine input records (COMBINE_INPUT_RECORDS)	The number of input records consumed by all the combiners (if any) in the job. Incremented every time a value is read from the combiner's iterator over values. Note that this count is the number of values consumed by the combiner, not the number of distinct key groups (which would not be a useful metric, since there is not necessarily one group per key for a combiner; see "Combiner Functions" on page 34, and also "Shuffle and Sort" on page 197).
Combine output records (COMBINE_OUTPUT_RECORDS)	The number of output records produced by all the combiners (if any) in the job. Incremented every time the collect() method is called on a combiner's OutputCollector.
Reduce input groups (REDUCE_INPUT_GROUPS)	The number of distinct key groups consumed by all the reducers in the job. Incremented every time the reducer's reduce() method is called by the framework.
Reduce input records (REDUCE_INPUT_RECORDS)	The number of input records consumed by all the reducers in the job. Incremented every time a value is read from the reducer's iterator over values. If reducers consume all of their inputs, this count should be the same as the count for map output records.
Reduce output records (REDUCE_OUTPUT_RECORDS)	The number of reduce output records produced by all the maps in the job. Incremented every time the collect() method is called on a reducer's OutputCollector.
Reduce shuffle bytes (REDUCE_SHUFFLE_BYTES)	The number of bytes of map output copied by the shuffle to reducers.
Spilled records (SPILLED_RECORDS)	The number of records spilled to disk in all map and reduce tasks in the job.
CPU milliseconds (CPU_MILLISECONDS)	The cumulative CPU time for a task in milliseconds, as reported by */proc/cpuinfo*.
Physical memory bytes (PHYSICAL_MEMORY_BYTES)	The physical memory being used by a task in bytes, as reported by */proc/meminfo*.

Counter	Description
Virtual memory bytes (`VIRTUAL_MEMORY_BYTES`)	The virtual memory being used by a task in bytes, as reported by */proc/meminfo*.
Committed heap bytes (`COMMITTED_HEAP_BYTES`)	The total amount of memory available in the JVM in bytes, as reported by `Runtime.getRuntime().totalMemory()`.
GC time milliseconds (`GC_TIME_MILLIS`)	The elapsed time for garbage collection in tasks in milliseconds, as reported by `GarbageCollectorMXBean.getCollectionTime()`.
Shuffled maps (`SHUFFLED_MAPS`)	The number of map output files transferred to reducers by the shuffle (see "Shuffle and Sort" on page 197).
Failed shuffle (`FAILED_SHUFFLE`)	The number of map output copy failures during the shuffle.
Merged map outputs (`MERGED_MAP_OUTPUTS`)	The number of map outputs that have been merged on the reduce side of the shuffle.

Table 9-3. Built-in filesystem task counters

Counter	Description
Filesystem bytes read (`BYTES_READ`)	The number of bytes read by the filesystem by map and reduce tasks. There is a counter for each filesystem, and *Filesystem* may be Local, HDFS, S3, etc.
Filesystem bytes written (`BYTES_WRITTEN`)	The number of bytes written by the filesystem by map and reduce tasks.
Filesystem read ops (`READ_OPS`)	The number of read operations (e.g., open, file status) by the filesystem by map and reduce tasks.
Filesystem large read ops (`LARGE_READ_OPS`)	The number of large read operations (e.g., list directory for a large directory) by the filesystem by map and reduce tasks.
Filesystem write ops (`WRITE_OPS`)	The number of write operations (e.g., create, append) by the filesystem by map and reduce tasks.

Table 9-4. Built-in FileInputFormat task counters

Counter	Description
Bytes read (`BYTES_READ`)	The number of bytes read by map tasks via the `FileInputFormat`.

Table 9-5. Built-in FileOutputFormat task counters

Counter	Description
Bytes written (`BYTES_WRITTEN`)	The number of bytes written by map tasks (for map-only jobs) or reduce tasks via the `FileOutputFormat`.

Job counters

Job counters (Table 9-6) are maintained by the application master, so they don't need to be sent across the network, unlike all other counters, including user-defined ones. They measure job-level statistics, not values that change while a task is running. For example, TOTAL_LAUNCHED_MAPS counts the number of map tasks that were launched over the course of a job (including tasks that failed).

Table 9-6. Built-in job counters

Counter	Description
Launched map tasks (TOTAL_LAUNCHED_MAPS)	The number of map tasks that were launched. Includes tasks that were started speculatively (see "Speculative Execution" on page 204).
Launched reduce tasks (TOTAL_LAUNCHED_REDUCES)	The number of reduce tasks that were launched. Includes tasks that were started speculatively.
Launched uber tasks (TOTAL_LAUNCHED_UBERTASKS)	The number of uber tasks (see "Anatomy of a MapReduce Job Run" on page 185) that were launched.
Maps in uber tasks (NUM_UBER_SUBMAPS)	The number of maps in uber tasks.
Reduces in uber tasks (NUM_UBER_SUBREDUCES)	The number of reduces in uber tasks.
Failed map tasks (NUM_FAILED_MAPS)	The number of map tasks that failed. See "Task Failure" on page 193 for potential causes.
Failed reduce tasks (NUM_FAILED_REDUCES)	The number of reduce tasks that failed.
Failed uber tasks (NUM_FAILED_UBERTASKS)	The number of uber tasks that failed.
Killed map tasks (NUM_KILLED_MAPS)	The number of map tasks that were killed. See "Task Failure" on page 193 for potential causes.
Killed reduce tasks (NUM_KILLED_REDUCES)	The number of reduce tasks that were killed.
Data-local map tasks (DATA_LOCAL_MAPS)	The number of map tasks that ran on the same node as their input data.
Rack-local map tasks (RACK_LOCAL_MAPS)	The number of map tasks that ran on a node in the same rack as their input data, but were not data-local.
Other local map tasks (OTHER_LOCAL_MAPS)	The number of map tasks that ran on a node in a different rack to their input data. Inter-rack bandwidth is scarce, and Hadoop tries to place map tasks close to their input data, so this count should be low. See Figure 2-2.
Total time in map tasks (MILLIS_MAPS)	The total time taken running map tasks, in milliseconds. Includes tasks that were started speculatively. See also corresponding counters for measuring core and memory usage (VCORES_MILLIS_MAPS and MB_MILLIS_MAPS).
Total time in reduce tasks (MILLIS_REDUCES)	The total time taken running reduce tasks, in milliseconds. Includes tasks that were started speculatively. See also corresponding counters for measuring core and memory usage (VCORES_MILLIS_REDUCES and MB_MILLIS_REDUCES).

User-Defined Java Counters

MapReduce allows user code to define a set of counters, which are then incremented as desired in the mapper or reducer. Counters are defined by a Java enum, which serves to group related counters. A job may define an arbitrary number of enums, each with an arbitrary number of fields. The name of the enum is the group name, and the enum's fields are the counter names. Counters are global: the MapReduce framework aggregates them across all maps and reduces to produce a grand total at the end of the job.

We created some counters in Chapter 6 for counting malformed records in the weather dataset. The program in Example 9-1 extends that example to count the number of missing records and the distribution of temperature quality codes.

Example 9-1. Application to run the maximum temperature job, including counting missing and malformed fields and quality codes

```java
public class MaxTemperatureWithCounters extends Configured implements Tool {

  enum Temperature {
    MISSING,
    MALFORMED
  }

  static class MaxTemperatureMapperWithCounters
      extends Mapper<LongWritable, Text, Text, IntWritable> {

    private NcdcRecordParser parser = new NcdcRecordParser();

    @Override
    protected void map(LongWritable key, Text value, Context context)
        throws IOException, InterruptedException {

      parser.parse(value);
      if (parser.isValidTemperature()) {
        int airTemperature = parser.getAirTemperature();
        context.write(new Text(parser.getYear()),
            new IntWritable(airTemperature));
      } else if (parser.isMalformedTemperature()) {
        System.err.println("Ignoring possibly corrupt input: " + value);
        context.getCounter(Temperature.MALFORMED).increment(1);
      } else if (parser.isMissingTemperature()) {
        context.getCounter(Temperature.MISSING).increment(1);
      }

      // dynamic counter
      context.getCounter("TemperatureQuality", parser.getQuality()).increment(1);
    }
  }

  @Override
  public int run(String[] args) throws Exception {
    Job job = JobBuilder.parseInputAndOutput(this, getConf(), args);
    if (job == null) {
      return -1;
    }

    job.setOutputKeyClass(Text.class);
    job.setOutputValueClass(IntWritable.class);
```

```
    job.setMapperClass(MaxTemperatureMapperWithCounters.class);
    job.setCombinerClass(MaxTemperatureReducer.class);
    job.setReducerClass(MaxTemperatureReducer.class);

    return job.waitForCompletion(true) ? 0 : 1;
  }

  public static void main(String[] args) throws Exception {
    int exitCode = ToolRunner.run(new MaxTemperatureWithCounters(), args);
    System.exit(exitCode);
  }
}
```

The best way to see what this program does is to run it over the complete dataset:

```
% hadoop jar hadoop-examples.jar MaxTemperatureWithCounters \
  input/ncdc/all output-counters
```

When the job has successfully completed, it prints out the counters at the end (this is done by the job client). Here are the ones we are interested in:

```
Air Temperature Records
  Malformed=3
  Missing=66136856
TemperatureQuality
  0=1
  1=973422173
  2=1246032
  4=10764500
  5=158291879
  6=40066
  9=66136858
```

Notice that the counters for temperature have been made more readable by using a resource bundle named after the enum (using an underscore as a separator for nested classes)—in this case *MaxTemperatureWithCounters_Temperature.properties*, which contains the display name mappings.

Dynamic counters

The code makes use of a dynamic counter—one that isn't defined by a Java enum. Because a Java enum's fields are defined at compile time, you can't create new counters on the fly using enums. Here we want to count the distribution of temperature quality codes, and though the format specification defines the values that the temperature quality code *can* take, it is more convenient to use a dynamic counter to emit the values that it *actually* takes. The method we use on the Context object takes a group and counter name using String names:

```
public Counter getCounter(String groupName, String counterName)
```

The two ways of creating and accessing counters—using enums and using strings—are actually equivalent because Hadoop turns enums into strings to send counters over RPC. Enums are slightly easier to work with, provide type safety, and are suitable for most jobs. For the odd occasion when you need to create counters dynamically, you can use the `String` interface.

Retrieving counters

In addition to using the web UI and the command line (using `mapred job -counter`), you can retrieve counter values using the Java API. You can do this while the job is running, although it is more usual to get counters at the end of a job run, when they are stable. Example 9-2 shows a program that calculates the proportion of records that have missing temperature fields.

Example 9-2. Application to calculate the proportion of records with missing temperature fields

```java
import org.apache.hadoop.conf.Configured;
import org.apache.hadoop.mapreduce.*;
import org.apache.hadoop.util.*;

public class MissingTemperatureFields extends Configured implements Tool {

  @Override
  public int run(String[] args) throws Exception {
    if (args.length != 1) {
      JobBuilder.printUsage(this, "<job ID>");
      return -1;
    }
    String jobID = args[0];
    Cluster cluster = new Cluster(getConf());
    Job job = cluster.getJob(JobID.forName(jobID));
    if (job == null) {
      System.err.printf("No job with ID %s found.\n", jobID);
      return -1;
    }
    if (!job.isComplete()) {
      System.err.printf("Job %s is not complete.\n", jobID);
      return -1;
    }

    Counters counters = job.getCounters();
    long missing = counters.findCounter(
        MaxTemperatureWithCounters.Temperature.MISSING).getValue();
    long total = counters.findCounter(TaskCounter.MAP_INPUT_RECORDS).getValue();

    System.out.printf("Records with missing temperature fields: %.2f%%\n",
        100.0 * missing / total);
    return 0;
  }
```

```
  public static void main(String[] args) throws Exception {
    int exitCode = ToolRunner.run(new MissingTemperatureFields(), args);
    System.exit(exitCode);
  }
}
```

First we retrieve a Job object from a Cluster by calling the getJob() method with the job ID. We check whether there is actually a job with the given ID by checking if it is null. There may not be, either because the ID was incorrectly specified or because the job is no longer in the job history.

After confirming that the job has completed, we call the Job's getCounters() method, which returns a Counters object encapsulating all the counters for the job. The Counters class provides various methods for finding the names and values of counters. We use the findCounter() method, which takes an enum to find the number of records that had a missing temperature field and also the total number of records processed (from a built-in counter).

Finally, we print the proportion of records that had a missing temperature field. Here's what we get for the whole weather dataset:

```
% hadoop jar hadoop-examples.jar MissingTemperatureFields job_1410450250506_0007
Records with missing temperature fields: 5.47%
```

User-Defined Streaming Counters

A Streaming MapReduce program can increment counters by sending a specially for-matted line to the standard error stream, which is co-opted as a control channel in this case. The line must have the following format:

```
reporter:counter:group,counter,amount
```

This snippet in Python shows how to increment the "Missing" counter in the "Tem-perature" group by 1:

```
sys.stderr.write("reporter:counter:Temperature,Missing,1\n")
```

In a similar way, a status message may be sent with a line formatted like this:

```
reporter:status:message
```

Sorting

The ability to sort data is at the heart of MapReduce. Even if your application isn't concerned with sorting per se, it may be able to use the sorting stage that MapReduce provides to organize its data. In this section, we examine different ways of sorting datasets and how you can control the sort order in MapReduce. Sorting Avro data is covered separately, in "Sorting Using Avro MapReduce" on page 363.

Preparation

We are going to sort the weather dataset by temperature. Storing temperatures as Text objects doesn't work for sorting purposes, because signed integers don't sort lexicographically.[1] Instead, we are going to store the data using sequence files whose IntWritable keys represent the temperatures (and sort correctly) and whose Text values are the lines of data.

The MapReduce job in Example 9-3 is a map-only job that also filters the input to remove records that don't have a valid temperature reading. Each map creates a single block-compressed sequence file as output. It is invoked with the following command:

```
% hadoop jar hadoop-examples.jar SortDataPreprocessor input/ncdc/all \
    input/ncdc/all-seq
```

Example 9-3. A MapReduce program for transforming the weather data into Sequence-File format

```
public class SortDataPreprocessor extends Configured implements Tool {

  static class CleanerMapper
      extends Mapper<LongWritable, Text, IntWritable, Text> {

    private NcdcRecordParser parser = new NcdcRecordParser();

    @Override
    protected void map(LongWritable key, Text value, Context context)
        throws IOException, InterruptedException {

      parser.parse(value);
      if (parser.isValidTemperature()) {
        context.write(new IntWritable(parser.getAirTemperature()), value);
      }
    }
  }

  @Override
  public int run(String[] args) throws Exception {
    Job job = JobBuilder.parseInputAndOutput(this, getConf(), args);
    if (job == null) {
      return -1;
    }

    job.setMapperClass(CleanerMapper.class);
    job.setOutputKeyClass(IntWritable.class);
    job.setOutputValueClass(Text.class);
```

---

1. One commonly used workaround for this problem—particularly in text-based Streaming applications—is to add an offset to eliminate all negative numbers and to left pad with zeros so all numbers are the same number of characters. However, see "Streaming" on page 266 for another approach.

```
    job.setNumReduceTasks(0);
    job.setOutputFormatClass(SequenceFileOutputFormat.class);
    SequenceFileOutputFormat.setCompressOutput(job, true);
    SequenceFileOutputFormat.setOutputCompressorClass(job, GzipCodec.class);
    SequenceFileOutputFormat.setOutputCompressionType(job,
        CompressionType.BLOCK);

    return job.waitForCompletion(true) ? 0 : 1;
  }
  public static void main(String[] args) throws Exception {
    int exitCode = ToolRunner.run(new SortDataPreprocessor(), args);
    System.exit(exitCode);
  }
}
```

Partial Sort

In "The Default MapReduce Job" on page 214, we saw that, by default, MapReduce will sort input records by their keys. Example 9-4 is a variation for sorting sequence files with IntWritable keys.

Example 9-4. A MapReduce program for sorting a SequenceFile with IntWritable keys using the default HashPartitioner

```
public class SortByTemperatureUsingHashPartitioner extends Configured
    implements Tool {

  @Override
  public int run(String[] args) throws Exception {
    Job job = JobBuilder.parseInputAndOutput(this, getConf(), args);
    if (job == null) {
      return -1;
    }

    job.setInputFormatClass(SequenceFileInputFormat.class);
    job.setOutputKeyClass(IntWritable.class);
    job.setOutputFormatClass(SequenceFileOutputFormat.class);
    SequenceFileOutputFormat.setCompressOutput(job, true);
    SequenceFileOutputFormat.setOutputCompressorClass(job, GzipCodec.class);
    SequenceFileOutputFormat.setOutputCompressionType(job,
        CompressionType.BLOCK);

    return job.waitForCompletion(true) ? 0 : 1;
  }

  public static void main(String[] args) throws Exception {
    int exitCode = ToolRunner.run(new SortByTemperatureUsingHashPartitioner(),
        args);
    System.exit(exitCode);
  }
}
```

Controlling Sort Order

The sort order for keys is controlled by a `RawComparator`, which is found as follows:

1. If the property `mapreduce.job.output.key.comparator.class` is set, either explicitly or by calling `setSortComparatorClass()` on `Job`, then an instance of that class is used. (In the old API, the equivalent method is `setOutputKeyComparatorClass()` on `JobConf`.)

2. Otherwise, keys must be a subclass of `WritableComparable`, and the registered comparator for the key class is used.

3. If there is no registered comparator, then a `RawComparator` is used. The `RawComparator` deserializes the byte streams being compared into objects and delegates to the `WritableComparable`'s `compareTo()` method.

These rules reinforce the importance of registering optimized versions of `RawComparators` for your own custom `Writable` classes (which is covered in "Implementing a RawComparator for speed" on page 123), and also show that it's straightforward to override the sort order by setting your own comparator (we do this in "Secondary Sort" on page 262).

Suppose we run this program using 30 reducers:[2]

```
% hadoop jar hadoop-examples.jar SortByTemperatureUsingHashPartitioner \
  -D mapreduce.job.reduces=30 input/ncdc/all-seq output-hashsort
```

This command produces 30 output files, each of which is sorted. However, there is no easy way to combine the files (by concatenation, for example, in the case of plain-text files) to produce a globally sorted file.

For many applications, this doesn't matter. For example, having a partially sorted set of files is fine when you want to do lookups by key. The `SortByTemperatureToMapFile` and `LookupRecordsByTemperature` classes in this book's example code explore this idea. By using a map file instead of a sequence file, it's possible to first find the relevant partition that a key belongs in (using the partitioner), then to do an efficient lookup of the record within the map file partition.

[2]. See "Sorting and merging SequenceFiles" on page 133 for how to do the same thing using the sort program example that comes with Hadoop.

Total Sort

How can you produce a globally sorted file using Hadoop? The naive answer is to use a single partition.[3] But this is incredibly inefficient for large files, because one machine has to process all of the output, so you are throwing away the benefits of the parallel architecture that MapReduce provides.

Instead, it is possible to produce a set of sorted files that, if concatenated, would form a globally sorted file. The secret to doing this is to use a partitioner that respects the total order of the output. For example, if we had four partitions, we could put keys for temperatures less than –10°C in the first partition, those between –10°C and 0°C in the second, those between 0°C and 10°C in the third, and those over 10°C in the fourth.

Although this approach works, you have to choose your partition sizes carefully to ensure that they are fairly even, so job times aren't dominated by a single reducer. For the partitioning scheme just described, the relative sizes of the partitions are as follows:

Temperature range	< –10°C	[–10°C, 0°C)	[0°C, 10°C)	>= 10°C
Proportion of records	11%	13%	17%	59%

These partitions are not very even. To construct more even partitions, we need to have a better understanding of the temperature distribution for the whole dataset. It's fairly easy to write a MapReduce job to count the number of records that fall into a collection of temperature buckets. For example, Figure 9-1 shows the distribution for buckets of size 1°C, where each point on the plot corresponds to one bucket.

Although we could use this information to construct a very even set of partitions, the fact that we needed to run a job that used the entire dataset to construct them is not ideal. It's possible to get a fairly even set of partitions by *sampling* the key space. The idea behind sampling is that you look at a small subset of the keys to approximate the key distribution, which is then used to construct partitions. Luckily, we don't have to write the code to do this ourselves, as Hadoop comes with a selection of samplers.

The InputSampler class defines a nested Sampler interface whose implementations return a sample of keys given an InputFormat and Job:

```
public interface Sampler<K, V> {
  K[] getSample(InputFormat<K, V> inf, Job job)
      throws IOException, InterruptedException;
}
```

---

3. A better answer is to use Pig ("Sorting Data" on page 465), Hive ("Sorting and Aggregating" on page 503), Crunch, or Spark, all of which can sort with a single command.

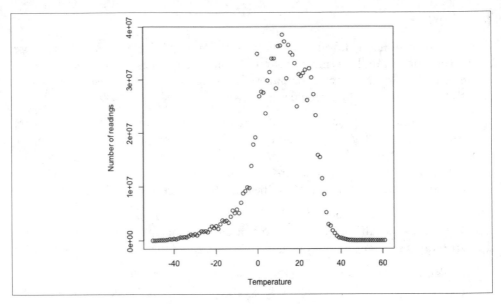

Figure 9-1. Temperature distribution for the weather dataset

This interface usually is not called directly by clients. Instead, the `writePartition File()` static method on `InputSampler` is used, which creates a sequence file to store the keys that define the partitions:

```
public static <K, V> void writePartitionFile(Job job, Sampler<K, V> sampler)
    throws IOException, ClassNotFoundException, InterruptedException
```

The sequence file is used by `TotalOrderPartitioner` to create partitions for the sort job. Example 9-5 puts it all together.

Example 9-5. A MapReduce program for sorting a SequenceFile with IntWritable keys using the TotalOrderPartitioner to globally sort the data

```
public class SortByTemperatureUsingTotalOrderPartitioner extends Configured
    implements Tool {

  @Override
  public int run(String[] args) throws Exception {
    Job job = JobBuilder.parseInputAndOutput(this, getConf(), args);
    if (job == null) {
      return -1;
    }

    job.setInputFormatClass(SequenceFileInputFormat.class);
    job.setOutputKeyClass(IntWritable.class);
    job.setOutputFormatClass(SequenceFileOutputFormat.class);
    SequenceFileOutputFormat.setCompressOutput(job, true);
    SequenceFileOutputFormat.setOutputCompressorClass(job, GzipCodec.class);
```

```
SequenceFileOutputFormat.setOutputCompressionType(job,
    CompressionType.BLOCK);

job.setPartitionerClass(TotalOrderPartitioner.class);

InputSampler.Sampler<IntWritable, Text> sampler =
    new InputSampler.RandomSampler<IntWritable, Text>(0.1, 10000, 10);

InputSampler.writePartitionFile(job, sampler);

// Add to DistributedCache
Configuration conf = job.getConfiguration();
String partitionFile = TotalOrderPartitioner.getPartitionFile(conf);
URI partitionUri = new URI(partitionFile);
job.addCacheFile(partitionUri);

    return job.waitForCompletion(true) ? 0 : 1;
  }

  public static void main(String[] args) throws Exception {
    int exitCode = ToolRunner.run(
        new SortByTemperatureUsingTotalOrderPartitioner(), args);
    System.exit(exitCode);
  }
}
```

We use a `RandomSampler`, which chooses keys with a uniform probability—here, 0.1. There are also parameters for the maximum number of samples to take and the maximum number of splits to sample (here, 10,000 and 10, respectively; these settings are the defaults when `InputSampler` is run as an application), and the sampler stops when the first of these limits is met. Samplers run on the client, making it important to limit the number of splits that are downloaded so the sampler runs quickly. In practice, the time taken to run the sampler is a small fraction of the overall job time.

The `InputSampler` writes a partition file that we need to share with the tasks running on the cluster by adding it to the distributed cache (see "Distributed Cache" on page 274).

On one run, the sampler chose –5.6°C, 13.9°C, and 22.0°C as partition boundaries (for four partitions), which translates into more even partition sizes than the earlier choice:

Temperature range	< –5.6°C	[–5.6°C, 13.9°C)	[13.9°C, 22.0°C)	>= 22.0°C
Proportion of records	29%	24%	23%	24%

Your input data determines the best sampler to use. For example, `SplitSampler`, which samples only the first *n* records in a split, is not so good for sorted data,[4] because it doesn't select keys from throughout the split.

On the other hand, `IntervalSampler` chooses keys at regular intervals through the split and makes a better choice for sorted data. `RandomSampler` is a good general-purpose sampler. If none of these suits your application (and remember that the point of sampling is to produce partitions that are *approximately* equal in size), you can write your own implementation of the `Sampler` interface.

One of the nice properties of `InputSampler` and `TotalOrderPartitioner` is that you are free to choose the number of partitions—that is, the number of reducers. However, `TotalOrderPartitioner` will work only if the partition boundaries are distinct. One problem with choosing a high number is that you may get collisions if you have a small key space.

Here's how we run it:

```
% hadoop jar hadoop-examples.jar SortByTemperatureUsingTotalOrderPartitioner \
  -D mapreduce.job.reduces=30 input/ncdc/all-seq output-totalsort
```

The program produces 30 output partitions, each of which is internally sorted; in addition, for these partitions, all the keys in partition *i* are less than the keys in partition *i* + 1.

Secondary Sort

The MapReduce framework sorts the records by key before they reach the reducers. For any particular key, however, the values are *not* sorted. The order in which the values appear is not even stable from one run to the next, because they come from different map tasks, which may finish at different times from run to run. Generally speaking, most MapReduce programs are written so as not to depend on the order in which the values appear to the reduce function. However, it is possible to impose an order on the values by sorting and grouping the keys in a particular way.

To illustrate the idea, consider the MapReduce program for calculating the maximum temperature for each year. If we arranged for the values (temperatures) to be sorted in descending order, we wouldn't have to iterate through them to find the maximum; instead, we could take the first for each year and ignore the rest. (This approach isn't the most efficient way to solve this particular problem, but it illustrates how secondary sort works in general.)

---

4. In some applications, it's common for some of the input to already be sorted, or at least partially sorted. For example, the weather dataset is ordered by time, which may introduce certain biases, making the `Random Sampler` a safer choice.

To achieve this, we change our keys to be composite: a combination of year and temperature. We want the sort order for keys to be by year (ascending) and then by temperature (descending):

```
1900 35°C
1900 34°C
1900 34°C
...
1901 36°C
1901 35°C
```

If all we did was change the key, this wouldn't help, because then records for the same year would have different keys and therefore would not (in general) go to the same reducer. For example, (1900, 35°C) and (1900, 34°C) could go to different reducers. By setting a partitioner to partition by the year part of the key, we can guarantee that records for the same year go to the same reducer. This still isn't enough to achieve our goal, however. A partitioner ensures only that one reducer receives all the records for a year; it doesn't change the fact that the reducer groups by key within the partition:

```
           Partition  Group
1900 35°C   |         |
1900 34°C   |         |
1900 34°C   |         |
   ...
1901 36°C   |         |
1901 35°C   |         |
```

The final piece of the puzzle is the setting to control the grouping. If we group values in the reducer by the year part of the key, we will see all the records for the same year in one reduce group. And because they are sorted by temperature in descending order, the first is the maximum temperature:

```
           Partition  Group
1900 35°C   |         |
1900 34°C   |         |
1900 34°C   |         |
   ...
1901 36°C   |         |
1901 35°C   |         |
```

To summarize, there is a recipe here to get the effect of sorting by value:

- Make the key a composite of the natural key and the natural value.
- The sort comparator should order by the composite key (i.e., the natural key *and* natural value).
- The partitioner and grouping comparator for the composite key should consider only the natural key for partitioning and grouping.

Java code

Putting this all together results in the code in Example 9-6. This program uses the plain-text input again.

Example 9-6. Application to find the maximum temperature by sorting temperatures in the key

```java
public class MaxTemperatureUsingSecondarySort
    extends Configured implements Tool {

  static class MaxTemperatureMapper
      extends Mapper<LongWritable, Text, IntPair, NullWritable> {

    private NcdcRecordParser parser = new NcdcRecordParser();

    @Override
    protected void map(LongWritable key, Text value,
        Context context) throws IOException, InterruptedException {

      parser.parse(value);
      if (parser.isValidTemperature()) {
        context.write(new IntPair(parser.getYearInt(),
            parser.getAirTemperature()), NullWritable.get());
      }
    }
  }

  static class MaxTemperatureReducer
      extends Reducer<IntPair, NullWritable, IntPair, NullWritable> {

    @Override
    protected void reduce(IntPair key, Iterable<NullWritable> values,
        Context context) throws IOException, InterruptedException {

      context.write(key, NullWritable.get());
    }
  }

  public static class FirstPartitioner
      extends Partitioner<IntPair, NullWritable> {

    @Override
    public int getPartition(IntPair key, NullWritable value, int numPartitions) {
      // multiply by 127 to perform some mixing
      return Math.abs(key.getFirst() * 127) % numPartitions;
    }
  }

  public static class KeyComparator extends WritableComparator {
    protected KeyComparator() {
      super(IntPair.class, true);
    }
```

```
    @Override
    public int compare(WritableComparable w1, WritableComparable w2) {
      IntPair ip1 = (IntPair) w1;
      IntPair ip2 = (IntPair) w2;
      int cmp = IntPair.compare(ip1.getFirst(), ip2.getFirst());
      if (cmp != 0) {
        return cmp;
      }
      return -IntPair.compare(ip1.getSecond(), ip2.getSecond()); //reverse
    }
  }

  public static class GroupComparator extends WritableComparator {
    protected GroupComparator() {
      super(IntPair.class, true);
    }
    @Override
    public int compare(WritableComparable w1, WritableComparable w2) {
      IntPair ip1 = (IntPair) w1;
      IntPair ip2 = (IntPair) w2;
      return IntPair.compare(ip1.getFirst(), ip2.getFirst());
    }
  }

  @Override
  public int run(String[] args) throws Exception {
    Job job = JobBuilder.parseInputAndOutput(this, getConf(), args);
    if (job == null) {
      return -1;
    }

    job.setMapperClass(MaxTemperatureMapper.class);
    job.setPartitionerClass(FirstPartitioner.class);
    job.setSortComparatorClass(KeyComparator.class);
    job.setGroupingComparatorClass(GroupComparator.class);
    job.setReducerClass(MaxTemperatureReducer.class);
    job.setOutputKeyClass(IntPair.class);
    job.setOutputValueClass(NullWritable.class);

    return job.waitForCompletion(true) ? 0 : 1;
  }

  public static void main(String[] args) throws Exception {
    int exitCode = ToolRunner.run(new MaxTemperatureUsingSecondarySort(), args);
    System.exit(exitCode);
  }
}
```

In the mapper, we create a key representing the year and temperature, using an IntPair Writable implementation. (IntPair is like the TextPair class we developed in "Implementing a Custom Writable" on page 121.) We don't need to carry any information in the value, because we can get the first (maximum) temperature in the reducer from the key, so we use a `NullWritable`. The reducer emits the first key, which, due to the secondary sorting, is an `IntPair` for the year and its maximum temperature. `IntPair`'s `toString()` method creates a tab-separated string, so the output is a set of tab-separated year-temperature pairs.

 Many applications need to access all the sorted values, not just the first value as we have provided here. To do this, you need to populate the value fields since in the reducer you can retrieve only the first key. This necessitates some unavoidable duplication of information between key and value.

We set the partitioner to partition by the first field of the key (the year) using a custom partitioner called `FirstPartitioner`. To sort keys by year (ascending) and temperature (descending), we use a custom sort comparator, using `setSortComparatorClass()`, that extracts the fields and performs the appropriate comparisons. Similarly, to group keys by year, we set a custom comparator, using `setGroupingComparatorClass()`, to extract the first field of the key for comparison.[5]

Running this program gives the maximum temperatures for each year:

```
% hadoop jar hadoop-examples.jar MaxTemperatureUsingSecondarySort \
  input/ncdc/all output-secondarysort
% hadoop fs -cat output-secondarysort/part-* | sort | head
1901  317
1902  244
1903  289
1904  256
1905  283
1906  294
1907  283
1908  289
1909  278
1910  294
```

Streaming

To do a secondary sort in Streaming, we can take advantage of a couple of library classes that Hadoop provides. Here's the driver that we can use to do a secondary sort:

```
% hadoop jar $HADOOP_HOME/share/hadoop/tools/lib/hadoop-streaming-*.jar \
  -D stream.num.map.output.key.fields=2 \
  -D mapreduce.partition.keypartitioner.options=-k1,1 \
  -D mapreduce.job.output.key.comparator.class=\
```

---

5. For simplicity, these custom comparators as shown are not optimized; see "Implementing a RawComparator for speed" on page 123 for the steps we would need to take to make them faster.

```
org.apache.hadoop.mapred.lib.KeyFieldBasedComparator \
  -D mapreduce.partition.keycomparator.options="-k1n -k2nr" \
  -files secondary_sort_map.py,secondary_sort_reduce.py \
  -input input/ncdc/all \
  -output output-secondarysort-streaming \
  -mapper ch09-mr-features/src/main/python/secondary_sort_map.py \
  -partitioner org.apache.hadoop.mapred.lib.KeyFieldBasedPartitioner \
  -reducer ch09-mr-features/src/main/python/secondary_sort_reduce.py
```

Our map function (Example 9-7) emits records with year and temperature fields. We want to treat the combination of both of these fields as the key, so we set `stream.num.map.output.key.fields` to 2. This means that values will be empty, just like in the Java case.

Example 9-7. Map function for secondary sort in Python

```
#!/usr/bin/env python

import re
import sys

for line in sys.stdin:
  val = line.strip()
  (year, temp, q) = (val[15:19], int(val[87:92]), val[92:93])
  if temp == 9999:
    sys.stderr.write("reporter:counter:Temperature,Missing,1\n")
  elif re.match("[01459]", q):
    print "%s\t%s" % (year, temp)
```

However, we don't want to partition by the entire key, so we use `KeyFieldBasedPartitioner`, which allows us to partition by a part of the key. The specification `mapreduce.partition.keypartitioner.options` configures the partitioner. The value `-k1,1` instructs the partitioner to use only the first field of the key, where fields are assumed to be separated by a string defined by the `mapreduce.map.output.key.field.separator` property (a tab character by default).

Next, we want a comparator that sorts the year field in ascending order and the temperature field in descending order, so that the reduce function can simply return the first record in each group. Hadoop provides `KeyFieldBasedComparator`, which is ideal for this purpose. The comparison order is defined by a specification that is like the one used for GNU *sort*. It is set using the `mapreduce.partition.keycomparator.options` property. The value `-k1n -k2nr` used in this example means "sort by the first field in numerical order, then by the second field in reverse numerical order." Like its partitioner cousin, `KeyFieldBasedPartitioner`, it uses the map output key separator to split a key into fields.

In the Java version, we had to set the grouping comparator; however, in Streaming, groups are not demarcated in any way, so in the reduce function we have to detect the group boundaries ourselves by looking for when the year changes (Example 9-8).

Example 9-8. Reduce function for secondary sort in Python

```
#!/usr/bin/env python

import sys

last_group = None
for line in sys.stdin:
  val = line.strip()
  (year, temp) = val.split("\t")
  group = year
  if last_group != group:
    print val
    last_group = group
```

When we run the Streaming program, we get the same output as the Java version.

Finally, note that `KeyFieldBasedPartitioner` and `KeyFieldBasedComparator` are not confined to use in Streaming programs; they are applicable to Java MapReduce programs, too.

Joins

MapReduce can perform joins between large datasets, but writing the code to do joins from scratch is fairly involved. Rather than writing MapReduce programs, you might consider using a higher-level framework such as Pig, Hive, Cascading, Cruc, or Spark, in which join operations are a core part of the implementation.

Let's briefly consider the problem we are trying to solve. We have two datasets—for example, the weather stations database and the weather records—and we want to reconcile the two. Let's say we want to see each station's history, with the station's metadata inlined in each output row. This is illustrated in Figure 9-2.

How we implement the join depends on how large the datasets are and how they are partitioned. If one dataset is large (the weather records) but the other one is small enough to be distributed to each node in the cluster (as the station metadata is), the join can be effected by a MapReduce job that brings the records for each station together (a partial sort on station ID, for example). The mapper or reducer uses the smaller dataset to look up the station metadata for a station ID, so it can be written out with each record. See "Side Data Distribution" on page 273 for a discussion of this approach, where we focus on the mechanics of distributing the data to nodes in the cluster.

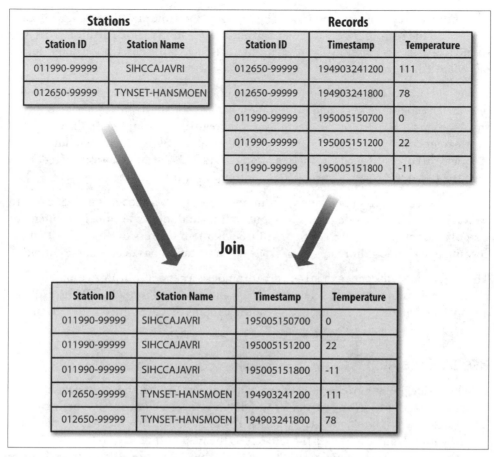

Figure 9-2. *Inner join of two datasets*

If the join is performed by the mapper it is called a *map-side join*, whereas if it is performed by the reducer it is called a *reduce-side join*.

If both datasets are too large for either to be copied to each node in the cluster, we can still join them using MapReduce with a map-side or reduce-side join, depending on how the data is structured. One common example of this case is a user database and a log of some user activity (such as access logs). For a popular service, it is not feasible to distribute the user database (or the logs) to all the MapReduce nodes.

Map-Side Joins

A map-side join between large inputs works by performing the join before the data reaches the map function. For this to work, though, the inputs to each map must be partitioned and sorted in a particular way. Each input dataset must be divided into the same number of partitions, and it must be sorted by the same key (the join key) in each source. All the records for a particular key must reside in the same partition. This may sound like a strict requirement (and it is), but it actually fits the description of the output of a MapReduce job.

A map-side join can be used to join the outputs of several jobs that had the same number of reducers, the same keys, and output files that are not splittable (by virtue of being smaller than an HDFS block or being gzip compressed, for example). In the context of the weather example, if we ran a partial sort on the stations file by station ID, and another identical sort on the records, again by station ID and with the same number of reducers, then the two outputs would satisfy the conditions for running a map-side join.

You use a `CompositeInputFormat` from the `org.apache.hadoop.mapreduce.join` package to run a map-side join. The input sources and join type (inner or outer) for `CompositeInputFormat` are configured through a join expression that is written according to a simple grammar. The package documentation has details and examples.

The `org.apache.hadoop.examples.Join` example is a general-purpose command-line program for running a map-side join, since it allows you to run a MapReduce job for any specified mapper and reducer over multiple inputs that are joined with a given join operation.

Reduce-Side Joins

A reduce-side join is more general than a map-side join, in that the input datasets don't have to be structured in any particular way, but it is less efficient because both datasets have to go through the MapReduce shuffle. The basic idea is that the mapper tags each record with its source and uses the join key as the map output key, so that the records with the same key are brought together in the reducer. We use several ingredients to make this work in practice:

Multiple inputs
> The input sources for the datasets generally have different formats, so it is very convenient to use the `MultipleInputs` class (see "Multiple Inputs" on page 237) to separate the logic for parsing and tagging each source.

Secondary sort
> As described, the reducer will see the records from both sources that have the same key, but they are not guaranteed to be in any particular order. However, to perform the join, it is important to have the data from one source before that from the other. For the weather data join, the station record must be the first of the values seen for each key, so the reducer can fill in the weather records with the station name and emit them straightaway. Of course, it would be possible to receive the records in any order if we buffered them in memory, but this should be avoided because the

number of records in any group may be very large and exceed the amount of memory available to the reducer.

We saw in "Secondary Sort" on page 262 how to impose an order on the values for each key that the reducers see, so we use this technique here.

To tag each record, we use TextPair (discussed in Chapter 5) for the keys (to store the station ID) and the tag. The only requirement for the tag values is that they sort in such a way that the station records come before the weather records. This can be achieved by tagging station records as 0 and weather records as 1. The mapper classes to do this are shown in Examples 9-9 and 9-10.

Example 9-9. Mapper for tagging station records for a reduce-side join

```
public class JoinStationMapper
    extends Mapper<LongWritable, Text, TextPair, Text> {
  private NcdcStationMetadataParser parser = new NcdcStationMetadataParser();

  @Override
  protected void map(LongWritable key, Text value, Context context)
      throws IOException, InterruptedException {
    if (parser.parse(value)) {
      context.write(new TextPair(parser.getStationId(), "0"),
          new Text(parser.getStationName()));
    }
  }
}
```

Example 9-10. Mapper for tagging weather records for a reduce-side join

```
public class JoinRecordMapper
    extends Mapper<LongWritable, Text, TextPair, Text> {
  private NcdcRecordParser parser = new NcdcRecordParser();

  @Override
  protected void map(LongWritable key, Text value, Context context)
      throws IOException, InterruptedException {
    parser.parse(value);
    context.write(new TextPair(parser.getStationId(), "1"), value);
  }

}
```

The reducer knows that it will receive the station record first, so it extracts its name from the value and writes it out as a part of every output record (Example 9-11).

Example 9-11. Reducer for joining tagged station records with tagged weather records

```
public class JoinReducer extends Reducer<TextPair, Text, Text, Text> {

  @Override
  protected void reduce(TextPair key, Iterable<Text> values, Context context)
```

```
      throws IOException, InterruptedException {
    Iterator<Text> iter = values.iterator();
    Text stationName = new Text(iter.next());
    while (iter.hasNext()) {
      Text record = iter.next();
      Text outValue = new Text(stationName.toString() + "\t" + record.toString());
      context.write(key.getFirst(), outValue);
    }
  }
}
```

The code assumes that every station ID in the weather records has exactly one matching record in the station dataset. If this were not the case, we would need to generalize the code to put the tag into the value objects, by using another TextPair. The reduce() method would then be able to tell which entries were station names and detect (and handle) missing or duplicate entries before processing the weather records.

 Because objects in the reducer's values iterator are reused (for efficiency purposes), it is vital that the code makes a copy of the first Text object from the values iterator:

```
Text stationName = new Text(iter.next());
```

If the copy is not made, the stationName reference will refer to the value just read when it is turned into a string, which is a bug.

Tying the job together is the driver class, shown in Example 9-12. The essential point here is that we partition and group on the first part of the key, the station ID, which we do with a custom Partitioner (KeyPartitioner) and a custom group comparator, FirstComparator (from TextPair).

Example 9-12. Application to join weather records with station names

```
public class JoinRecordWithStationName extends Configured implements Tool {

  public static class KeyPartitioner extends Partitioner<TextPair, Text> {
    @Override
    public int getPartition(TextPair key, Text value, int numPartitions) {
      return (key.getFirst().hashCode() & Integer.MAX_VALUE) % numPartitions;
    }
  }

  @Override
  public int run(String[] args) throws Exception {
    if (args.length != 3) {
      JobBuilder.printUsage(this, "<ncdc input> <station input> <output>");
      return -1;
    }

    Job job = new Job(getConf(), "Join weather records with station names");
```

```
job.setJarByClass(getClass());

Path ncdcInputPath = new Path(args[0]);
Path stationInputPath = new Path(args[1]);
Path outputPath = new Path(args[2]);

MultipleInputs.addInputPath(job, ncdcInputPath,
    TextInputFormat.class, JoinRecordMapper.class);
MultipleInputs.addInputPath(job, stationInputPath,
    TextInputFormat.class, JoinStationMapper.class);
FileOutputFormat.setOutputPath(job, outputPath);

job.setPartitionerClass(KeyPartitioner.class);
job.setGroupingComparatorClass(TextPair.FirstComparator.class);

job.setMapOutputKeyClass(TextPair.class);

job.setReducerClass(JoinReducer.class);

job.setOutputKeyClass(Text.class);

return job.waitForCompletion(true) ? 0 : 1;
}

public static void main(String[] args) throws Exception {
  int exitCode = ToolRunner.run(new JoinRecordWithStationName(), args);
  System.exit(exitCode);
}
}
```

Running the program on the sample data yields the following output:

```
011990-99999    SIHCCAJAVRI         0067011990099999991950051507004...
011990-99999    SIHCCAJAVRI         0043011990099999991950051512004...
011990-99999    SIHCCAJAVRI         0043011990099999991950051518004...
012650-99999    TYNSET-HANSMOEN     0043012650099999991949032412004...
012650-99999    TYNSET-HANSMOEN     0043012650099999991949032418004...
```

Side Data Distribution

Side data can be defined as extra read-only data needed by a job to process the main dataset. The challenge is to make side data available to all the map or reduce tasks (which are spread across the cluster) in a convenient and efficient fashion.

Using the Job Configuration

You can set arbitrary key-value pairs in the job configuration using the various setter methods on Configuration (or JobConf in the old MapReduce API). This is very useful when you need to pass a small piece of metadata to your tasks.

In the task, you can retrieve the data from the configuration returned by Context's `getConfiguration()` method. (In the old API, it's a little more involved: override the `configure()` method in the Mapper or Reducer and use a getter method on the JobConf object passed in to retrieve the data. It's very common to store the data in an instance field so it can be used in the `map()` or `reduce()` method.)

Usually a primitive type is sufficient to encode your metadata, but for arbitrary objects you can either handle the serialization yourself (if you have an existing mechanism for turning objects to strings and back) or use Hadoop's `Stringifier` class. The `DefaultStringifier` uses Hadoop's serialization framework to serialize objects (see "Serialization" on page 109).

You shouldn't use this mechanism for transferring more than a few kilobytes of data, because it can put pressure on the memory usage in MapReduce components. The job configuration is always read by the client, the application master, and the task JVM, and each time the configuration is read, all of its entries are read into memory, even if they are not used.

Distributed Cache

Rather than serializing side data in the job configuration, it is preferable to distribute datasets using Hadoop's distributed cache mechanism. This provides a service for copying files and archives to the task nodes in time for the tasks to use them when they run. To save network bandwidth, files are normally copied to any particular node once per job.

Usage

For tools that use `GenericOptionsParser` (this includes many of the programs in this book; see "GenericOptionsParser, Tool, and ToolRunner" on page 148), you can specify the files to be distributed as a comma-separated list of URIs as the argument to the `-files` option. Files can be on the local filesystem, on HDFS, or on another Hadoop-readable filesystem (such as S3). If no scheme is supplied, then the files are assumed to be local. (This is true even when the default filesystem is not the local filesystem.)

You can also copy archive files (JAR files, ZIP files, tar files, and gzipped tar files) to your tasks using the `-archives` option; these are unarchived on the task node. The `-libjars` option will add JAR files to the classpath of the mapper and reducer tasks. This is useful if you haven't bundled library JAR files in your job JAR file.

Let's see how to use the distributed cache to share a metadata file for station names. The command we will run is:

```
% hadoop jar hadoop-examples.jar \
  MaxTemperatureByStationNameUsingDistributedCacheFile \
  -files input/ncdc/metadata/stations-fixed-width.txt input/ncdc/all output
```

This command will copy the local file *stations-fixed-width.txt* (no scheme is supplied, so the path is automatically interpreted as a local file) to the task nodes, so we can use it to look up station names. The listing for `MaxTemperatureByStationNameUs ingDistributedCacheFile` appears in Example 9-13.

Example 9-13. Application to find the maximum temperature by station, showing station names from a lookup table passed as a distributed cache file

```java
public class MaxTemperatureByStationNameUsingDistributedCacheFile
    extends Configured implements Tool {

  static class StationTemperatureMapper
      extends Mapper<LongWritable, Text, Text, IntWritable> {

    private NcdcRecordParser parser = new NcdcRecordParser();

    @Override
    protected void map(LongWritable key, Text value, Context context)
        throws IOException, InterruptedException {

      parser.parse(value);
      if (parser.isValidTemperature()) {
        context.write(new Text(parser.getStationId()),
            new IntWritable(parser.getAirTemperature()));
      }
    }
  }

  static class MaxTemperatureReducerWithStationLookup
      extends Reducer<Text, IntWritable, Text, IntWritable> {

    private NcdcStationMetadata metadata;

    @Override
    protected void setup(Context context)
        throws IOException, InterruptedException {
      metadata = new NcdcStationMetadata();
      metadata.initialize(new File("stations-fixed-width.txt"));
    }

    @Override
    protected void reduce(Text key, Iterable<IntWritable> values,
        Context context) throws IOException, InterruptedException {

      String stationName = metadata.getStationName(key.toString());

      int maxValue = Integer.MIN_VALUE;
      for (IntWritable value : values) {
        maxValue = Math.max(maxValue, value.get());
      }
      context.write(new Text(stationName), new IntWritable(maxValue));
    }
```

```
  }

  @Override
  public int run(String[] args) throws Exception {
    Job job = JobBuilder.parseInputAndOutput(this, getConf(), args);
    if (job == null) {
      return -1;
    }

    job.setOutputKeyClass(Text.class);
    job.setOutputValueClass(IntWritable.class);

    job.setMapperClass(StationTemperatureMapper.class);
    job.setCombinerClass(MaxTemperatureReducer.class);
    job.setReducerClass(MaxTemperatureReducerWithStationLookup.class);

    return job.waitForCompletion(true) ? 0 : 1;
  }

  public static void main(String[] args) throws Exception {
    int exitCode = ToolRunner.run(
        new MaxTemperatureByStationNameUsingDistributedCacheFile(), args);
    System.exit(exitCode);
  }
}
```

The program finds the maximum temperature by weather station, so the mapper (StationTemperatureMapper) simply emits (station ID, temperature) pairs. For the combiner, we reuse MaxTemperatureReducer (from Chapters 2 and 6) to pick the maximum temperature for any given group of map outputs on the map side. The reducer (MaxTemperatureReducerWithStationLookup) is different from the combiner, since in addition to finding the maximum temperature, it uses the cache file to look up the station name.

We use the reducer's setup() method to retrieve the cache file using its original name, relative to the working directory of the task.

 You can use the distributed cache for copying files that do not fit in memory. Hadoop map files are very useful in this regard, since they serve as an on-disk lookup format (see "MapFile" on page 135). Because map files are collections of files with a defined directory structure, you should put them into an archive format (JAR, ZIP, tar, or gzipped tar) and add them to the cache using the -archives option.

Here's a snippet of the output, showing some maximum temperatures for a few weather stations:

```
    PEATS RIDGE WARATAH         372
    STRATHALBYN RACECOU         410
```

```
SHEOAKS AWS              399
WANGARATTA AERO         409
MOOGARA                 334
MACKAY AERO             331
```

How it works

When you launch a job, Hadoop copies the files specified by the `-files`, `-archives`, and `-libjars` options to the distributed filesystem (normally HDFS). Then, before a task is run, the node manager copies the files from the distributed filesystem to a local disk—the cache—so the task can access the files. The files are said to be *localized* at this point. From the task's point of view, the files are just there, symbolically linked from the task's working directory. In addition, files specified by `-libjars` are added to the task's classpath before it is launched.

The node manager also maintains a reference count for the number of tasks using each file in the cache. Before the task has run, the file's reference count is incremented by 1; then, after the task has run, the count is decreased by 1. Only when the file is not being used (when the count reaches zero) is it eligible for deletion. Files are deleted to make room for a new file when the node's cache exceeds a certain size—10 GB by default—using a least-recently used policy. The cache size may be changed by setting the configuration property `yarn.nodemanager.localizer.cache.target-size-mb`.

Although this design doesn't guarantee that subsequent tasks from the same job running on the same node will find the file they need in the cache, it is very likely that they will: tasks from a job are usually scheduled to run at around the same time, so there isn't the opportunity for enough other jobs to run to cause the original task's file to be deleted from the cache.

The distributed cache API

Most applications don't need to use the distributed cache API, because they can use the cache via `GenericOptionsParser`, as we saw in Example 9-13. However, if `GenericOptionsParser` is not being used, then the API in `Job` can be used to put objects into the distributed cache.[6] Here are the pertinent methods in `Job`:

```
public void addCacheFile(URI uri)
public void addCacheArchive(URI uri)
public void setCacheFiles(URI[] files)
public void setCacheArchives(URI[] archives)
public void addFileToClassPath(Path file)
public void addArchiveToClassPath(Path archive)
```

6. If you are using the old MapReduce API, the same methods can be found in `org.apache.ha doop.filecache.DistributedCache`.

Recall that there are two types of objects that can be placed in the cache: files and archives. Files are left intact on the task node, whereas archives are unarchived on the task node. For each type of object, there are three methods: an addCache*XXXX*() method to add the file or archive to the distributed cache, a setCache*XXXX*s() method to set the entire list of files or archives to be added to the cache in a single call (replacing those set in any previous calls), and an add*XXXX*ToClassPath() method to add the file or archive to the MapReduce task's classpath. Table 9-7 compares these API methods to the GenericOptionsParser options described in Table 6-1.

Table 9-7. Distributed cache API

Job API method	GenericOptionsParser equivalent	Description
addCacheFile(URI uri) setCacheFiles(URI[] files)	-files *file1,file2,...*	Add files to the distributed cache to be copied to the task node.
addCacheArchive(URI uri) setCacheArchives(URI[] files)	-archives *archive1,archive2,...*	Add archives to the distributed cache to be copied to the task node and unarchived there.
addFileToClassPath(Path file)	-libjars *jar1,jar2,...*	Add files to the distributed cache to be added to the MapReduce task's classpath. The files are not unarchived, so this is a useful way to add JAR files to the classpath.
addArchiveToClassPath(Path archive)	None	Add archives to the distributed cache to be unarchived and added to the MapReduce task's classpath. This can be useful when you want to add a directory of files to the classpath, since you can create an archive containing the files. Alternatively, you could create a JAR file and use addFileToClassPath(), which works equally well.

The URIs referenced in the add or set methods must be files in a shared filesystem that exist when the job is run. On the other hand, the filenames specified as a GenericOptionsParser option (e.g., -files) may refer to local files, in which case they get copied to the default shared filesystem (normally HDFS) on your behalf.

This is the key difference between using the Java API directly and using GenericOptionsParser: the Java API does *not* copy the file specified in the add or set method to the shared filesystem, whereas the GenericOptionsParser does.

Retrieving distributed cache files from the task works in the same way as before: you access the localized file directly by name, as we did in Example 9-13. This works because MapReduce will always create a symbolic link from the task's working directory to every file or archive added to the distributed cache.[7] Archives are unarchived so you can access the files in them using the nested path.

MapReduce Library Classes

Hadoop comes with a library of mappers and reducers for commonly used functions. They are listed with brief descriptions in Table 9-8. For further information on how to use them, consult their Java documentation.

Table 9-8. MapReduce library classes

Classes	Description
`ChainMapper`, `ChainReducer`	Run a chain of mappers in a single mapper and a reducer followed by a chain of mappers in a single reducer, respectively. (Symbolically, M+RM*, where M is a mapper and R is a reducer.) This can substantially reduce the amount of disk I/O incurred compared to running multiple MapReduce jobs.
`FieldSelectionMapReduce` (old API): `FieldSelectionMapper` and `FieldSelectionReducer` (new API)	A mapper and reducer that can select fields (like the Unix `cut` command) from the input keys and values and emit them as output keys and values.
`IntSumReducer`, `LongSumReducer`	Reducers that sum integer values to produce a total for every key.
`InverseMapper`	A mapper that swaps keys and values.
`MultithreadedMapRunner` (old API), `MultithreadedMapper` (new API)	A mapper (or map runner in the old API) that runs mappers concurrently in separate threads. Useful for mappers that are not CPU-bound.
`TokenCounterMapper`	A mapper that tokenizes the input value into words (using Java's `StringTokenizer`) and emits each word along with a count of 1.
`RegexMapper`	A mapper that finds matches of a regular expression in the input value and emits the matches along with a count of 1.

---

7. In Hadoop 1, localized files were not always symlinked, so it was sometimes necessary to retrieve localized file paths using methods on `JobContext`. This limitation was removed in Hadoop 2.

## PART III

Hadoop Operations

Setting Up a Hadoop Cluster

This chapter explains how to set up Hadoop to run on a cluster of machines. Running HDFS, MapReduce, and YARN on a single machine is great for learning about these systems, but to do useful work, they need to run on multiple nodes.

There are a few options when it comes to getting a Hadoop cluster, from building your own, to running on rented hardware or using an offering that provides Hadoop as a hosted service in the cloud. The number of hosted options is too large to list here, but even if you choose to build a Hadoop cluster yourself, there are still a number of installation options:

Apache tarballs

> The Apache Hadoop project and related projects provide binary (and source) tarballs for each release. Installation from binary tarballs gives you the most flexibility but entails the most amount of work, since you need to decide on where the installation files, configuration files, and logfiles are located on the filesystem, set their file permissions correctly, and so on.

Packages

> RPM and Debian packages are available from the Apache Bigtop project (*http://bigtop.apache.org/*), as well as from all the Hadoop vendors. Packages bring a number of advantages over tarballs: they provide a consistent filesystem layout, they are tested together as a stack (so you know that the versions of Hadoop and Hive, say, will work together), and they work well with configuration management tools like Puppet.

Hadoop cluster management tools

> Cloudera Manager and Apache Ambari are examples of dedicated tools for installing and managing a Hadoop cluster over its whole lifecycle. They provide a simple web UI, and are the recommended way to set up a Hadoop cluster for most users and operators. These tools encode a lot of operator knowledge about running

Hadoop. For example, they use heuristics based on the hardware profile (among other factors) to choose good defaults for Hadoop configuration settings. For more complex setups, like HA, or secure Hadoop, the management tools provide well-tested wizards for getting a working cluster in a short amount of time. Finally, they add extra features that the other installation options don't offer, such as unified monitoring and log search, and rolling upgrades (so you can upgrade the cluster without experiencing downtime).

This chapter and the next give you enough information to set up and operate your own basic cluster, but even if you are using Hadoop cluster management tools or a service in which a lot of the routine setup and maintenance are done for you, these chapters still offer valuable information about how Hadoop works from an operations point of view. For more in-depth information, I highly recommend *Hadoop Operations* by Eric Sammer (O'Reilly, 2012).

Cluster Specification

Hadoop is designed to run on commodity hardware. That means that you are not tied to expensive, proprietary offerings from a single vendor; rather, you can choose standardized, commonly available hardware from any of a large range of vendors to build your cluster.

"Commodity" does not mean "low-end." Low-end machines often have cheap components, which have higher failure rates than more expensive (but still commodity-class) machines. When you are operating tens, hundreds, or thousands of machines, cheap components turn out to be a false economy, as the higher failure rate incurs a greater maintenance cost. On the other hand, large database-class machines are not recommended either, since they don't score well on the price/performance curve. And even though you would need fewer of them to build a cluster of comparable performance to one built of mid-range commodity hardware, when one did fail, it would have a bigger impact on the cluster because a larger proportion of the cluster hardware would be unavailable.

Hardware specifications rapidly become obsolete, but for the sake of illustration, a typical choice of machine for running an HDFS datanode and a YARN node manager in 2014 would have had the following specifications:

Processor
Two hex/octo-core 3 GHz CPUs

Memory
64–512 GB ECC RAM[1]

---

1. ECC memory is strongly recommended, as several Hadoop users have reported seeing many checksum errors when using non-ECC memory on Hadoop clusters.

Storage

12–24 × 1–4 TB SATA disks

Network

Gigabit Ethernet with link aggregation

Although the hardware specification for your cluster will assuredly be different, Hadoop is designed to use multiple cores and disks, so it will be able to take full advantage of more powerful hardware.

Why Not Use RAID?

HDFS clusters do not benefit from using RAID (redundant array of independent disks) for datanode storage (although RAID is recommended for the namenode's disks, to protect against corruption of its metadata). The redundancy that RAID provides is not needed, since HDFS handles it by replication between nodes.

Furthermore, RAID striping (RAID 0), which is commonly used to increase performance, turns out to be *slower* than the JBOD (just a bunch of disks) configuration used by HDFS, which round-robins HDFS blocks between all disks. This is because RAID 0 read and write operations are limited by the speed of the slowest-responding disk in the RAID array. In JBOD, disk operations are independent, so the average speed of operations is greater than that of the slowest disk. Disk performance often shows considerable variation in practice, even for disks of the same model. In some benchmarking carried out on a Yahoo! cluster (*http://markmail.org/message/xmzc45zi25htr7ry*), JBOD performed 10% faster than RAID 0 in one test (Gridmix) and 30% better in another (HDFS write throughput).

Finally, if a disk fails in a JBOD configuration, HDFS can continue to operate without the failed disk, whereas with RAID, failure of a single disk causes the whole array (and hence the node) to become unavailable.

Cluster Sizing

How large should your cluster be? There isn't an exact answer to this question, but the beauty of Hadoop is that you can start with a small cluster (say, 10 nodes) and grow it as your storage and computational needs grow. In many ways, a better question is this: how fast does your cluster need to grow? You can get a good feel for this by considering storage capacity.

For example, if your data grows by 1 TB a day and you have three-way HDFS replication, you need an additional 3 TB of raw storage per day. Allow some room for intermediate files and logfiles (around 30%, say), and this is in the range of one (2014-vintage) machine per week. In practice, you wouldn't buy a new machine each week and add it to the cluster. The value of doing a back-of-the-envelope calculation like this is that it gives you a feel for how big your cluster should be. In this example, a cluster that holds two years' worth of data needs 100 machines.

Master node scenarios

Depending on the size of the cluster, there are various configurations for running the master daemons: the namenode, secondary namenode, resource manager, and history server. For a small cluster (on the order of 10 nodes), it is usually acceptable to run the namenode and the resource manager on a single master machine (as long as at least one copy of the namenode's metadata is stored on a remote filesystem). However, as the cluster gets larger, there are good reasons to separate them.

The namenode has high memory requirements, as it holds file and block metadata for the entire namespace in memory. The secondary namenode, although idle most of the time, has a comparable memory footprint to the primary when it creates a checkpoint. (This is explained in detail in "The filesystem image and edit log" on page 318.) For filesystems with a large number of files, there may not be enough physical memory on one machine to run both the primary and secondary namenode.

Aside from simple resource requirements, the main reason to run masters on separate machines is for high availability. Both HDFS and YARN support configurations where they can run masters in active-standby pairs. If the active master fails, then the standby, running on separate hardware, takes over with little or no interruption to the service. In the case of HDFS, the standby performs the checkpointing function of the secondary namenode (so you don't need to run a standby and a secondary namenode).

Configuring and running Hadoop HA is not covered in this book. Refer to the Hadoop website or vendor documentation for details.

Network Topology

A common Hadoop cluster architecture consists of a two-level network topology, as illustrated in Figure 10-1. Typically there are 30 to 40 servers per rack (only 3 are shown in the diagram), with a 10 Gb switch for the rack and an uplink to a core switch or router (at least 10 Gb or better). The salient point is that the aggregate bandwidth between nodes on the same rack is much greater than that between nodes on different racks.

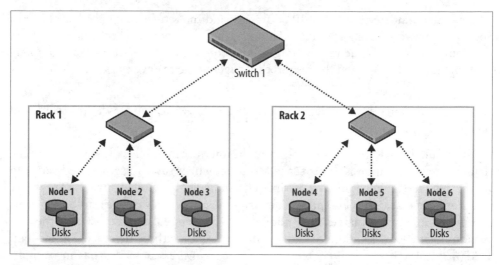

Figure 10-1. Typical two-level network architecture for a Hadoop cluster

Rack awareness

To get maximum performance out of Hadoop, it is important to configure Hadoop so that it knows the topology of your network. If your cluster runs on a single rack, then there is nothing more to do, since this is the default. However, for multirack clusters, you need to map nodes to racks. This allows Hadoop to prefer within-rack transfers (where there is more bandwidth available) to off-rack transfers when placing MapReduce tasks on nodes. HDFS will also be able to place replicas more intelligently to trade off performance and resilience.

Network locations such as nodes and racks are represented in a tree, which reflects the network "distance" between locations. The namenode uses the network location when determining where to place block replicas (see "Network Topology and Hadoop" on page 70); the MapReduce scheduler uses network location to determine where the closest replica is for input to a map task.

For the network in Figure 10-1, the rack topology is described by two network locations —say, */switch1/rack1* and */switch1/rack2*. Because there is only one top-level switch in this cluster, the locations can be simplified to */rack1* and */rack2*.

The Hadoop configuration must specify a map between node addresses and network locations. The map is described by a Java interface, `DNSToSwitchMapping`, whose signature is:

```
public interface DNSToSwitchMapping {
  public List<String> resolve(List<String> names);
}
```

The `names` parameter is a list of IP addresses, and the return value is a list of corresponding network location strings. The `net.topology.node.switch.mapping.impl` configuration property defines an implementation of the `DNSToSwitchMapping` interface that the namenode and the resource manager use to resolve worker node network locations.

For the network in our example, we would map *node1*, *node2*, and *node3* to */rack1*, and *node4*, *node5*, and *node6* to */rack2*.

Most installations don't need to implement the interface themselves, however, since the default implementation is `ScriptBasedMapping`, which runs a user-defined script to determine the mapping. The script's location is controlled by the property `net.topology.script.file.name`. The script must accept a variable number of arguments that are the hostnames or IP addresses to be mapped, and it must emit the corresponding network locations to standard output, separated by whitespace. The Hadoop wiki (*http://wiki.apache.org/hadoop/topology_rack_awareness_scripts*) has an example.

If no script location is specified, the default behavior is to map all nodes to a single network location, called */default-rack*.

Cluster Setup and Installation

This section describes how to install and configure a basic Hadoop cluster from scratch using the Apache Hadoop distribution on a Unix operating system. It provides background information on the things you need to think about when setting up Hadoop. For a production installation, most users and operators should consider one of the Hadoop cluster management tools listed at the beginning of this chapter.

Installing Java

Hadoop runs on both Unix and Windows operating systems, and requires Java to be installed. For a production installation, you should select a combination of operating system, Java, and Hadoop that has been certified by the vendor of the Hadoop distribution you are using. There is also a page on the Hadoop wiki (*http://wiki.apache.org/hadoop/HadoopJavaVersions*) that lists combinations that community members have run with success.

Creating Unix User Accounts

It's good practice to create dedicated Unix user accounts to separate the Hadoop processes from each other, and from other services running on the same machine. The HDFS, MapReduce, and YARN services are usually run as separate users, named `hdfs`, `mapred`, and `yarn`, respectively. They all belong to the same `hadoop` group.

Installing Hadoop

Download Hadoop from the Apache Hadoop releases page (*http://hadoop.apache.org/core/releases.html*), and unpack the contents of the distribution in a sensible location, such as */usr/local* (*/opt* is another standard choice; note that Hadoop should not be installed in a user's home directory, as that may be an NFS-mounted directory):

```
% cd /usr/local
% sudo tar xzf hadoop-x.y.z.tar.gz
```

You also need to change the owner of the Hadoop files to be the hadoop user and group:

```
% sudo chown -R hadoop:hadoop hadoop-x.y.z
```

It's convenient to put the Hadoop binaries on the shell path too:

```
% export HADOOP_HOME=/usr/local/hadoop-x.y.z
% export PATH=$PATH:$HADOOP_HOME/bin:$HADOOP_HOME/sbin
```

Configuring SSH

The Hadoop control scripts (but not the daemons) rely on SSH to perform cluster-wide operations. For example, there is a script for stopping and starting all the daemons in the cluster. Note that the control scripts are optional—cluster-wide operations can be performed by other mechanisms, too, such as a distributed shell or dedicated Hadoop management applications.

To work seamlessly, SSH needs to be set up to allow passwordless login for the hdfs and yarn users from machines in the cluster.[2] The simplest way to achieve this is to generate a public/private key pair and place it in an NFS location that is shared across the cluster.

First, generate an RSA key pair by typing the following. You need to do this twice, once as the hdfs user and once as the yarn user:

```
% ssh-keygen -t rsa -f ~/.ssh/id_rsa
```

Even though we want passwordless logins, keys without passphrases are not considered good practice (it's OK to have an empty passphrase when running a local pseudo-distributed cluster, as described in Appendix A), so we specify a passphrase when prompted for one. We use *ssh-agent* to avoid the need to enter a password for each connection.

The private key is in the file specified by the -f option, *~/.ssh/id_rsa*, and the public key is stored in a file with the same name but with *.pub* appended, *~/.ssh/id_rsa.pub*.

---

2. The mapred user doesn't use SSH, as in Hadoop 2 and later, the only MapReduce daemon is the job history server.

Next, we need to make sure that the public key is in the *~/.ssh/authorized_keys* file on all the machines in the cluster that we want to connect to. If the users' home directories are stored on an NFS filesystem, the keys can be shared across the cluster by typing the following (first as `hdfs` and then as `yarn`):

```
% cat ~/.ssh/id_rsa.pub >> ~/.ssh/authorized_keys
```

If the home directory is not shared using NFS, the public keys will need to be shared by some other means (such as *ssh-copy-id*).

Test that you can SSH from the master to a worker machine by making sure *ssh-agent* is running,[3] and then run *ssh-add* to store your passphrase. You should be able to SSH to a worker without entering the passphrase again.

Configuring Hadoop

Hadoop must have its configuration set appropriately to run in distributed mode on a cluster. The important configuration settings to achieve this are discussed in "Hadoop Configuration" on page 292.

Formatting the HDFS Filesystem

Before it can be used, a brand-new HDFS installation needs to be formatted. The formatting process creates an empty filesystem by creating the storage directories and the initial versions of the namenode's persistent data structures. Datanodes are not involved in the initial formatting process, since the namenode manages all of the filesystem's metadata, and datanodes can join or leave the cluster dynamically. For the same reason, you don't need to say how large a filesystem to create, since this is determined by the number of datanodes in the cluster, which can be increased as needed, long after the filesystem is formatted.

Formatting HDFS is a fast operation. Run the following command as the `hdfs` user:

```
% hdfs namenode -format
```

Starting and Stopping the Daemons

Hadoop comes with scripts for running commands and starting and stopping daemons across the whole cluster. To use these scripts (which can be found in the *sbin* directory), you need to tell Hadoop which machines are in the cluster. There is a file for this purpose, called *slaves*, which contains a list of the machine hostnames or IP addresses, one per line. The *slaves* file lists the machines that the datanodes and node managers should run on. It resides in Hadoop's configuration directory, although it may be placed elsewhere

---

3. See its man page for instructions on how to start *ssh-agent*.

(and given another name) by changing the HADOOP_SLAVES setting in *hadoop-env.sh*. Also, this file does not need to be distributed to worker nodes, since they are used only by the control scripts running on the namenode or resource manager.

The HDFS daemons are started by running the following command as the hdfs user:

```
% start-dfs.sh
```

The machine (or machines) that the namenode and secondary namenode run on is determined by interrogating the Hadoop configuration for their hostnames. For example, the script finds the namenode's hostname by executing the following:

```
% hdfs getconf -namenodes
```

By default, this finds the namenode's hostname from fs.defaultFS. In slightly more detail, the *start-dfs.sh* script does the following:

- Starts a namenode on each machine returned by executing hdfs getconf -namenodes[4]
- Starts a datanode on each machine listed in the *slaves* file
- Starts a secondary namenode on each machine returned by executing hdfs get conf -secondarynamenodes

The YARN daemons are started in a similar way, by running the following command as the yarn user on the machine hosting the resource manager:

```
% start-yarn.sh
```

In this case, the resource manager is always run on the machine from which the *start-yarn.sh* script was run. More specifically, the script:

- Starts a resource manager on the local machine
- Starts a node manager on each machine listed in the *slaves* file

Also provided are *stop-dfs.sh* and *stop-yarn.sh* scripts to stop the daemons started by the corresponding start scripts.

These scripts start and stop Hadoop daemons using the *hadoop-daemon.sh* script (or the *yarn-daemon.sh* script, in the case of YARN). If you use the aforementioned scripts, you shouldn't call *hadoop-daemon.sh* directly. But if you need to control Hadoop daemons from another system or from your own scripts, the *hadoop-daemon.sh* script is a good integration point. Likewise, *hadoop-daemons.sh* (with an "s") is handy for starting the same daemon on a set of hosts.

---

4. There can be more than one namenode when running HDFS HA.

Finally, there is only one MapReduce daemon—the job history server, which is started as follows, as the `mapred` user:

```
% mr-jobhistory-daemon.sh start historyserver
```

Creating User Directories

Once you have a Hadoop cluster up and running, you need to give users access to it. This involves creating a home directory for each user and setting ownership permissions on it:

```
% hadoop fs -mkdir /user/username
% hadoop fs -chown username:username /user/username
```

This is a good time to set space limits on the directory. The following sets a 1 TB limit on the given user directory:

```
% hdfs dfsadmin -setSpaceQuota 1t /user/username
```

Hadoop Configuration

There are a handful of files for controlling the configuration of a Hadoop installation; the most important ones are listed in Table 10-1.

Table 10-1. Hadoop configuration files

Filename	Format	Description
hadoop-env.sh	Bash script	Environment variables that are used in the scripts to run Hadoop
mapred-env.sh	Bash script	Environment variables that are used in the scripts to run MapReduce (overrides variables set in *hadoop-env.sh*)
yarn-env.sh	Bash script	Environment variables that are used in the scripts to run YARN (overrides variables set in *hadoop-env.sh*)
core-site.xml	Hadoop configuration XML	Configuration settings for Hadoop Core, such as I/O settings that are common to HDFS, MapReduce, and YARN
hdfs-site.xml	Hadoop configuration XML	Configuration settings for HDFS daemons: the namenode, the secondary namenode, and the datanodes
mapred-site.xml	Hadoop configuration XML	Configuration settings for MapReduce daemons: the job history server
yarn-site.xml	Hadoop configuration XML	Configuration settings for YARN daemons: the resource manager, the web app proxy server, and the node managers
slaves	Plain text	A list of machines (one per line) that each run a datanode and a node manager
hadoop-metrics2 .properties	Java properties	Properties for controlling how metrics are published in Hadoop (see "Metrics and JMX" on page 331)
log4j.properties	Java properties	Properties for system logfiles, the namenode audit log, and the task log for the task JVM process ("Hadoop Logs" on page 172)

Filename	Format	Description
hadoop-policy.xml	Hadoop configuration XML	Configuration settings for access control lists when running Hadoop in secure mode

These files are all found in the *etc/hadoop* directory of the Hadoop distribution. The configuration directory can be relocated to another part of the filesystem (outside the Hadoop installation, which makes upgrades marginally easier) as long as daemons are started with the `--config` option (or, equivalently, with the `HADOOP_CONF_DIR` environment variable set) specifying the location of this directory on the local filesystem.

Configuration Management

Hadoop does not have a single, global location for configuration information. Instead, each Hadoop node in the cluster has its own set of configuration files, and it is up to administrators to ensure that they are kept in sync across the system. There are parallel shell tools that can help do this, such as *dsh* or *pdsh*. This is an area where Hadoop cluster management tools like Cloudera Manager and Apache Ambari really shine, since they take care of propagating changes across the cluster.

Hadoop is designed so that it is possible to have a single set of configuration files that are used for all master and worker machines. The great advantage of this is simplicity, both conceptually (since there is only one configuration to deal with) and operationally (as the Hadoop scripts are sufficient to manage a single configuration setup).

For some clusters, the one-size-fits-all configuration model breaks down. For example, if you expand the cluster with new machines that have a different hardware specification from the existing ones, you need a different configuration for the new machines to take advantage of their extra resources.

In these cases, you need to have the concept of a *class* of machine and maintain a separate configuration for each class. Hadoop doesn't provide tools to do this, but there are several excellent tools for doing precisely this type of configuration management, such as Chef, Puppet, CFEngine, and Bcfg2.

For a cluster of any size, it can be a challenge to keep all of the machines in sync. Consider what happens if the machine is unavailable when you push out an update. Who ensures it gets the update when it becomes available? This is a big problem and can lead to divergent installations, so even if you use the Hadoop control scripts for managing Hadoop, it may be a good idea to use configuration management tools for maintaining the cluster. These tools are also excellent for doing regular maintenance, such as patching security holes and updating system packages.

Environment Settings

In this section, we consider how to set the variables in *hadoop-env.sh*. There are also analogous configuration files for MapReduce and YARN (but not for HDFS), called *mapred-env.sh* and *yarn-env.sh*, where variables pertaining to those components can be set. Note that the MapReduce and YARN files override the values set in *hadoop-env.sh*.

Java

The location of the Java implementation to use is determined by the JAVA_HOME setting in *hadoop-env.sh* or the JAVA_HOME shell environment variable, if not set in *hadoop-env.sh*. It's a good idea to set the value in *hadoop-env.sh*, so that it is clearly defined in one place and to ensure that the whole cluster is using the same version of Java.

Memory heap size

By default, Hadoop allocates 1,000 MB (1 GB) of memory to each daemon it runs. This is controlled by the HADOOP_HEAPSIZE setting in *hadoop-env.sh*. There are also environment variables to allow you to change the heap size for a single daemon. For example, you can set YARN_RESOURCEMANAGER_HEAPSIZE in *yarn-env.sh* to override the heap size for the resource manager.

Surprisingly, there are no corresponding environment variables for HDFS daemons, despite it being very common to give the namenode more heap space. There is another way to set the namenode heap size, however; this is discussed in the following sidebar.

How Much Memory Does a Namenode Need?

A namenode can eat up memory, since a reference to every block of every file is maintained in memory. It's difficult to give a precise formula because memory usage depends on the number of blocks per file, the filename length, and the number of directories in the filesystem; plus, it can change from one Hadoop release to another.

The default of 1,000 MB of namenode memory is normally enough for a few million files, but as a rule of thumb for sizing purposes, you can conservatively allow 1,000 MB per million blocks of storage.

For example, a 200-node cluster with 24 TB of disk space per node, a block size of 128 MB, and a replication factor of 3 has room for about 2 million blocks (or more): 200 × 24,000,000 MB/(128 MB × 3). So in this case, setting the namenode memory to 12,000 MB would be a good starting point.

You can increase the namenode's memory without changing the memory allocated to other Hadoop daemons by setting HADOOP_NAMENODE_OPTS in *hadoop-env.sh* to include a JVM option for setting the memory size. HADOOP_NAMENODE_OPTS allows you to pass extra options to the namenode's JVM. So, for example, if you were using a Sun JVM,

---

-Xmx2000m would specify that 2,000 MB of memory should be allocated to the namenode.

If you change the namenode's memory allocation, don't forget to do the same for the secondary namenode (using the HADOOP_SECONDARYNAMENODE_OPTS variable), since its memory requirements are comparable to the primary namenode's.

In addition to the memory requirements of the daemons, the node manager allocates containers to applications, so we need to factor these into the total memory footprint of a worker machine; see "Memory settings in YARN and MapReduce" on page 301.

System logfiles

System logfiles produced by Hadoop are stored in *$HADOOP_HOME/logs* by default. This can be changed using the HADOOP_LOG_DIR setting in *hadoop-env.sh*. It's a good idea to change this so that logfiles are kept out of the directory that Hadoop is installed in. Changing this keeps logfiles in one place, even after the installation directory changes due to an upgrade. A common choice is */var/log/hadoop*, set by including the following line in *hadoop-env.sh*:

```
export HADOOP_LOG_DIR=/var/log/hadoop
```

The log directory will be created if it doesn't already exist. (If it does not exist, confirm that the relevant Unix Hadoop user has permission to create it.) Each Hadoop daemon running on a machine produces two logfiles. The first is the log output written via log4j. This file, whose name ends in *.log*, should be the first port of call when diagnosing problems because most application log messages are written here. The standard Hadoop log4j configuration uses a daily rolling file appender to rotate logfiles. Old logfiles are never deleted, so you should arrange for them to be periodically deleted or archived, so as to not run out of disk space on the local node.

The second logfile is the combined standard output and standard error log. This logfile, whose name ends in *.out*, usually contains little or no output, since Hadoop uses log4j for logging. It is rotated only when the daemon is restarted, and only the last five logs are retained. Old logfiles are suffixed with a number between 1 and 5, with 5 being the oldest file.

Logfile names (of both types) are a combination of the name of the user running the daemon, the daemon name, and the machine hostname. For example, *hadoop-hdfs-datanode-ip-10-45-174-112.log.2014-09-20* is the name of a logfile after it has been rotated. This naming structure makes it possible to archive logs from all machines in the cluster in a single directory, if needed, since the filenames are unique.

The username in the logfile name is actually the default for the HADOOP_IDENT_STRING setting in *hadoop-env.sh*. If you wish to give the Hadoop instance a different identity for the purposes of naming the logfiles, change HADOOP_IDENT_STRING to be the identifier you want.

SSH settings

The control scripts allow you to run commands on (remote) worker nodes from the master node using SSH. It can be useful to customize the SSH settings, for various reasons. For example, you may want to reduce the connection timeout (using the ConnectTimeout option) so the control scripts don't hang around waiting to see whether a dead node is going to respond. Obviously, this can be taken too far. If the timeout is too low, then busy nodes will be skipped, which is bad.

Another useful SSH setting is StrictHostKeyChecking, which can be set to no to automatically add new host keys to the known hosts files. The default, ask, prompts the user to confirm that the key fingerprint has been verified, which is not a suitable setting in a large cluster environment.[5]

To pass extra options to SSH, define the HADOOP_SSH_OPTS environment variable in *hadoop-env.sh*. See the ssh and ssh_config manual pages for more SSH settings.

Important Hadoop Daemon Properties

Hadoop has a bewildering number of configuration properties. In this section, we address the ones that you need to define (or at least understand why the default is appropriate) for any real-world working cluster. These properties are set in the Hadoop site files: *core-site.xml*, *hdfs-site.xml*, and *yarn-site.xml*. Typical instances of these files are shown in Examples 10-1, 10-2, and 10-3.[6] You can learn more about the format of Hadoop's configuration files in "The Configuration API" on page 141.

To find the actual configuration of a running daemon, visit the */conf* page on its web server. For example, *http://resource-manager-host:8088/conf* shows the configuration that the resource manager is running with. This page shows the combined site and default configuration files that the daemon is running with, and also shows which file each property was picked up from.

Example 10-1. A typical core-site.xml configuration file

```
<?xml version="1.0"?>
<!-- core-site.xml -->
<configuration>
  <property>
```

---

5. For more discussion on the security implications of SSH host keys, consult the article "SSH Host Key Protection" (*http://www.securityfocus.com/infocus/1806*) by Brian Hatch.

6. Notice that there is no site file for MapReduce shown here. This is because the only MapReduce daemon is the job history server, and the defaults are sufficient.

```
    <name>fs.defaultFS</name>
    <value>hdfs://namenode/</value>
  </property>
</configuration>
```

Example 10-2. A typical hdfs-site.xml configuration file

```
<?xml version="1.0"?>
<!-- hdfs-site.xml -->
<configuration>
  <property>
    <name>dfs.namenode.name.dir</name>
    <value>/disk1/hdfs/name,/remote/hdfs/name</value>
  </property>

  <property>
    <name>dfs.datanode.data.dir</name>
    <value>/disk1/hdfs/data,/disk2/hdfs/data</value>
  </property>

  <property>
    <name>dfs.namenode.checkpoint.dir</name>
    <value>/disk1/hdfs/namesecondary,/disk2/hdfs/namesecondary</value>
  </property>
</configuration>
```

Example 10-3. A typical yarn-site.xml configuration file

```
<?xml version="1.0"?>
<!-- yarn-site.xml -->
<configuration>
  <property>
    <name>yarn.resourcemanager.hostname</name>
    <value>resourcemanager</value>
  </property>

  <property>
    <name>yarn.nodemanager.local-dirs</name>
    <value>/disk1/nm-local-dir,/disk2/nm-local-dir</value>
  </property>

  <property>
    <name>yarn.nodemanager.aux-services</name>
    <value>mapreduce.shuffle</value>
  </property>

  <property>
    <name>yarn.nodemanager.resource.memory-mb</name>
    <value>16384</value>
  </property>

  <property>
    <name>yarn.nodemanager.resource.cpu-vcores</name>
```

```
      <value>16</value>
  </property>
</configuration>
```

HDFS

To run HDFS, you need to designate one machine as a namenode. In this case, the property `fs.defaultFS` is an HDFS filesystem URI whose host is the namenode's hostname or IP address and whose port is the port that the namenode will listen on for RPCs. If no port is specified, the default of 8020 is used.

The `fs.defaultFS` property also doubles as specifying the default filesystem. The default filesystem is used to resolve relative paths, which are handy to use because they save typing (and avoid hardcoding knowledge of a particular namenode's address). For example, with the default filesystem defined in Example 10-1, the relative URI */a/b* is resolved to *hdfs://namenode/a/b*.

 If you are running HDFS, the fact that `fs.defaultFS` is used to specify both the HDFS namenode *and* the default filesystem means HDFS has to be the default filesystem in the server configuration. Bear in mind, however, that it is possible to specify a different filesystem as the default in the client configuration, for convenience.

For example, if you use both HDFS and S3 filesystems, then you have a choice of specifying either as the default in the client configuration, which allows you to refer to the default with a relative URI and the other with an absolute URI.

There are a few other configuration properties you should set for HDFS: those that set the storage directories for the namenode and for datanodes. The property `dfs.name node.name.dir` specifies a list of directories where the namenode stores persistent filesystem metadata (the edit log and the filesystem image). A copy of each metadata file is stored in each directory for redundancy. It's common to configure `dfs.name node.name.dir` so that the namenode metadata is written to one or two local disks, as well as a remote disk, such as an NFS-mounted directory. Such a setup guards against failure of a local disk and failure of the entire namenode, since in both cases the files can be recovered and used to start a new namenode. (The secondary namenode takes only periodic checkpoints of the namenode, so it does not provide an up-to-date backup of the namenode.)

You should also set the `dfs.datanode.data.dir` property, which specifies a list of directories for a datanode to store its blocks in. Unlike the namenode, which uses multiple directories for redundancy, a datanode round-robins writes between its storage directories, so for performance you should specify a storage directory for each local disk. Read performance also benefits from having multiple disks for storage, because blocks will be spread across them and concurrent reads for distinct blocks will be correspondingly spread across disks.

 For maximum performance, you should mount storage disks with the noatime option. This setting means that last accessed time information is not written on file reads, which gives significant performance gains.

Finally, you should configure where the secondary namenode stores its checkpoints of the filesystem. The dfs.namenode.checkpoint.dir property specifies a list of directories where the checkpoints are kept. Like the storage directories for the namenode, which keep redundant copies of the namenode metadata, the checkpointed filesystem image is stored in each checkpoint directory for redundancy.

Table 10-2 summarizes the important configuration properties for HDFS.

Table 10-2. Important HDFS daemon properties

Property name	Type	Default value	Description
fs.defaultFS	URI	file:///	The default filesystem. The URI defines the hostname and port that the namenode's RPC server runs on. The default port is 8020. This property is set in *core-site.xml*.
dfs.namenode.name.dir	Comma-separated directory names	file://${hadoop.tmp.dir}/dfs/name	The list of directories where the namenode stores its persistent metadata. The namenode stores a copy of the metadata in each directory in the list.
dfs.datanode.data.dir	Comma-separated directory names	file://${hadoop.tmp.dir}/dfs/data	A list of directories where the datanode stores blocks. Each block is stored in only one of these directories.
dfs.namenode.checkpoint.dir	Comma-separated directory names	file://${hadoop.tmp.dir}/dfs/namesecondary	A list of directories where the secondary namenode stores checkpoints. It stores a copy of the checkpoint in each directory in the list.

Note that the storage directories for HDFS are under Hadoop's temporary directory by default (this is configured via the `hadoop.tmp.dir` property, whose default is `/tmp/hadoop-${user.name}`). Therefore, it is critical that these properties are set so that data is not lost by the system when it clears out temporary directories.

YARN

To run YARN, you need to designate one machine as a resource manager. The simplest way to do this is to set the property `yarn.resourcemanager.hostname` to the hostname or IP address of the machine running the resource manager. Many of the resource manager's server addresses are derived from this property. For example, `yarn.resourcemanager.address` takes the form of a host-port pair, and the host defaults to `yarn.resourcemanager.hostname`. In a MapReduce client configuration, this property is used to connect to the resource manager over RPC.

During a MapReduce job, intermediate data and working files are written to temporary local files. Because this data includes the potentially very large output of map tasks, you need to ensure that the `yarn.nodemanager.local-dirs` property, which controls the location of local temporary storage for YARN containers, is configured to use disk partitions that are large enough. The property takes a comma-separated list of directory names, and you should use all available local disks to spread disk I/O (the directories are used in round-robin fashion). Typically, you will use the same disks and partitions (but different directories) for YARN local storage as you use for datanode block storage, as governed by the `dfs.datanode.data.dir` property, which was discussed earlier.

Unlike MapReduce 1, YARN doesn't have tasktrackers to serve map outputs to reduce tasks, so for this function it relies on shuffle handlers, which are long-running auxiliary services running in node managers. Because YARN is a general-purpose service, the MapReduce shuffle handlers need to be enabled explicitly in *yarn-site.xml* by setting the `yarn.nodemanager.aux-services` property to `mapreduce_shuffle`.

Table 10-3 summarizes the important configuration properties for YARN. The resource-related settings are covered in more detail in the next sections.

Table 10-3. Important YARN daemon properties

Property name	Type	Default value	Description
`yarn.resourcemanager.hostname`	Hostname	`0.0.0.0`	The hostname of the machine the resource manager runs on. Abbreviated `${y.rm.hostname}` below.
`yarn.resourcemanager.address`	Hostname and port	`${y.rm.hostname}:8032`	The hostname and port that the resource manager's RPC server runs on.

Property name	Type	Default value	Description
yarn.nodemanager.local-dirs	Comma-separated directory names	${hadoop.tmp.dir}/nm-local-dir	A list of directories where node managers allow containers to store intermediate data. The data is cleared out when the application ends.
yarn.nodemanager.aux-services	Comma-separated service names		A list of auxiliary services run by the node manager. A service is implemented by the class defined by the property yarn.nodemanager.aux-services.*service-name*.class. By default, no auxiliary services are specified.
yarn.nodemanager.resource.memory-mb	int	8192	The amount of physical memory (in MB) that may be allocated to containers being run by the node manager.
yarn.nodemanager.vmem-pmem-ratio	float	2.1	The ratio of virtual to physical memory for containers. Virtual memory usage may exceed the allocation by this amount.
yarn.nodemanager.resource.cpu-vcores	int	8	The number of CPU cores that may be allocated to containers being run by the node manager.

Memory settings in YARN and MapReduce

YARN treats memory in a more fine-grained manner than the slot-based model used in MapReduce 1. Rather than specifying a fixed maximum number of map and reduce slots that may run on a node at once, YARN allows applications to request an arbitrary amount of memory (within limits) for a task. In the YARN model, node managers allocate memory from a pool, so the number of tasks that are running on a particular node depends on the sum of their memory requirements, and not simply on a fixed number of slots.

The calculation for how much memory to dedicate to a node manager for running containers depends on the amount of physical memory on the machine. Each Hadoop daemon uses 1,000 MB, so for a datanode and a node manager, the total is 2,000 MB. Set aside enough for other processes that are running on the machine, and the remainder can be dedicated to the node manager's containers by setting the configuration property yarn.nodemanager.resource.memory-mb to the total allocation in MB. (The default is 8,192 MB, which is normally too low for most setups.)

The next step is to determine how to set memory options for individual jobs. There are two main controls: one for the size of the container allocated by YARN, and another for the heap size of the Java process run in the container.

 The memory controls for MapReduce are all set by the client in the job configuration. The YARN settings are cluster settings and cannot be modified by the client.

Container sizes are determined by `mapreduce.map.memory.mb` and `mapreduce.re duce.memory.mb`; both default to 1,024 MB. These settings are used by the application master when negotiating for resources in the cluster, and also by the node manager, which runs and monitors the task containers. The heap size of the Java process is set by `mapred.child.java.opts`, and defaults to 200 MB. You can also set the Java options separately for map and reduce tasks (see Table 10-4).

Table 10-4. MapReduce job memory properties (set by the client)

Property name	Type	Default value	Description
`mapreduce.map.memory.mb`	`int`	1024	The amount of memory for map containers.
`mapreduce.reduce.memory.mb`	`int`	1024	The amount of memory for reduce containers.
`mapred.child.java.opts`	`String`	`-Xmx200m`	The JVM options used to launch the container process that runs map and reduce tasks. In addition to memory settings, this property can include JVM properties for debugging, for example.
`mapreduce.map.java.opts`	`String`	`-Xmx200m`	The JVM options used for the child process that runs map tasks.
`mapreduce.reduce.java.opts`	`String`	`-Xmx200m`	The JVM options used for the child process that runs reduce tasks.

For example, suppose `mapred.child.java.opts` is set to `-Xmx800m` and `mapre duce.map.memory.mb` is left at its default value of 1,024 MB. When a map task is run, the node manager will allocate a 1,024 MB container (decreasing the size of its pool by that amount for the duration of the task) and will launch the task JVM configured with an 800 MB maximum heap size. Note that the JVM process will have a larger memory footprint than the heap size, and the overhead will depend on such things as the native libraries that are in use, the size of the permanent generation space, and so on. The important thing is that the physical memory used by the JVM process, including any processes that it spawns, such as Streaming processes, does not exceed its allocation (1,024 MB). If a container uses more memory than it has been allocated, then it may be terminated by the node manager and marked as failed.

YARN schedulers impose a minimum or maximum on memory allocations. The default minimum is 1,024 MB (set by `yarn.scheduler.minimum-allocation-mb`), and the default maximum is 8,192 MB (set by `yarn.scheduler.maximum-allocation-mb`).

There are also virtual memory constraints that a container must meet. If a container's virtual memory usage exceeds a given multiple of the allocated physical memory, the node manager may terminate the process. The multiple is expressed by the `yarn.nodemanager.vmem-pmem-ratio` property, which defaults to 2.1. In the example used earlier, the virtual memory threshold above which the task may be terminated is 2,150 MB, which is 2.1 × 1,024 MB.

When configuring memory parameters it's very useful to be able to monitor a task's actual memory usage during a job run, and this is possible via MapReduce task counters. The counters `PHYSICAL_MEMORY_BYTES`, `VIRTUAL_MEMORY_BYTES`, and `COMMITTED_HEAP_BYTES` (described in Table 9-2) provide snapshot values of memory usage and are therefore suitable for observation during the course of a task attempt.

Hadoop also provides settings to control how much memory is used for MapReduce operations. These can be set on a per-job basis and are covered in "Shuffle and Sort" on page 197.

CPU settings in YARN and MapReduce

In addition to memory, YARN treats CPU usage as a managed resource, and applications can request the number of cores they need. The number of cores that a node manager can allocate to containers is controlled by the `yarn.nodemanager.resource.cpu-vcores` property. It should be set to the total number of cores on the machine, minus a core for each daemon process running on the machine (datanode, node manager, and any other long-running processes).

MapReduce jobs can control the number of cores allocated to map and reduce containers by setting `mapreduce.map.cpu.vcores` and `mapreduce.reduce.cpu.vcores`. Both default to 1, an appropriate setting for normal single-threaded MapReduce tasks, which can only saturate a single core.

While the number of cores is tracked during scheduling (so a container won't be allocated on a machine where there are no spare cores, for example), the node manager will not, by default, limit actual CPU usage of running containers. This means that a container can abuse its allocation by using more CPU than it was given, possibly starving other containers running on the same host. YARN has support for enforcing CPU limits using Linux cgroups. The node manager's container executor class (`yarn.nodemanager.container-executor.class`) must be set to use the `LinuxContainerExecutor` class, which in turn must be configured to use cgroups (see the properties under `yarn.nodemanager.linux-container-executor`).

Hadoop Daemon Addresses and Ports

Hadoop daemons generally run both an RPC server for communication between daemons (Table 10-5) and an HTTP server to provide web pages for human consumption (Table 10-6). Each server is configured by setting the network address and port number to listen on. A port number of 0 instructs the server to start on a free port, but this is generally discouraged because it is incompatible with setting cluster-wide firewall policies.

In general, the properties for setting a server's RPC and HTTP addresses serve double duty: they determine the network interface that the server will bind to, and they are used by clients or other machines in the cluster to connect to the server. For example, node managers use the `yarn.resourcemanager.resource-tracker.address` property to find the address of their resource manager.

It is often desirable for servers to bind to multiple network interfaces, but setting the network address to `0.0.0.0`, which works for the server, breaks the second case, since the address is not resolvable by clients or other machines in the cluster. One solution is to have separate configurations for clients and servers, but a better way is to set the bind host for the server. By setting `yarn.resourcemanager.hostname` to the (externally resolvable) hostname or IP address and `yarn.resourcemanager.bind-host` to `0.0.0.0`, you ensure that the resource manager will bind to all addresses on the machine, while at the same time providing a resolvable address for node managers and clients.

In addition to an RPC server, datanodes run a TCP/IP server for block transfers. The server address and port are set by the `dfs.datanode.address` property , which has a default value of `0.0.0.0:50010`.

Table 10-5. RPC server properties

Property name	Default value	Description
`fs.defaultFS`	`file:///`	When set to an HDFS URI, this property determines the namenode's RPC server address and port. The default port is 8020 if not specified.
`dfs.namenode.rpc-bind-host`		The address the namenode's RPC server will bind to. If not set (the default), the bind address is determined by `fs.defaultFS`. It can be set to `0.0.0.0` to make the namenode listen on all interfaces.
`dfs.datanode.ipc.address`	`0.0.0.0:50020`	The datanode's RPC server address and port.
`mapreduce.jobhistory.address`	`0.0.0.0:10020`	The job history server's RPC server address and port. This is used by the client (typically outside the cluster) to query job history.
`mapreduce.jobhistory.bind-host`		The address the job history server's RPC and HTTP servers will bind to.
`yarn.resourcemanager.hostname`	`0.0.0.0`	The hostname of the machine the resource manager runs on. Abbreviated `${y.rm.hostname}` below.
`yarn.resourcemanager.bind-host`		The address the resource manager's RPC and HTTP servers will bind to.
`yarn.resourcemanager.address`	`${y.rm.hostname}:8032`	The resource manager's RPC server address and port. This is used by the client (typically outside the cluster) to communicate with the resource manager.
`yarn.resourcemanager.admin.address`	`${y.rm.hostname}:8033`	The resource manager's admin RPC server address and port. This is used by the admin client (invoked with `yarn rmadmin`, typically run outside the cluster) to communicate with the resource manager.
`yarn.resourcemanager.scheduler.address`	`${y.rm.hostname}:8030`	The resource manager scheduler's RPC server address and port. This is used by (in-cluster) application masters to communicate with the resource manager.
`yarn.resourcemanager.resource-tracker.address`	`${y.rm.hostname}:8031`	The resource manager resource tracker's RPC server address and port. This is used by (in-cluster) node managers to communicate with the resource manager.
`yarn.nodemanager.hostname`	`0.0.0.0`	The hostname of the machine the node manager runs on. Abbreviated `${y.nm.hostname}` below.
`yarn.nodemanager.bind-host`		The address the node manager's RPC and HTTP servers will bind to.

Property name	Default value	Description
`yarn.nodemanager.address`	`${y.nm.host name}:0`	The node manager's RPC server address and port. This is used by (in-cluster) application masters to communicate with node managers.
`yarn.nodemanager.localizer.address`	`${y.nm.host name}:8040`	The node manager localizer's RPC server address and port.

Table 10-6. HTTP server properties

Property name	Default value	Description
`dfs.namenode.http-address`	`0.0.0.0:50070`	The namenode's HTTP server address and port.
`dfs.namenode.http-bind-host`		The address the namenode's HTTP server will bind to.
`dfs.namenode.secondary.http-address`	`0.0.0.0:50090`	The secondary namenode's HTTP server address and port.
`dfs.datanode.http.address`	`0.0.0.0:50075`	The datanode's HTTP server address and port. (Note that the property name is inconsistent with the ones for the namenode.)
`mapreduce.jobhistory.webapp.ad dress`	`0.0.0.0:19888`	The MapReduce job history server's address and port. This property is set in *mapred-site.xml*.
`mapreduce.shuffle.port`	`13562`	The shuffle handler's HTTP port number. This is used for serving map outputs, and is not a user-accessible web UI. This property is set in *mapred-site.xml*.
`yarn.resourcemanager.webapp.ad dress`	`${y.rm.host name}:8088`	The resource manager's HTTP server address and port.
`yarn.nodemanager.webapp.address`	`${y.nm.host name}:8042`	The node manager's HTTP server address and port.
`yarn.web-proxy.address`		The web app proxy server's HTTP server address and port. If not set (the default), then the web app proxy server will run in the resource manager process.

There is also a setting for controlling which network interfaces the datanodes use as their IP addresses (for HTTP and RPC servers). The relevant property is `dfs.data node.dns.interface`, which is set to `default` to use the default network interface. You can set this explicitly to report the address of a particular interface (`eth0`, for example).

Other Hadoop Properties

This section discusses some other properties that you might consider setting.

Cluster membership

To aid in the addition and removal of nodes in the future, you can specify a file containing a list of authorized machines that may join the cluster as datanodes or node managers. The file is specified using the dfs.hosts and yarn.resourcemanager.nodes.include-path properties (for datanodes and node managers, respectively), and the corresponding dfs.hosts.exclude and yarn.resourcemanager.nodes.exclude-path properties specify the files used for decommissioning. See "Commissioning and Decommissioning Nodes" on page 334 for further discussion.

Buffer size

Hadoop uses a buffer size of 4 KB (4,096 bytes) for its I/O operations. This is a conservative setting, and with modern hardware and operating systems, you will likely see performance benefits by increasing it; 128 KB (131,072 bytes) is a common choice. Set the value in bytes using the io.file.buffer.size property in *core-site.xml.*

HDFS block size

The HDFS block size is 128 MB by default, but many clusters use more (e.g., 256 MB, which is 268,435,456 bytes) to ease memory pressure on the namenode and to give mappers more data to work on. Use the dfs.blocksize property in *hdfs-site.xml* to specify the size in bytes.

Reserved storage space

By default, datanodes will try to use all of the space available in their storage directories. If you want to reserve some space on the storage volumes for non-HDFS use, you can set dfs.datanode.du.reserved to the amount, in bytes, of space to reserve.

Trash

Hadoop filesystems have a trash facility, in which deleted files are not actually deleted but rather are moved to a trash folder, where they remain for a minimum period before being permanently deleted by the system. The minimum period in minutes that a file will remain in the trash is set using the fs.trash.interval configuration property in *core-site.xml.* By default, the trash interval is zero, which disables trash.

Like in many operating systems, Hadoop's trash facility is a user-level feature, meaning that only files that are deleted using the filesystem shell are put in the trash. Files deleted programmatically are deleted immediately. It is possible to use the trash programmatically, however, by constructing a Trash instance, then calling its moveTo Trash() method with the Path of the file intended for deletion. The method returns a value indicating success; a value of false means either that trash is not enabled or that the file is already in the trash.

When trash is enabled, users each have their own trash directories called *.Trash* in their home directories. File recovery is simple: you look for the file in a subdirectory of *.Trash* and move it out of the trash subtree.

HDFS will automatically delete files in trash folders, but other filesystems will not, so you have to arrange for this to be done periodically. You can *expunge* the trash, which will delete files that have been in the trash longer than their minimum period, using the filesystem shell:

```
% hadoop fs -expunge
```

The Trash class exposes an expunge() method that has the same effect.

Job scheduler

Particularly in a multiuser setting, consider updating the job scheduler queue configuration to reflect your organizational needs. For example, you can set up a queue for each group using the cluster. See "Scheduling in YARN" on page 85.

Reduce slow start

By default, schedulers wait until 5% of the map tasks in a job have completed before scheduling reduce tasks for the same job. For large jobs, this can cause problems with cluster utilization, since they take up reduce containers while waiting for the map tasks to complete. Setting mapreduce.job.reduce.slowstart.completedmaps to a higher value, such as 0.80 (80%), can help improve throughput.

Short-circuit local reads

When reading a file from HDFS, the client contacts the datanode and the data is sent to the client via a TCP connection. If the block being read is on the same node as the client, then it is more efficient for the client to bypass the network and read the block data directly from the disk. This is termed a *short-circuit local read*, and can make applications like HBase perform better.

You can enable short-circuit local reads by setting dfs.client.read.shortcircuit to true. Short-circuit local reads are implemented using Unix domain sockets, which use a local path for client-datanode communication. The path is set using the property dfs.domain.socket.path, and must be a path that only the datanode user (typically hdfs) or root can create, such as */var/run/hadoop-hdfs/dn_socket*.

Security

Early versions of Hadoop assumed that HDFS and MapReduce clusters would be used by a group of cooperating users within a secure environment. The measures for restricting access were designed to prevent accidental data loss, rather than to prevent unauthorized access to data. For example, the file permissions system in HDFS prevents one user from accidentally wiping out the whole filesystem because of a bug in a program, or by mistakenly typing `hadoop fs -rmr /`, but it doesn't prevent a malicious user from assuming root's identity to access or delete any data in the cluster.

In security parlance, what was missing was a secure *authentication* mechanism to assure Hadoop that the user seeking to perform an operation on the cluster is who he claims to be and therefore can be trusted. HDFS file permissions provide only a mechanism for *authorization*, which controls what a particular user can do to a particular file. For example, a file may be readable only by a certain group of users, so anyone not in that group is not authorized to read it. However, authorization is not enough by itself, because the system is still open to abuse via spoofing by a malicious user who can gain network access to the cluster.

It's common to restrict access to data that contains personally identifiable information (such as an end user's full name or IP address) to a small set of users (of the cluster) within the organization who are authorized to access such information. Less sensitive (or anonymized) data may be made available to a larger set of users. It is convenient to host a mix of datasets with different security levels on the same cluster (not least because it means the datasets with lower security levels can be shared). However, to meet regulatory requirements for data protection, secure authentication must be in place for shared clusters.

This is the situation that Yahoo! faced in 2009, which led a team of engineers there to implement secure authentication for Hadoop. In their design, Hadoop itself does not manage user credentials; instead, it relies on Kerberos, a mature open-source network authentication protocol, to authenticate the user. However, Kerberos doesn't manage permissions. Kerberos says that a user is who she says she is; it's Hadoop's job to determine whether that user has permission to perform a given action.

There's a lot to security in Hadoop, and this section only covers the highlights. For more, readers are referred to *Hadoop Security* by Ben Spivey and Joey Echeverria (O'Reilly, 2014).

Kerberos and Hadoop

At a high level, there are three steps that a client must take to access a service when using Kerberos, each of which involves a message exchange with a server:

1. *Authentication.* The client authenticates itself to the Authentication Server and receives a timestamped Ticket-Granting Ticket (TGT).

2. *Authorization.* The client uses the TGT to request a service ticket from the Ticket-Granting Server.

3. *Service request.* The client uses the service ticket to authenticate itself to the server that is providing the service the client is using. In the case of Hadoop, this might be the namenode or the resource manager.

Together, the Authentication Server and the Ticket Granting Server form the *Key Distribution Center* (KDC). The process is shown graphically in Figure 10-2.

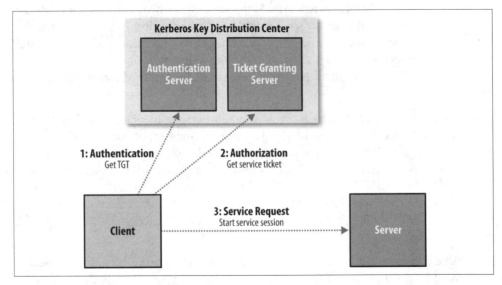

Figure 10-2. The three-step Kerberos ticket exchange protocol

The authorization and service request steps are not user-level actions; the client performs these steps on the user's behalf. The authentication step, however, is normally carried out explicitly by the user using the kinit command, which will prompt for a password. However, this doesn't mean you need to enter your password every time you run a job or access HDFS, since TGTs last for 10 hours by default (and can be renewed for up to a week). It's common to automate authentication at operating system login time, thereby providing *single sign-on* to Hadoop.

In cases where you don't want to be prompted for a password (for running an unattended MapReduce job, for example), you can create a Kerberos *keytab* file using the ktutil command. A keytab is a file that stores passwords and may be supplied to kinit with the -t option.

An example

Let's look at an example of the process in action. The first step is to enable Kerberos authentication by setting the `hadoop.security.authentication` property in *core-site.xml* to `kerberos`.[7] The default setting is `simple`, which signifies that the old backward-compatible (but insecure) behavior of using the operating system username to determine identity should be employed.

We also need to enable service-level authorization by setting `hadoop.security.author``ization` to `true` in the same file. You may configure access control lists (ACLs) in the *hadoop-policy.xml* configuration file to control which users and groups have permission to connect to each Hadoop service. Services are defined at the protocol level, so there are ones for MapReduce job submission, namenode communication, and so on. By default, all ACLs are set to `*`, which means that all users have permission to access each service; however, on a real cluster you should lock the ACLs down to only those users and groups that should have access.

The format for an ACL is a comma-separated list of usernames, followed by whitespace, followed by a comma-separated list of group names. For example, the ACL `preston,howard directors,inventors` would authorize access to users named `preston` or `howard`, or in groups `directors` or `inventors`.

With Kerberos authentication turned on, let's see what happens when we try to copy a local file to HDFS:

```
% hadoop fs -put quangle.txt .
10/07/03 15:44:58 WARN ipc.Client: Exception encountered while connecting to the
server: javax.security.sasl.SaslException: GSS initiate failed [Caused by
GSSException: No valid credentials provided (Mechanism level: Failed to find
any Kerberos tgt)]
Bad connection to FS. command aborted. exception: Call to localhost/
127.0.0.1:8020 failed on local exception: java.io.IOException:
javax.security.sasl.SaslException: GSS initiate failed [Caused by GSSException:
No valid credentials provided
(Mechanism level: Failed to find any Kerberos tgt)]
```

The operation fails because we don't have a Kerberos ticket. We can get one by authenticating to the KDC, using `kinit`:

```
% kinit
Password for hadoop-user@LOCALDOMAIN: password
% hadoop fs -put quangle.txt .
% hadoop fs -stat %n quangle.txt
quangle.txt
```

---

7. To use Kerberos authentication with Hadoop, you need to install, configure, and run a KDC (Hadoop does not come with one). Your organization may already have a KDC you can use (an Active Directory installation, for example); if not, you can set up an MIT Kerberos 5 KDC.

And we see that the file is successfully written to HDFS. Notice that even though we carried out two filesystem commands, we only needed to call kinit once, since the Kerberos ticket is valid for 10 hours (use the klist command to see the expiry time of your tickets and kdestroy to invalidate your tickets). After we get a ticket, everything works just as it normally would.

Delegation Tokens

In a distributed system such as HDFS or MapReduce, there are many client-server interactions, each of which must be authenticated. For example, an HDFS read operation will involve multiple calls to the namenode and calls to one or more datanodes. Instead of using the three-step Kerberos ticket exchange protocol to authenticate each call, which would present a high load on the KDC on a busy cluster, Hadoop uses *delegation tokens* to allow later authenticated access without having to contact the KDC again. Delegation tokens are created and used transparently by Hadoop on behalf of users, so there's no action you need to take as a user beyond using kinit to sign in, but it's useful to have a basic idea of how they are used.

A delegation token is generated by the server (the namenode, in this case) and can be thought of as a shared secret between the client and the server. On the first RPC call to the namenode, the client has no delegation token, so it uses Kerberos to authenticate. As a part of the response, it gets a delegation token from the namenode. In subsequent calls it presents the delegation token, which the namenode can verify (since it generated it using a secret key), and hence the client is authenticated to the server.

When it wants to perform operations on HDFS blocks, the client uses a special kind of delegation token, called a *block access token*, that the namenode passes to the client in response to a metadata request. The client uses the block access token to authenticate itself to datanodes. This is possible only because the namenode shares its secret key used to generate the block access token with datanodes (sending it in heartbeat messages), so that they can verify block access tokens. Thus, an HDFS block may be accessed only by a client with a valid block access token from a namenode. This closes the security hole in unsecured Hadoop where only the block ID was needed to gain access to a block. This property is enabled by setting dfs.block.access.token.enable to true.

In MapReduce, job resources and metadata (such as JAR files, input splits, and configuration files) are shared in HDFS for the application master to access, and user code runs on the node managers and accesses files on HDFS (the process is explained in "Anatomy of a MapReduce Job Run" on page 185). Delegation tokens are used by these components to access HDFS during the course of the job. When the job has finished, the delegation tokens are invalidated.

Delegation tokens are automatically obtained for the default HDFS instance, but if your job needs to access other HDFS clusters, you can load the delegation tokens for these by setting the `mapreduce.job.hdfs-servers` job property to a comma-separated list of HDFS URIs.

Other Security Enhancements

Security has been tightened throughout the Hadoop stack to protect against unauthorized access to resources. The more notable features are listed here:

- Tasks can be run using the operating system account for the user who submitted the job, rather than the user running the node manager. This means that the operating system is used to isolate running tasks, so they can't send signals to each other (to kill another user's tasks, for example) and so local information, such as task data, is kept private via local filesystem permissions.

  This feature is enabled by setting `yarn.nodemanager.container-executor.class` to `org.apache.hadoop.yarn.server.nodemanager.LinuxContainerExecutor`.[8] In addition, administrators need to ensure that each user is given an account on every node in the cluster (typically using LDAP).

- When tasks are run as the user who submitted the job, the distributed cache (see "Distributed Cache" on page 274) is secure. Files that are world-readable are put in a shared cache (the insecure default); otherwise, they go in a private cache, readable only by the owner.

- Users can view and modify only their own jobs, not others. This is enabled by setting `mapreduce.cluster.acls.enabled` to `true`. There are two job configuration properties, `mapreduce.job.acl-view-job` and `mapreduce.job.acl-modify-job`, which may be set to a comma-separated list of users to control who may view or modify a particular job.

- The shuffle is secure, preventing a malicious user from requesting another user's map outputs.

- When appropriately configured, it's no longer possible for a malicious user to run a rogue secondary namenode, datanode, or node manager that can join the cluster and potentially compromise data stored in the cluster. This is enforced by requiring daemons to authenticate with the master node they are connecting to.

  To enable this feature, you first need to configure Hadoop to use a keytab previously generated with the `ktutil` command. For a datanode, for example, you would set the `dfs.datanode.keytab.file` property to the keytab filename and `dfs.datanode.kerberos.principal` to the username to use for the datanode. Finally, the ACL for the `DataNodeProtocol` (which is used by datanodes to communicate with

---

8. `LinuxTaskController` uses a setuid executable called *container-executor*, found in the *bin* directory. You should ensure that this binary is owned by root and has the setuid bit set (with `chmod +s`).

the namenode) must be set in *hadoop-policy.xml*, by restricting `security.data node.protocol.acl` to the datanode's username.

- A datanode may be run on a privileged port (one lower than 1024), so a client may be reasonably sure that it was started securely.

- A task may communicate only with its parent application master, thus preventing an attacker from obtaining MapReduce data from another user's job.

- Various parts of Hadoop can be configured to encrypt network data, including RPC (`hadoop.rpc.protection`), HDFS block transfers (`dfs.encrypt.data.transfer`), the MapReduce shuffle (`mapreduce.shuffle.ssl.enabled`), and the web UIs (`hadokop.ssl.enabled`). Work is ongoing to encrypt data "at rest," too, so that HDFS blocks can be stored in encrypted form, for example.

Benchmarking a Hadoop Cluster

Is the cluster set up correctly? The best way to answer this question is empirically: run some jobs and confirm that you get the expected results. Benchmarks make good tests because you also get numbers that you can compare with other clusters as a sanity check on whether your new cluster is performing roughly as expected. And you can tune a cluster using benchmark results to squeeze the best performance out of it. This is often done with monitoring systems in place (see "Monitoring" on page 330), so you can see how resources are being used across the cluster.

To get the best results, you should run benchmarks on a cluster that is not being used by others. In practice, this will be just before it is put into service and users start relying on it. Once users have scheduled periodic jobs on a cluster, it is generally impossible to find a time when the cluster is not being used (unless you arrange downtime with users), so you should run benchmarks to your satisfaction before this happens.

Experience has shown that most hardware failures for new systems are hard drive failures. By running I/O-intensive benchmarks—such as the ones described next—you can "burn in" the cluster before it goes live.

Hadoop Benchmarks

Hadoop comes with several benchmarks that you can run very easily with minimal setup cost. Benchmarks are packaged in the tests JAR file, and you can get a list of them, with descriptions, by invoking the JAR file with no arguments:

```
% hadoop jar $HADOOP_HOME/share/hadoop/mapreduce/hadoop-mapreduce-*-tests.jar
```

Most of the benchmarks show usage instructions when invoked with no arguments. For example:

```
% hadoop jar $HADOOP_HOME/share/hadoop/mapreduce/hadoop-mapreduce-*-tests.jar \
  TestDFSIO
TestDFSIO.1.7
Missing arguments.
Usage: TestDFSIO [genericOptions] -read [-random | -backward |
-skip [-skipSize Size]] | -write | -append | -clean [-compression codecClassName]
[-nrFiles N] [-size Size[B|KB|MB|GB|TB]] [-resFile resultFileName]
[-bufferSize Bytes] [-rootDir]
```

Benchmarking MapReduce with TeraSort

Hadoop comes with a MapReduce program called *TeraSort* that does a total sort of its input.[9] It is very useful for benchmarking HDFS and MapReduce together, as the full input dataset is transferred through the shuffle. The three steps are: generate some random data, perform the sort, then validate the results.

First, we generate some random data using teragen (found in the examples JAR file, not the tests one). It runs a map-only job that generates a specified number of rows of binary data. Each row is 100 bytes long, so to generate one terabyte of data using 1,000 maps, run the following (10t is short for 10 trillion):

```
% hadoop jar \
  $HADOOP_HOME/share/hadoop/mapreduce/hadoop-mapreduce-examples-*.jar \
  teragen -Dmapreduce.job.maps=1000 10t random-data
```

Next, run terasort:

```
% hadoop jar \
  $HADOOP_HOME/share/hadoop/mapreduce/hadoop-mapreduce-examples-*.jar \
  terasort random-data sorted-data
```

The overall execution time of the sort is the metric we are interested in, but it's instructive to watch the job's progress via the web UI (*http://resource-manager-host:8088/*), where you can get a feel for how long each phase of the job takes. Adjusting the parameters mentioned in "Tuning a Job" on page 175 is a useful exercise, too.

As a final sanity check, we validate that the data in *sorted-data* is, in fact, correctly sorted:

```
% hadoop jar \
  $HADOOP_HOME/share/hadoop/mapreduce/hadoop-mapreduce-examples-*.jar \
  teravalidate sorted-data report
```

This command runs a short MapReduce job that performs a series of checks on the sorted data to check whether the sort is accurate. Any errors can be found in the *report/part-r-00000* output file.

---

9. In 2008, TeraSort was used to break the world record for sorting 1 TB of data; see "A Brief History of Apache Hadoop" on page 12.

Other benchmarks

There are many more Hadoop benchmarks, but the following are widely used:

- *TestDFSIO* tests the I/O performance of HDFS. It does this by using a MapReduce job as a convenient way to read or write files in parallel.
- *MRBench* (invoked with mrbench) runs a small job a number of times. It acts as a good counterpoint to TeraSort, as it checks whether small job runs are responsive.
- *NNBench* (invoked with nnbench) is useful for load-testing namenode hardware.
- *Gridmix* is a suite of benchmarks designed to model a realistic cluster workload by mimicking a variety of data-access patterns seen in practice. See the documentation in the distribution for how to run Gridmix.
- *SWIM*, or the Statistical Workload Injector for MapReduce (*https://github.com/ SWIMProjectUCB/SWIM/wiki*), is a repository of real-life MapReduce workloads that you can use to generate representative test workloads for your system.
- *TPCx-HS* (*http://www.tpc.org/tpcx-hs/*) is a standardized benchmark based on Ter- aSort from the Transaction Processing Performance Council.

User Jobs

For tuning, it is best to include a few jobs that are representative of the jobs that your users run, so your cluster is tuned for these and not just for the standard benchmarks. If this is your first Hadoop cluster and you don't have any user jobs yet, then either Gridmix or SWIM is a good substitute.

When running your own jobs as benchmarks, you should select a dataset for your user jobs and use it each time you run the benchmarks to allow comparisons between runs. When you set up a new cluster or upgrade a cluster, you will be able to use the same dataset to compare the performance with previous runs.

Administering Hadoop

The previous chapter was devoted to setting up a Hadoop cluster. In this chapter, we look at the procedures to keep a cluster running smoothly.

HDFS

Persistent Data Structures

As an administrator, it is invaluable to have a basic understanding of how the components of HDFS—the namenode, the secondary namenode, and the datanodes—organize their persistent data on disk. Knowing which files are which can help you diagnose problems or spot that something is awry.

Namenode directory structure

A running namenode has a directory structure like this:

```
${dfs.namenode.name.dir}/
├── current
│   ├── VERSION
│   ├── edits_0000000000000000001-0000000000000000019
│   ├── edits_inprogress_0000000000000000020
│   ├── fsimage_0000000000000000000
│   ├── fsimage_0000000000000000000.md5
│   ├── fsimage_0000000000000000019
│   ├── fsimage_0000000000000000019.md5
│   └── seen_txid
└── in_use.lock
```

Recall from Chapter 10 that the dfs.namenode.name.dir property is a list of directories, with the same contents mirrored in each directory. This mechanism provides resilience, particularly if one of the directories is an NFS mount, as is recommended.

The *VERSION* file is a Java properties file that contains information about the version of HDFS that is running. Here are the contents of a typical file:

```
#Mon Sep 29 09:54:36 BST 2014
namespaceID=1342387246
clusterID=CID-01b5c398-959c-4ea8-aae6-1e0d9bd8b142
cTime=0
storageType=NAME_NODE
blockpoolID=BP-526805057-127.0.0.1-1411980876842
layoutVersion=-57
```

The layoutVersion is a negative integer that defines the version of HDFS's persistent data structures. This version number has no relation to the release number of the Hadoop distribution. Whenever the layout changes, the version number is decremented (for example, the version after −57 is −58). When this happens, HDFS needs to be upgraded, since a newer namenode (or datanode) will not operate if its storage layout is an older version. Upgrading HDFS is covered in "Upgrades" on page 337.

The namespaceID is a unique identifier for the filesystem namespace, which is created when the namenode is first formatted. The clusterID is a unique identifier for the HDFS cluster as a whole; this is important for HDFS federation (see "HDFS Federation" on page 48), where a cluster is made up of multiple namespaces and each namespace is managed by one namenode. The blockpoolID is a unique identifier for the block pool containing all the files in the namespace managed by this namenode.

The cTime property marks the creation time of the namenode's storage. For newly formatted storage, the value is always zero, but it is updated to a timestamp whenever the filesystem is upgraded.

The storageType indicates that this storage directory contains data structures for a namenode.

The *in_use.lock* file is a lock file that the namenode uses to lock the storage directory. This prevents another namenode instance from running at the same time with (and possibly corrupting) the same storage directory.

The other files in the namenode's storage directory are the *edits* and *fsimage* files, and *seen_txid*. To understand what these files are for, we need to dig into the workings of the namenode a little more.

The filesystem image and edit log

When a filesystem client performs a write operation (such as creating or moving a file), the transaction is first recorded in the edit log. The namenode also has an in-memory representation of the filesystem metadata, which it updates after the edit log has been modified. The in-memory metadata is used to serve read requests.

Conceptually the edit log is a single entity, but it is represented as a number of files on disk. Each file is called a *segment*, and has the prefix *edits* and a suffix that indicates the transaction IDs contained in it. Only one file is open for writes at any one time (*edits_inprogress_0000000000000000020* in the preceding example), and it is flushed and synced after every transaction before a success code is returned to the client. For namenodes that write to multiple directories, the write must be flushed and synced to every copy before returning successfully. This ensures that no transaction is lost due to machine failure.

Each *fsimage* file is a complete persistent checkpoint of the filesystem metadata. (The suffix indicates the last transaction in the image.) However, it is *not* updated for every filesystem write operation, because writing out the *fsimage* file, which can grow to be gigabytes in size, would be very slow. This does not compromise resilience because if the namenode fails, then the latest state of its metadata can be reconstructed by loading the latest *fsimage* from disk into memory, and then applying each of the transactions from the relevant point onward in the edit log. In fact, this is precisely what the namenode does when it starts up (see "Safe Mode" on page 322).

Each *fsimage* file contains a serialized form of all the directory and file inodes in the filesystem. Each inode is an internal representation of a file or directory's metadata and contains such information as the file's replication level, modification and access times, access permissions, block size, and the blocks the file is made up of. For directories, the modification time, permissions, and quota metadata are stored.

An *fsimage* file does *not* record the datanodes on which the blocks are stored. Instead, the namenode keeps this mapping in memory, which it constructs by asking the datanodes for their block lists when they join the cluster and periodically afterward to ensure the namenode's block mapping is up to date.

As described, the edit log would grow without bound (even if it was spread across several physical *edits* files). Though this state of affairs would have no impact on the system while the namenode is running, if the namenode were restarted, it would take a long time to apply each of the transactions in its (very long) edit log. During this time, the filesystem would be offline, which is generally undesirable.

The solution is to run the secondary namenode, whose purpose is to produce checkpoints of the primary's in-memory filesystem metadata.[1] The checkpointing process proceeds as follows (and is shown schematically in Figure 11-1 for the edit log and image files shown earlier):

1. The secondary asks the primary to roll its in-progress *edits* file, so new edits go to a new file. The primary also updates the *seen_txid* file in all its storage directories.

2. The secondary retrieves the latest *fsimage* and *edits* files from the primary (using HTTP GET).

3. The secondary loads *fsimage* into memory, applies each transaction from *edits*, then creates a new merged *fsimage* file.

4. The secondary sends the new *fsimage* back to the primary (using HTTP PUT), and the primary saves it as a temporary *.ckpt* file.

5. The primary renames the temporary *fsimage* file to make it available.

At the end of the process, the primary has an up-to-date *fsimage* file and a short in-progress *edits* file (it is not necessarily empty, as it may have received some edits while the checkpoint was being taken). It is possible for an administrator to run this process manually while the namenode is in safe mode, using the `hdfs dfsadmin -saveNamespace` command.

This procedure makes it clear why the secondary has similar memory requirements to the primary (since it loads the *fsimage* into memory), which is the reason that the secondary needs a dedicated machine on large clusters.

The schedule for checkpointing is controlled by two configuration parameters. The secondary namenode checkpoints every hour (`dfs.namenode.checkpoint.period` in seconds), or sooner if the edit log has reached one million transactions since the last checkpoint (`dfs.namenode.checkpoint.txns`), which it checks every minute (`dfs.namenode.checkpoint.check.period` in seconds).

---

1. It is actually possible to start a namenode with the `-checkpoint` option so that it runs the checkpointing process against another (primary) namenode. This is functionally equivalent to running a secondary namenode, but at the time of this writing offers no advantages over the secondary namenode (and indeed, the secondary namenode is the most tried and tested option). When running in a high-availability environment (see "HDFS High Availability" on page 48), the standby node performs checkpointing.

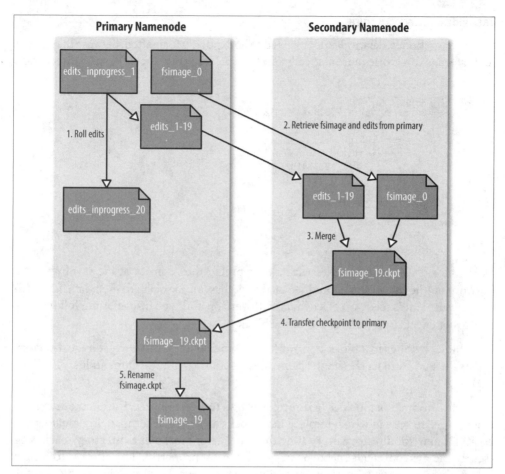

Figure 11-1. The checkpointing process

Secondary namenode directory structure

The layout of the secondary's checkpoint directory (dfs.namenode.checkpoint.dir) is identical to the namenode's. This is by design, since in the event of total namenode failure (when there are no recoverable backups, even from NFS), it allows recovery from a secondary namenode. This can be achieved either by copying the relevant storage directory to a new namenode or, if the secondary is taking over as the new primary namenode, by using the -importCheckpoint option when starting the namenode daemon. The -importCheckpoint option will load the namenode metadata from the latest checkpoint in the directory defined by the dfs.namenode.checkpoint.dir property, but only if there is no metadata in the dfs.namenode.name.dir directory, to ensure that there is no risk of overwriting precious metadata.

Datanode directory structure

Unlike namenodes, datanodes do not need to be explicitly formatted, because they create their storage directories automatically on startup. Here are the key files and directories:

```
${dfs.datanode.data.dir}/
├── current
│   ├── BP-526805057-127.0.0.1-1411980876842
│   │   └── current
│   │       ├── VERSION
│   │       ├── finalized
│   │       │   ├── blk_1073741825
│   │       │   ├── blk_1073741825_1001.meta
│   │       │   ├── blk_1073741826
│   │       │   └── blk_1073741826_1002.meta
│   │       └── rbw
│   └── VERSION
└── in_use.lock
```

HDFS blocks are stored in files with a *blk_* prefix; they consist of the raw bytes of a portion of the file being stored. Each block has an associated metadata file with a *.meta* suffix. It is made up of a header with version and type information, followed by a series of checksums for sections of the block.

Each block belongs to a block pool, and each block pool has its own storage directory that is formed from its ID (it's the same block pool ID from the namenode's *VERSION* file).

When the number of blocks in a directory grows to a certain size, the datanode creates a new subdirectory in which to place new blocks and their accompanying metadata. It creates a new subdirectory every time the number of blocks in a directory reaches 64 (set by the dfs.datanode.numblocks configuration property). The effect is to have a tree with high fan-out, so even for systems with a very large number of blocks, the directories will be only a few levels deep. By taking this measure, the datanode ensures that there is a manageable number of files per directory, which avoids the problems that most operating systems encounter when there are a large number of files (tens or hundreds of thousands) in a single directory.

If the configuration property dfs.datanode.data.dir specifies multiple directories on different drives, blocks are written in a round-robin fashion. Note that blocks are *not* replicated on each drive on a single datanode; instead, block replication is across distinct datanodes.

Safe Mode

When the namenode starts, the first thing it does is load its image file (*fsimage*) into memory and apply the edits from the edit log. Once it has reconstructed a consistent in-memory image of the filesystem metadata, it creates a new *fsimage* file (effectively doing the checkpoint itself, without recourse to the secondary namenode) and an empty edit log. During this process, the namenode is running in *safe mode*, which means that it offers only a read-only view of the filesystem to clients.

 Strictly speaking, in safe mode, only filesystem operations that access the filesystem metadata (such as producing a directory listing) are guaranteed to work. Reading a file will work only when the blocks are available on the current set of datanodes in the cluster, and file modifications (writes, deletes, or renames) will always fail.

Recall that the locations of blocks in the system are not persisted by the namenode; this information resides with the datanodes, in the form of a list of the blocks each one is storing. During normal operation of the system, the namenode has a map of block locations stored in memory. Safe mode is needed to give the datanodes time to check in to the namenode with their block lists, so the namenode can be informed of enough block locations to run the filesystem effectively. If the namenode didn't wait for enough datanodes to check in, it would start the process of replicating blocks to new datanodes, which would be unnecessary in most cases (because it only needed to wait for the extra datanodes to check in) and would put a great strain on the cluster's resources. Indeed, while in safe mode, the namenode does not issue any block-replication or deletion instructions to datanodes.

Safe mode is exited when the *minimal replication condition* is reached, plus an extension time of 30 seconds. The minimal replication condition is when 99.9% of the blocks in the whole filesystem meet their minimum replication level (which defaults to 1 and is set by dfs.namenode.replication.min; see Table 11-1).

When you are starting a newly formatted HDFS cluster, the namenode does not go into safe mode, since there are no blocks in the system.

Table 11-1. Safe mode properties

Property name	Type	Default value	Description
dfs.namenode.replication.min	int	1	The minimum number of replicas that have to be written for a write to be successful.
dfs.namenode.safemode.threshold-pct	float	0.999	The proportion of blocks in the system that must meet the minimum replication level defined by dfs.namenode.replication.min before the namenode will exit safe mode. Setting this value to 0 or less forces the namenode not to start in safe mode. Setting this value to more than 1 means the namenode never exits safe mode.

Property name	Type	Default value	Description
dfs.namenode.safemode.extension	int	30000	The time, in milliseconds, to extend safe mode after the minimum replication condition defined by dfs.namenode.safemode.threshold-pct has been satisfied. For small clusters (tens of nodes), it can be set to 0.

Entering and leaving safe mode

To see whether the namenode is in safe mode, you can use the dfsadmin command:

```
% hdfs dfsadmin -safemode get
Safe mode is ON
```

The front page of the HDFS web UI provides another indication of whether the namenode is in safe mode.

Sometimes you want to wait for the namenode to exit safe mode before carrying out a command, particularly in scripts. The wait option achieves this:

```
% hdfs dfsadmin -safemode wait
# command to read or write a file
```

An administrator has the ability to make the namenode enter or leave safe mode at any time. It is sometimes necessary to do this when carrying out maintenance on the cluster or after upgrading a cluster, to confirm that data is still readable. To enter safe mode, use the following command:

```
% hdfs dfsadmin -safemode enter
Safe mode is ON
```

You can use this command when the namenode is still in safe mode while starting up to ensure that it never leaves safe mode. Another way of making sure that the namenode stays in safe mode indefinitely is to set the property dfs.namenode.safemode .threshold-pct to a value over 1.

You can make the namenode leave safe mode by using the following:

```
% hdfs dfsadmin -safemode leave
Safe mode is OFF
```

Audit Logging

HDFS can log all filesystem access requests, a feature that some organizations require for auditing purposes. Audit logging is implemented using log4j logging at the INFO level. In the default configuration it is disabled, but it's easy to enable by adding the following line to *hadoop-env.sh*:

```
export HDFS_AUDIT_LOGGER="INFO,RFAAUDIT"
```

A log line is written to the audit log (*hdfs-audit.log*) for every HDFS event. Here's an example for a list status request on */user/tom*:

```
2014-09-30 21:35:30,484 INFO FSNamesystem.audit: allowed=true   ugi=tom
(auth:SIMPLE)   ip=/127.0.0.1   cmd=listStatus  src=/user/tom   dst=null
perm=null       proto=rpc
```

Tools

dfsadmin

The *dfsadmin* tool is a multipurpose tool for finding information about the state of HDFS, as well as for performing administration operations on HDFS. It is invoked as `hdfs dfsadmin` and requires superuser privileges.

Some of the available commands to *dfsadmin* are described in Table 11-2. Use the `-help` command to get more information.

Table 11-2. dfsadmin commands

Command	Description
-help	Shows help for a given command, or all commands if no command is specified.
-report	Shows filesystem statistics (similar to those shown in the web UI) and information on connected datanodes.
-metasave	Dumps information to a file in Hadoop's log directory about blocks that are being replicated or deleted, as well as a list of connected datanodes.
-safemode	Changes or queries the state of safe mode. See "Safe Mode" on page 322.
-saveNamespace	Saves the current in-memory filesystem image to a new *fsimage* file and resets the *edits* file. This operation may be performed only in safe mode.
-fetchImage	Retrieves the latest *fsimage* from the namenode and saves it in a local file.
-refreshNodes	Updates the set of datanodes that are permitted to connect to the namenode. See "Commissioning and Decommissioning Nodes" on page 334.
-upgradeProgress	Gets information on the progress of an HDFS upgrade or forces an upgrade to proceed. See "Upgrades" on page 337.
-finalizeUpgrade	Removes the previous version of the namenode and datanode storage directories. Used after an upgrade has been applied and the cluster is running successfully on the new version. See "Upgrades" on page 337.
-setQuota	Sets directory quotas. Directory quotas set a limit on the number of names (files or directories) in the directory tree. Directory quotas are useful for preventing users from creating large numbers of small files, a measure that helps preserve the namenode's memory (recall that accounting information for every file, directory, and block in the filesystem is stored in memory).
-clrQuota	Clears specified directory quotas.
-setSpaceQuota	Sets space quotas on directories. Space quotas set a limit on the size of files that may be stored in a directory tree. They are useful for giving users a limited amount of storage.
-clrSpaceQuota	Clears specified space quotas.

Command	Description
`-refreshServiceAcl`	Refreshes the namenode's service-level authorization policy file.
`-allowSnapshot`	Allows snapshot creation for the specified directory.
`-disallowSnapshot`	Disallows snapshot creation for the specified directory.

Filesystem check (fsck)

Hadoop provides an *fsck* utility for checking the health of files in HDFS. The tool looks for blocks that are missing from all datanodes, as well as under- or over-replicated blocks. Here is an example of checking the whole filesystem for a small cluster:

```
% hdfs fsck /
.....................Status: HEALTHY
 Total size: 511799225 B
 Total dirs: 10
 Total files: 22
 Total blocks (validated): 22 (avg. block size 23263601 B)
 Minimally replicated blocks: 22 (100.0 %)
 Over-replicated blocks: 0 (0.0 %)
 Under-replicated blocks: 0 (0.0 %)
 Mis-replicated blocks:  0 (0.0 %)
 Default replication factor: 3
 Average block replication: 3.0
 Corrupt blocks:  0
 Missing replicas:  0 (0.0 %)
 Number of data-nodes:  4
 Number of racks:  1


 The filesystem under path '/' is HEALTHY
```

fsck recursively walks the filesystem namespace, starting at the given path (here the filesystem root), and checks the files it finds. It prints a dot for every file it checks. To check a file, *fsck* retrieves the metadata for the file's blocks and looks for problems or inconsistencies. Note that *fsck* retrieves all of its information from the namenode; it does not communicate with any datanodes to actually retrieve any block data.

Most of the output from *fsck* is self-explanatory, but here are some of the conditions it looks for:

Over-replicated blocks

These are blocks that exceed their target replication for the file they belong to. Normally, over-replication is not a problem, and HDFS will automatically delete excess replicas.

Under-replicated blocks

These are blocks that do not meet their target replication for the file they belong to. HDFS will automatically create new replicas of under-replicated blocks until they meet the target replication. You can get information about the blocks being replicated (or waiting to be replicated) using `hdfs dfsadmin -metasave`.

Misreplicated blocks

These are blocks that do not satisfy the block replica placement policy (see "Replica Placement" on page 73). For example, for a replication level of three in a multirack cluster, if all three replicas of a block are on the same rack, then the block is misreplicated because the replicas should be spread across at least two racks for resilience. HDFS will automatically re-replicate misreplicated blocks so that they satisfy the rack placement policy.

Corrupt blocks

These are blocks whose replicas are all corrupt. Blocks with at least one noncorrupt replica are not reported as corrupt; the namenode will replicate the noncorrupt replica until the target replication is met.

Missing replicas

These are blocks with no replicas anywhere in the cluster.

Corrupt or missing blocks are the biggest cause for concern, as they mean data has been lost. By default, *fsck* leaves files with corrupt or missing blocks, but you can tell it to perform one of the following actions on them:

- *Move* the affected files to the */lost+found* directory in HDFS, using the `-move` option. Files are broken into chains of contiguous blocks to aid any salvaging efforts you may attempt.

- *Delete* the affected files, using the `-delete` option. Files cannot be recovered after being deleted.

Finding the blocks for a file. The *fsck* tool provides an easy way to find out which blocks are in any particular file. For example:

```
% hdfs fsck /user/tom/part-00007 -files -blocks -racks
/user/tom/part-00007 25582428 bytes, 1 block(s):  OK
0. blk_-3724870485760122836_1035 len=25582428 repl=3 [/default-rack/10.251.43.2:
50010,/default-rack/10.251.27.178:50010, /default-rack/10.251.123.163:50010]
```

This says that the file */user/tom/part-00007* is made up of one block and shows the datanodes where the block is located. The *fsck* options used are as follows:

- The `-files` option shows the line with the filename, size, number of blocks, and its health (whether there are any missing blocks).

- The `-blocks` option shows information about each block in the file, one line per block.

- The -racks option displays the rack location and the datanode addresses for each block.

Running hdfs fsck without any arguments displays full usage instructions.

Datanode block scanner

Every datanode runs a *block scanner*, which periodically verifies all the blocks stored on the datanode. This allows bad blocks to be detected and fixed before they are read by clients. The scanner maintains a list of blocks to verify and scans them one by one for checksum errors. It employs a throttling mechanism to preserve disk bandwidth on the datanode.

Blocks are verified every three weeks to guard against disk errors over time (this period is controlled by the dfs.datanode.scan.period.hours property, which defaults to 504 hours). Corrupt blocks are reported to the namenode to be fixed.

You can get a block verification report for a datanode by visiting the datanode's web interface at *http://datanode:50075/blockScannerReport*. Here's an example of a report, which should be self-explanatory:

```
Total Blocks                   :  21131
Verified in last hour          :     70
Verified in last day           :   1767
Verified in last week          :   7360
Verified in last four weeks    :  20057
Verified in SCAN_PERIOD        :  20057
Not yet verified               :   1074
Verified since restart         :  35912
Scans since restart            :   6541
Scan errors since restart      :      0
Transient scan errors          :      0
Current scan rate limit KBps   :   1024
Progress this period           :    109%
Time left in cur period        :  53.08%
```

If you specify the listblocks parameter, *http://datanode:50075/blockScannerReport?listblocks*, the report is preceded by a list of all the blocks on the datanode along with their latest verification status. Here is a snippet of the block list (lines are split to fit the page):

```
blk_6035596358209321442    : status : ok     type : none    scan time :
 0                    not yet verified
blk_3065580480714947643    : status : ok     type : remote scan time :
 1215755306400       2008-07-11 05:48:26,400
blk_8729669677359108508    : status : ok     type : local   scan time :
 1215755727345       2008-07-11 05:55:27,345
```

The first column is the block ID, followed by some key-value pairs. The status can be one of failed or ok, according to whether the last scan of the block detected a checksum error. The type of scan is `local` if it was performed by the background thread, `remote` if it was performed by a client or a remote datanode, or `none` if a scan of this block has yet to be made. The last piece of information is the scan time, which is displayed as the number of milliseconds since midnight on January 1, 1970, and also as a more readable value.

Balancer

Over time, the distribution of blocks across datanodes can become unbalanced. An unbalanced cluster can affect locality for MapReduce, and it puts a greater strain on the highly utilized datanodes, so it's best avoided.

The *balancer* program is a Hadoop daemon that redistributes blocks by moving them from overutilized datanodes to underutilized datanodes, while adhering to the block replica placement policy that makes data loss unlikely by placing block replicas on different racks (see "Replica Placement" on page 73). It moves blocks until the cluster is deemed to be balanced, which means that the utilization of every datanode (ratio of used space on the node to total capacity of the node) differs from the utilization of the cluster (ratio of used space on the cluster to total capacity of the cluster) by no more than a given threshold percentage. You can start the balancer with:

```
% start-balancer.sh
```

The `-threshold` argument specifies the threshold percentage that defines what it means for the cluster to be balanced. The flag is optional; if omitted, the threshold is 10%. At any one time, only one balancer may be running on the cluster.

The balancer runs until the cluster is balanced, it cannot move any more blocks, or it loses contact with the namenode. It produces a logfile in the standard log directory, where it writes a line for every iteration of redistribution that it carries out. Here is the output from a short run on a small cluster (slightly reformatted to fit the page):

```
Time Stamp          Iteration# Bytes Already Moved  ...Left To Move  ...Being Moved
Mar 18, 2009 5:23:42 PM  0               0 KB         219.21 MB        150.29 MB
Mar 18, 2009 5:27:14 PM  1          195.24 MB          22.45 MB        150.29 MB
The cluster is balanced. Exiting...
Balancing took 6.072933333333333 minutes
```

The balancer is designed to run in the background without unduly taxing the cluster or interfering with other clients using the cluster. It limits the bandwidth that it uses to copy a block from one node to another. The default is a modest 1 MB/s, but this can be changed by setting the `dfs.datanode.balance.bandwidthPerSec` property in *hdfs-site.xml*, specified in bytes.

Monitoring

Monitoring is an important part of system administration. In this section, we look at the monitoring facilities in Hadoop and how they can hook into external monitoring systems.

The purpose of monitoring is to detect when the cluster is not providing the expected level of service. The master daemons are the most important to monitor: the namenodes (primary and secondary) and the resource manager. Failure of datanodes and node managers is to be expected, particularly on larger clusters, so you should provide extra capacity so that the cluster can tolerate having a small percentage of dead nodes at any time.

In addition to the facilities described next, some administrators run test jobs on a periodic basis as a test of the cluster's health.

Logging

All Hadoop daemons produce logfiles that can be very useful for finding out what is happening in the system. "System logfiles" on page 295 explains how to configure these files.

Setting log levels

When debugging a problem, it is very convenient to be able to change the log level temporarily for a particular component in the system.

Hadoop daemons have a web page for changing the log level for any log4j log name, which can be found at */logLevel* in the daemon's web UI. By convention, log names in Hadoop correspond to the names of the classes doing the logging, although there are exceptions to this rule, so you should consult the source code to find log names.

It's also possible to enable logging for all packages that start with a given prefix. For example, to enable debug logging for all classes related to the resource manager, we would visit the its web UI at *http://resource-manager-host:8088/logLevel* and set the log name org.apache.hadoop.yarn.server.resourcemanager to level DEBUG.

The same thing can be achieved from the command line as follows:

```
% hadoop daemonlog -setlevel resource-manager-host:8088 \
    org.apache.hadoop.yarn.server.resourcemanager DEBUG
```

Log levels changed in this way are reset when the daemon restarts, which is usually what you want. However, to make a persistent change to a log level, you can simply change the *log4j.properties* file in the configuration directory. In this case, the line to add is:

```
log4j.logger.org.apache.hadoop.yarn.server.resourcemanager=DEBUG
```

Getting stack traces

Hadoop daemons expose a web page (*/stacks* in the web UI) that produces a thread dump for all running threads in the daemon's JVM. For example, you can get a thread dump for a resource manager from *http://resource-manager-host:8088/stacks*.

Metrics and JMX

The Hadoop daemons collect information about events and measurements that are collectively known as *metrics*. For example, datanodes collect the following metrics (and many more): the number of bytes written, the number of blocks replicated, and the number of read requests from clients (both local and remote).

> The metrics system in Hadoop 2 and later is sometimes referred to as *metrics2* to distinguish it from the older (now deprecated) metrics system in earlier versions of Hadoop.

Metrics belong to a *context*; "dfs," "mapred," "yarn," and "rpc" are examples of different contexts. Hadoop daemons usually collect metrics under several contexts. For example, datanodes collect metrics for the "dfs" and "rpc" contexts.

How Do Metrics Differ from Counters?

The main difference is their scope: metrics are collected by Hadoop daemons, whereas counters (see "Counters" on page 247) are collected for MapReduce tasks and aggregated for the whole job. They have different audiences, too: broadly speaking, metrics are for administrators, and counters are for MapReduce users.

The way they are collected and aggregated is also different. Counters are a MapReduce feature, and the MapReduce system ensures that counter values are propagated from the task JVMs where they are produced back to the application master, and finally back to the client running the MapReduce job. (Counters are propagated via RPC heartbeats; see "Progress and Status Updates" on page 190.) Both the task process and the application master perform aggregation.

The collection mechanism for metrics is decoupled from the component that receives the updates, and there are various pluggable outputs, including local files, Ganglia, and JMX. The daemon collecting the metrics performs aggregation on them before they are sent to the output.

All Hadoop metrics are published to JMX (Java Management Extensions), so you can use standard JMX tools like JConsole (which comes with the JDK) to view them. For remote monitoring, you must set the JMX system property `com.sun.management.jmxremote.port` (and others for security) to allow access. To do this for the namenode, say, you would set the following in *hadoop-env.sh*:

```
HADOOP_NAMENODE_OPTS="-Dcom.sun.management.jmxremote.port=8004"
```

You can also view JMX metrics (in JSON format) gathered by a particular Hadoop daemon by connecting to its */jmx* web page. This is handy for debugging. For example, you can view namenode metrics at *http://namenode-host:50070/jmx*.

Hadoop comes with a number of metrics sinks for publishing metrics to external systems, such as local files or the Ganglia monitoring system. Sinks are configured in the *hadoop-metrics2.properties* file; see that file for sample configuration settings.

Maintenance

Routine Administration Procedures

Metadata backups

If the namenode's persistent metadata is lost or damaged, the entire filesystem is rendered unusable, so it is critical that backups are made of these files. You should keep multiple copies of different ages (one hour, one day, one week, and one month, say) to protect against corruption, either in the copies themselves or in the live files running on the namenode.

A straightforward way to make backups is to use the `dfsadmin` command to download a copy of the namenode's most recent *fsimage*:

```
% hdfs dfsadmin -fetchImage fsimage.backup
```

You can write a script to run this command from an offsite location to store archive copies of the *fsimage*. The script should additionally test the integrity of the copy. This can be done by starting a local namenode daemon and verifying that it has successfully read the *fsimage* and *edits* files into memory (by scanning the namenode log for the appropriate success message, for example).[2]

Data backups

Although HDFS is designed to store data reliably, data loss can occur, just like in any storage system; thus, a backup strategy is essential. With the large data volumes that

---

2. Hadoop comes with an Offline Image Viewer and an Offline Edits Viewer, which can be used to check the integrity of the *fsimage* and *edits* files. Note that both viewers support older formats of these files, so you can use them to diagnose problems in these files generated by previous releases of Hadoop. Type `hdfs oiv` and `hdfs oev` to invoke these tools.

Hadoop can store, deciding what data to back up and where to store it is a challenge. The key here is to prioritize your data. The highest priority is the data that cannot be regenerated and that is critical to the business; however, data that is either straightforward to regenerate or essentially disposable because it is of limited business value is the lowest priority, and you may choose not to make backups of this low-priority data.

 Do not make the mistake of thinking that HDFS replication is a substitute for making backups. Bugs in HDFS can cause replicas to be lost, and so can hardware failures. Although Hadoop is expressly designed so that hardware failure is very unlikely to result in data loss, the possibility can never be completely ruled out, particularly when combined with software bugs or human error.

When it comes to backups, think of HDFS in the same way as you would RAID. Although the data will survive the loss of an individual RAID disk, it may not survive if the RAID controller fails or is buggy (perhaps overwriting some data), or the entire array is damaged.

It's common to have a policy for user directories in HDFS. For example, they may have space quotas and be backed up nightly. Whatever the policy, make sure your users know what it is, so they know what to expect.

The *distcp* tool is ideal for making backups to other HDFS clusters (preferably running on a different version of the software, to guard against loss due to bugs in HDFS) or other Hadoop filesystems (such as S3) because it can copy files in parallel. Alternatively, you can employ an entirely different storage system for backups, using one of the methods for exporting data from HDFS described in "Hadoop Filesystems" on page 53.

HDFS allows administrators and users to take *snapshots* of the filesystem. A snapshot is a read-only copy of a filesystem subtree at a given point in time. Snapshots are very efficient since they do not copy data; they simply record each file's metadata and block list, which is sufficient to reconstruct the filesystem contents at the time the snapshot was taken.

Snapshots are not a replacement for data backups, but they are a useful tool for point-in-time data recovery for files that were mistakenly deleted by users. You might have a policy of taking periodic snapshots and keeping them for a specific period of time according to age. For example, you might keep hourly snapshots for the previous day and daily snapshots for the previous month.

Filesystem check (fsck)

It is advisable to run HDFS's *fsck* tool regularly (i.e., daily) on the whole filesystem to proactively look for missing or corrupt blocks. See "Filesystem check (fsck)" on page 326.

Filesystem balancer

Run the balancer tool (see "Balancer" on page 329) regularly to keep the filesystem datanodes evenly balanced.

Commissioning and Decommissioning Nodes

As an administrator of a Hadoop cluster, you will need to add or remove nodes from time to time. For example, to grow the storage available to a cluster, you commission new nodes. Conversely, sometimes you may wish to shrink a cluster, and to do so, you decommission nodes. Sometimes it is necessary to decommission a node if it is misbehaving, perhaps because it is failing more often than it should or its performance is noticeably slow.

Nodes normally run both a datanode and a node manager, and both are typically commissioned or decommissioned in tandem.

Commissioning new nodes

Although commissioning a new node can be as simple as configuring the *hdfs-site.xml* file to point to the namenode, configuring the *yarn-site.xml* file to point to the resource manager, and starting the datanode and resource manager daemons, it is generally best to have a list of authorized nodes.

It is a potential security risk to allow any machine to connect to the namenode and act as a datanode, because the machine may gain access to data that it is not authorized to see. Furthermore, because such a machine is not a real datanode, it is not under your control and may stop at any time, potentially causing data loss. (Imagine what would happen if a number of such nodes were connected and a block of data was present only on the "alien" nodes.) This scenario is a risk even inside a firewall, due to the possibility of misconfiguration, so datanodes (and node managers) should be explicitly managed on all production clusters.

Datanodes that are permitted to connect to the namenode are specified in a file whose name is specified by the `dfs.hosts` property. The file resides on the namenode's local filesystem, and it contains a line for each datanode, specified by network address (as reported by the datanode; you can see what this is by looking at the namenode's web UI). If you need to specify multiple network addresses for a datanode, put them on one line, separated by whitespace.

Similarly, node managers that may connect to the resource manager are specified in a file whose name is specified by the `yarn.resourcemanager.nodes.include-path` property. In most cases, there is one shared file, referred to as the *include file*, that both `dfs.hosts` and `yarn.resourcemanager.nodes.include-path` refer to, since nodes in the cluster run both datanode and node manager daemons.

 The file (or files) specified by the `dfs.hosts` and `yarn.resourcemanager.nodes.include-path` properties is different from the *slaves* file. The former is used by the namenode and resource manager to determine which worker nodes may connect. The *slaves* file is used by the Hadoop control scripts to perform cluster-wide operations, such as cluster restarts. It is never used by the Hadoop daemons.

To add new nodes to the cluster:

1. Add the network addresses of the new nodes to the include file.
2. Update the namenode with the new set of permitted datanodes using this command:

   ```
   % hdfs dfsadmin -refreshNodes
   ```

3. Update the resource manager with the new set of permitted node managers using:

   ```
   % yarn rmadmin -refreshNodes
   ```

4. Update the *slaves* file with the new nodes, so that they are included in future operations performed by the Hadoop control scripts.
5. Start the new datanodes and node managers.
6. Check that the new datanodes and node managers appear in the web UI.

HDFS will not move blocks from old datanodes to new datanodes to balance the cluster. To do this, you should run the balancer described in "Balancer" on page 329.

Decommissioning old nodes

Although HDFS is designed to tolerate datanode failures, this does not mean you can just terminate datanodes en masse with no ill effect. With a replication level of three, for example, the chances are very high that you will lose data by simultaneously shutting down three datanodes if they are on different racks. The way to decommission datanodes is to inform the namenode of the nodes that you wish to take out of circulation, so that it can replicate the blocks to other datanodes before the datanodes are shut down.

With node managers, Hadoop is more forgiving. If you shut down a node manager that is running MapReduce tasks, the application master will notice the failure and reschedule the tasks on other nodes.

The decommissioning process is controlled by an *exclude file*, which is set for HDFS iby the `dfs.hosts.exclude` property and for YARN by the `yarn.resourcemanager.nodes.exclude-path` property. It is often the case that these properties refer to the same file. The exclude file lists the nodes that are not permitted to connect to the cluster.

The rules for whether a node manager may connect to the resource manager are simple: a node manager may connect only if it appears in the include file and does *not* appear in the exclude file. An unspecified or empty include file is taken to mean that all nodes are in the include file.

For HDFS, the rules are slightly different. If a datanode appears in both the include and the exclude file, then it may connect, but only to be decommissioned. Table 11-3 summarizes the different combinations for datanodes. As for node managers, an unspecified or empty include file means all nodes are included.

Table 11-3. HDFS include and exclude file precedence

Node appears in include file	Node appears in exclude file	Interpretation
No	No	Node may not connect.
No	Yes	Node may not connect.
Yes	No	Node may connect.
Yes	Yes	Node may connect and will be decommissioned.

To remove nodes from the cluster:

1. Add the network addresses of the nodes to be decommissioned to the exclude file. Do not update the include file at this point.

2. Update the namenode with the new set of permitted datanodes, using this command:

   ```
   % hdfs dfsadmin -refreshNodes
   ```

3. Update the resource manager with the new set of permitted node managers using:

   ```
   % yarn rmadmin -refreshNodes
   ```

4. Go to the web UI and check whether the admin state has changed to "Decommission In Progress" for the datanodes being decommissioned. They will start copying their blocks to other datanodes in the cluster.

5. When all the datanodes report their state as "Decommissioned," all the blocks have been replicated. Shut down the decommissioned nodes.

6. Remove the nodes from the include file, and run:

   ```
   % hdfs dfsadmin -refreshNodes
   % yarn rmadmin -refreshNodes
   ```

7. Remove the nodes from the *slaves* file.

Upgrades

Upgrading a Hadoop cluster requires careful planning. The most important consideration is the HDFS upgrade. If the layout version of the filesystem has changed, then the upgrade will automatically migrate the filesystem data and metadata to a format that is compatible with the new version. As with any procedure that involves data migration, there is a risk of data loss, so you should be sure that both your data and the metadata are backed up (see "Routine Administration Procedures" on page 332).

Part of the planning process should include a trial run on a small test cluster with a copy of data that you can afford to lose. A trial run will allow you to familiarize yourself with the process, customize it to your particular cluster configuration and toolset, and iron out any snags before running the upgrade procedure on a production cluster. A test cluster also has the benefit of being available to test client upgrades on. You can read about general compatibility concerns for clients in the following sidebar.

Compatibility

When moving from one release to another, you need to think about the upgrade steps that are needed. There are several aspects to consider: API compatibility, data compatibility, and wire compatibility.

API compatibility concerns the contract between user code and the published Hadoop APIs, such as the Java MapReduce APIs. Major releases (e.g., from 1.x.y to 2.0.0) are allowed to break API compatibility, so user programs may need to be modified and recompiled. Minor releases (e.g., from 1.0.x to 1.1.0) and point releases (e.g., from 1.0.1 to 1.0.2) should not break compatibility.

 Hadoop uses a classification scheme for API elements to denote their stability. The preceding rules for API compatibility cover those elements that are marked `InterfaceStability.Stable`. Some elements of the public Hadoop APIs, however, are marked with the `InterfaceStability.Evolving` or `InterfaceStabili ty.Unstable` annotations (all these annotations are in the `org.apache.hadoop.classification` package), which mean they are allowed to break compatibility on minor and point releases, respectively.

Data compatibility concerns persistent data and metadata formats, such as the format in which the HDFS namenode stores its persistent data. The formats can change across minor or major releases, but the change is transparent to users because the upgrade will

---

automatically migrate the data. There may be some restrictions about upgrade paths, and these are covered in the release notes. For example, it may be necessary to upgrade via an intermediate release rather than upgrading directly to the later final release in one step.

Wire compatibility concerns the interoperability between clients and servers via wire protocols such as RPC and HTTP. The rule for wire compatibility is that the client must have the same major release number as the server, but may differ in its minor or point release number (e.g., client version 2.0.2 will work with server 2.0.1 or 2.1.0, but not necessarily with server 3.0.0).

 This rule for wire compatibility differs from earlier versions of Hadoop, where internal clients (like datanodes) had to be upgraded in lockstep with servers. The fact that internal client and server versions can be mixed allows Hadoop 2 to support rolling upgrades.

The full set of compatibility rules that Hadoop adheres to are documented at the Apache Software Foundation's website (*http://bit.ly/hadoop_compatibility*).

Upgrading a cluster when the filesystem layout has not changed is fairly straightforward: install the new version of Hadoop on the cluster (and on clients at the same time), shut down the old daemons, update the configuration files, and then start up the new daemons and switch clients to use the new libraries. This process is reversible, so rolling back an upgrade is also straightforward.

After every successful upgrade, you should perform a couple of final cleanup steps:

1. Remove the old installation and configuration files from the cluster.

2. Fix any deprecation warnings in your code and configuration.

Upgrades are where Hadoop cluster management tools like Cloudera Manager and Apache Ambari come into their own. They simplify the upgrade process and also make it easy to do rolling upgrades, where nodes are upgraded in batches (or one at a time for master nodes), so that clients don't experience service interruptions.

HDFS data and metadata upgrades

If you use the procedure just described to upgrade to a new version of HDFS and it expects a different layout version, then the namenode will refuse to run. A message like the following will appear in its log:

```
File system image contains an old layout version -16.
An upgrade to version -18 is required.
Please restart NameNode with -upgrade option.
```

The most reliable way of finding out whether you need to upgrade the filesystem is by performing a trial on a test cluster.

An upgrade of HDFS makes a copy of the previous version's metadata and data. Doing an upgrade does not double the storage requirements of the cluster, as the datanodes use hard links to keep two references (for the current and previous version) to the same block of data. This design makes it straightforward to roll back to the previous version of the filesystem, if you need to. You should understand that any changes made to the data on the upgraded system will be lost after the rollback completes, however.

You can keep only the previous version of the filesystem, which means you can't roll back several versions. Therefore, to carry out another upgrade to HDFS data and metadata, you will need to delete the previous version, a process called *finalizing the upgrade*. Once an upgrade is finalized, there is no procedure for rolling back to a previous version.

In general, you can skip releases when upgrading, but in some cases, you may have to go through intermediate releases. The release notes make it clear when this is required.

You should only attempt to upgrade a healthy filesystem. Before running the upgrade, do a full *fsck* (see "Filesystem check (fsck)" on page 326). As an extra precaution, you can keep a copy of the *fsck* output that lists all the files and blocks in the system, so you can compare it with the output of running *fsck* after the upgrade.

It's also worth clearing out temporary files before doing the upgrade—both local temporary files and those in the MapReduce system directory on HDFS.

With these preliminaries out of the way, here is the high-level procedure for upgrading a cluster when the filesystem layout needs to be migrated:

1. Ensure that any previous upgrade is finalized before proceeding with another upgrade.

2. Shut down the YARN and MapReduce daemons.

3. Shut down HDFS, and back up the namenode directories.

4. Install the new version of Hadoop on the cluster and on clients.

5. Start HDFS with the `-upgrade` option.

6. Wait until the upgrade is complete.

7. Perform some sanity checks on HDFS.

8. Start the YARN and MapReduce daemons.

9. Roll back or finalize the upgrade (optional).

While running the upgrade procedure, it is a good idea to remove the Hadoop scripts from your PATH environment variable. This forces you to be explicit about which version of the scripts you are running. It can be convenient to define two environment variables for the new installation directories; in the following instructions, we have defined OLD_HADOOP_HOME and NEW_HADOOP_HOME.

Start the upgrade. To perform the upgrade, run the following command (this is step 5 in the high-level upgrade procedure):

```
% $NEW_HADOOP_HOME/bin/start-dfs.sh -upgrade
```

This causes the namenode to upgrade its metadata, placing the previous version in a new directory called *previous* under dfs.namenode.name.dir. Similarly, datanodes upgrade their storage directories, preserving the old copy in a directory called *previous*.

Wait until the upgrade is complete. The upgrade process is not instantaneous, but you can check the progress of an upgrade using *dfsadmin* (step 6; upgrade events also appear in the daemons' logfiles):

```
% $NEW_HADOOP_HOME/bin/hdfs dfsadmin -upgradeProgress status
Upgrade for version -18 has been completed.
Upgrade is not finalized.
```

Check the upgrade. This shows that the upgrade is complete. At this stage, you should run some sanity checks (step 7) on the filesystem (e.g., check files and blocks using *fsck*, test basic file operations). You might choose to put HDFS into safe mode while you are running some of these checks (the ones that are read-only) to prevent others from making changes; see "Safe Mode" on page 322.

Roll back the upgrade (optional). If you find that the new version is not working correctly, you may choose to roll back to the previous version (step 9). This is possible only if you have not finalized the upgrade.

 A rollback reverts the filesystem state to before the upgrade was performed, so any changes made in the meantime will be lost. In other words, it rolls back to the previous state of the filesystem, rather than downgrading the current state of the filesystem to a former version.

First, shut down the new daemons:

```
% $NEW_HADOOP_HOME/bin/stop-dfs.sh
```

Then start up the old version of HDFS with the -rollback option:

```
% $OLD_HADOOP_HOME/bin/start-dfs.sh -rollback
```

This command gets the namenode and datanodes to replace their current storage directories with their previous copies. The filesystem will be returned to its previous state.

Finalize the upgrade (optional). When you are happy with the new version of HDFS, you can finalize the upgrade (step 9) to remove the previous storage directories.

 After an upgrade has been finalized, there is no way to roll back to the previous version.

This step is required before performing another upgrade:

```
% $NEW_HADOOP_HOME/bin/hdfs dfsadmin -finalizeUpgrade
% $NEW_HADOOP_HOME/bin/hdfs dfsadmin -upgradeProgress status
There are no upgrades in progress.
```

HDFS is now fully upgraded to the new version.

## PART IV

Related Projects

Avro

Apache Avro (*http://avro.apache.org/*)[1] is a language-neutral data serialization system. The project was created by Doug Cutting (the creator of Hadoop) to address the major downside of Hadoop Writables: lack of language portability. Having a data format that can be processed by many languages (currently C, C++, C#, Java, JavaScript, Perl, PHP, Python, and Ruby) makes it easier to share datasets with a wider audience than one tied to a single language. It is also more future-proof, allowing data to potentially outlive the language used to read and write it.

But why a new data serialization system? Avro has a set of features that, taken together, differentiate it from other systems such as Apache Thrift or Google's Protocol Buffers.[2] Like in these systems and others, Avro data is described using a language-independent *schema*. However, unlike in some other systems, code generation is optional in Avro, which means you can read and write data that conforms to a given schema even if your code has not seen that particular schema before. To achieve this, Avro assumes that the schema is always present—at both read and write time—which makes for a very compact encoding, since encoded values do not need to be tagged with a field identifier.

Avro schemas are usually written in JSON, and data is usually encoded using a binary format, but there are other options, too. There is a higher-level language called *Avro IDL* for writing schemas in a C-like language that is more familiar to developers. There is also a JSON-based data encoder, which, being human readable, is useful for prototyping and debugging Avro data.

---

1. Named after the British aircraft manufacturer from the 20th century.

2. Avro also performs favorably compared to other serialization libraries, as the benchmarks (*http://code.google.com/p/thrift-protobuf-compare/*) demonstrate.

The *Avro specification (http://avro.apache.org/docs/current/spec.html)* precisely defines the binary format that all implementations must support. It also specifies many of the other features of Avro that implementations should support. One area that the specification does not rule on, however, is APIs: implementations have complete latitude in the APIs they expose for working with Avro data, since each one is necessarily language specific. The fact that there is only one binary format is significant, because it means the barrier for implementing a new language binding is lower and avoids the problem of a combinatorial explosion of languages and formats, which would harm interoperability.

Avro has rich *schema resolution* capabilities. Within certain carefully defined constraints, the schema used to read data need not be identical to the schema that was used to write the data. This is the mechanism by which Avro supports schema evolution. For example, a new, optional field may be added to a record by declaring it in the schema used to read the old data. New and old clients alike will be able to read the old data, while new clients can write new data that uses the new field. Conversely, if an old client sees newly encoded data, it will gracefully ignore the new field and carry on processing as it would have done with old data.

Avro specifies an *object container format* for sequences of objects, similar to Hadoop's sequence file. An *Avro datafile* has a metadata section where the schema is stored, which makes the file self-describing. Avro datafiles support compression and are splittable, which is crucial for a MapReduce data input format. In fact, support goes beyond MapReduce: all of the data processing frameworks in this book (Pig, Hive, Crunch, Spark) can read and write Avro datafiles.

Avro can be used for RPC, too, although this isn't covered here. More information is in the specification.

Avro Data Types and Schemas

Avro defines a small number of primitive data types, which can be used to build application-specific data structures by writing schemas. For interoperability, implementations must support all Avro types.

Avro's primitive types are listed in Table 12-1. Each primitive type may also be specified using a more verbose form by using the `type` attribute, such as:

```
{ "type": "null" }
```

Table 12-1. Avro primitive types

Type	Description	Schema
null	The absence of a value	"null"
boolean	A binary value	"boolean"
int	32-bit signed integer	"int"

Type	Description	Schema
long	64-bit signed integer	`"long"`
float	Single-precision (32-bit) IEEE 754 floating-point number	`"float"`
double	Double-precision (64-bit) IEEE 754 floating-point number	`"double"`
bytes	Sequence of 8-bit unsigned bytes	`"bytes"`
string	Sequence of Unicode characters	`"string"`

Avro also defines the complex types listed in Table 12-2, along with a representative example of a schema of each type.

Table 12-2. Avro complex types

Type	Description	Schema example

array	An ordered collection of objects. All objects in a particular array must have the same schema.	<pre>{
		  "type": "array",
		  "items": "long"
		}</pre>

map	An unordered collection of key-value pairs. Keys must be strings and values may be any type, although within a particular map, all values must have the same schema.	<pre>{
		  "type": "map",
		  "values": "string"
		}</pre>

record	A collection of named fields of any type.	<pre>{
		  "type": "record",
		  "name": "WeatherRecord",
		  "doc": "A weather reading.",
		  "fields": [
		    {"name": "year", "type": "int"},
		    {"name": "temperature", "type": "int"},
		    {"name": "stationId", "type": "string"}
		  ]
		}</pre>

enum	A set of named values.	<pre>{
		  "type": "enum",
		  "name": "Cutlery",
		  "doc": "An eating utensil.",
		  "symbols": ["KNIFE", "FORK", "SPOON"]
		}</pre>

fixed	A fixed number of 8-bit unsigned bytes.	<pre>{
		  "type": "fixed",
		  "name": "Md5Hash",
		  "size": 16
		}</pre>

Type	Description	Schema example

union	A union of schemas. A union is represented by a JSON array, where each element in the array is a schema. Data represented by a union must match one of the schemas in the union.	```
		[
		  "null",
		  "string",
		  {"type": "map", "values": "string"}
		]
		``

Each Avro language API has a representation for each Avro type that is specific to the language. For example, Avro's double type is represented in C, C++, and Java by a double, in Python by a float, and in Ruby by a Float.

What's more, there may be more than one representation, or mapping, for a language. All languages support a dynamic mapping, which can be used even when the schema is not known ahead of runtime. Java calls this the *Generic* mapping.

In addition, the Java and C++ implementations can generate code to represent the data for an Avro schema. Code generation, which is called the *Specific* mapping in Java, is an optimization that is useful when you have a copy of the schema before you read or write data. Generated classes also provide a more domain-oriented API for user code than Generic ones.

Java has a third mapping, the *Reflect* mapping, which maps Avro types onto preexisting Java types using reflection. It is slower than the Generic and Specific mappings but can be a convenient way of defining a type, since Avro can infer a schema automatically.

Java's type mappings are shown in Table 12-3. As the table shows, the Specific mapping is the same as the Generic one unless otherwise noted (and the Reflect one is the same as the Specific one unless noted). The Specific mapping differs from the Generic one only for record, enum, and fixed, all of which have generated classes (the names of which are controlled by the name and optional namespace attributes).

Table 12-3. Avro Java type mappings

Avro type	Generic Java mapping	Specific Java mapping	Reflect Java mapping
null	null type		
boolean	boolean		
int	int		byte, short, int, or char
long	long		
float	float		
double	double		
bytes	java.nio.ByteBuffer		Array of bytes
string	org.apache.avro.util.Utf8 or java.lang.String		java.lang.String
array	org.apache.avro.generic.GenericArray		Array or java.util.Collection
map	java.util.Map		

Avro type	Generic Java mapping	Specific Java mapping	Reflect Java mapping
record	`org.apache.avro.gener ic.GenericRecord`	Generated class implementing `org.apache.avro.spe cific.SpecificRe cord`	Arbitrary user class with a zero-argument constructor; all inherited nontransient instance fields are used
enum	`java.lang.String`	Generated Java enum	Arbitrary Java enum
fixed	`org.apache.avro. generic.GenericFixed`	Generated class implementing `org.apache.avro.spe cific.SpecificFixed`	`org.apache.avro.generic.Ge nericFixed`
union	`java.lang.Object`		

 Avro `string` can be represented by either Java `String` or the Avro `Utf8` Java type. The reason to use `Utf8` is efficiency: because it is mutable, a single `Utf8` instance may be reused for reading or writing a series of values. Also, Java `String` decodes UTF-8 at object construction time, whereas Avro `Utf8` does it lazily, which can increase performance in some cases.

`Utf8` implements Java's `java.lang.CharSequence` interface, which allows some interoperability with Java libraries. In other cases, it may be necessary to convert `Utf8` instances to `String` objects by calling its `toString()` method.

`Utf8` is the default for Generic and Specific, but it's possible to use `String` for a particular mapping. There are a couple of ways to achieve this. The first is to set the `avro.java.string` property in the schema to `String`:

```
{ "type": "string", "avro.java.string": "String" }
```

Alternatively, for the Specific mapping, you can generate classes that have `String`-based getters and setters. When using the Avro Maven plug-in, this is done by setting the configuration property `string Type` to `String` ("The Specific API" on page 351 has a demonstration of this).

Finally, note that the Java Reflect mapping always uses `String` objects, since it is designed for Java compatibility, not performance.

In-Memory Serialization and Deserialization

Avro provides APIs for serialization and deserialization that are useful when you want to integrate Avro with an existing system, such as a messaging system where the framing format is already defined. In other cases, consider using Avro's datafile format.

Let's write a Java program to read and write Avro data from and to streams. We'll start with a simple Avro schema for representing a pair of strings as a record:

```
{
  "type": "record",
  "name": "StringPair",
  "doc": "A pair of strings.",
  "fields": [
    {"name": "left", "type": "string"},
    {"name": "right", "type": "string"}
  ]
}
```

If this schema is saved in a file on the classpath called *StringPair.avsc* (*.avsc* is the conventional extension for an Avro schema), we can load it using the following two lines of code:

```
Schema.Parser parser = new Schema.Parser();
Schema schema = parser.parse(
    getClass().getResourceAsStream("StringPair.avsc"));
```

We can create an instance of an Avro record using the Generic API as follows:

```
GenericRecord datum = new GenericData.Record(schema);
datum.put("left", "L");
datum.put("right", "R");
```

Next, we serialize the record to an output stream:

```
ByteArrayOutputStream out = new ByteArrayOutputStream();
DatumWriter<GenericRecord> writer =
    new GenericDatumWriter<GenericRecord>(schema);
Encoder encoder = EncoderFactory.get().binaryEncoder(out, null);
writer.write(datum, encoder);
encoder.flush();
out.close();
```

There are two important objects here: the DatumWriter and the Encoder. A DatumWriter translates data objects into the types understood by an Encoder, which the latter writes to the output stream. Here we are using a GenericDatumWriter, which passes the fields of GenericRecord to the Encoder. We pass a null to the encoder factory because we are not reusing a previously constructed encoder here.

In this example, only one object is written to the stream, but we could call write() with more objects before closing the stream if we wanted to.

The GenericDatumWriter needs to be passed the schema because it follows the schema to determine which values from the data objects to write out. After we have called the writer's write() method, we flush the encoder, then close the output stream.

We can reverse the process and read the object back from the byte buffer:

```
DatumReader<GenericRecord> reader =
    new GenericDatumReader<GenericRecord>(schema);
Decoder decoder = DecoderFactory.get().binaryDecoder(out.toByteArray(),
    null);
GenericRecord result = reader.read(null, decoder);
assertThat(result.get("left").toString(), is("L"));
assertThat(result.get("right").toString(), is("R"));
```

We pass null to the calls to binaryDecoder() and read() because we are not reusing objects here (the decoder or the record, respectively).

The objects returned by result.get("left") and result.get("left") are of type Utf8, so we convert them into Java String objects by calling their toString() methods.

The Specific API

Let's look now at the equivalent code using the Specific API. We can generate the StringPair class from the schema file by using Avro's Maven plug-in for compiling schemas. The following is the relevant part of the Maven Project Object Model (POM):

```
<project>
  ...
  <build>
    <plugins>
      <plugin>
        <groupId>org.apache.avro</groupId>
        <artifactId>avro-maven-plugin</artifactId>
        <version>${avro.version}</version>
        <executions>
          <execution>
            <id>schemas</id>
            <phase>generate-sources</phase>
            <goals>
              <goal>schema</goal>
            </goals>
            <configuration>
              <includes>
                <include>StringPair.avsc</include>
              </includes>
              <stringType>String</stringType>
              <sourceDirectory>src/main/resources</sourceDirectory>
              <outputDirectory>${project.build.directory}/generated-sources/java
              </outputDirectory>
            </configuration>
          </execution>
        </executions>
      </plugin>
    </plugins>
  </build>
  ...
</project>
```

As an alternative to Maven, you can use Avro's Ant task, `org.apache.avro.specific` `.SchemaTask`, or the Avro command-line tools[3] to generate Java code for a schema.

In the code for serializing and deserializing, instead of a `GenericRecord` we construct a `StringPair` instance, which we write to the stream using a `SpecificDatumWriter` and read back using a `SpecificDatumReader`:

```
StringPair datum = new StringPair();
datum.setLeft("L");
datum.setRight("R");

ByteArrayOutputStream out = new ByteArrayOutputStream();
DatumWriter<StringPair> writer =
    new SpecificDatumWriter<StringPair>(StringPair.class);
Encoder encoder = EncoderFactory.get().binaryEncoder(out, null);
writer.write(datum, encoder);
encoder.flush();
out.close();

DatumReader<StringPair> reader =
    new SpecificDatumReader<StringPair>(StringPair.class);
Decoder decoder = DecoderFactory.get().binaryDecoder(out.toByteArray(),
    null);
StringPair result = reader.read(null, decoder);
assertThat(result.getLeft(), is("L"));
assertThat(result.getRight(), is("R"));
```

Avro Datafiles

Avro's object container file format is for storing sequences of Avro objects. It is very similar in design to Hadoop's sequence file format, described in "SequenceFile" on page 127. The main difference is that Avro datafiles are designed to be portable across languages, so, for example, you can write a file in Python and read it in C (we will do exactly this in the next section).

A datafile has a header containing metadata, including the Avro schema and a *sync marker*, followed by a series of (optionally compressed) blocks containing the serialized Avro objects. Blocks are separated by a sync marker that is unique to the file (the marker for a particular file is found in the header) and that permits rapid resynchronization with a block boundary after seeking to an arbitrary point in the file, such as an HDFS block boundary. Thus, Avro datafiles are splittable, which makes them amenable to efficient MapReduce processing.

---

3. Avro can be downloaded in both source and binary forms (*http://avro.apache.org/releases.html*). Get usage instructions for the Avro tools by typing `java -jar avro-tools-*.jar`.

Writing Avro objects to a datafile is similar to writing to a stream. We use a `DatumWriter` as before, but instead of using an `Encoder`, we create a `DataFileWriter` instance with the `DatumWriter`. Then we can create a new datafile (which, by convention, has a *.avro* extension) and append objects to it:

```
File file = new File("data.avro");
DatumWriter<GenericRecord> writer =
    new GenericDatumWriter<GenericRecord>(schema);
DataFileWriter<GenericRecord> dataFileWriter =
    new DataFileWriter<GenericRecord>(writer);
dataFileWriter.create(schema, file);
dataFileWriter.append(datum);
dataFileWriter.close();
```

The objects that we write to the datafile must conform to the file's schema; otherwise, an exception will be thrown when we call `append()`.

This example demonstrates writing to a local file (`java.io.File` in the previous snippet), but we can write to any `java.io.OutputStream` by using the overloaded `create()` method on `DataFileWriter`. To write a file to HDFS, for example, we get an `Output Stream` by calling `create()` on `FileSystem` (see "Writing Data" on page 61).

Reading back objects from a datafile is similar to the earlier case of reading objects from an in-memory stream, with one important difference: we don't have to specify a schema, since it is read from the file metadata. Indeed, we can get the schema from the `DataFi leReader` instance, using `getSchema()`, and verify that it is the same as the one we used to write the original object:

```
DatumReader<GenericRecord> reader = new GenericDatumReader<GenericRecord>();
DataFileReader<GenericRecord> dataFileReader =
    new DataFileReader<GenericRecord>(file, reader);
assertThat("Schema is the same", schema, is(dataFileReader.getSchema()));
```

`DataFileReader` is a regular Java iterator, so we can iterate through its data objects by calling its `hasNext()` and `next()` methods. The following snippet checks that there is only one record and that it has the expected field values:

```
assertThat(dataFileReader.hasNext(), is(true));
GenericRecord result = dataFileReader.next();
assertThat(result.get("left").toString(), is("L"));
assertThat(result.get("right").toString(), is("R"));
assertThat(dataFileReader.hasNext(), is(false));
```

Rather than using the usual `next()` method, however, it is preferable to use the overloaded form that takes an instance of the object to be returned (in this case, `Gener icRecord`), since it will reuse the object and save allocation and garbage collection costs for files containing many objects. The following is idiomatic:

```
GenericRecord record = null;
while (dataFileReader.hasNext()) {
  record = dataFileReader.next(record);
```

```
    // process record
}
```

If object reuse is not important, you can use this shorter form:

```
for (GenericRecord record : dataFileReader) {
    // process record
}
```

For the general case of reading a file on a Hadoop filesystem, use Avro's `FsInput` to specify the input file using a Hadoop `Path` object. `DataFileReader` actually offers random access to Avro datafiles (via its `seek()` and `sync()` methods); however, in many cases, sequential streaming access is sufficient, for which `DataFileStream` should be used. `DataFileStream` can read from any Java `InputStream`.

Interoperability

To demonstrate Avro's language interoperability, let's write a datafile using one language (Python) and read it back with another (Java).

Python API

The program in Example 12-1 reads comma-separated strings from standard input and writes them as `StringPair` records to an Avro datafile. Like in the Java code for writing a datafile, we create a `DatumWriter` and a `DataFileWriter` object. Notice that we have embedded the Avro schema in the code, although we could equally well have read it from a file.

Python represents Avro records as dictionaries; each line that is read from standard in is turned into a `dict` object and appended to the `DataFileWriter`.

Example 12-1. A Python program for writing Avro record pairs to a datafile

```python
import os
import string
import sys

from avro import schema
from avro import io
from avro import datafile

if __name__ == '__main__':
    if len(sys.argv) != 2:
        sys.exit('Usage: %s <data_file>' % sys.argv[0])
    avro_file = sys.argv[1]
    writer = open(avro_file, 'wb')
    datum_writer = io.DatumWriter()
    schema_object = schema.parse("\
{ "type": "record",
  "name": "StringPair",
```

```
    "doc": "A pair of strings.",
    "fields": [
      {"name": "left", "type": "string"},
      {"name": "right", "type": "string"}
    ]
}")
  dfw = datafile.DataFileWriter(writer, datum_writer, schema_object)
  for line in sys.stdin.readlines():
    (left, right) = string.split(line.strip(), ',')
    dfw.append({'left':left, 'right':right});
  dfw.close()
```

Before we can run the program, we need to install Avro for Python:

```
% easy_install avro
```

To run the program, we specify the name of the file to write output to (*pairs.avro*) and send input pairs over standard in, marking the end of file by typing Ctrl-D:

```
% python ch12-avro/src/main/py/write_pairs.py pairs.avro
a,1
c,2
b,3
b,2
^D
```

Avro Tools

Next, we'll use the Avro tools (written in Java) to display the contents of *pairs.avro*. The tools JAR is available from the Avro website; here we assume it's been placed in a local directory called *$AVRO_HOME*. The `tojson` command converts an Avro datafile to JSON and prints it to the console:

```
% java -jar $AVRO_HOME/avro-tools-*.jar tojson pairs.avro
{"left":"a","right":"1"}
{"left":"c","right":"2"}
{"left":"b","right":"3"}
{"left":"b","right":"2"}
```

We have successfully exchanged complex data between two Avro implementations (Python and Java).

Schema Resolution

We can choose to use a different schema for reading the data back (the *reader's schema*) from the one we used to write it (the *writer's schema*). This is a powerful tool because it enables schema evolution. To illustrate, consider a new schema for string pairs with an added `description` field:

```
{
  "type": "record",
  "name": "StringPair",
  "doc": "A pair of strings with an added field.",
  "fields": [
    {"name": "left", "type": "string"},
    {"name": "right", "type": "string"},
    {"name": "description", "type": "string", "default": ""}
  ]
}
```

We can use this schema to read the data we serialized earlier because, crucially, we have given the description field a default value (the empty string),[4] which Avro will use when there is no such field defined in the records it is reading. Had we omitted the default attribute, we would get an error when trying to read the old data.

> To make the default value null rather than the empty string, we would instead define the description field using a union with the null Avro type:
>
> ```
> {"name": "description", "type": ["null", "string"], "default": null}
> ```

When the reader's schema is different from the writer's, we use the constructor for GenericDatumReader that takes two schema objects, the writer's and the reader's, in that order:

```
DatumReader<GenericRecord> reader =
    new GenericDatumReader<GenericRecord>(schema, newSchema);
Decoder decoder = DecoderFactory.get().binaryDecoder(out.toByteArray(),
    null);
GenericRecord result = reader.read(null, decoder);
assertThat(result.get("left").toString(), is("L"));
assertThat(result.get("right").toString(), is("R"));
assertThat(result.get("description").toString(), is(""));
```

For datafiles, which have the writer's schema stored in the metadata, we only need to specify the reader's schema explicitly, which we can do by passing null for the writer's schema:

```
DatumReader<GenericRecord> reader =
    new GenericDatumReader<GenericRecord>(null, newSchema);
```

Another common use of a different reader's schema is to drop fields in a record, an operation called *projection*. This is useful when you have records with a large number of fields and you want to read only some of them. For example, this schema can be used to get only the right field of a StringPair:

---

4. Default values for fields are encoded using JSON. See the Avro specification for a description of this encoding for each data type.

```
{
  "type": "record",
  "name": "StringPair",
  "doc": "The right field of a pair of strings.",
  "fields": [
    {"name": "right", "type": "string"}
  ]
}
```

The rules for schema resolution have a direct bearing on how schemas may evolve from one version to the next, and are spelled out in the Avro specification for all Avro types. A summary of the rules for record evolution from the point of view of readers and writers (or servers and clients) is presented in Table 12-4.

Table 12-4. Schema resolution of records

New schema	Writer	Reader	Action
Added field	Old	New	The reader uses the default value of the new field, since it is not written by the writer.
	New	Old	The reader does not know about the new field written by the writer, so it is ignored (projection).
Removed field	Old	New	The reader ignores the removed field (projection).
	New	Old	The removed field is not written by the writer. If the old schema had a default defined for the field, the reader uses this; otherwise, it gets an error. In this case, it is best to update the reader's schema, either at the same time as or before the writer's.

Another useful technique for evolving Avro schemas is the use of name *aliases*. Aliases allow you to use different names in the schema used to read the Avro data than in the schema originally used to write the data. For example, the following reader's schema can be used to read StringPair data with the new field names first and second instead of left and right (which are what it was written with):

```
{
  "type": "record",
  "name": "StringPair",
  "doc": "A pair of strings with aliased field names.",
  "fields": [
    {"name": "first", "type": "string", "aliases": ["left"]},
    {"name": "second", "type": "string", "aliases": ["right"]}
  ]
}
```

Note that the aliases are used to translate (at read time) the writer's schema into the reader's, but the alias names are not available to the reader. In this example, the reader cannot use the field names left and right, because they have already been translated to first and second.

Sort Order

Avro defines a sort order for objects. For most Avro types, the order is the natural one you would expect—for example, numeric types are ordered by ascending numeric value. Others are a little more subtle. For instance, enums are compared by the order in which the symbols are defined and not by the values of the symbol strings.

All types except record have preordained rules for their sort order, as described in the Avro specification, that cannot be overridden by the user. For records, however, you can control the sort order by specifying the order attribute for a field. It takes one of three values: ascending (the default), descending (to reverse the order), or ignore (so the field is skipped for comparison purposes).

For example, the following schema (*SortedStringPair.avsc*) defines an ordering of StringPair records by the right field in descending order. The left field is ignored for the purposes of ordering, but it is still present in the projection:

```
{
  "type": "record",
  "name": "StringPair",
  "doc": "A pair of strings, sorted by right field descending.",
  "fields": [
    {"name": "left", "type": "string", "order": "ignore"},
    {"name": "right", "type": "string", "order": "descending"}
  ]
}
```

The record's fields are compared pairwise in the document order of the reader's schema. Thus, by specifying an appropriate reader's schema, you can impose an arbitrary ordering on data records. This schema (*SwitchedStringPair.avsc*) defines a sort order by the right field, then the left:

```
{
  "type": "record",
  "name": "StringPair",
  "doc": "A pair of strings, sorted by right then left.",
  "fields": [
    {"name": "right", "type": "string"},
    {"name": "left", "type": "string"}
  ]
}
```

Avro implements efficient binary comparisons. That is to say, Avro does not have to deserialize binary data into objects to perform the comparison, because it can instead work directly on the byte streams.[5] In the case of the original `StringPair` schema (with no `order` attributes), for example, Avro implements the binary comparison as follows.

The first field, `left`, is a UTF-8-encoded string, for which Avro can compare the bytes lexicographically. If they differ, the order is determined, and Avro can stop the comparison there. Otherwise, if the two byte sequences are the same, it compares the second two (`right`) fields, again lexicographically at the byte level because the field is another UTF-8 string.

Notice that this description of a comparison function has exactly the same logic as the binary comparator we wrote for Writables in "Implementing a RawComparator for speed" on page 123. The great thing is that Avro provides the comparator for us, so we don't have to write and maintain this code. It's also easy to change the sort order just by changing the reader's schema. For the *SortedStringPair.avsc* and *SwitchedString Pair.avsc* schemas, the comparison function Avro uses is essentially the same as the one just described. The differences are which fields are considered, the order in which they are considered, and whether the sort order is ascending or descending.

Later in the chapter, we'll use Avro's sorting logic in conjunction with MapReduce to sort Avro datafiles in parallel.

Avro MapReduce

Avro provides a number of classes for making it easy to run MapReduce programs on Avro data. We'll use the new MapReduce API classes from the `org.apache.avro.map reduce` package, but you can find (old-style) MapReduce classes in the `org.apache.avro.mapred` package.

Let's rework the MapReduce program for finding the maximum temperature for each year in the weather dataset, this time using the Avro MapReduce API. We will represent weather records using the following schema:

```
{
  "type": "record",
  "name": "WeatherRecord",
  "doc": "A weather reading.",
  "fields": [
    {"name": "year", "type": "int"},
    {"name": "temperature", "type": "int"},
    {"name": "stationId", "type": "string"}
  ]
}
```

---

5. A useful consequence of this property is that you can compute an Avro datum's hash code from either the object or the binary representation (the latter by using the static `hashCode()` method on `BinaryData`) and get the same result in both cases.

The program in Example 12-2 reads text input (in the format we saw in earlier chapters) and writes Avro datafiles containing weather records as output.

Example 12-2. MapReduce program to find the maximum temperature, creating Avro output

```java
public class AvroGenericMaxTemperature extends Configured implements Tool {

  private static final Schema SCHEMA = new Schema.Parser().parse(
      "{" +
      "  \"type\": \"record\"," +
      "  \"name\": \"WeatherRecord\"," +
      "  \"doc\": \"A weather reading.\"," +
      "  \"fields\": [" +
      "    {\"name\": \"year\", \"type\": \"int\"}," +
      "    {\"name\": \"temperature\", \"type\": \"int\"}," +
      "    {\"name\": \"stationId\", \"type\": \"string\"}" +
      "  ]" +
      "}"
  );

  public static class MaxTemperatureMapper
      extends Mapper<LongWritable, Text, AvroKey<Integer>,
          AvroValue<GenericRecord>> {
    private NcdcRecordParser parser = new NcdcRecordParser();
    private GenericRecord record = new GenericData.Record(SCHEMA);

    @Override
    protected void map(LongWritable key, Text value, Context context)
        throws IOException, InterruptedException {
      parser.parse(value.toString());
      if (parser.isValidTemperature()) {
        record.put("year", parser.getYearInt());
        record.put("temperature", parser.getAirTemperature());
        record.put("stationId", parser.getStationId());
        context.write(new AvroKey<Integer>(parser.getYearInt()),
            new AvroValue<GenericRecord>(record));
      }
    }
  }

  public static class MaxTemperatureReducer
      extends Reducer<AvroKey<Integer>, AvroValue<GenericRecord>,
          AvroKey<GenericRecord>, NullWritable> {

    @Override
    protected void reduce(AvroKey<Integer> key, Iterable<AvroValue<GenericRecord>>
        values, Context context) throws IOException, InterruptedException {
      GenericRecord max = null;
      for (AvroValue<GenericRecord> value : values) {
        GenericRecord record = value.datum();
        if (max == null ||
```

```
          (Integer) record.get("temperature") > (Integer) max.get("temperature")) {
        max = newWeatherRecord(record);
      }
    }
    context.write(new AvroKey(max), NullWritable.get());
  }
  private GenericRecord newWeatherRecord(GenericRecord value) {
    GenericRecord record = new GenericData.Record(SCHEMA);
    record.put("year", value.get("year"));
    record.put("temperature", value.get("temperature"));
    record.put("stationId", value.get("stationId"));
    return record;
  }
}

@Override
public int run(String[] args) throws Exception {
  if (args.length != 2) {
    System.err.printf("Usage: %s [generic options] <input> <output>\n",
        getClass().getSimpleName());
    ToolRunner.printGenericCommandUsage(System.err);
    return -1;
  }

  Job job = new Job(getConf(), "Max temperature");
  job.setJarByClass(getClass());

  job.getConfiguration().setBoolean(
      Job.MAPREDUCE_JOB_USER_CLASSPATH_FIRST, true);

  FileInputFormat.addInputPath(job, new Path(args[0]));
  FileOutputFormat.setOutputPath(job, new Path(args[1]));

  AvroJob.setMapOutputKeySchema(job, Schema.create(Schema.Type.INT));
  AvroJob.setMapOutputValueSchema(job, SCHEMA);
  AvroJob.setOutputKeySchema(job, SCHEMA);

  job.setInputFormatClass(TextInputFormat.class);
  job.setOutputFormatClass(AvroKeyOutputFormat.class);

  job.setMapperClass(MaxTemperatureMapper.class);
  job.setReducerClass(MaxTemperatureReducer.class);

  return job.waitForCompletion(true) ? 0 : 1;
}

public static void main(String[] args) throws Exception {
  int exitCode = ToolRunner.run(new AvroGenericMaxTemperature(), args);
  System.exit(exitCode);
}
}
```

This program uses the Generic Avro mapping. This frees us from generating code to represent records, at the expense of type safety (field names are referred to by string value, such as `"temperature"`).[6] The schema for weather records is inlined in the code for convenience (and read into the `SCHEMA` constant), although in practice it might be more maintainable to read the schema from a local file in the driver code and pass it to the mapper and reducer via the Hadoop job configuration. (Techniques for achieving this are discussed in "Side Data Distribution" on page 273.)

There are a couple of differences from the regular Hadoop MapReduce API. The first is the use of wrappers around Avro Java types. For this MapReduce program, the key is the year (an integer), and the value is the weather record, which is represented by Avro's `GenericRecord`. This translates to `AvroKey<Integer>` for the key type and `AvroValue<GenericRecord>` for the value type in the map output (and reduce input).

The `MaxTemperatureReducer` iterates through the records for each key (year) and finds the one with the maximum temperature. It is necessary to make a copy of the record with the highest temperature found so far, since the iterator reuses the instance for reasons of efficiency (and only the fields are updated).

The second major difference from regular MapReduce is the use of `AvroJob` for configuring the job. `AvroJob` is a convenience class for specifying the Avro schemas for the input, map output, and final output data. In this program, no input schema is set, because we are reading from a text file. The map output key schema is an Avro `int` and the value schema is the weather record schema. The final output key schema is the weather record schema, and the output format is `AvroKeyOutputFormat`, which writes keys to Avro datafiles and ignores the values (which are `NullWritable`).

The following commands show how to run the program on a small sample dataset:

```
% export HADOOP_CLASSPATH=avro-examples.jar
% export HADOOP_USER_CLASSPATH_FIRST=true # override version of Avro in Hadoop
% hadoop jar avro-examples.jar AvroGenericMaxTemperature \
  input/ncdc/sample.txt output
```

On completion we can look at the output using the Avro tools JAR to render the Avro datafile as JSON, one record per line:

```
% java -jar $AVRO_HOME/avro-tools-*.jar tojson output/part-r-00000.avro
{"year":1949,"temperature":111,"stationId":"012650-99999"}
{"year":1950,"temperature":22,"stationId":"011990-99999"}
```

In this example we read a text file and created an Avro datafile, but other combinations are possible, which is useful for converting between Avro formats and other formats

---

6. For an example that uses the Specific mapping with generated classes, see the `AvroSpecificMaxTemperature` class in the example code.

(such as SequenceFiles). See the documentation for the Avro MapReduce package for details.

Sorting Using Avro MapReduce

In this section, we use Avro's sort capabilities and combine them with MapReduce to write a program to sort an Avro datafile (Example 12-3).

Example 12-3. A MapReduce program to sort an Avro datafile

```java
public class AvroSort extends Configured implements Tool {

  static class SortMapper<K> extends Mapper<AvroKey<K>, NullWritable,
      AvroKey<K>, AvroValue<K>> {
    @Override
    protected void map(AvroKey<K> key, NullWritable value,
        Context context) throws IOException, InterruptedException {
      context.write(key, new AvroValue<K>(key.datum()));
    }
  }

  static class SortReducer<K> extends Reducer<AvroKey<K>, AvroValue<K>,
      AvroKey<K>, NullWritable> {
    @Override
    protected void reduce(AvroKey<K> key, Iterable<AvroValue<K>> values,
        Context context) throws IOException, InterruptedException {
      for (AvroValue<K> value : values) {
        context.write(new AvroKey(value.datum()), NullWritable.get());
      }
    }
  }

  @Override
  public int run(String[] args) throws Exception {

    if (args.length != 3) {
      System.err.printf(
          "Usage: %s [generic options] <input> <output> <schema-file>\n",
          getClass().getSimpleName());
      ToolRunner.printGenericCommandUsage(System.err);
      return -1;
    }

    String input = args[0];
    String output = args[1];
    String schemaFile = args[2];

    Job job = new Job(getConf(), "Avro sort");
    job.setJarByClass(getClass());

    job.getConfiguration().setBoolean(
```

```
        Job.MAPREDUCE_JOB_USER_CLASSPATH_FIRST, true);

    FileInputFormat.addInputPath(job, new Path(input));
    FileOutputFormat.setOutputPath(job, new Path(output));

    AvroJob.setDataModelClass(job, GenericData.class);

    Schema schema = new Schema.Parser().parse(new File(schemaFile));
    AvroJob.setInputKeySchema(job, schema);
    AvroJob.setMapOutputKeySchema(job, schema);
    AvroJob.setMapOutputValueSchema(job, schema);
    AvroJob.setOutputKeySchema(job, schema);

    job.setInputFormatClass(AvroKeyInputFormat.class);
    job.setOutputFormatClass(AvroKeyOutputFormat.class);

    job.setOutputKeyClass(AvroKey.class);
    job.setOutputValueClass(NullWritable.class);

    job.setMapperClass(SortMapper.class);
    job.setReducerClass(SortReducer.class);

    return job.waitForCompletion(true) ? 0 : 1;
  }

  public static void main(String[] args) throws Exception {
    int exitCode = ToolRunner.run(new AvroSort(), args);
    System.exit(exitCode);
  }
}
```

This program (which uses the Generic Avro mapping and hence does not require any code generation) can sort Avro records of any type, represented in Java by the generic type parameter K. We choose a value that is the same as the key, so that when the values are grouped by key we can emit all of the values in the case that more than one of them share the same key (according to the sorting function). This means we don't lose any records.[7] The mapper simply emits the input key wrapped in an AvroKey and an Avro Value. The reducer acts as an identity, passing the values through as output keys, which will get written to an Avro datafile.

The sorting happens in the MapReduce shuffle, and the sort function is determined by the Avro schema that is passed to the program. Let's use the program to sort the *pairs.av ro* file created earlier, using the *SortedStringPair.avsc* schema to sort by the right field in descending order. First, we inspect the input using the Avro tools JAR:

---

7. If we had used the identity mapper and reducer here, the program would sort and remove duplicate keys at the same time. We encounter this idea of duplicating information from the key in the value object again in "Secondary Sort" on page 262.

```
% java -jar $AVRO_HOME/avro-tools-*.jar tojson input/avro/pairs.avro
{"left":"a","right":"1"}
{"left":"c","right":"2"}
{"left":"b","right":"3"}
{"left":"b","right":"2"}
```

Then we run the sort:

```
% hadoop jar avro-examples.jar AvroSort input/avro/pairs.avro output \
  ch12-avro/src/main/resources/SortedStringPair.avsc
```

Finally, we inspect the output and see that it is sorted correctly:

```
% java -jar $AVRO_HOME/avro-tools-*.jar tojson output/part-r-00000.avro
{"left":"b","right":"3"}
{"left":"b","right":"2"}
{"left":"c","right":"2"}
{"left":"a","right":"1"}
```

Avro in Other Languages

For languages and frameworks other than Java, there are a few choices for working with Avro data.

AvroAsTextInputFormat is designed to allow Hadoop Streaming programs to read Avro datafiles. Each datum in the file is converted to a string, which is the JSON representation of the datum, or just to the raw bytes if the type is Avro bytes. Going the other way, you can specify AvroTextOutputFormat as the output format of a Streaming job to create Avro datafiles with a bytes schema, where each datum is the tab-delimited key-value pair written from the Streaming output. Both of these classes can be found in the org.apache.avro.mapred package.

It's also worth considering other frameworks like Pig, Hive, Crunch, and Spark for doing Avro processing, since they can all read and write Avro datafiles by specifying the appropriate storage formats. See the relevant chapters in this book for details.

Parquet

Apache Parquet (*http://parquet.incubator.apache.org/*) is a columnar storage format that can efficiently store nested data.

Columnar formats are attractive since they enable greater efficiency, in terms of both *file size* and *query performance*. File sizes are usually smaller than row-oriented equivalents since in a columnar format the values from one column are stored next to each other, which usually allows a very efficient encoding. A column storing a timestamp, for example, can be encoded by storing the first value and the differences between subsequent values (which tend to be small due to temporal locality: records from around the same time are stored next to each other). Query performance is improved too since a query engine can skip over columns that are not needed to answer a query. (This idea is illustrated in Figure 5-4.) This chapter looks at Parquet in more depth, but there are other columnar formats that work with Hadoop—notably ORCFile (Optimized Record Columnar File), which is a part of the Hive project.

A key strength of Parquet is its ability to store data that has a deeply *nested* structure in true columnar fashion. This is important since schemas with several levels of nesting are common in real-world systems. Parquet uses a novel technique for storing nested structures in a flat columnar format with little overhead, which was introduced by Google engineers in the Dremel paper.[1] The result is that even nested fields can be read independently of other fields, resulting in significant performance improvements.

Another feature of Parquet is the large number of tools that support it as a format. The engineers at Twitter and Cloudera who created Parquet wanted it to be easy to try new tools to process existing data, so to facilitate this they divided the project into a specification (*parquet-format*), which defines the file format in a language-neutral way, and

---

1. Sergey Melnik et al., *Dremel: Interactive Analysis of Web-Scale Datasets*, (*http://research.google.com/pubs/pub36632.html*) Proceedings of the 36th International Conference on Very Large Data Bases, 2010.

implementations of the specification for different languages (Java and C++) that made it easy for tools to read or write Parquet files. In fact, most of the data processing components covered in this book understand the Parquet format (MapReduce, Pig, Hive, Cascading, Crunch, and Spark). This flexibility also extends to the in-memory representation: the Java implementation is not tied to a single representation, so you can use in-memory data models for Avro, Thrift, or Protocol Buffers to read your data from and write it to Parquet files.

Data Model

Parquet defines a small number of primitive types, listed in Table 13-1.

Table 13-1. Parquet primitive types

Type	Description
boolean	Binary value
int32	32-bit signed integer
int64	64-bit signed integer
int96	96-bit signed integer
float	Single-precision (32-bit) IEEE 754 floating-point number
double	Double-precision (64-bit) IEEE 754 floating-point number
binary	Sequence of 8-bit unsigned bytes
fixed_len_byte_array	Fixed number of 8-bit unsigned bytes

The data stored in a Parquet file is described by a schema, which has at its root a message containing a group of fields. Each field has a repetition (required, optional, or repeated), a type, and a name. Here is a simple Parquet schema for a weather record:

```
message WeatherRecord {
  required int32 year;
  required int32 temperature;
  required binary stationId (UTF8);
}
```

Notice that there is no primitive string type. Instead, Parquet defines logical types that specify how primitive types should be interpreted, so there is a separation between the serialized representation (the primitive type) and the semantics that are specific to the application (the logical type). Strings are represented as binary primitives with a UTF8 annotation. Some of the logical types defined by Parquet are listed in Table 13-2, along with a representative example schema of each. Among those not listed in the table are signed integers, unsigned integers, more date/time types, and JSON and BSON document types. See the Parquet specification for details.

Table 13-2. Parquet logical types

Logical type annotation	Description	Schema example
UTF8	A UTF-8 character string. Annotates `binary`.	```message m { required binary a (UTF8); }```
ENUM	A set of named values. Annotates `binary`.	```message m { required binary a (ENUM); }```
DECIMAL(*preci sion,scale*)	An arbitrary-precision signed decimal number. Annotates `int32`, `int64`, `binary`, or `fixed_len_byte_array`.	```message m { required int32 a (DECIMAL(5,2)); }```
DATE	A date with no time value. Annotates `int32`. Represented by the number of days since the Unix epoch (January 1, 1970).	```message m { required int32 a (DATE); }```
LIST	An ordered collection of values. Annotates `group`.	```message m { required group a (LIST) { repeated group list { required int32 element; } } }```
MAP	An unordered collection of key-value pairs. Annotates `group`.	```message m { required group a (MAP) { repeated group key_value { required binary key (UTF8); optional int32 value; } } }```

Complex types in Parquet are created using the `group` type, which adds a layer of nesting.[2] A group with no annotation is simply a nested record.

Lists and maps are built from groups with a particular two-level group structure, as shown in Table 13-2. A list is represented as a `LIST` group with a nested repeating group (called `list`) that contains an element field. In this example, a list of 32-bit integers has a required `int32` element field. For maps, the outer group `a` (annotated `MAP`) contains an inner repeating group `key_value` that contains the key and value fields. In this example, the values have been marked `optional` so that it's possible to have `null` values in the map.

---

2. This is based on the model used in Protocol Buffers (*https://developers.google.com/protocol-buffers/*), where groups are used to define complex types like lists and maps.

Nested Encoding

In a column-oriented store, a column's values are stored together. For a flat table where there is no nesting and no repetition—such as the weather record schema—this is simple enough since each column has the same number of values, making it straightforward to determine which row each value belongs to.

In the general case where there is nesting or repetition—such as the map schema—it is more challenging, since the structure of the nesting needs to be encoded too. Some columnar formats avoid the problem by flattening the structure so that only the top-level columns are stored in column-major fashion (this is the approach that Hive's RCFile takes, for example). A map with nested columns would be stored in such a way that the keys and values are interleaved, so it would not be possible to read only the keys, say, without also reading the values into memory.

Parquet uses the encoding from Dremel, where every primitive type field in the schema is stored in a separate column, and for each value written, the structure is encoded by means of two integers: the definition level and the repetition level. The details are intricate,[3] but you can think of storing definition and repetition levels like this as a generalization of using a bit field to encode nulls for a flat record, where the non-null values are written one after another.

The upshot of this encoding is that any column (even nested ones) can be read independently of the others. In the case of a Parquet map, for example, the keys can be read without accessing any of the values, which can result in significant performance improvements, especially if the values are large (such as nested records with many fields).

Parquet File Format

A Parquet file consists of a header followed by one or more blocks, terminated by a footer. The header contains only a 4-byte magic number, PAR1, that identifies the file as being in Parquet format, and all the file metadata is stored in the footer. The footer's metadata includes the format version, the schema, any extra key-value pairs, and metadata for every block in the file. The final two fields in the footer are a 4-byte field encoding the length of the footer metadata, and the magic number again (PAR1).

The consequence of storing the metadata in the footer is that reading a Parquet file requires an initial seek to the end of the file (minus 8 bytes) to read the footer metadata length, then a second seek backward by that length to read the footer metadata. Unlike sequence files and Avro datafiles, where the metadata is stored in the header and sync markers are used to separate blocks, Parquet files don't need sync markers since the block boundaries are stored in the footer metadata. (This is possible because the

---

3. Julien Le Dem's exposition (*http://bit.ly/dremel_parquet*) is excellent.

---

metadata is written after all the blocks have been written, so the writer can retain the block boundary positions in memory until the file is closed.) Therefore, Parquet files are splittable, since the blocks can be located after reading the footer and can then be processed in parallel (by MapReduce, for example).

Each block in a Parquet file stores a *row group*, which is made up of *column chunks* containing the column data for those rows. The data for each column chunk is written in *pages*; this is illustrated in Figure 13-1.

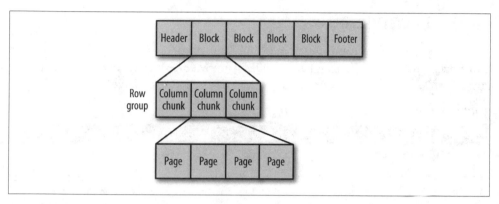

Figure 13-1. The internal structure of a Parquet file

Each page contains values from the same column, making a page a very good candidate for compression since the values are likely to be similar. The first level of compression is achieved through how the values are encoded. The simplest encoding is plain encoding, where values are written in full (e.g., an int32 is written using a 4-byte little-endian representation), but this doesn't afford any compression in itself.

Parquet also uses more compact encodings, including delta encoding (the difference between values is stored), run-length encoding (sequences of identical values are encoded as a single value and the count), and dictionary encoding (a dictionary of values is built and itself encoded, then values are encoded as integers representing the indexes in the dictionary). In most cases, it also applies techniques such as bit packing to save space by storing several small values in a single byte.

When writing files, Parquet will choose an appropriate encoding automatically, based on the column type. For example, Boolean values will be written using a combination of run-length encoding and bit packing. Most types are encoded using dictionary encoding by default; however, a plain encoding will be used as a fallback if the dictionary becomes too large. The threshold size at which this happens is referred to as the *dictionary page size* and is the same as the page size by default (so the dictionary has to fit into one page if it is to be used). Note that the encoding that is actually used is stored in the file metadata to ensure that readers use the correct encoding.

In addition to the encoding, a second level of compression can be applied using a standard compression algorithm on the encoded page bytes. By default, no compression is applied, but Snappy, gzip, and LZO compressors are all supported.

For nested data, each page will also store the definition and repetition levels for all the values in the page. Since levels are small integers (the maximum is determined by the amount of nesting specified in the schema), they can be very efficiently encoded using a bit-packed run-length encoding.

Parquet Configuration

Parquet file properties are set at write time. The properties listed in Table 13-3 are appropriate if you are creating Parquet files from MapReduce (using the formats discussed in "Parquet MapReduce" on page 377), Crunch, Pig, or Hive.

Table 13-3. ParquetOutputFormat properties

Property name	Type	Default value	Description
parquet.block.size	int	134217728 (128 MB)	The size in bytes of a block (row group).
parquet.page.size	int	1048576 (1 MB)	The size in bytes of a page.
parquet.dictio nary.page.size	int	1048576 (1 MB)	The maximum allowed size in bytes of a dictionary before falling back to plain encoding for a page.
parquet.enable.dictio nary	boolean	true	Whether to use dictionary encoding.
parquet.compression	String	UNCOMPRESSED	The type of compression to use for Parquet files: UN COMPRESSED, SNAPPY, GZIP, or LZO. Used instead of mapreduce.output.fileoutput format.compress.

Setting the block size is a trade-off between scanning efficiency and memory usage. Larger blocks are more efficient to scan through since they contain more rows, which improves sequential I/O (as there's less overhead in setting up each column chunk). However, each block is buffered in memory for both reading and writing, which limits how large blocks can be. The default block size is 128 MB.

The Parquet file block size should be no larger than the HDFS block size for the file so that each Parquet block can be read from a single HDFS block (and therefore from a single datanode). It is common to set them to be the same, and indeed both defaults are for 128 MB block sizes.

A page is the smallest unit of storage in a Parquet file, so retrieving an arbitrary row (with a single column, for the sake of illustration) requires that the page containing the row be decompressed and decoded. Thus, for single-row lookups, it is more efficient to have smaller pages, so there are fewer values to read through before reaching the target value. However, smaller pages incur a higher storage and processing overhead, due to the extra metadata (offsets, dictionaries) resulting from more pages. The default page size is 1 MB.

Writing and Reading Parquet Files

Most of the time Parquet files are processed using higher-level tools like Pig, Hive, or Impala, but sometimes low-level sequential access may be required, which we cover in this section.

Parquet has a pluggable in-memory data model to facilitate integration of the Parquet file format with a wide range of tools and components. `ReadSupport` and `WriteSupport` are the integration points in Java, and implementations of these classes do the conversion between the objects used by the tool or component and the objects used to represent each Parquet type in the schema.

To demonstrate, we'll use a simple in-memory model that comes bundled with Parquet in the `parquet.example.data` and `parquet.example.data.simple` packages. Then, in the next section, we'll use an Avro representation to do the same thing.

> As the names suggest, the example classes that come with Parquet are an object model for demonstrating how to work with Parquet files; for production, one of the supported frameworks should be used (Avro, Protocol Buffers, or Thrift).

To write a Parquet file, we need to define a Parquet schema, represented by an instance of `parquet.schema.MessageType`:

```
MessageType schema = MessageTypeParser.parseMessageType(
    "message Pair {\n" +
    "  required binary left (UTF8);\n" +
    "  required binary right (UTF8);\n" +
    "}");
```

Next, we need to create an instance of a Parquet message for each record to be written to the file. For the `parquet.example.data` package, a message is represented by an instance of `Group`, constructed using a `GroupFactory`:

```
GroupFactory groupFactory = new SimpleGroupFactory(schema);
Group group = groupFactory.newGroup()
    .append("left", "L")
    .append("right", "R");
```

Notice that the values in the message are UTF8 logical types, and `Group` provides a natural conversion from a Java `String` for us.

The following snippet of code shows how to create a Parquet file and write a message to it. The write() method would normally be called in a loop to write multiple messages to the file, but this only writes one here:

```
Configuration conf = new Configuration();
Path path = new Path("data.parquet");
GroupWriteSupport writeSupport = new GroupWriteSupport();
GroupWriteSupport.setSchema(schema, conf);
ParquetWriter<Group> writer = new ParquetWriter<Group>(path, writeSupport,
    ParquetWriter.DEFAULT_COMPRESSION_CODEC_NAME,
    ParquetWriter.DEFAULT_BLOCK_SIZE,
    ParquetWriter.DEFAULT_PAGE_SIZE,
    ParquetWriter.DEFAULT_PAGE_SIZE, /* dictionary page size */
    ParquetWriter.DEFAULT_IS_DICTIONARY_ENABLED,
    ParquetWriter.DEFAULT_IS_VALIDATING_ENABLED,
    ParquetProperties.WriterVersion.PARQUET_1_0, conf);
writer.write(group);
writer.close();
```

The ParquetWriter constructor needs to be provided with a WriteSupport instance, which defines how the message type is translated to Parquet's types. In this case, we are using the Group message type, so GroupWriteSupport is used. Notice that the Parquet schema is set on the Configuration object by calling the setSchema() static method on GroupWriteSupport, and then the Configuration object is passed to ParquetWrit er. This example also illustrates the Parquet file properties that may be set, corresponding to the ones listed in Table 13-3.

Reading a Parquet file is simpler than writing one, since the schema does not need to be specified as it is stored in the Parquet file. (It is, however, possible to set a *read schema* to return a subset of the columns in the file, via projection.) Also, there are no file properties to be set since they are set at write time:

```
GroupReadSupport readSupport = new GroupReadSupport();
ParquetReader<Group> reader = new ParquetReader<Group>(path, readSupport);
```

ParquetReader has a read() method to read the next message. It returns null when the end of the file is reached:

```
Group result = reader.read();
assertNotNull(result);
assertThat(result.getString("left", 0), is("L"));
assertThat(result.getString("right", 0), is("R"));
assertNull(reader.read());
```

Note that the 0 parameter passed to the getString() method specifies the index of the field to retrieve, since fields may have repeated values.

Avro, Protocol Buffers, and Thrift

Most applications will prefer to define models using a framework like Avro, Protocol Buffers, or Thrift, and Parquet caters to all of these cases. Instead of `ParquetWriter` and `ParquetReader`, use `AvroParquetWriter`, `ProtoParquetWriter`, or `ThriftParquetWriter`, and the respective reader classes. These classes take care of translating between Avro, Protocol Buffers, or Thrift schemas and Parquet schemas (as well as performing the equivalent mapping between the framework types and Parquet types), which means you don't need to deal with Parquet schemas directly.

Let's repeat the previous example but using the Avro Generic API, just like we did in "In-Memory Serialization and Deserialization" on page 349. The Avro schema is:

```
{
  "type": "record",
  "name": "StringPair",
  "doc": "A pair of strings.",
  "fields": [
    {"name": "left", "type": "string"},
    {"name": "right", "type": "string"}
  ]
}
```

We create a schema instance and a generic record with:

```
Schema.Parser parser = new Schema.Parser();
Schema schema = parser.parse(getClass().getResourceAsStream("StringPair.avsc"));

GenericRecord datum = new GenericData.Record(schema);
datum.put("left", "L");
datum.put("right", "R");
```

Then we can write a Parquet file:

```
Path path = new Path("data.parquet");
AvroParquetWriter<GenericRecord> writer =
    new AvroParquetWriter<GenericRecord>(path, schema);
writer.write(datum);
writer.close();
```

`AvroParquetWriter` converts the Avro schema into a Parquet schema, and also translates each Avro `GenericRecord` instance into the corresponding Parquet types to write to the Parquet file. The file is a regular Parquet file—it is identical to the one written in the previous section using `ParquetWriter` with `GroupWriteSupport`, except for an extra piece of metadata to store the Avro schema. We can see this by inspecting the file's metadata using Parquet's command-line tools:[4]

---

4. The Parquet tools can be downloaded as a binary tarball from the Parquet Maven repository. Search for "parquet-tools" on *http://search.maven.org*.

```
% parquet-tools meta data.parquet
...
extra:          avro.schema = {"type":"record","name":"StringPair", ...
...
```

Similarly, to see the Parquet schema that was generated from the Avro schema, we can use the following:

```
% parquet-tools schema data.parquet
message StringPair {
  required binary left (UTF8);
  required binary right (UTF8);
}
```

To read the Parquet file back, we use an AvroParquetReader and get back Avro Gener icRecord objects:

```
AvroParquetReader<GenericRecord> reader =
    new AvroParquetReader<GenericRecord>(path);
GenericRecord result = reader.read();
assertNotNull(result);
assertThat(result.get("left").toString(), is("L"));
assertThat(result.get("right").toString(), is("R"));
assertNull(reader.read());
```

Projection and read schemas

It's often the case that you only need to read a few columns in the file, and indeed this is the *raison d'être* of a columnar format like Parquet: to save time and I/O. You can use a projection schema to select the columns to read. For example, the following schema will read only the right field of a StringPair:

```
{
  "type": "record",
  "name": "StringPair",
  "doc": "The right field of a pair of strings.",
  "fields": [
    {"name": "right", "type": "string"}
  ]
}
```

In order to use a projection schema, set it on the configuration using the setReques tedProjection() static convenience method on AvroReadSupport:

```
Schema projectionSchema = parser.parse(
    getClass().getResourceAsStream("ProjectedStringPair.avsc"));
Configuration conf = new Configuration();
AvroReadSupport.setRequestedProjection(conf, projectionSchema);
```

Then pass the configuration into the constructor for AvroParquetReader:

```
AvroParquetReader<GenericRecord> reader =
    new AvroParquetReader<GenericRecord>(conf, path);
GenericRecord result = reader.read();
```

```
        assertNull(result.get("left"));
        assertThat(result.get("right").toString(), is("R"));
```

Both the Protocol Buffers and Thrift implementations support projection in a similar manner. In addition, the Avro implementation allows you to specify a reader's schema by calling `setReadSchema()` on `AvroReadSupport`. This schema is used to resolve Avro records according to the rules listed in Table 12-4.

The reason that Avro has both a projection schema and a reader's schema is that the projection must be a subset of the schema used to write the Parquet file, so it cannot be used to evolve a schema by adding new fields.

The two schemas serve different purposes, and you can use both together. The projection schema is used to filter the columns to read from the Parquet file. Although it is expressed as an Avro schema, it can be viewed simply as a list of Parquet columns to read back. The reader's schema, on the other hand, is used only to resolve Avro records. It is never translated to a Parquet schema, since it has no bearing on which columns are read from the Parquet file. For example, if we added a `description` field to our Avro schema (like in "Schema Resolution" on page 355) and used it as the Avro reader's schema, then the records would contain the default value of the field, even though the Parquet file has no such field.

Parquet MapReduce

Parquet comes with a selection of MapReduce input and output formats for reading and writing Parquet files from MapReduce jobs, including ones for working with Avro, Protocol Buffers, and Thrift schemas and data.

The program in Example 13-1 is a map-only job that reads text files and writes Parquet files where each record is the line's offset in the file (represented by an `int64`—converted from a `long` in Avro) and the line itself (a string). It uses the Avro Generic API for its in-memory data model.

Example 13-1. MapReduce program to convert text files to Parquet files using AvroParquetOutputFormat

```
public class TextToParquetWithAvro extends Configured implements Tool {

  private static final Schema SCHEMA = new Schema.Parser().parse(
      "{\n" +
      "  \"type\": \"record\",\n" +
      "  \"name\": \"Line\",\n" +
      "  \"fields\": [\n" +
      "    {\"name\": \"offset\", \"type\": \"long\"},\n" +
      "    {\"name\": \"line\", \"type\": \"string\"}\n" +
      "  ]\n" +
      "}");
```

```
public static class TextToParquetMapper
    extends Mapper<LongWritable, Text, Void, GenericRecord> {

  private GenericRecord record = new GenericData.Record(SCHEMA);

  @Override
  protected void map(LongWritable key, Text value, Context context)
      throws IOException, InterruptedException {
    record.put("offset", key.get());
    record.put("line", value.toString());
    context.write(null, record);
  }
}

@Override
public int run(String[] args) throws Exception {
  if (args.length != 2) {
    System.err.printf("Usage: %s [generic options] <input> <output>\n",
        getClass().getSimpleName());
    ToolRunner.printGenericCommandUsage(System.err);
    return -1;
  }

  Job job = new Job(getConf(), "Text to Parquet");
  job.setJarByClass(getClass());

  FileInputFormat.addInputPath(job, new Path(args[0]));
  FileOutputFormat.setOutputPath(job, new Path(args[1]));

  job.setMapperClass(TextToParquetMapper.class);
  job.setNumReduceTasks(0);

  job.setOutputFormatClass(AvroParquetOutputFormat.class);
  AvroParquetOutputFormat.setSchema(job, SCHEMA);

  job.setOutputKeyClass(Void.class);
  job.setOutputValueClass(Group.class);

  return job.waitForCompletion(true) ? 0 : 1;
}

public static void main(String[] args) throws Exception {
  int exitCode = ToolRunner.run(new TextToParquetWithAvro(), args);
  System.exit(exitCode);
}
}
```

The job's output format is set to `AvroParquetOutputFormat`, and the output key and value types are set to `Void` and `GenericRecord` to match, since we are using Avro's Generic API. `Void` simply means that the key is always set to `null`.

Like `AvroParquetWriter` from the previous section, `AvroParquetOutputFormat` converts the Avro schema to a Parquet schema automatically. The Avro schema is set on the `Job` instance so that the MapReduce tasks can find the schema when writing the files.

The mapper is straightforward; it takes the file offset (key) and line (value) and builds an Avro `GenericRecord` object with them, which it writes out to the MapReduce context object as the value (the key is always `null`). `AvroParquetOutputFormat` takes care of the conversion of the Avro `GenericRecord` to the Parquet file format encoding.

 Parquet is a columnar format, so it buffers rows in memory. Even though the mapper in this example just passes values through, it must have sufficient memory for the Parquet writer to buffer each block (row group), which is by default 128 MB. If you get job failures due to out of memory errors, you can adjust the Parquet file block size for the writer with `parquet.block.size` (see Table 13-3). You may also need to change the MapReduce task memory allocation (when reading or writing) using the settings discussed in "Memory settings in YARN and MapReduce" on page 301.

The following command runs the program on the four-line text file *quangle.txt*:

```
% hadoop jar parquet-examples.jar TextToParquetWithAvro \
  input/docs/quangle.txt output
```

We can use the Parquet command-line tools to dump the output Parquet file for inspection:

```
% parquet-tools dump output/part-m-00000.parquet
INT64 offset
--------------------------------------------------------------------------------
*** row group 1 of 1, values 1 to 4 ***
value 1: R:0 D:0 V:0
value 2: R:0 D:0 V:33
value 3: R:0 D:0 V:57
value 4: R:0 D:0 V:89

BINARY line
--------------------------------------------------------------------------------
*** row group 1 of 1, values 1 to 4 ***
value 1: R:0 D:0 V:On the top of the Crumpetty Tree
value 2: R:0 D:0 V:The Quangle Wangle sat,
value 3: R:0 D:0 V:But his face you could not see,
value 4: R:0 D:0 V:On account of his Beaver Hat.
```

Notice how the values within a row group are shown together. `V` indicates the value, `R` the repetition level, and `D` the definition level. For this schema, the latter two are zero since there is no nesting.

Flume

Hadoop is built for processing very large datasets. Often it is assumed that the data is already in HDFS, or can be copied there in bulk. However, there are many systems that don't meet this assumption. They produce streams of data that we would like to aggregate, store, and analyze using Hadoop—and these are the systems that Apache Flume (*http://flume.apache.org/*) is an ideal fit for.

Flume is designed for high-volume ingestion into Hadoop of event-based data. The canonical example is using Flume to collect logfiles from a bank of web servers, then moving the log events from those files into new aggregated files in HDFS for processing. The usual destination (or *sink* in Flume parlance) is HDFS. However, Flume is flexible enough to write to other systems, like HBase or Solr.

To use Flume, we need to run a Flume *agent*, which is a long-lived Java process that runs *sources* and *sinks*, connected by *channels*. A source in Flume produces *events* and delivers them to the channel, which stores the events until they are forwarded to the sink. You can think of the source-channel-sink combination as a basic Flume building block.

A Flume installation is made up of a collection of connected agents running in a distributed topology. Agents on the edge of the system (co-located on web server machines, for example) collect data and forward it to agents that are responsible for aggregating and then storing the data in its final destination. Agents are configured to run a collection of particular sources and sinks, so using Flume is mainly a configuration exercise in wiring the pieces together. In this chapter, we'll see how to build Flume topologies for data ingestion that you can use as a part of your own Hadoop pipeline.

Installing Flume

Download a stable release of the Flume binary distribution from the download page (*http://flume.apache.org/download.html*), and unpack the tarball in a suitable location:

```
% tar xzf apache-flume-x.y.z-bin.tar.gz
```

It's useful to put the Flume binary on your path:

```
% export FLUME_HOME=~/sw/apache-flume-x.y.z-bin
% export PATH=$PATH:$FLUME_HOME/bin
```

A Flume agent can then be started with the flume-ng command, as we'll see next.

An Example

To show how Flume works, let's start with a setup that:

1. Watches a local directory for new text files
2. Sends each line of each file to the console as files are added

We'll add the files by hand, but it's easy to imagine a process like a web server creating new files that we want to continuously ingest with Flume. Also, in a real system, rather than just logging the file contents we would write the contents to HDFS for subsequent processing—we'll see how to do that later in the chapter.

In this example, the Flume agent runs a single source-channel-sink, configured using a Java properties file. The configuration controls the types of sources, sinks, and channels that are used, as well as how they are connected together. For this example, we'll use the configuration in Example 14-1.

Example 14-1. Flume configuration using a spooling directory source and a logger sink

```
agent1.sources = source1
agent1.sinks = sink1
agent1.channels = channel1

agent1.sources.source1.channels = channel1
agent1.sinks.sink1.channel = channel1

agent1.sources.source1.type = spooldir
agent1.sources.source1.spoolDir = /tmp/spooldir

agent1.sinks.sink1.type = logger

agent1.channels.channel1.type = file
```

Property names form a hierarchy with the agent name at the top level. In this example, we have a single agent, called agent1. The names for the different components in an agent are defined at the next level, so for example agent1.sources lists the names of the sources that should be run in agent1 (here it is a single source, source1). Similarly, agent1 has a sink (sink1) and a channel (channel1).

The properties for each component are defined at the next level of the hierarchy. The configuration properties that are available for a component depend on the type of the component. In this case, `agent1.sources.source1.type` is set to `spooldir`, which is a spooling directory source that monitors a spooling directory for new files. The spooling directory source defines a `spoolDir` property, so for `source1` the full key is `agent1.sources.source1.spoolDir`. The source's channels are set with `agent1.sources.source1.channels`.

The sink is a `logger` sink for logging events to the console. It too must be connected to the channel (with the `agent1.sinks.sink1.channel` property).[1] The channel is a `file` channel, which means that events in the channel are persisted to disk for durability. The system is illustrated in Figure 14-1.

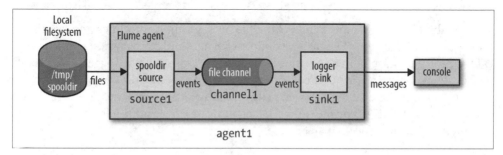

Figure 14-1. Flume agent with a spooling directory source and a logger sink connected by a file channel

Before running the example, we need to create the spooling directory on the local file-system:

```
% mkdir /tmp/spooldir
```

Then we can start the Flume agent using the `flume-ng` command:

```
% flume-ng agent \
  --conf-file spool-to-logger.properties \
  --name agent1 \
  --conf $FLUME_HOME/conf \
  -Dflume.root.logger=INFO,console
```

The Flume properties file from Example 14-1 is specified with the `--conf-file` flag. The agent name must also be passed in with `--name` (since a Flume properties file can

---

1. Note that a source has a `channels` property (plural) but a sink has a `channel` property (singular). This is because a source can feed more than one channel (see "Fan Out" on page 388), but a sink can only be fed by one channel. It's also possible for a channel to feed multiple sinks. This is covered in "Sink Groups" on page 395.

define several agents, we have to say which one to run). The `--conf` flag tells Flume where to find its general configuration, such as environment settings.

In a new terminal, create a file in the spooling directory. The spooling directory source expects files to be immutable. To prevent partially written files from being read by the source, we write the full contents to a hidden file. Then, we do an atomic rename so the source can read it:[2]

```
% echo "Hello Flume" > /tmp/spooldir/.file1.txt
% mv /tmp/spooldir/.file1.txt /tmp/spooldir/file1.txt
```

Back in the agent's terminal, we see that Flume has detected and processed the file:

```
Preparing to move file /tmp/spooldir/file1.txt to
 /tmp/spooldir/file1.txt.COMPLETED
Event: { headers:{} body: 48 65 6C 6C 6F 20 46 6C 75 6D 65         Hello Flume }
```

The spooling directory source ingests the file by splitting it into lines and creating a Flume event for each line. Events have optional headers and a binary body, which is the UTF-8 representation of the line of text. The body is logged by the logger sink in both hexadecimal and string form. The file we placed in the spooling directory was only one line long, so only one event was logged in this case. We also see that the file was renamed to *file1.txt.COMPLETED* by the source, which indicates that Flume has completed processing it and won't process it again.

Transactions and Reliability

Flume uses separate transactions to guarantee delivery from the source to the channel and from the channel to the sink. In the example in the previous section, the spooling directory source creates an event for each line in the file. The source will only mark the file as completed once the transactions encapsulating the delivery of the events to the channel have been successfully committed.

Similarly, a transaction is used for the delivery of the events from the channel to the sink. If for some unlikely reason the events could not be logged, the transaction would be rolled back and the events would remain in the channel for later redelivery.

The channel we are using is a *file channel,* which has the property of being durable: once an event has been written to the channel, it will not be lost, even if the agent restarts. (Flume also provides a *memory channel* that does not have this property, since events are stored in memory. With this channel, events are lost if the agent restarts. Depending on the application, this might be acceptable. The trade-off is that the memory channel has higher throughput than the file channel.)

---

2. For a logfile that is continually appended to, you would periodically roll the logfile and move the old file to the spooling directory for Flume to read it.

The overall effect is that every event produced by the source will reach the sink. The major caveat here is that every event will reach the sink *at least once*—that is, duplicates are possible. Duplicates can be produced in sources or sinks: for example, after an agent restart, the spooling directory source will redeliver events for an uncompleted file, even if some or all of them had been committed to the channel before the restart. After a restart, the logger sink will re-log any event that was logged but not committed (which could happen if the agent was shut down between these two operations).

At-least-once semantics might seem like a limitation, but in practice it is an acceptable performance trade-off. The stronger semantics of *exactly once* require a two-phase commit protocol, which is expensive. This choice is what differentiates Flume (at-least-once semantics) as a high-volume parallel event ingest system from more traditional enterprise messaging systems (exactly-once semantics). With at-least-once semantics, duplicate events can be removed further down the processing pipeline. Usually this takes the form of an application-specific deduplication job written in MapReduce or Hive.

Batching

For efficiency, Flume tries to process events in batches for each transaction, where possible, rather than one by one. Batching helps file channel performance in particular, since every transaction results in a local disk write and `fsync` call.

The batch size used is determined by the component in question, and is configurable in many cases. For example, the spooling directory source will read files in batches of 100 lines. (This can be changed by setting the `batchSize` property.) Similarly, the Avro sink (discussed in "Distribution: Agent Tiers" on page 390) will try to read 100 events from the channel before sending them over RPC, although it won't block if fewer are available.

The HDFS Sink

The point of Flume is to deliver large amounts of data into a Hadoop data store, so let's look at how to configure a Flume agent to deliver events to an HDFS sink. The configuration in Example 14-2 updates the previous example to use an HDFS sink. The only two settings that are required are the sink's type (`hdfs`) and `hdfs.path`, which specifies the directory where files will be placed (if, like here, the filesystem is not specified in the path, it's determined in the usual way from Hadoop's `fs.defaultFS` property). We've also specified a meaningful file prefix and suffix, and instructed Flume to write events to the files in text format.

Example 14-2. Flume configuration using a spooling directory source and an HDFS sink

```
agent1.sources = source1
agent1.sinks = sink1
```

```
agent1.channels = channel1

agent1.sources.source1.channels = channel1
agent1.sinks.sink1.channel = channel1

agent1.sources.source1.type = spooldir
agent1.sources.source1.spoolDir = /tmp/spooldir

agent1.sinks.sink1.type = hdfs
agent1.sinks.sink1.hdfs.path = /tmp/flume
agent1.sinks.sink1.hdfs.filePrefix = events
agent1.sinks.sink1.hdfs.fileSuffix = .log
agent1.sinks.sink1.hdfs.inUsePrefix = _
agent1.sinks.sink1.hdfs.fileType = DataStream

agent1.channels.channel1.type = file
```

Restart the agent to use the *spool-to-hdfs.properties* configuration, and create a new file in the spooling directory:

```
% echo -e "Hello\nAgain" > /tmp/spooldir/.file2.txt
% mv /tmp/spooldir/.file2.txt /tmp/spooldir/file2.txt
```

Events will now be delivered to the HDFS sink and written to a file. Files in the process of being written to have a *.tmp* in-use suffix added to their name to indicate that they are not yet complete. In this example, we have also set `hdfs.inUsePrefix` to be _ (underscore; by default it is empty), which causes files in the process of being written to have that prefix added to their names. This is useful since MapReduce will ignore files that have a _ prefix. So, a typical temporary filename would be *_events. 1399295780136.log.tmp*; the number is a timestamp generated by the HDFS sink.

A file is kept open by the HDFS sink until it has either been open for a given time (default 30 seconds, controlled by the `hdfs.rollInterval` property), has reached a given size (default 1,024 bytes, set by `hdfs.rollSize`), or has had a given number of events written to it (default 10, set by `hdfs.rollCount`). If any of these criteria are met, the file is closed and its in-use prefix and suffix are removed. New events are written to a new file (which will have an in-use prefix and suffix until it is rolled).

After 30 seconds, we can be sure that the file has been rolled and we can take a look at its contents:

```
% hadoop fs -cat /tmp/flume/events.1399295780136.log
Hello
Again
```

The HDFS sink writes files as the user who is running the Flume agent, unless the `hdfs.proxyUser` property is set, in which case files will be written as that user.

Partitioning and Interceptors

Large datasets are often organized into partitions, so that processing can be restricted to particular partitions if only a subset of the data is being queried. For Flume event data, it's very common to partition by time. A process can be run periodically that transforms completed partitions (to remove duplicate events, for example).

It's easy to change the example to store data in partitions by setting hdfs.path to include subdirectories that use time format escape sequences:

```
agent1.sinks.sink1.hdfs.path = /tmp/flume/year=%Y/month=%m/day=%d
```

Here we have chosen to have day-sized partitions, but other levels of granularity are possible, as are other directory layout schemes. (If you are using Hive, see "Partitions and Buckets" on page 491 for how Hive lays out partitions on disk.) The full list of format escape sequences is provided in the documentation for the HDFS sink in the Flume User Guide (*http://flume.apache.org/FlumeUserGuide.html*).

The partition that a Flume event is written to is determined by the timestamp header on the event. Events don't have this header by default, but it can be added using a Flume *interceptor*. Interceptors are components that can modify or drop events in the flow; they are attached to sources, and are run on events before the events have been placed in a channel.[3] The following extra configuration lines add a timestamp interceptor to source1, which adds a timestamp header to every event produced by the source:

```
agent1.sources.source1.interceptors = interceptor1
agent1.sources.source1.interceptors.interceptor1.type = timestamp
```

Using the timestamp interceptor ensures that the timestamps closely reflect the times at which the events were created. For some applications, using a timestamp for when the event was written to HDFS might be sufficient—although, be aware that when there are multiple tiers of Flume agents there can be a significant difference between creation time and write time, especially in the event of agent downtime (see "Distribution: Agent Tiers" on page 390). For these cases, the HDFS sink has a setting, hdfs.useLocal TimeStamp, that will use a timestamp generated by the Flume agent running the HDFS sink.

File Formats

It's normally a good idea to use a binary format for storing your data in, since the resulting files are smaller than they would be if you used text. For the HDFS sink, the file format used is controlled using hdfs.fileType and a combination of a few other properties.

---

3. Table 14-1 describes the interceptors that Flume provides.

If unspecified, `hdfs.fileType` defaults to `SequenceFile`, which will write events to a sequence file with `LongWritable` keys that contain the event timestamp (or the current time if the `timestamp` header is not present) and `BytesWritable` values that contain the event body. It's possible to use `Text` Writable values in the sequence file instead of `BytesWritable` by setting `hdfs.writeFormat` to `Text`.

The configuration is a little different for Avro files. The `hdfs.fileType` property is set to `DataStream`, just like for plain text. Additionally, `serializer` (note the lack of an `hdfs.` prefix) must be set to `avro_event`. To enable compression, set the `serializer.compressionCodec` property. Here is an example of an HDFS sink configured to write Snappy-compressed Avro files:

```
agent1.sinks.sink1.type = hdfs
agent1.sinks.sink1.hdfs.path = /tmp/flume
agent1.sinks.sink1.hdfs.filePrefix = events
agent1.sinks.sink1.hdfs.fileSuffix = .avro
agent1.sinks.sink1.hdfs.fileType = DataStream
agent1.sinks.sink1.serializer = avro_event
agent1.sinks.sink1.serializer.compressionCodec = snappy
```

An event is represented as an Avro record with two fields: `headers`, an Avro map with string values, and `body`, an Avro bytes field.

If you want to use a custom Avro schema, there are a couple of options. If you have Avro in-memory objects that you want to send to Flume, then the `Log4jAppender` is appropriate. It allows you to log an Avro Generic, Specific, or Reflect object using a log4j `Logger` and send it to an Avro source running in a Flume agent (see "Distribution: Agent Tiers" on page 390). In this case, the `serializer` property for the HDFS sink should be set to `org.apache.flume.sink.hdfs.AvroEventSerializer$Builder`, and the Avro schema set in the header (see the class documentation).

Alternatively, if the events are not originally derived from Avro objects, you can write a custom serializer to convert a Flume event into an Avro object with a custom schema. The helper class `AbstractAvroEventSerializer` in the `org.apache.flume.seriali zation` package is a good starting point.

Fan Out

Fan out is the term for delivering events from one source to multiple channels, so they reach multiple sinks. For example, the configuration in Example 14-3 delivers events to both an HDFS sink (`sink1a` via `channel1a`) and a logger sink (`sink1b` via `channel1b`).

Example 14-3. Flume configuration using a spooling directory source, fanning out to an HDFS sink and a logger sink

```
agent1.sources = source1
agent1.sinks = sink1a sink1b
agent1.channels = channel1a channel1b
```

```
agent1.sources.source1.channels = channel1a channel1b
agent1.sinks.sink1a.channel = channel1a
agent1.sinks.sink1b.channel = channel1b

agent1.sources.source1.type = spooldir
agent1.sources.source1.spoolDir = /tmp/spooldir

agent1.sinks.sink1a.type = hdfs
agent1.sinks.sink1a.hdfs.path = /tmp/flume
agent1.sinks.sink1a.hdfs.filePrefix = events
agent1.sinks.sink1a.hdfs.fileSuffix = .log
agent1.sinks.sink1a.hdfs.fileType = DataStream

agent1.sinks.sink1b.type = logger

agent1.channels.channel1a.type = file
agent1.channels.channel1b.type = memory
```

The key change here is that the source is configured to deliver to multiple channels by setting agent1.sources.source1.channels to a space-separated list of channel names, channel1a and channel1b. This time, the channel feeding the logger sink (channel1b) is a memory channel, since we are logging events for debugging purposes and don't mind losing events on agent restart. Also, each channel is configured to feed one sink, just like in the previous examples. The flow is illustrated in Figure 14-2.

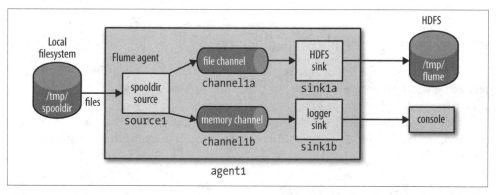

Figure 14-2. Flume agent with a spooling directory source and fanning out to an HDFS sink and a logger sink

Delivery Guarantees

Flume uses a separate transaction to deliver each batch of events from the spooling directory source to each channel. In this example, one transaction will be used to deliver to the channel feeding the HDFS sink, and then another transaction will be used to deliver the same batch of events to the channel for the logger sink. If either of these transactions fails (if a channel is full, for example), then the events will not be removed from the source, and will be retried later.

In this case, since we don't mind if some events are not delivered to the logger sink, we can designate its channel as an *optional* channel, so that if the transaction associated with it fails, this will not cause events to be left in the source and tried again later. (Note that if the agent fails before *both* channel transactions have committed, then the affected events will be redelivered after the agent restarts—this is true even if the uncommitted channels are marked as optional.) To do this, we set the `selector.optional` property on the source, passing it a space-separated list of channels:

```
agent1.sources.source1.selector.optional = channel1b
```

Near-Real-Time Indexing

Indexing events for search is a good example of where fan out is used in practice. A single source of events is sent to both an HDFS sink (this is the main repository of events, so a required channel is used) and a Solr (or Elasticsearch) sink, to build a search index (using an optional channel).

The `MorphlineSolrSink` extracts fields from Flume events and transforms them into a Solr document (using a Morphline configuration file), which is then loaded into a live Solr search server. The process is called *near real time* since ingested data appears in search results in a matter of seconds.

Replicating and Multiplexing Selectors

In normal fan-out flow, events are replicated to all channels—but sometimes more selective behavior might be desirable, so that some events are sent to one channel and others to another. This can be achieved by setting a *multiplexing* selector on the source, and defining routing rules that map particular event header values to channels. See the Flume User Guide (*http://flume.apache.org/FlumeUserGuide.html*) for configuration details.

Distribution: Agent Tiers

How do we scale a set of Flume agents? If there is one agent running on every node producing raw data, then with the setup described so far, at any particular time each file being written to HDFS will consist entirely of the events from one node. It would be better if we could aggregate the events from a group of nodes in a single file, since this would result in fewer, larger files (with the concomitant reduction in pressure on HDFS, and more efficient processing in MapReduce; see "Small files and CombineFileInput-Format" on page 226). Also, if needed, files can be rolled more often since they are being fed by a larger number of nodes, leading to a reduction between the time when an event is created and when it's available for analysis.

Aggregating Flume events is achieved by having *tiers* of Flume agents. The first tier collects events from the original sources (such as web servers) and sends them to a smaller set of agents in the second tier, which aggregate events from the first tier before writing them to HDFS (see Figure 14-3). Further tiers may be warranted for very large numbers of source nodes.

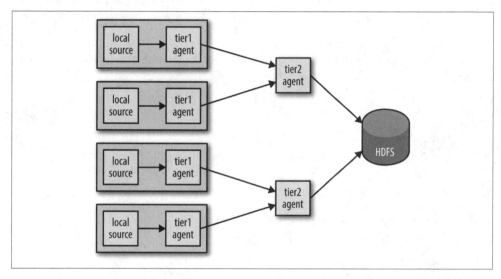

Figure 14-3. Using a second agent tier to aggregate Flume events from the first tier

Tiers are constructed by using a special sink that sends events over the network, and a corresponding source that receives events. The Avro sink sends events over Avro RPC to an Avro source running in another Flume agent. There is also a Thrift sink that does the same thing using Thrift RPC, and is paired with a Thrift source.[4]

 Don't be confused by the naming: Avro sinks and sources do not provide the ability to write (or read) Avro files. They are used only to distribute events between agent tiers, and to do so they use Avro RPC to communicate (hence the name). If you need to write events to Avro files, use the HDFS sink, described in "File Formats" on page 387.

---

4. The Avro sink-source pair is older than the Thrift equivalent, and (at the time of writing) has some features that the Thrift one doesn't provide, such as encryption.

Example 14-4 shows a two-tier Flume configuration. Two agents are defined in the file, named agent1 and agent2. An agent of type agent1 runs in the first tier, and has a spooldir source and an Avro sink connected by a file channel. The agent2 agent runs in the second tier, and has an Avro source that listens on the port that agent1's Avro sink sends events to. The sink for agent2 uses the same HDFS sink configuration from Example 14-2.

Notice that since there are two file channels running on the same machine, they are configured to point to different data and checkpoint directories (they are in the user's home directory by default). This way, they don't try to write their files on top of one another.

Example 14-4. A two-tier Flume configuration using a spooling directory source and an HDFS sink

```
# First-tier agent

agent1.sources = source1
agent1.sinks = sink1
agent1.channels = channel1

agent1.sources.source1.channels = channel1
agent1.sinks.sink1.channel = channel1

agent1.sources.source1.type = spooldir
agent1.sources.source1.spoolDir = /tmp/spooldir

agent1.sinks.sink1.type = avro
agent1.sinks.sink1.hostname = localhost
agent1.sinks.sink1.port = 10000

agent1.channels.channel1.type = file
agent1.channels.channel1.checkpointDir=/tmp/agent1/file-channel/checkpoint
agent1.channels.channel1.dataDirs=/tmp/agent1/file-channel/data

# Second-tier agent

agent2.sources = source2
agent2.sinks = sink2
agent2.channels = channel2

agent2.sources.source2.channels = channel2
agent2.sinks.sink2.channel = channel2

agent2.sources.source2.type = avro
agent2.sources.source2.bind = localhost
agent2.sources.source2.port = 10000

agent2.sinks.sink2.type = hdfs
agent2.sinks.sink2.hdfs.path = /tmp/flume
agent2.sinks.sink2.hdfs.filePrefix = events
```

```
agent2.sinks.sink2.hdfs.fileSuffix = .log
agent2.sinks.sink2.hdfs.fileType = DataStream

agent2.channels.channel2.type = file
agent2.channels.channel2.checkpointDir=/tmp/agent2/file-channel/checkpoint
agent2.channels.channel2.dataDirs=/tmp/agent2/file-channel/data
```

The system is illustrated in Figure 14-4.

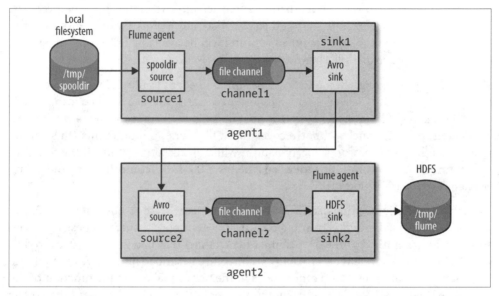

Figure 14-4. Two Flume agents connected by an Avro sink-source pair

Each agent is run independently, using the same `--conf-file` parameter but different agent `--name` parameters:

```
% flume-ng agent --conf-file spool-to-hdfs-tiered.properties --name agent1 ...
```

and:

```
% flume-ng agent --conf-file spool-to-hdfs-tiered.properties --name agent2 ...
```

Delivery Guarantees

Flume uses transactions to ensure that each batch of events is reliably delivered from a source to a channel, and from a channel to a sink. In the context of the Avro sink-source connection, transactions ensure that events are reliably delivered from one agent to the next.

The operation to read a batch of events from the file channel in `agent1` by the Avro sink will be wrapped in a transaction. The transaction will only be committed once the Avro sink has received the (synchronous) confirmation that the write to the Avro source's RPC endpoint was successful. This confirmation will only be sent once agent2's transaction wrapping the operation to write the batch of events to its file channel has been successfully committed. Thus, the Avro sink-source pair guarantees that an event is delivered from one Flume agent's channel to another Flume agent's channel (at least once).

If either agent is not running, then clearly events cannot be delivered to HDFS. For example, if agent1 stops running, then files will accumulate in the spooling directory, to be processed once agent1 starts up again. Also, any events in an agent's own file channel at the point the agent stopped running will be available on restart, due to the durability guarantee that file channel provides.

If agent2 stops running, then events will be stored in agent1's file channel until agent2 starts again. Note, however, that channels necessarily have a limited capacity; if agent1's channel fills up while agent2 is not running, then any new events will be lost. By default, a file channel will not recover more than one million events (this can be overridden by its capacity property), and it will stop accepting events if the free disk space for its checkpoint directory falls below 500 MB (controlled by the mini mumRequiredSpace property).

Both these scenarios assume that the agent will eventually recover, but that is not always the case (if the hardware it is running on fails, for example). If agent1 doesn't recover, then the loss is limited to the events in its file channel that had not been delivered to agent2 before agent1 shut down. In the architecture described here, there are multiple first-tier agents like agent1, so other nodes in the tier can take over the function of the failed node. For example, if the nodes are running load-balanced web servers, then other nodes will absorb the failed web server's traffic, and they will generate new Flume events that are delivered to agent2. Thus, no new events are lost.

An unrecoverable agent2 failure is more serious, however. Any events in the channels of upstream first-tier agents (agent1 instances) will be lost, and all new events generated by these agents will not be delivered either. The solution to this problem is for agent1 to have multiple redundant Avro sinks, arranged in a *sink group*, so that if the destination agent2 Avro endpoint is unavailable, it can try another sink from the group. We'll see how to do this in the next section.

Sink Groups

A sink group allows multiple sinks to be treated as one, for failover or load-balancing purposes (see Figure 14-5). If a second-tier agent is unavailable, then events will be delivered to another second-tier agent and on to HDFS without disruption.

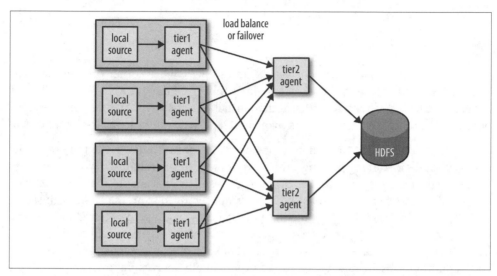

Figure 14-5. Using multiple sinks for load balancing or failover

To configure a sink group, the agent's `sinkgroups` property is set to define the sink group's name; then the sink group lists the sinks in the group, and also the type of the sink processor, which sets the policy for choosing a sink. Example 14-5 shows the configuration for load balancing between two Avro endpoints.

Example 14-5. A Flume configuration for load balancing between two Avro endpoints using a sink group

```
agent1.sources = source1
agent1.sinks = sink1a sink1b
agent1.sinkgroups = sinkgroup1
agent1.channels = channel1

agent1.sources.source1.channels = channel1
agent1.sinks.sink1a.channel = channel1
agent1.sinks.sink1b.channel = channel1

agent1.sinkgroups.sinkgroup1.sinks = sink1a sink1b
agent1.sinkgroups.sinkgroup1.processor.type = load_balance
agent1.sinkgroups.sinkgroup1.processor.backoff = true
```

```
agent1.sources.source1.type = spooldir
agent1.sources.source1.spoolDir = /tmp/spooldir

agent1.sinks.sink1a.type = avro
agent1.sinks.sink1a.hostname = localhost
agent1.sinks.sink1a.port = 10000

agent1.sinks.sink1b.type = avro
agent1.sinks.sink1b.hostname = localhost
agent1.sinks.sink1b.port = 10001

agent1.channels.channel1.type = file
```

There are two Avro sinks defined, sink1a and sink1b, which differ only in the Avro endpoint they are connected to (since we are running all the examples on localhost, it is the port that is different; for a distributed install, the hosts would differ and the ports would be the same). We also define sinkgroup1, and set its sinks to sink1a and sink1b.

The processor type is set to load_balance, which attempts to distribute the event flow over both sinks in the group, using a round-robin selection mechanism (you can change this using the processor.selector property). If a sink is unavailable, then the next sink is tried; if they are all unavailable, the event is not removed from the channel, just like in the single sink case. By default, sink unavailability is not remembered by the sink processor, so failing sinks are retried for every batch of events being delivered. This can be inefficient, so we have set the processor.backoff property to change the behavior so that failing sinks are blacklisted for an exponentially increasing timeout period (up to a maximum period of 30 seconds, controlled by processor.selector.maxTimeOut).

 There is another type of processor, failover, that instead of load balancing events across sinks uses a preferred sink if it is available, and fails over to another sink in the case that the preferred sink is down. The failover sink processor maintains a priority order for sinks in the group, and attempts delivery in order of priority. If the sink with the highest priority is unavailable the one with the next highest priority is tried, and so on. Failed sinks are blacklisted for an increasing timeout period (up to a maximum period of 30 seconds, controlled by processor.maxpenalty).

The configuration for one of the second-tier agents, agent2a, is shown in Example 14-6.

Example 14-6. Flume configuration for second-tier agent in a load balancing scenario

```
agent2a.sources = source2a
agent2a.sinks = sink2a
agent2a.channels = channel2a

agent2a.sources.source2a.channels = channel2a
agent2a.sinks.sink2a.channel = channel2a

agent2a.sources.source2a.type = avro
agent2a.sources.source2a.bind = localhost
agent2a.sources.source2a.port = 10000

agent2a.sinks.sink2a.type = hdfs
agent2a.sinks.sink2a.hdfs.path = /tmp/flume
agent2a.sinks.sink2a.hdfs.filePrefix = events-a
agent2a.sinks.sink2a.hdfs.fileSuffix = .log
agent2a.sinks.sink2a.hdfs.fileType = DataStream

agent2a.channels.channel2a.type = file
```

The configuration for `agent2b` is the same, except for the Avro source port (since we are running the examples on localhost) and the file prefix for the files created by the HDFS sink. The file prefix is used to ensure that HDFS files created by second-tier agents at the same time don't collide.

In the more usual case of agents running on different machines, the hostname can be used to make the filename unique by configuring a host interceptor (see Table 14-1) and including the `%{host}` escape sequence in the file path, or prefix:

```
agent2.sinks.sink2.hdfs.filePrefix = events-%{host}
```

A diagram of the whole system is shown in Figure 14-6.

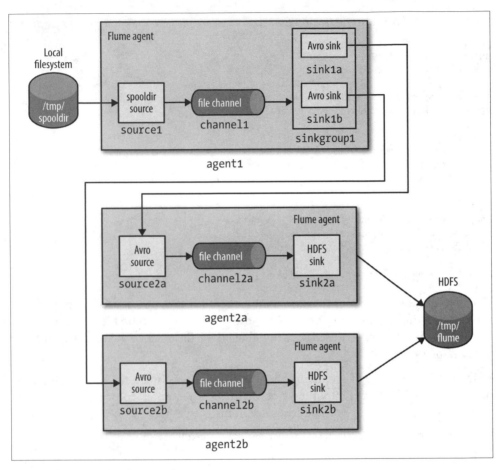

Figure 14-6. Load balancing between two agents

Integrating Flume with Applications

An Avro source is an RPC endpoint that accepts Flume events, making it possible to write an RPC client to send events to the endpoint, which can be embedded in any application that wants to introduce events into Flume.

The *Flume SDK* is a module that provides a Java `RpcClient` class for sending `Event` objects to an Avro endpoint (an Avro source running in a Flume agent, usually in another tier). Clients can be configured to fail over or load balance between endpoints, and Thrift endpoints (Thrift sources) are supported too.

The Flume *embedded agent* offers similar functionality: it is a cut-down Flume agent that runs in a Java application. It has a single special source that your application sends Flume `Event` objects to by calling a method on the `EmbeddedAgent` object; the only sinks that are supported are Avro sinks, but it can be configured with multiple sinks for failover or load balancing.

Both the SDK and the embedded agent are described in more detail in the Flume Developer Guide (*http://flume.apache.org/FlumeDeveloperGuide.html*).

Component Catalog

We've only used a handful of Flume components in this chapter. Flume comes with many more, which are briefly described in Table 14-1. Refer to the Flume User Guide (*http://flume.apache.org/FlumeUserGuide.html*) for further information on how to configure and use them.

Table 14-1. Flume components

Category	Component	Description
Source	Avro	Listens on a port for events sent over Avro RPC by an Avro sink or the Flume SDK.
	Exec	Runs a Unix command (e.g., `tail -F/path/to/file`) and converts lines read from standard output into events. Note that this source cannot guarantee delivery of events to the channel; see the spooling directory source or the Flume SDK for better alternatives.
	HTTP	Listens on a port and converts HTTP requests into events using a pluggable handler (e.g., a JSON handler or binary blob handler).
	JMS	Reads messages from a JMS queue or topic and converts them into events.
	Netcat	Listens on a port and converts each line of text into an event.
	Sequence generator	Generates events from an incrementing counter. Useful for testing.
	Spooling directory	Reads lines from files placed in a spooling directory and converts them into events.
	Syslog	Reads lines from syslog and converts them into events.
	Thrift	Listens on a port for events sent over Thrift RPC by a Thrift sink or the Flume SDK.
	Twitter	Connects to Twitter's streaming API (1% of the firehose) and converts tweets into events.
Sink	Avro	Sends events over Avro RPC to an Avro source.
	Elasticsearch	Writes events to an Elasticsearch cluster using the Logstash format.
	File roll	Writes events to the local filesystem.
	HBase	Writes events to HBase using a choice of serializer.
	HDFS	Writes events to HDFS in text, sequence file, Avro, or a custom format.
	IRC	Sends events to an IRC channel.
	Logger	Logs events at `INFO` level using SLF4J. Useful for testing.
	Morphline (Solr)	Runs events through an in-process chain of Morphline commands. Typically used to load data into Solr.
	Null	Discards all events.
	Thrift	Sends events over Thrift RPC to a Thrift source.

Category	Component	Description
Channel	File	Stores events in a transaction log stored on the local filesystem.
	JDBC	Stores events in a database (embedded Derby).
	Memory	Stores events in an in-memory queue.
Interceptor	Host	Sets a `host` header containing the agent's hostname or IP address on all events.
	Morphline	Filters events through a Morphline configuration file. Useful for conditionally dropping events or adding headers based on pattern matching or content extraction.
	Regex extractor	Sets headers extracted from the event body as text using a specified regular expression.
	Regex filtering	Includes or excludes events by matching the event body as text against a specified regular expression.
	Static	Sets a fixed header and value on all events.
	Timestamp	Sets a `timestamp` header containing the time in milliseconds at which the agent processes the event.
	UUID	Sets an `id` header containing a universally unique identifier on all events. Useful for later deduplication.

Further Reading

This chapter has given a short overview of Flume. For more detail, see *Using Flume* by Hari Shreedharan (O'Reilly, 2014). There is also a lot of practical information about designing ingest pipelines (and building Hadoop applications in general) in *Hadoop Application Architectures* by Mark Grover, Ted Malaska, Jonathan Seidman, and Gwen Shapira (O'Reilly, 2014).

Sqoop

Aaron Kimball

A great strength of the Hadoop platform is its ability to work with data in several different forms. HDFS can reliably store logs and other data from a plethora of sources, and MapReduce programs can parse diverse ad hoc data formats, extracting relevant information and combining multiple datasets into powerful results.

But to interact with data in storage repositories outside of HDFS, MapReduce programs need to use external APIs. Often, valuable data in an organization is stored in structured data stores such as relational database management systems (RDBMSs). Apache Sqoop (*http://sqoop.apache.org/*) is an open source tool that allows users to extract data from a structured data store into Hadoop for further processing. This processing can be done with MapReduce programs or other higher-level tools such as Hive. (It's even possible to use Sqoop to move data from a database into HBase.) When the final results of an analytic pipeline are available, Sqoop can export these results back to the data store for consumption by other clients.

In this chapter, we'll take a look at how Sqoop works and how you can use it in your data processing pipeline.

Getting Sqoop

Sqoop is available in a few places. The primary home of the project is the Apache Software Foundation (*http://sqoop.apache.org/*). This repository contains all the Sqoop source code and documentation. Official releases are available at this site, as well as the source code for the version currently under development. The repository itself contains instructions for compiling the project. Alternatively, you can get Sqoop from a Hadoop vendor distribution.

If you download a release from Apache, it will be placed in a directory such as */home/yourname/sqoop-x.y.z/*. We'll call this directory $SQOOP_HOME. You can run Sqoop by running the executable script $SQOOP_HOME/bin/sqoop.

If you've installed a release from a vendor, the package will have placed Sqoop's scripts in a standard location such as */usr/bin/sqoop*. You can run Sqoop by simply typing sqoop at the command line. (Regardless of how you install Sqoop, we'll refer to this script as just *sqoop* from here on.)

Sqoop 2

Sqoop 2 is a rewrite of Sqoop that addresses the architectural limitations of Sqoop 1. For example, Sqoop 1 is a command-line tool and does not provide a Java API, so it's difficult to embed it in other programs. Also, in Sqoop 1 every connector has to know about every output format, so it is a lot of work to write new connectors. Sqoop 2 has a server component that runs jobs, as well as a range of clients: a command-line interface (CLI), a web UI, a REST API, and a Java API. Sqoop 2 also will be able to use alternative execution engines, such as Spark. Note that Sqoop 2's CLI is not compatible with Sqoop 1's CLI.

The Sqoop 1 release series is the current stable release series, and is what is used in this chapter. Sqoop 2 is under active development but does not yet have feature parity with Sqoop 1, so you should check that it can support your use case before using it in production.

Running Sqoop with no arguments does not do much of interest:

```
% sqoop
Try sqoop help for usage.
```

Sqoop is organized as a set of tools or commands. If you don't select a tool, Sqoop does not know what to do. help is the name of one such tool; it can print out the list of available tools, like this:

```
% sqoop help
usage: sqoop COMMAND [ARGS]

Available commands:
  codegen            Generate code to interact with database records
  create-hive-table  Import a table definition into Hive
  eval               Evaluate a SQL statement and display the results
  export             Export an HDFS directory to a database table
  help               List available commands
  import             Import a table from a database to HDFS
  import-all-tables  Import tables from a database to HDFS
  job                Work with saved jobs
  list-databases     List available databases on a server
```

```
    list-tables        List available tables in a database
    merge              Merge results of incremental imports
    metastore          Run a standalone Sqoop metastore
    version            Display version information

See 'sqoop help COMMAND' for information on a specific command.
```

As it explains, the `help` tool can also provide specific usage instructions on a particular tool when you provide that tool's name as an argument:

```
% sqoop help import
usage: sqoop import [GENERIC-ARGS] [TOOL-ARGS]

Common arguments:
    --connect <jdbc-uri>        Specify JDBC connect string
    --driver <class-name>       Manually specify JDBC driver class to use
    --hadoop-home <dir>         Override $HADOOP_HOME
    --help                      Print usage instructions
-P                              Read password from console
    --password <password>       Set authentication password
    --username <username>       Set authentication username
    --verbose                   Print more information while working
...
```

An alternate way of running a Sqoop tool is to use a tool-specific script. This script will be named *sqoop-toolname* (e.g., *sqoop-help*, *sqoop-import*, etc.). Running these scripts from the command line is identical to running `sqoop help` or `sqoop import`.

Sqoop Connectors

Sqoop has an extension framework that makes it possible to import data from—and export data to—any external storage system that has bulk data transfer capabilities. A Sqoop *connector* is a modular component that uses this framework to enable Sqoop imports and exports. Sqoop ships with connectors for working with a range of popular databases, including MySQL, PostgreSQL, Oracle, SQL Server, DB2, and Netezza. There is also a generic JDBC connector for connecting to any database that supports Java's JDBC protocol. Sqoop provides optimized MySQL, PostgreSQL, Oracle, and Netezza connectors that use database-specific APIs to perform bulk transfers more efficiently (this is discussed more in "Direct-Mode Imports" on page 411).

As well as the built-in Sqoop connectors, various third-party connectors are available for data stores, ranging from enterprise data warehouses (such as Teradata) to NoSQL stores (such as Couchbase). These connectors must be downloaded separately and can be added to an existing Sqoop installation by following the instructions that come with the connector.

A Sample Import

After you install Sqoop, you can use it to import data to Hadoop. For the examples in this chapter, we'll use MySQL, which is easy to use and available for a large number of platforms.

To install and configure MySQL, follow the online documentation (*http://dev.mysql.com/doc*). Chapter 2 ("Installing and Upgrading MySQL") in particular should help. Users of Debian-based Linux systems (e.g., Ubuntu) can type `sudo apt-get install mysql-client mysql-server`. Red Hat users can type `sudo yum install mysql mysql-server`.

Now that MySQL is installed, let's log in and create a database (Example 15-1).

Example 15-1. Creating a new MySQL database schema

```
% mysql -u root -p
Enter password:
Welcome to the MySQL monitor.  Commands end with ; or \g.
Your MySQL connection id is 235
Server version: 5.6.21 MySQL Community Server (GPL)

Type 'help;' or '\h' for help. Type '\c' to clear the current input
statement.

mysql> CREATE DATABASE hadoopguide;
Query OK, 1 row affected (0.00 sec)

mysql> GRANT ALL PRIVILEGES ON hadoopguide.* TO ''@'localhost';
Query OK, 0 rows affected (0.00 sec)

mysql> quit;
Bye
```

The password prompt shown in this example asks for your root user password. This is likely the same as the password for the root shell login. If you are running Ubuntu or another variant of Linux where root cannot log in directly, enter the password you picked at MySQL installation time. (If you didn't set a password, then just press Return.)

In this session, we created a new database schema called hadoopguide, which we'll use throughout this chapter. We then allowed any local user to view and modify the contents of the hadoopguide schema, and closed our session.[1]

---

1. Of course, in a production deployment we'd need to be much more careful about access control, but this serves for demonstration purposes. The grant privilege shown in the example also assumes you're running a pseudodistributed Hadoop instance. If you're working with a distributed Hadoop cluster, you'd need to enable remote access by at least one user, whose account would be used to perform imports and exports via Sqoop.

Now let's log back into the database (do this as yourself this time, not as root) and create a table to import into HDFS (Example 15-2).

Example 15-2. Populating the database

```
% mysql hadoopguide
Welcome to the MySQL monitor.  Commands end with ; or \g.
Your MySQL connection id is 257
Server version: 5.6.21 MySQL Community Server (GPL)

Type 'help;' or '\h' for help. Type '\c' to clear the current input statement.

mysql> CREATE TABLE widgets(id INT NOT NULL PRIMARY KEY AUTO_INCREMENT,
    -> widget_name VARCHAR(64) NOT NULL,
    -> price DECIMAL(10,2),
    -> design_date DATE,
    -> version INT,
    -> design_comment VARCHAR(100));
Query OK, 0 rows affected (0.00 sec)

mysql> INSERT INTO widgets VALUES (NULL, 'sprocket', 0.25, '2010-02-10',
    -> 1, 'Connects two gizmos');
Query OK, 1 row affected (0.00 sec)

mysql> INSERT INTO widgets VALUES (NULL, 'gizmo', 4.00, '2009-11-30', 4,
    -> NULL);
Query OK, 1 row affected (0.00 sec)

mysql> INSERT INTO widgets VALUES (NULL, 'gadget', 99.99, '1983-08-13',
    -> 13, 'Our flagship product');
Query OK, 1 row affected (0.00 sec)

mysql> quit;
```

In this listing, we created a new table called widgets. We'll be using this fictional product database in further examples in this chapter. The widgets table contains several fields representing a variety of data types.

Before going any further, you need to download the JDBC driver JAR file for MySQL (Connector/J) and add it to Sqoop's classpath, which is simply achieved by placing it in Sqoop's *lib* directory.

Now let's use Sqoop to import this table into HDFS:

```
% sqoop import --connect jdbc:mysql://localhost/hadoopguide \
> --table widgets -m 1
...
14/10/28 21:36:23 INFO tool.CodeGenTool: Beginning code generation
...
14/10/28 21:36:28 INFO mapreduce.Job: Running job: job_1413746845532_0008
14/10/28 21:36:35 INFO mapreduce.Job: Job job_1413746845532_0008 running in
uber mode : false
```

```
14/10/28 21:36:35 INFO mapreduce.Job:  map 0% reduce 0%
14/10/28 21:36:41 INFO mapreduce.Job:  map 100% reduce 0%
14/10/28 21:36:41 INFO mapreduce.Job: Job job_1413746845532_0008 completed
successfully
...
14/10/28 21:36:41 INFO mapreduce.ImportJobBase: Retrieved 3 records.
```

Sqoop's `import` tool will run a MapReduce job that connects to the MySQL database and reads the table. By default, this will use four map tasks in parallel to speed up the import process. Each task will write its imported results to a different file, but all in a common directory. Because we knew that we had only three rows to import in this example, we specified that Sqoop should use a single map task (`-m 1`) so we get a single file in HDFS.

We can inspect this file's contents like so:

```
% hadoop fs -cat widgets/part-m-00000
1,sprocket,0.25,2010-02-10,1,Connects two gizmos
2,gizmo,4.00,2009-11-30,4,null
3,gadget,99.99,1983-08-13,13,Our flagship product
```

The connect string (`jdbc:mysql://localhost/hadoopguide`) shown in the example will read from a database on the local machine. If a distributed Hadoop cluster is being used, `localhost` should not be specified in the connect string, because map tasks not running on the same machine as the database will fail to connect. Even if Sqoop is run from the same host as the database sever, the full hostname should be specified.

By default, Sqoop will generate comma-delimited text files for our imported data. Delimiters can be specified explicitly, as well as field enclosing and escape characters, to allow the presence of delimiters in the field contents. The command-line arguments that specify delimiter characters, file formats, compression, and more fine-grained control of the import process are described in the Sqoop User Guide distributed with Sqoop,[2] as well as in the online help (`sqoop help import`, or `man sqoop-import` in CDH).

Text and Binary File Formats

Sqoop is capable of importing into a few different file formats. Text files (the default) offer a human-readable representation of data, platform independence, and the simplest structure. However, they cannot hold binary fields (such as database columns of type `VARBINARY`), and distinguishing between `null` values and `String`-based fields contain-

---

2. Available from the Apache Software Foundation website (*http://sqoop.apache.org/*).

ing the value "null" can be problematic (although using the --null-string import option allows you to control the representation of null values).

To handle these conditions, Sqoop also supports SequenceFiles, Avro datafiles, and Parquet files. These binary formats provide the most precise representation possible of the imported data. They also allow data to be compressed while retaining MapReduce's ability to process different sections of the same file in parallel. However, current versions of Sqoop cannot load Avro datafiles or SequenceFiles into Hive (although you can load Avro into Hive manually, and Parquet can be loaded directly into Hive by Sqoop). Another disadvantage of SequenceFiles is that they are Java specific, whereas Avro and Parquet files can be processed by a wide range of languages.

Generated Code

In addition to writing the contents of the database table to HDFS, Sqoop also provides you with a generated Java source file (*widgets.java*) written to the current local directory. (After running the sqoop import command shown earlier, you can see this file by running ls widgets.java.)

As you'll learn in "Imports: A Deeper Look" on page 408, Sqoop can use generated code to handle the deserialization of table-specific data from the database source before writing it to HDFS.

The generated class (widgets) is capable of holding a single record retrieved from the imported table. It can manipulate such a record in MapReduce or store it in a Sequen ceFile in HDFS. (SequenceFiles written by Sqoop during the import process will store each imported row in the "value" element of the SequenceFile's key-value pair format, using the generated class.)

It is likely that you don't want to name your generated class widgets, since each instance of the class refers to only a single record. We can use a different Sqoop tool to generate source code without performing an import; this generated code will still examine the database table to determine the appropriate data types for each field:

```
% sqoop codegen --connect jdbc:mysql://localhost/hadoopguide \
> --table widgets --class-name Widget
```

The codegen tool simply generates code; it does not perform the full import. We specified that we'd like it to generate a class named Widget; this will be written to *Widget.java*. We also could have specified --class-name and other code-generation arguments during the import process we performed earlier. This tool can be used to regenerate code if you accidentally remove the source file, or generate code with different settings than were used during the import.

If you're working with records imported to SequenceFiles, it is inevitable that you'll need to use the generated classes (to deserialize data from the SequenceFile storage).

You can work with text-file-based records without using generated code, but as we'll see in "Working with Imported Data" on page 412, Sqoop's generated code can handle some tedious aspects of data processing for you.

Additional Serialization Systems

Recent versions of Sqoop support Avro-based serialization and schema generation as well (see Chapter 12), allowing you to use Sqoop in your project without integrating with generated code.

Imports: A Deeper Look

As mentioned earlier, Sqoop imports a table from a database by running a MapReduce job that extracts rows from the table, and writes the records to HDFS. How does Map-Reduce read the rows? This section explains how Sqoop works under the hood.

At a high level, Figure 15-1 demonstrates how Sqoop interacts with both the database source and Hadoop. Like Hadoop itself, Sqoop is written in Java. Java provides an API called Java Database Connectivity, or JDBC, that allows applications to access data stored in an RDBMS as well as to inspect the nature of this data. Most database vendors provide a JDBC *driver* that implements the JDBC API and contains the necessary code to connect to their database servers.

 Based on the URL in the connect string used to access the database, Sqoop attempts to predict which driver it should load. You still need to download the JDBC driver itself and install it on your Sqoop client. For cases where Sqoop does not know which JDBC driver is appropriate, users can specify the JDBC driver explicitly with the --driver argument. This capability allows Sqoop to work with a wide variety of database platforms.

Before the import can start, Sqoop uses JDBC to examine the table it is to import. It retrieves a list of all the columns and their SQL data types. These SQL types (VARCHAR, INTEGER, etc.) can then be mapped to Java data types (String, Integer, etc.), which will hold the field values in MapReduce applications. Sqoop's code generator will use this information to create a table-specific class to hold a record extracted from the table.

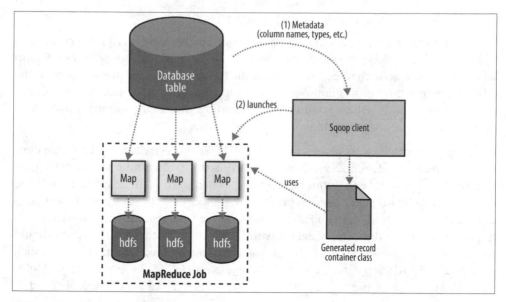

Figure 15-1. Sqoop's import process

The Widget class from earlier, for example, contains the following methods that retrieve each column from an extracted record:

```
public Integer get_id();
public String get_widget_name();
public java.math.BigDecimal get_price();
public java.sql.Date get_design_date();
public Integer get_version();
public String get_design_comment();
```

More critical to the import system's operation, though, are the serialization methods that form the DBWritable interface, which allow the Widget class to interact with JDBC:

```
public void readFields(ResultSet __dbResults) throws SQLException;
public void write(PreparedStatement __dbStmt) throws SQLException;
```

JDBC's ResultSet interface provides a cursor that retrieves records from a query; the readFields() method here will populate the fields of the Widget object with the columns from one row of the ResultSet's data. The write() method shown here allows Sqoop to insert new Widget rows into a table, a process called *exporting*. Exports are discussed in "Performing an Export" on page 417.

The MapReduce job launched by Sqoop uses an InputFormat that can read sections of a table from a database via JDBC. The DataDrivenDBInputFormat provided with Hadoop partitions a query's results over several map tasks.

Reading a table is typically done with a simple query such as:

```
SELECT col1,col2,col3,... FROM tableName
```

But often, better import performance can be gained by dividing this query across multiple nodes. This is done using a *splitting column*. Using metadata about the table, Sqoop will guess a good column to use for splitting the table (typically the primary key for the table, if one exists). The minimum and maximum values for the primary key column are retrieved, and then these are used in conjunction with a target number of tasks to determine the queries that each map task should issue.

For example, suppose the `widgets` table had 100,000 entries, with the `id` column containing values 0 through 99,999. When importing this table, Sqoop would determine that `id` is the primary key column for the table. When starting the MapReduce job, the `DataDrivenDBInputFormat` used to perform the import would issue a statement such as `SELECT MIN(id), MAX(id) FROM widgets`. These values would then be used to interpolate over the entire range of data. Assuming we specified that five map tasks should run in parallel (with `-m 5`), this would result in each map task executing queries such as `SELECT id, widget_name, ... FROM widgets WHERE id >= 0 AND id < 20000`, `SELECT id, widget_name, ... FROM widgets WHERE id >= 20000 AND id < 40000`, and so on.

The choice of splitting column is essential to parallelizing work efficiently. If the `id` column were not uniformly distributed (perhaps there are no widgets with IDs between 50,000 and 75,000), then some map tasks might have little or no work to perform, whereas others would have a great deal. Users can specify a particular splitting column when running an import job (via the `--split-by` argument), to tune the job to the data's actual distribution. If an import job is run as a single (sequential) task with `-m 1`, this split process is not performed.

After generating the deserialization code and configuring the `InputFormat`, Sqoop sends the job to the MapReduce cluster. Map tasks execute the queries and deserialize rows from the `ResultSet` into instances of the generated class, which are either stored directly in `SequenceFiles` or transformed into delimited text before being written to HDFS.

Controlling the Import

Sqoop does not need to import an entire table at a time. For example, a subset of the table's columns can be specified for import. Users can also specify a `WHERE` clause to include in queries via the `--where` argument, which bounds the rows of the table to import. For example, if widgets 0 through 99,999 were imported last month, but this month our vendor catalog included 1,000 new types of widget, an import could be configured with the clause `WHERE id >= 100000`; this will start an import job to retrieve all the new rows added to the source database since the previous import run. User-supplied `WHERE` clauses are applied before task splitting is performed, and are pushed down into the queries executed by each task.

For more control—to perform column transformations, for example—users can specify a `--query` argument.

Imports and Consistency

When importing data to HDFS, it is important that you ensure access to a consistent snapshot of the source data. (Map tasks reading from a database in parallel are running in separate processes. Thus, they cannot share a single database transaction.) The best way to do this is to ensure that any processes that update existing rows of a table are disabled during the import.

Incremental Imports

It's common to run imports on a periodic basis so that the data in HDFS is kept synchronized with the data stored in the database. To do this, there needs to be some way of identifying the new data. Sqoop will import rows that have a column value (for the column specified with `--check-column`) that is greater than some specified value (set via `--last-value`).

The value specified as `--last-value` can be a row ID that is strictly increasing, such as an `AUTO_INCREMENT` primary key in MySQL. This is suitable for the case where new rows are added to the database table, but existing rows are not updated. This mode is called *append* mode, and is activated via `--incremental append`. Another option is time-based incremental imports (specified by `--incremental lastmodified`), which is appropriate when existing rows may be updated, and there is a column (the check column) that records the last modified time of the update.

At the end of an incremental import, Sqoop will print out the value to be specified as `--last-value` on the next import. This is useful when running incremental imports manually, but for running periodic imports it is better to use Sqoop's saved job facility, which automatically stores the last value and uses it on the next job run. Type `sqoop job --help` for usage instructions for saved jobs.

Direct-Mode Imports

Sqoop's architecture allows it to choose from multiple available strategies for performing an import. Most databases will use the `DataDrivenDBInputFormat`-based approach described earlier. Some databases, however, offer specific tools designed to extract data quickly. For example, MySQL's `mysqldump` application can read from a table with greater throughput than a JDBC channel. The use of these external tools is referred to as *direct mode* in Sqoop's documentation. Direct mode must be specifically enabled by the user (via the `--direct` argument), as it is not as general purpose as the JDBC approach. (For example, MySQL's direct mode cannot handle large objects, such as `CLOB` or `BLOB` columns, and that's why Sqoop needs to use a JDBC-specific API to load these columns into HDFS.)

For databases that provide such tools, Sqoop can use these to great effect. A direct-mode import from MySQL is usually much more efficient (in terms of map tasks and time required) than a comparable JDBC-based import. Sqoop will still launch multiple map tasks in parallel. These tasks will then spawn instances of the `mysqldump` program and read its output. Sqoop can also perform direct-mode imports from PostgreSQL, Oracle, and Netezza.

Even when direct mode is used to access the contents of a database, the metadata is still queried through JDBC.

Working with Imported Data

Once data has been imported to HDFS, it is ready for processing by custom MapReduce programs. Text-based imports can easily be used in scripts run with Hadoop Streaming or in MapReduce jobs run with the default `TextInputFormat`.

To use individual fields of an imported record, though, the field delimiters (and any escape/enclosing characters) must be parsed and the field values extracted and converted to the appropriate data types. For example, the ID of the "sprocket" widget is represented as the string `"1"` in the text file, but should be parsed into an `Integer` or `int` variable in Java. The generated table class provided by Sqoop can automate this process, allowing you to focus on the actual MapReduce job to run. Each autogenerated class has several overloaded methods named `parse()` that operate on the data represented as `Text`, `CharSequence`, `char[]`, or other common types.

The MapReduce application called `MaxWidgetId` (available in the example code) will find the widget with the highest ID. The class can be compiled into a JAR file along with *Widget.java* using the Maven POM that comes with the example code. The JAR file is called *sqoop-examples.jar*, and is executed like so:

```
% HADOOP_CLASSPATH=$SQOOP_HOME/sqoop-version.jar hadoop jar \
> sqoop-examples.jar MaxWidgetId -libjars $SQOOP_HOME/sqoop-version.jar
```

This command line ensures that Sqoop is on the classpath locally (via $HADOOP_CLASS PATH) when running the `MaxWidgetId.run()` method, as well as when map tasks are running on the cluster (via the `-libjars` argument).

When run, the *maxwidget* path in HDFS will contain a file named *part-r-00000* with the following expected result:

```
3,gadget,99.99,1983-08-13,13,Our flagship product
```

It is worth noting that in this example MapReduce program, a `Widget` object was emitted from the mapper to the reducer; the autogenerated `Widget` class implements the

`Writable` interface provided by Hadoop, which allows the object to be sent via Hadoop's serialization mechanism, as well as written to and read from `SequenceFiles`.

The `MaxWidgetId` example is built on the new MapReduce API. MapReduce applications that rely on Sqoop-generated code can be built on the new or old APIs, though some advanced features (such as working with large objects) are more convenient to use in the new API.

Avro-based imports can be processed using the APIs described in "Avro MapReduce" on page 359. With the Generic Avro mapping, the MapReduce program does not need to use schema-specific generated code (although this is an option too, by using Avro's Specific compiler; Sqoop does not do the code generation in this case). The example code includes a program called `MaxWidgetIdGenericAvro`, which finds the widget with the highest ID and writes out the result in an Avro datafile.

Imported Data and Hive

As we'll see in Chapter 17, for many types of analysis, using a system such as Hive to handle relational operations can dramatically ease the development of the analytic pipeline. Especially for data originally from a relational data source, using Hive makes a lot of sense. Hive and Sqoop together form a powerful toolchain for performing analysis.

Suppose we had another log of data in our system, coming from a web-based widget purchasing system. This might return logfiles containing a widget ID, a quantity, a shipping address, and an order date.

Here is a snippet from an example log of this type:

```
1,15,120 Any St.,Los Angeles,CA,90210,2010-08-01
3,4,120 Any St.,Los Angeles,CA,90210,2010-08-01
2,5,400 Some Pl.,Cupertino,CA,95014,2010-07-30
2,7,88 Mile Rd.,Manhattan,NY,10005,2010-07-18
```

By using Hadoop to analyze this purchase log, we can gain insight into our sales operation. By combining this data with the data extracted from our relational data source (the `widgets` table), we can do better. In this example session, we will compute which zip code is responsible for the most sales dollars, so we can better focus our sales team's operations. Doing this requires data from both the sales log and the `widgets` table.

The table shown in the previous code snippet should be in a local file named *sales.log* for this to work.

First, let's load the sales data into Hive:

```
hive> CREATE TABLE sales(widget_id INT, qty INT,
    > street STRING, city STRING, state STRING,
    > zip INT, sale_date STRING)
    > ROW FORMAT DELIMITED FIELDS TERMINATED BY ',';
```

```
OK
Time taken: 5.248 seconds
hive> LOAD DATA LOCAL INPATH "ch15-sqoop/sales.log" INTO TABLE sales;
...
Loading data to table default.sales
Table default.sales stats: [numFiles=1, numRows=0, totalSize=189, rawDataSize=0]
OK
Time taken: 0.6 seconds
```

Sqoop can generate a Hive table based on a table from an existing relational data source. We've already imported the widgets data to HDFS, so we can generate the Hive table definition and then load in the HDFS-resident data:

```
% sqoop create-hive-table --connect jdbc:mysql://localhost/hadoopguide \
> --table widgets --fields-terminated-by ','
...
14/10/29 11:54:52 INFO hive.HiveImport: OK
14/10/29 11:54:52 INFO hive.HiveImport: Time taken: 1.098 seconds
14/10/29 11:54:52 INFO hive.HiveImport: Hive import complete.
% hive
hive> LOAD DATA INPATH "widgets" INTO TABLE widgets;
Loading data to table widgets
OK
Time taken: 3.265 seconds
```

When creating a Hive table definition with a specific already imported dataset in mind, we need to specify the delimiters used in that dataset. Otherwise, Sqoop will allow Hive to use its default delimiters (which are different from Sqoop's default delimiters).

 Hive's type system is less rich than that of most SQL systems. Many SQL types do not have direct analogues in Hive. When Sqoop generates a Hive table definition for an import, it uses the best Hive type available to hold a column's values. This may result in a decrease in precision. When this occurs, Sqoop will provide you with a warning message such as this one:

```
14/10/29 11:54:43 WARN hive.TableDefWriter:
Column design_date had to be
cast to a less precise type in Hive
```

This three-step process of importing data to HDFS, creating the Hive table, and then loading the HDFS-resident data into Hive can be shortened to one step if you know that you want to import straight from a database directly into Hive. During an import, Sqoop can generate the Hive table definition and then load in the data. Had we not already performed the import, we could have executed this command, which creates the widgets table in Hive based on the copy in MySQL:

```
% sqoop import --connect jdbc:mysql://localhost/hadoopguide \
> --table widgets -m 1 --hive-import
```

Running sqoop import with the --hive-import argument will load the data directly from the source database into Hive; it infers a Hive schema automatically based on the schema for the table in the source database. Using this, you can get started working with your data in Hive with only one command.

Regardless of which data import route we chose, we can now use the widgets dataset and the sales dataset together to calculate the most profitable zip code. Let's do so, and also save the result of this query in another table for later:

```
hive> CREATE TABLE zip_profits
    > AS
    > SELECT SUM(w.price * s.qty) AS sales_vol, s.zip  FROM SALES s
    > JOIN widgets w ON (s.widget_id = w.id) GROUP BY s.zip;
...
Moving data to: hdfs://localhost/user/hive/warehouse/zip_profits
...
OK

hive> SELECT * FROM zip_profits ORDER BY sales_vol DESC;
...
OK
403.71  90210
28.0    10005
20.0    95014
```

Importing Large Objects

Most databases provide the capability to store large amounts of data in a single field. Depending on whether this data is textual or binary in nature, it is usually represented as a CLOB or BLOB column in the table. These "large objects" are often handled specially by the database itself. In particular, most tables are physically laid out on disk as in Figure 15-2. When scanning through rows to determine which rows match the criteria for a particular query, this typically involves reading all columns of each row from disk. If large objects were stored "inline" in this fashion, they would adversely affect the performance of such scans. Therefore, large objects are often stored externally from their rows, as in Figure 15-3. Accessing a large object often requires "opening" it through the reference contained in the row.

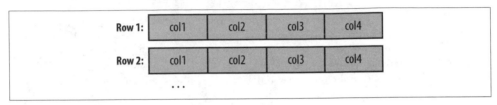

Figure 15-2. Database tables are typically physically represented as an array of rows, with all the columns in a row stored adjacent to one another

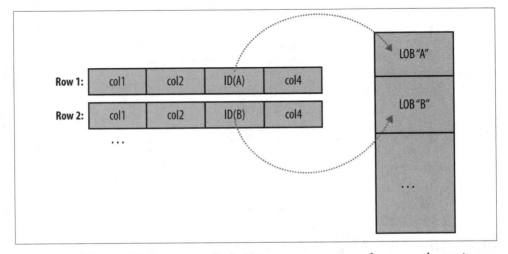

Figure 15-3. Large objects are usually held in a separate area of storage; the main row storage contains indirect references to the large objects

The difficulty of working with large objects in a database suggests that a system such as Hadoop, which is much better suited to storing and processing large, complex data objects, is an ideal repository for such information. Sqoop can extract large objects from tables and store them in HDFS for further processing.

As in a database, MapReduce typically *materializes* every record before passing it along to the mapper. If individual records are truly large, this can be very inefficient.

As shown earlier, records imported by Sqoop are laid out on disk in a fashion very similar to a database's internal structure: an array of records with all fields of a record concatenated together. When running a MapReduce program over imported records, each map task must fully materialize all fields of each record in its input split. If the contents of a large object field are relevant only for a small subset of the total number of records used as input to a MapReduce program, it would be inefficient to fully materialize all these records. Furthermore, depending on the size of the large object, full materialization in memory may be impossible.

To overcome these difficulties, Sqoop will store imported large objects in a separate file called a LobFile, if they are larger than a threshold size of 16 MB (configurable via the sqoop.inline.lob.length.max setting, in bytes). The LobFile format can store individual records of very large size (a 64-bit address space is used). Each record in a LobFile holds a single large object. The LobFile format allows clients to hold a reference to a record without accessing the record contents. When records are accessed, this is done through a java.io.InputStream (for binary objects) or java.io.Reader (for character-based objects).

When a record is imported, the "normal" fields will be materialized together in a text file, along with a reference to the LobFile where a CLOB or BLOB column is stored. For example, suppose our widgets table contained a BLOB field named schematic holding the actual schematic diagram for each widget.

An imported record might then look like:

```
2,gizmo,4.00,2009-11-30,4,null,externalLob(lf,lobfile0,100,5011714)
```

The externalLob(...) text is a reference to an externally stored large object, stored in LobFile format (lf) in a file named *lobfile0*, with the specified byte offset and length inside that file.

When working with this record, the Widget.get_schematic() method would return an object of type BlobRef referencing the schematic column, but not actually containing its contents. The BlobRef.getDataStream() method actually opens the LobFile and returns an InputStream, allowing you to access the schematic field's contents.

When running a MapReduce job processing many Widget records, you might need to access the schematic fields of only a handful of records. This system allows you to incur the I/O costs of accessing only the required large object entries—a big savings, as individual schematics may be several megabytes or more of data.

The BlobRef and ClobRef classes cache references to underlying LobFiles within a map task. If you do access the schematic fields of several sequentially ordered records, they will take advantage of the existing file pointer's alignment on the next record body.

Performing an Export

In Sqoop, an *import* refers to the movement of data from a database system into HDFS. By contrast, an *export* uses HDFS as the source of data and a remote database as the destination. In the previous sections, we imported some data and then performed some analysis using Hive. We can export the results of this analysis to a database for consumption by other tools.

Before exporting a table from HDFS to a database, we must prepare the database to receive the data by creating the target table. Although Sqoop can infer which Java types are appropriate to hold SQL data types, this translation does not work in both directions (for example, there are several possible SQL column definitions that can hold data in a Java String; this could be CHAR(64), VARCHAR(200), or something else entirely). Consequently, you must determine which types are most appropriate.

We are going to export the zip_profits table from Hive. We need to create a table in MySQL that has target columns in the same order, with the appropriate SQL types:

```
% mysql hadoopguide
mysql> CREATE TABLE sales_by_zip (volume DECIMAL(8,2), zip INTEGER);
Query OK, 0 rows affected (0.01 sec)
```

Then we run the export command:

```
% sqoop export --connect jdbc:mysql://localhost/hadoopguide -m 1 \
> --table sales_by_zip --export-dir /user/hive/warehouse/zip_profits \
> --input-fields-terminated-by '\0001'
...
14/10/29 12:05:08 INFO mapreduce.ExportJobBase: Transferred 176 bytes in 13.5373
seconds (13.0011 bytes/sec)
14/10/29 12:05:08 INFO mapreduce.ExportJobBase: Exported 3 records.
```

Finally, we can verify that the export worked by checking MySQL:

```
% mysql hadoopguide -e 'SELECT * FROM sales_by_zip'
+--------+-------+
| volume | zip   |
+--------+-------+
|  28.00 | 10005 |
| 403.71 | 90210 |
|  20.00 | 95014 |
+--------+-------+
```

When we created the zip_profits table in Hive, we did not specify any delimiters. So Hive used its default delimiters: a Ctrl-A character (Unicode 0x0001) between fields and a newline at the end of each record. When we used Hive to access the contents of this table (in a SELECT statement), Hive converted this to a tab-delimited representation for display on the console. But when reading the tables directly from files, we need to tell Sqoop which delimiters to use. Sqoop assumes records are newline-delimited by default, but needs to be told about the Ctrl-A field delimiters. The --input-fields-terminated-by argument to sqoop export specified this information. Sqoop supports several escape sequences, which start with a backslash (\) character, when specifying delimiters.

In the example syntax, the escape sequence is enclosed in single quotes to ensure that the shell processes it literally. Without the quotes, the leading backslash itself may need to be escaped (e.g., --input-fields-terminated-by \\0001). The escape sequences supported by Sqoop are listed in Table 15-1.

Table 15-1. Escape sequences that can be used to specify nonprintable characters as field and record delimiters in Sqoop

Escape	Description
\b	Backspaces.
\n	Newline.
\r	Carriage return.
\t	Tab.
\'	Single quote.
\"	Double quote.
\\	Backslash.
\0	NUL. This will insert NUL characters between fields or lines, or will disable enclosing/escaping if used for one of the `--enclosed-by`, `--optionally-enclosed-by`, or `--escaped-by` arguments.
\0*ooo*	The octal representation of a Unicode character's code point. The actual character is specified by the octal value ooo.
\0x*hhh*	The hexadecimal representation of a Unicode character's code point. This should be of the form \0x*hhh*, where *hhh* is the hex value. For example, `--fields-terminated-by '\0x10'` specifies the carriage return character.

Exports: A Deeper Look

The Sqoop performs exports is very similar in nature to how Sqoop performs imports (see Figure 15-4). Before performing the export, Sqoop picks a strategy based on the database connect string. For most systems, Sqoop uses JDBC. Sqoop then generates a Java class based on the target table definition. This generated class has the ability to parse records from text files and insert values of the appropriate types into a table (in addition to the ability to read the columns from a ResultSet). A MapReduce job is then launched that reads the source datafiles from HDFS, parses the records using the generated class, and executes the chosen export strategy.

The JDBC-based export strategy builds up batch INSERT statements that will each add multiple records to the target table. Inserting many records per statement performs much better than executing many single-row INSERT statements on most database systems. Separate threads are used to read from HDFS and communicate with the database, to ensure that I/O operations involving different systems are overlapped as much as possible.

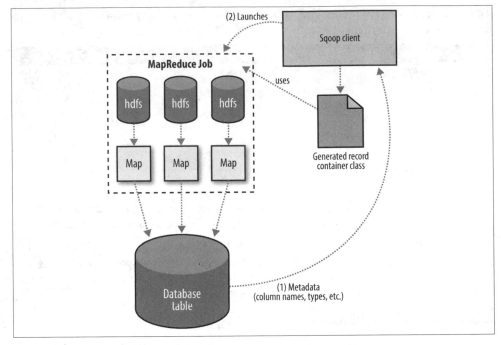

Figure 15-4. Exports are performed in parallel using MapReduce

For MySQL, Sqoop can employ a direct-mode strategy using `mysqlimport`. Each map task spawns a `mysqlimport` process that it communicates with via a named FIFO file on the local filesystem. Data is then streamed into `mysqlimport` via the FIFO channel, and from there into the database.

Whereas most MapReduce jobs reading from HDFS pick the degree of parallelism (number of map tasks) based on the number and size of the files to process, Sqoop's export system allows users explicit control over the number of tasks. The performance of the export can be affected by the number of parallel writers to the database, so Sqoop uses the `CombineFileInputFormat` class to group the input files into a smaller number of map tasks.

Exports and Transactionality

Due to the parallel nature of the process, often an export is not an atomic operation. Sqoop will spawn multiple tasks to export slices of the data in parallel. These tasks can complete at different times, meaning that even though transactions are used inside tasks, results from one task may be visible before the results of another task. Moreover, databases often use fixed-size buffers to store transactions. As a result, one transaction cannot necessarily contain the entire set of operations performed by a task. Sqoop commits results every few thousand rows, to ensure that it does not run out of memory. These intermediate results are visible while the export continues. Applications that will use the results of an export should not be started until the export process is complete, or they may see partial results.

To solve this problem, Sqoop can export to a temporary staging table and then, at the end of the job—if the export has succeeded—move the staged data into the destination table in a single transaction. You can specify a staging table with the `--staging-table` option. The staging table must already exist and have the same schema as the destination. It must also be empty, unless the `--clear-staging-table` option is also supplied.

 Using a staging table is slower, since the data must be written twice: first to the staging table, then to the destination table. The export process also uses more space while it is running, since there are two copies of the data while the staged data is being copied to the destination.

Exports and SequenceFiles

The example export reads source data from a Hive table, which is stored in HDFS as a delimited text file. Sqoop can also export delimited text files that were not Hive tables. For example, it can export text files that are the output of a MapReduce job.

Sqoop can export records stored in `SequenceFiles` to an output table too, although some restrictions apply. A `SequenceFile` cannot contain arbitrary record types. Sqoop's export tool will read objects from `SequenceFiles` and send them directly to the `Output Collector`, which passes the objects to the database export `OutputFormat`. To work with Sqoop, the record must be stored in the "value" portion of the `SequenceFile`'s key-value pair format and must subclass the `org.apache.sqoop.lib.SqoopRecord` abstract class (as is done by all classes generated by Sqoop).

If you use the codegen tool (*sqoop-codegen*) to generate a `SqoopRecord` implementation for a record based on your export target table, you can write a MapReduce program that populates instances of this class and writes them to `SequenceFiles`. `sqoop-export` can then export these `SequenceFiles` to the table. Another means by which data may be in `SqoopRecord` instances in `SequenceFiles` is if data is imported from a database table to HDFS and modified in some fashion, and then the results are stored in `SequenceFiles` holding records of the same data type.

In this case, Sqoop should reuse the existing class definition to read data from `Sequenceces`, rather than generating a new (temporary) record container class to perform the export, as is done when converting text-based records to database rows. You can suppress code generation and instead use an existing record class and JAR by providing the `--class-name` and `--jar-file` arguments to Sqoop. Sqoop will use the specified class, loaded from the specified JAR, when exporting records.

In the following example, we reimport the widgets table as SequenceFiles, and then export it back to the database in a different table:

```
% sqoop import --connect jdbc:mysql://localhost/hadoopguide \
> --table widgets -m 1 --class-name WidgetHolder --as-sequencefile \
> --target-dir widget_sequence_files --bindir .
...
14/10/29 12:25:03 INFO mapreduce.ImportJobBase: Retrieved 3 records.

% mysql hadoopguide
mysql> CREATE TABLE widgets2(id INT, widget_name VARCHAR(100),
    -> price DOUBLE, designed DATE, version INT, notes VARCHAR(200));
Query OK, 0 rows affected (0.03 sec)

mysql> exit;

% sqoop export --connect jdbc:mysql://localhost/hadoopguide \
> --table widgets2 -m 1 --class-name WidgetHolder \
> --jar-file WidgetHolder.jar --export-dir widget_sequence_files
...
14/10/29 12:28:17 INFO mapreduce.ExportJobBase: Exported 3 records.
```

During the import, we specified the SequenceFile format and indicated that we wanted the JAR file to be placed in the current directory (with --bindir) so we can reuse it. Otherwise, it would be placed in a temporary directory. We then created a destination table for the export, which had a slightly different schema (albeit one that is compatible with the original data). Finally, we ran an export that used the existing generated code to read the records from the SequenceFile and write them to the database.

Further Reading

For more information on using Sqoop, consult the *Apache Sqoop Cookbook* by Kathleen Ting and Jarek Jarcec Cecho (O'Reilly, 2013).

Pig

Apache Pig (*http://pig.apache.org/*) raises the level of abstraction for processing large datasets. MapReduce allows you, as the programmer, to specify a map function followed by a reduce function, but working out how to fit your data processing into this pattern, which often requires multiple MapReduce stages, can be a challenge. With Pig, the data structures are much richer, typically being multivalued and nested, and the transformations you can apply to the data are much more powerful. They include joins, for example, which are not for the faint of heart in MapReduce.

Pig is made up of two pieces:

- The language used to express data flows, called *Pig Latin*.
- The execution environment to run Pig Latin programs. There are currently two environments: local execution in a single JVM and distributed execution on a Hadoop cluster.

A Pig Latin program is made up of a series of operations, or transformations, that are applied to the input data to produce output. Taken as a whole, the operations describe a data flow, which the Pig execution environment translates into an executable representation and then runs. Under the covers, Pig turns the transformations into a series of MapReduce jobs, but as a programmer you are mostly unaware of this, which allows you to focus on the data rather than the nature of the execution.

Pig is a scripting language for exploring large datasets. One criticism of MapReduce is that the development cycle is very long. Writing the mappers and reducers, compiling and packaging the code, submitting the job(s), and retrieving the results is a time-consuming business, and even with Streaming, which removes the compile and package step, the experience is still involved. Pig's sweet spot is its ability to process terabytes of data in response to a half-dozen lines of Pig Latin issued from the console. Indeed, it was created at Yahoo! to make it easier for researchers and engineers to mine the huge datasets there. Pig is very supportive of a programmer writing a query, since it provides several commands for introspecting the data structures in your program as it is written. Even more useful, it can perform a sample run on a representative subset of your input data, so you can see whether there are errors in the processing before unleashing it on the full dataset.

Pig was designed to be extensible. Virtually all parts of the processing path are customizable: loading, storing, filtering, grouping, and joining can all be altered by user-defined functions (UDFs). These functions operate on Pig's nested data model, so they can integrate very deeply with Pig's operators. As another benefit, UDFs tend to be more reusable than the libraries developed for writing MapReduce programs.

In some cases, Pig doesn't perform as well as programs written in MapReduce. However, the gap is narrowing with each release, as the Pig team implements sophisticated algorithms for applying Pig's relational operators. It's fair to say that unless you are willing to invest a lot of effort optimizing Java MapReduce code, writing queries in Pig Latin will save you time.

Installing and Running Pig

Pig runs as a client-side application. Even if you want to run Pig on a Hadoop cluster, there is nothing extra to install on the cluster: Pig launches jobs and interacts with HDFS (or other Hadoop filesystems) from your workstation.

Installation is straightforward. Download a stable release from *http://pig.apache.org/releases.html*, and unpack the tarball in a suitable place on your workstation:

```
% tar xzf pig-x.y.z.tar.gz
```

It's convenient to add Pig's binary directory to your command-line path. For example:

```
% export PIG_HOME=~/sw/pig-x.y.z
% export PATH=$PATH:$PIG_HOME/bin
```

You also need to set the JAVA_HOME environment variable to point to a suitable Java installation.

Try typing pig -help to get usage instructions.

Execution Types

Pig has two execution types or modes: local mode and MapReduce mode. Execution modes for Apache Tez and Spark (see Chapter 19) were both under development at the time of writing. Both promise significant performance gains over MapReduce mode, so try them if they are available in the version of Pig you are using.

Local mode

In local mode, Pig runs in a single JVM and accesses the local filesystem. This mode is suitable only for small datasets and when trying out Pig.

The execution type is set using the `-x` or `-exectype` option. To run in local mode, set the option to `local`:

```
% pig -x local
grunt>
```

This starts Grunt, the Pig interactive shell, which is discussed in more detail shortly.

MapReduce mode

In MapReduce mode, Pig translates queries into MapReduce jobs and runs them on a Hadoop cluster. The cluster may be a pseudo- or fully distributed cluster. MapReduce mode (with a fully distributed cluster) is what you use when you want to run Pig on large datasets.

To use MapReduce mode, you first need to check that the version of Pig you downloaded is compatible with the version of Hadoop you are using. Pig releases will only work against particular versions of Hadoop; this is documented in the release notes.

Pig honors the `HADOOP_HOME` environment variable for finding which Hadoop client to run. However, if it is not set, Pig will use a bundled copy of the Hadoop libraries. Note that these may not match the version of Hadoop running on your cluster, so it is best to explicitly set `HADOOP_HOME`.

Next, you need to point Pig at the cluster's namenode and resource manager. If the installation of Hadoop at `HADOOP_HOME` is already configured for this, then there is nothing more to do. Otherwise, you can set `HADOOP_CONF_DIR` to a directory containing the Hadoop site file (or files) that define `fs.defaultFS`, `yarn.resourcemanager.address`, and `mapreduce.framework.name` (the latter should be set to `yarn`).

Alternatively, you can set these properties in the *pig.properties* file in Pig's *conf* directory (or the directory specified by `PIG_CONF_DIR`). Here's an example for a pseudo-distributed setup:

```
fs.defaultFS=hdfs://localhost/
mapreduce.framework.name=yarn
yarn.resourcemanager.address=localhost:8032
```

Once you have configured Pig to connect to a Hadoop cluster, you can launch Pig, setting the `-x` option to `mapreduce` or omitting it entirely, as MapReduce mode is the default. We've used the `-brief` option to stop timestamps from being logged:

```
% pig -brief
Logging error messages to: /Users/tom/pig_1414246949680.log
Default bootup file /Users/tom/.pigbootup not found
```

```
Connecting to hadoop file system at: hdfs://localhost/
grunt>
```

As you can see from the output, Pig reports the filesystem (but not the YARN resource manager) that it has connected to.

In MapReduce mode, you can optionally enable *auto-local mode* (by setting `pig.auto.local.enabled` to `true`), which is an optimization that runs small jobs locally if the input is less than 100 MB (set by `pig.auto.local.input.maxbytes`, default 100,000,000) and no more than one reducer is being used.

Running Pig Programs

There are three ways of executing Pig programs, all of which work in both local and MapReduce mode:

Script

> Pig can run a script file that contains Pig commands. For example, `pig script.pig` runs the commands in the local file *script.pig*. Alternatively, for very short scripts, you can use the `-e` option to run a script specified as a string on the command line.

Grunt

> Grunt is an interactive shell for running Pig commands. Grunt is started when no file is specified for Pig to run and the `-e` option is not used. It is also possible to run Pig scripts from within Grunt using `run` and `exec`.

Embedded

> You can run Pig programs from Java using the `PigServer` class, much like you can use JDBC to run SQL programs from Java. For programmatic access to Grunt, use `PigRunner`.

Grunt

Grunt has line-editing facilities like those found in GNU Readline (used in the bash shell and many other command-line applications). For instance, the Ctrl-E key combination will move the cursor to the end of the line. Grunt remembers command history, too,[1] and you can recall lines in the history buffer using Ctrl-P or Ctrl-N (for previous and next), or equivalently, the up or down cursor keys.

Another handy feature is Grunt's completion mechanism, which will try to complete Pig Latin keywords and functions when you press the Tab key. For example, consider the following incomplete line:

```
grunt> a = foreach b ge
```

---

1. History is stored in a file called *.pig_history* in your home directory.

If you press the Tab key at this point, ge will expand to generate, a Pig Latin keyword:

```
grunt> a = foreach b generate
```

You can customize the completion tokens by creating a file named *autocomplete* and placing it on Pig's classpath (such as in the *conf* directory in Pig's *install* directory) or in the directory you invoked Grunt from. The file should have one token per line, and tokens must not contain any whitespace. Matching is case sensitive. It can be very handy to add commonly used file paths (especially because Pig does not perform filename completion) or the names of any user-defined functions you have created.

You can get a list of commands using the help command. When you've finished your Grunt session, you can exit with the quit command, or the equivalent shortcut \q.

Pig Latin Editors

There are Pig Latin syntax highlighters available for a variety of editors, including Eclipse, IntelliJ IDEA, Vim, Emacs, and TextMate. Details are available on the Pig wiki (*https://cwiki.apache.org/confluence/display/PIG/PigTools*).

Many Hadoop distributions come with the Hue web interface (*http://gethue.com/*), which has a Pig script editor and launcher.

An Example

Let's look at a simple example by writing the program to calculate the maximum recorded temperature by year for the weather dataset in Pig Latin (just like we did using MapReduce in Chapter 2). The complete program is only a few lines long:

```
-- max_temp.pig: Finds the maximum temperature by year
records = LOAD 'input/ncdc/micro-tab/sample.txt'
  AS (year:chararray, temperature:int, quality:int);
filtered_records = FILTER records BY temperature != 9999 AND
  quality IN (0, 1, 4, 5, 9);
grouped_records = GROUP filtered_records BY year;
max_temp = FOREACH grouped_records GENERATE group,
  MAX(filtered_records.temperature);
DUMP max_temp;
```

To explore what's going on, we'll use Pig's Grunt interpreter, which allows us to enter lines and interact with the program to understand what it's doing. Start up Grunt in local mode, and then enter the first line of the Pig script:

```
grunt> records = LOAD 'input/ncdc/micro-tab/sample.txt'
>>    AS (year:chararray, temperature:int, quality:int);
```

For simplicity, the program assumes that the input is tab-delimited text, with each line having just year, temperature, and quality fields. (Pig actually has more flexibility than this with regard to the input formats it accepts, as we'll see later.) This line describes the input data we want to process. The year:chararray notation describes the field's name and type; chararray is like a Java String, and an int is like a Java int. The LOAD operator takes a URI argument; here we are just using a local file, but we could refer to an HDFS URI. The AS clause (which is optional) gives the fields names to make it convenient to refer to them in subsequent statements.

The result of the LOAD operator, and indeed any operator in Pig Latin, is a *relation*, which is just a set of tuples. A *tuple* is just like a row of data in a database table, with multiple fields in a particular order. In this example, the LOAD function produces a set of (year, temperature, quality) tuples that are present in the input file. We write a relation with one tuple per line, where tuples are represented as comma-separated items in parentheses:

```
(1950,0,1)
(1950,22,1)
(1950,-11,1)
(1949,111,1)
```

Relations are given names, or *aliases*, so they can be referred to. This relation is given the records alias. We can examine the contents of an alias using the DUMP operator:

```
grunt> DUMP records;
(1950,0,1)
(1950,22,1)
(1950,-11,1)
(1949,111,1)
(1949,78,1)
```

We can also see the structure of a relation—the relation's *schema*—using the DESCRIBE operator on the relation's alias:

```
grunt> DESCRIBE records;
records: {year: chararray,temperature: int,quality: int}
```

This tells us that records has three fields, with aliases year, temperature, and quality, which are the names we gave them in the AS clause. The fields have the types given to them in the AS clause, too. We examine types in Pig in more detail later.

The second statement removes records that have a missing temperature (indicated by a value of 9999) or an unsatisfactory quality reading. For this small dataset, no records are filtered out:

```
grunt> filtered_records = FILTER records BY temperature != 9999 AND
>>   quality IN (0, 1, 4, 5, 9);
grunt> DUMP filtered_records;
(1950,0,1)
(1950,22,1)
(1950,-11,1)
(1949,111,1)
(1949,78,1)
```

The third statement uses the GROUP function to group the records relation by the year field. Let's use DUMP to see what it produces:

```
grunt> grouped_records = GROUP filtered_records BY year;
grunt> DUMP grouped_records;
(1949,{(1949,78,1),(1949,111,1)})
(1950,{(1950,-11,1),(1950,22,1),(1950,0,1)})
```

We now have two rows, or tuples: one for each year in the input data. The first field in each tuple is the field being grouped by (the year), and the second field has a bag of tuples for that year. A *bag* is just an unordered collection of tuples, which in Pig Latin is represented using curly braces.

By grouping the data in this way, we have created a row per year, so now all that remains is to find the maximum temperature for the tuples in each bag. Before we do this, let's understand the structure of the grouped_records relation:

```
grunt> DESCRIBE grouped_records;
grouped_records: {group: chararray,filtered_records: {year: chararray,
temperature: int,quality: int}}
```

This tells us that the grouping field is given the alias group by Pig, and the second field is the same structure as the filtered_records relation that was being grouped. With this information, we can try the fourth transformation:

```
grunt> max_temp = FOREACH grouped_records GENERATE group,
>>    MAX(filtered_records.temperature);
```

FOREACH processes every row to generate a derived set of rows, using a GENERATE clause to define the fields in each derived row. In this example, the first field is group, which is just the year. The second field is a little more complex. The filtered_records.temperature reference is to the temperature field of the filtered_records bag in the grouped_records relation. MAX is a built-in function for calculating the maximum value of fields in a bag. In this case, it calculates the maximum temperature for the fields in each filtered_records bag. Let's check the result:

```
grunt> DUMP max_temp;
(1949,111)
(1950,22)
```

We've successfully calculated the maximum temperature for each year.

Generating Examples

In this example, we've used a small sample dataset with just a handful of rows to make it easier to follow the data flow and aid debugging. Creating a cut-down dataset is an art, as ideally it should be rich enough to cover all the cases to exercise your queries (the *completeness* property), yet small enough to make sense to the programmer (the *conciseness* property). Using a random sample doesn't work well in general because join and filter operations tend to remove all random data, leaving an empty result, which is not illustrative of the general data flow.

With the ILLUSTRATE operator, Pig provides a tool for generating a reasonably complete and concise sample dataset. Here is the output from running ILLUSTRATE on our dataset (slightly reformatted to fit the page):

```
grunt> ILLUSTRATE max_temp;
```

records	year:chararray	temperature:int	quality:int
	1949	78	1
	1949	111	1
	1949	9999	1

filtered_records	year:chararray	temperature:int	quality:int
	1949	78	1
	1949	111	1

grouped_records	group:chararray	filtered_records:bag{:tuple(year:chararray,temperature:int, quality:int)}
	1949	{(1949, 78, 1), (1949, 111, 1)}

max_temp	group:chararray	:int
	1949	111

Notice that Pig used some of the original data (this is important to keep the generated dataset realistic), as well as creating some new data. It noticed the special value 9999 in the query and created a tuple containing this value to exercise the FILTER statement.

In summary, the output of ILLUSTRATE is easy to follow and can help you understand what your query is doing.

Comparison with Databases

Having seen Pig in action, it might seem that Pig Latin is similar to SQL. The presence of such operators as GROUP BY and DESCRIBE reinforces this impression. However, there are several differences between the two languages, and between Pig and relational database management systems (RDBMSs) in general.

The most significant difference is that Pig Latin is a data flow programming language, whereas SQL is a declarative programming language. In other words, a Pig Latin program is a step-by-step set of operations on an input relation, in which each step is a single transformation. By contrast, SQL statements are a set of constraints that, taken together, define the output. In many ways, programming in Pig Latin is like working at the level of an RDBMS query planner, which figures out how to turn a declarative statement into a system of steps.

RDBMSs store data in tables, with tightly predefined schemas. Pig is more relaxed about the data that it processes: you can define a schema at runtime, but it's optional. Essentially, it will operate on any source of tuples (although the source should support being read in parallel, by being in multiple files, for example), where a UDF is used to read the tuples from their raw representation.[2] The most common representation is a text file with tab-separated fields, and Pig provides a built-in load function for this format. Unlike with a traditional database, there is no data import process to load the data into the RDBMS. The data is loaded from the filesystem (usually HDFS) as the first step in the processing.

Pig's support for complex, nested data structures further differentiates it from SQL, which operates on flatter data structures. Also, Pig's ability to use UDFs and streaming operators that are tightly integrated with the language and Pig's nested data structures makes Pig Latin more customizable than most SQL dialects.

RDBMSs have several features to support online, low-latency queries, such as transactions and indexes, that are absent in Pig. Pig does not support random reads or queries on the order of tens of milliseconds. Nor does it support random writes to update small portions of data; all writes are bulk streaming writes, just like with MapReduce.

Hive (covered in Chapter 17) sits between Pig and conventional RDBMSs. Like Pig, Hive is designed to use HDFS for storage, but otherwise there are some significant differences. Its query language, HiveQL, is based on SQL, and anyone who is familiar with SQL will have little trouble writing queries in HiveQL. Like RDBMSs, Hive mandates that all data be stored in tables, with a schema under its management; however, it can associate a schema with preexisting data in HDFS, so the load step is optional. Pig is able to work with Hive tables using HCatalog; this is discussed further in "Using Hive tables with HCatalog" on page 442.

---

2. Or as the Pig Philosophy (*http://pig.apache.org/philosophy.html*) has it, "Pigs eat anything."

Pig Latin

This section gives an informal description of the syntax and semantics of the Pig Latin programming language.[3] It is not meant to offer a complete reference to the language,[4] but there should be enough here for you to get a good understanding of Pig Latin's constructs.

Structure

A Pig Latin program consists of a collection of statements. A statement can be thought of as an operation or a command.[5] For example, a GROUP operation is a type of statement:

```
grouped_records = GROUP records BY year;
```

The command to list the files in a Hadoop filesystem is another example of a statement:

```
ls /
```

Statements are usually terminated with a semicolon, as in the example of the GROUP statement. In fact, this is an example of a statement that must be terminated with a semicolon; it is a syntax error to omit it. The ls command, on the other hand, does not have to be terminated with a semicolon. As a general guideline, statements or commands for interactive use in Grunt do not need the terminating semicolon. This group includes the interactive Hadoop commands, as well as the diagnostic operators such as DE SCRIBE. It's never an error to add a terminating semicolon, so if in doubt, it's simplest to add one.

Statements that have to be terminated with a semicolon can be split across multiple lines for readability:

```
records = LOAD 'input/ncdc/micro-tab/sample.txt'
  AS (year:chararray, temperature:int, quality:int);
```

Pig Latin has two forms of comments. Double hyphens are used for single-line comments. Everything from the first hyphen to the end of the line is ignored by the Pig Latin interpreter:

```
-- My program
DUMP A; -- What's in A?
```

---

3. Not to be confused with Pig Latin, the language game. English words are translated into Pig Latin by moving the initial consonant sound to the end of the word and adding an "ay" sound. For example, "pig" becomes "ig-pay," and "Hadoop" becomes "Adoop-hay."

4. Pig Latin does not have a formal language definition as such, but there is a comprehensive guide to the language that you can find through a link on the Pig website (*http://pig.apache.org/*).

5. You sometimes see these terms being used interchangeably in documentation on Pig Latin: for example, "GROUP command," "GROUP operation," "GROUP statement."

C-style comments are more flexible since they delimit the beginning and end of the comment block with /* and */ markers. They can span lines or be embedded in a single line:

```
/*
 * Description of my program spanning
 * multiple lines.
 */
A = LOAD 'input/pig/join/A';
B = LOAD 'input/pig/join/B';
C = JOIN A BY $0, /* ignored */ B BY $1;
DUMP C;
```

Pig Latin has a list of keywords that have a special meaning in the language and cannot be used as identifiers. These include the operators (LOAD, ILLUSTRATE), commands (cat, ls), expressions (matches, FLATTEN), and functions (DIFF, MAX)—all of which are covered in the following sections.

Pig Latin has mixed rules on case sensitivity. Operators and commands are not case sensitive (to make interactive use more forgiving); however, aliases and function names are case sensitive.

Statements

As a Pig Latin program is executed, each statement is parsed in turn. If there are syntax errors or other (semantic) problems, such as undefined aliases, the interpreter will halt and display an error message. The interpreter builds a *logical plan* for every relational operation, which forms the core of a Pig Latin program. The logical plan for the statement is added to the logical plan for the program so far, and then the interpreter moves on to the next statement.

It's important to note that no data processing takes place while the logical plan of the program is being constructed. For example, consider again the Pig Latin program from the first example:

```
-- max_temp.pig: Finds the maximum temperature by year
records = LOAD 'input/ncdc/micro-tab/sample.txt'
  AS (year:chararray, temperature:int, quality:int);
filtered_records = FILTER records BY temperature != 9999 AND
  quality IN (0, 1, 4, 5, 9);
grouped_records = GROUP filtered_records BY year;
max_temp = FOREACH grouped_records GENERATE group,
  MAX(filtered_records.temperature);
DUMP max_temp;
```

When the Pig Latin interpreter sees the first line containing the LOAD statement, it confirms that it is syntactically and semantically correct and adds it to the logical plan, but it does *not* load the data from the file (or even check whether the file exists). Indeed, where would it load it? Into memory? Even if it did fit into memory, what would it do with the data? Perhaps not all the input data is needed (because later statements filter it, for example), so it would be pointless to load it. The point is that it makes no sense to start any processing until the whole flow is defined. Similarly, Pig validates the GROUP and FOREACH...GENERATE statements, and adds them to the logical plan without executing them. The trigger for Pig to start execution is the DUMP statement. At that point, the logical plan is compiled into a physical plan and executed.

Multiquery Execution

Because DUMP is a diagnostic tool, it will always trigger execution. However, the STORE command is different. In interactive mode, STORE acts like DUMP and will always trigger execution (this includes the run command), but in batch mode it will not (this includes the exec command). The reason for this is efficiency. In batch mode, Pig will parse the whole script to see whether there are any optimizations that could be made to limit the amount of data to be written to or read from disk. Consider the following simple example:

```
A = LOAD 'input/pig/multiquery/A';
B = FILTER A BY $1 == 'banana';
C = FILTER A BY $1 != 'banana';
STORE B INTO 'output/b';
STORE C INTO 'output/c';
```

Relations B and C are both derived from A, so to save reading A twice, Pig can run this script as single MapReduce job by reading A once and writing two output files from the job, one for each of B and C. This feature is called *multiquery execution*.

In previous versions of Pig that did not have multiquery execution, each STORE statement in a script run in batch mode triggered execution, resulting in a job for each STORE statement. It is possible to restore the old behavior by disabling multiquery execution with the -M or -no_multiquery option to pig.

The physical plan that Pig prepares is a series of MapReduce jobs, which in local mode Pig runs in the local JVM and in MapReduce mode Pig runs on a Hadoop cluster.

You can see the logical and physical plans created by Pig using the EXPLAIN command on a relation (EXPLAIN max_temp;, for example).

EXPLAIN will also show the MapReduce plan, which shows how the physical operators are grouped into MapReduce jobs. This is a good way to find out how many MapReduce jobs Pig will run for your query.

The relational operators that can be a part of a logical plan in Pig are summarized in Table 16-1. We go through the operators in more detail in "Data Processing Operators" on page 457.

Table 16-1. Pig Latin relational operators

Category	Operator	Description
Loading and storing	LOAD	Loads data from the filesystem or other storage into a relation
	STORE	Saves a relation to the filesystem or other storage
	DUMP (\d)	Prints a relation to the console
Filtering	FILTER	Removes unwanted rows from a relation
	DISTINCT	Removes duplicate rows from a relation
	FOREACH...GENERATE	Adds or removes fields to or from a relation
	MAPREDUCE	Runs a MapReduce job using a relation as input
	STREAM	Transforms a relation using an external program
	SAMPLE	Selects a random sample of a relation
	ASSERT	Ensures a condition is true for all rows in a relation; otherwise, fails
Grouping and joining	JOIN	Joins two or more relations
	COGROUP	Groups the data in two or more relations
	GROUP	Groups the data in a single relation
	CROSS	Creates the cross product of two or more relations
	CUBE	Creates aggregations for all combinations of specified columns in a relation
Sorting	ORDER	Sorts a relation by one or more fields
	RANK	Assign a rank to each tuple in a relation, optionally sorting by fields first
	LIMIT	Limits the size of a relation to a maximum number of tuples
Combining and splitting	UNION	Combines two or more relations into one
	SPLIT	Splits a relation into two or more relations

There are other types of statements that are not added to the logical plan. For example, the diagnostic operators—DESCRIBE, EXPLAIN, and ILLUSTRATE—are provided to allow the user to interact with the logical plan for debugging purposes (see Table 16-2). DUMP is a sort of diagnostic operator, too, since it is used only to allow interactive debugging of small result sets or in combination with LIMIT to retrieve a few rows from a larger relation. The STORE statement should be used when the size of the output is more than a few lines, as it writes to a file rather than to the console.

Table 16-2. Pig Latin diagnostic operators

Operator (Shortcut)	Description
DESCRIBE (\de)	Prints a relation's schema
EXPLAIN (\e)	Prints the logical and physical plans
ILLUSTRATE (\i)	Shows a sample execution of the logical plan, using a generated subset of the input

Pig Latin also provides three statements—REGISTER, DEFINE, and IMPORT—that make it possible to incorporate macros and user-defined functions into Pig scripts (see Table 16-3).

Table 16-3. Pig Latin macro and UDF statements

Statement	Description
REGISTER	Registers a JAR file with the Pig runtime
DEFINE	Creates an alias for a macro, UDF, streaming script, or command specification
IMPORT	Imports macros defined in a separate file into a script

Because they do not process relations, commands are not added to the logical plan; instead, they are executed immediately. Pig provides commands to interact with Hadoop filesystems (which are very handy for moving data around before or after processing with Pig) and MapReduce, as well as a few utility commands (described in Table 16-4).

Table 16-4. Pig Latin commands

Category	Command	Description
Hadoop filesystem	cat	Prints the contents of one or more files
	cd	Changes the current directory
	copyFromLocal	Copies a local file or directory to a Hadoop filesystem
	copyToLocal	Copies a file or directory on a Hadoop filesystem to the local filesystem
	cp	Copies a file or directory to another directory
	fs	Accesses Hadoop's filesystem shell
	ls	Lists files
	mkdir	Creates a new directory
	mv	Moves a file or directory to another directory
	pwd	Prints the path of the current working directory
	rm	Deletes a file or directory
	rmf	Forcibly deletes a file or directory (does not fail if the file or directory does not exist)
Hadoop MapReduce	kill	Kills a MapReduce job

Category	Command	Description
Utility	clear	Clears the screen in Grunt
	exec	Runs a script in a new Grunt shell in batch mode
	help	Shows the available commands and options
	history	Prints the query statements run in the current Grunt session
	quit (\q)	Exits the interpreter
	run	Runs a script within the existing Grunt shell
	set	Sets Pig options and MapReduce job properties
	sh	Runs a shell command from within Grunt

The filesystem commands can operate on files or directories in any Hadoop filesystem, and they are very similar to the hadoop fs commands (which is not surprising, as both are simple wrappers around the Hadoop FileSystem interface). You can access all of the Hadoop filesystem shell commands using Pig's fs command. For example, fs -ls will show a file listing, and fs -help will show help on all the available commands.

Precisely which Hadoop filesystem is used is determined by the fs.defaultFS property in the site file for Hadoop Core. See "The Command-Line Interface" on page 50 for more details on how to configure this property.

These commands are mostly self-explanatory, except set, which is used to set options that control Pig's behavior (including arbitrary MapReduce job properties). The debug option is used to turn debug logging on or off from within a script (you can also control the log level when launching Pig, using the -d or -debug option):

```
grunt> set debug on
```

Another useful option is the job.name option, which gives a Pig job a meaningful name, making it easier to pick out your Pig MapReduce jobs when running on a shared Hadoop cluster. If Pig is running a script (rather than operating as an interactive query from Grunt), its job name defaults to a value based on the script name.

There are two commands in Table 16-4 for running a Pig script, exec and run. The difference is that exec runs the script in batch mode in a new Grunt shell, so any aliases defined in the script are not accessible to the shell after the script has completed. On the other hand, when running a script with run, it is as if the contents of the script had been entered manually, so the command history of the invoking shell contains all the statements from the script. Multiquery execution, where Pig executes a batch of statements in one go (see "Multiquery Execution" on page 434), is used only by exec, not run.

Control Flow

By design, Pig Latin lacks native control flow statements. The recommended approach for writing programs that have conditional logic or loop constructs is to embed Pig Latin in another language, such as Python, JavaScript, or Java, and manage the control flow from there. In this model, the host script uses a compile-bind-run API to execute Pig scripts and retrieve their status. Consult the Pig documentation for details of the API.

Embedded Pig programs always run in a JVM, so for Python and JavaScript you use the `pig` command followed by the name of your script, and the appropriate Java scripting engine will be selected (Jython for Python, Rhino for JavaScript).

Expressions

An expression is something that is evaluated to yield a value. Expressions can be used in Pig as a part of a statement containing a relational operator. Pig has a rich variety of expressions, many of which will be familiar from other programming languages. They are listed in Table 16-5, with brief descriptions and examples. We will see examples of many of these expressions throughout the chapter.

Table 16-5. Pig Latin expressions

Category	Expressions	Description	Examples
Constant	Literal	Constant value (see also the "Literal example" column in Table 16-6)	`1.0, 'a'`
Field (by position)	$n	Field in position n (zero-based)	`$0`
Field (by name)	f	Field named f	`year`
Field (disambiguate)	r::f	Field named f from relation r after grouping or joining	`A::year`
Projection	c.$n, c.f	Field in container c (relation, bag, or tuple) by position, by name	`records.$0, records.year`
Map lookup	m#k	Value associated with key k in map m	`items#'Coat'`
Cast	(t) f	Cast of field f to type t	`(int) year`
Arithmetic	x + y, x - y	Addition, subtraction	`$1 + $2, $1 - $2`
	x * y, x / y	Multiplication, division	`$1 * $2, $1 / $2`
	x % y	Modulo, the remainder of x divided by y	`$1 % $2`
	+x, -x	Unary positive, negation	`+1, -1`
Conditional	x ? y : z	Bincond/ternary; y if x evaluates to true, z otherwise	`quality == 0 ? 0 : 1`
	CASE	Multi-case conditional	`CASE q WHEN 0 THEN 'good' ELSE 'bad' END`

Category	Expressions	Description	Examples
Comparison	$x == y, x != y$	Equals, does not equal	`quality == 0, tempera ture != 9999`
	$x > y, x < y$	Greater than, less than	`quality > 0, quality < 10`
	$x >= y, x <= y$	Greater than or equal to, less than or equal to	`quality >= 1, quality <= 9`
	`x matches y`	Pattern matching with regular expression	`quality matches '[01459]'`
	`x is null`	Is null	`temperature is null`
	`x is not null`	Is not null	`temperature is not null`
Boolean	`x OR y`	Logical OR	`q == 0 OR q == 1`
	`x AND y`	Logical AND	`q == 0 AND r == 0`
	`NOT x`	Logical negation	`NOT q matches '[01459]'`
	`IN x`	Set membership	`q IN (0, 1, 4, 5, 9)`
Functional	`fn(f1,f2,...)`	Invocation of function fn on fields f1, f2, etc.	`isGood(quality)`
Flatten	`FLATTEN(f)`	Removal of a level of nesting from bags and tuples	`FLATTEN(group)`

Types

So far you have seen some of the simple types in Pig, such as int and chararray. Here we will discuss Pig's built-in types in more detail.

Pig has a boolean type and six numeric types: int, long, float, double, biginteger, and bigdecimal, which are identical to their Java counterparts. There is also a bytearray type, like Java's byte array type for representing a blob of binary data, and chararray, which, like java.lang.String, represents textual data in UTF-16 format (although it can be loaded or stored in UTF-8 format). The datetime type is for storing a date and time with millisecond precision and including a time zone.

Pig does not have types corresponding to Java's byte, short, or char primitive types. These are all easily represented using Pig's int type, or chararray for char.

The Boolean, numeric, textual, binary, and temporal types are simple atomic types. Pig Latin also has three complex types for representing nested structures: tuple, bag, and map. All of Pig Latin's types are listed in Table 16-6.

Table 16-6. Pig Latin types

Category	Type	Description	Literal example
Boolean	boolean	True/false value	`true`
Numeric	int	32-bit signed integer	`1`
	long	64-bit signed integer	`1L`
	float	32-bit floating-point number	`1.0F`
	double	64-bit floating-point number	`1.0`
	biginteger	Arbitrary-precision integer	`'10000000000'`
	bigdecimal	Arbitrary-precision signed decimal number	`'0.110001000000000000000001'`
Text	chararray	Character array in UTF-16 format	`'a'`
Binary	bytearray	Byte array	Not supported
Temporal	datetime	Date and time with time zone	Not supported, use `ToDate` built-in function
Complex	tuple	Sequence of fields of any type	`(1,'pomegranate')`
	bag	Unordered collection of tuples, possibly with duplicates	`{(1,'pomegranate'),(2)}`
	map	Set of key-value pairs; keys must be character arrays, but values may be any type	`['a'#'pomegranate']`

The complex types are usually loaded from files or constructed using relational operators. Be aware, however, that the literal form in Table 16-6 is used when a constant value
is created from within a Pig Latin program. The raw form in a file is usually different
when using the standard `PigStorage` loader. For example, the representation in a file
of the bag in Table 16-6 would be `{(1,pomegranate),(2)}` (note the lack of quotation
marks), and with a suitable schema, this would be loaded as a relation with a single field
and row, whose value was the bag.

Pig provides the built-in functions `TOTUPLE`, `TOBAG`, and `TOMAP`, which are used for turning expressions into tuples, bags, and maps.

Although relations and bags are conceptually the same (unordered collections of tuples),
in practice Pig treats them slightly differently. A relation is a top-level construct, whereas
a bag has to be contained in a relation. Normally you don't have to worry about this,
but there are a few restrictions that can trip up the uninitiated. For example, it's not
possible to create a relation from a bag literal. So, the following statement fails:

```
A = {(1,2),(3,4)}; -- Error
```

The simplest workaround in this case is to load the data from a file using the `LOAD`
statement.

As another example, you can't treat a relation like a bag and project a field into a new
relation (`$0` refers to the first field of `A`, using the positional notation):

```
B = A.$0;
```

Instead, you have to use a relational operator to turn the relation A into relation B:

```
B = FOREACH A GENERATE $0;
```

It's possible that a future version of Pig Latin will remove these inconsistencies and treat relations and bags in the same way.

Schemas

A relation in Pig may have an associated schema, which gives the fields in the relation names and types. We've seen how an AS clause in a LOAD statement is used to attach a schema to a relation:

```
grunt> records = LOAD 'input/ncdc/micro-tab/sample.txt'
>>    AS (year:int, temperature:int, quality:int);
grunt> DESCRIBE records;
records: {year: int,temperature: int,quality: int}
```

This time we've declared the year to be an integer rather than a chararray, even though the file it is being loaded from is the same. An integer may be more appropriate if we need to manipulate the year arithmetically (to turn it into a timestamp, for example), whereas the chararray representation might be more appropriate when it's being used as a simple identifier. Pig's flexibility in the degree to which schemas are declared contrasts with schemas in traditional SQL databases, which are declared before the data is loaded into the system. Pig is designed for analyzing plain input files with no associated type information, so it is quite natural to choose types for fields later than you would with an RDBMS.

It's possible to omit type declarations completely, too:

```
grunt> records = LOAD 'input/ncdc/micro-tab/sample.txt'
>>    AS (year, temperature, quality);
grunt> DESCRIBE records;
records: {year: bytearray,temperature: bytearray,quality: bytearray}
```

In this case, we have specified only the names of the fields in the schema: year, temperature, and quality. The types default to bytearray, the most general type, representing a binary string.

You don't need to specify types for every field; you can leave some to default to bytearray, as we have done for year in this declaration:

```
grunt> records = LOAD 'input/ncdc/micro-tab/sample.txt'
>>    AS (year, temperature:int, quality:int);
grunt> DESCRIBE records;
records: {year: bytearray,temperature: int,quality: int}
```

However, if you specify a schema in this way, you do need to specify every field. Also, there's no way to specify the type of a field without specifying the name. On the other hand, the schema is entirely optional and can be omitted by not specifying an AS clause:

```
grunt> records = LOAD 'input/ncdc/micro-tab/sample.txt';
grunt> DESCRIBE records;
Schema for records unknown.
```

Fields in a relation with no schema can be referenced using only positional notation: $0 refers to the first field in a relation, $1 to the second, and so on. Their types default to bytearray:

```
grunt> projected_records = FOREACH records GENERATE $0, $1, $2;
grunt> DUMP projected_records;
(1950,0,1)
(1950,22,1)
(1950,-11,1)
(1949,111,1)
(1949,78,1)
grunt> DESCRIBE projected_records;
projected_records: {bytearray,bytearray,bytearray}
```

Although it can be convenient not to assign types to fields (particularly in the first stages of writing a query), doing so can improve the clarity and efficiency of Pig Latin programs and is generally recommended.

Using Hive tables with HCatalog

Declaring a schema as a part of the query is flexible but doesn't lend itself to schema reuse. A set of Pig queries over the same input data will often have the same schema repeated in each query. If the query processes a large number of fields, this repetition can become hard to maintain.

HCatalog (which is a component of Hive) solves this problem by providing access to Hive's metastore, so that Pig queries can reference schemas by name, rather than specifying them in full each time. For example, after running through "An Example" on page 474 to load data into a Hive table called records, Pig can access the table's schema and data as follows:

```
% pig -useHCatalog
grunt> records = LOAD 'records' USING org.apache.hcatalog.pig.HCatLoader();
grunt> DESCRIBE records;
records: {year: chararray,temperature: int,quality: int}
grunt> DUMP records;
(1950,0,1)
(1950,22,1)
(1950,-11,1)
(1949,111,1)
(1949,78,1)
```

Validation and nulls

A SQL database will enforce the constraints in a table's schema at load time; for example, trying to load a string into a column that is declared to be a numeric type will fail. In

Pig, if the value cannot be cast to the type declared in the schema, it will substitute a null value. Let's see how this works when we have the following input for the weather data, which has an "e" character in place of an integer:

```
1950 0   1
1950 22  1
1950 e   1
1949 111 1
1949 78  1
```

Pig handles the corrupt line by producing a null for the offending value, which is displayed as the absence of a value when dumped to screen (and also when saved using STORE):

```
grunt> records = LOAD 'input/ncdc/micro-tab/sample_corrupt.txt'
>>    AS (year:chararray, temperature:int, quality:int);
grunt> DUMP records;
(1950,0,1)
(1950,22,1)
(1950,,1)
(1949,111,1)
(1949,78,1)
```

Pig produces a warning for the invalid field (not shown here) but does not halt its processing. For large datasets, it is very common to have corrupt, invalid, or merely unexpected data, and it is generally infeasible to incrementally fix every unparsable record. Instead, we can pull out all of the invalid records in one go so we can take action on them, perhaps by fixing our program (because they indicate that we have made a mistake) or by filtering them out (because the data is genuinely unusable):

```
grunt> corrupt_records = FILTER records BY temperature is null;
grunt> DUMP corrupt_records;
(1950,,1)
```

Note the use of the is null operator, which is analogous to SQL. In practice, we would include more information from the original record, such as an identifier and the value that could not be parsed, to help our analysis of the bad data.

We can find the number of corrupt records using the following idiom for counting the number of rows in a relation:

```
grunt> grouped = GROUP corrupt_records ALL;
grunt> all_grouped = FOREACH grouped GENERATE group, COUNT(corrupt_records);
grunt> DUMP all_grouped;
(all,1)
```

("GROUP" on page 464 explains grouping and the ALL operation in more detail.)

Another useful technique is to use the SPLIT operator to partition the data into "good" and "bad" relations, which can then be analyzed separately:

```
grunt> SPLIT records INTO good_records IF temperature is not null,
>>    bad_records OTHERWISE;
grunt> DUMP good_records;
(1950,0,1)
(1950,22,1)
(1949,111,1)
(1949,78,1)
grunt> DUMP bad_records;
(1950,,1)
```

Going back to the case in which temperature's type was left undeclared, the corrupt data cannot be detected easily, since it doesn't surface as a null:

```
grunt> records = LOAD 'input/ncdc/micro-tab/sample_corrupt.txt'
>>    AS (year:chararray, temperature, quality:int);
grunt> DUMP records;
(1950,0,1)
(1950,22,1)
(1950,e,1)
(1949,111,1)
(1949,78,1)
grunt> filtered_records = FILTER records BY temperature != 9999 AND
>>    quality IN (0, 1, 4, 5, 9);
grunt> grouped_records = GROUP filtered_records BY year;
grunt> max_temp = FOREACH grouped_records GENERATE group,
>>    MAX(filtered_records.temperature);
grunt> DUMP max_temp;
(1949,111.0)
(1950,22.0)
```

What happens in this case is that the temperature field is interpreted as a bytearray, so the corrupt field is not detected when the input is loaded. When passed to the MAX function, the temperature field is cast to a double, since MAX works only with numeric types. The corrupt field cannot be represented as a double, so it becomes a null, which MAX silently ignores. The best approach is generally to declare types for your data on loading and look for missing or corrupt values in the relations themselves before you do your main processing.

Sometimes corrupt data shows up as smaller tuples because fields are simply missing. You can filter these out by using the SIZE function as follows:

```
grunt> A = LOAD 'input/pig/corrupt/missing_fields';
grunt> DUMP A;
(2,Tie)
(4,Coat)
(3)
(1,Scarf)
grunt> B = FILTER A BY SIZE(TOTUPLE(*)) > 1;
grunt> DUMP B;
(2,Tie)
(4,Coat)
(1,Scarf)
```

Schema merging

In Pig, you don't declare the schema for every new relation in the data flow. In most cases, Pig can figure out the resulting schema for the output of a relational operation by considering the schema of the input relation.

How are schemas propagated to new relations? Some relational operators don't change the schema, so the relation produced by the LIMIT operator (which restricts a relation to a maximum number of tuples), for example, has the same schema as the relation it operates on. For other operators, the situation is more complicated. UNION, for example, combines two or more relations into one and tries to merge the input relations' schemas. If the schemas are incompatible, due to different types or number of fields, then the schema of the result of the UNION is unknown.

You can find out the schema for any relation in the data flow using the DESCRIBE operator. If you want to redefine the schema for a relation, you can use the FORE ACH...GENERATE operator with AS clauses to define the schema for some or all of the fields of the input relation.

See "User-Defined Functions" on page 448 for a further discussion of schemas.

Functions

Functions in Pig come in four types:

Eval function
> A function that takes one or more expressions and returns another expression. An example of a built-in eval function is MAX, which returns the maximum value of the entries in a bag. Some eval functions are *aggregate functions*, which means they operate on a bag of data to produce a scalar value; MAX is an example of an aggregate function. Furthermore, many aggregate functions are *algebraic*, which means that the result of the function may be calculated incrementally. In MapReduce terms, algebraic functions make use of the combiner and are much more efficient to calculate (see "Combiner Functions" on page 34). MAX is an algebraic function, whereas a function to calculate the median of a collection of values is an example of a function that is not algebraic.

Filter function
> A special type of eval function that returns a logical Boolean result. As the name suggests, filter functions are used in the FILTER operator to remove unwanted rows. They can also be used in other relational operators that take Boolean conditions, and in general, in expressions using Boolean or conditional expressions. An example of a built-in filter function is IsEmpty, which tests whether a bag or a map contains any items.

Load function

A function that specifies how to load data into a relation from external storage.

Store function

A function that specifies how to save the contents of a relation to external storage. Often, load and store functions are implemented by the same type. For example, `PigStorage`, which loads data from delimited text files, can store data in the same format.

Pig comes with a collection of built-in functions, a selection of which are listed in Table 16-7. The complete list of built-in functions, which includes a large number of standard math, string, date/time, and collection functions, can be found in the documentation for each Pig release.

Table 16-7. A selection of Pig's built-in functions

Category	Function	Description
Eval	AVG	Calculates the average (mean) value of entries in a bag.
	CONCAT	Concatenates byte arrays or character arrays together.
	COUNT	Calculates the number of non-null entries in a bag.
	COUNT_STAR	Calculates the number of entries in a bag, including those that are null.
	DIFF	Calculates the set difference of two bags. If the two arguments are not bags, returns a bag containing both if they are equal; otherwise, returns an empty bag.
	MAX	Calculates the maximum value of entries in a bag.
	MIN	Calculates the minimum value of entries in a bag.
	SIZE	Calculates the size of a type. The size of numeric types is always 1; for character arrays, it is the number of characters; for byte arrays, the number of bytes; and for containers (tuple, bag, map), it is the number of entries.
	SUM	Calculates the sum of the values of entries in a bag.
	TOBAG	Converts one or more expressions to individual tuples, which are then put in a bag. A synonym for ( ).
	TOKENIZE	Tokenizes a character array into a bag of its constituent words.
	TOMAP	Converts an even number of expressions to a map of key-value pairs. A synonym for [ ].
	TOP	Calculates the top *n* tuples in a bag.
	TOTUPLE	Converts one or more expressions to a tuple. A synonym for {}.
Filter	IsEmpty	Tests whether a bag or map is empty.
Load/Store	PigStorage	Loads or stores relations using a field-delimited text format. Each line is broken into fields using a configurable field delimiter (defaults to a tab character) to be stored in the tuple's fields. It is the default storage when none is specified.[a]
	TextLoader	Loads relations from a plain-text format. Each line corresponds to a tuple whose single field is the line of text.

Category	Function	Description
	`JsonLoader, JsonStorage`	Loads or stores relations from or to a (Pig-defined) JSON format. Each tuple is stored on one line.
	`AvroStorage`	Loads or stores relations from or to Avro datafiles.
	`ParquetLoader, ParquetStorer`	Loads or stores relations from or to Parquet files.
	`OrcStorage`	Loads or stores relations from or to Hive ORCFiles.
	`HBaseStorage`	Loads or stores relations from or to HBase tables.

[a] The default storage can be changed by setting `pig.default.load.func` and `pig.default.store.func` to the fully qualified load and store function classnames.

Other libraries

If the function you need is not available, you can write your own user-defined function (or UDF for short), as explained in "User-Defined Functions" on page 448. Before you do that, however, have a look in the Piggy Bank (*https://cwiki.apache.org/confluence/display/PIG/PiggyBank?*), a library of Pig functions shared by the Pig community and distributed as a part of Pig. For example, there are load and store functions in the Piggy Bank for CSV files, Hive RCFiles, sequence files, and XML files. The Piggy Bank JAR file comes with Pig, and you can use it with no further configuration. Pig's API documentation includes a list of functions provided by the Piggy Bank.

Apache DataFu (*http://datafu.incubator.apache.org/*) is another rich library of Pig UDFs. In addition to general utility functions, it includes functions for computing basic statistics, performing sampling and estimation, hashing, and working with web data (sessionization, link analysis).

Macros

Macros provide a way to package reusable pieces of Pig Latin code from within Pig Latin itself. For example, we can extract the part of our Pig Latin program that performs grouping on a relation and then finds the maximum value in each group by defining a macro as follows:

```
DEFINE max_by_group(X, group_key, max_field) RETURNS Y {
  A = GROUP $X by $group_key;
  $Y = FOREACH A GENERATE group, MAX($X.$max_field);
};
```

The macro, called `max_by_group`, takes three parameters: a relation, X, and two field names, `group_key` and `max_field`. It returns a single relation, Y. Within the macro body, parameters and return aliases are referenced with a $ prefix, such as $X.

The macro is used as follows:

```
records = LOAD 'input/ncdc/micro-tab/sample.txt'
  AS (year:chararray, temperature:int, quality:int);
filtered_records = FILTER records BY temperature != 9999 AND
  quality IN (0, 1, 4, 5, 9);
max_temp = max_by_group(filtered_records, year, temperature);
DUMP max_temp
```

At runtime, Pig will expand the macro using the macro definition. After expansion, the program looks like the following, with the expanded section in bold:

```
records = LOAD 'input/ncdc/micro-tab/sample.txt'
  AS (year:chararray, temperature:int, quality:int);
filtered_records = FILTER records BY temperature != 9999 AND
  quality IN (0, 1, 4, 5, 9);
macro_max_by_group_A_0 = GROUP filtered_records by (year);
max_temp = FOREACH macro_max_by_group_A_0 GENERATE group,
  MAX(filtered_records.(temperature));
DUMP max_temp
```

Normally you don't see the expanded form, because Pig creates it internally; however, in some cases it is useful to see it when writing and debugging macros. You can get Pig to perform macro expansion only (without executing the script) by passing the -dryrun argument to pig.

Notice that the parameters that were passed to the macro (filtered_records, year, and temperature) have been substituted for the names in the macro definition. Aliases in the macro definition that don't have a $ prefix, such as A in this example, are local to the macro definition and are rewritten at expansion time to avoid conflicts with aliases in other parts of the program. In this case, A becomes macro_max_by_group_A_0 in the expanded form.

To foster reuse, macros can be defined in separate files to Pig scripts, in which case they need to be imported into any script that uses them. An import statement looks like this:

```
IMPORT './ch16-pig/src/main/pig/max_temp.macro';
```

User-Defined Functions

Pig's designers realized that the ability to plug in custom code is crucial for all but the most trivial data processing jobs. For this reason, they made it easy to define and use user-defined functions. We only cover Java UDFs in this section, but be aware that you can also write UDFs in Python, JavaScript, Ruby, or Groovy, all of which are run using the Java Scripting API.

A Filter UDF

Let's demonstrate by writing a filter function for filtering out weather records that do not have a temperature quality reading of satisfactory (or better). The idea is to change this line:

```
filtered_records = FILTER records BY temperature != 9999 AND
  quality IN (0, 1, 4, 5, 9);
```

to:

```
filtered_records = FILTER records BY temperature != 9999 AND isGood(quality);
```

This achieves two things: it makes the Pig script a little more concise, and it encapsulates the logic in one place so that it can be easily reused in other scripts. If we were just writing an ad hoc query, we probably wouldn't bother to write a UDF. It's when you start doing the same kind of processing over and over again that you see opportunities for reusable UDFs.

Filter UDFs are all subclasses of FilterFunc, which itself is a subclass of EvalFunc. We'll look at EvalFunc in more detail later, but for the moment just note that, in essence, EvalFunc looks like the following class:

```
public abstract class EvalFunc<T> {
  public abstract T exec(Tuple input) throws IOException;
}
```

EvalFunc's only abstract method, exec(), takes a tuple and returns a single value, the (parameterized) type T. The fields in the input tuple consist of the expressions passed to the function—in this case, a single integer. For FilterFunc, T is Boolean, so the method should return true only for those tuples that should not be filtered out.

For the quality filter, we write a class, IsGoodQuality, that extends FilterFunc and implements the exec() method (see Example 16-1). The Tuple class is essentially a list of objects with associated types. Here we are concerned only with the first field (since the function only has a single argument), which we extract by index using the get() method on Tuple. The field is an integer, so if it's not null, we cast it and check whether the value is one that signifies the temperature was a good reading, returning the appropriate value, true or false.

Example 16-1. A FilterFunc UDF to remove records with unsatisfactory temperature quality readings

```
package com.hadoopbook.pig;

import java.io.IOException;
import java.util.ArrayList;
import java.util.List;

import org.apache.pig.FilterFunc;

import org.apache.pig.backend.executionengine.ExecException;
import org.apache.pig.data.DataType;
import org.apache.pig.data.Tuple;
import org.apache.pig.impl.logicalLayer.FrontendException;

public class IsGoodQuality extends FilterFunc {
```

```
@Override
public Boolean exec(Tuple tuple) throws IOException {
  if (tuple == null || tuple.size() == 0) {
    return false;
  }
  try {
    Object object = tuple.get(0);
    if (object == null) {
      return false;
    }
    int i = (Integer) object;
    return i == 0 || i == 1 || i == 4 || i == 5 || i == 9;
  } catch (ExecException e) {
    throw new IOException(e);
  }
}

}
```

To use the new function, we first compile it and package it in a JAR file (the example code that accompanies this book comes with build instructions for how to do this). Then we tell Pig about the JAR file with the REGISTER operator, which is given the local path to the filename (and is *not* enclosed in quotes):

```
grunt> REGISTER pig-examples.jar;
```

Finally, we can invoke the function:

```
grunt> filtered_records = FILTER records BY temperature != 9999 AND
>>   com.hadoopbook.pig.IsGoodQuality(quality);
```

Pig resolves function calls by treating the function's name as a Java classname and attempting to load a class of that name. (This, incidentally, is why function names are case sensitive: because Java classnames are.) When searching for classes, Pig uses a classloader that includes the JAR files that have been registered. When running in distributed mode, Pig will ensure that your JAR files get shipped to the cluster.

For the UDF in this example, Pig looks for a class with the name com.hadoop book.pig.IsGoodQuality, which it finds in the JAR file we registered.

Resolution of built-in functions proceeds in the same way, except for one difference: Pig has a set of built-in package names that it searches, so the function call does not have to be a fully qualified name. For example, the function MAX is actually implemented by a class MAX in the package org.apache.pig.builtin. This is one of the packages that Pig looks in, so we can write MAX rather than org.apache.pig.builtin.MAX in our Pig programs.

We can add our package name to the search path by invoking Grunt with this command-line argument: `-Dudf.import.list=com.hadoopbook.pig`. Alternatively, we can shorten the function name by defining an alias, using the `DEFINE` operator:

```
grunt> DEFINE isGood com.hadoopbook.pig.IsGoodQuality();
grunt> filtered_records = FILTER records BY temperature != 9999 AND
>>    isGood(quality);
```

Defining an alias is a good idea if you want to use the function several times in the same script. It's also necessary if you want to pass arguments to the constructor of the UDF's implementation class.

 If you add the lines to register JAR files and define function aliases to the *.pigbootup* file in your home directory, they will be run whenever you start Pig.

Leveraging types

The filter works when the quality field is declared to be of type `int`, but if the type information is absent, the UDF fails! This happens because the field is the default type, `bytearray`, represented by the `DataByteArray` class. Because `DataByteArray` is not an `Integer`, the cast fails.

The obvious way to fix this is to convert the field to an integer in the `exec()` method. However, there is a better way, which is to tell Pig the types of the fields that the function expects. The `getArgToFuncMapping()` method on `EvalFunc` is provided for precisely this reason. We can override it to tell Pig that the first field should be an integer:

```
@Override
public List<FuncSpec> getArgToFuncMapping() throws FrontendException {
  List<FuncSpec> funcSpecs = new ArrayList<FuncSpec>();
  funcSpecs.add(new FuncSpec(this.getClass().getName(),
      new Schema(new Schema.FieldSchema(null, DataType.INTEGER))));

  return funcSpecs;
}
```

This method returns a `FuncSpec` object corresponding to each of the fields of the tuple that are passed to the `exec()` method. Here there is a single field, and we construct an anonymous `FieldSchema` (the name is passed as `null`, since Pig ignores the name when doing type conversion). The type is specified using the `INTEGER` constant on Pig's `DataType` class.

With the amended function, Pig will attempt to convert the argument passed to the function to an integer. If the field cannot be converted, then a `null` is passed for the field. The `exec()` method always returns `false` when the field is `null`. For this application, this behavior is appropriate, as we want to filter out records whose quality field is unintelligible.

An Eval UDF

Writing an eval function is a small step up from writing a filter function. Consider the UDF in Example 16-2, which trims the leading and trailing whitespace from chararray values using the trim() method on java.lang.String.[6]

Example 16-2. An EvalFunc UDF to trim leading and trailing whitespace from chararray values

```java
public class Trim extends PrimitiveEvalFunc<String, String> {
  @Override
  public String exec(String input) {
    return input.trim();
  }
}
```

In this case, we have taken advantage of PrimitiveEvalFunc, which is a specialization of EvalFunc for when the input is a single primitive (atomic) type. For the Trim UDF, the input and output types are both of type String.[7]

In general, when you write an eval function, you need to consider what the output's schema looks like. In the following statement, the schema of B is determined by the function udf:

```
B = FOREACH A GENERATE udf($0);
```

If udf creates tuples with scalar fields, then Pig can determine B's schema through reflection. For complex types such as bags, tuples, or maps, Pig needs more help, and you should implement the outputSchema() method to give Pig the information about the output schema.

The Trim UDF returns a string, which Pig translates as a chararray, as can be seen from the following session:

```
grunt> DUMP A;
( pomegranate)
(banana   )
(apple)
(  lychee )
grunt> DESCRIBE A;
A: {fruit: chararray}
grunt> B = FOREACH A GENERATE com.hadoopbook.pig.Trim(fruit);
```

---

6. Pig actually comes with an equivalent built-in function called TRIM.

7. Although not relevant for this example, eval functions that operate on a bag may additionally implement Pig's Algebraic or Accumulator interfaces for more efficient processing of the bag in chunks.

```
grunt> DUMP B;
(pomegranate)
(banana)
(apple)
(lychee)
grunt> DESCRIBE B;
B: {chararray}
```

A has chararray fields that have leading and trailing spaces. We create B from A by applying the Trim function to the first field in A (named fruit). B's fields are correctly inferred to be of type chararray.

Dynamic invokers

Sometimes you want to use a function that is provided by a Java library, but without going to the effort of writing a UDF. Dynamic invokers allow you to do this by calling Java methods directly from a Pig script. The trade-off is that method calls are made via reflection, which can impose significant overhead when calls are made for every record in a large dataset. So for scripts that are run repeatedly, a dedicated UDF is normally preferred.

The following snippet shows how we could define and use a trim UDF that uses the Apache Commons Lang StringUtils class:

```
grunt> DEFINE trim InvokeForString('org.apache.commons.lang.StringUtils.trim',
>>   'String');
grunt> B = FOREACH A GENERATE trim(fruit);
grunt> DUMP B;
(pomegranate)
(banana)
(apple)
(lychee)
```

The InvokeForString invoker is used because the return type of the method is a String. (There are also InvokeForInt, InvokeForLong, InvokeForDouble, and Invoke ForFloat invokers.) The first argument to the invoker constructor is the fully qualified method to be invoked. The second is a space-separated list of the method argument classes.

A Load UDF

We'll demonstrate a custom load function that can read plain-text column ranges as fields, very much like the Unix cut command.[8] It is used as follows:

```
grunt> records = LOAD 'input/ncdc/micro/sample.txt'
>>   USING com.hadoopbook.pig.CutLoadFunc('16-19,88-92,93-93')
>>   AS (year:int, temperature:int, quality:int);
```

---

8. There is a more fully featured UDF for doing the same thing in the Piggy Bank called FixedWidthLoader.

```
grunt> DUMP records;
(1950,0,1)
(1950,22,1)
(1950,-11,1)
(1949,111,1)
(1949,78,1)
```

The string passed to CutLoadFunc is the column specification; each comma-separated range defines a field, which is assigned a name and type in the AS clause. Let's examine the implementation of CutLoadFunc, shown in Example 16-3.

Example 16-3. A LoadFunc UDF to load tuple fields as column ranges

```java
public class CutLoadFunc extends LoadFunc {

  private static final Log LOG = LogFactory.getLog(CutLoadFunc.class);

  private final List<Range> ranges;
  private final TupleFactory tupleFactory = TupleFactory.getInstance();
  private RecordReader reader;

  public CutLoadFunc(String cutPattern) {
    ranges = Range.parse(cutPattern);
  }

  @Override
  public void setLocation(String location, Job job)
      throws IOException {
    FileInputFormat.setInputPaths(job, location);
  }

  @Override
  public InputFormat getInputFormat() {
    return new TextInputFormat();
  }

  @Override
  public void prepareToRead(RecordReader reader, PigSplit split) {
    this.reader = reader;
  }

  @Override
  public Tuple getNext() throws IOException {
    try {
      if (!reader.nextKeyValue()) {
        return null;
      }
      Text value = (Text) reader.getCurrentValue();
      String line = value.toString();
      Tuple tuple = tupleFactory.newTuple(ranges.size());
      for (int i = 0; i < ranges.size(); i++) {
        Range range = ranges.get(i);
        if (range.getEnd() > line.length()) {
```

```
            LOG.warn(String.format(
                "Range end (%s) is longer than line length (%s)",
                range.getEnd(), line.length()));
            continue;
          }
          tuple.set(i, new DataByteArray(range.getSubstring(line)));
        }
        return tuple;
      } catch (InterruptedException e) {
        throw new ExecException(e);
      }
    }
  }
}
```

In Pig, like in Hadoop, data loading takes place before the mapper runs, so it is important that the input can be split into portions that are handled independently by each mapper (see "Input Splits and Records" on page 220 for background). A LoadFunc will typically use an existing underlying Hadoop InputFormat to create records, with the LoadFunc providing the logic for turning the records into Pig tuples.

CutLoadFunc is constructed with a string that specifies the column ranges to use for each field. The logic for parsing this string and creating a list of internal Range objects that encapsulates these ranges is contained in the Range class, and is not shown here (it is available in the example code that accompanies this book).

Pig calls setLocation() on a LoadFunc to pass the input location to the loader. Since CutLoadFunc uses a TextInputFormat to break the input into lines, we just pass the location to set the input path using a static method on FileInputFormat.

Pig uses the new MapReduce API, so we use the input and output formats and associated classes from the org.apache.hadoop.mapre duce package.

Next, Pig calls the getInputFormat() method to create a RecordReader for each split, just like in MapReduce. Pig passes each RecordReader to the prepareToRead() method of CutLoadFunc, which we store a reference to, so we can use it in the getNext() method for iterating through the records.

The Pig runtime calls getNext() repeatedly, and the load function reads tuples from the reader until the reader reaches the last record in its split. At this point, it returns null to signal that there are no more tuples to be read.

It is the responsibility of the getNext() implementation to turn lines of the input file into Tuple objects. It does this by means of a TupleFactory, a Pig class for creating Tuple instances. The newTuple() method creates a new tuple with the required number of fields, which is just the number of Range classes, and the fields are populated using substrings of the line, which are determined by the Range objects.

We need to think about what to do when the line is shorter than the range asked for. One option is to throw an exception and stop further processing. This is appropriate if your application cannot tolerate incomplete or corrupt records. In many cases, it is better to return a tuple with null fields and let the Pig script handle the incomplete data as it sees fit. This is the approach we take here; by exiting the for loop if the range end is past the end of the line, we leave the current field and any subsequent fields in the tuple with their default values of null.

Using a schema

Let's now consider the types of the fields being loaded. If the user has specified a schema, then the fields need to be converted to the relevant types. However, this is performed lazily by Pig, so the loader should always construct tuples of type bytearrary, using the DataByteArray type. The load function still has the opportunity to do the conversion, however, by overriding getLoadCaster() to return a custom implementation of the LoadCaster interface, which provides a collection of conversion methods for this purpose.

CutLoadFunc doesn't override getLoadCaster() because the default implementation returns Utf8StorageConverter, which provides standard conversions between UTF-8–encoded data and Pig data types.

In some cases, the load function itself can determine the schema. For example, if we were loading self-describing data such as XML or JSON, we could create a schema for Pig by looking at the data. Alternatively, the load function may determine the schema in another way, such as from an external file, or by being passed information in its constructor. To support such cases, the load function should implement the LoadMeta data interface (in addition to the LoadFunc interface) so it can supply a schema to the Pig runtime. Note, however, that if a user supplies a schema in the AS clause of LOAD, then it takes precedence over the schema specified through the LoadMetadata interface.

A load function may additionally implement the LoadPushDown interface as a means for finding out which columns the query is asking for. This can be a useful optimization for column-oriented storage, so that the loader loads only the columns that are needed by the query. There is no obvious way for CutLoadFunc to load only a subset of columns, because it reads the whole line for each tuple, so we don't use this optimization.

Data Processing Operators

Loading and Storing Data

Throughout this chapter, we have seen how to load data from external storage for processing in Pig. Storing the results is straightforward, too. Here's an example of using `PigStorage` to store tuples as plain-text values separated by a colon character:

```
grunt> STORE A INTO 'out' USING PigStorage(':');
grunt> cat out
Joe:cherry:2
Ali:apple:3
Joe:banana:2
Eve:apple:7
```

Other built-in storage functions were described in Table 16-7.

Filtering Data

Once you have some data loaded into a relation, often the next step is to filter it to remove the data that you are not interested in. By filtering early in the processing pipeline, you minimize the amount of data flowing through the system, which can improve efficiency.

FOREACH...GENERATE

We have already seen how to remove rows from a relation using the `FILTER` operator with simple expressions and a UDF. The `FOREACH...GENERATE` operator is used to act on every row in a relation. It can be used to remove fields or to generate new ones. In this example, we do both:

```
grunt> DUMP A;
(Joe,cherry,2)
(Ali,apple,3)
(Joe,banana,2)
(Eve,apple,7)
grunt> B = FOREACH A GENERATE $0, $2+1, 'Constant';
grunt> DUMP B;
(Joe,3,Constant)
(Ali,4,Constant)
(Joe,3,Constant)
(Eve,8,Constant)
```

Here we have created a new relation, B, with three fields. Its first field is a projection of the first field ($0) of A. B's second field is the third field of A ($2) with 1 added to it. B's third field is a constant field (every row in B has the same third field) with the `charar ray` value `Constant`.

The FOREACH...GENERATE operator has a nested form to support more complex processing. In the following example, we compute various statistics for the weather dataset:

```
-- year_stats.pig
REGISTER pig-examples.jar;
DEFINE isGood com.hadoopbook.pig.IsGoodQuality();
records = LOAD 'input/ncdc/all/19{1,2,3,4,5}0*'
  USING com.hadoopbook.pig.CutLoadFunc('5-10,11-15,16-19,88-92,93-93')
  AS (usaf:chararray, wban:chararray, year:int, temperature:int, quality:int);

grouped_records = GROUP records BY year PARALLEL 30;

year_stats = FOREACH grouped_records {
  uniq_stations = DISTINCT records.usaf;
  good_records = FILTER records BY isGood(quality);
  GENERATE FLATTEN(group), COUNT(uniq_stations) AS station_count,
    COUNT(good_records) AS good_record_count, COUNT(records) AS record_count;
}

DUMP year_stats;
```

Using the cut UDF we developed earlier, we load various fields from the input dataset into the records relation. Next, we group records by year. Notice the PARALLEL keyword for setting the number of reducers to use; this is vital when running on a cluster. Then we process each group using a nested FOREACH...GENERATE operator. The first nested statement creates a relation for the distinct USAF identifiers for stations using the DISTINCT operator. The second nested statement creates a relation for the records with "good" readings using the FILTER operator and a UDF. The final nested statement is a GENERATE statement (a nested FOREACH...GENERATE must always have a GENERATE statement as the last nested statement) that generates the summary fields of interest using the grouped records, as well as the relations created in the nested block.

Running it on a few years' worth of data, we get the following:

```
(1920,8L,8595L,8595L)
(1950,1988L,8635452L,8641353L)
(1930,121L,89245L,89262L)
(1910,7L,7650L,7650L)
(1940,732L,1052333L,1052976L)
```

The fields are year, number of unique stations, total number of good readings, and total number of readings. We can see how the number of weather stations and readings grew over time.

STREAM

The STREAM operator allows you to transform data in a relation using an external program or script. It is named by analogy with Hadoop Streaming, which provides a similar capability for MapReduce (see "Hadoop Streaming" on page 37).

STREAM can use built-in commands with arguments. Here is an example that uses the Unix cut command to extract the second field of each tuple in A. Note that the command and its arguments are enclosed in backticks:

```
grunt> C = STREAM A THROUGH `cut -f 2`;
grunt> DUMP C;
(cherry)
(apple)
(banana)
(apple)
```

The STREAM operator uses PigStorage to serialize and deserialize relations to and from the program's standard input and output streams. Tuples in A are converted to tab-delimited lines that are passed to the script. The output of the script is read one line at a time and split on tabs to create new tuples for the output relation C. You can provide a custom serializer and deserializer by subclassing PigStreamingBase (in the org.apache.pig package), then using the DEFINE operator.

Pig streaming is most powerful when you write custom processing scripts. The following Python script filters out bad weather records:

```
#!/usr/bin/env python

import re
import sys

for line in sys.stdin:
  (year, temp, q) = line.strip().split()
  if (temp != "9999" and re.match("[01459]", q)):
    print "%s\t%s" % (year, temp)
```

To use the script, you need to ship it to the cluster. This is achieved via a DEFINE clause, which also creates an alias for the STREAM command. The STREAM statement can then refer to the alias, as the following Pig script shows:

```
-- max_temp_filter_stream.pig
DEFINE is_good_quality `is_good_quality.py`
  SHIP ('ch16-pig/src/main/python/is_good_quality.py');
records = LOAD 'input/ncdc/micro-tab/sample.txt'
  AS (year:chararray, temperature:int, quality:int);
filtered_records = STREAM records THROUGH is_good_quality
  AS (year:chararray, temperature:int);
grouped_records = GROUP filtered_records BY year;
max_temp = FOREACH grouped_records GENERATE group,
  MAX(filtered_records.temperature);
DUMP max_temp;
```

Grouping and Joining Data

Joining datasets in MapReduce takes some work on the part of the programmer (see "Joins" on page 268), whereas Pig has very good built-in support for join operations, making it much more approachable. Since the large datasets that are suitable for analysis by Pig (and MapReduce in general) are not normalized, however, joins are used more infrequently in Pig than they are in SQL.

JOIN

Let's look at an example of an inner join. Consider the relations A and B:

```
grunt> DUMP A;
(2,Tie)
(4,Coat)
(3,Hat)
(1,Scarf)
grunt> DUMP B;
(Joe,2)
(Hank,4)
(Ali,0)
(Eve,3)
(Hank,2)
```

We can join the two relations on the numerical (identity) field in each:

```
grunt> C = JOIN A BY $0, B BY $1;
grunt> DUMP C;
(2,Tie,Hank,2)
(2,Tie,Joe,2)
(3,Hat,Eve,3)
(4,Coat,Hank,4)
```

This is a classic inner join, where each match between the two relations corresponds to a row in the result. (It's actually an equijoin because the join predicate is equality.) The result's fields are made up of all the fields of all the input relations.

You should use the general join operator when all the relations being joined are too large to fit in memory. If one of the relations is small enough to fit in memory, you can use a special type of join called a *fragment replicate join*, which is implemented by distributing the small input to all the mappers and performing a map-side join using an in-memory lookup table against the (fragmented) larger relation. There is a special syntax for telling Pig to use a fragment replicate join:[9]

```
grunt> C = JOIN A BY $0, B BY $1 USING 'replicated';
```

The first relation must be the large one, followed by one or more small ones (all of which must fit in memory).

---

9. There are more keywords that may be used in the USING clause, including 'skewed' (for large datasets with a skewed keyspace), 'merge' (to effect a merge join for inputs that are already sorted on the join key), and 'merge-sparse' (where 1% or less of data is matched). See Pig's documentation for details on how to use these specialized joins.

Pig also supports outer joins using a syntax that is similar to SQL's (this is covered for Hive in "Outer joins" on page 506). For example:

```
grunt> C = JOIN A BY $0 LEFT OUTER, B BY $1;
grunt> DUMP C;
(1,Scarf,,)
(2,Tie,Hank,2)
(2,Tie,Joe,2)
(3,Hat,Eve,3)
(4,Coat,Hank,4)
```

COGROUP

JOIN always gives a flat structure: a set of tuples. The COGROUP statement is similar to JOIN, but instead creates a nested set of output tuples. This can be useful if you want to exploit the structure in subsequent statements:

```
grunt> D = COGROUP A BY $0, B BY $1;
grunt> DUMP D;
(0,{},{(Ali,0)})
(1,{(1,Scarf)},{})
(2,{(2,Tie)},{(Hank,2),(Joe,2)})
(3,{(3,Hat)},{(Eve,3)})
(4,{(4,Coat)},{(Hank,4)})
```

COGROUP generates a tuple for each unique grouping key. The first field of each tuple is the key, and the remaining fields are bags of tuples from the relations with a matching key. The first bag contains the matching tuples from relation A with the same key. Similarly, the second bag contains the matching tuples from relation B with the same key.

If for a particular key a relation has no matching key, the bag for that relation is empty. For example, since no one has bought a scarf (with ID 1), the second bag in the tuple for that row is empty. This is an example of an outer join, which is the default type for COGROUP. It can be made explicit using the OUTER keyword, making this COGROUP statement the same as the previous one:

```
D = COGROUP A BY $0 OUTER, B BY $1 OUTER;
```

You can suppress rows with empty bags by using the INNER keyword, which gives the COGROUP inner join semantics. The INNER keyword is applied per relation, so the following suppresses rows only when relation A has no match (dropping the unknown product 0 here):

```
grunt> E = COGROUP A BY $0 INNER, B BY $1;
grunt> DUMP E;
(1,{(1,Scarf)},{})
(2,{(2,Tie)},{(Hank,2),(Joe,2)})
(3,{(3,Hat)},{(Eve,3)})
(4,{(4,Coat)},{(Hank,4)})
```

We can flatten this structure to discover who bought each of the items in relation A:

```
grunt> F = FOREACH E GENERATE FLATTEN(A), B.$0;
grunt> DUMP F;
(1,Scarf,{})
(2,Tie,{(Hank),(Joe)})
(3,Hat,{(Eve)})
(4,Coat,{(Hank)})
```

Using a combination of COGROUP, INNER, and FLATTEN (which removes nesting) it's possible to simulate an (inner) JOIN:

```
grunt> G = COGROUP A BY $0 INNER, B BY $1 INNER;
grunt> H = FOREACH G GENERATE FLATTEN($1), FLATTEN($2);
grunt> DUMP H;
(2,Tie,Hank,2)
(2,Tie,Joe,2)
(3,Hat,Eve,3)
(4,Coat,Hank,4)
```

This gives the same result as JOIN A BY $0, B BY $1.

If the join key is composed of several fields, you can specify them all in the BY clauses of the JOIN or COGROUP statement. Make sure that the number of fields in each BY clause is the same.

Here's another example of a join in Pig, in a script for calculating the maximum temperature for every station over a time period controlled by the input:

```
-- max_temp_station_name.pig
REGISTER pig-examples.jar;
DEFINE isGood com.hadoopbook.pig.IsGoodQuality();

stations = LOAD 'input/ncdc/metadata/stations-fixed-width.txt'
  USING com.hadoopbook.pig.CutLoadFunc('1-6,8-12,14-42')
  AS (usaf:chararray, wban:chararray, name:chararray);

trimmed_stations = FOREACH stations GENERATE usaf, wban, TRIM(name);

records = LOAD 'input/ncdc/all/191*'
  USING com.hadoopbook.pig.CutLoadFunc('5-10,11-15,88-92,93-93')
  AS (usaf:chararray, wban:chararray, temperature:int, quality:int);

filtered_records = FILTER records BY temperature != 9999 AND isGood(quality);
grouped_records = GROUP filtered_records BY (usaf, wban) PARALLEL 30;
max_temp = FOREACH grouped_records GENERATE FLATTEN(group),
  MAX(filtered_records.temperature);
max_temp_named = JOIN max_temp BY (usaf, wban), trimmed_stations BY (usaf, wban)
  PARALLEL 30;
max_temp_result = FOREACH max_temp_named GENERATE $0, $1, $5, $2;

STORE max_temp_result INTO 'max_temp_by_station';
```

We use the cut UDF we developed earlier to load one relation holding the station IDs (USAF and WBAN identifiers) and names, and one relation holding all the weather records, keyed by station ID. We group the filtered weather records by station ID and aggregate by maximum temperature before joining with the stations. Finally, we project out the fields we want in the final result: USAF, WBAN, station name, and maximum temperature.

Here are a few results for the 1910s:

```
228020        99999        SORTAVALA       322
029110        99999        VAASA AIRPORT   300
040650        99999        GRIMSEY         378
```

This query could be made more efficient by using a fragment replicate join, as the station metadata is small.

CROSS

Pig Latin includes the cross-product operator (also known as the Cartesian product), CROSS, which joins every tuple in a relation with every tuple in a second relation (and with every tuple in further relations, if supplied). The size of the output is the product of the size of the inputs, potentially making the output very large:

```
grunt> I = CROSS A, B;
grunt> DUMP I;
(2,Tie,Joe,2)
(2,Tie,Hank,4)
(2,Tie,Ali,0)
(2,Tie,Eve,3)
(2,Tie,Hank,2)
(4,Coat,Joe,2)
(4,Coat,Hank,4)
(4,Coat,Ali,0)
(4,Coat,Eve,3)
(4,Coat,Hank,2)
(3,Hat,Joe,2)
(3,Hat,Hank,4)
(3,Hat,Ali,0)
(3,Hat,Eve,3)
(3,Hat,Hank,2)
(1,Scarf,Joe,2)
(1,Scarf,Hank,4)
(1,Scarf,Ali,0)
(1,Scarf,Eve,3)
(1,Scarf,Hank,2)
```

When dealing with large datasets, you should try to avoid operations that generate intermediate representations that are quadratic (or worse) in size. Computing the cross product of the whole input dataset is rarely needed, if ever.

For example, at first blush, one might expect that calculating pairwise document similarity in a corpus of documents would require every document pair to be generated before calculating their similarity. However, if we start with the insight that most document pairs have a similarity score of zero (i.e., they are unrelated), then we can find a way to a better algorithm.

In this case, the key idea is to focus on the entities that we are using to calculate similarity (terms in a document, for example) and make them the center of the algorithm. In practice, we also remove terms that don't help discriminate between documents (stopwords), and this reduces the problem space still further. Using this technique to analyze a set of roughly one million (10^6) documents generates on the order of one billion (10^9) intermediate pairs,[10] rather than the one trillion (10^{12}) produced by the naive approach (generating the cross product of the input) or the approach with no stopword removal.

GROUP

Where COGROUP groups the data in two or more relations, the GROUP statement groups the data in a single relation. GROUP supports grouping by more than equality of keys: you can use an expression or user-defined function as the group key. For example, consider the following relation A:

```
grunt> DUMP A;
(Joe,cherry)
(Ali,apple)
(Joe,banana)
(Eve,apple)
```

Let's group by the number of characters in the second field:

```
grunt> B = GROUP A BY SIZE($1);
grunt> DUMP B;
(5,{(Eve,apple),(Ali,apple)})
(6,{(Joe,banana),(Joe,cherry)})
```

GROUP creates a relation whose first field is the grouping field, which is given the alias group. The second field is a bag containing the grouped fields with the same schema as the original relation (in this case, A).

There are also two special grouping operations: ALL and ANY. ALL groups all the tuples in a relation in a single group, as if the GROUP function were a constant:

```
grunt> C = GROUP A ALL;
grunt> DUMP C;
(all,{(Eve,apple),(Joe,banana),(Ali,apple),(Joe,cherry)})
```

Note that there is no BY in this form of the GROUP statement. The ALL grouping is commonly used to count the number of tuples in a relation, as shown in "Validation and nulls" on page 442.

---

10. Tamer Elsayed, Jimmy Lin, and Douglas W. Oard, "Pairwise Document Similarity in Large Collections with MapReduce," (*http://bit.ly/doc_similarity*) *Proceedings of the 46th Annual Meeting of the Association of Computational Linguistics*, June 2008.

The ANY keyword is used to group the tuples in a relation randomly, which can be useful for sampling.

Sorting Data

Relations are unordered in Pig. Consider a relation A:

```
grunt> DUMP A;
(2,3)
(1,2)
(2,4)
```

There is no guarantee which order the rows will be processed in. In particular, when retrieving the contents of A using DUMP or STORE, the rows may be written in any order. If you want to impose an order on the output, you can use the ORDER operator to sort a relation by one or more fields. The default sort order compares fields of the same type using the natural ordering, and different types are given an arbitrary, but deterministic, ordering (a tuple is always "less than" a bag, for example).

The following example sorts A by the first field in ascending order and by the second field in descending order:

```
grunt> B = ORDER A BY $0, $1 DESC;
grunt> DUMP B;
(1,2)
(2,4)
(2,3)
```

Any further processing on a sorted relation is not guaranteed to retain its order. For example:

```
grunt> C = FOREACH B GENERATE *;
```

Even though relation C has the same contents as relation B, its tuples may be emitted in any order by a DUMP or a STORE. It is for this reason that it is usual to perform the ORDER operation just before retrieving the output.

The LIMIT statement is useful for limiting the number of results as a quick-and-dirty way to get a sample of a relation. (Although random sampling using the SAMPLE operator, or prototyping with the ILLUSTRATE command, should be preferred for generating more representative samples of the data.) It can be used immediately after the ORDER statement to retrieve the first *n* tuples. Usually, LIMIT will select any *n* tuples from a relation, but when used immediately after an ORDER statement, the order is retained (in an exception to the rule that processing a relation does not retain its order):

```
grunt> D = LIMIT B 2;
grunt> DUMP D;
(1,2)
(2,4)
```

If the limit is greater than the number of tuples in the relation, all tuples are returned (so LIMIT has no effect).

Using LIMIT can improve the performance of a query because Pig tries to apply the limit as early as possible in the processing pipeline, to minimize the amount of data that needs to be processed. For this reason, you should always use LIMIT if you are not interested in the entire output.

Combining and Splitting Data

Sometimes you have several relations that you would like to combine into one. For this, the UNION statement is used. For example:

```
grunt> DUMP A;
(2,3)
(1,2)
(2,4)
grunt> DUMP B;
(z,x,8)
(w,y,1)
grunt> C = UNION A, B;
grunt> DUMP C;
(2,3)
(z,x,8)
(1,2)
(w,y,1)
(2,4)
```

C is the union of relations A and B, and because relations are unordered, the order of the tuples in C is undefined. Also, it's possible to form the union of two relations with different schemas or with different numbers of fields, as we have done here. Pig attempts to merge the schemas from the relations that UNION is operating on. In this case, they are incompatible, so C has no schema:

```
grunt> DESCRIBE A;
A: {f0: int,f1: int}
grunt> DESCRIBE B;
B: {f0: chararray,f1: chararray,f2: int}
grunt> DESCRIBE C;
Schema for C unknown.
```

If the output relation has no schema, your script needs to be able to handle tuples that vary in the number of fields and/or types.

The SPLIT operator is the opposite of UNION: it partitions a relation into two or more relations. See "Validation and nulls" on page 442 for an example of how to use it.

Pig in Practice

There are some practical techniques that are worth knowing about when you are developing and running Pig programs. This section covers some of them.

Parallelism

When running in MapReduce mode, it's important that the degree of parallelism matches the size of the dataset. By default, Pig sets the number of reducers by looking at the size of the input and using one reducer per 1 GB of input, up to a maximum of 999 reducers. You can override these parameters by setting `pig.exec.reducers` `.bytes.per.reducer` (the default is 1,000,000,000 bytes) and `pig.exec.reducers` `.max` (the default is 999).

To explicitly set the number of reducers you want for each job, you can use a `PARALLEL` clause for operators that run in the reduce phase. These include all the grouping and joining operators (`GROUP`, `COGROUP`, `JOIN`, `CROSS`), as well as `DISTINCT` and `ORDER`. The following line sets the number of reducers to 30 for the `GROUP`:

```
grouped_records = GROUP records BY year PARALLEL 30;
```

Alternatively, you can set the `default_parallel` option, and it will take effect for all subsequent jobs:

```
grunt> set default_parallel 30
```

See "Choosing the Number of Reducers" on page 217 for further discussion.

The number of map tasks is set by the size of the input (with one map per HDFS block) and is not affected by the `PARALLEL` clause.

Anonymous Relations

You usually apply a diagnostic operator like `DUMP` or `DESCRIBE` to the most recently defined relation. Since this is so common, Pig has a shortcut to refer to the previous relation: @. Similarly, it can be tiresome to have to come up with a name for each relation when using the interpreter. Pig allows you to use the special syntax => to create a relation with no alias, which can only be referred to with @. For example:

```
grunt> => LOAD 'input/ncdc/micro-tab/sample.txt';
grunt> DUMP @
(1950,0,1)
(1950,22,1)
(1950,-11,1)
(1949,111,1)
(1949,78,1)
```

Parameter Substitution

If you have a Pig script that you run on a regular basis, it's quite common to want to be able to run the same script with different parameters. For example, a script that runs daily may use the date to determine which input files it runs over. Pig supports *parameter substitution*, where parameters in the script are substituted with values supplied at run-time. Parameters are denoted by identifiers prefixed with a $ character; for example, $input and $output are used in the following script to specify the input and output paths:

```
-- max_temp_param.pig
records = LOAD '$input' AS (year:chararray, temperature:int, quality:int);
filtered_records = FILTER records BY temperature != 9999 AND
  quality IN (0, 1, 4, 5, 9);
grouped_records = GROUP filtered_records BY year;
max_temp = FOREACH grouped_records GENERATE group,
  MAX(filtered_records.temperature);
STORE max_temp into '$output';
```

Parameters can be specified when launching Pig using the -param option, once for each parameter:

```
% pig -param input=/user/tom/input/ncdc/micro-tab/sample.txt \
>     -param output=/tmp/out \
>     ch16-pig/src/main/pig/max_temp_param.pig
```

You can also put parameters in a file and pass them to Pig using the -param_file option. For example, we can achieve the same result as the previous command by placing the parameter definitions in a file:

```
# Input file
input=/user/tom/input/ncdc/micro-tab/sample.txt
# Output file
output=/tmp/out
```

The *pig* invocation then becomes:

```
% pig -param_file ch16-pig/src/main/pig/max_temp_param.param \
>     ch16-pig/src/main/pig/max_temp_param.pig
```

You can specify multiple parameter files by using -param_file repeatedly. You can also use a combination of -param and -param_file options; if any parameter is defined both in a parameter file and on the command line, the last value on the command line takes precedence.

Dynamic parameters

For parameters that are supplied using the -param option, it is easy to make the value dynamic by running a command or script. Many Unix shells support command substitution for a command enclosed in backticks, and we can use this to make the output directory date-based:

```
% pig -param input=/user/tom/input/ncdc/micro-tab/sample.txt \
>      -param output=/tmp/`date "+%Y-%m-%d"`/out \
>      ch16-pig/src/main/pig/max_temp_param.pig
```

Pig also supports backticks in parameter files by executing the enclosed command in a shell and using the shell output as the substituted value. If the command or script exits with a nonzero exit status, then the error message is reported and execution halts. Backtick support in parameter files is a useful feature; it means that parameters can be defined in the same way in a file or on the command line.

Parameter substitution processing

Parameter substitution occurs as a preprocessing step before the script is run. You can see the substitutions that the preprocessor made by executing Pig with the -dryrun option. In dry run mode, Pig performs parameter substitution (and macro expansion) and generates a copy of the original script with substituted values, but does not execute the script. You can inspect the generated script and check that the substitutions look sane (because they are dynamically generated, for example) before running it in normal mode.

Further Reading

This chapter provided a basic introduction to using Pig. For a more detailed guide, see *Programming Pig* by Alan Gates (O'Reilly, 2011).

Hive

In "Information Platforms and the Rise of the Data Scientist,"[1] Jeff Hammerbacher describes Information Platforms as "the locus of their organization's efforts to ingest, process, and generate information," and how they "serve to accelerate the process of learning from empirical data."

One of the biggest ingredients in the Information Platform built by Jeff's team at Facebook was Apache Hive (*https://hive.apache.org/*), a framework for data warehousing on top of Hadoop. Hive grew from a need to manage and learn from the huge volumes of data that Facebook was producing every day from its burgeoning social network. After trying a few different systems, the team chose Hadoop for storage and processing, since it was cost effective and met the scalability requirements.

Hive was created to make it possible for analysts with strong SQL skills (but meager Java programming skills) to run queries on the huge volumes of data that Facebook stored in HDFS. Today, Hive is a successful Apache project used by many organizations as a general-purpose, scalable data processing platform.

Of course, SQL isn't ideal for every big data problem—it's not a good fit for building complex machine-learning algorithms, for example—but it's great for many analyses, and it has the huge advantage of being very well known in the industry. What's more, SQL is the *lingua franca* in business intelligence tools (ODBC is a common bridge, for example), so Hive is well placed to integrate with these products.

This chapter is an introduction to using Hive. It assumes that you have working knowledge of SQL and general database architecture; as we go through Hive's features, we'll often compare them to the equivalent in a traditional RDBMS.

---

1. Toby Segaran and Jeff Hammerbacher, *Beautiful Data: The Stories Behind Elegant Data Solutions* (O'Reilly, 2009).

Installing Hive

In normal use, Hive runs on your workstation and converts your SQL query into a series of jobs for execution on a Hadoop cluster. Hive organizes data into tables, which provide a means for attaching structure to data stored in HDFS. Metadata—such as table schemas—is stored in a database called the *metastore*.

When starting out with Hive, it is convenient to run the metastore on your local machine. In this configuration, which is the default, the Hive table definitions that you create will be local to your machine, so you can't share them with other users. We'll see how to configure a shared remote metastore, which is the norm in production environments, in "The Metastore" on page 480.

Installation of Hive is straightforward. As a prerequisite, you need to have the same version of Hadoop installed locally that your cluster is running.[2] Of course, you may choose to run Hadoop locally, either in standalone or pseudodistributed mode, while getting started with Hive. These options are all covered in Appendix A.

Which Versions of Hadoop Does Hive Work With?

Any given release of Hive is designed to work with multiple versions of Hadoop. Generally, Hive works with the latest stable release of Hadoop, as well as supporting a number of older versions, listed in the release notes. You don't need to do anything special to tell Hive which version of Hadoop you are using, beyond making sure that the *hadoop* executable is on the path or setting the HADOOP_HOME environment variable.

Download a release (*http://hive.apache.org/downloads.html*), and unpack the tarball in a suitable place on your workstation:

```
% tar xzf apache-hive-x.y.z-bin.tar.gz
```

It's handy to put Hive on your path to make it easy to launch:

```
% export HIVE_HOME=~/sw/apache-hive-x.y.z-bin
% export PATH=$PATH:$HIVE_HOME/bin
```

Now type hive to launch the Hive shell:

```
% hive
hive>
```

---

2. It is assumed that you have network connectivity from your workstation to the Hadoop cluster. You can test this before running Hive by installing Hadoop locally and performing some HDFS operations with the hadoop fs command.

The Hive Shell

The shell is the primary way that we will interact with Hive, by issuing commands in *HiveQL*. HiveQL is Hive's query language, a dialect of SQL. It is heavily influenced by MySQL, so if you are familiar with MySQL, you should feel at home using Hive.

When starting Hive for the first time, we can check that it is working by listing its tables —there should be none. The command must be terminated with a semicolon to tell Hive to execute it:

```
hive> SHOW TABLES;
OK
Time taken: 0.473 seconds
```

Like SQL, HiveQL is generally case insensitive (except for string comparisons), so `show tables;` works equally well here. The Tab key will autocomplete Hive keywords and functions.

For a fresh install, the command takes a few seconds to run as it lazily creates the metastore database on your machine. (The database stores its files in a directory called *metastore_db*, which is relative to the location from which you ran the `hive` command.)

You can also run the Hive shell in noninteractive mode. The `-f` option runs the commands in the specified file, which is *script.q* in this example:

```
% hive -f script.q
```

For short scripts, you can use the `-e` option to specify the commands inline, in which case the final semicolon is not required:

```
% hive -e 'SELECT * FROM dummy'
OK
X
Time taken: 1.22 seconds, Fetched: 1 row(s)
```

 It's useful to have a small table of data to test queries against, such as trying out functions in `SELECT` expressions using literal data (see "Operators and Functions" on page 488). Here's one way of populating a single-row table:

```
% echo 'X' > /tmp/dummy.txt
% hive -e "CREATE TABLE dummy (value STRING); \
    LOAD DATA LOCAL INPATH '/tmp/dummy.txt' \
    OVERWRITE INTO TABLE dummy"
```

In both interactive and noninteractive mode, Hive will print information to standard error—such as the time taken to run a query—during the course of operation. You can suppress these messages using the `-S` option at launch time, which has the effect of showing only the output result for queries:

```
% hive -S -e 'SELECT * FROM dummy'
X
```

Other useful Hive shell features include the ability to run commands on the host operating system by using a ! prefix to the command and the ability to access Hadoop filesystems using the dfs command.

An Example

Let's see how to use Hive to run a query on the weather dataset we explored in earlier chapters. The first step is to load the data into Hive's managed storage. Here we'll have Hive use the local filesystem for storage; later we'll see how to store tables in HDFS.

Just like an RDBMS, Hive organizes its data into tables. We create a table to hold the weather data using the CREATE TABLE statement:

```
CREATE TABLE records (year STRING, temperature INT, quality INT)
ROW FORMAT DELIMITED
  FIELDS TERMINATED BY '\t';
```

The first line declares a records table with three columns: year, temperature, and quality. The type of each column must be specified, too. Here the year is a string, while the other two columns are integers.

So far, the SQL is familiar. The ROW FORMAT clause, however, is particular to HiveQL. This declaration is saying that each row in the data file is tab-delimited text. Hive expects there to be three fields in each row, corresponding to the table columns, with fields separated by tabs and rows by newlines.

Next, we can populate Hive with the data. This is just a small sample, for exploratory purposes:

```
LOAD DATA LOCAL INPATH 'input/ncdc/micro-tab/sample.txt'
OVERWRITE INTO TABLE records;
```

Running this command tells Hive to put the specified local file in its warehouse directory. This is a simple filesystem operation. There is no attempt, for example, to parse the file and store it in an internal database format, because Hive does not mandate any particular file format. Files are stored verbatim; they are not modified by Hive.

In this example, we are storing Hive tables on the local filesystem (fs.defaultFS is set to its default value of file:///). Tables are stored as directories under Hive's warehouse directory, which is controlled by the hive.metastore.warehouse.dir property and defaults to */user/hive/warehouse*.

Thus, the files for the records table are found in the */user/hive/warehouse/records* directory on the local filesystem:

```
% ls /user/hive/warehouse/records/
sample.txt
```

In this case, there is only one file, *sample.txt*, but in general there can be more, and Hive will read all of them when querying the table.

The OVERWRITE keyword in the LOAD DATA statement tells Hive to delete any existing files in the directory for the table. If it is omitted, the new files are simply added to the table's directory (unless they have the same names, in which case they replace the old files).

Now that the data is in Hive, we can run a query against it:

```
hive> SELECT year, MAX(temperature)
    > FROM records
    > WHERE temperature != 9999 AND quality IN (0, 1, 4, 5, 9)
    > GROUP BY year;
1949    111
1950    22
```

This SQL query is unremarkable. It is a SELECT statement with a GROUP BY clause for grouping rows into years, which uses the MAX aggregate function to find the maximum temperature for each year group. The remarkable thing is that Hive transforms this query into a job, which it executes on our behalf, then prints the results to the console. There are some nuances, such as the SQL constructs that Hive supports and the format of the data that we can query—and we explore some of these in this chapter—but it is the ability to execute SQL queries against our raw data that gives Hive its power.

Running Hive

In this section, we look at some more practical aspects of running Hive, including how to set up Hive to run against a Hadoop cluster and a shared metastore. In doing so, we'll see Hive's architecture in some detail.

Configuring Hive

Hive is configured using an XML configuration file like Hadoop's. The file is called *hive-site.xml* and is located in Hive's *conf* directory. This file is where you can set properties that you want to set every time you run Hive. The same directory contains *hive-default.xml*, which documents the properties that Hive exposes and their default values.

You can override the configuration directory that Hive looks for in *hive-site.xml* by passing the --config option to the hive command:

```
% hive --config /Users/tom/dev/hive-conf
```

Note that this option specifies the containing directory, not *hive-site.xml* itself. It can be useful when you have multiple site files—for different clusters, say—that you switch between on a regular basis. Alternatively, you can set the HIVE_CONF_DIR environment variable to the configuration directory for the same effect.

The *hive-site.xml* file is a natural place to put the cluster connection details: you can specify the filesystem and resource manager using the usual Hadoop properties, `fs.defaultFS` and `yarn.resourcemanager.address` (see Appendix A for more details on configuring Hadoop). If not set, they default to the local filesystem and the local (in-process) job runner—just like they do in Hadoop—which is very handy when trying out Hive on small trial datasets. Metastore configuration settings (covered in "The Metastore" on page 480) are commonly found in *hive-site.xml*, too.

Hive also permits you to set properties on a per-session basis, by passing the `-hiveconf` option to the `hive` command. For example, the following command sets the cluster (in this case, to a pseudodistributed cluster) for the duration of the session:

```
% hive -hiveconf fs.defaultFS=hdfs://localhost \
  -hiveconf mapreduce.framework.name=yarn \
  -hiveconf yarn.resourcemanager.address=localhost:8032
```

> If you plan to have more than one Hive user sharing a Hadoop cluster, you need to make the directories that Hive uses writable by all users. The following commands will create the directories and set their permissions appropriately:
>
> ```
> % hadoop fs -mkdir /tmp
> % hadoop fs -chmod a+w /tmp
> % hadoop fs -mkdir -p /user/hive/warehouse
> % hadoop fs -chmod a+w /user/hive/warehouse
> ```
>
> If all users are in the same group, then permissions g+w are sufficient on the warehouse directory.

You can change settings from within a session, too, using the SET command. This is useful for changing Hive settings for a particular query. For example, the following command ensures buckets are populated according to the table definition (see "Buckets" on page 493):

```
hive> SET hive.enforce.bucketing=true;
```

To see the current value of any property, use SET with just the property name:

```
hive> SET hive.enforce.bucketing;
hive.enforce.bucketing=true
```

By itself, SET will list all the properties (and their values) set by Hive. Note that the list will not include Hadoop defaults, unless they have been explicitly overridden in one of the ways covered in this section. Use SET -v to list all the properties in the system, including Hadoop defaults.

There is a precedence hierarchy to setting properties. In the following list, lower numbers take precedence over higher numbers:

1. The Hive SET command
2. The command-line -hiveconf option
3. *hive-site.xml* and the Hadoop site files (*core-site.xml, hdfs-site.xml, mapred-site.xml*, and *yarn-site.xml*)
4. The Hive defaults and the Hadoop default files (*core-default.xml, hdfs-default.xml, mapred-default.xml*, and *yarn-default.xml*)

Setting configuration properties for Hadoop is covered in more detail in "Which Properties Can I Set?" on page 150.

Execution engines

Hive was originally written to use MapReduce as its execution engine, and that is still the default. It is now also possible to run Hive using Apache Tez (*http://tez.apache.org/*) as its execution engine, and work is underway to support Spark (see Chapter 19), too. Both Tez and Spark are general directed acyclic graph (DAG) engines that offer more flexibility and higher performance than MapReduce. For example, unlike MapReduce, where intermediate job output is materialized to HDFS, Tez and Spark can avoid replication overhead by writing the intermediate output to local disk, or even store it in memory (at the request of the Hive planner).

The execution engine is controlled by the `hive.execution.engine` property, which defaults to `mr` (for MapReduce). It's easy to switch the execution engine on a per-query basis, so you can see the effect of a different engine on a particular query. Set Hive to use Tez as follows:

```
hive> SET hive.execution.engine=tez;
```

Note that Tez needs to be installed on the Hadoop cluster first; see the Hive documentation for up-to-date details on how to do this.

Logging

You can find Hive's error log on the local filesystem at *${java.io.tmpdir}/${user.name}/hive.log*. It can be very useful when trying to diagnose configuration problems or other types of error. Hadoop's MapReduce task logs are also a useful resource for troubleshooting; see "Hadoop Logs" on page 172 for where to find them.

On many systems, `${java.io.tmpdir}` is */tmp*, but if it's not, or if you want to set the logging directory to be another location, then use the following:

```
% hive -hiveconf hive.log.dir='/tmp/${user.name}'
```

The logging configuration is in *conf/hive-log4j.properties*, and you can edit this file to change log levels and other logging-related settings. However, often it's more convenient to set logging configuration for the session. For example, the following handy invocation will send debug messages to the console:

```
% hive -hiveconf hive.root.logger=DEBUG,console
```

Hive Services

The Hive shell is only one of several services that you can run using the hive command. You can specify the service to run using the --service option. Type hive --service help to get a list of available service names; some of the most useful ones are described in the following list:

cli

> The command-line interface to Hive (the shell). This is the default service.

hiveserver2

> Runs Hive as a server exposing a Thrift service, enabling access from a range of clients written in different languages. HiveServer 2 improves on the original Hive-Server by supporting authentication and multiuser concurrency. Applications using the Thrift, JDBC, and ODBC connectors need to run a Hive server to communicate with Hive. Set the hive.server2.thrift.port configuration property to specify the port the server will listen on (defaults to 10000).

beeline

> A command-line interface to Hive that works in embedded mode (like the regular CLI), or by connecting to a HiveServer 2 process using JDBC.

hwi

> The Hive Web Interface. A simple web interface that can be used as an alternative to the CLI without having to install any client software. See also Hue (*http://gethue.com/*) for a more fully featured Hadoop web interface that includes applications for running Hive queries and browsing the Hive metastore.

jar

> The Hive equivalent of hadoop jar, a convenient way to run Java applications that includes both Hadoop and Hive classes on the classpath.

metastore

> By default, the metastore is run in the same process as the Hive service. Using this service, it is possible to run the metastore as a standalone (remote) process. Set the METASTORE_PORT environment variable (or use the -p command-line option) to specify the port the server will listen on (defaults to 9083).

Hive clients

If you run Hive as a server (`hive --service hiveserver2`), there are a number of different mechanisms for connecting to it from applications (the relationship between Hive clients and Hive services is illustrated in Figure 17-1):

Thrift Client

The Hive server is exposed as a Thrift service, so it's possible to interact with it using any programming language that supports Thrift. There are third-party projects providing clients for Python and Ruby; for more details, see the Hive wiki (*http://bit.ly/hive_server*).

JDBC driver

Hive provides a Type 4 (pure Java) JDBC driver, defined in the class `org.apache.hadoop.hive.jdbc.HiveDriver`. When configured with a JDBC URI of the form `jdbc:hive2://host:port/dbname`, a Java application will connect to a Hive server running in a separate process at the given host and port. (The driver makes calls to an interface implemented by the Hive Thrift Client using the Java Thrift bindings.)

You may alternatively choose to connect to Hive via JDBC in *embedded mode* using the URI `jdbc:hive2://`. In this mode, Hive runs in the same JVM as the application invoking it; there is no need to launch it as a standalone server, since it does not use the Thrift service or the Hive Thrift Client.

The Beeline CLI uses the JDBC driver to communicate with Hive.

ODBC driver

An ODBC driver allows applications that support the ODBC protocol (such as business intelligence software) to connect to Hive. The Apache Hive distribution does not ship with an ODBC driver, but several vendors make one freely available. (Like the JDBC driver, ODBC drivers use Thrift to communicate with the Hive server.)

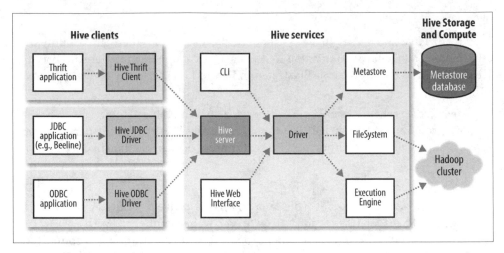

Figure 17-1. Hive architecture

The Metastore

The *metastore* is the central repository of Hive metadata. The metastore is divided into two pieces: a service and the backing store for the data. By default, the metastore service runs in the same JVM as the Hive service and contains an embedded Derby database instance backed by the local disk. This is called the *embedded metastore* configuration (see Figure 17-2).

Using an embedded metastore is a simple way to get started with Hive; however, only one embedded Derby database can access the database files on disk at any one time, which means you can have only one Hive session open at a time that accesses the same metastore. Trying to start a second session produces an error when it attempts to open a connection to the metastore.

The solution to supporting multiple sessions (and therefore multiple users) is to use a standalone database. This configuration is referred to as a *local metastore*, since the metastore service still runs in the same process as the Hive service but connects to a database running in a separate process, either on the same machine or on a remote machine. Any JDBC-compliant database may be used by setting the `javax.jdo`
`.option.*` configuration properties listed in Table 17-1.[3]

---

3. The properties have the `javax.jdo` prefix because the metastore implementation uses the Java Data Objects (JDO) API for persisting Java objects. Specifically, it uses the DataNucleus implementation of JDO.

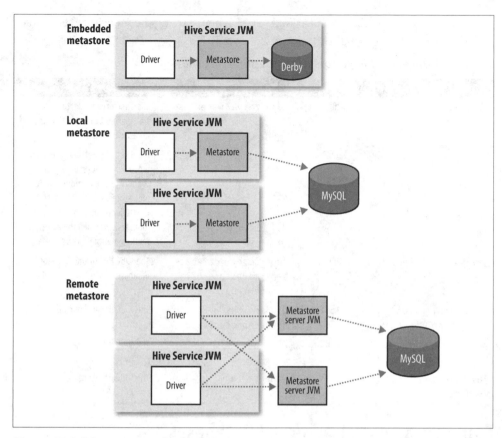

Figure 17-2. Metastore configurations

MySQL is a popular choice for the standalone metastore. In this case, the `javax.jdo.op tion.ConnectionURL` property is set to `jdbc:mysql://host/dbname?createDataba seIfNotExist=true`, and `javax.jdo.option.ConnectionDriverName` is set to `com.mysql.jdbc.Driver`. (The username and password should be set too, of course.) The JDBC driver JAR file for MySQL (Connector/J) must be on Hive's classpath, which is simply achieved by placing it in Hive's *lib* directory.

Going a step further, there's another metastore configuration called a *remote metastore*, where one or more metastore servers run in separate processes to the Hive service. This brings better manageability and security because the database tier can be completely firewalled off, and the clients no longer need the database credentials.

A Hive service is configured to use a remote metastore by setting `hive.meta store.uris` to the metastore server URI(s), separated by commas if there is more than one. Metastore server URIs are of the form `thrift://host:port`, where the port corresponds to the one set by METASTORE_PORT when starting the metastore server (see "Hive Services" on page 478).

Table 17-1. Important metastore configuration properties

Property name	Type	Default value	Description
hive.metastore.warehouse.dir	URI	/user/hive/warehouse	The directory relative to fs.defaultFS where managed tables are stored.
hive.metastore.uris	Comma-separated URIs	Not set	If not set (the default), use an in-process metastore; otherwise, connect to one or more remote metastores, specified by a list of URIs. Clients connect in a round-robin fashion when there are multiple remote servers.
javax.jdo.option.ConnectionURL	URI	jdbc:derby:;databaseName=metastore_db;create=true	The JDBC URL of the metastore database.
javax.jdo.option.ConnectionDriverName	String	org.apache.derby.jdbc.EmbeddedDriver	The JDBC driver classname.
javax.jdo.option.ConnectionUserName	String	APP	The JDBC username.
javax.jdo.option.ConnectionPassword	String	mine	The JDBC password.

Comparison with Traditional Databases

Although Hive resembles a traditional database in many ways (such as supporting a SQL interface), its original HDFS and MapReduce underpinnings mean that there are a number of architectural differences that have directly influenced the features that Hive supports. Over time, however, these limitations have been (and continue to be) removed, with the result that Hive looks and feels more like a traditional database with every year that passes.

Schema on Read Versus Schema on Write

In a traditional database, a table's schema is enforced at data load time. If the data being loaded doesn't conform to the schema, then it is rejected. This design is sometimes called *schema on write* because the data is checked against the schema when it is written into the database.

Hive, on the other hand, doesn't verify the data when it is loaded, but rather when a query is issued. This is called *schema on read*.

There are trade-offs between the two approaches. Schema on read makes for a very fast initial load, since the data does not have to be read, parsed, and serialized to disk in the database's internal format. The load operation is just a file copy or move. It is more flexible, too: consider having two schemas for the same underlying data, depending on the analysis being performed. (This is possible in Hive using external tables; see "Managed Tables and External Tables" on page 490.)

Schema on write makes query time performance faster because the database can index columns and perform compression on the data. The trade-off, however, is that it takes longer to load data into the database. Furthermore, there are many scenarios where the schema is not known at load time, so there are no indexes to apply, because the queries have not been formulated yet. These scenarios are where Hive shines.

Updates, Transactions, and Indexes

Updates, transactions, and indexes are mainstays of traditional databases. Yet, until recently, these features have not been considered a part of Hive's feature set. This is because Hive was built to operate over HDFS data using MapReduce, where full-table scans are the norm and a table update is achieved by transforming the data into a new table. For a data warehousing application that runs over large portions of the dataset, this works well.

Hive has long supported adding new rows in bulk to an existing table by using INSERT INTO to add new data files to a table. From release 0.14.0, finer-grained changes are possible, so you can call INSERT INTO TABLE...VALUES to insert small batches of values computed in SQL. In addition, it is possible to UPDATE and DELETE rows in a table.

HDFS does not provide in-place file updates, so changes resulting from inserts, updates, and deletes are stored in small delta files. Delta files are periodically merged into the base table files by MapReduce jobs that are run in the background by the metastore. These features only work in the context of transactions (introduced in Hive 0.13.0), so the table they are being used on needs to have transactions enabled on it. Queries reading the table are guaranteed to see a consistent snapshot of the table.

Hive also has support for table- and partition-level locking. Locks prevent, for example, one process from dropping a table while another is reading from it. Locks are managed transparently using ZooKeeper, so the user doesn't have to acquire or release them, although it is possible to get information about which locks are being held via the SHOW LOCKS statement. By default, locks are not enabled.

Hive indexes can speed up queries in certain cases. A query such as SELECT * from t WHERE x = a, for example, can take advantage of an index on column x, since only a small portion of the table's files need to be scanned. There are currently two index types: *compact* and *bitmap*. (The index implementation was designed to be pluggable, so it's expected that a variety of implementations will emerge for different use cases.)

Compact indexes store the HDFS block numbers of each value, rather than each file offset, so they don't take up much disk space but are still effective for the case where values are clustered together in nearby rows. Bitmap indexes use compressed bitsets to efficiently store the rows that a particular value appears in, and they are usually appropriate for low-cardinality columns (such as gender or country).

SQL-on-Hadoop Alternatives

In the years since Hive was created, many other SQL-on-Hadoop engines have emerged to address some of Hive's limitations. Cloudera Impala (*http://impala.io/*), an open source interactive SQL engine, was one of the first, giving an order of magnitude performance boost compared to Hive running on MapReduce. Impala uses a dedicated daemon that runs on each datanode in the cluster. When a client runs a query it contacts an arbitrary node running an Impala daemon, which acts as a coordinator node for the query. The coordinator sends work to other Impala daemons in the cluster and combines their results into the full result set for the query. Impala uses the Hive metastore and supports Hive formats and most HiveQL constructs (plus SQL-92), so in practice it is straightforward to migrate between the two systems, or to run both on the same cluster.

Hive has not stood still, though, and since Impala was launched, the "Stinger" initiative by Hortonworks has improved the performance of Hive through support for Tez as an execution engine, and the addition of a vectorized query engine among other improvements.

Other prominent open source Hive alternatives include Presto from Facebook (*http://prestodb.io/*), Apache Drill (*http://drill.apache.org/*), and Spark SQL (*https://spark.apache.org/sql/*). Presto and Drill have similar architectures to Impala, although Drill targets SQL:2011 rather than HiveQL. Spark SQL uses Spark as its underlying engine, and lets you embed SQL queries in Spark programs.

> Spark SQL is different to using the Spark execution engine from within Hive ("Hive on Spark," see "Execution engines" on page 477). Hive, on Spark provides all the features of Hive since it is a part of the Hive project. Spark SQL, on the other hand, is a new SQL engine that offers some level of Hive compatibility.

Apache Phoenix (*http://phoenix.apache.org/*) takes a different approach entirely: it provides SQL on HBase. SQL access is through a JDBC driver that turns queries into HBase scans and takes advantage of HBase coprocessors to perform server-side aggregation. Metadata is stored in HBase, too.

HiveQL

Hive's SQL dialect, called HiveQL, is a mixture of SQL-92, MySQL, and Oracle's SQL dialect. The level of SQL-92 support has improved over time, and will likely continue to get better. HiveQL also provides features from later SQL standards, such as window functions (also known as analytic functions) from SQL:2003. Some of Hive's non-standard extensions to SQL were inspired by MapReduce, such as multitable inserts (see "Multitable insert" on page 501) and the TRANSFORM, MAP, and REDUCE clauses (see "MapReduce Scripts" on page 503).

This chapter does not provide a complete reference to HiveQL; for that, see the Hive documentation (*http://bit.ly/languagemanual*). Instead, we focus on commonly used features and pay particular attention to features that diverge from either SQL-92 or popular databases such as MySQL. Table 17-2 provides a high-level comparison of SQL and HiveQL.

Table 17-2. A high-level comparison of SQL and HiveQL

Feature	SQL	HiveQL	References
Updates	UPDATE, INSERT, DELETE	UPDATE, INSERT, DELETE	"Inserts" on page 500; "Updates, Transactions, and Indexes" on page 483
Transactions	Supported	Limited support	
Indexes	Supported	Supported	
Data types	Integral, floating-point, fixed-point, text and binary strings, temporal	Boolean, integral, floating-point, fixed-point, text and binary strings, temporal, array, map, struct	"Data Types" on page 486
Functions	Hundreds of built-in functions	Hundreds of built-in functions	"Operators and Functions" on page 488
Multitable inserts	Not supported	Supported	"Multitable insert" on page 501
CREATE TABLE...AS SELECT	Not valid SQL-92, but found in some databases	Supported	"CREATE TABLE...AS SELECT" on page 501
SELECT	SQL-92	SQL-92. SORT BY for partial ordering, LIMIT to limit number of rows returned	"Querying Data" on page 503
Joins	SQL-92, or variants (join tables in the FROM clause, join condition in the WHERE clause)	Inner joins, outer joins, semi joins, map joins, cross joins	"Joins" on page 505
Subqueries	In any clause (correlated or noncorrelated)	In the FROM, WHERE, or HAVING clauses (uncorrelated subqueries not supported)	"Subqueries" on page 508
Views	Updatable (materialized or nonmaterialized)	Read-only (materialized views not supported)	"Views" on page 509

Feature	SQL	HiveQL	References
Extension points	User-defined functions, stored procedures	User-defined functions, MapReduce scripts	"User-Defined Functions" on page 510; "MapReduce Scripts" on page 503

Data Types

Hive supports both primitive and complex data types. Primitives include numeric, Boolean, string, and timestamp types. The complex data types include arrays, maps, and structs. Hive's data types are listed in Table 17-3. Note that the literals shown are those used from within HiveQL; they are not the serialized forms used in the table's storage format (see "Storage Formats" on page 496).

Table 17-3. Hive data types

Category	Type	Description	Literal examples
Primitive	BOOLEAN	True/false value.	TRUE
	TINYINT	1-byte (8-bit) signed integer, from −128 to 127.	1Y
	SMALLINT	2-byte (16-bit) signed integer, from −32,768 to 32,767.	1S
	INT	4-byte (32-bit) signed integer, from −2,147,483,648 to 2,147,483,647.	1
	BIGINT	8-byte (64-bit) signed integer, from −9,223,372,036,854,775,808 to 9,223,372,036,854,775,807.	1L
	FLOAT	4-byte (32-bit) single-precision floating-point number.	1.0
	DOUBLE	8-byte (64-bit) double-precision floating-point number.	1.0
	DECIMAL	Arbitrary-precision signed decimal number.	1.0
	STRING	Unbounded variable-length character string.	'a', "a"
	VARCHAR	Variable-length character string.	'a', "a"
	CHAR	Fixed-length character string.	'a', "a"
	BINARY	Byte array.	Not supported
	TIMESTAMP	Timestamp with nanosecond precision.	1325502245000, '2012-01-02 03:04:05.123456789'
	DATE	Date.	'2012-01-02'

Category	Type	Description	Literal examples
Complex	ARRAY	An ordered collection of fields. The fields must all be of the same type.	`array(1, 2)` [a]
	MAP	An unordered collection of key-value pairs. Keys must be primitives; values may be any type. For a particular map, the keys must be the same type, and the values must be the same type.	`map('a', 1, 'b', 2)`
	STRUCT	A collection of named fields. The fields may be of different types.	`struct('a', 1, 1.0)`,[b] `named_struct('col1', 'a', 'col2', 1, 'col3', 1.0)`
	UNION	A value that may be one of a number of defined data types. The value is tagged with an integer (zero-indexed) representing its data type in the union.	`create_union(1, 'a', 63)`

[a] The literal forms for arrays, maps, structs, and unions are provided as functions. That is, `array`, `map`, `struct`, and `create_union` are built-in Hive functions.

[b] The columns are named `col1`, `col2`, `col3`, etc.

Primitive types

Hive's primitive types correspond roughly to Java's, although some names are influenced by MySQL's type names (some of which, in turn, overlap with SQL-92's). There is a `BOOLEAN` type for storing true and false values. There are four signed integral types: `TINYINT`, `SMALLINT`, `INT`, and `BIGINT`, which are equivalent to Java's `byte`, `short`, `int`, and `long` primitive types, respectively (they are 1-byte, 2-byte, 4-byte, and 8-byte signed integers).

Hive's floating-point types, `FLOAT` and `DOUBLE`, correspond to Java's `float` and `double`, which are 32-bit and 64-bit floating-point numbers.

The `DECIMAL` data type is used to represent arbitrary-precision decimals, like Java's `BigDecimal`, and are commonly used for representing currency values. `DECIMAL` values are stored as unscaled integers. The *precision* is the number of digits in the unscaled value, and the *scale* is the number of digits to the right of the decimal point. So, for example, `DECIMAL(5,2)` stores numbers between −999.99 and 999.99. If the scale is omitted then it defaults to 0, so `DECIMAL(5)` stores numbers in the range −99,999 to 99,999 (i.e., integers). If the precision is omitted then it defaults to 10, so `DECIMAL` is equivalent to `DECIMAL(10,0)`. The maximum allowed precision is 38, and the scale must be no larger than the precision.

There are three Hive data types for storing text. `STRING` is a variable-length character string with no declared maximum length. (The theoretical maximum size `STRING` that may be stored is 2 GB, although in practice it may be inefficient to materialize such large values. Sqoop has large object support; see "Importing Large Objects" on page 415.) `VARCHAR` types are similar except they are declared with a maximum length between 1 and 65355; for example, VARCHAR(100). CHAR types are fixed-length strings that are padded with trailing spaces if necessary; for example, CHAR(100). Trailing spaces are ignored for the purposes of string comparison of CHAR values.

The BINARY data type is for storing variable-length binary data.

The TIMESTAMP data type stores timestamps with nanosecond precision. Hive comes with UDFs for converting between Hive timestamps, Unix timestamps (seconds since the Unix epoch), and strings, which makes most common date operations tractable. TIMESTAMP does not encapsulate a time zone; however, the to_utc_timestamp and from_utc_timestamp functions make it possible to do time zone conversions.

The DATE data type stores a date with year, month, and day components.

Complex types

Hive has four complex types: ARRAY, MAP, STRUCT, and UNION. ARRAY and MAP are like their namesakes in Java, whereas a STRUCT is a record type that encapsulates a set of named fields. A UNION specifies a choice of data types; values must match exactly one of these types.

Complex types permit an arbitrary level of nesting. Complex type declarations must specify the type of the fields in the collection, using an angled bracket notation, as illustrated in this table definition with three columns (one for each complex type):

```
CREATE TABLE complex (
  c1 ARRAY<INT>,
  c2 MAP<STRING, INT>,
  c3 STRUCT<a:STRING, b:INT, c:DOUBLE>,
  c4 UNIONTYPE<STRING, INT>
);
```

If we load the table with one row of data for ARRAY, MAP, STRUCT, and UNION, as shown in the "Literal examples" column in Table 17-3 (we'll see the file format needed to do this in "Storage Formats" on page 496), the following query demonstrates the field accessor operators for each type:

```
hive> SELECT c1[0], c2['b'], c3.c, c4 FROM complex;
1    2    1.0    {1:63}
```

Operators and Functions

The usual set of SQL operators is provided by Hive: relational operators (such as x = 'a' for testing equality, x IS NULL for testing nullity, and x LIKE 'a%' for pattern matching), arithmetic operators (such as x + 1 for addition), and logical operators (such as x OR y for logical OR). The operators match those in MySQL, which deviates from SQL-92 because || is logical OR, not string concatenation. Use the concat function for the latter in both MySQL and Hive.

Hive comes with a large number of built-in functions—too many to list here—divided into categories that include mathematical and statistical functions, string functions, date functions (for operating on string representations of dates), conditional functions, aggregate functions, and functions for working with XML (using the `xpath` function) and JSON.

You can retrieve a list of functions from the Hive shell by typing SHOW FUNCTIONS.[4] To get brief usage instructions for a particular function, use the DESCRIBE command:

```
hive> DESCRIBE FUNCTION length;
length(str | binary) - Returns the length of str or number of bytes in binary
  data
```

In the case when there is no built-in function that does what you want, you can write your own; see "User-Defined Functions" on page 510.

Conversions

Primitive types form a hierarchy that dictates the implicit type conversions Hive will perform in function and operator expressions. For example, a TINYINT will be converted to an INT if an expression expects an INT; however, the reverse conversion will not occur, and Hive will return an error unless the CAST operator is used.

The implicit conversion rules can be summarized as follows. Any numeric type can be implicitly converted to a wider type, or to a text type (STRING, VARCHAR, CHAR). All the text types can be implicitly converted to another text type. Perhaps surprisingly, they can also be converted to DOUBLE or DECIMAL. BOOLEAN types cannot be converted to any other type, and they cannot be implicitly converted to any other type in expressions. TIMESTAMP and DATE can be implicitly converted to a text type.

You can perform explicit type conversion using CAST. For example, CAST('1' AS INT) will convert the string '1' to the integer value 1. If the cast fails—as it does in CAST('X' AS INT), for example—the expression returns NULL.

Tables

A Hive table is logically made up of the data being stored and the associated metadata describing the layout of the data in the table. The data typically resides in HDFS, although it may reside in any Hadoop filesystem, including the local filesystem or S3. Hive stores the metadata in a relational database and not in, say, HDFS (see "The Metastore" on page 480).

In this section, we look in more detail at how to create tables, the different physical storage formats that Hive offers, and how to import data into tables.

---

4. Or see the Hive function reference (*http://bit.ly/languagemanual_udf*).

Managed Tables and External Tables

When you create a table in Hive, by default Hive will manage the data, which means that Hive moves the data into its warehouse directory. Alternatively, you may create an *external table*, which tells Hive to refer to the data that is at an existing location outside the warehouse directory.

The difference between the two table types is seen in the LOAD and DROP semantics. Let's consider a managed table first.

When you load data into a managed table, it is moved into Hive's warehouse directory. For example, this:

```
CREATE TABLE managed_table (dummy STRING);
LOAD DATA INPATH '/user/tom/data.txt' INTO table managed_table;
```

will *move* the file *hdfs://user/tom/data.txt* into Hive's warehouse directory for the managed_table table, which is *hdfs://user/hive/warehouse/managed_table*.[5]

> The load operation is very fast because it is just a move or rename within a filesystem. However, bear in mind that Hive does not check that the files in the table directory conform to the schema declared for the table, even for managed tables. If there is a mismatch, this will become apparent at query time, often by the query returning NULL for a missing field. You can check that the data is being parsed correctly by issuing a simple SELECT statement to retrieve a few rows directly from the table.

If the table is later dropped, using:

```
DROP TABLE managed_table;
```

---

5. The move will succeed only if the source and target filesystems are the same. Also, there is a special case when the LOCAL keyword is used, where Hive will *copy* the data from the local filesystem into Hive's warehouse directory (even if it, too, is on the same local filesystem). In all other cases, though, LOAD is a move operation and is best thought of as such.

the table, including its metadata *and its data*, is deleted. It bears repeating that since the initial LOAD performed a move operation, and the DROP performed a delete operation, the data no longer exists anywhere. This is what it means for Hive to manage the data.

An external table behaves differently. You control the creation and deletion of the data. The location of the external data is specified at table creation time:

```
CREATE EXTERNAL TABLE external_table (dummy STRING)
  LOCATION '/user/tom/external_table';
LOAD DATA INPATH '/user/tom/data.txt' INTO TABLE external_table;
```

With the EXTERNAL keyword, Hive knows that it is not managing the data, so it doesn't move it to its warehouse directory. Indeed, it doesn't even check whether the external location exists at the time it is defined. This is a useful feature because it means you can create the data lazily after creating the table.

When you drop an external table, Hive will leave the data untouched and only delete the metadata.

So how do you choose which type of table to use? In most cases, there is not much difference between the two (except of course for the difference in DROP semantics), so it is a just a matter of preference. As a rule of thumb, if you are doing all your processing with Hive, then use managed tables, but if you wish to use Hive and other tools on the same dataset, then use external tables. A common pattern is to use an external table to access an initial dataset stored in HDFS (created by another process), then use a Hive transform to move the data into a managed Hive table. This works the other way around, too; an external table (not necessarily on HDFS) can be used to export data from Hive for other applications to use.[6]

Another reason for using external tables is when you wish to associate multiple schemas with the same dataset.

Partitions and Buckets

Hive organizes tables into *partitions*—a way of dividing a table into coarse-grained parts based on the value of a *partition column*, such as a date. Using partitions can make it faster to do queries on slices of the data.

Tables or partitions may be subdivided further into *buckets* to give extra structure to the data that may be used for more efficient queries. For example, bucketing by user ID means we can quickly evaluate a user-based query by running it on a randomized sample of the total set of users.

---

6. You can also use INSERT OVERWRITE DIRECTORY to export data to a Hadoop filesystem.

Partitions

To take an example where partitions are commonly used, imagine logfiles where each record includes a timestamp. If we partition by date, then records for the same date will be stored in the same partition. The advantage to this scheme is that queries that are restricted to a particular date or set of dates can run much more efficiently, because they only need to scan the files in the partitions that the query pertains to. Notice that partitioning doesn't preclude more wide-ranging queries: it is still feasible to query the entire dataset across many partitions.

A table may be partitioned in multiple dimensions. For example, in addition to partitioning logs by date, we might also *subpartition* each date partition by country to permit efficient queries by location.

Partitions are defined at table creation time using the PARTITIONED BY clause,[7] which takes a list of column definitions. For the hypothetical logfiles example, we might define a table with records comprising a timestamp and the log line itself:

```
CREATE TABLE logs (ts BIGINT, line STRING)
PARTITIONED BY (dt STRING, country STRING);
```

When we load data into a partitioned table, the partition values are specified explicitly:

```
LOAD DATA LOCAL INPATH 'input/hive/partitions/file1'
INTO TABLE logs
PARTITION (dt='2001-01-01', country='GB');
```

At the filesystem level, partitions are simply nested subdirectories of the table directory. After loading a few more files into the logs table, the directory structure might look like this:

```
/user/hive/warehouse/logs
├── dt=2001-01-01/
│   ├── country=GB/
│   │   ├── file1
│   │   └── file2
│   └── country=US/
│       └── file3
└── dt=2001-01-02/
    ├── country=GB/
    │   └── file4
    └── country=US/
        ├── file5
        └── file6
```

The logs table has two date partitions (2001-01-01 and 2001-01-02, corresponding to subdirectories called *dt=2001-01-01* and *dt=2001-01-02*); and two country subparti-

---

7. However, partitions may be added to or removed from a table after creation using an ALTER TABLE statement.

tions (GB and US, corresponding to nested subdirectories called *country=GB* and *country=US*). The datafiles reside in the leaf directories.

We can ask Hive for the partitions in a table using SHOW PARTITIONS:

```
hive> SHOW PARTITIONS logs;
dt=2001-01-01/country=GB
dt=2001-01-01/country=US
dt=2001-01-02/country=GB
dt=2001-01-02/country=US
```

One thing to bear in mind is that the column definitions in the PARTITIONED BY clause are full-fledged table columns, called *partition columns*; however, the datafiles do not contain values for these columns, since they are derived from the directory names.

You can use partition columns in SELECT statements in the usual way. Hive performs *input pruning* to scan only the relevant partitions. For example:

```
SELECT ts, dt, line
FROM logs
WHERE country='GB';
```

will only scan *file1*, *file2*, and *file4*. Notice, too, that the query returns the values of the dt partition column, which Hive reads from the directory names since they are not in the datafiles.

Buckets

There are two reasons why you might want to organize your tables (or partitions) into buckets. The first is to enable more efficient queries. Bucketing imposes extra structure on the table, which Hive can take advantage of when performing certain queries. In particular, a join of two tables that are bucketed on the same columns—which include the join columns—can be efficiently implemented as a map-side join.

The second reason to bucket a table is to make sampling more efficient. When working with large datasets, it is very convenient to try out queries on a fraction of your dataset while you are in the process of developing or refining them. We will see how to do efficient sampling at the end of this section.

First, let's see how to tell Hive that a table should be bucketed. We use the CLUSTERED BY clause to specify the columns to bucket on and the number of buckets:

```
CREATE TABLE bucketed_users (id INT, name STRING)
CLUSTERED BY (id) INTO 4 BUCKETS;
```

Here we are using the user ID to determine the bucket (which Hive does by hashing the value and reducing modulo the number of buckets), so any particular bucket will effectively have a random set of users in it.

In the map-side join case, where the two tables are bucketed in the same way, a mapper processing a bucket of the left table knows that the matching rows in the right table are in its corresponding bucket, so it need only retrieve that bucket (which is a small fraction of all the data stored in the right table) to effect the join. This optimization also works when the number of buckets in the two tables are multiples of each other; they do not have to have exactly the same number of buckets. The HiveQL for joining two bucketed tables is shown in "Map joins" on page 507.

The data within a bucket may additionally be sorted by one or more columns. This allows even more efficient map-side joins, since the join of each bucket becomes an efficient merge sort. The syntax for declaring that a table has sorted buckets is:

```
CREATE TABLE bucketed_users (id INT, name STRING)
CLUSTERED BY (id) SORTED BY (id ASC) INTO 4 BUCKETS;
```

How can we make sure the data in our table is bucketed? Although it's possible to load data generated outside Hive into a bucketed table, it's often easier to get Hive to do the bucketing, usually from an existing table.

 Hive does not check that the buckets in the datafiles on disk are consistent with the buckets in the table definition (either in number or on the basis of bucketing columns). If there is a mismatch, you may get an error or undefined behavior at query time. For this reason, it is advisable to get Hive to perform the bucketing.

Take an unbucketed users table:

```
hive> SELECT * FROM users;
0       Nat
2       Joe
3       Kay
4       Ann
```

To populate the bucketed table, we need to set the hive.enforce.bucketing property to true so that Hive knows to create the number of buckets declared in the table definition. Then it is just a matter of using the INSERT command:

```
INSERT OVERWRITE TABLE bucketed_users
SELECT * FROM users;
```

Physically, each bucket is just a file in the table (or partition) directory. The filename is not important, but bucket *n* is the *n*th file when arranged in lexicographic order. In fact, buckets correspond to MapReduce output file partitions: a job will produce as many buckets (output files) as reduce tasks. We can see this by looking at the layout of the bucketed_users table we just created. Running this command:

```
hive> dfs -ls /user/hive/warehouse/bucketed_users;
```

shows that four files were created, with the following names (the names are generated by Hive):

```
000000_0
000001_0
000002_0
000003_0
```

The first bucket contains the users with IDs 0 and 4, since for an `INT` the hash is the integer itself, and the value is reduced modulo the number of buckets—four, in this case:[8]

```
hive> dfs -cat /user/hive/warehouse/bucketed_users/000000_0;
0Nat
4Ann
```

We can see the same thing by sampling the table using the `TABLESAMPLE` clause, which restricts the query to a fraction of the buckets in the table rather than the whole table:

```
hive> SELECT * FROM bucketed_users
    > TABLESAMPLE(BUCKET 1 OUT OF 4 ON id);
4   Ann
0   Nat
```

Bucket numbering is 1-based, so this query retrieves all the users from the first of four buckets. For a large, evenly distributed dataset, approximately one-quarter of the table's rows would be returned. It's possible to sample a number of buckets by specifying a different proportion (which need not be an exact multiple of the number of buckets, as sampling is not intended to be a precise operation). For example, this query returns half of the buckets:

```
hive> SELECT * FROM bucketed_users
    > TABLESAMPLE(BUCKET 1 OUT OF 2 ON id);
4   Ann
0   Nat
2   Joe
```

Sampling a bucketed table is very efficient because the query only has to read the buckets that match the `TABLESAMPLE` clause. Contrast this with sampling a nonbucketed table using the `rand()` function, where the whole input dataset is scanned, even if only a very small sample is needed:

```
hive> SELECT * FROM users
    > TABLESAMPLE(BUCKET 1 OUT OF 4 ON rand());
2   Joe
```

---

8. The fields appear to run together when displaying the raw file because the separator character in the output is a nonprinting control character. The control characters used are explained in the next section.

Storage Formats

There are two dimensions that govern table storage in Hive: the *row format* and the *file format*. The row format dictates how rows, and the fields in a particular row, are stored. In Hive parlance, the row format is defined by a *SerDe*, a portmanteau word for a *Ser*ializer-*De*serializer.

When acting as a deserializer, which is the case when querying a table, a SerDe will deserialize a row of data from the bytes in the file to objects used internally by Hive to operate on that row of data. When used as a serializer, which is the case when performing an INSERT or CTAS (see "Importing Data" on page 500), the table's SerDe will serialize Hive's internal representation of a row of data into the bytes that are written to the output file.

The file format dictates the container format for fields in a row. The simplest format is a plain-text file, but there are row-oriented and column-oriented binary formats available, too.

The default storage format: Delimited text

When you create a table with no ROW FORMAT or STORED AS clauses, the default format is delimited text with one row per line.[9]

The default row delimiter is not a tab character, but the Ctrl-A character from the set of ASCII control codes (it has ASCII code 1). The choice of Ctrl-A, sometimes written as ^A in documentation, came about because it is less likely to be a part of the field text than a tab character. There is no means for escaping delimiter characters in Hive, so it is important to choose ones that don't occur in data fields.

The default collection item delimiter is a Ctrl-B character, used to delimit items in an ARRAY or STRUCT, or in key-value pairs in a MAP. The default map key delimiter is a Ctrl-C character, used to delimit the key and value in a MAP. Rows in a table are delimited by a newline character.

---

9. The default format can be changed by setting the property hive.default.fileformat.

The preceding description of delimiters is correct for the usual case of flat data structures, where the complex types contain only primitive types. For nested types, however, this isn't the whole story, and in fact the *level* of the nesting determines the delimiter.

For an array of arrays, for example, the delimiters for the outer array are Ctrl-B characters, as expected, but for the inner array they are Ctrl-C characters, the next delimiter in the list. If you are unsure which delimiters Hive uses for a particular nested structure, you can run a command like:

```
CREATE TABLE nested
AS
SELECT array(array(1, 2), array(3, 4))
FROM dummy;
```

and then use hexdump or something similar to examine the delimiters in the output file.

Hive actually supports eight levels of delimiters, corresponding to ASCII codes 1, 2, ... 8, but you can override only the first three.

Thus, the statement:

```
CREATE TABLE ...;
```

is identical to the more explicit:

```
CREATE TABLE ...
ROW FORMAT DELIMITED
  FIELDS TERMINATED BY '\001'
  COLLECTION ITEMS TERMINATED BY '\002'
  MAP KEYS TERMINATED BY '\003'
  LINES TERMINATED BY '\n'
STORED AS TEXTFILE;
```

Notice that the octal form of the delimiter characters can be used—001 for Ctrl-A, for instance.

Internally, Hive uses a SerDe called LazySimpleSerDe for this delimited format, along with the line-oriented MapReduce text input and output formats we saw in Chapter 8. The "lazy" prefix comes about because it deserializes fields lazily—only as they are accessed. However, it is not a compact format because fields are stored in a verbose textual format, so a Boolean value, for instance, is written as the literal string true or false.

The simplicity of the format has a lot going for it, such as making it easy to process with other tools, including MapReduce programs or Streaming, but there are more compact and performant binary storage formats that you might consider using. These are discussed next.

Binary storage formats: Sequence files, Avro datafiles, Parquet files, RCFiles, and ORCFiles

Using a binary format is as simple as changing the STORED AS clause in the CREATE TABLE statement. In this case, the ROW FORMAT is not specified, since the format is controlled by the underlying binary file format.

Binary formats can be divided into two categories: row-oriented formats and column-oriented formats. Generally speaking, column-oriented formats work well when queries access only a small number of columns in the table, whereas row-oriented formats are appropriate when a large number of columns of a single row are needed for processing at the same time.

The two row-oriented formats supported natively in Hive are Avro datafiles (see Chapter 12) and sequence files (see "SequenceFile" on page 127). Both are general-purpose, splittable, compressible formats; in addition, Avro supports schema evolution and multiple language bindings. From Hive 0.14.0, a table can be stored in Avro format using:

```
SET hive.exec.compress.output=true;
SET avro.output.codec=snappy;
CREATE TABLE ... STORED AS AVRO;
```

Notice that compression is enabled on the table by setting the relevant properties.

Similarly, the declaration STORED AS SEQUENCEFILE can be used to store sequence files in Hive. The properties for compression are listed in "Using Compression in MapReduce" on page 107.

Hive has native support for the Parquet (see Chapter 13), RCFile, and ORCFile column-oriented binary formats (see "Other File Formats and Column-Oriented Formats" on page 136). Here is an example of creating a copy of a table in Parquet format using CREATE TABLE...AS SELECT (see "CREATE TABLE...AS SELECT" on page 501):

```
CREATE TABLE users_parquet STORED AS PARQUET
AS
SELECT * FROM users;
```

Using a custom SerDe: RegexSerDe

Let's see how to use a custom SerDe for loading data. We'll use a contrib SerDe that uses a regular expression for reading the fixed-width station metadata from a text file:

```
CREATE TABLE stations (usaf STRING, wban STRING, name STRING)
ROW FORMAT SERDE 'org.apache.hadoop.hive.contrib.serde2.RegexSerDe'
WITH SERDEPROPERTIES (
  "input.regex" = "(\\d{6}) (\\d{5}) (.{29}) .*"
);
```

In previous examples, we have used the DELIMITED keyword to refer to delimited text in the ROW FORMAT clause. In this example, we instead specify a SerDe with the SERDE keyword and the fully qualified classname of the Java class that implements the SerDe, `org.apache.hadoop.hive.contrib.serde2.RegexSerDe`.

SerDes can be configured with extra properties using the `WITH SERDEPROPERTIES` clause. Here we set the `input.regex` property, which is specific to `RegexSerDe`.

`input.regex` is the regular expression pattern to be used during deserialization to turn the line of text forming the row into a set of columns. Java regular expression syntax (*http://bit.ly/java_regex*) is used for the matching, and columns are formed from capturing groups of parentheses.[10] In this example, there are three capturing groups for `usaf` (a six-digit identifier), `wban` (a five-digit identifier), and `name` (a fixed-width column of 29 characters).

To populate the table, we use a `LOAD DATA` statement as before:

```
LOAD DATA LOCAL INPATH "input/ncdc/metadata/stations-fixed-width.txt"
INTO TABLE stations;
```

Recall that `LOAD DATA` copies or moves the files to Hive's warehouse directory (in this case, it's a copy because the source is the local filesystem). The table's SerDe is not used for the load operation.

When we retrieve data from the table the SerDe is invoked for deserialization, as we can see from this simple query, which correctly parses the fields for each row:

```
hive> SELECT * FROM stations LIMIT 4;
010000   99999     BOGUS NORWAY
010003   99999     BOGUS NORWAY
010010   99999     JAN MAYEN
010013   99999     ROST
```

As this example demonstrates, `RegexSerDe` can be useful for getting data into Hive, but due to its inefficiency it should not be used for general-purpose storage. Consider copying the data into a binary storage format instead.

Storage handlers

Storage handlers are used for storage systems that Hive cannot access natively, such as HBase. Storage handlers are specified using a `STORED BY` clause, instead of the `ROW FORMAT` and `STORED AS` clauses. For more information on HBase integration, see the Hive wiki (*http://bit.ly/hbase_int*).

---

10. Sometimes you need to use parentheses for regular expression constructs that you don't want to count as a capturing group—for example, the pattern (ab)+ for matching a string of one or more ab characters. The solution is to use a noncapturing group, which has a ? character after the first parenthesis. There are various noncapturing group constructs (see the Java documentation), but in this example we could use (?:ab)+ to avoid capturing the group as a Hive column.

Importing Data

We've already seen how to use the LOAD DATA operation to import data into a Hive table (or partition) by copying or moving files to the table's directory. You can also populate a table with data from another Hive table using an INSERT statement, or at creation time using the *CTAS* construct, which is an abbreviation used to refer to CREATE TABLE...AS SELECT.

If you want to import data from a relational database directly into Hive, have a look at Sqoop; this is covered in "Imported Data and Hive" on page 413.

Inserts

Here's an example of an INSERT statement:

```
INSERT OVERWRITE TABLE target
SELECT col1, col2
  FROM source;
```

For partitioned tables, you can specify the partition to insert into by supplying a PARTITION clause:

```
INSERT OVERWRITE TABLE target
PARTITION (dt='2001-01-01')
SELECT col1, col2
  FROM source;
```

The OVERWRITE keyword means that the contents of the target table (for the first example) or the 2001-01-01 partition (for the second example) are replaced by the results of the SELECT statement. If you want to add records to an already populated nonpartitioned table or partition, use INSERT INTO TABLE.

You can specify the partition dynamically by determining the partition value from the SELECT statement:

```
INSERT OVERWRITE TABLE target
PARTITION (dt)
SELECT col1, col2, dt
  FROM source;
```

This is known as a *dynamic partition insert*.

 From Hive 0.14.0, you can use the INSERT INTO TABLE...VALUES statement for inserting a small collection of records specified in literal form.

Multitable insert

In HiveQL, you can turn the INSERT statement around and start with the FROM clause
for the same effect:

```
FROM source
INSERT OVERWRITE TABLE target
  SELECT col1, col2;
```

The reason for this syntax becomes clear when you see that it's possible to have multiple
INSERT clauses in the same query. This so-called *multitable insert* is more efficient than
multiple INSERT statements because the source table needs to be scanned only once to
produce the multiple disjoint outputs.

Here's an example that computes various statistics over the weather dataset:

```
FROM records2
INSERT OVERWRITE TABLE stations_by_year
  SELECT year, COUNT(DISTINCT station)
  GROUP BY year
INSERT OVERWRITE TABLE records_by_year
  SELECT year, COUNT(1)
  GROUP BY year
INSERT OVERWRITE TABLE good_records_by_year
  SELECT year, COUNT(1)
  WHERE temperature != 9999 AND quality IN (0, 1, 4, 5, 9)
  GROUP BY year;
```

There is a single source table (records2), but three tables to hold the results from three
different queries over the source.

CREATE TABLE...AS SELECT

It's often very convenient to store the output of a Hive query in a new table, perhaps
because it is too large to be dumped to the console or because there are further processing
steps to carry out on the result.

The new table's column definitions are derived from the columns retrieved by the
SELECT clause. In the following query, the target table has two columns named col1
and col2 whose types are the same as the ones in the source table:

```
CREATE TABLE target
AS
SELECT col1, col2
FROM source;
```

A CTAS operation is atomic, so if the SELECT query fails for some reason, the table is
not created.

Altering Tables

Because Hive uses the schema-on-read approach, it's flexible in permitting a table's definition to change after the table has been created. The general caveat, however, is that in many cases, it is up to you to ensure that the data is changed to reflect the new structure.

You can rename a table using the ALTER TABLE statement:

```
ALTER TABLE source RENAME TO target;
```

In addition to updating the table metadata, ALTER TABLE moves the underlying table directory so that it reflects the new name. In the current example, */user/hive/warehouse/source* is renamed to */user/hive/warehouse/target*. (An external table's underlying directory is not moved; only the metadata is updated.)

Hive allows you to change the definition for columns, add new columns, or even replace all existing columns in a table with a new set.

For example, consider adding a new column:

```
ALTER TABLE target ADD COLUMNS (col3 STRING);
```

The new column col3 is added after the existing (nonpartition) columns. The datafiles are not updated, so queries will return null for all values of col3 (unless of course there were extra fields already present in the files). Because Hive does not permit updating existing records, you will need to arrange for the underlying files to be updated by another mechanism. For this reason, it is more common to create a new table that defines new columns and populates them using a SELECT statement.

Changing a column's metadata, such as a column's name or data type, is more straightforward, assuming that the old data type can be interpreted as the new data type.

To learn more about how to alter a table's structure, including adding and dropping partitions, changing and replacing columns, and changing table and SerDe properties, see the Hive wiki (*http://bit.ly/data_def_lang*).

Dropping Tables

The DROP TABLE statement deletes the data and metadata for a table. In the case of external tables, only the metadata is deleted; the data is left untouched.

If you want to delete all the data in a table but keep the table definition, use TRUNCATE TABLE. For example:

```
TRUNCATE TABLE my_table;
```

This doesn't work for external tables; instead, use dfs -rmr (from the Hive shell) to remove the external table directory directly.

In a similar vein, if you want to create a new, empty table with the same schema as another table, then use the LIKE keyword:

```
CREATE TABLE new_table LIKE existing_table;
```

Querying Data

This section discusses how to use various forms of the SELECT statement to retrieve data from Hive.

Sorting and Aggregating

Sorting data in Hive can be achieved by using a standard ORDER BY clause. ORDER BY performs a parallel total sort of the input (like that described in "Total Sort" on page 259). When a globally sorted result is not required—and in many cases it isn't—you can use Hive's nonstandard extension, SORT BY, instead. SORT BY produces a sorted file per reducer.

In some cases, you want to control which reducer a particular row goes to—typically so you can perform some subsequent aggregation. This is what Hive's DISTRIBUTE BY clause does. Here's an example to sort the weather dataset by year and temperature, in such a way as to ensure that all the rows for a given year end up in the same reducer partition:[11]

```
hive> FROM records2
    > SELECT year, temperature
    > DISTRIBUTE BY year
    > SORT BY year ASC, temperature DESC;
1949    111
1949    78
1950    22
1950    0
1950    -11
```

A follow-on query (or a query that nests this query as a subquery; see "Subqueries" on page 508) would be able to use the fact that each year's temperatures were grouped and sorted (in descending order) in the same file.

If the columns for SORT BY and DISTRIBUTE BY are the same, you can use CLUSTER BY as a shorthand for specifying both.

MapReduce Scripts

Using an approach like Hadoop Streaming, the TRANSFORM, MAP, and REDUCE clauses make it possible to invoke an external script or program from Hive. Suppose we want

---

11. This is a reworking in Hive of the discussion in "Secondary Sort" on page 262.

to use a script to filter out rows that don't meet some condition, such as the script in Example 17-1, which removes poor-quality readings.

Example 17-1. Python script to filter out poor-quality weather records

```
#!/usr/bin/env python

import re
import sys

for line in sys.stdin:
  (year, temp, q) = line.strip().split()
  if (temp != "9999" and re.match("[01459]", q)):
    print "%s\t%s" % (year, temp)
```

We can use the script as follows:

```
hive> ADD FILE /Users/tom/book-workspace/hadoop-book/ch17-hive/
src/main/python/is_good_quality.py;
hive> FROM records2
    > SELECT TRANSFORM(year, temperature, quality)
    > USING 'is_good_quality.py'
    > AS year, temperature;
1950    0
1950    22
1950    -11
1949    111
1949    78
```

Before running the query, we need to register the script with Hive. This is so Hive knows to ship the file to the Hadoop cluster (see "Distributed Cache" on page 274).

The query itself streams the year, temperature, and quality fields as a tab-separated line to the *is_good_quality.py* script, and parses the tab-separated output into year and temperature fields to form the output of the query.

This example has no reducers. If we use a nested form for the query, we can specify a map and a reduce function. This time we use the MAP and REDUCE keywords, but SELECT TRANSFORM in both cases would have the same result. (Example 2-10 includes the source for the *max_temperature_reduce.py* script):

```
FROM (
  FROM records2
  MAP year, temperature, quality
  USING 'is_good_quality.py'
  AS year, temperature) map_output
REDUCE year, temperature
USING 'max_temperature_reduce.py'
AS year, temperature;
```

Joins

One of the nice things about using Hive, rather than raw MapReduce, is that Hive makes performing commonly used operations very simple. Join operations are a case in point, given how involved they are to implement in MapReduce (see "Joins" on page 268).

Inner joins

The simplest kind of join is the inner join, where each match in the input tables results in a row in the output. Consider two small demonstration tables, sales (which lists the names of people and the IDs of the items they bought) and things (which lists the item IDs and their names):

```
hive> SELECT * FROM sales;
Joe     2
Hank    4
Ali     0
Eve     3
Hank    2
hive> SELECT * FROM things;
2       Tie
4       Coat
3       Hat
1       Scarf
```

We can perform an inner join on the two tables as follows:

```
hive> SELECT sales.*, things.*
    > FROM sales JOIN things ON (sales.id = things.id);
Joe     2   2   Tie
Hank    4   4   Coat
Eve     3   3   Hat
Hank    2   2   Tie
```

The table in the FROM clause (sales) is joined with the table in the JOIN clause (things), using the predicate in the ON clause. Hive only supports equijoins, which means that only equality can be used in the join predicate, which here matches on the id column in both tables.

In Hive, you can join on multiple columns in the join predicate by specifying a series of expressions, separated by AND keywords. You can also join more than two tables by supplying additional JOIN...ON... clauses in the query. Hive is intelligent about trying to minimize the number of MapReduce jobs to perform the joins.

Hive (like MySQL and Oracle) allows you to list the join tables in the FROM clause and specify the join condition in the WHERE clause of a SELECT statement. For example, the following is another way of expressing the query we just saw:

```
SELECT sales.*, things.*
FROM sales, things
WHERE sales.id = things.id;
```

A single join is implemented as a single MapReduce job, but multiple joins can be performed in less than one MapReduce job per join if the same column is used in the join condition.[12] You can see how many MapReduce jobs Hive will use for any particular query by prefixing it with the EXPLAIN keyword:

```
EXPLAIN
SELECT sales.*, things.*
FROM sales JOIN things ON (sales.id = things.id);
```

The EXPLAIN output includes many details about the execution plan for the query, including the abstract syntax tree, the dependency graph for the stages that Hive will execute, and information about each stage. Stages may be MapReduce jobs or operations such as file moves. For even more detail, prefix the query with EXPLAIN EXTENDED.

Hive currently uses a rule-based query optimizer for determining how to execute a query, but a cost-based optimizer is available from Hive 0.14.0.

Outer joins

Outer joins allow you to find nonmatches in the tables being joined. In the current example, when we performed an inner join, the row for Ali did not appear in the output, because the ID of the item she purchased was not present in the things table. If we change the join type to LEFT OUTER JOIN, the query will return a row for every row in the left table (sales), even if there is no corresponding row in the table it is being joined to (things):

```
hive> SELECT sales.*, things.*
    > FROM sales LEFT OUTER JOIN things ON (sales.id = things.id);
Joe     2    2     Tie
Hank    4    4     Coat
Ali     0    NULL  NULL
Eve     3    3     Hat
Hank    2    2     Tie
```

---

12. The order of the tables in the JOIN clauses is significant. It's generally best to have the largest table last, but see the Hive wiki (*http://bit.ly/hive_joins_docs*) for more details, including how to give hints to the Hive planner.

Notice that the row for Ali is now returned, and the columns from the `things` table are `NULL` because there is no match.

Hive also supports right outer joins, which reverses the roles of the tables relative to the left join. In this case, all items from the `things` table are included, even those that weren't purchased by anyone (a scarf):

```
hive> SELECT sales.*, things.*
    > FROM sales RIGHT OUTER JOIN things ON (sales.id = things.id);
Joe     2     2    Tie
Hank    2     2    Tie
Hank    4     4    Coat
Eve     3     3    Hat
NULL    NULL  1    Scarf
```

Finally, there is a full outer join, where the output has a row for each row from both tables in the join:

```
hive> SELECT sales.*, things.*
    > FROM sales FULL OUTER JOIN things ON (sales.id = things.id);
Ali     0     NULL NULL
NULL    NULL  1    Scarf
Hank    2     2    Tie
Joe     2     2    Tie
Eve     3     3    Hat
Hank    4     4    Coat
```

Semi joins

Consider this `IN` subquery, which finds all the items in the `things` table that are in the `sales` table:

```
SELECT *
FROM things
WHERE things.id IN (SELECT id from sales);
```

We can also express it as follows:

```
hive> SELECT *
    > FROM things LEFT SEMI JOIN sales ON (sales.id = things.id);
2     Tie
4     Coat
3     Hat
```

There is a restriction that we must observe for LEFT SEMI JOIN queries: the right table (`sales`) may appear only in the ON clause. It cannot be referenced in a SELECT expression, for example.

Map joins

Consider the original inner join again:

```
SELECT sales.*, things.*
FROM sales JOIN things ON (sales.id = things.id);
```

If one table is small enough to fit in memory, as things is here, Hive can load it into memory to perform the join in each of the mappers. This is called a map join.

The job to execute this query has no reducers, so this query would not work for a RIGHT or FULL OUTER JOIN, since absence of matching can be detected only in an aggregating (reduce) step across all the inputs.

Map joins can take advantage of bucketed tables (see "Buckets" on page 493), since a mapper working on a bucket of the left table needs to load only the corresponding buckets of the right table to perform the join. The syntax for the join is the same as for the in-memory case shown earlier; however, you also need to enable the optimization with the following:

```
SET hive.optimize.bucketmapjoin=true;
```

Subqueries

A subquery is a SELECT statement that is embedded in another SQL statement. Hive has limited support for subqueries, permitting a subquery in the FROM clause of a SELECT statement, or in the WHERE clause in certain cases.

Hive allows uncorrelated subqueries, where the subquery is a self-contained query referenced by an IN or EXISTS statement in the WHERE clause. Correlated subqueries, where the subquery references the outer query, are not currently supported.

The following query finds the mean maximum temperature for every year and weather station:

```
SELECT station, year, AVG(max_temperature)
FROM (
  SELECT station, year, MAX(temperature) AS max_temperature
  FROM records2
  WHERE temperature != 9999 AND quality IN (0, 1, 4, 5, 9)
  GROUP BY station, year
) mt
GROUP BY station, year;
```

The FROM subquery is used to find the maximum temperature for each station/date combination, and then the outer query uses the AVG aggregate function to find the average of the maximum temperature readings for each station/date combination.

The outer query accesses the results of the subquery like it does a table, which is why the subquery must be given an alias (mt). The columns of the subquery have to be given unique names so that the outer query can refer to them.

Views

A view is a sort of "virtual table" that is defined by a SELECT statement. Views can be used to present data to users in a way that differs from the way it is actually stored on disk. Often, the data from existing tables is simplified or aggregated in a particular way that makes it convenient for further processing. Views may also be used to restrict users' access to particular subsets of tables that they are authorized to see.

In Hive, a view is not materialized to disk when it is created; rather, the view's SELECT statement is executed when the statement that refers to the view is run. If a view performs extensive transformations on the base tables or is used frequently, you may choose to manually materialize it by creating a new table that stores the contents of the view (see "CREATE TABLE...AS SELECT" on page 501).

We can use views to rework the query from the previous section for finding the mean maximum temperature for every year and weather station. First, let's create a view for valid records—that is, records that have a particular quality value:

```
CREATE VIEW valid_records
AS
SELECT *
FROM records2
WHERE temperature != 9999 AND quality IN (0, 1, 4, 5, 9);
```

When we create a view, the query is not run; it is simply stored in the metastore. Views are included in the output of the SHOW TABLES command, and you can see more details about a particular view, including the query used to define it, by issuing the DESCRIBE EXTENDED *view_name* command.

Next, let's create a second view of maximum temperatures for each station and year. It is based on the valid_records view:

```
CREATE VIEW max_temperatures (station, year, max_temperature)
AS
SELECT station, year, MAX(temperature)
FROM valid_records
GROUP BY station, year;
```

In this view definition, we list the column names explicitly. We do this because the maximum temperature column is an aggregate expression, and otherwise Hive would create a column alias for us (such as _c2). We could equally well have used an AS clause in the SELECT to name the column.

With the views in place, we can now use them by running a query:

```
SELECT station, year, AVG(max_temperature)
FROM max_temperatures
GROUP BY station, year;
```

The result of the query is the same as that of running the one that uses a subquery. In particular, Hive creates the same number of MapReduce jobs for both: two in each case, one for each GROUP BY. This example shows that Hive can combine a query on a view into a sequence of jobs that is equivalent to writing the query without using a view. In other words, Hive won't needlessly materialize a view, even at execution time.

Views in Hive are read-only, so there is no way to load or insert data into an underlying base table via a view.

User-Defined Functions

Sometimes the query you want to write can't be expressed easily (or at all) using the built-in functions that Hive provides. By allowing you to write a *user-defined function* (UDF), Hive makes it easy to plug in your own processing code and invoke it from a Hive query.

UDFs have to be written in Java, the language that Hive itself is written in. For other languages, consider using a SELECT TRANSFORM query, which allows you to stream data through a user-defined script ("MapReduce Scripts" on page 503).

There are three types of UDF in Hive: (regular) UDFs, user-defined aggregate functions (UDAFs), and user-defined table-generating functions (UDTFs). They differ in the number of rows that they accept as input and produce as output:

- A UDF operates on a single row and produces a single row as its output. Most functions, such as mathematical functions and string functions, are of this type.

- A UDAF works on multiple input rows and creates a single output row. Aggregate functions include such functions as COUNT and MAX.

- A UDTF operates on a single row and produces multiple rows—a table—as output.

Table-generating functions are less well known than the other two types, so let's look at an example. Consider a table with a single column, x, which contains arrays of strings. It's instructive to take a slight detour to see how the table is defined and populated:

```
CREATE TABLE arrays (x ARRAY<STRING>)
ROW FORMAT DELIMITED
  FIELDS TERMINATED BY '\001'
  COLLECTION ITEMS TERMINATED BY '\002';
```

Notice that the ROW FORMAT clause specifies that the entries in the array are delimited by Ctrl-B characters. The example file that we are going to load has the following contents, where ^B is a representation of the Ctrl-B character to make it suitable for printing:

```
a^Bb
c^Bd^Be
```

After running a `LOAD DATA` command, the following query confirms that the data was loaded correctly:

```
hive> SELECT * FROM arrays;
["a","b"]
["c","d","e"]
```

Next, we can use the `explode` UDTF to transform this table. This function emits a row for each entry in the array, so in this case the type of the output column y is `STRING`. The result is that the table is flattened into five rows:

```
hive> SELECT explode(x) AS y FROM arrays;
a
b
c
d
e
```

`SELECT` statements using UDTFs have some restrictions (e.g., they cannot retrieve additional column expressions), which make them less useful in practice. For this reason, Hive supports `LATERAL VIEW` queries, which are more powerful. `LATERAL VIEW` queries are not covered here, but you may find out more about them in the Hive wiki (*http://bit.ly/lateral_view*).

Writing a UDF

To illustrate the process of writing and using a UDF, we'll write a simple UDF to trim characters from the ends of strings. Hive already has a built-in function called `trim`, so we'll call ours `strip`. The code for the `Strip` Java class is shown in Example 17-2.

Example 17-2. A UDF for stripping characters from the ends of strings

```
package com.hadoopbook.hive;

import org.apache.commons.lang.StringUtils;
import org.apache.hadoop.hive.ql.exec.UDF;
import org.apache.hadoop.io.Text;

public class Strip extends UDF {
  private Text result = new Text();

  public Text evaluate(Text str) {
    if (str == null) {
      return null;
    }
    result.set(StringUtils.strip(str.toString()));
    return result;
  } public Text evaluate(Text str, String stripChars) {
    if (str == null) {
      return null;
    }
```

```
        result.set(StringUtils.strip(str.toString(), stripChars));
        return result;
    }
}
```

A UDF must satisfy the following two properties:

- A UDF must be a subclass of `org.apache.hadoop.hive.ql.exec.UDF`.
- A UDF must implement at least one `evaluate()` method.

The `evaluate()` method is not defined by an interface, since it may take an arbitrary number of arguments, of arbitrary types, and it may return a value of arbitrary type. Hive introspects the UDF to find the `evaluate()` method that matches the Hive function that was invoked.

The `Strip` class has two `evaluate()` methods. The first strips leading and trailing whitespace from the input, and the second can strip any of a set of supplied characters from the ends of the string. The actual string processing is delegated to the `StringUtils` class from the Apache Commons project, which makes the only noteworthy part of the code the use of `Text` from the Hadoop Writable library. Hive actually supports Java primitives in UDFs (and a few other types, such as `java.util.List` and `java.util.Map`), so a signature like:

```
public String evaluate(String str)
```

would work equally well. However, by using `Text` we can take advantage of object reuse, which can bring efficiency savings, so this is preferred in general.

To use the UDF in Hive, we first need to package the compiled Java class in a JAR file. You can do this by typing `mvn package` with the book's example code. Next, we register the function in the metastore and give it a name using the `CREATE FUNCTION` statement:

```
CREATE FUNCTION strip AS 'com.hadoopbook.hive.Strip'
USING JAR '/path/to/hive-examples.jar';
```

When using Hive locally, a local file path is sufficient, but on a cluster you should copy the JAR file into HDFS and use an HDFS URI in the `USING JAR` clause.

The UDF is now ready to be used, just like a built-in function:

```
hive> SELECT strip('  bee   ') FROM dummy;
bee
hive> SELECT strip('banana', 'ab') FROM dummy;
nan
```

Notice that the UDF's name is not case sensitive:

```
hive> SELECT STRIP('  bee   ') FROM dummy;
bee
```

If you want to remove the function, use the `DROP FUNCTION` statement:

```
DROP FUNCTION strip;
```

It's also possible to create a function for the duration of the Hive session, so it is not persisted in the metastore, using the TEMPORARY keyword:

```
ADD JAR /path/to/hive-examples.jar;
CREATE TEMPORARY FUNCTION strip AS 'com.hadoopbook.hive.Strip';
```

When using temporary functions, it may be useful to create a *.hiverc* file in your home directory containing the commands to define your UDFs. The file will be automatically run at the beginning of each Hive session.

As an alternative to calling ADD JAR at launch time, you can specify a path where Hive looks for auxiliary JAR files to put on its classpath (including the task classpath). This technique is useful for automatically adding your own library of UDFs every time you run Hive.

There are two ways of specifying the path. Either pass the --auxpath option to the hive command:

```
% hive --auxpath /path/to/hive-examples.jar
```

or set the HIVE_AUX_JARS_PATH environment variable before invoking Hive. The auxiliary path may be a comma-separated list of JAR file paths or a directory containing JAR files.

Writing a UDAF

An aggregate function is more difficult to write than a regular UDF. Values are aggregated in chunks (potentially across many tasks), so the implementation has to be capable of combining partial aggregations into a final result. The code to achieve this is best explained by example, so let's look at the implementation of a simple UDAF for calculating the maximum of a collection of integers (Example 17-3).

Example 17-3. A UDAF for calculating the maximum of a collection of integers

```
package com.hadoopbook.hive;

import org.apache.hadoop.hive.ql.exec.UDAF;
import org.apache.hadoop.hive.ql.exec.UDAFEvaluator;
import org.apache.hadoop.io.IntWritable;

public class Maximum extends UDAF {

  public static class MaximumIntUDAFEvaluator implements UDAFEvaluator {

    private IntWritable result;

    public void init() {
      result = null;
    }
```

```
    public boolean iterate(IntWritable value) {
      if (value == null) {
        return true;
      }
      if (result == null) {
        result = new IntWritable(value.get());
      } else {
        result.set(Math.max(result.get(), value.get()));
      }
      return true;
    }

    public IntWritable terminatePartial() {
      return result;
    }

    public boolean merge(IntWritable other) {
      return iterate(other);
    }

    public IntWritable terminate() {
      return result;
    }
  }
}
```

The class structure is slightly different from the one for UDFs. A UDAF must be a subclass of org.apache.hadoop.hive.ql.exec.UDAF (note the "A" in UDAF) and contain one or more nested static classes implementing org.apache.hadoop.hive.ql.exec.UDAFEvaluator. In this example, there is a single nested class, MaximumIntUDAFEvaluator, but we could add more evaluators, such as MaximumLongUDAFEvaluator, MaximumFloatUDAFEvaluator, and so on, to provide overloaded forms of the UDAF for finding the maximum of a collection of longs, floats, and so on.

An evaluator must implement five methods, described in turn here (the flow is illustrated in Figure 17-3):

init()

The init() method initializes the evaluator and resets its internal state. In MaximumIntUDAFEvaluator, we set the IntWritable object holding the final result to null. We use null to indicate that no values have been aggregated yet, which has the desirable effect of making the maximum value of an empty set NULL.

iterate()

The iterate() method is called every time there is a new value to be aggregated. The evaluator should update its internal state with the result of performing the aggregation. The arguments that iterate() takes correspond to those in the Hive function from which it was called. In this example, there is only one argument. The value is first checked to see whether it is null, and if it is, it is ignored. Otherwise, the result instance variable is set either to value's integer value (if this is the first value that has been seen) or to the larger of the current result and value (if one or more values have already been seen). We return true to indicate that the input value was valid.

terminatePartial()

The terminatePartial() method is called when Hive wants a result for the partial aggregation. The method must return an object that encapsulates the state of the aggregation. In this case, an IntWritable suffices because it encapsulates either the maximum value seen or null if no values have been processed.

merge()

The merge() method is called when Hive decides to combine one partial aggregation with another. The method takes a single object, whose type must correspond to the return type of the terminatePartial() method. In this example, the merge() method can simply delegate to the iterate() method because the partial aggregation is represented in the same way as a value being aggregated. This is not generally the case (we'll see a more general example later), and the method should implement the logic to combine the evaluator's state with the state of the partial aggregation.

terminate()

The terminate() method is called when the final result of the aggregation is needed. The evaluator should return its state as a value. In this case, we return the result instance variable.

Let's exercise our new function:

```
hive> CREATE TEMPORARY FUNCTION maximum AS 'com.hadoopbook.hive.Maximum';
hive> SELECT maximum(temperature) FROM records;
111
```

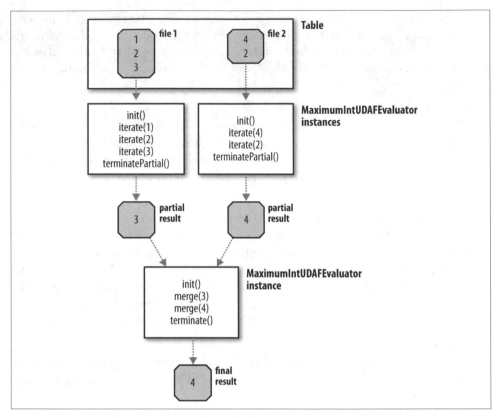

Figure 17-3. Data flow with partial results for a UDAF

A more complex UDAF

The previous example is unusual in that a partial aggregation can be represented using the same type (IntWritable) as the final result. This is not generally the case for more complex aggregate functions, as can be seen by considering a UDAF for calculating the mean (average) of a collection of double values. It's not mathematically possible to combine partial means into a final mean value (see "Combiner Functions" on page 34). Instead, we can represent the partial aggregation as a pair of numbers: the cumulative sum of the double values processed so far, and the number of values.

This idea is implemented in the UDAF shown in Example 17-4. Notice that the partial aggregation is implemented as a "struct" nested static class, called PartialResult, which Hive is intelligent enough to serialize and deserialize, since we are using field types that Hive can handle (Java primitives in this case).

In this example, the merge() method is different from iterate() because it combines the partial sums and partial counts by pairwise addition. In addition to this, the return type of terminatePartial() is PartialResult—which, of course, is never seen by the

user calling the function—whereas the return type of `terminate()` is `DoubleWrita`
ble, the final result seen by the user.

Example 17-4. A UDAF for calculating the mean of a collection of doubles

```java
package com.hadoopbook.hive;

import org.apache.hadoop.hive.ql.exec.UDAF;
import org.apache.hadoop.hive.ql.exec.UDAFEvaluator;
import org.apache.hadoop.hive.serde2.io.DoubleWritable;

public class Mean extends UDAF {

  public static class MeanDoubleUDAFEvaluator implements UDAFEvaluator {
    public static class PartialResult {
      double sum;
      long count;
    }

    private PartialResult partial;

    public void init() {
      partial = null;
    }

    public boolean iterate(DoubleWritable value) {
      if (value == null) {
        return true;
      }
      if (partial == null) {
        partial = new PartialResult();
      }
      partial.sum += value.get();
      partial.count++;
      return true;
    }

    public PartialResult terminatePartial() {
      return partial;
    }

    public boolean merge(PartialResult other) {
      if (other == null) {
        return true;
      }
      if (partial == null) {
        partial = new PartialResult();
      }
      partial.sum += other.sum;
      partial.count += other.count;
      return true;
    }
```

```
    public DoubleWritable terminate() {
      if (partial == null) {
        return null;
      }
      return new DoubleWritable(partial.sum / partial.count);
    }
  }
}
```

Further Reading

For more information about Hive, see *Programming Hive* by Edward Capriolo, Dean
Wampler, and Jason Rutherglen (O'Reilly, 2012).

Crunch

Apache Crunch (*https://crunch.apache.org/*) is a higher-level API for writing MapReduce pipelines. The main advantages it offers over plain MapReduce are its focus on programmer-friendly Java types like String and plain old Java objects, a richer set of data transformation operations, and multistage pipelines (no need to explicitly manage individual MapReduce jobs in a workflow).

In these respects, Crunch looks a lot like a Java version of Pig. One day-to-day source of friction in using Pig, which Crunch avoids, is that the language used to write user-defined functions (Java or Python) is different from the language used to write Pig scripts (Pig Latin), which makes for a disjointed development experience as one switches between the two different representations and languages. By contrast, Crunch programs and UDFs are written in a single language (Java or Scala), and UDFs can be embedded right in the programs. The overall experience feels very like writing a non-distributed program. Although it has many parallels with Pig, Crunch was inspired by FlumeJava, the Java library developed at Google for building MapReduce pipelines.

 FlumeJava is not to be confused with Apache Flume, covered in Chapter 14, which is a system for collecting streaming event data. You can read more about FlumeJava in "FlumeJava: Easy, Efficient Data-Parallel Pipelines" (*http://bit.ly/data-parallel_pipelines*) by Craig Chambers et al.

Because they are high level, Crunch pipelines are highly composable and common functions can be extracted into libraries and reused in other programs. This is different from MapReduce, where it is very difficult to reuse code: most programs have custom mapper and reducer implementations, apart from simple cases such as where an identity function or a simple sum (LongSumReducer) is called for. Writing a library of mappers and reducers for different types of transformations, like sorting and joining operations, is not easy in MapReduce, whereas in Crunch it is very natural. For example, there is a library class, `org.apache.crunch.lib.Sort`, with a `sort()` method that will sort any Crunch collection that is passed to it.

Although Crunch was initially written to run using Hadoop's MapReduce execution engine, it is not tied to it, and in fact you can run a Crunch pipeline using Apache Spark (see Chapter 19) as the distributed execution engine. Different engines have different characteristics: Spark, for example, is more efficient than MapReduce if there is a lot of intermediate data to be passed between jobs, since it can retain the data in memory rather than materializing it to disk like MapReduce does. Being able to try a pipeline on different engines without rewriting the program is a powerful property, since it allows you to treat what the program *does* separately from matters of runtime efficiency (which generally improve over time as the engines are tuned).

This chapter is an introduction to writing data processing programs in Crunch. You can find more information in the Crunch User Guide (*http://crunch.apache.org/user-guide.html*).

An Example

We'll start with a simple Crunch pipeline to illustrate the basic concepts. Example 18-1 shows a Crunch version of the program to calculate the maximum temperature by year for the weather dataset, which we first met in Chapter 2.

Example 18-1. Application to find the maximum temperature, using Crunch

```
public class MaxTemperatureCrunch {

  public static void main(String[] args) throws Exception {
    if (args.length != 2) {
      System.err.println("Usage: MaxTemperatureCrunch <input path> <output path>");
      System.exit(-1);
    }

    Pipeline pipeline = new MRPipeline(getClass());
    PCollection<String> records = pipeline.readTextFile(args[0]);

    PTable<String, Integer> yearTemperatures = records
        .parallelDo(toYearTempPairsFn(), tableOf(strings(), ints()));
    PTable<String, Integer> maxTemps = yearTemperatures
        .groupByKey()
        .combineValues(Aggregators.MAX_INTS());

    maxTemps.write(To.textFile(args[1]));
    PipelineResult result = pipeline.done();
    System.exit(result.succeeded() ? 0 : 1);
  }

  static DoFn<String, Pair<String, Integer>> toYearTempPairsFn() {
    return new DoFn<String, Pair<String, Integer>>() {
```

```
  NcdcRecordParser parser = new NcdcRecordParser();
  @Override
  public void process(String input, Emitter<Pair<String, Integer>> emitter) {
    parser.parse(input);
    if (parser.isValidTemperature()) {
      emitter.emit(Pair.of(parser.getYear(), parser.getAirTemperature()));
    }
  }
};
}


}
```

After the customary checking of command-line arguments, the program starts by constructing a Crunch `Pipeline` object, which represents the computation that we want to run. As the name suggests, a pipeline can have multiple stages; pipelines with multiple inputs and outputs, branches, and iteration are all possible, although in this example we start with a single-stage pipeline. We're going to use MapReduce to run the pipeline, so we create an `MRPipeline`, but we could have chosen to use a `MemPipeline` for running the pipeline in memory for testing purposes, or a `SparkPipeline` to run the same computation using Spark.

A pipeline receives data from one or more input sources, and in this example the source is a single text file whose name is specified by the first command-line argument, `args[0]`. The `Pipeline` class has a convenience method, `readTextFile()`, to convert a text file into a `PCollection` of `String` objects, where each `String` is a line from the text file. `PCollection<S>` is the most fundamental data type in Crunch, and represents an immutable, unordered, distributed collection of elements of type S. You can think of `PCollection<S>` as an unmaterialized analog of `java.util.Collection`—unmaterialized since its elements are not read into memory. In this example, the input is a distributed collection of the lines of a text file, and is represented by `PCollection<String>`.

A Crunch computation operates on a `PCollection`, and produces a new `PCollection`. The first thing we need to do is parse each line of the input file, and filter out any bad records. We do this by using the `parallelDo()` method on `PCollection`, which applies a function to every element in the `PCollection` and returns a new `PCollection`. The method signature looks like this:

```
<T> PCollection<T> parallelDo(DoFn<S,T> doFn, PType<T> type);
```

The idea is that we write a `DoFn` implementation that transforms an instance of type S into one or more instances of type T, and Crunch will apply the function to every element in the `PCollection`. It should be clear that the operation can be performed in parallel in the map task of a MapReduce job. The second argument to the `parallelDo()` method is a `PType<T>` object, which gives Crunch information about both the Java type used for T and how to serialize that type.

We are actually going to use an overloaded version of `parallelDo()` that creates an extension of `PCollection` called `PTable<K, V>`, which is a distributed *multi-map* of key-value pairs. (A multi-map is a map that can have duplicate key-value pairs.) This is so we can represent the year as the key and the temperature as the value, which will enable us to do grouping and aggregation later in the pipeline. The method signature is:

```
<K, V> PTable<K, V> parallelDo(DoFn<S, Pair<K, V>> doFn, PTableType<K, V> type);
```

In this example, the `DoFn` parses a line of input and emits a year-temperature pair:

```
static DoFn<String, Pair<String, Integer>> toYearTempPairsFn() {
  return new DoFn<String, Pair<String, Integer>>() {
    NcdcRecordParser parser = new NcdcRecordParser();
    @Override
    public void process(String input, Emitter<Pair<String, Integer>> emitter) {
      parser.parse(input);
      if (parser.isValidTemperature()) {
        emitter.emit(Pair.of(parser.getYear(), parser.getAirTemperature()));
      }
    }
  };
}
```

After applying the function we get a table of year-temperature pairs:

```
PTable<String, Integer> yearTemperatures = records
    .parallelDo(toYearTempPairsFn(), tableOf(strings(), ints()));
```

The second argument to `parallelDo()` is a `PTableType<K, V>` instance, which is constructed using static methods on Crunch's `Writables` class (since we have chosen to use Hadoop Writable serialization for any intermediate data that Crunch will write). The `tableOf()` method creates a `PTableType` with the given key and value types. The `strings()` method declares that keys are represented by Java `String` objects in memory, and serialized as Hadoop `Text`. The values are Java `int` types and are serialized as Hadoop `IntWritables`.

At this point, we have a more structured representation of the data, but the number of records is still the same since every line in the input file corresponds to an entry in the `yearTemperatures` table. To calculate the maximum temperature reading for each year in the dataset, we need to group the table entries by year, then find the maximum temperature value for each year. Fortunately, Crunch provides exactly these operations as a part of `PTable`'s API. The `groupByKey()` method performs a MapReduce shuffle to group entries by key and returns the third type of `PCollection`, called `PGrou pedTable<K, V>`, which has a `combineValues()` method for performing aggregation of all the values for a key, just like a MapReduce reducer:

```
PTable<String, Integer> maxTemps = yearTemperatures
    .groupByKey()
    .combineValues(Aggregators.MAX_INTS());
```

The `combineValues()` method accepts an instance of a Crunch `Aggregator`, a simple interface for expressing any kind of aggregation of a stream of values, and here we can take advantage of a built-in aggregator from the `Aggregators` class called `MAX_INTS` that finds the maximum value from a set of integers.

The final step in the pipeline is writing the `maxTemps` table to a file by calling `write()` with a text file target object constructed using the `To` static factory. Crunch actually uses Hadoop's `TextOutputFormat` for this operation, which means that the key and value in each line of output are separated by a tab:

```
maxTemps.write(To.textFile(args[1]));
```

The program so far has only been concerned with pipeline construction. To execute a pipeline, we have to call the `done()` method, at which point the program blocks until the pipeline completes. Crunch returns a `PipelineResult` object that encapsulates various statistics about the different jobs that were run in the pipeline, as well as whether the pipeline succeeded or not. We use the latter information to set the program's exit code appropriately.

When we run the program on the sample dataset, we get the following result:

```
% hadoop jar crunch-examples.jar crunch.MaxTemperatureCrunch \
  input/ncdc/sample.txt output
% cat output/part-r-00000
1949 111
1950 22
```

The Core Crunch API

This section presents the core interfaces in Crunch. Crunch's API is high level by design, so the programmer can concentrate on the logical operations of the computation, rather than the details of how it is executed.

Primitive Operations

The core data structure in Crunch is `PCollection<S>`, an immutable, unordered, distributed collection of elements of type S. In this section, we examine the primitive operations on `PCollection` and its derived types, `PTable` and `PGroupedTable`.

union()

The simplest primitive Crunch operation is `union()`, which returns a `PCollection` that contains all the elements of the `PCollection` it is invoked on and the `PCollection` supplied as an argument. For example:

```
PCollection<Integer> a = MemPipeline.collectionOf(1, 3);
PCollection<Integer> b = MemPipeline.collectionOf(2);
```

```
PCollection<Integer> c = a.union(b);
assertEquals("{2,1,3}", dump(c));
```

MemPipeline's collectionOf() method is used to create a PCollection instance from a small number of elements, normally for the purposes of testing or demonstration. The dump() method is a utility method introduced here for rendering the contents of a small PCollection as a string (it's not a part of Crunch, but you can find the implementation in the PCollections class in the example code that accompanies this book). Since PCollections are unordered, the order of the elements in c is undefined.

When forming the union of two PCollections, they must have been created from the same pipeline (or the operation will fail at runtime), and they must have the same type. The latter condition is enforced at compile time, since PCollection is a parameterized type and the type arguments for the PCollections in the union must match.

parallelDo()

The second primitive operation is parallelDo() for calling a function on every element in an input PCollection<S> and returning a new output PCollection<T> containing the results of the function calls. In its simplest form, parallelDo() takes two arguments: a DoFn<S, T> implementation that defines a function transforming elements of type S to type T, and a PType<T> instance to describe the output type T. (PTypes are explained in more detail in the section "Types" on page 528.)

The following code snippet shows how to use parallelDo() to apply a string length function to a PCollection of strings:

```
PCollection<String> a = MemPipeline.collectionOf("cherry", "apple", "banana");
PCollection<Integer> b = a.parallelDo(new DoFn<String, Integer>() {
  @Override
  public void process(String input, Emitter<Integer> emitter) {
    emitter.emit(input.length());
  }
}, ints());
assertEquals("{6,5,6}", dump(b));
```

In this case, the output PCollection of integers has the same number of elements as the input, so we could have used the MapFn subclass of DoFn for 1:1 mappings:

```
PCollection<Integer> b = a.parallelDo(new MapFn<String, Integer>() {
  @Override
  public Integer map(String input) {
    return input.length();
  }
}, ints());
assertEquals("{6,5,6}", dump(b));
```

One common use of parallelDo() is for filtering out data that is not needed in later processing steps. Crunch provides a filter() method for this purpose that takes a special DoFn called FilterFn. Implementors need only implement the accept() method to indicate whether an element should be in the output. For example, this code retains only those strings with an even number of characters:

```
PCollection<String> b = a.filter(new FilterFn<String>() {
  @Override
  public boolean accept(String input) {
    return input.length() % 2 == 0; // even
  }
});
assertEquals("{cherry,banana}", dump(b));
```

Notice that there is no PType in the method signature for filter(), since the output PCollection has the same type as the input.

If your DoFn significantly changes the size of the PCollection it is operating on, you can override its scaleFactor() method to give a hint to the Crunch planner about the estimated relative size of the output, which may improve its efficiency.

FilterFn's scaleFactor() method returns 0.5; in other words, the assumption is that implementations will filter out about half of the elements in a PCollection. You can override this method if your filter function is significantly more or less selective than this.

There is an overloaded form of parallelDo() for generating a PTable from a PCollection. Recall from the opening example that a PTable<K, V> is a multi-map of key-value pairs; or, in the language of Java types, PTable<K, V> is a PCollection<Pair<K, V>>, where Pair<K, V> is Crunch's pair class.

The following code creates a PTable by using a DoFn that turns an input string into a key-value pair (the key is the length of the string, and the value is the string itself):

```
PTable<Integer, String> b = a.parallelDo(
    new DoFn<String, Pair<Integer, String>>() {
  @Override
  public void process(String input, Emitter<Pair<Integer, String>> emitter) {
    emitter.emit(Pair.of(input.length(), input));
  }
}, tableOf(ints(), strings()));
assertEquals("{(6,cherry),(5,apple),(6,banana)}", dump(b));
```

Extracting keys from a PCollection of values to form a PTable is a common enough task that Crunch provides a method for it, called by(). This method takes a MapFn<S, K> to map the input value S to its key K:

```
PTable<Integer, String> b = a.by(new MapFn<String, Integer>() {
  @Override
  public Integer map(String input) {
    return input.length();
  }
```

```
        }, ints());
        assertEquals("{(6,cherry),(5,apple),(6,banana)}", dump(b));
```

groupByKey()

The third primitive operation is groupByKey(), for bringing together all the values in a
PTable<K, V> that have the same key. This operation can be thought of as the MapReduce shuffle, and indeed that's how it's implemented for the MapReduce execution engine. In terms of Crunch types, groupByKey() returns a PGroupedTable<K, V>, which
is a PCollection<Pair<K, Iterable<V>>>, or a multi-map where each key is paired
with an iterable collection over its values.

Continuing from the previous code snippet, if we group the PTable of length-string
mappings by key, we get the following (where the items in square brackets indicate an
iterable collection):

```
        PGroupedTable<Integer, String> c = b.groupByKey();
        assertEquals("{(5,[apple]),(6,[banana,cherry])}", dump(c));
```

Crunch uses information on the size of the table to set the number of partitions (reduce
tasks in MapReduce) to use for the groupByKey() operation. Most of the time the default
is fine, but you can explicitly set the number of partitions by using the overloaded form,
groupByKey(int), if needed.

combineValues()

Despite the suggestive naming, PGroupedTable is not actually a subclass of PTable, so
you can't call methods like groupByKey() on it. This is because there is no reason to
group by key on a PTable that was already grouped by key. Another way of thinking
about PGroupedTable is as an intermediate representation before generating another
PTable. After all, the reason to group by key is so you can do something to the values
for each key. This is the basis of the fourth primitive operation, combineValues().

In its most general form, combineValues() takes a combining function CombineFn<K,
V>, which is a more concise name for DoFn<Pair<K, Iterable<V>>, Pair<K, V>>, and
returns a PTable<K, V>. To see it in action, consider a combining function that concatenates all the string values together for a key, using a semicolon as a separator:

```
        PTable<Integer, String> d = c.combineValues(new CombineFn<Integer, String>() {
          @Override
          public void process(Pair<Integer, Iterable<String>> input,
              Emitter<Pair<Integer, String>> emitter) {
            StringBuilder sb = new StringBuilder();
            for (Iterator i = input.second().iterator(); i.hasNext(); ) {
              sb.append(i.next());
              if (i.hasNext()) { sb.append(";"); }
            }
            emitter.emit(Pair.of(input.first(), sb.toString()));
          }
```

```
});
assertEquals("{(5,apple),(6,banana;cherry)}", dump(d));
```

 String concatenation is not commutative, so the result is not deterministic. This may or may not be important in your application!

The code is cluttered somewhat by the use of Pair objects in the process() method signature; they have to be unwrapped with calls to first() and second(), and a new Pair object is created to emit the new key-value pair. This combining function does not alter the key, so we can use an overloaded form of combineValues() that takes an Aggregator object for operating only on the values and passes the keys through unchanged. Even better, we can use a built-in Aggregator implementation for performing string concatenation found in the Aggregators class. The code becomes:

```
PTable<Integer, String> e = c.combineValues(Aggregators.STRING_CONCAT(";",
    false));
assertEquals("{(5,apple),(6,banana;cherry)}", dump(e));
```

Sometimes you may want to aggregate the values in a PGroupedTable and return a result with a different type from the values being grouped. This can be achieved using the mapValues() method with a MapFn for converting the iterable collection into another object. For example, the following calculates the number of values for each key:

```
PTable<Integer, Integer> f = c.mapValues(new MapFn<Iterable<String>, Integer>() {
  @Override
  public Integer map(Iterable<String> input) {
    return Iterables.size(input);
  }
}, ints());
assertEquals("{(5,1),(6,2)}", dump(f));
```

Notice that the values are strings, but the result of applying the map function is an integer, the size of the iterable collection computed using Guava's Iterables class.

You might wonder why the combineValues() operation exists at all, given that the mapValues() method is more powerful. The reason is that combineValues() can be run as a MapReduce combiner, and therefore it can improve performance by being run on the map side, which has the effect of reducing the amount of data that has to be transferred in the shuffle (see "Combiner Functions" on page 34). The mapValues() method is translated into a parallelDo() operation, and in this context it can only run on the reduce side, so there is no possibility for using a combiner to improve its performance.

Finally, the other operation on PGroupedTable is ungroup(), which turns a PGrou pedTable<K, V> back into a PTable<K, V>—the reverse of groupByKey(). (It's not a primitive operation though, since it is implemented with a parallelDo().) Calling groupByKey() then ungroup() on a PTable has the effect of performing a partial sort on the table by its keys, although it's normally more convenient to use the Sort library, which implements a total sort (which is usually what you want) and also offers options for ordering.

Types

Every PCollection<S> has an associated class, PType<S>, that encapsulates type information about the elements in the PCollection. The PType<S> determines the Java class, S, of the elements in the PCollection, as well as the serialization format used to read data from persistent storage into the PCollection and, conversely, write data from the PCollection to persistent storage.

There are two PType families in Crunch: Hadoop Writables and Avro. The choice of which to use broadly corresponds to the file format that you are using in your pipeline; Writables for sequence files, and Avro for Avro data files. Either family can be used with text files. Pipelines can use a mixture of PTypes from different families (since the PType is associated with the PCollection, not the pipeline), but this is usually unnecessary unless you are doing something that spans families, like file format conversion.

In general, Crunch strives to hide the differences between different serialization formats, so that the types used in code are familiar to Java programmers. (Another benefit is that it's easier to write libraries and utilities to work with Crunch collections, regardless of the serialization family they belong to.) Lines read from a text file, for instance, are presented as regular Java String objects, rather than the Writable Text variant or Avro Utf8 objects.

The PType used by a PCollection is specified when the PCollection is created, although sometimes it is implicit. For example, reading a text file will use Writables by default, as this test shows:

```
PCollection<String> lines = pipeline.read(From.textFile(inputPath));
assertEquals(WritableTypeFamily.getInstance(), lines.getPType().getFamily());
```

However, it is possible to explicitly use Avro serialization by passing the appropriate PType to the textFile() method. Here we use the static factory method on Avros to create an Avro representation of PType<String>:

```
PCollection<String> lines = pipeline.read(From.textFile(inputPath,
    Avros.strings()));
```

Similarly, operations that create new PCollections require that the PType is specified and matches the type parameters of the PCollection.[1] For instance, in our earlier ex-

---

[1]. Some operations do not require a PType, since they can infer it from the PCollection they are applied to. For example, filter() returns a PCollection with the same PType as the original.

ample the `parallelDo()` operation to extract an integer key from a `PCollec tion<String>`, turning it into a `PTable<Integer, String>`, specified a matching `PType` of:

```
tableOf(ints(), strings())
```

where all three methods are statically imported from `Writables`.

Records and tuples

When it comes to working with complex objects with multiple fields, you can choose between records or tuples in Crunch. A record is a class where fields are accessed by name, such as Avro's `GenericRecord`, a plain old Java object (corresponding to Avro Specific or Reflect), or a custom `Writable`. For a tuple, on the other hand, field access is by position, and Crunch provides a `Tuple` interface as well as a few convenience classes for tuples with a small number of elements: `Pair<K, V>`, `Tuple3<V1, V2, V3>`, `Tuple4<V1, V2, V3, V4>`, and `TupleN` for tuples with an arbitrary but fixed number of values.

Where possible, you should prefer records over tuples, since the resulting Crunch programs are more readable and understandable. If a weather record is represented by a `WeatherRecord` class with year, temperature, and station ID fields, then it is easier to work with this type:

```
Emitter<Pair<Integer, WeatherRecord>>
```

than this:

```
Emitter<Pair<Integer, Tuple3<Integer, Integer, String>>
```

The latter does not convey any semantic information through its type names, unlike `WeatherRecord`, which clearly describes what it is.

As this example hints, it's is not possible to entirely avoid using Crunch `Pair` objects, since they are a fundamental part of the way Crunch represents table collections (recall that a `PTable<K, V>` is a `PCollection<Pair<K, V>>`). However, there are opportunities to limit the use of `Pair` objects in many cases, which will make your code more readable. For example, use `PCollection`'s `by()` method in favor of `parallelDo()` when creating a table where the values are the same as the ones in the `PCollection` (as discussed in "parallelDo()" on page 524), or use `PGroupedTable`'s `combineValues()` with an `Aggre gator` in preference to a `CombineFn` (see "combineValues()" on page 526).

The fastest path to using records in a Crunch pipeline is to define a Java class that has fields that Avro Reflect can serialize and a no-arg constructor, like this `WeatherRe cord` class:

```
public class WeatherRecord {
  private int year;
  private int temperature;
```

```
    private String stationId;

    public WeatherRecord() {
    }

    public WeatherRecord(int year, int temperature, String stationId) {
      this.year = year;
      this.temperature = temperature;
      this.stationId = stationId;
    }

    // ... getters elided
  }
```

From there, it's straightforward to generate a PCollection<WeatherRecord> from a
PCollection<String>, using parallelDo() to parse each line into a WeatherRecord
object:

```
PCollection<String> lines = pipeline.read(From.textFile(inputPath));
PCollection<WeatherRecord> records = lines.parallelDo(
    new DoFn<String, WeatherRecord>() {
  NcdcRecordParser parser = new NcdcRecordParser();
  @Override
  public void process(String input, Emitter<WeatherRecord> emitter) {
    parser.parse(input);
    if (parser.isValidTemperature()) {
      emitter.emit(new WeatherRecord(parser.getYearInt(),
          parser.getAirTemperature(), parser.getStationId()));
    }
  }
}, Avros.records(WeatherRecord.class));
```

The records() factory method returns a Crunch PType for the Avro Reflect data model,
as we have used it here; but it also supports Avro Specific and Generic data models. If
you wanted to use Avro Specific instead, then you would define your custom type using
an Avro schema file, generate the Java class for it, and call records() with the generated
class. For Avro Generic, you would declare the class to be a GenericRecord.

Writables also provides a records() factory method for using custom Writable types;
however, they are more cumbersome to define since you have to write serialization logic
yourself (see "Implementing a Custom Writable" on page 121).

With a collection of records in hand, we can use Crunch libraries or our own processing
functions to perform computations on it. For example, this will perform a total sort of
the weather records by the fields in the order they are declared (by year, then by temperature, then by station ID):

```
PCollection<WeatherRecord> sortedRecords = Sort.sort(records);
```

Sources and Targets

This section covers the different types of sources and targets in Crunch, and how to use them.

Reading from a source

Crunch pipelines start with one or more `Source<T>` instances specifying the storage location and `PType<T>` of the input data. For the simple case of reading text files, the `readTextFile()` method on `Pipeline` works well; for other types of source, use the `read()` method that takes a `Source<T>` object. In fact, this:

```
PCollection<String> lines = pipeline.readTextFile(inputPath);
```

is shorthand for:

```
PCollection<String> lines = pipeline.read(From.textFile(inputPath));
```

The `From` class (in the `org.apache.crunch.io` package) acts as a collection of static factory methods for file sources, of which text files are just one example.

Another common case is reading sequence files of `Writable` key-value pairs. In this case, the source is a `TableSource<K, V>`, to accommodate key-value pairs, and it returns a `PTable<K, V>`. For example, a sequence file containing `IntWritable` keys and `Text` values yields a `PTable<Integer, String>`:

```
TableSource<Integer, String> source =
    From.sequenceFile(inputPath, Writables.ints(), Writables.strings());
PTable<Integer, String> table = pipeline.read(source);
```

You can also read Avro datafiles into a `PCollection` as follows:

```
Source<WeatherRecord> source =
    From.avroFile(inputPath, Avros.records(WeatherRecord.class));
PCollection<WeatherRecord> records = pipeline.read(source);
```

Any MapReduce `FileInputFormat` (in the new MapReduce API) can be used as a `TableSource` by means of the `formattedFile()` method on `From`, providing Crunch access to the large number of different Hadoop-supported file formats. There are also more source implementations in Crunch than the ones exposed in the `From` class, including:

- `AvroParquetFileSource` for reading Parquet files as Avro `PTypes`.
- `FromHBase`, which has a `table()` method for reading rows from HBase tables into `PTable<ImmutableBytesWritable, Result>` collections. `ImmutableBytesWritable` is an HBase class for representing a row key as bytes, and `Result` contains the cells from the row scan, which can be configured to return only cells in particular columns or column families.

Writing to a target

Writing a PCollection to a Target is as simple as calling PCollection's write() method with the desired Target. Most commonly, the target is a file, and the file type can be selected with the static factory methods on the To class. For example, the following line writes Avro files to a directory called *output* in the default filesystem:

```
collection.write(To.avroFile("output"));
```

This is just a slightly more convenient way of saying:

```
pipeline.write(collection, To.avroFile("output"));
```

Since the PCollection is being written to an Avro file, it must have a PType belonging to the Avro family, or the pipeline will fail.

The To factory also has methods for creating text files, sequence files, and any MapReduce FileOutputFormat. Crunch also has built-in Target implementations for the Parquet file format (AvroParquetFileTarget) and HBase (ToHBase).

 Crunch tries to write the type of collection to the target file in the most natural way. For example, a PTable is written to an Avro file using a Pair record schema with key and value fields that match the PTable. Similarly, a PCollection's values are written to a sequence file's values (the keys are null), and a PTable is written to a text file with tab-separated keys and values.

Existing outputs

If a file-based target already exists, Crunch will throw a CrunchRuntimeException when the write() method is called. This preserves the behavior of MapReduce, which is to be conservative and not overwrite existing outputs unless explicitly directed to by the user (see "Java MapReduce" on page 24).

A flag may be passed to the write() method indicating that outputs should be overwritten as follows:

```
collection.write(To.avroFile("output"), Target.WriteMode.OVERWRITE);
```

If *output* already exists, then it will be deleted before the pipeline runs.

There is another write mode, APPEND, which will add new files[2] to the output directory, leaving any existing ones from previous runs intact. Crunch takes care to use a unique identifier in filenames to avoid the possibility of a new run overwriting files from a previous run.[3]

---

2. Despite the name, APPEND does not append to existing output files.

3. HBaseTarget does not check for existing outputs, so it behaves as if APPEND mode is used.

The final write mode is CHECKPOINT, which is for saving work to a file so that a new pipeline can start from that point rather than from the beginning of the pipeline. This mode is covered in "Checkpointing a Pipeline" on page 545.

Combined sources and targets

Sometimes you want to write to a target and then read from it as a source (i.e., in another pipeline in the same program). For this case, Crunch provides the SourceTarget<T> interface, which is both a Source<T> and a Target. The At class provides static factory methods for creating SourceTarget instances for text files, sequence files, and Avro files.

Functions

At the heart of any Crunch program are the functions (represented by DoFn) that transform one PCollection into another. In this section, we examine some of the considerations in writing your own custom functions.

Serialization of functions

When writing MapReduce programs, it is up to you to package the code for mappers and reducers into a job JAR file so that Hadoop can make the user code available on the task classpath (see "Packaging a Job" on page 160). Crunch takes a different approach. When a pipeline is executed, all the DoFn instances are serialized to a file that is distributed to task nodes using Hadoop's distributed cache mechanism (described in "Distributed Cache" on page 274), and then deserialized by the task itself so that the DoFn can be invoked.

The upshot for you, the user, is that you don't need to do any packaging work; instead, you only need to make sure that your DoFn implementations are serializable according to the standard Java serialization mechanism.[4]

In most cases, no extra work is required, since the DoFn base class is declared as implementing the java.io.Serializable interface. Thus, if your function is stateless, there are no fields to serialize, and it will be serialized without issue.

There are a couple of problems to watch out for, however. One problem occurs if your DoFn is defined as an inner class (also called a nonstatic nested class), such as an anonymous class, in an outer class that doesn't implement Serializable:

```
public class NonSerializableOuterClass {

    public void runPipeline() throws IOException {
        // ...
```

---

4. See the documentation (*http://bit.ly/interface_serializable*).

```
    PCollection<String> lines = pipeline.readTextFile(inputPath);
    PCollection<String> lower = lines.parallelDo(new DoFn<String, String>() {
      @Override
      public void process(String input, Emitter<String> emitter) {
        emitter.emit(input.toLowerCase());
      }
    }, strings());
    // ...
  }
}
```

Since inner classes have an implicit reference to their enclosing instance, if the enclosing class is not serializable, then the function will not be serializable and the pipeline will fail with a CrunchRuntimeException. You can easily fix this by making the function a (named) static nested class or a top-level class, or you can make the enclosing class implement Serializable.

Another problem is when a function depends on nonserializable state in the form of an instance variable whose class is not Serializable. In this case, you can mark the non-serializable instance variable as transient so Java doesn't try to serialize it, then set it in the initialize() method of DoFn. Crunch will call the initialize() method before the process() method is invoked for the first time:

```
public class CustomDoFn<S, T> extends DoFn<S, T> {

  transient NonSerializableHelper helper;

  @Override
  public void initialize() {
    helper = new NonSerializableHelper();
  }

  @Override
  public void process(S input, Emitter<T> emitter) {
    // use helper here
  }
}
```

Although not shown here, it's possible to pass state to initialize the transient instance variable using other, nontransient instance variables, such as strings.

Object reuse

In MapReduce, the objects in the reducer's values iterator are reused for efficiency (to avoid the overhead of object allocation). Crunch has the same behavior for the iterators used in the combineValues() and mapValues() methods on PGroupedTable. Therefore, if you retain a reference to an object outside the body of the iterator, you should make a copy to avoid object identity errors.

We can see how to go about this by writing a general-purpose utility for finding the set of unique values for each key in a PTable; see Example 18-2.

Example 18-2. Finding the set of unique values for each key in a PTable

```java
public static <K, V> PTable<K, Collection<V>> uniqueValues(PTable<K, V> table) {
  PTypeFamily tf = table.getTypeFamily();
  final PType<V> valueType = table.getValueType();
  return table.groupByKey().mapValues("unique",
      new MapFn<Iterable<V>, Collection<V>>() {
        @Override
        public void initialize() {
          valueType.initialize(getConfiguration());
        }

    @Override
    public Set<V> map(Iterable<V> values) {
      Set<V> collected = new HashSet<V>();
      for (V value : values) {
        collected.add(valueType.getDetachedValue(value));
      }
      return collected;
    }
  }, tf.collections(table.getValueType()));
}
```

The idea is to group by key, then iterate over each value associated with a key and collect the unique values in a Set, which will automatically remove duplicates. Since we want to retain the values outside the iteration, we need to make a copy of each value before we put it in the set.

Fortunately, we don't need to write code that knows how to perform the copy for each possible Java class; we can use the getDetachedValue() method that Crunch provides for exactly this purpose on PType, which we get from the table's value type. Notice that we also have to initialize the PType in the DoFn's initialize() method so that the PType can access the configuration in order to perform the copying.

For immutable objects like Strings or Integers, calling getDetachedValue() is actually a no-op, but for mutable Avro or Writable types, a deep copy of each value is made.

Materialization

Materialization is the process of making the values in a PCollection available so they can be read in your program. For example, you might want to read all the values from a (typically small) PCollection and display them, or send them to another part of your program, rather than writing them to a Crunch target. Another reason to materialize a PCollection is to use the contents as the basis for determining further processing steps—for example, to test for convergence in an iterative algorithm (see "Iterative Algorithms" on page 543).

There are a few ways of materializing a PCollection; the most direct way to accomplish this is to call materialize(), which returns an Iterable collection of its values. If the PCollection has not already been materialized, then Crunch will have to run the pipeline to ensure that the objects in the PCollection have been computed and stored in a temporary intermediate file so they can be iterated over.[5]

Consider the following Crunch program for lowercasing lines in a text file:

```
Pipeline pipeline = new MRPipeline(getClass());
PCollection<String> lines = pipeline.readTextFile(inputPath);
PCollection<String> lower = lines.parallelDo(new ToLowerFn(), strings());

Iterable<String> materialized = lower.materialize();
for (String s : materialized) { // pipeline is run
  System.out.println(s);
}
pipeline.done();
```

The lines from the text file are transformed using the ToLowerFn function, which is defined separately so we can use it again later:

```
public class ToLowerFn extends DoFn<String, String> {
  @Override
  public void process(String input, Emitter<String> emitter) {
    emitter.emit(input.toLowerCase());
  }
}
```

The call to materialize() on the variable lower returns an Iterable<String>, but it is not this method call that causes the pipeline to be run. It is only once an Iterator is created from the Iterable (implicitly by the for each loop) that Crunch runs the pipeline. When the pipeline has completed, the iteration can proceed over the materialized PCollection, and in this example the lowercase lines are printed to the console.

PTable has a materializeToMap() method, which might be expected to behave in a similar way to materialize(). However, there are two important differences. First, since it returns a Map<K, V> rather than an iterator, the whole table is loaded into memory at once, which should be avoided for large collections. Second, although a PTable is a multi-map, the Map interface does not support multiple values for a single key, so if the table has multiple values for the same key, all but one will be lost in the returned Map.

To avoid these limitations, simply call materialize() on the table in order to obtain an Iterable<Pair<K, V>>.

---

5. This is an example of where a pipeline gets executed without an explicit call to run() or done(), but it is still good practice to call done() when the pipeline is finished with so that intermediate files are disposed of.

PObject

Another way to materialize a PCollection is to use PObjects. A PObject<T> is a *future*, a computation of a value of type T that may not have been completed at the time when the PObject is created in the running program. The computed value can be retrieved by calling getValue() on the PObject, which will block until the computation is completed (by running the Crunch pipeline) before returning the value.

Calling getValue() on a PObject is analogous to calling materialize() on a PCollection, since both calls will trigger execution of the pipeline to materialize the necessary collections. Indeed, we can rewrite the program to lowercase lines in a text file to use a PObject as follows:

```
Pipeline pipeline = new MRPipeline(getClass());
PCollection<String> lines = pipeline.readTextFile(inputPath);
PCollection<String> lower = lines.parallelDo(new ToLowerFn(), strings());

PObject<Collection<String>> po = lower.asCollection();
for (String s : po.getValue()) { // pipeline is run
  System.out.println(s);
}
pipeline.done();
```

The asCollection() method converts a PCollection<T> into a regular Java Collection<T>.[6] This is done by way of a PObject, so that the conversion can be deferred to a later point in the program's execution if necessary. In this case, we call PObject's getValue() immediately after getting the PObject so that we can iterate over the resulting Collection.

 asCollection() will materialize all the objects in the PCollection into memory, so you should only call it on small PCollection instances, such as the results of a computation that contain only a few objects. There is no such restriction on the use of materialize(), which iterates over the collection, rather than holding the entire collection in memory at once.

At the time of writing, Crunch does not provide a way to evaluate a PObject during pipeline execution, such as from within a DoFn. A PObject may only be inspected after the pipeline execution has finished.

---

6. There is also an asMap() method on PTable<K, V> that returns an object of type PObject<Map<K, V>>.

Pipeline Execution

During pipeline construction, Crunch builds an internal execution plan, which is either run explicitly by the user or implicitly by Crunch (as discussed in "Materialization" on page 535). An execution plan is a directed acyclic graph of operations on PCollections, where each PCollection in the plan holds a reference to the operation that produces it, along with the PCollections that are arguments to the operation. In addition, each PCollection has an internal state that records whether it has been materialized or not.

Running a Pipeline

A pipeline's operations can be explicitly executed by calling Pipeline's run() method, which performs the following steps.

First, it optimizes the execution plan as a number of stages. The details of the optimization depend on the execution engine—a plan optimized for MapReduce will be different from the same plan optimized for Spark.

Second, it executes each stage in the optimized plan (in parallel, where possible) to materialize the resulting PCollection. PCollections that are to be written to a Target are materialized as the target itself—this might be an output file in HDFS or a table in HBase. Intermediate PCollections are materialized by writing the serialized objects in the collection to a temporary intermediate file in HDFS.

Finally, the run() method returns a PipelineResult object to the caller, with information about each stage that was run (duration and MapReduce counters[7]), as well as whether the pipeline was successful or not (via the succeeded() method).

The clean() method removes all of the temporary intermediate files that were created to materialize PCollections. It should be called after the pipeline is finished with to free up disk space on HDFS. The method takes a Boolean parameter to indicate whether the temporary files should be forcibly deleted. If false, the temporary files will only be deleted if all the targets in the pipeline have been created.

Rather than calling run() followed by clean(false), it is more convenient to call done(), which has the same effect; it signals that the pipeline should be run and then cleaned up since it will not be needed any more.

---

7. You can increment your own custom counters from Crunch using DoFn's increment() method.

Asynchronous execution

The run() method is a blocking call that waits until the pipeline has completed before returning. There is a companion method, runAsync(), that returns immediately after the pipeline has been started. You can think of run() as being implemented as follows:

```
public PipelineResult run() {
  PipelineExecution execution = runAsync();
  execution.waitUntilDone();
  return execution.getResult();
}
```

There are times when you may want to use the runAsync() method directly; most obviously if you want to run other code while waiting for the pipeline to complete, but also to take advantage of the methods exposed by PipelineExecution, like the ones to inspect the execution plan, find the status of the execution, or stop the pipeline midway through.

PipelineExecution implements Future<PipelineResult> (from java.util.concur rent), offering the following simple idiom for performing background work:

```
PipelineExecution execution = pipeline.runAsync();
// meanwhile, do other things here
PipelineResult result = execution.get(); // blocks
```

Debugging

To get more debug information in the MapReduce task logs in the event of a failure, you can call enableDebug() on the Pipeline instance.

Another useful setting is the configuration property crunch.log.job.progress, which, if set to true, will log the MapReduce job progress of each stage to the console:

```
pipeline.getConfiguration().setBoolean("crunch.log.job.progress", true);
```

Stopping a Pipeline

Sometimes you might need to stop a pipeline before it completes. Perhaps only moments after starting a pipeline you realized that there's a programming error in the code, so you'd like to stop the pipeline, fix the problem, and then restart.

If the pipeline was run using the blocking run() or done() calls, then using the standard Java thread interrupt mechanism will cause the run() or done() method to return. However, any jobs running on the cluster will continue running—they will *not* be killed by Crunch.

Instead, to stop a pipeline properly, it needs to be launched asynchronously in order to retain a reference to the PipelineExecution object:

```
PipelineExecution execution = pipeline.runAsync();
```

Stopping the pipeline and its jobs is then just a question of calling the `kill()` method on `PipelineExecution`, and waiting for the pipeline to complete:

```
execution.kill();
execution.waitUntilDone();
```

At this point, the `PipelineExecution`'s status will be `PipelineExecution.Status.KILLED`, and any previously running jobs on the cluster from this pipeline will have been killed. An example of where this pattern could be effectively applied is in a Java VM shutdown hook to safely stop a currently executing pipeline when the Java application is shut down using Ctrl-C.

> `PipelineExecution` implements `Future<PipelineResult>`, so calling `kill()` can achieve the same effect as calling `cancel(true)`.

Inspecting a Crunch Plan

Sometimes it is useful, or at least enlightening, to inspect the optimized execution plan. The following snippet shows how to obtain a DOT file representation of the graph of operations in a pipeline as a string, and write it to a file (using Guava's `Files` utility class). It relies on having access to the `PipelineExecution` returned from running the pipeline asynchronously:

```
PipelineExecution execution = pipeline.runAsync();
String dot = execution.getPlanDotFile();
Files.write(dot, new File("pipeline.dot"), Charsets.UTF_8);
execution.waitUntilDone();
pipeline.done();
```

The *dot* command-line tool converts the DOT file into a graphical format, such as PNG, for easy inspection. The following invocation converts all DOT files in the current directory to PNG format, so *pipeline.dot* is converted to a file called *pipeline.dot.png*:

```
% dot -Tpng -O *.dot
```

> There is a trick for obtaining the DOT file when you don't have a `PipelineExecution` object, such as when the pipeline is run synchronously or implicitly (see "Materialization" on page 535). Crunch stores the DOT file representation in the job configuration, so it can be retrieved after the pipeline has finished:
>
> ```
> PipelineResult result = pipeline.done();
> String dot = pipeline.getConfiguration().get("crunch.planner.dotfile");
> Files.write(dot, new File("pipeline.dot"), Charsets.UTF_8);
> ```

Let's look at a plan for a nontrivial pipeline for calculating a histogram of word counts for text files stored in `inputPath` (see Example 18-3). Production pipelines can grow to be much longer than this one, with dozens of MapReduce jobs, but this illustrates some of the characteristics of the Crunch planner.

Example 18-3. A Crunch pipeline for calculating a histogram of word counts

```
PCollection<String> lines = pipeline.readTextFile(inputPath);
PCollection<String> lower = lines.parallelDo("lower", new ToLowerFn(), strings());
PTable<String, Long> counts = lower.count();
PTable<Long, String> inverseCounts = counts.parallelDo("inverse",
    new InversePairFn<String, Long>(), tableOf(longs(), strings()));
PTable<Long, Integer> hist = inverseCounts
    .groupByKey()
    .mapValues("count values", new CountValuesFn<String>(), ints());
hist.write(To.textFile(outputPath), Target.WriteMode.OVERWRITE);
pipeline.done();
```

The plan diagram generated from this pipeline is shown in Figure 18-1.

Sources and targets are rendered as folder icons. The top of the diagram shows the input source, and the output target is shown at the bottom. We can see that there are two MapReduce jobs (labeled *Crunch Job 1* and *Crunch Job 2*), and a temporary sequence file that Crunch generates to write the output of one job to so that the other can read it as input. The temporary file is deleted when `clean()` is called at the end of the pipeline execution.

Crunch Job 2 (which is actually the one that runs first; it was just produced by the planner second) consists of a map phase and a reduce phase, depicted by labeled boxes in the diagram. Each map and reduce is decomposed into smaller operations, shown by boxes labeled with names that correspond to the names of primitive Crunch operations in the code. For example, the first `parallelDo()` operation in the map phase is the one labeled *lower*, which simply lowercases each string in a `PCollection`.

> Use the overloaded methods of `PCollection` and related classes that take a name to give meaningful names to the operations in your pipeline. This makes it easier to follow plan diagrams.

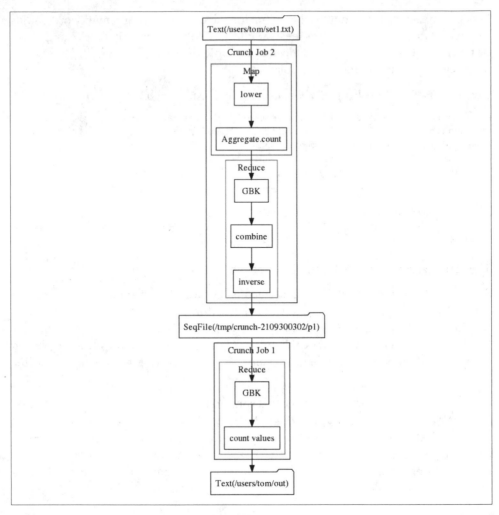

Figure 18-1. Plan diagram for a Crunch pipeline for calculating a histogram of word counts

After the lowercasing operation, the next transformation in the program is to produce a PTable of counts of each unique string, using the built-in convenience method count(). This method actually performs three primitive Crunch operations: a paral lelDo() named *Aggregate.count*, a groupByKey() operation labeled *GBK* in the diagram, and a combineValues() operation labeled *combine*.

Each *GBK* operation is realized as a MapReduce shuffle step, with the groupByKey() and combineValues() operations running in the reduce phase. The *Aggregate.count* parallelDo() operation runs in the map phase, but notice that it is run in the same map as the *lower* operation: the Crunch planner attempts to minimize the number of

MapReduce jobs that it needs to run for a pipeline. In a similar way, the *inverse* `paral lelDo()` operation is run as a part of the preceding reduce.[8]

The last transformation is to take the inverted counts `PTable` and find the frequency of each count. For example, if the strings that occur three times are `apple` and `orange`, then the count of 3 has a frequency of 2. This transformation is another *GBK* operation, which forces a new MapReduce job (Crunch Job 1), followed by a `mapValues()` operation that we named *count values*. The `mapValues()` operation is simply a `parallel Do()` operation that can therefore be run in the reduce.

Notice that the map phase for Crunch Job 1 is omitted from the diagram since no primitive Crunch operations are run in it.

Iterative Algorithms

A common use of `PObjects` is to check for convergence in an iterative algorithm. The classic example of a distributed iterative algorithm is the PageRank algorithm for ranking the relative importance of each of a set of linked pages, such as the World Wide Web. [9] The control flow for a Crunch implementation of PageRank looks like this:

```
PTable<String, PageRankData> scores = readUrls(pipeline, urlInput);
Float delta = 1.0f;
while (delta > 0.01) {
  scores = pageRank(scores, 0.5f);
  PObject<Float> pDelta = computeDelta(scores);
  delta = pDelta.getValue();
}
```

Without going into detail on the operation of the PageRank algorithm itself, we can understand how the higher-level program execution works in Crunch.

The input is a text file with two URLs per line: a page and an outbound link from that page. For example, the following file encodes the fact that A has links to B and C, and B has a link to D:

```
www.A.com www.B.com
www.A.com www.C.com
www.B.com www.D.com
```

Going back to the code, the first line reads the input and computes an initial `PageRank Data` object for each unique page. `PageRankData` is a simple Java class with fields for the

---

8. This optimization is called `parallelDo` *fusion*; it explained in more detail in the FlumeJava paper (*http:// bit.ly/data-parallel_pipelines*) referenced at the beginning of the chapter, along with some of the other optimizations used by Crunch. Note that `parallelDo` fusion is what allows you to decompose pipeline operations into small, logically separate functions without any loss of efficiency, since Crunch fuses them into as few MapReduce stages as possible.

9. For details, see Wikipedia (*http://en.wikipedia.org/wiki/PageRank*).

score, the previous score (this will be used to check for convergence), and a list of outbound links:

```
public static class PageRankData {
    public float score;
    public float lastScore;
    public List<String> urls;

    // ... methods elided
}
```

The goal of the algorithm is to compute a score for each page, representing its relative importance. All pages start out equal, so the initial score is set to be 1 for each page, and the previous score is 0. Creating the list of outbound links is achieved using the Crunch operations of grouping the input by the first field (page), then aggregating the values (outbound links) into a list.[10]

The iteration is carried out using a regular Java `while` loop. The scores are updated in each iteration of the loop by calling the `pageRank()` method, which encapsulates the PageRank algorithm as a series of Crunch operations. If the delta between the last set of scores and the new set of scores is below a small enough value (0.01), then the scores have converged and the algorithm terminates. The delta is computed by the `compute Delta()` method, a Crunch aggregation that finds the largest absolute difference in page score for all the pages in the collection.

So when is the pipeline run? The answer is each time `pDelta.getValue()` is called. The first time through the loop, no `PCollections` have been materialized yet, so the jobs for `readUrls()`, `pageRank()`, and `computeDelta()` must be run in order to compute `delta`. On subsequent iterations only the jobs to compute the new scores (`pageRank()`) and delta (`computeDelta()`) need be run.

> For this pipeline, Crunch's planner does a better job of optimizing the execution plan if `scores.materialize().iterator()` is called immediately after the `pageRank()` call. This ensures that the `scores` table is explicitly materialized, so it is available for the next execution plan in the next iteration of the loop. Without the call to `mate rialize()`, the program still produces the same result, but it's less efficient: the planner may choose to materialize different intermediate results, and so for the next iteration of the loop some of the computation must be re-executed to get the `scores` to pass to the `pageRank()` call.

10. You can find the full source code in the Crunch integration tests in a class called `PageRankIT`.

Checkpointing a Pipeline

In the previous section, we saw that Crunch will reuse any PCollections that were materialized in any previous runs of the same pipeline. However, if you create a new pipeline instance, then it will not automatically share any materialized PCollections from other pipelines, even if the input source is the same. This can make developing a pipeline rather time consuming, since even a small change to a computation toward the end of the pipeline means Crunch will run the new pipeline from the beginning.

The solution is to *checkpoint* a PCollection to persistent storage (typically HDFS) so that Crunch can start from the checkpoint in the new pipeline.

Consider the Crunch program for calculating a histogram of word counts for text files back in Example 18-3. We saw that the Crunch planner translates this pipeline into two MapReduce jobs. If the program is run for a second time, then Crunch will run the two MapReduce jobs again and overwrite the original output, since WriteMode is set to OVERWRITE.

If instead we checkpointed inverseCounts, a subsequent run would only launch one MapReduce job (the one for computing hist, since it is entirely derived from inverse Counts). Checkpointing is simply a matter of writing a PCollection to a target with the WriteMode set to CHECKPOINT:

```
PCollection<String> lines = pipeline.readTextFile(inputPath);
PTable<String, Long> counts = lines.count();
PTable<Long, String> inverseCounts = counts.parallelDo(
    new InversePairFn<String, Long>(), tableOf(longs(), strings()));
inverseCounts.write(To.sequenceFile(checkpointPath),
    Target.WriteMode.CHECKPOINT);
PTable<Long, Integer> hist = inverseCounts
    .groupByKey()
    .mapValues(new CountValuesFn<String>(), ints()));
hist.write(To.textFile(outputPath), Target.WriteMode.OVERWRITE);
pipeline.done();
```

Crunch compares the timestamps of the input files with those of the checkpoint files; if any inputs have later timestamps than the checkpoints, then it will recompute the dependent checkpoints automatically, so there is no risk of using out-of-date data in the pipeline.

Since they are persistent between pipeline runs, checkpoints are not cleaned up by Crunch, so you will need to delete them once you are happy that the code is producing the expected results.

Crunch Libraries

Crunch comes with a powerful set of library functions in the org.apache.crunch.lib package—they are summarized in Table 18-1.

Table 18-1. Crunch libraries

Class	Method name(s)	Description
Aggregate	length()	Returns the number of elements in a PCollection wrapped in a PObject.
	min()	Returns the smallest value element in a PCollection wrapped in a PObject.
	max()	Returns the largest value element in a PCollection wrapped in a PObject.
	count()	Returns a table of the unique elements of the input PCollection mapped to their counts.
	top()	Returns a table of the top or bottom *N* key-value pairs in a PTable, ordered by value.
	collectValues()	Groups the values for each unique key in a table into a Java Collection, returning a PTable<K, Collection<V>>.
Cartesian	cross()	Calculates the cross product of two PCollections or PTables.
Channels	split()	Splits a collection of pairs (PCollection<Pair<T, U>>) into a pair of collections (Pair<PCollection<T>, PCollection<U>>).
Cogroup	cogroup()	Groups the elements in two or more PTables by key.
Distinct	distinct()	Creates a new PCollection or PTable with duplicate elements removed.
Join	join()	Performs an inner join on two PTables by key. There are also methods for left, right, and full joins.
Mapred	map()	Runs a mapper (old API) on a PTable<K1, V1> to produce a PTable<K2, V2>.
	reduce()	Runs a reducer (old API) on a PGroupedTable<K1, V1> to produce a PTable<K2, V2>.
Mapreduce	map(), reduce()	Like Mapred, but for the new MapReduce API.
PTables	asPTable()	Converts a PCollection<Pair<K, V>> to a PTable<K, V>.
	keys()	Returns a PTable's keys as a PCollection.
	values()	Returns a PTable's values as a PCollection.
	mapKeys()	Applies a map function to all the keys in a PTable, leaving the values unchanged.
	mapValues()	Applies a map function to all the values in a PTable or PGroupedTable, leaving the keys unchanged.
Sample	sample()	Creates a sample of a PCollection by choosing each element independently with a specified probability.
	reservoirSample()	Creates a sample of a PCollection of a specified size, where each element is equally likely to be included.
Secondary Sort	sortAndApply()	Sorts a PTable<K, Pair<V1, V2>> by K then V1, then applies a function to give an output PCollection or PTable.

Class	Method name(s)	Description
Set	difference()	Returns a PCollection that is the set difference of two PCollections.
	intersection()	Returns a PCollection that is the set intersection of two PCollections.
	comm()	Returns a PCollection of triples that classifies each element from two PCollections by whether it is only in the first collection, only in the second collection, or in both collections. (Similar to the Unix comm command.)
Shard	shard()	Creates a PCollection that contains exactly the same elements as the input PCollection, but is partitioned (sharded) across a specified number of files.
Sort	sort()	Performs a total sort on a PCollection in the natural order of its elements in ascending (the default) or descending order. There are also methods to sort PTables by key, and collections of Pairs or tuples by a subset of their columns in a specified order.

One of the most powerful things about Crunch is that if the function you need is not provided, then it is simple to write it yourself, typically in a few lines of Java. For an example of a general-purpose function (for finding the unique values in a PTable), see Example 18-2.

The methods length(), min(), max(), and count() from Aggregate have convenience method equivalents on PCollection. Similarly, top() (as well as the derived method bottom()) and collectValues() from Aggregate, all the methods from PTables, join() from Join, and cogroup() from Cogroup are all duplicated on PTable.

The code in Example 18-4 walks through the behavior of some of the aggregation methods.

Example 18-4. Using the aggregation methods on PCollection and PTable

```
PCollection<String> a = MemPipeline.typedCollectionOf(strings(),
    "cherry", "apple", "banana", "banana");

assertEquals((Long) 4L, a.length().getValue());
assertEquals("apple", a.min().getValue());
assertEquals("cherry", a.max().getValue());

PTable<String, Long> b = a.count();
assertEquals("{(apple,1),(banana,2),(cherry,1)}", dump(b));

PTable<String, Long> c = b.top(1);
assertEquals("{(banana,2)}", dump(c));

PTable<String, Long> d = b.bottom(2);
assertEquals("{(apple,1),(cherry,1)}", dump(d));
```

Further Reading

This chapter has given a short introduction to Crunch. To find out more, consult the Crunch User Guide (*http://crunch.apache.org/user-guide.html*).

Spark

Apache Spark (*https://spark.apache.org/*) is a cluster computing framework for large-scale data processing. Unlike most of the other processing frameworks discussed in this book, Spark does not use MapReduce as an execution engine; instead, it uses its own distributed runtime for executing work on a cluster. However, Spark has many parallels with MapReduce, in terms of both API and runtime, as we will see in this chapter. Spark is closely integrated with Hadoop: it can run on YARN and works with Hadoop file formats and storage backends like HDFS.

Spark is best known for its ability to keep large working datasets in memory *between jobs*. This capability allows Spark to outperform the equivalent MapReduce workflow (by an order of magnitude or more in some cases[1]), where datasets are always loaded from disk. Two styles of application that benefit greatly from Spark's processing model are iterative algorithms (where a function is applied to a dataset repeatedly until an exit condition is met) and interactive analysis (where a user issues a series of ad hoc exploratory queries on a dataset).

Even if you don't need in-memory caching, Spark is very attractive for a couple of other reasons: its DAG engine and its user experience. Unlike MapReduce, Spark's DAG engine can process arbitrary pipelines of operators and translate them into a single job for the user.

Spark's user experience is also second to none, with a rich set of APIs for performing many common data processing tasks, such as joins. At the time of writing, Spark provides APIs in three languages: Scala, Java, and Python. We'll use the Scala API for most of the examples in this chapter, but they should be easy to translate to the other

---

1. See Matei Zaharia et al., "Resilient Distributed Datasets: A Fault-Tolerant Abstraction for In-Memory Cluster Computing," (*http://bit.ly/resilient_dist_datasets*) *NSDI '12 Proceedings of the 9th USENIX Conference on Networked Systems Design and Implementation*, 2012.

languages. Spark also comes with a REPL (read—eval—print loop) for both Scala and Python, which makes it quick and easy to explore datasets.

Spark is proving to be a good platform on which to build analytics tools, too, and to this end the Apache Spark project includes modules for machine learning (MLlib), graph processing (GraphX), stream processing (Spark Streaming), and SQL (Spark SQL). These modules are not covered in this chapter; the interested reader should refer to the Apache Spark website (*http://spark.apache.org/*).

Installing Spark

Download a stable release of the Spark binary distribution from the downloads page (*https://spark.apache.org/downloads.html*) (choose the one that matches the Hadoop distribution you are using), and unpack the tarball in a suitable location:

```
% tar xzf spark-x.y.z-bin-distro.tgz
```

It's convenient to put the Spark binaries on your path as follows:

```
% export SPARK_HOME=~/sw/spark-x.y.z-bin-distro
% export PATH=$PATH:$SPARK_HOME/bin
```

We're now ready to run an example in Spark.

An Example

To introduce Spark, let's run an interactive session using *spark-shell*, which is a Scala REPL with a few Spark additions. Start up the shell with the following:

```
% spark-shell
Spark context available as sc.

scala>
```

From the console output, we can see that the shell has created a Scala variable, sc, to store the SparkContext instance. This is our entry point to Spark, and allows us to load a text file as follows:

```
scala> val lines = sc.textFile("input/ncdc/micro-tab/sample.txt")
lines: org.apache.spark.rdd.RDD[String] = MappedRDD[1] at textFile at
  <console>:12
```

The lines variable is a reference to a *Resilient Distributed Dataset*, abbreviated to *RDD*, which is the central abstraction in Spark: a read-only collection of objects that is partitioned across multiple machines in a cluster. In a typical Spark program, one or more RDDs are loaded as input and through a series of transformations are turned into a set of target RDDs, which have an action performed on them (such as computing a result or writing them to persistent storage). The term "resilient" in "Resilient Distributed Dataset" refers to the fact that Spark can automatically reconstruct a lost partition by recomputing it from the RDDs that it was computed from.

 Loading an RDD or performing a transformation on one does not trigger any data processing; it merely creates a plan for performing a computation. The computation is only triggered when an action (like foreach()) is performed on an RDD.

Let's continue with the program. The first transformation we want to perform is to split the lines into fields:

```
scala> val records = lines.map(_.split("\t"))
records: org.apache.spark.rdd.RDD[Array[String]] = MappedRDD[2] at map at
  <console>:14
```

This uses the map() method on RDD to apply a function to every element in the RDD. In this case, we split each line (a String) into a Scala Array of Strings.

Next, we apply a filter to remove any bad records:

```
scala> val filtered = records.filter(rec => (rec(1) != "9999"
  && rec(2).matches("[01459]")))
filtered: org.apache.spark.rdd.RDD[Array[String]] = FilteredRDD[3] at filter at
  <console>:16
```

The filter() method on RDD takes a predicate, a function that returns a Boolean. This one tests for records that don't have a missing temperature (indicated by 9999) or a bad quality reading.

To find the maximum temperatures for each year, we need to perform a grouping operation on the year field so we can process all the temperature values for each year. Spark provides a reduceByKey() method to do this, but it needs an RDD of key-value pairs, represented by a Scala Tuple2. So, first we need to transform our RDD into the correct form using another map:

```
scala> val tuples = filtered.map(rec => (rec(0).toInt, rec(1).toInt))
tuples: org.apache.spark.rdd.RDD[(Int, Int)] = MappedRDD[4] at map at
  <console>:18
```

Then we can perform the aggregation. The reduceByKey() method's argument is a function that takes a pair of values and combines them into a single value; in this case, we use Java's Math.max function:

```
scala> val maxTemps = tuples.reduceByKey((a, b) => Math.max(a, b))
maxTemps: org.apache.spark.rdd.RDD[(Int, Int)] = MapPartitionsRDD[7] at
  reduceByKey at <console>:21
```

We can display the contents of maxTemps by invoking the foreach() method and passing println() to print each element to the console:

```
scala> maxTemps.foreach(println(_))
(1950,22)
(1949,111)
```

The foreach() method is the same as the equivalent on standard Scala collections, like List, and applies a function (that has some side effect) to each element in the RDD. It is this operation that causes Spark to run a job to compute the values in the RDD, so they can be run through the println() method.

Alternatively, we can save the RDD to the filesystem with:

```
scala> maxTemps.saveAsTextFile("output")
```

which creates a directory called *output* containing the partition files:

```
% cat output/part-*
(1950,22)
(1949,111)
```

The saveAsTextFile() method also triggers a Spark job. The main difference is that no value is returned, and instead the RDD is computed and its partitions are written to files in the *output* directory.

Spark Applications, Jobs, Stages, and Tasks

As we've seen in the example, like MapReduce, Spark has the concept of a *job*. A Spark job is more general than a MapReduce job, though, since it is made up of an arbitrary directed acyclic graph (DAG) of *stages*, each of which is roughly equivalent to a map or reduce phase in MapReduce.

Stages are split into *tasks* by the Spark runtime and are run in parallel on partitions of an RDD spread across the cluster—just like tasks in MapReduce.

A job always runs in the context of an *application* (represented by a SparkContext instance) that serves to group RDDs and shared variables. An application can run more than one job, in series or in parallel, and provides the mechanism for a job to access an RDD that was cached by a previous job in the same application. (We will see how to cache RDDs in "Persistence" on page 560.) An interactive Spark session, such as a *spark-shell* session, is just an instance of an application.

A Scala Standalone Application

After working with the Spark shell to refine a program, you may want to package it into a self-contained application that can be run more than once. The Scala program in Example 19-1 shows how to do this.

Example 19-1. Scala application to find the maximum temperature, using Spark

```
import org.apache.spark.SparkContext._
import org.apache.spark.{SparkConf, SparkContext}
```

```
object MaxTemperature {
  def main(args: Array[String]) {
    val conf = new SparkConf().setAppName("Max Temperature")
    val sc = new SparkContext(conf)

    sc.textFile(args(0))
      .map(_.split("\t"))
      .filter(rec => (rec(1) != "9999" && rec(2).matches("[01459]")))
      .map(rec => (rec(0).toInt, rec(1).toInt))
      .reduceByKey((a, b) => Math.max(a, b))
      .saveAsTextFile(args(1))
  }
}
```

When running a standalone program, we need to create the `SparkContext` since there is no shell to provide it. We create a new instance with a `SparkConf`, which allows us to pass various Spark properties to the application; here we just set the application name.

There are a couple of other minor changes. The first is that we've used the command-line arguments to specify the input and output paths. We've also used method chaining to avoid having to create intermediate variables for each RDD. This makes the program more compact, and we can still view the type information for each transformation in the Scala IDE if needed.

 Not all the transformations that Spark defines are available on the RDD class itself. In this case, `reducebyKey()` (which acts only on RDDs of key-value pairs) is actually defined in the `PairRDDFunctions` class, but we can get Scala to implicitly convert `RDD[(Int, Int)]` to `PairRDDFunctions` with the following import:

```
import org.apache.spark.SparkContext._
```

This imports various implicit conversion functions used in Spark, so it is worth including in programs as a matter of course.

This time we use *spark-submit* to run the program, passing as arguments the application JAR containing the compiled Scala program, followed by our program's command-line arguments (the input and output paths):

```
% spark-submit --class MaxTemperature --master local \
  spark-examples.jar input/ncdc/micro-tab/sample.txt output
% cat output/part-*
(1950,22)
(1949,111)
```

We also specified two options: `--class` to tell Spark the name of the application class, and `--master` to specify where the job should run. The value `local` tells Spark to run everything in a single JVM on the local machine. We'll learn about the options for running on a cluster in "Executors and Cluster Managers" on page 570. Next, let's see how to use other languages with Spark, starting with Java.

A Java Example

Spark is implemented in Scala, which as a JVM-based language has excellent integration with Java. It is straightforward—albeit verbose—to express the same example in Java (see Example 19-2).[2]

Example 19-2. Java application to find the maximum temperature, using Spark

```java
public class MaxTemperatureSpark {

  public static void main(String[] args) throws Exception {
    if (args.length != 2) {
      System.err.println("Usage: MaxTemperatureSpark <input path> <output path>");
      System.exit(-1);
    }

    SparkConf conf = new SparkConf();
    JavaSparkContext sc = new JavaSparkContext("local", "MaxTemperatureSpark", conf);
    JavaRDD<String> lines = sc.textFile(args[0]);
    JavaRDD<String[]> records = lines.map(new Function<String, String[]>() {
      @Override public String[] call(String s) {
        return s.split("\t");
      }
    });
    JavaRDD<String[]> filtered = records.filter(new Function<String[], Boolean>() {
      @Override public Boolean call(String[] rec) {
        return rec[1] != "9999" && rec[2].matches("[01459]");
      }
    });
    JavaPairRDD<Integer, Integer> tuples = filtered.mapToPair(
      new PairFunction<String[], Integer, Integer>() {
        @Override public Tuple2<Integer, Integer> call(String[] rec) {
          return new Tuple2<Integer, Integer>(
              Integer.parseInt(rec[0]), Integer.parseInt(rec[1]));
        }
      }
    );
    JavaPairRDD<Integer, Integer> maxTemps = tuples.reduceByKey(
      new Function2<Integer, Integer, Integer>() {
        @Override public Integer call(Integer i1, Integer i2) {
          return Math.max(i1, i2);
        }
      }
    );
    maxTemps.saveAsTextFile(args[1]);
```

2. The Java version is much more compact when written using Java 8 lambda expressions.

```
    }
}
```

In Spark's Java API, an RDD is represented by an instance of JavaRDD, or Java PairRDD for the special case of an RDD of key-value pairs. Both of these classes implement the JavaRDDLike interface, where most of the methods for working with RDDs can be found (when viewing class documentation, for example).

Running the program is identical to running the Scala version, except the classname is MaxTemperatureSpark.

A Python Example

Spark also has language support for Python, in an API called *PySpark*. By taking advantage of Python's lambda expressions, we can rewrite the example program in a way that closely mirrors the Scala equivalent, as shown in Example 19-3.

Example 19-3. Python application to find the maximum temperature, using PySpark

```python
from pyspark import SparkContext
import re, sys

sc = SparkContext("local", "Max Temperature")
sc.textFile(sys.argv[1]) \
  .map(lambda s: s.split("\t")) \
  .filter(lambda rec: (rec[1] != "9999" and re.match("[01459]", rec[2]))) \
  .map(lambda rec: (int(rec[0]), int(rec[1]))) \
  .reduceByKey(max) \
  .saveAsTextFile(sys.argv[2])
```

Notice that for the reduceByKey() transformation we can use Python's built-in max function.

The important thing to note is that this program is written in regular CPython. Spark will fork Python subprocesses to run the user's Python code (both in the launcher program and on *executors* that run user tasks in the cluster), and uses a socket to connect the two processes so the parent can pass RDD partition data to be processed by the Python code.

To run, we specify the Python file rather than the application JAR:

```
% spark-submit --master local \
  ch19-spark/src/main/python/MaxTemperature.py \
  input/ncdc/micro-tab/sample.txt output
```

Spark can also be run with Python in interactive mode using the pyspark command.

Resilient Distributed Datasets

RDDs are at the heart of every Spark program, so in this section we look at how to work with them in more detail.

Creation

There are three ways of creating RDDs: from an in-memory collection of objects (known as *parallelizing* a collection), using a dataset from external storage (such as HDFS), or transforming an existing RDD. The first way is useful for doing CPU-intensive computations on small amounts of input data in parallel. For example, the following runs separate computations on the numbers from 1 to 10:[3]

```
val params = sc.parallelize(1 to 10)
val result = params.map(performExpensiveComputation)
```

The performExpensiveComputation function is run on input values in parallel. The level of parallelism is determined from the spark.default.parallelism property, which has a default value that depends on where the Spark job is running. When running locally it is the number of cores on the machine, while for a cluster it is the total number of cores on all executor nodes in the cluster.

You can also override the level of parallelism for a particular computation by passing it as the second argument to parallelize():

```
sc.parallelize(1 to 10, 10)
```

The second way to create an RDD is by creating a reference to an external dataset. We have already seen how to create an RDD of String objects for a text file:

```
val text: RDD[String] = sc.textFile(inputPath)
```

The path may be any Hadoop filesystem path, such as a file on the local filesystem or on HDFS. Internally, Spark uses TextInputFormat from the old MapReduce API to read the file (see "TextInputFormat" on page 232). This means that the file-splitting behavior is the same as in Hadoop itself, so in the case of HDFS there is one Spark partition per HDFS block. The default can be changed by passing a second argument to request a particular number of splits:

```
sc.textFile(inputPath, 10)
```

Another variant permits text files to be processed as whole files (similar to "Processing a whole file as a record" on page 228) by returning an RDD of string pairs, where the first string is the file path and the second is the file contents. Since each file is loaded into memory, this is only suitable for small files:

---

3. This is like performing a parameter sweep using NLineInputFormat in MapReduce, as described in "NLineInputFormat" on page 234.

```
val files: RDD[(String, String)] = sc.wholeTextFiles(inputPath)
```

Spark can work with other file formats besides text. For example, sequence files can be read with:

```
sc.sequenceFile[IntWritable, Text](inputPath)
```

Notice how the sequence file's key and value Writable types have been specified. For common Writable types, Spark can map them to the Java equivalents, so we could use the equivalent form:

```
sc.sequenceFile[Int, String](inputPath)
```

There are two methods for creating RDDs from an arbitrary Hadoop InputFormat: hadoopFile() for file-based formats that expect a path, and hadoopRDD() for those that don't, such as HBase's TableInputFormat. These methods are for the old MapReduce API; for the new one, use newAPIHadoopFile() and newAPIHadoopRDD(). Here is an example of reading an Avro datafile using the Specific API with a WeatherRecord class:

```
val job = new Job()
AvroJob.setInputKeySchema(job, WeatherRecord.getClassSchema)
val data = sc.newAPIHadoopFile(inputPath,
    classOf[AvroKeyInputFormat[WeatherRecord]],
    classOf[AvroKey[WeatherRecord]], classOf[NullWritable],
    job.getConfiguration)
```

In addition to the path, the newAPIHadoopFile() method expects the InputFormat type, the key type, and the value type, plus the Hadoop configuration. The configuration carries the Avro schema, which we set in the second line using the AvroJob helper class.

The third way of creating an RDD is by transforming an existing RDD. We look at transformations next.

Transformations and Actions

Spark provides two categories of operations on RDDs: *transformations* and *actions*. A transformation generates a new RDD from an existing one, while an action triggers a computation on an RDD and does something with the results—either returning them to the user, or saving them to external storage.

Actions have an immediate effect, but transformations do not—they are lazy, in the sense that they don't perform any work until an action is performed on the transformed RDD. For example, the following lowercases lines in a text file:

```
val text = sc.textFile(inputPath)
val lower: RDD[String] = text.map(_.toLowerCase())
lower.foreach(println(_))
```

The map() method is a transformation, which Spark represents internally as a function (toLowerCase()) to be called at some later time on each element in the input RDD (text). The function is not actually called until the foreach() method (which is an action) is invoked and Spark runs a job to read the input file and call `toLowerCase()` on each line in it, before writing the result to the console.

One way of telling if an operation is a transformation or an action is by looking at its return type: if the return type is RDD, then it's a transformation; otherwise, it's an action. It's useful to know this when looking at the documentation for RDD (in the `org.apache.spark.rdd` package), where most of the operations that can be performed on RDDs can be found. More operations can be found in `PairRDDFunctions`, which contains transformations and actions for working with RDDs of key-value pairs.

Spark's library contains a rich set of operators, including transformations for mapping, grouping, aggregating, repartitioning, sampling, and joining RDDs, and for treating RDDs as sets. There are also actions for materializing RDDs as collections, computing statistics on RDDs, sampling a fixed number of elements from an RDD, and saving RDDs to external storage. For details, consult the class documentation.

MapReduce in Spark

Despite the suggestive naming, Spark's `map()` and `reduce()` operations do not directly correspond to the functions of the same name in Hadoop MapReduce. The general form of map and reduce in Hadoop MapReduce is (from Chapter 8):

```
map: (K1, V1) → list(K2, V2)
reduce: (K2, list(V2)) → list(K3, V3)
```

Notice that both functions can return multiple output pairs, indicated by the `list` notation. This is implemented by the `flatMap()` operation in Spark (and Scala in general), which is like `map()`, but removes a layer of nesting:

```
scala> val l = List(1, 2, 3)
l: List[Int] = List(1, 2, 3)

scala> l.map(a => List(a))
res0: List[List[Int]] = List(List(1), List(2), List(3))

scala> l.flatMap(a => List(a))
res1: List[Int] = List(1, 2, 3)
```

One naive way to try to emulate Hadoop MapReduce in Spark is with two `flatMap()` operations, separated by a `groupByKey()` and a `sortByKey()` to perform a MapReduce shuffle and sort:

```
val input: RDD[(K1, V1)] = ...
val mapOutput: RDD[(K2, V2)] = input.flatMap(mapFn)
val shuffled: RDD[(K2, Iterable[V2])] = mapOutput.groupByKey().sortByKey()
val output: RDD[(K3, V3)] = shuffled.flatMap(reduceFn)
```

Here the key type K2 needs to inherit from Scala's `Ordering` type to satisfy `sortByKey()`.

This example may be useful as a way to help understand the relationship between Map-Reduce and Spark, but it should not be applied blindly. For one thing, the semantics are slightly different from Hadoop's MapReduce, since `sortByKey()` performs a total sort. This issue can be avoided by using `repartitionAndSortWithinPartitions()` to perform a partial sort. However, even this isn't as efficient, since Spark uses two shuffles (one for the `groupByKey()` and one for the sort).

Rather than trying to reproduce MapReduce, it is better to use only the operations that you actually need. For example, if you don't need keys to be sorted, you can omit the `sortByKey()` call (something that is not possible in regular Hadoop MapReduce).

Similarly, `groupByKey()` is too general in most cases. Usually you only need the shuffle to aggregate values, so you should use `reduceByKey()`, `foldByKey()`, or `aggregateByKey()` (covered in the next section), which are more efficient than `groupByKey()` since they can also run as combiners in the map task. Finally, `flatMap()` may not always be needed either, with `map()` being preferred if there is always one return value, and `filter()` if there is zero or one.

Aggregation transformations

The three main transformations for aggregating RDDs of pairs by their keys are `reduceByKey()`, `foldByKey()`, and `aggregateByKey()`. They work in slightly different ways, but they all aggregate the values for a given key to produce a single value for each key. (The equivalent actions are `reduce()`, `fold()`, and `aggregate()`, which operate in an analogous way, resulting in a single value for the whole RDD.)

The simplest is `reduceByKey()`, which repeatedly applies a binary function to values in pairs until a single value is produced. For example:

```
val pairs: RDD[(String, Int)] =
    sc.parallelize(Array(("a", 3), ("a", 1), ("b", 7), ("a", 5)))
val sums: RDD[(String, Int)] = pairs.reduceByKey(_+_)
assert(sums.collect().toSet === Set(("a", 9), ("b", 7)))
```

The values for key a are aggregated using the addition function (_+_) as *(3 + 1) + 5 = 9*, while there is only one value for key b, so no aggregation is needed. Since in general the operations are distributed and performed in different tasks for different partitions of the RDD, the function should be commutative and associative. In other words, the order and grouping of the operations should not matter; in this case, the aggregation could be *5 + (3 + 1)*, or *3 + (1 + 5)*, which both return the same result.

The triple equals operator (===) used in the `assert` statement is from ScalaTest, and provides more informative failure messages than using the regular == operator.

Here's how we would perform the same operation using `foldByKey()`:

```scala
val sums: RDD[(String, Int)] = pairs.foldByKey(0)(_+_)
assert(sums.collect().toSet === Set(("a", 9), ("b", 7)))
```

Notice that this time we had to supply a *zero value*, which is just 0 when adding integers, but would be something different for other types and operations. This time, values for a are aggregated as $((0 + 3) + 1) + 5) = 9$ (or possibly some other order, although adding to 0 is always the first operation). For b it is $0 + 7 = 7$.

Using `foldByKey()` is no more or less powerful than using `reduceByKey()`. In particular, neither can change the type of the value that is the result of the aggregation. For that we need `aggregateByKey()`. For example, we can aggregate the integer values into a set:

```scala
val sets: RDD[(String, HashSet[Int])] =
    pairs.aggregateByKey(new HashSet[Int])(_+=_, _++=_)
assert(sets.collect().toSet === Set(("a", Set(1, 3, 5)), ("b", Set(7))))
```

For set addition, the zero value is the empty set, so we create a new mutable set with `new HashSet[Int]`. We have to supply two functions to `aggregateByKey()`. The first controls how an `Int` is combined with a `HashSet[Int]`, and in this case we use the addition and assignment function `_+=_` to add the integer to the set (`_+_` would return a new set and leave the first set unchanged).

The second function controls how two `HashSet[Int]` values are combined (this happens after the combiner runs in the map task, while the two partitions are being aggregated in the reduce task), and here we use `_++=_` to add all the elements of the second set to the first.

For key a, the sequence of operations might be:

$$((\varnothing + 3) + 1) + 5) = (1, 3, 5)$$

or:

$$(\varnothing + 3) + 1) ++ (\varnothing + 5) = (1, 3) ++ (5) = (1, 3, 5)$$

if Spark uses a combiner.

A transformed RDD can be persisted in memory so that subsequent operations on it are more efficient. We look at that next.

Persistence

Going back to the introductory example in "An Example" on page 550, we can cache the intermediate dataset of year-temperature pairs in memory with the following:

```scala
scala> tuples.cache()
res1: tuples.type = MappedRDD[4] at map at <console>:18
```

Calling cache() does not cache the RDD in memory straightaway. Instead, it marks the RDD with a flag indicating it should be cached when the Spark job is run. So let's first force a job run:

```
scala> tuples.reduceByKey((a, b) => Math.max(a, b)).foreach(println(_))
INFO BlockManagerInfo: Added rdd_4_0 in memory on 192.168.1.90:64640
INFO BlockManagerInfo: Added rdd_4_1 in memory on 192.168.1.90:64640
(1950,22)
(1949,111)
```

The log lines for BlockManagerInfo show that the RDD's partitions have been kept in memory as a part of the job run. The log shows that the RDD's number is 4 (this was shown in the console after calling the cache() method), and it has two partitions labeled 0 and 1. If we run another job on the cached dataset, we'll see that the RDD is loaded from memory. This time we'll compute minimum temperatures:

```
scala> tuples.reduceByKey((a, b) => Math.min(a, b)).foreach(println(_))
INFO BlockManager: Found block rdd_4_0 locally
INFO BlockManager: Found block rdd_4_1 locally
(1949,78)
(1950,-11)
```

This is a simple example on a tiny dataset, but for larger jobs the time savings can be impressive. Compare this to MapReduce, where to perform another calculation the input dataset has to be loaded from disk again. Even if an intermediate dataset can be used as input (such as a cleaned-up dataset with invalid rows and unnecessary fields removed), there is no getting away from the fact that it must be loaded from disk, which is slow. Spark will cache datasets in a cross-cluster in-memory cache, which means that any computation performed on those datasets will be very fast.

This turns out to be tremendously useful for interactive exploration of data. It's also a natural fit for certain styles of algorithm, such as iterative algorithms where a result computed in one iteration can be cached in memory and used as input for the next iteration. These algorithms can be expressed in MapReduce, but each iteration runs as a single MapReduce job, so the result from each iteration must be written to disk and then read back in the next iteration.

Cached RDDs can be retrieved only by jobs in the same application. To share datasets between applications, they must be written to external storage using one of the saveAs*() methods (saveAsText File(), saveAsHadoopFile(), etc.) in the first application, then loaded using the corresponding method in SparkContext (textFile(), hadoopFile(), etc.) in the second application. Likewise, when the application terminates, all its cached RDDs are destroyed and cannot be accessed again unless they have been explicitly saved.

Persistence levels

Calling `cache()` will persist each partition of the RDD in the executor's memory. If an executor does not have enough memory to store the RDD partition, the computation will not fail, but instead the partition will be recomputed as needed. For complex programs with lots of transformations, this may be expensive, so Spark offers different types of persistence behavior that may be selected by calling `persist()` with an argument to specify the `StorageLevel`.

By default, the level is `MEMORY_ONLY`, which uses the regular in-memory representation of objects. A more compact representation can be used by serializing the elements in a partition as a byte array. This level is `MEMORY_ONLY_SER`; it incurs CPU overhead compared to `MEMORY_ONLY`, but is worth it if the resulting serialized RDD partition fits in memory when the regular in-memory representation doesn't. `MEMORY_ONLY_SER` also reduces garbage collection pressure, since each RDD is stored as one byte array rather than lots of objects.

 You can see if an RDD partition doesn't fit in memory by inspecting the driver logfile for messages from the `BlockManager`. Also, every driver's `SparkContext` runs an HTTP server (on port 4040) that provides useful information about its environment and the jobs it is running, including information about cached RDD partitions.

By default, regular Java serialization is used to serialize RDD partitions, but Kryo serialization (covered in the next section) is normally a better choice, both in terms of size and speed. Further space savings can be achieved (again at the expense of CPU) by compressing the serialized partitions by setting the `spark.rdd.compress` property to `true`, and optionally setting `spark.io.compression.codec`.

If recomputing a dataset is expensive, then either `MEMORY_AND_DISK` (spill to disk if the dataset doesn't fit in memory) or `MEMORY_AND_DISK_SER` (spill to disk if the serialized dataset doesn't fit in memory) is appropriate.

There are also some more advanced and experimental persistence levels for replicating partitions on more than one node in the cluster, or using off-heap memory—see the Spark documentation for details.

Serialization

There are two aspects of serialization to consider in Spark: serialization of data and serialization of functions (or closures).

Data

Let's look at data serialization first. By default, Spark will use Java serialization to send data over the network from one executor to another, or when caching (persisting) data in serialized form as described in "Persistence levels" on page 562. Java serialization is well understood by programmers (you make sure the class you are using implements `java.io.Serializable` or `java.io.Externalizable`), but it is not particularly efficient from a performance or size perspective.

A better choice for most Spark programs is Kryo serialization (*https://github.com/EsotericSoftware/kryo*). Kryo is a more efficient general-purpose serialization library for Java. In order to use Kryo serialization, set the `spark.serializer` as follows on the `SparkConf` in your driver program:

```
conf.set("spark.serializer", "org.apache.spark.serializer.KryoSerializer")
```

Kryo does not require that a class implement a particular interface (like `java.io.Serializable`) to be serialized, so plain old Java objects can be used in RDDs without any further work beyond enabling Kryo serialization. Having said that, it is much more efficient to register classes with Kryo before using them. This is because Kryo writes a reference to the class of the object being serialized (one reference is written for every object written), which is just an integer identifier if the class has been registered but is the full classname otherwise. This guidance only applies to your own classes; Spark registers Scala classes and many other framework classes (like Avro Generic or Thrift classes) on your behalf.

Registering classes with Kryo is straightforward. Create a subclass of `KryoRegistrator`, and override the `registerClasses()` method:

```
class CustomKryoRegistrator extends KryoRegistrator {
  override def registerClasses(kryo: Kryo) {
    kryo.register(classOf[WeatherRecord])
  }
}
```

Finally, in your driver program, set the `spark.kryo.registrator` property to the fully qualified classname of your `KryoRegistrator` implementation:

```
conf.set("spark.kryo.registrator", "CustomKryoRegistrator")
```

Functions

Generally, serialization of functions will "just work": in Scala, functions are serializable using the standard Java serialization mechanism, which is what Spark uses to send functions to remote executor nodes. Spark will serialize functions even when running in local mode, so if you inadvertently introduce a function that is not serializable (such as one converted from a method on a nonserializable class), you will catch it early on in the development process.

Shared Variables

Spark programs often need to access data that is not part of an RDD. For example, this program uses a lookup table in a `map()` operation:

```
val lookup = Map(1 -> "a", 2 -> "e", 3 -> "i", 4 -> "o", 5 -> "u")
val result = sc.parallelize(Array(2, 1, 3)).map(lookup(_))
assert(result.collect().toSet === Set("a", "e", "i"))
```

While it works correctly (the variable `lookup` is serialized as a part of the closure passed to `map()`), there is a more efficient way to achieve the same thing using *broadcast variables*.

Broadcast Variables

A broadcast variable is serialized and sent to each executor, where it is cached so that later tasks can access it if needed. This is unlike a regular variable that is serialized as part of the closure, which is transmitted over the network once per task. Broadcast variables play a similar role to the distributed cache in MapReduce (see "Distributed Cache" on page 274), although the implementation in Spark stores the data in memory, only spilling to disk when memory is exhausted.

A broadcast variable is created by passing the variable to be broadcast to the `broad cast()` method on `SparkContext`. It returns a `Broadcast[T]` wrapper around the variable of type `T`:

```
val lookup: Broadcast[Map[Int, String]] =
    sc.broadcast(Map(1 -> "a", 2 -> "e", 3 -> "i", 4 -> "o", 5 -> "u"))
val result = sc.parallelize(Array(2, 1, 3)).map(lookup.value(_))
assert(result.collect().toSet === Set("a", "e", "i"))
```

Notice that the variable is accessed in the RDD `map()` operation by calling `value` on the broadcast variable.

As the name suggests, broadcast variables are sent one way, from driver to task—there is no way to update a broadcast variable and have the update propagate back to the driver. For that, we need an *accumulator*.

Accumulators

An accumulator is a shared variable that tasks can only add to, like counters in Map-Reduce (see "Counters" on page 247). After a job has completed, the accumulator's final value can be retrieved from the driver program. Here is an example that counts the number of elements in an RDD of integers using an accumulator, while at the same time summing the values in the RDD using a `reduce()` action:

```
val count: Accumulator[Int] = sc.accumulator(0)
val result = sc.parallelize(Array(1, 2, 3))
```

```
    .map(i => { count += 1; i })
    .reduce((x, y) => x + y)
assert(count.value === 3)
assert(result === 6)
```

An accumulator variable, count, is created in the first line using the accumulator()
method on SparkContext. The map() operation is an identity function with a side effect
that increments count. When the result of the Spark job has been computed, the value
of the accumulator is accessed by calling value on it.

In this example, we used an Int for the accumulator, but any numeric value type can be
used. Spark also provides a way to use accumulators whose result type is different to the
type being added (see the accumulable() method on SparkContext), and a way to
accumulate values in mutable collections (via accumulableCollection()).

Anatomy of a Spark Job Run

Let's walk through what happens when we run a Spark job. At the highest level, there
are two independent entities: the *driver*, which hosts the application (SparkContext)
and schedules tasks for a job; and the *executors*, which are exclusive to the application,
run for the duration of the application, and execute the application's tasks. Usually the
driver runs as a client that is not managed by the cluster manager and the executors run
on machines in the cluster, but this isn't always the case (as we'll see in "Executors and
Cluster Managers" on page 570). For the remainder of this section, we assume that the
application's executors are already running.

Job Submission

Figure 19-1 illustrates how Spark runs a job. A Spark job is submitted automatically
when an action (such as count()) is performed on an RDD. Internally, this causes
runJob() to be called on the SparkContext (step 1 in Figure 19-1), which passes the
call on to the scheduler that runs as a part of the driver (step 2). The scheduler is made
up of two parts: a DAG scheduler that breaks down the job into a DAG of stages, and a
task scheduler that is responsible for submitting the tasks from each stage to the cluster.

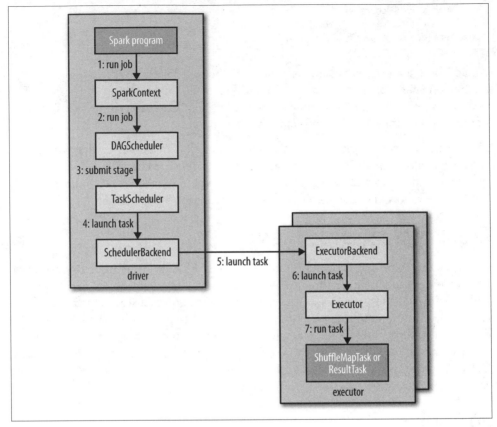

Figure 19-1. How Spark runs a job

Next, let's take a look at how the DAG scheduler constructs a DAG.

DAG Construction

To understand how a job is broken up into stages, we need to look at the type of tasks that can run in a stage. There are two types: *shuffle map tasks* and *result tasks*. The name of the task type indicates what Spark does with the task's output:

Shuffle map tasks

As the name suggests, shuffle map tasks are like the map-side part of the shuffle in MapReduce. Each shuffle map task runs a computation on one RDD partition and, based on a partitioning function, writes its output to a new set of partitions, which are then fetched in a later stage (which could be composed of either shuffle map tasks or result tasks). Shuffle map tasks run in all stages except the final stage.

Result tasks

Result tasks run in the final stage that returns the result to the user's program (such as the result of a `count()`). Each result task runs a computation on its RDD partition, then sends the result back to the driver, and the driver assembles the results from each partition into a final result (which may be `Unit`, in the case of actions like `saveAsTextFile()`).

The simplest Spark job is one that does not need a shuffle and therefore has just a single stage composed of result tasks. This is like a map-only job in MapReduce.

More complex jobs involve grouping operations and require one or more shuffle stages. For example, consider the following job for calculating a histogram of word counts for text files stored in `inputPath` (one word per line):

```
val hist: Map[Int, Long] = sc.textFile(inputPath)
  .map(word => (word.toLowerCase(), 1))
  .reduceByKey((a, b) => a + b)
  .map(_.swap)
  .countByKey()
```

The first two transformations, `map()` and `reduceByKey()`, perform a word count. The third transformation is a `map()` that swaps the key and value in each pair, to give *(count, word)* pairs, and the final operation is the `countByKey()` action, which returns the number of words with each count (i.e., a frequency distribution of word counts).

Spark's DAG scheduler turns this job into two stages since the `reduceByKey()` operation forces a shuffle stage.[4] The resulting DAG is illustrated in Figure 19-2.

The RDDs within each stage are also, in general, arranged in a DAG. The diagram shows the type of the RDD and the operation that created it. `RDD[String]` was created by `textFile()`, for instance. To simplify the diagram, some intermediate RDDs generated internally by Spark have been omitted. For example, the RDD returned by `text File()` is actually a `MappedRDD[String]` whose parent is a `HadoopRDD[LongWritable, Text]`.

Notice that the `reduceByKey()` transformation spans two stages; this is because it is implemented using a shuffle, and the reduce function runs as a combiner on the map side (stage 1) and as a reducer on the reduce side (stage 2)—just like in MapReduce. Also like MapReduce, Spark's shuffle implementation writes its output to partitioned

---

4. Note that `countByKey()` performs its final aggregation locally on the driver rather than using a second shuffle step. This is unlike the equivalent Crunch program in Example 18-3, which uses a second MapReduce job for the count.

files on local disk (even for in-memory RDDs), and the files are fetched by the RDD in the next stage.[5]

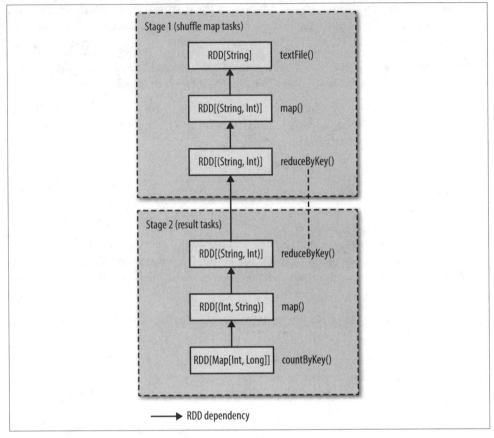

Figure 19-2. The stages and RDDs in a Spark job for calculating a histogram of word counts

If an RDD has been persisted from a previous job in the same application (SparkCon text), then the DAG scheduler will save work and not create stages for recomputing it (or the RDDs it was derived from).

The DAG scheduler is responsible for splitting a stage into tasks for submission to the task scheduler. In this example, in the first stage one shuffle map task is run for each partition of the input file. The level of parallelism for a reduceByKey() operation can

---

5. There is scope for tuning the performance of the shuffle through configuration (*http://bit.ly/shuffle_behav ior*). Note also that Spark uses its own custom implementation for the shuffle, and does not share any code with the MapReduce shuffle implementation.

be set explicitly by passing it as the second parameter. If not set, it will be determined from the parent RDD, which in this case is the number of partitions in the input data.

Each task is given a placement preference by the DAG scheduler to allow the task scheduler to take advantage of data locality. A task that processes a partition of an input RDD stored on HDFS, for example, will have a placement preference for the datanode hosting the partition's block (known as *node local*), while a task that processes a partition of an RDD that is cached in memory will prefer the executor storing the RDD partition (*process local*).

Going back to Figure 19-1, once the DAG scheduler has constructed the complete DAG of stages, it submits each stage's set of tasks to the task scheduler (step 3). Child stages are only submitted once their parents have completed successfully.

Task Scheduling

When the task scheduler is sent a set of tasks, it uses its list of executors that are running for the application and constructs a mapping of tasks to executors that takes placement preferences into account. Next, the task scheduler assigns tasks to executors that have free cores (this may not be the complete set if another job in the same application is running), and it continues to assign more tasks as executors finish running tasks, until the task set is complete. Each task is allocated one core by default, although this can be changed by setting `spark.task.cpus`.

Note that for a given executor the scheduler will first assign process-local tasks, then node-local tasks, then rack-local tasks, before assigning an arbitrary (nonlocal) task, or a speculative task if there are no other candidates.[6]

Assigned tasks are launched through a scheduler backend (step 4 in Figure 19-1), which sends a remote launch task message (step 5) to the executor backend to tell the executor to run the task (step 6).

 Rather than using Hadoop RPC for remote calls, Spark uses Akka (*http://akka.io/*), an actor-based platform for building highly scalable, event-driven distributed applications.

Executors also send status update messages to the driver when a task has finished or if a task fails. In the latter case, the task scheduler will resubmit the task on another executor. It will also launch speculative tasks for tasks that are running slowly, if this is enabled (it is not by default).

---

6. Speculative tasks are duplicates of existing tasks, which the scheduler may run as a backup if a task is running more slowly than expected. See "Speculative Execution" on page 204.

Task Execution

An executor runs a task as follows (step 7). First, it makes sure that the JAR and file dependencies for the task are up to date. The executor keeps a local cache of all the dependencies that previous tasks have used, so that it only downloads them when they have changed. Second, it deserializes the task code (which includes the user's functions) from the serialized bytes that were sent as a part of the launch task message. Third, the task code is executed. Note that tasks are run in the same JVM as the executor, so there is no process overhead for task launch.[7]

Tasks can return a result to the driver. The result is serialized and sent to the executor backend, and then back to the driver as a status update message. A shuffle map task returns information that allows the next stage to retrieve the output partitions, while a result task returns the value of the result for the partition it ran on, which the driver assembles into a final result to return to the user's program.

Executors and Cluster Managers

We have seen how Spark relies on executors to run the tasks that make up a Spark job, but we glossed over how the executors actually get started. Managing the lifecycle of executors is the responsibility of the *cluster manager*, and Spark provides a variety of cluster managers with different characteristics:

Local
> In local mode there is a single executor running in the same JVM as the driver. This mode is useful for testing or running small jobs. The master URL for this mode is local (use one thread), local[*n*] (*n* threads), or local(*) (one thread per core on the machine).

Standalone
> The standalone cluster manager is a simple distributed implementation that runs a single Spark master and one or more workers. When a Spark application starts, the master will ask the workers to spawn executor processes on behalf of the application. The master URL is spark://*host*:*port*.

Mesos
> Apache Mesos is a general-purpose cluster resource manager that allows fine-grained sharing of resources across different applications according to an organizational policy. By default (fine-grained mode), each Spark task is run as a Mesos task. This uses the cluster resources more efficiently, but at the cost of additional process launch overhead. In coarse-grained mode, executors run their tasks in-

---

7. This is not true for Mesos fine-grained mode, where each task runs as a separate process. See the following section for details.

process, so the cluster resources are held by the executor processes for the duration of the Spark application. The master URL is mesos://*host:port*.

YARN

YARN is the resource manager used in Hadoop (see Chapter 4). Each running Spark application corresponds to an instance of a YARN application, and each executor runs in its own YARN container. The master URL is yarn-client or yarn-cluster.

The Mesos and YARN cluster managers are superior to the standalone manager since they take into account the resource needs of other applications running on the cluster (MapReduce jobs, for example) and enforce a scheduling policy across all of them. The standalone cluster manager uses a static allocation of resources from the cluster, and therefore is not able to adapt to the varying needs of other applications over time. Also, YARN is the only cluster manager that is integrated with Hadoop's Kerberos security mechanisms (see "Security" on page 309).

Spark on YARN

Running Spark on YARN provides the tightest integration with other Hadoop components and is the most convenient way to use Spark when you have an existing Hadoop cluster. Spark offers two deploy modes for running on YARN: *YARN client* mode, where the driver runs in the client, and *YARN cluster* mode, where the driver runs on the cluster in the YARN application master.

YARN client mode is required for programs that have any interactive component, such as *spark-shell* or *pyspark*. Client mode is also useful when building Spark programs, since any debugging output is immediately visible.

YARN cluster mode, on the other hand, is appropriate for production jobs, since the entire application runs on the cluster, which makes it much easier to retain logfiles (including those from the driver program) for later inspection. YARN will also retry the application if the application master fails (see "Application Master Failure" on page 194).

YARN client mode

In YARN client mode, the interaction with YARN starts when a new SparkContext instance is constructed by the driver program (step 1 in Figure 19-3). The context submits a YARN application to the YARN resource manager (step 2), which starts a YARN container on a node manager in the cluster and runs a Spark ExecutorLauncher application master in it (step 3). The job of the ExecutorLauncher is to start executors in YARN containers, which it does by requesting resources from the resource manager (step 4), then launching ExecutorBackend processes as the containers are allocated to it (step 5).

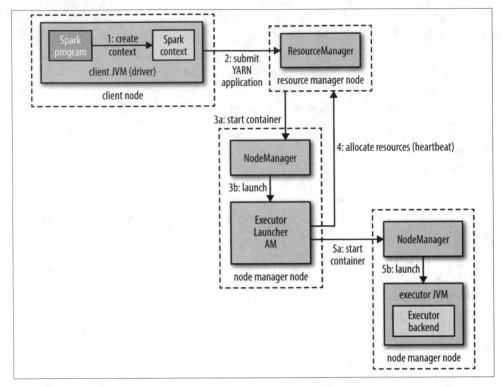

Figure 19-3. How Spark executors are started in YARN client mode

As each executor starts, it connects back to the SparkContext and registers itself. This gives the SparkContext information about the number of executors available for running tasks and their locations, which is used for making task placement decisions (described in "Task Scheduling" on page 569).

The number of executors that are launched is set in *spark-shell*, *spark-submit*, or *pyspark* (if not set, it defaults to two), along with the number of cores that each executor uses (the default is one) and the amount of memory (the default is 1,024 MB). Here's an example showing how to run *spark-shell* on YARN with four executors, each using one core and 2 GB of memory:

```
% spark-shell --master yarn-client \
  --num-executors 4 \
  --executor-cores 1 \
  --executor-memory 2g
```

The YARN resource manager address is not specified in the master URL (unlike when using the standalone or Mesos cluster managers), but is picked up from Hadoop configuration in the directory specified by the HADOOP_CONF_DIR environment variable.

YARN cluster mode

In YARN cluster mode, the user's driver program runs in a YARN application master process. The `spark-submit` command is used with a master URL of `yarn-cluster`:

```
% spark-submit --master yarn-cluster ...
```

All other parameters, like `--num-executors` and the application JAR (or Python file), are the same as for YARN client mode (use `spark-submit --help` for usage).

The *spark-submit* client will launch the YARN application (step 1 in Figure 19-4), but it doesn't run any user code. The rest of the process is the same as client mode, except the application master starts the driver program (step 3b) before allocating resources for executors (step 4).

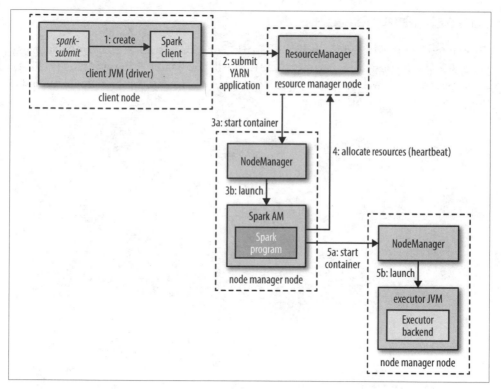

Figure 19-4. How Spark executors are started in YARN cluster mode

In both YARN modes, the executors are launched before there is any data locality information available, so it could be that they end up not being co-located on the datanodes hosting the files that the jobs access. For interactive sessions, this may be acceptable, particularly as it may not be known which datasets are going to be accessed before the session starts. This is less true of production jobs, however, so Spark provides a way to give placement hints to improve data locality when running in YARN cluster mode.

The `SparkContext` constructor can take a second argument of preferred locations, computed from the input format and path using the `InputFormatInfo` helper class. For example, for text files, we use `TextInputFormat`:

```
val preferredLocations = InputFormatInfo.computePreferredLocations(
    Seq(new InputFormatInfo(new Configuration(), classOf[TextInputFormat],
    inputPath)))
val sc = new SparkContext(conf, preferredLocations)
```

The preferred locations are used by the application master when making allocation requests to the resource manager (step 4).[8]

Further Reading

This chapter only covered the basics of Spark. For more detail, see *Learning Spark* by Holden Karau, Andy Konwinski, Patrick Wendell, and Matei Zaharia (O'Reilly, 2014). The Apache Spark website (*http://spark.apache.org/*) also has up-to-date documentation about the latest Spark release.

---

8. The preferred locations API is not stable (in Spark 1.2.0, the latest release as of this writing) and may change in a later release.

HBase

Jonathan Gray
Michael Stack

HBasics

HBase is a distributed column-oriented database built on top of HDFS. HBase is the Hadoop application to use when you require real-time read/write random access to very large datasets.

Although there are countless strategies and implementations for database storage and retrieval, most solutions—especially those of the relational variety—are not built with very large scale and distribution in mind. Many vendors offer replication and partitioning solutions to grow the database beyond the confines of a single node, but these add-ons are generally an afterthought and are complicated to install and maintain. They also severely compromise the RDBMS feature set. Joins, complex queries, triggers, views, and foreign-key constraints become prohibitively expensive to run on a scaled RDBMS, or do not work at all.

HBase approaches the scaling problem from the opposite direction. It is built from the ground up to scale linearly just by adding nodes. HBase is not relational and does not support SQL,[1] but given the proper problem space, it is able to do what an RDBMS cannot: host very large, sparsely populated tables on clusters made from commodity hardware.

The canonical HBase use case is the *webtable*, a table of crawled web pages and their attributes (such as language and MIME type) keyed by the web page URL. The webtable is large, with row counts that run into the billions. Batch analytic and parsing

---

1. But see the Apache Phoenix project, mentioned in "SQL-on-Hadoop Alternatives" on page 484, and Trafodion (*https://wiki.trafodion.org/*), a transactional SQL database built on HBase.

MapReduce jobs are continuously run against the webtable, deriving statistics and adding new columns of verified MIME-type and parsed-text content for later indexing by a search engine. Concurrently, the table is randomly accessed by crawlers running at various rates and updating random rows while random web pages are served in real time as users click on a website's cached-page feature.

Backdrop

The HBase project was started toward the end of 2006 by Chad Walters and Jim Kellerman at Powerset. It was modeled after Google's Bigtable, which had just been published.[2] In February 2007, Mike Cafarella made a code drop of a mostly working system that Jim Kellerman then carried forward.

The first HBase release was bundled as part of Hadoop 0.15.0 in October 2007. In May 2010, HBase graduated from a Hadoop subproject to become an Apache Top Level Project. Today, HBase is a mature technology used in production across a wide range of industries.

Concepts

In this section, we provide a quick overview of core HBase concepts. At a minimum, a passing familiarity will ease the digestion of all that follows.

Whirlwind Tour of the Data Model

Applications store data in labeled tables. Tables are made of rows and columns. Table cells—the intersection of row and column coordinates—are versioned. By default, their version is a timestamp auto-assigned by HBase at the time of cell insertion. A cell's content is an uninterpreted array of bytes. An example HBase table for storing photos is shown in Figure 20-1.

---

2. Fay Chang et al., "Bigtable: A Distributed Storage System for Structured Data," (*http://research.google.com/archive/bigtable.html*) November 2006.

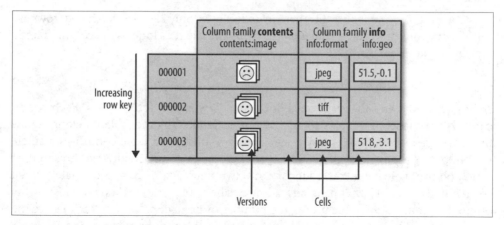

Figure 20-1. The HBase data model, illustrated for a table storing photos

Table row keys are also byte arrays, so theoretically anything can serve as a row key, from strings to binary representations of long or even serialized data structures. Table rows are sorted by row key, aka the table's primary key. The sort is byte-ordered. All table accesses are via the primary key.[3]

Row columns are grouped into *column families*. All column family members have a common prefix, so, for example, the columns info:format and info:geo are both members of the info column family, whereas contents:image belongs to the contents family. The column family prefix must be composed of *printable* characters. The qualifying tail, the column family *qualifier*, can be made of any arbitrary bytes. The column family and the qualifier are always separated by a colon character (:).

A table's column families must be specified up front as part of the table schema definition, but new column family members can be added on demand. For example, a new column info:camera can be offered by a client as part of an update, and its value persisted, as long as the column family info already exists on the table.

Physically, all column family members are stored together on the filesystem. So although earlier we described HBase as a column-oriented store, it would be more accurate if it were described as a column-*family*-oriented store. Because tuning and storage specifications are done at the column family level, it is advised that all column family members have the same general access pattern and size characteristics. For the photos table, the image data, which is large (megabytes), is stored in a separate column family from the metadata, which is much smaller in size (kilobytes).

---

3. HBase doesn't support indexing of other columns in the table (also known as *secondary indexes*). However, there are several strategies for supporting the types of query that secondary indexes provide, each with different trade-offs between storage space, processing load, and query execution time; see the HBase Reference Guide (*http://hbase.apache.org/book.html*) for a discussion.

In synopsis, HBase tables are like those in an RDBMS, only cells are versioned, rows are sorted, and columns can be added on the fly by the client as long as the column family they belong to preexists.

Regions

Tables are automatically partitioned horizontally by HBase into *regions*. Each region comprises a subset of a table's rows. A region is denoted by the table it belongs to, its first row (inclusive), and its last row (exclusive). Initially, a table comprises a single region, but as the region grows it eventually crosses a configurable size threshold, at which point it splits at a row boundary into two new regions of approximately equal size. Until this first split happens, all loading will be against the single server hosting the original region. As the table grows, the number of its regions grows. Regions are the units that get distributed over an HBase cluster. In this way, a table that is too big for any one server can be carried by a cluster of servers, with each node hosting a subset of the table's total regions. This is also the means by which the loading on a table gets distributed. The online set of sorted regions comprises the table's total content.

Locking

Row updates are atomic, no matter how many row columns constitute the row-level transaction. This keeps the locking model simple.

Implementation

Just as HDFS and YARN are built of clients, workers, and a coordinating master—the *namenode* and *datanodes* in HDFS and *resource manager* and *node managers* in YARN—so is HBase made up of an HBase *master* node orchestrating a cluster of one or more *regionserver* workers (see Figure 20-2). The HBase master is responsible for bootstrapping a virgin install, for assigning regions to registered regionservers, and for recovering regionserver failures. The master node is lightly loaded. The regionservers carry zero or more regions and field client read/write requests. They also manage region splits, informing the HBase master about the new daughter regions so it can manage the offlining of parent regions and assignment of the replacement daughters.

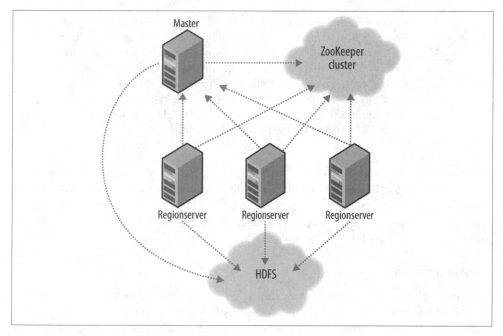

Figure 20-2. HBase cluster members

HBase depends on ZooKeeper (Chapter 21), and by default it manages a ZooKeeper instance as the authority on cluster state, although it can be configured to use an existing ZooKeeper cluster instead. The ZooKeeper ensemble hosts vitals such as the location of the `hbase:meta` catalog table and the address of the current cluster master. Assignment of regions is mediated via ZooKeeper in case participating servers crash mid-assignment. Hosting the assignment transaction state in ZooKeeper makes it so recovery can pick up on the assignment where the crashed server left off. At a minimum, when bootstrapping a client connection to an HBase cluster, the client must be passed the location of the ZooKeeper ensemble. Thereafter, the client navigates the ZooKeeper hierarchy to learn cluster attributes such as server locations.

Regionserver worker nodes are listed in the HBase *conf/regionservers* file, as you would list datanodes and node managers in the Hadoop *etc/hadoop/slaves* file. Start and stop scripts are like those in Hadoop and use the same SSH-based mechanism for running remote commands. A cluster's site-specific configuration is done in the HBase *conf/hbase-site.xml* and *conf/hbase-env.sh* files, which have the same format as their equivalents in the Hadoop parent project (see Chapter 10).

Where there is commonality to be found, whether in a service or type, HBase typically directly uses or subclasses the parent Hadoop implementation. When this is not possible, HBase will follow the Hadoop model where it can. For example, HBase uses the Hadoop configuration system, so configuration files have the same format. What this means for you, the user, is that you can leverage any Hadoop familiarity in your exploration of HBase. HBase deviates from this rule only when adding its specializations.

HBase persists data via the Hadoop filesystem API. Most people using HBase run it on HDFS for storage, though by default, and unless told otherwise, HBase writes to the local filesystem. The local filesystem is fine for experimenting with your initial HBase install, but thereafter, the first configuration made in an HBase cluster usually involves pointing HBase at the HDFS cluster it should use.

HBase in operation

Internally, HBase keeps a special catalog table named `hbase:meta`, within which it maintains the current list, state, and locations of all user-space regions afloat on the cluster. Entries in `hbase:meta` are keyed by region name, where a region name is made up of the name of the table the region belongs to, the region's start row, its time of creation, and finally, an MD5 hash of all of these (i.e., a hash of table name, start row, and creation timestamp). Here is an example region name for a region in the table `TestTable` whose start row is `xyz`:

```
TestTable,xyz,1279729913622.1b6e176fb8d8aa88fd4ab6bc80247ece.
```

Commas delimit the table name, start row, and timestamp. The MD5 hash is surrounded by a leading and trailing period.

As noted previously, row keys are sorted, so finding the region that hosts a particular row is a matter of a lookup to find the largest entry whose key is less than or equal to that of the requested row key. As regions transition—are split, disabled, enabled, deleted, or redeployed by the region load balancer, or redeployed due to a regionserver crash—the catalog table is updated so the state of all regions on the cluster is kept current.

Fresh clients connect to the ZooKeeper cluster first to learn the location of `hbase:meta`. The client then does a lookup against the appropriate `hbase:meta` region to figure out the hosting user-space region and its location. Thereafter, the client interacts directly with the hosting regionserver.

To save on having to make three round-trips per row operation, clients cache all they learn while doing lookups for `hbase:meta`. They cache locations as well as user-space region start and stop rows, so they can figure out hosting regions themselves without having to go back to the `hbase:meta` table. Clients continue to use the cached entries as they work, until there is a fault. When this happens—i.e., when the region has moved—

the client consults the `hbase:meta` table again to learn the new location. If the consulted `hbase:meta` region has moved, then ZooKeeper is reconsulted.

Writes arriving at a regionserver are first appended to a commit log and then added to an in-memory *memstore*. When a memstore fills, its content is flushed to the filesystem.

The commit log is hosted on HDFS, so it remains available through a regionserver crash. When the master notices that a regionserver is no longer reachable, usually because the server's znode has expired in ZooKeeper, it splits the dead regionserver's commit log by region. On reassignment and before they reopen for business, regions that were on the dead regionserver will pick up their just-split files of not-yet-persisted edits and replay them to bring themselves up to date with the state they had just before the failure.

When reading, the region's memstore is consulted first. If sufficient versions are found reading memstore alone, the query completes there. Otherwise, flush files are consulted in order, from newest to oldest, either until versions sufficient to satisfy the query are found or until we run out of flush files.

A background process compacts flush files once their number has exceeded a threshold, rewriting many files as one, because the fewer files a read consults, the more performant it will be. On compaction, the process cleans out versions beyond the schema-configured maximum and removes deleted and expired cells. A separate process running in the regionserver monitors flush file sizes, splitting the region when they grow in excess of the configured maximum.

Installation

Download a stable release from an Apache Download Mirror (*http://www.apache.org/dyn/closer.cgi/hbase/*) and unpack it on your local filesystem. For example:

```
% tar xzf hbase-x.y.z.tar.gz
```

As with Hadoop, you first need to tell HBase where Java is located on your system. If you have the `JAVA_HOME` environment variable set to point to a suitable Java installation, then that will be used, and you don't have to configure anything further. Otherwise, you can set the Java installation that HBase uses by editing HBase's *conf/hbase-env.sh* file and specifying the `JAVA_HOME` variable (see Appendix A for some examples).

For convenience, add the HBase binary directory to your command-line path. For example:

```
% export HBASE_HOME=~/sw/hbase-x.y.z
% export PATH=$PATH:$HBASE_HOME/bin
```

To get the list of HBase options, use the following:

```
% hbase
Options:
  --config DIR    Configuration direction to use. Default: ./conf
  --hosts HOSTS   Override the list in 'regionservers' file

Commands:
Some commands take arguments. Pass no args or -h for usage.
  shell           Run the HBase shell
  hbck            Run the hbase 'fsck' tool
  hlog            Write-ahead-log analyzer
  hfile           Store file analyzer
  zkcli           Run the ZooKeeper shell
  upgrade         Upgrade hbase
  master          Run an HBase HMaster node
  regionserver    Run an HBase HRegionServer node
  zookeeper       Run a Zookeeper server
  rest            Run an HBase REST server
  thrift          Run the HBase Thrift server
  thrift2         Run the HBase Thrift2 server
  clean           Run the HBase clean up script
  classpath       Dump hbase CLASSPATH
  mapredcp        Dump CLASSPATH entries required by mapreduce
  pe              Run PerformanceEvaluation
  ltt             Run LoadTestTool
  version         Print the version
  CLASSNAME       Run the class named CLASSNAME
```

Test Drive

To start a standalone instance of HBase that uses a temporary directory on the local filesystem for persistence, use this:

```
% start-hbase.sh
```

By default, HBase writes to */${java.io.tmpdir}/hbase-${user.name}*. `${java.io.tmpdir}` usually maps to */tmp*, but you should configure HBase to use a more permanent location by setting `hbase.tmp.dir` in *hbase-site.xml*. In standalone mode, the HBase master, the regionserver, and a `ZooKeeper` instance are all run in the same JVM.

To administer your HBase instance, launch the HBase shell as follows:

```
% hbase shell
HBase Shell; enter 'help<RETURN>' for list of supported commands.
Type "exit<RETURN>" to leave the HBase Shell
Version 0.98.7-hadoop2, r800c23e2207aa3f9bddb7e9514d8340bcfb89277, Wed Oct  8
15:58:11 PDT 2014

hbase(main):001:0>
```

This will bring up a JRuby IRB interpreter that has had some HBase-specific commands added to it. Type `help` and then press Return to see the list of shell commands grouped into categories. Type `help "COMMAND_GROUP"` for help by category or `help "COMMAND"` for help on a specific command and example usage. Commands use Ruby formatting to specify lists and dictionaries. See the end of the main help screen for a quick tutorial.

Now let's create a simple table, add some data, and then clean up.

To create a table, you must name your table and define its schema. A table's schema comprises table attributes and the list of table column families. Column families themselves have attributes that you in turn set at schema definition time. Examples of column family attributes include whether the family content should be compressed on the filesystem and how many versions of a cell to keep. Schemas can be edited later by offlining the table using the shell disable command, making the necessary alterations using alter, then putting the table back online with enable.

To create a table named test with a single column family named data using defaults for table and column family attributes, enter:

```
hbase(main):001:0> create 'test', 'data'
0 row(s) in 0.9810 seconds
```

 If the previous command does not complete successfully, and the shell displays an error and a stack trace, your install was not successful. Check the master logs under the HBase *logs* directory—the default location for the logs directory is *${HBASE_HOME}/logs*—for a clue as to where things went awry.

See the help output for examples of adding table and column family attributes when specifying a schema.

To prove the new table was created successfully, run the list command. This will output all tables in user space:

```
hbase(main):002:0> list
TABLE
test
1 row(s) in 0.0260 seconds
```

To insert data into three different rows and columns in the data column family, get the first row, and then list the table content, do the following:

```
hbase(main):003:0> put 'test', 'row1', 'data:1', 'value1'
hbase(main):004:0> put 'test', 'row2', 'data:2', 'value2'
hbase(main):005:0> put 'test', 'row3', 'data:3', 'value3'
hbase(main):006:0> get 'test', 'row1'
COLUMN                        CELL
 data:1                       timestamp=1414927084811, value=value1
1 row(s) in 0.0240 seconds
hbase(main):007:0> scan 'test'
ROW                           COLUMN+CELL
 row1                         column=data:1, timestamp=1414927084811, value=value1
```

```
row2                      column=data:2, timestamp=1414927125174, value=value2
row3                      column=data:3, timestamp=1414927131931, value=value3
3 row(s) in 0.0240 seconds
```

Notice how we added three new columns without changing the schema.

To remove the table, you must first disable it before dropping it:

```
hbase(main):009:0> disable 'test'
0 row(s) in 5.8420 seconds
hbase(main):010:0> drop 'test'
0 row(s) in 5.2560 seconds
hbase(main):011:0> list
TABLE
0 row(s) in 0.0200 seconds
```

Shut down your HBase instance by running:

```
% stop-hbase.sh
```

To learn how to set up a distributed HBase cluster and point it at a running HDFS, see the configuration section of the HBase documentation (*http://hbase.apache.org/book/ configuration.html*).

Clients

There are a number of client options for interacting with an HBase cluster.

Java

HBase, like Hadoop, is written in Java. Example 20-1 shows the Java version of how you would do the shell operations listed in the previous section.

Example 20-1. Basic table administration and access

```java
public class ExampleClient {

  public static void main(String[] args) throws IOException {
    Configuration config = HBaseConfiguration.create();
    // Create table
    HBaseAdmin admin = new HBaseAdmin(config);
    try {
      TableName tableName = TableName.valueOf("test");
      HTableDescriptor htd = new HTableDescriptor(tableName);
      HColumnDescriptor hcd = new HColumnDescriptor("data");
      htd.addFamily(hcd);
      admin.createTable(htd);
      HTableDescriptor[] tables = admin.listTables();
      if (tables.length != 1 &&
          Bytes.equals(tableName.getName(), tables[0].getTableName().getName())) {
        throw new IOException("Failed create of table");
      }
```

```
    // Run some operations -- three puts, a get, and a scan -- against the table.
    HTable table = new HTable(config, tableName);
    try {
      for (int i = 1; i <= 3; i++) {
        byte[] row = Bytes.toBytes("row" + i);
        Put put = new Put(row);
        byte[] columnFamily = Bytes.toBytes("data");
        byte[] qualifier = Bytes.toBytes(String.valueOf(i));
        byte[] value = Bytes.toBytes("value" + i);
        put.add(columnFamily, qualifier, value);
        table.put(put);
      }
      Get get = new Get(Bytes.toBytes("row1"));
      Result result = table.get(get);
      System.out.println("Get: " + result);
      Scan scan = new Scan();
      ResultScanner scanner = table.getScanner(scan);
      try {
        for (Result scannerResult : scanner) {
          System.out.println("Scan: " + scannerResult);
        }
      } finally {
        scanner.close();
      }
      // Disable then drop the table
      admin.disableTable(tableName);
      admin.deleteTable(tableName);
    } finally {
      table.close();
    }
  } finally {
    admin.close();
  }
  }
}
```

This class has a `main()` method only. For the sake of brevity, we do not include the package name, nor imports. Most of the HBase classes are found in the `org.apache.ha doop.hbase` and `org.apache.hadoop.hbase.client` packages.

In this class, we first ask the `HBaseConfiguration` class to create a `Configuration` object. It will return a `Configuration` that has read the HBase configuration from the *hbase-site.xml* and *hbase-default.xml* files found on the program's classpath. This `Configura tion` is subsequently used to create instances of `HBaseAdmin` and `HTable`. `HBaseAdmin` is used for administering your HBase cluster, specifically for adding and dropping tables. `HTable` is used to access a specific table. The `Configuration` instance points these classes at the cluster the code is to work against.

From HBase 1.0, there is a new client API that is cleaner and more intuitive. The constructors of `HBaseAdmin` and `HTable` have been deprecated, and clients are discouraged from making explicit reference to these old classes. In their place, clients should use the new `ConnectionFactory` class to create a `Connection` object, then call `getAdmin()` or `getTable()` to retrieve an `Admin` or `Table` instance, as appropriate. Connection management was previously done for the user under the covers, but is now the responsibility of the client. You can find versions of the examples in this chapter updated to use the new API on this book's accompanying website.

To create a table, we need to create an instance of `HBaseAdmin` and then ask it to create the table named `test` with a single column family named `data`. In our example, our table schema is the default. We could use methods on `HTableDescriptor` and `HColumnDescriptor` to change the table schema. Next, the code asserts the table was actually created, and throws an exception if it wasn't.

To operate on a table, we will need an instance of `HTable`, which we construct by passing it our `Configuration` instance and the name of the table. We then create `Put` objects in a loop to insert data into the table. Each `Put` puts a single cell value of `valuen` into a row named `rown` on the column named `data:n`, where `n` is from 1 to 3. The column name is specified in two parts: the column family name, and the column family qualifier. The code makes liberal use of HBase's `Bytes` utility class (found in the `org.apache.hadoop.hbase.util` package) to convert identifiers and values to the byte arrays that HBase requires.

Next, we create a `Get` object to retrieve and print the first row that we added. Then we use a `Scan` object to scan over the table, printing out what we find.

At the end of the program, we clean up by first disabling the table and then deleting it (recall that a table must be disabled before it can be dropped).

Scanners

HBase scanners are like cursors in a traditional database or Java iterators, except—unlike the latter—they have to be closed after use. Scanners return rows in order. Users obtain a scanner on a `Table` object by calling `getScanner()`, passing a configured instance of a `Scan` object as a parameter. In the `Scan` instance, you can pass the row at which to start and stop the scan, which columns in a row to return in the row result, and a filter to run on the server side. The `ResultScanner` interface, which is returned when you call `getScanner()`, is as follows:

```
public interface ResultScanner extends Closeable, Iterable<Result> {
  public Result next() throws IOException;
  public Result[] next(int nbRows) throws IOException;
```

```
    public void close();
  }
```

You can ask for the next row's results, or a number of rows. Scanners will, under the covers, fetch batches of 100 rows at a time, bringing them client-side and returning to the server to fetch the next batch only after the current batch has been exhausted. The number of rows to fetch and cache in this way is determined by the `hbase.cli ent.scanner.caching` configuration option. Alternatively, you can set how many rows to cache on the `Scan` instance itself via the `setCaching()` method.

Higher caching values will enable faster scanning but will eat up more memory in the client. Also, avoid setting the caching so high that the time spent processing the batch client-side exceeds the scanner timeout period. If a client fails to check back with the server before the scanner timeout expires, the server will go ahead and garbage collect resources consumed by the scanner server-side. The default scanner timeout is 60 seconds, and can be changed by setting `hbase.client.scanner.timeout.period`. Clients will see an `UnknownScannerException` if the scanner timeout has expired.

The simplest way to compile the program is to use the Maven POM that comes with the book's example code. Then we can use the `hbase` command followed by the classname to run the program. Here's a sample run:

```
% mvn package
% export HBASE_CLASSPATH=hbase-examples.jar
% hbase ExampleClient
Get: keyvalues={row1/data:1/1414932826551/Put/vlen=6/mvcc=0}
Scan: keyvalues={row1/data:1/1414932826551/Put/vlen=6/mvcc=0}
Scan: keyvalues={row2/data:2/1414932826564/Put/vlen=6/mvcc=0}
Scan: keyvalues={row3/data:3/1414932826566/Put/vlen=6/mvcc=0}
```

Each line of output shows an HBase row, rendered using the `toString()` method from `Result`. The fields are separated by a slash character, and are as follows: the row name, the column name, the cell timestamp, the cell type, the length of the value's byte array (`vlen`), and an internal HBase field (`mvcc`). We'll see later how to get the value from a `Result` object using its `getValue()` method.

MapReduce

HBase classes and utilities in the `org.apache.hadoop.hbase.mapreduce` package facilitate using HBase as a source and/or sink in MapReduce jobs. The `TableInputFor mat` class makes splits on region boundaries so maps are handed a single region to work on. The `TableOutputFormat` will write the result of the reduce into HBase.

The `SimpleRowCounter` class in Example 20-2 (which is a simplified version of `Row Counter` in the HBase `mapreduce` package) runs a map task to count rows using `TableInputFormat`.

Example 20-2. A MapReduce application to count the number of rows in an HBase table

```
public class SimpleRowCounter extends Configured implements Tool {

  static class RowCounterMapper extends TableMapper<ImmutableBytesWritable, Result> {
    public static enum Counters { ROWS }

    @Override
    public void map(ImmutableBytesWritable row, Result value, Context context) {
      context.getCounter(Counters.ROWS).increment(1);
    }
  }

  @Override
  public int run(String[] args) throws Exception {
    if (args.length != 1) {
      System.err.println("Usage: SimpleRowCounter <tablename>");
      return -1;
    }
    String tableName = args[0];
    Scan scan = new Scan();
    scan.setFilter(new FirstKeyOnlyFilter());

    Job job = new Job(getConf(), getClass().getSimpleName());
    job.setJarByClass(getClass());
    TableMapReduceUtil.initTableMapperJob(tableName, scan,
        RowCounterMapper.class, ImmutableBytesWritable.class, Result.class, job);
    job.setNumReduceTasks(0);
    job.setOutputFormatClass(NullOutputFormat.class);
    return job.waitForCompletion(true) ? 0 : 1;
  }

  public static void main(String[] args) throws Exception {
    int exitCode = ToolRunner.run(HBaseConfiguration.create(),
        new SimpleRowCounter(), args);
    System.exit(exitCode);
  }
}
```

The `RowCounterMapper` nested class is a subclass of the HBase `TableMapper` abstract class, a specialization of `org.apache.hadoop.mapreduce.Mapper` that sets the map input types passed by `TableInputFormat`. Input keys are `ImmutableBytesWritable` objects (row keys), and values are `Result` objects (row results from a scan). Since this job counts rows and does not emit any output from the map, we just increment `Counters.ROWS` by 1 for every row we see.

In the `run()` method, we create a scan object that is used to configure the job by invoking the `TableMapReduceUtil.initTableMapJob()` utility method, which, among other things (such as setting the map class to use), sets the input format to `TableInputFormat`.

Notice how we set a filter, an instance of `FirstKeyOnlyFilter`, on the scan. This filter instructs the server to short-circuit when running server-side, populating the `Result` object in the mapper with only the first cell in each row. Since the mapper ignores the cell values, this is a useful optimization.

 You can also find the number of rows in a table by typing `count 'tablename'` in the HBase shell. It's not distributed, though, so for large tables the MapReduce program is preferable.

REST and Thrift

HBase ships with REST and Thrift interfaces. These are useful when the interacting application is written in a language other than Java. In both cases, a Java server hosts an instance of the HBase client brokering REST and Thrift application requests into and out of the HBase cluster. Consult the Reference Guide (*http://hbase.apache.org/book.html*) for information on running the services, and the client interfaces.

Building an Online Query Application

Although HDFS and MapReduce are powerful tools for processing batch operations over large datasets, they do not provide ways to read or write individual records efficiently. In this example, we'll explore using HBase as the tool to fill this gap.

The existing weather dataset described in previous chapters contains observations for tens of thousands of stations over 100 years, and this data is growing without bound. In this example, we will build a simple online (as opposed to batch) interface that allows a user to navigate the different stations and page through their historical temperature observations in time order. We'll build simple command-line Java applications for this, but it's easy to see how the same techniques could be used to build a web application to do the same thing.

For the sake of this example, let us allow that the dataset is massive, that the observations run to the billions, and that the rate at which temperature updates arrive is significant —say, hundreds to thousands of updates per second from around the world and across the whole range of weather stations. Also, let us allow that it is a requirement that the online application must display the most up-to-date observation within a second or so of receipt.

The first size requirement should preclude our use of a simple RDBMS instance and make HBase a candidate store. The second latency requirement rules out plain HDFS. A MapReduce job could build initial indices that allowed random access over all of the observation data, but keeping up this index as the updates arrive is not what HDFS and MapReduce are good at.

Schema Design

In our example, there will be two tables:

stations

> This table holds station data. Let the row key be the `stationid`. Let this table have a column family `info` that acts as a key-value dictionary for station information. Let the dictionary keys be the column names `info:name`, `info:location`, and `info:description`. This table is static, and in this case, the `info` family closely mirrors a typical RDBMS table design.

observations

> This table holds temperature observations. Let the row key be a composite key of `stationid` plus a reverse-order timestamp. Give this table a column family `data` that will contain one column, `airtemp`, with the observed temperature as the column value.

Our choice of schema is derived from knowing the most efficient way we can read from HBase. Rows and columns are stored in increasing lexicographical order. Though there are facilities for secondary indexing and regular expression matching, they come at a performance penalty. It is vital that you understand the most efficient way to query your data in order to choose the most effective setup for storing and accessing.

For the `stations` table, the choice of `stationid` as the key is obvious because we will always access information for a particular station by its ID. The `observations` table, however, uses a composite key that adds the observation timestamp at the end. This will group all observations for a particular station together, and by using a reverse-order timestamp (`Long.MAX_VALUE - timestamp`) and storing it as binary, observations for each station will be ordered with most recent observation first.

 We rely on the fact that station IDs are a fixed length. In some cases, you will need to zero-pad number components so row keys sort properly. Otherwise, you will run into the issue where 10 sorts before 2, say, when only the byte order is considered (02 sorts before 10).

Also, if your keys are integers, use a binary representation rather than persisting the string version of a number. The former consumes less space.

In the shell, define the tables as follows:

```
hbase(main):001:0> create 'stations', {NAME => 'info'}
0 row(s) in 0.9600 seconds
```

```
hbase(main):002:0> create 'observations', {NAME => 'data'}
0 row(s) in 0.1770 seconds
```

Wide Tables

All access in HBase is via primary key, so the key design should lend itself to how the data is going to be queried. One thing to keep in mind when designing schemas is that a defining attribute of column(-family)-oriented stores (*http://en.wikipedia.org/wiki/ Column-oriented_DBMS*), such as HBase, is the ability to host wide and sparsely populated tables at no incurred cost.[4]

There is no native database join facility in HBase, but wide tables can make it so that there is no need for database joins to pull from secondary or tertiary tables. A wide row can sometimes be made to hold all data that pertains to a particular primary key.

Loading Data

There are a relatively small number of stations, so their static data is easily inserted using any of the available interfaces. The example code includes a Java application for doing this, which is run as follows:

```
% hbase HBaseStationImporter input/ncdc/metadata/stations-fixed-width.txt
```

However, let's assume that there are billions of individual observations to be loaded. This kind of import is normally an extremely complex and long-running database operation, but MapReduce and HBase's distribution model allow us to make full use of the cluster. We'll copy the raw input data onto HDFS, and then run a MapReduce job that can read the input and write to HBase.

Example 20-3 shows an example MapReduce job that imports observations to HBase from the same input files used in the previous chapters' examples.

Example 20-3. A MapReduce application to import temperature data from HDFS into an HBase table

```
public class HBaseTemperatureImporter extends Configured implements Tool {

  static class HBaseTemperatureMapper<K> extends Mapper<LongWritable, Text, K, Put> {
    private NcdcRecordParser parser = new NcdcRecordParser();

    @Override
    public void map(LongWritable key, Text value, Context context) throws
        IOException, InterruptedException {
      parser.parse(value.toString());
      if (parser.isValidTemperature()) {
```

---

4. See Daniel J. Abadi, "Column-Stores for Wide and Sparse Data," (*http://bit.ly/column-stores*) January 2007.

```
          byte[] rowKey = RowKeyConverter.makeObservationRowKey(parser.getStationId(),
              parser.getObservationDate().getTime());
          Put p = new Put(rowKey);
          p.add(HBaseTemperatureQuery.DATA_COLUMNFAMILY,
              HBaseTemperatureQuery.AIRTEMP_QUALIFIER,
              Bytes.toBytes(parser.getAirTemperature()));
          context.write(null, p);
        }
      }
    }

    @Override
    public int run(String[] args) throws Exception {
      if (args.length != 1) {
        System.err.println("Usage: HBaseTemperatureImporter <input>");
        return -1;
      }
      Job job = new Job(getConf(), getClass().getSimpleName());
      job.setJarByClass(getClass());
      FileInputFormat.addInputPath(job, new Path(args[0]));
      job.getConfiguration().set(TableOutputFormat.OUTPUT_TABLE, "observations");
      job.setMapperClass(HBaseTemperatureMapper.class);
      job.setNumReduceTasks(0);
      job.setOutputFormatClass(TableOutputFormat.class);
      return job.waitForCompletion(true) ? 0 : 1;
    }

    public static void main(String[] args) throws Exception {
      int exitCode = ToolRunner.run(HBaseConfiguration.create(),
          new HBaseTemperatureImporter(), args);
      System.exit(exitCode);
    }
  }
```

HBaseTemperatureImporter has a nested class named HBaseTemperatureMapper that is like the MaxTemperatureMapper class from Chapter 6. The outer class implements Tool and does the setup to launch the map-only job. HBaseTemperatureMapper takes the same input as MaxTemperatureMapper and does the same parsing—using the NcdcRecordParser introduced in Chapter 6—to check for valid temperatures. But rather than writing valid temperatures to the output context, as MaxTemperatureMapper does, it creates a Put object to add those temperatures to the observations HBase table, in the data:airtemp column. (We are using static constants for data and airtemp, imported from the HBaseTemperatureQuery class described later.)

The row key for each observation is created in the makeObservationRowKey() method on RowKeyConverter from the station ID and observation time:

```
    public class RowKeyConverter {

      private static final int STATION_ID_LENGTH = 12;
```

```
/**
 * @return A row key whose format is: <station_id> <reverse_order_timestamp>
 */
public static byte[] makeObservationRowKey(String stationId,
    long observationTime) {
  byte[] row = new byte[STATION_ID_LENGTH + Bytes.SIZEOF_LONG];
  Bytes.putBytes(row, 0, Bytes.toBytes(stationId), 0, STATION_ID_LENGTH);
  long reverseOrderTimestamp = Long.MAX_VALUE - observationTime;
  Bytes.putLong(row, STATION_ID_LENGTH, reverseOrderTimestamp);
  return row;
}
}
```

The conversion takes advantage of the fact that the station ID is a fixed-length ASCII string. Like in the earlier example, we use HBase's `Bytes` class for converting between byte arrays and common Java types. The `Bytes.SIZEOF_LONG` constant is used for calculating the size of the timestamp portion of the row key byte array. The `putBytes()` and `putLong()` methods are used to fill the station ID and timestamp portions of the key at the relevant offsets in the byte array.

The job is configured in the `run()` method to use HBase's `TableOutputFormat`. The table to write to must be specified by setting the `TableOutputFormat.OUTPUT_TABLE` property in the job configuration.

It's convenient to use `TableOutputFormat` since it manages the creation of an `HTable` instance for us, which otherwise we would do in the mapper's `setup()` method (along with a call to `close()` in the `cleanup()` method). `TableOutputFormat` also disables the `HTable` auto-flush feature, so that calls to `put()` are buffered for greater efficiency.

The example code includes a class called `HBaseTemperatureDirectImporter` to demonstrate how to use an `HTable` directly from a MapReduce program. We can run the program with the following:

```
% hbase HBaseTemperatureImporter input/ncdc/all
```

Load distribution

Watch for the phenomenon where an import walks in lockstep through the table, with all clients in concert pounding one of the table's regions (and thus, a single node), then moving on to the next, and so on, rather than evenly distributing the load over all regions. This is usually brought on by some interaction between sorted input and how the splitter works. Randomizing the ordering of your row keys prior to insertion may help. In our example, given the distribution of `stationid` values and how `TextInput Format` makes splits, the upload should be sufficiently distributed.

If a table is new, it will have only one region, and all updates will be to this single region until it splits. This will happen even if row keys are randomly distributed. This startup phenomenon means uploads run slowly at first, until there are sufficient regions distributed so all cluster members are able to participate in the uploads. Do not confuse this phenomenon with that noted in the previous paragraph.

Both of these problems can be avoided by using bulk loads, discussed next.

Bulk load

HBase has an efficient facility for bulk loading HBase by writing its internal data format directly into the filesystem from MapReduce. Going this route, it's possible to load an HBase instance at rates that are an order of magnitude or more beyond those attainable by writing via the HBase client API.

Bulk loading is a two-step process. The first step uses `HFileOutputFormat2` to write HFiles to an HDFS directory using a MapReduce job. Since rows have to be written in order, the job must perform a total sort (see "Total Sort" on page 259) of the row keys. The `configureIncrementalLoad()` method of `HFileOutputFormat2` does all the necessary configuration for you.

The second step of the bulk load involves moving the HFiles from HDFS into an existing HBase table. The table can be live during this process. The example code includes a class called `HBaseTemperatureBulkImporter` for loading the observation data using a bulk load.

Online Queries

To implement the online query application, we will use the HBase Java API directly. Here it becomes clear how important your choice of schema and storage format is.

Station queries

The simplest query will be to get the static station information. This is a single row lookup, performed using a `get()` operation. This type of query is simple in a traditional database, but HBase gives you additional control and flexibility. Using the `info` family as a key-value dictionary (column names as keys, column values as values), the code from `HBaseStationQuery` looks like this:

```
static final byte[] INFO_COLUMNFAMILY = Bytes.toBytes("info");
static final byte[] NAME_QUALIFIER = Bytes.toBytes("name");
static final byte[] LOCATION_QUALIFIER = Bytes.toBytes("location");
static final byte[] DESCRIPTION_QUALIFIER = Bytes.toBytes("description");

public Map<String, String> getStationInfo(HTable table, String stationId)
    throws IOException {
  Get get = new Get(Bytes.toBytes(stationId));
  get.addFamily(INFO_COLUMNFAMILY);
  Result res = table.get(get);
  if (res == null) {
    return null;
```

```
    }
    Map<String, String> resultMap = new LinkedHashMap<String, String>();
    resultMap.put("name", getValue(res, INFO_COLUMNFAMILY, NAME_QUALIFIER));
    resultMap.put("location", getValue(res, INFO_COLUMNFAMILY,
        LOCATION_QUALIFIER));
    resultMap.put("description", getValue(res, INFO_COLUMNFAMILY,
        DESCRIPTION_QUALIFIER));
    return resultMap;
  }

  private static String getValue(Result res, byte[] cf, byte[] qualifier) {
    byte[] value = res.getValue(cf, qualifier);
    return value == null? "": Bytes.toString(value);
  }
```

In this example, getStationInfo() takes an HTable instance and a station ID. To get the station info, we use get(), passing a Get instance configured to retrieve all the column values for the row identified by the station ID in the defined column family, INFO_COLUMNFAMILY.

The get() results are returned in a Result. It contains the row, and you can fetch cell values by stipulating the column cell you want. The getStationInfo() method converts the Result into a more friendly Map of String keys and values.

We can already see how there is a need for utility functions when using HBase. There are an increasing number of abstractions being built atop HBase to deal with this low-level interaction, but it's important to understand how this works and how storage choices make a difference.

One of the strengths of HBase over a relational database is that you don't have to specify all the columns up front. So, if each station now has at least these three attributes but there are hundreds of optional ones, in the future we can just insert them without modifying the schema. (Our application's reading and writing code would, of course, need to be changed. The example code might change in this case to looping through Result rather than grabbing each value explicitly.)

Here's an example of a station query:

```
% hbase HBaseStationQuery 011990-99999
name     SIHCCAJAVRI
location         (unknown)
description      (unknown)
```

Observation queries

Queries of the observations table take the form of a station ID, a start time, and a maximum number of rows to return. Since the rows are stored in reverse chronological order by station, queries will return observations that preceded the start time. The getStationObservations() method in Example 20-4 uses an HBase scanner to iterate over the table rows. It returns a NavigableMap<Long, Integer>, where the key is the timestamp and the value is the temperature. Since the map sorts by key in ascending order, its entries are in chronological order.

Example 20-4. An application for retrieving a range of rows of weather station observations from an HBase table

```
public class HBaseTemperatureQuery extends Configured implements Tool {
  static final byte[] DATA_COLUMNFAMILY = Bytes.toBytes("data");
  static final byte[] AIRTEMP_QUALIFIER = Bytes.toBytes("airtemp");

  public NavigableMap<Long, Integer> getStationObservations(HTable table,
      String stationId, long maxStamp, int maxCount) throws IOException {
    byte[] startRow = RowKeyConverter.makeObservationRowKey(stationId, maxStamp);
    NavigableMap<Long, Integer> resultMap = new TreeMap<Long, Integer>();
    Scan scan = new Scan(startRow);
    scan.addColumn(DATA_COLUMNFAMILY, AIRTEMP_QUALIFIER);
    ResultScanner scanner = table.getScanner(scan);
    try {
      Result res;
      int count = 0;
      while ((res = scanner.next()) != null && count++ < maxCount) {
        byte[] row = res.getRow();
        byte[] value = res.getValue(DATA_COLUMNFAMILY, AIRTEMP_QUALIFIER);
        Long stamp = Long.MAX_VALUE -
            Bytes.toLong(row, row.length - Bytes.SIZEOF_LONG, Bytes.SIZEOF_LONG);
        Integer temp = Bytes.toInt(value);
        resultMap.put(stamp, temp);
      }
    } finally {
      scanner.close();
    }
    return resultMap;
  }

  public int run(String[] args) throws IOException {
    if (args.length != 1) {
      System.err.println("Usage: HBaseTemperatureQuery <station_id>");
      return -1;
    }

    HTable table = new HTable(HBaseConfiguration.create(getConf()), "observations");
    try {
      NavigableMap<Long, Integer> observations =
          getStationObservations(table, args[0], Long.MAX_VALUE, 10).descendingMap();
      for (Map.Entry<Long, Integer> observation : observations.entrySet()) {
        // Print the date, time, and temperature
        System.out.printf("%1$tF %1$tR\t%2$s\n", observation.getKey(),
            observation.getValue());
      }
      return 0;
    } finally {
```

```
      table.close();
    }
  }

  public static void main(String[] args) throws Exception {
    int exitCode = ToolRunner.run(HBaseConfiguration.create(),
        new HBaseTemperatureQuery(), args);
    System.exit(exitCode);
  }
}
```

The run() method calls getStationObservations(), asking for the 10 most recent observations, which it turns back into descending order by calling descendingMap(). The observations are formatted and printed to the console (remember that the temperatures are in tenths of a degree). For example:

```
% hbase HBaseTemperatureQuery 011990-99999
1902-12-31 20:00    -106
1902-12-31 13:00    -83
1902-12-30 20:00    -78
1902-12-30 13:00    -100
1902-12-29 20:00    -128
1902-12-29 13:00    -111
1902-12-29 06:00    -111
1902-12-28 20:00    -117
1902-12-28 13:00    -61
1902-12-27 20:00    -22
```

The advantage of storing timestamps in reverse chronological order is that it lets us get the newest observations, which is often what we want in online applications. If the observations were stored with the actual timestamps, we would be able to get only the oldest observations for a given offset and limit efficiently. Getting the newest would mean getting all of the rows and then grabbing the newest off the end. It's much more efficient to get the first *n* rows, then exit the scanner (this is sometimes called an "early-out" scenario).

 HBase 0.98 added the ability to do reverse scans, which means it is now possible to store observations in chronological order and scan backward from a given starting row. Reverse scans are a few percent slower than forward scans. To reverse a scan, call setReversed(true) on the Scan object before starting the scan.

HBase Versus RDBMS

HBase and other column-oriented databases are often compared to more traditional and popular relational databases, or RDBMSs. Although they differ dramatically in their implementations and in what they set out to accomplish, the fact that they are potential solutions to the same problems means that despite their enormous differences, the comparison is a fair one to make.

As described previously, HBase is a distributed, column-oriented data storage system. It picks up where Hadoop left off by providing random reads and writes on top of HDFS. It has been designed from the ground up with a focus on scale in every direction: tall in numbers of rows (billions), wide in numbers of columns (millions), and able to be horizontally partitioned and replicated across thousands of commodity nodes automatically. The table schemas mirror the physical storage, creating a system for efficient data structure serialization, storage, and retrieval. The burden is on the application developer to make use of this storage and retrieval in the right way.

Strictly speaking, an RDBMS is a database that follows Codd's 12 rules (*http://en.wiki pedia.org/wiki/Codd%27s_12_rules*). Typical RDBMSs are fixed-schema, row-oriented databases with ACID properties and a sophisticated SQL query engine. The emphasis is on strong consistency, referential integrity, abstraction from the physical layer, and complex queries through the SQL language. You can easily create secondary indexes; perform complex inner and outer joins; and count, sum, sort, group, and page your data across a number of tables, rows, and columns.

For a majority of small- to medium-volume applications, there is no substitute for the ease of use, flexibility, maturity, and powerful feature set of available open source RDBMS solutions such as MySQL and PostgreSQL. However, if you need to scale up in terms of dataset size, read/write concurrency, or both, you'll soon find that the conveniences of an RDBMS come at an enormous performance penalty and make distribution inherently difficult. The scaling of an RDBMS usually involves breaking Codd's rules, loosening ACID restrictions, forgetting conventional DBA wisdom, and, on the way, losing most of the desirable properties that made relational databases so convenient in the first place.

Successful Service

Here is a synopsis of how the typical RDBMS scaling story runs. The following list presumes a successful growing service:

Initial public launch
> Move from local workstation to a shared, remotely hosted MySQL instance with a well-defined schema.

Service becomes more popular; too many reads hitting the database
> Add memcached to cache common queries. Reads are now no longer strictly ACID; cached data must expire.

Service continues to grow in popularity; too many writes hitting the database
> Scale MySQL vertically by buying a beefed-up server with 16 cores, 128 GB of RAM, and banks of 15k RPM hard drives. Costly.

New features increase query complexity; now we have too many joins
> Denormalize your data to reduce joins. (That's not what they taught me in DBA school!)

Rising popularity swamps the server; things are too slow
> Stop doing any server-side computations.

Some queries are still too slow
> Periodically prematerialize the most complex queries, and try to stop joining in most cases.

Reads are OK, but writes are getting slower and slower
> Drop secondary indexes and triggers (no indexes?).

At this point, there are no clear solutions for how to solve your scaling problems. In any case, you'll need to begin to scale horizontally. You can attempt to build some type of partitioning on your largest tables, or look into some of the commercial solutions that provide multiple master capabilities.

Countless applications, businesses, and websites have successfully achieved scalable, fault-tolerant, and distributed data systems built on top of RDBMSs and are likely using many of the previous strategies. But what you end up with is something that is no longer a true RDBMS, sacrificing features and conveniences for compromises and complexities. Any form of slave replication or external caching introduces weak consistency into your now denormalized data. The inefficiency of joins and secondary indexes means almost all queries become primary key lookups. A multiwriter setup likely means no real joins at all, and distributed transactions are a nightmare. There's now an incredibly complex network topology to manage with an entirely separate cluster for caching. Even with this system and the compromises made, you will still worry about your primary master crashing and the daunting possibility of having 10 times the data and 10 times the load in a few months.

HBase

Enter HBase, which has the following characteristics:

No real indexes
> Rows are stored sequentially, as are the columns within each row. Therefore, no issues with index bloat, and insert performance is independent of table size.

Automatic partitioning
> As your tables grow, they will automatically be split into regions and distributed across all available nodes.

Scale linearly and automatically with new nodes
> Add a node, point it to the existing cluster, and run the regionserver. Regions will automatically rebalance, and load will spread evenly.

Commodity hardware

Clusters are built on $1,000–$5,000 nodes rather than $50,000 nodes. RDBMSs are I/O hungry, requiring more costly hardware.

Fault tolerance

Lots of nodes means each is relatively insignificant. No need to worry about individual node downtime.

Batch processing

MapReduce integration allows fully parallel, distributed jobs against your data with locality awareness.

If you stay up at night worrying about your database (uptime, scale, or speed), you should seriously consider making a jump from the RDBMS world to HBase. Use a solution that was intended to scale rather than a solution based on stripping down and throwing money at what used to work. With HBase, the software is free, the hardware is cheap, and the distribution is intrinsic.

Praxis

In this section, we discuss some of the common issues users run into when running an HBase cluster under load.

HDFS

HBase's use of HDFS is very different from how it's used by MapReduce. In MapReduce, generally, HDFS files are opened with their content streamed through a map task and then closed. In HBase, datafiles are opened on cluster startup and kept open so that we avoid paying the costs associated with opening files on each access. Because of this, HBase tends to see issues not normally encountered by MapReduce clients:

Running out of file descriptors

Because we keep files open, on a loaded cluster it doesn't take long before we run into system- and Hadoop-imposed limits. For instance, say we have a cluster that has three nodes, each running an instance of a datanode and a regionserver, and we're running an upload into a table that is currently at 100 regions and 10 column families. Allow that each column family has on average two flush files. Doing the math, we can have $100 \times 10 \times 2$, or 2,000, files open at any one time. Add to this total other miscellaneous descriptors consumed by outstanding scanners and Java libraries. Each open file consumes at least one descriptor over on the remote datanode.

The default limit on the number of file descriptors per process is 1,024. When we exceed the filesystem *ulimit*, we'll see the complaint about "Too many open files" in logs, but often we'll first see indeterminate behavior in HBase. The fix requires increasing the file descriptor ulimit count; 10,240 is a common setting. Consult the HBase Reference Guide (*http://hbase.apache.org/book.html*) for how to increase the ulimit on your cluster.

Running out of datanode threads

Similarly, the Hadoop datanode has an upper bound on the number of threads it can run at any one time. Hadoop 1 had a low default of 256 for this setting (`dfs.da tanode.max.xcievers`), which would cause HBase to behave erratically. Hadoop 2 increased the default to 4,096, so you are much less likely to see a problem for recent versions of HBase (which only run on Hadoop 2 and later). You can change the setting by configuring `dfs.datanode.max.transfer.threads` (the new name for this property) in *hdfs-site.xml*.

UI

HBase runs a web server on the master to present a view on the state of your running cluster. By default, it listens on port 60010. The master UI displays a list of basic attributes such as software versions, cluster load, request rates, lists of cluster tables, and participating regionservers. Click on a regionserver in the master UI, and you are taken to the web server running on the individual regionserver. It lists the regions this server is carrying and basic metrics such as resources consumed and request rates.

Metrics

Hadoop has a metrics system that can be used to emit vitals over a period to a *context* (this is covered in "Metrics and JMX" on page 331). Enabling Hadoop metrics, and in particular tying them to Ganglia or emitting them via JMX, will give you views on what is happening on your cluster, both currently and in the recent past. HBase also adds metrics of its own—request rates, counts of vitals, resources used. See the file *hadoop-metrics2-hbase.properties* under the HBase *conf* directory.

Counters

At StumbleUpon (*https://www.stumbleupon.com/*), the first production feature deployed on HBase was keeping counters for the *stumbleupon.com* frontend. Counters were previously kept in MySQL, but the rate of change was such that drops were frequent, and the load imposed by the counter writes was such that web designers self imposed limits on what was counted. Using the `incrementColumnValue()` method on `HTable`, counters can be incremented many thousands of times a second.

Further Reading

In this chapter, we only scratched the surface of what's possible with HBase. For more in-depth information, consult the project's Reference Guide (*http://hbase.apache.org/*

book.html), *HBase: The Definitive Guide* by Lars George (O'Reilly, 2011, new edition forthcoming), or *HBase in Action (http://www.manning.com/dimidukkhurana/)* by Nick Dimiduk and Amandeep Khurana (Manning, 2012).

ZooKeeper

So far in this book, we have been studying large-scale data processing. This chapter is different: it is about building general distributed applications using Hadoop's distributed coordination service, called ZooKeeper.

Writing distributed applications is hard. It's hard primarily because of partial failure. When a message is sent across the network between two nodes and the network fails, the sender does not know whether the receiver got the message. It may have gotten through before the network failed, or it may not have. Or perhaps the receiver's process died. The only way that the sender can find out what happened is to reconnect to the receiver and ask it. This is partial failure: when we don't even know if an operation failed.

ZooKeeper can't make partial failures go away, since they are intrinsic to distributed systems. It certainly does not hide partial failures, either.[1] But what ZooKeeper does do is give you a set of tools to build distributed applications that can safely handle partial failures.

ZooKeeper also has the following characteristics:

ZooKeeper is simple

> ZooKeeper is, at its core, a stripped-down filesystem that exposes a few simple operations and some extra abstractions, such as ordering and notifications.

ZooKeeper is expressive

> The ZooKeeper primitives are a rich set of building blocks that can be used to build a large class of coordination data structures and protocols. Examples include distributed queues, distributed locks, and leader election among a group of peers.

---

1. This is the message of Jim Waldo et al. in "A Note on Distributed Computing" (*http://www.eecs.harvard.edu/~waldo/Readings/waldo-94.pdf*) (Sun Microsystems, November 1994). Distributed programming is fundamentally different from local programming, and the differences cannot simply be papered over.

ZooKeeper is highly available

> ZooKeeper runs on a collection of machines and is designed to be highly available, so applications can depend on it. ZooKeeper can help you avoid introducing single points of failure into your system, so you can build a reliable application.

ZooKeeper facilitates loosely coupled interactions

> ZooKeeper interactions support participants that do not need to know about one another. For example, ZooKeeper can be used as a rendezvous mechanism so that processes that otherwise don't know of each other's existence (or network details) can discover and interact with one another. Coordinating parties may not even be contemporaneous, since one process may leave a message in ZooKeeper that is read by another after the first has shut down.

ZooKeeper is a library

> ZooKeeper provides an open source, shared repository of implementations and recipes of common coordination patterns. Individual programmers are spared the burden of writing common protocols themselves (which is often difficult to get right). Over time, the community can add to and improve the libraries, which is to everyone's benefit.

ZooKeeper is highly performant, too. At Yahoo!, where it was created, the throughput for a ZooKeeper cluster has been benchmarked at over 10,000 operations per second for write-dominant workloads generated by hundreds of clients. For workloads where reads dominate, which is the norm, the throughput is several times higher.[2]

Installing and Running ZooKeeper

When trying out ZooKeeper for the first time, it's simplest to run it in standalone mode with a single ZooKeeper server. You can do this on a development machine, for example. ZooKeeper requires Java to run, so make sure you have it installed first.

Download a stable release of ZooKeeper from the Apache ZooKeeper releases page (*http://zookeeper.apache.org/releases.html*), and unpack the tarball in a suitable location:

```
% tar xzf zookeeper-x.y.z.tar.gz
```

ZooKeeper provides a few binaries to run and interact with the service, and it's convenient to put the directory containing the binaries on your command-line path:

```
% export ZOOKEEPER_HOME=~/sw/zookeeper-x.y.z
% export PATH=$PATH:$ZOOKEEPER_HOME/bin
```

---

2. Detailed benchmarks are available in the excellent paper "ZooKeeper: Wait-free coordination for Internet-scale systems," (*http://bit.ly/wait-free_coordination*) by Patrick Hunt et al. (USENIX Annual Technology Conference, 2010).

Before running the ZooKeeper service, we need to set up a configuration file. The configuration file is conventionally called *zoo.cfg* and placed in the *conf* subdirectory (although you can also place it in */etc/zookeeper*, or in the directory defined by the ZOOCFGDIR environment variable, if set). Here's an example:

```
tickTime=2000
dataDir=/Users/tom/zookeeper
clientPort=2181
```

This is a standard Java properties file, and the three properties defined in this example are the minimum required for running ZooKeeper in standalone mode. Briefly, tickTime is the basic time unit in ZooKeeper (specified in milliseconds), dataDir is the local filesystem location where ZooKeeper stores persistent data, and clientPort is the port ZooKeeper listens on for client connections (2181 is a common choice). You should change dataDir to an appropriate setting for your system.

With a suitable configuration defined, we are now ready to start a local ZooKeeper server:

```
% zkServer.sh start
```

To check whether ZooKeeper is running, send the ruok command ("Are you OK?") to the client port using nc (telnet works, too):

```
% echo ruok | nc localhost 2181
imok
```

That's ZooKeeper saying, "I'm OK." Table 21-1 lists the commands, known as the "four-letter words," for managing ZooKeeper.

Table 21-1. ZooKeeper commands: the four-letter words

Category	Command	Description
Server status	ruok	Prints imok if the server is running and not in an error state.
	conf	Prints the server configuration (from *zoo.cfg*).
	envi	Prints the server environment, including ZooKeeper version, Java version, and other system properties.
	srvr	Prints server statistics, including latency statistics, the number of znodes, and the server mode (standalone, leader, or follower).
	stat	Prints server statistics and connected clients.
	srst	Resets server statistics.
	isro	Shows whether the server is in read-only (ro) mode (due to a network partition) or read/write mode (rw).
Client connections	dump	Lists all the sessions and ephemeral znodes for the ensemble. You must connect to the leader (see srvr) for this command.
	cons	Lists connection statistics for all the server's clients.
	crst	Resets connection statistics.

Category	Command	Description
Watches	wchs	Lists summary information for the server's watches.
	wchc	Lists all the server's watches by connection. Caution: may impact server performance for a large number of watches.
	wchp	Lists all the server's watches by znode path. Caution: may impact server performance for a large number of watches.
Monitoring	mntr	Lists server statistics in Java properties format, suitable as a source for monitoring systems such as Ganglia and Nagios.

In addition to the mntr command, ZooKeeper exposes statistics via JMX. For more details, see the ZooKeeper documentation (*http://zookeeper.apache.org/*). There are also monitoring tools and recipes in the *src/contrib* directory of the distribution.

From version 3.5.0 of ZooKeeper, there is an inbuilt web server for providing the same information as the four-letter words. Visit *http://localhost:8080/commands* for a list of commands.

An Example

Imagine a group of servers that provide some service to clients. We want clients to be able to locate one of the servers so they can use the service. One of the challenges is maintaining the list of servers in the group.

The membership list clearly cannot be stored on a single node in the network, as the failure of that node would mean the failure of the whole system (we would like the list to be highly available). Suppose for a moment that we had a robust way of storing the list. We would still have the problem of how to remove a server from the list if it failed. Some process needs to be responsible for removing failed servers, but note that it can't be the servers themselves, because they are no longer running!

What we are describing is not a passive distributed data structure, but an active one, and one that can change the state of an entry when some external event occurs. Zoo-Keeper provides this service, so let's see how to build this group membership application (as it is known) with it.

Group Membership in ZooKeeper

One way of understanding ZooKeeper is to think of it as providing a high-availability filesystem. It doesn't have files and directories, but a unified concept of a node, called a *znode*, that acts both as a container of data (like a file) and a container of other znodes (like a directory). Znodes form a hierarchical namespace, and a natural way to build a membership list is to create a parent znode with the name of the group and child znodes with the names of the group members (servers). This is shown in Figure 21-1.

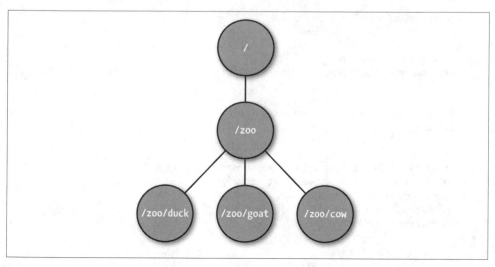

Figure 21-1. ZooKeeper znodes

In this example we won't store data in any of the znodes, but in a real application you could imagine storing data about the members, such as hostnames, in their znodes.

Creating the Group

Let's introduce ZooKeeper's Java API by writing a program to create a znode for the group, which is */zoo* in Example 21-1.

Example 21-1. A program to create a znode representing a group in ZooKeeper

```java
public class CreateGroup implements Watcher {

  private static final int SESSION_TIMEOUT = 5000;

  private ZooKeeper zk;
  private CountDownLatch connectedSignal = new CountDownLatch(1);

  public void connect(String hosts) throws IOException, InterruptedException {
    zk = new ZooKeeper(hosts, SESSION_TIMEOUT, this);
    connectedSignal.await();
  }

  @Override
  public void process(WatchedEvent event) { // Watcher interface
    if (event.getState() == KeeperState.SyncConnected) {
      connectedSignal.countDown();
    }
  }

  public void create(String groupName) throws KeeperException,
```

```
    InterruptedException {
  String path = "/" + groupName;
  String createdPath = zk.create(path, null/*data*/, Ids.OPEN_ACL_UNSAFE,
      CreateMode.PERSISTENT);
  System.out.println("Created " + createdPath);
}

public void close() throws InterruptedException {
  zk.close();
}

public static void main(String[] args) throws Exception {
  CreateGroup createGroup = new CreateGroup();
  createGroup.connect(args[0]);
  createGroup.create(args[1]);
  createGroup.close();
}
}
```

When the main() method is run, it creates a CreateGroup instance and then calls its connect() method. This method instantiates a new ZooKeeper object, which is the central class of the client API and the one that maintains the connection between the client and the ZooKeeper service. The constructor takes three arguments: the first is the host address (and optional port, which defaults to 2181) of the ZooKeeper service;[3] the second is the session timeout in milliseconds (which we set to 5 seconds), explained in more detail later; and the third is an instance of a Watcher object. The Watcher object receives callbacks from ZooKeeper to inform it of various events. In this scenario, CreateGroup is a Watcher, so we pass this to the ZooKeeper constructor.

When a ZooKeeper instance is created, it starts a thread to connect to the ZooKeeper service. The call to the constructor returns immediately, so it is important to wait for the connection to be established before using the ZooKeeper object. We make use of Java's CountDownLatch class (in the java.util.concurrent package) to block until the ZooKeeper instance is ready. This is where the Watcher comes in. The Watcher interface has a single method:

```
public void process(WatchedEvent event);
```

When the client has connected to ZooKeeper, the Watcher receives a call to its process() method with an event indicating that it has connected. On receiving a connection event (represented by the Watcher.Event.KeeperState enum, with value SyncConnected), we decrement the counter in the CountDownLatch, using its countDown() method. The latch was created with a count of one, representing the number of events that need to

---

3. For a replicated ZooKeeper service, this parameter is the comma-separated list of servers (host and optional port) in the ensemble.

occur before it releases all waiting threads. After calling `countDown()` once, the counter reaches zero and the `await()` method returns.

The `connect()` method has now returned, and the next method to be invoked on the `CreateGroup` is the `create()` method. In this method, we create a new ZooKeeper znode using the `create()` method on the `ZooKeeper` instance. The arguments it takes are the path (represented by a string), the contents of the znode (a byte array `null` here), an access control list (or ACL for short, which here is completely open, allowing any client to read from or write to the znode), and the nature of the znode to be created.

Znodes may be ephemeral or persistent. An *ephemeral* znode will be deleted by the ZooKeeper service when the client that created it disconnects, either explicitly or because the client terminates for whatever reason. A *persistent* znode, on the other hand, is not deleted when the client disconnects. We want the znode representing a group to live longer than the lifetime of the program that creates it, so we create a persistent znode.

The return value of the `create()` method is the path that was created by ZooKeeper. We use it to print a message that the path was successfully created. We will see how the path returned by `create()` may differ from the one passed into the method when we look at sequential znodes.

To see the program in action, we need to have ZooKeeper running on the local machine, and then we can use the following:

```
% export CLASSPATH=ch21-zk/target/classes/:$ZOOKEEPER_HOME/*:\
  $ZOOKEEPER_HOME/lib/*:$ZOOKEEPER_HOME/conf
% java CreateGroup localhost zoo
Created /zoo
```

Joining a Group

The next part of the application is a program to register a member in a group. Each member will run as a program and join a group. When the program exits, it should be removed from the group, which we can do by creating an ephemeral znode that represents it in the ZooKeeper namespace.

The `JoinGroup` program implements this idea, and its listing is in Example 21-2. The logic for creating and connecting to a `ZooKeeper` instance has been refactored into a base class, `ConnectionWatcher`, and appears in Example 21-3.

Example 21-2. A program that joins a group

```
public class JoinGroup extends ConnectionWatcher {

  public void join(String groupName, String memberName) throws KeeperException,
      InterruptedException {
    String path = "/" + groupName + "/" + memberName;
    String createdPath = zk.create(path, null/*data*/, Ids.OPEN_ACL_UNSAFE,
```

```
    CreateMode.EPHEMERAL);
    System.out.println("Created " + createdPath);
  }

  public static void main(String[] args) throws Exception {
    JoinGroup joinGroup = new JoinGroup();
    joinGroup.connect(args[0]);
    joinGroup.join(args[1], args[2]);

    // stay alive until process is killed or thread is interrupted
    Thread.sleep(Long.MAX_VALUE);
  }
}
```

Example 21-3. A helper class that waits for the ZooKeeper connection to be established

```
public class ConnectionWatcher implements Watcher {

  private static final int SESSION_TIMEOUT = 5000;

  protected ZooKeeper zk;
  private CountDownLatch connectedSignal = new CountDownLatch(1);

  public void connect(String hosts) throws IOException, InterruptedException {
    zk = new ZooKeeper(hosts, SESSION_TIMEOUT, this);
    connectedSignal.await();
  }

  @Override
  public void process(WatchedEvent event) {
    if (event.getState() == KeeperState.SyncConnected) {
      connectedSignal.countDown();
    }
  }

  public void close() throws InterruptedException {
    zk.close();
  }
}
```

The code for JoinGroup is very similar to CreateGroup. It creates an ephemeral znode as a child of the group znode in its join() method, then simulates doing work of some kind by sleeping until the process is forcibly terminated. Later, you will see that upon termination, the ephemeral znode is removed by ZooKeeper.

Listing Members in a Group

Now we need a program to find the members in a group (see Example 21-4).

Example 21-4. A program to list the members in a group

```java
public class ListGroup extends ConnectionWatcher {

  public void list(String groupName) throws KeeperException,
      InterruptedException {
    String path = "/" + groupName;

    try {
      List<String> children = zk.getChildren(path, false);
      if (children.isEmpty()) {
        System.out.printf("No members in group %s\n", groupName);
        System.exit(1);
      }
      for (String child : children) {
        System.out.println(child);
      }
    } catch (KeeperException.NoNodeException e) {
      System.out.printf("Group %s does not exist\n", groupName);
      System.exit(1);
    }
  }

  public static void main(String[] args) throws Exception {
    ListGroup listGroup = new ListGroup();
    listGroup.connect(args[0]);
    listGroup.list(args[1]);
    listGroup.close();
  }
}
```

In the `list()` method, we call `getChildren()` with a znode path and a watch flag to retrieve a list of child paths for the znode, which we print out. Placing a watch on a znode causes the registered `Watcher` to be triggered if the znode changes state. Although we're not using it here, watching a znode's children would permit a program to get notifications of members joining or leaving the group, or of the group being deleted.

We catch `KeeperException.NoNodeException`, which is thrown in the case when the group's znode does not exist.

Let's see `ListGroup` in action. As expected, the zoo group is empty, since we haven't added any members yet:

```
% java ListGroup localhost zoo
No members in group zoo
```

We can use `JoinGroup` to add some members. We launch them as background processes, since they don't terminate on their own (due to the sleep statement):

```
% java JoinGroup localhost zoo duck &
% java JoinGroup localhost zoo cow &
```

```
% java JoinGroup localhost zoo goat &
% goat_pid=$!
```

The last line saves the process ID of the Java process running the program that adds goat as a member. We need to remember the ID so that we can kill the process in a moment, after checking the members:

```
% java ListGroup localhost zoo
goat
duck
cow
```

To remove a member, we kill its process:

```
% kill $goat_pid
```

And a few seconds later, it has disappeared from the group because the process's Zoo-Keeper session has terminated (the timeout was set to 5 seconds) and its associated ephemeral node has been removed:

```
% java ListGroup localhost zoo
duck
cow
```

Let's stand back and see what we've built here. We have a way of building up a list of a group of nodes that are participating in a distributed system. The nodes may have no knowledge of each other. A client that wants to use the nodes in the list to perform some work, for example, can discover the nodes without them being aware of the client's existence.

Finally, note that group membership is not a substitution for handling network errors when communicating with a node. Even if a node is a group member, communications with it may fail, and such failures must be handled in the usual ways (retrying, trying a different member of the group, etc.).

ZooKeeper command-line tools

ZooKeeper comes with a command-line tool for interacting with the ZooKeeper name-space. We can use it to list the znodes under the /zoo znode as follows:

```
% zkCli.sh -server localhost ls /zoo
[cow, duck]
```

You can run the command without arguments to display usage instructions.

Deleting a Group

To round off the example, let's see how to delete a group. The ZooKeeper class provides a delete() method that takes a path and a version number. ZooKeeper will delete a znode only if the version number specified is the same as the version number of the znode it is trying to delete—an optimistic locking mechanism that allows clients to

---

```
```

detect conflicts over znode modification. You can bypass the version check, however, by using a version number of –1 to delete the znode regardless of its version number.

There is no recursive delete operation in ZooKeeper, so you have to delete child znodes before parents. This is what we do in the DeleteGroup class, which will remove a group and all its members (Example 21-5).

Example 21-5. A program to delete a group and its members

```
public class DeleteGroup extends ConnectionWatcher {

  public void delete(String groupName) throws KeeperException,
      InterruptedException {
    String path = "/" + groupName;

    try {
      List<String> children = zk.getChildren(path, false);
      for (String child : children) {
        zk.delete(path + "/" + child, -1);
      }
      zk.delete(path, -1);
    } catch (KeeperException.NoNodeException e) {
      System.out.printf("Group %s does not exist\n", groupName);
      System.exit(1);
    }
  }

  public static void main(String[] args) throws Exception {
    DeleteGroup deleteGroup = new DeleteGroup();
    deleteGroup.connect(args[0]);
    deleteGroup.delete(args[1]);
    deleteGroup.close();
  }
}
```

Finally, we can delete the zoo group that we created earlier:

```
% java DeleteGroup localhost zoo
% java ListGroup localhost zoo
Group zoo does not exist
```

The ZooKeeper Service

ZooKeeper is a highly available, high-performance coordination service. In this section, we look at the nature of the service it provides: its model, operations, and implementation.

Data Model

ZooKeeper maintains a hierarchical tree of nodes called znodes. A znode stores data and has an associated ACL. ZooKeeper is designed for coordination (which typically uses small datafiles), not high-volume data storage, so there is a limit of 1 MB on the amount of data that may be stored in any znode.

Data access is atomic. A client reading the data stored in a znode will never receive only some of the data; either the data will be delivered in its entirety or the read will fail. Similarly, a write will replace all the data associated with a znode. ZooKeeper guarantees that the write will either succeed or fail; there is no such thing as a partial write, where only some of the data written by the client is stored. ZooKeeper does not support an append operation. These characteristics contrast with HDFS, which is designed for high-volume data storage with streaming data access and provides an append operation.

Znodes are referenced by paths, which in ZooKeeper are represented as slash-delimited Unicode character strings, like filesystem paths in Unix. Paths must be absolute, so they must begin with a slash character. Furthermore, they are canonical, which means that each path has a single representation, and so paths do not undergo resolution. For example, in Unix, a file with the path /a/b can equivalently be referred to by the path /a/./b because "." refers to the current directory at the point it is encountered in the path. In ZooKeeper, "." does not have this special meaning and is actually illegal as a path component (as is ".." for the parent of the current directory).

Path components are composed of Unicode characters, with a few restrictions (these are spelled out in the ZooKeeper reference documentation). The string "zookeeper" is a reserved word and may not be used as a path component. In particular, ZooKeeper uses the /zookeeper subtree to store management information, such as information on quotas.

Note that paths are not URIs, and they are represented in the Java API by a `java.lang.String`, rather than the Hadoop `Path` class (or the `java.net.URI` class, for that matter).

Znodes have some properties that are very useful for building distributed applications, which we discuss in the following sections.

Ephemeral znodes

As we've seen, znodes can be one of two types: ephemeral or persistent. A znode's type is set at creation time and may not be changed later. An ephemeral znode is deleted by ZooKeeper when the creating client's session ends. By contrast, a persistent znode is not tied to the client's session and is deleted only when explicitly deleted by a client (not necessarily the one that created it). An ephemeral znode may not have children, not even ephemeral ones.

Even though ephemeral nodes are tied to a client session, they are visible to all clients (subject to their ACL policies, of course).

Ephemeral znodes are ideal for building applications that need to know when certain distributed resources are available. The example earlier in this chapter uses ephemeral znodes to implement a group membership service, so any process can discover the members of the group at any particular time.

Sequence numbers

A *sequential* znode is given a sequence number by ZooKeeper as a part of its name. If a znode is created with the sequential flag set, then the value of a monotonically increasing counter (maintained by the parent znode) is appended to its name.

If a client asks to create a sequential znode with the name /a/b-, for example, the znode created may actually have the name /a/b-3.[4] If, later on, another sequential znode with the name /a/b- is created, it will be given a unique name with a larger value of the counter —for example, /a/b-5. In the Java API, the actual path given to sequential znodes is communicated back to the client as the return value of the create() call.

Sequence numbers can be used to impose a global ordering on events in a distributed system and may be used by the client to infer the ordering. In "A Lock Service" on page 634, you will learn how to use sequential znodes to build a shared lock.

Watches

Watches allow clients to get notifications when a znode changes in some way. Watches are set by operations on the ZooKeeper service and are triggered by other operations on the service. For example, a client might call the exists operation on a znode, placing a watch on it at the same time. If the znode doesn't exist, the exists operation will return false. If, some time later, the znode is created by a second client, the watch is triggered, notifying the first client of the znode's creation. You will see precisely which operations trigger others in the next section.

Watchers are triggered only once.[5] To receive multiple notifications, a client needs to reregister the watch. So, if the client in the previous example wishes to receive further notifications for the znode's existence (to be notified when it is deleted, for example), it needs to call the exists operation again to set a new watch.

There is an example in "A Configuration Service" on page 627 demonstrating how to use watches to update configuration across a cluster.

---

4. It is conventional (but not required) to have a trailing dash on pathnames for sequential nodes, to make their sequence numbers easy to read and parse (by the application).

5. Except for callbacks for connection events, which do not need reregistration.

Operations

There are nine basic operations in ZooKeeper, listed in Table 21-2.

Table 21-2. Operations in the ZooKeeper service

Operation	Description
create	Creates a znode (the parent znode must already exist)
delete	Deletes a znode (the znode must not have any children)
exists	Tests whether a znode exists and retrieves its metadata
getACL, setACL	Gets/sets the ACL for a znode
getChildren	Gets a list of the children of a znode
getData, setData	Gets/sets the data associated with a znode
sync	Synchronizes a client's view of a znode with ZooKeeper

Update operations in ZooKeeper are conditional. A `delete` or `setData` operation has to specify the version number of the znode that is being updated (which is found from a previous `exists` call). If the version number does not match, the update will fail. Updates are a nonblocking operation, so a client that loses an update (because another process updated the znode in the meantime) can decide whether to try again or take some other action, and it can do so without blocking the progress of any other process.

Although ZooKeeper can be viewed as a filesystem, there are some filesystem primitives that it does away with in the name of simplicity. Because files are small and are written and read in their entirety, there is no need to provide open, close, or seek operations.

The `sync` operation is not like `fsync()` in POSIX filesystems. As mentioned earlier, writes in ZooKeeper are atomic, and a successful write operation is guaranteed to have been written to persistent storage on a majority of ZooKeeper servers. However, it is permissible for reads to lag the latest state of the ZooKeeper service, and the `sync` operation exists to allow a client to bring itself up to date. This topic is covered in more detail in "Consistency" on page 622.

Multiupdate

There is another ZooKeeper operation, called `multi`, that batches together multiple primitive operations into a single unit that either succeeds or fails in its entirety. The situation where some of the primitive operations succeed and some fail can never arise.

Multiupdate is very useful for building structures in ZooKeeper that maintain some global invariant. One example is an undirected graph. Each vertex in the graph is naturally represented as a znode in ZooKeeper, and to add or remove an edge we need to update the two znodes corresponding to its vertices because each has a reference to the other. If we used only primitive ZooKeeper operations, it would be possible for another client to observe the graph in an inconsistent state, where one vertex is connected to another but the reverse connection is absent. Batching the updates on the two znodes into one `multi` operation ensures that the update is atomic, so a pair of vertices can never have a dangling connection.

APIs

There are two core language bindings for ZooKeeper clients, one for Java and one for C; there are also `contrib` bindings for Perl, Python, and REST clients. For each binding, there is a choice between performing operations synchronously or asynchronously. We've already seen the synchronous Java API. Here's the signature for the `exists` operation, which returns either a `Stat` object that encapsulates the znode's metadata or `null` if the znode doesn't exist:

```
public Stat exists(String path, Watcher watcher) throws KeeperException,
    InterruptedException
```

The asynchronous equivalent, which is also found in the `ZooKeeper` class, looks like this:

```
public void exists(String path, Watcher watcher, StatCallback cb, Object ctx)
```

In the Java API, all the asynchronous methods have `void` return types, since the result of the operation is conveyed via a callback. The caller passes a callback implementation whose method is invoked when a response is received from ZooKeeper. In this case, the callback is the `StatCallback` interface, which has the following method:

```
public void processResult(int rc, String path, Object ctx, Stat stat);
```

The `rc` argument is the return code, corresponding to the codes defined by `Keep erException`. A nonzero code represents an exception, in which case the `stat` parameter will be `null`. The `path` and `ctx` arguments correspond to the equivalent arguments passed by the client to the `exists()` method, and can be used to identify the request for which this callback is a response. The `ctx` parameter can be an arbitrary object that may be used by the client when the path does not give enough context to disambiguate the request. If not needed, it may be set to `null`.

There are actually two C shared libraries. The single-threaded library, `zookeeper_st`, supports only the asynchronous API and is intended for platforms where the `pthread` library is not available or stable. Most developers will use the multithreaded library, `zookeeper_mt`, as it supports both the synchronous and asynchronous APIs. For details on how to build and use the C API, refer to the *README* file in the *src/c* directory of the ZooKeeper distribution.

Should I Use the Synchronous or Asynchronous API?

Both APIs offer the same functionality, so the one you use is largely a matter of style. The asynchronous API is appropriate if you have an event-driven programming model, for example.

The asynchronous API allows you to pipeline requests, which in some scenarios can offer better throughput. Imagine that you want to read a large batch of znodes and process them independently. Using the synchronous API, each read would block until it returned, whereas with the asynchronous API, you can fire off all the asynchronous reads very quickly and process the responses in a separate thread as they come back.

Watch triggers

The read operations `exists`, `getChildren`, and `getData` may have watches set on them, and the watches are triggered by write operations: `create`, `delete`, and `setData`. ACL operations do not participate in watches. When a watch is triggered, a watch event is generated, and the watch event's type depends both on the watch and the operation that triggered it:

- A watch set on an `exists` operation will be triggered when the znode being watched is created, deleted, or has its data updated.

- A watch set on a `getData` operation will be triggered when the znode being watched is deleted or has its data updated. No trigger can occur on creation because the znode must already exist for the `getData` operation to succeed.

- A watch set on a `getChildren` operation will be triggered when a child of the znode being watched is created or deleted, or when the znode itself is deleted. You can tell whether the znode or its child was deleted by looking at the watch event type: `NodeDeleted` shows the znode was deleted, and `NodeChildrenChanged` indicates that it was a child that was deleted.

The combinations are summarized in Table 21-3.

Table 21-3. Watch creation operations and their corresponding triggers

	Watch trigger				
Watch creation	create znode	create child	delete znode	delete child	setData
exists	NodeCreated		NodeDeleted		NodeData Changed
getData			NodeDeleted		NodeData Changed
getChildren		NodeChildren Changed	NodeDeleted	NodeChildren Changed	

A watch event includes the path of the znode that was involved in the event, so for NodeCreated and NodeDeleted events, you can tell which node was created or deleted simply by inspecting the path. To discover which children have changed after a Node ChildrenChanged event, you need to call getChildren again to retrieve the new list of children. Similarly, to discover the new data for a NodeDataChanged event, you need to call getData. In both of these cases, the state of the znodes may have changed between receiving the watch event and performing the read operation, so you should bear this in mind when writing applications.

ACLs

A znode is created with a list of ACLs, which determine who can perform certain operations on it.

ACLs depend on authentication, the process by which the client identifies itself to Zoo-Keeper. There are a few authentication schemes that ZooKeeper provides:

digest
: The client is authenticated by a username and password.

sasl
: The client is authenticated using Kerberos.

ip
: The client is authenticated by its IP address.

Clients may authenticate themselves after establishing a ZooKeeper session. Authentication is optional, although a znode's ACL may require an authenticated client, in which case the client must authenticate itself to access the znode. Here is an example of using the digest scheme to authenticate with a username and password:

```
zk.addAuthInfo("digest", "tom:secret".getBytes());
```

An ACL is the combination of an authentication scheme, an identity for that scheme, and a set of permissions. For example, if we wanted to give a client with the IP address

10.0.0.1 read access to a znode, we would set an ACL on the znode with the `ip` scheme, an ID of 10.0.0.1, and READ permission. In Java, we would create the ACL object as follows:

```
new ACL(Perms.READ,
  new Id("ip", "10.0.0.1"));
```

The full set of permissions are listed in Table 21-4. Note that the `exists` operation is not governed by an ACL permission, so any client may call `exists` to find the `Stat` for a znode or to discover that a znode does not in fact exist.

Table 21-4. ACL permissions

ACL permission	Permitted operations
CREATE	create (a child znode)
READ	getChildren
	getData
WRITE	setData
DELETE	delete (a child znode)
ADMIN	setACL

There are a number of predefined ACLs in the `ZooDefs.Ids` class, including OPEN_ACL_UNSAFE, which gives all permissions (except ADMIN permission) to everyone.

In addition, ZooKeeper has a pluggable authentication mechanism, which makes it possible to integrate third-party authentication systems if needed.

Implementation

The ZooKeeper service can run in two modes. In *standalone mode*, there is a single ZooKeeper server, which is useful for testing due to its simplicity (it can even be embedded in unit tests) but provides no guarantees of high availability or resilience. In production, ZooKeeper runs in *replicated mode* on a cluster of machines called an *ensemble*. ZooKeeper achieves high availability through replication, and can provide a service as long as a majority of the machines in the ensemble are up. For example, in a five-node ensemble, any two machines can fail and the service will still work because a majority of three remain. Note that a six-node ensemble can also tolerate only two machines failing, because if three machines fail, the remaining three do not constitute a majority of the six. For this reason, it is usual to have an odd number of machines in an ensemble.

Conceptually, ZooKeeper is very simple: all it has to do is ensure that every modification to the tree of znodes is replicated to a majority of the ensemble. If a minority of the machines fail, then a minimum of one machine will survive with the latest state. The other remaining replicas will eventually catch up with this state.

The implementation of this simple idea, however, is nontrivial. ZooKeeper uses a protocol called *Zab* that runs in two phases, which may be repeated indefinitely:

Phase 1: Leader election

The machines in an ensemble go through a process of electing a distinguished member, called the *leader*. The other machines are termed *followers*. This phase is finished once a majority (or *quorum*) of followers have synchronized their state with the leader.

Phase 2: Atomic broadcast

All write requests are forwarded to the leader, which broadcasts the update to the followers. When a majority have persisted the change, the leader commits the update, and the client gets a response saying the update succeeded. The protocol for achieving consensus is designed to be atomic, so a change either succeeds or fails. It resembles a two-phase commit.

Does ZooKeeper Use Paxos?

No. ZooKeeper's Zab protocol is not the same as the well-known Paxos algorithm.[6] Zab is similar, but it differs in several aspects of its operation, such as relying on TCP for its message ordering guarantees.[7]

Google's Chubby Lock Service,[8] which shares similar goals with ZooKeeper, is based on Paxos.

If the leader fails, the remaining machines hold another leader election and continue as before with the new leader. If the old leader later recovers, it then starts as a follower. Leader election is very fast, around 200 ms according to one published result (*http://bit.ly/dist_coordination*), so performance does not noticeably degrade during an election.

All machines in the ensemble write updates to disk before updating their in-memory copies of the znode tree. Read requests may be serviced from any machine, and because they involve only a lookup from memory, they are very fast.

---

6. Leslie Lamport, "Paxos Made Simple," (*http://bit.ly/simple-paxos*) *ACM SIGACT News* December 2001.

7. Zab is described in Benjamin Reed and Flavio Junqueira's "A simple totally ordered broadcast protocol," (*http://bit.ly/ordered_protocol*) *LADIS '08 Proceedings of the 2nd Workshop on Large-Scale Distributed Systems and Middleware*, 2008.

8. Mike Burrows, "The Chubby Lock Service for Loosely-Coupled Distributed Systems," (*http://research.google.com/archive/chubby.html*) November 2006.

Consistency

Understanding the basis of ZooKeeper's implementation helps in understanding the consistency guarantees that the service makes. The terms "leader" and "follower" for the machines in an ensemble are apt because they make the point that a follower may lag the leader by a number of updates. This is a consequence of the fact that only a majority and not all members of the ensemble need to have persisted a change before it is committed. A good mental model for ZooKeeper is of clients connected to ZooKeeper servers that are following the leader. A client may actually be connected to the leader, but it has no control over this and cannot even know if this is the case.[9] See Figure 21-2.

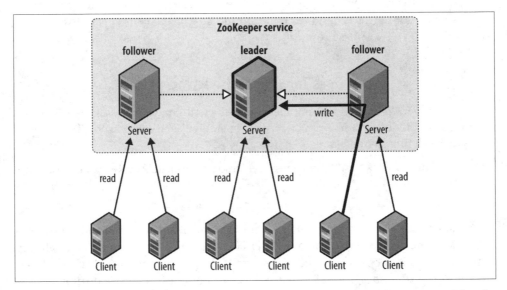

Figure 21-2. Reads are satisfied by followers, whereas writes are committed by the leader

Every update made to the znode tree is given a globally unique identifier, called a *zxid* (which stands for "ZooKeeper transaction ID"). Updates are ordered, so if *zxid* z_1 is less than z_2, then z_1 happened before z_2, according to ZooKeeper (which is the single authority on ordering in the distributed system).

The following guarantees for data consistency flow from ZooKeeper's design:

---

9. It is possible to configure ZooKeeper so that the leader does not accept client connections. In this case, its only job is to coordinate updates. Do this by setting the leaderServes property to no. This is recommended for ensembles of more than three servers.

Sequential consistency

Updates from any particular client are applied in the order that they are sent. This means that if a client updates the znode z to the value a, and in a later operation, it updates z to the value b, then no client will ever see z with value a after it has seen it with value b (if no other updates are made to z).

Atomicity

Updates either succeed or fail. This means that if an update fails, no client will ever see it.

Single system image

A client will see the same view of the system, regardless of the server it connects to. This means that if a client connects to a new server during the same session, it will not see an older state of the system than the one it saw with the previous server. When a server fails and a client tries to connect to another in the ensemble, a server that is behind the one that failed will not accept connections from the client until it has caught up with the failed server.

Durability

Once an update has succeeded, it will persist and will not be undone. This means updates will survive server failures.

Timeliness

The lag in any client's view of the system is bounded, so it will not be out of date by more than some multiple of tens of seconds. This means that rather than allow a client to see data that is very stale, a server will shut down, forcing the client to switch to a more up-to-date server.

For performance reasons, reads are satisfied from a ZooKeeper server's memory and do not participate in the global ordering of writes. This property can lead to the appearance of inconsistent ZooKeeper states from clients that communicate through a mechanism outside ZooKeeper: for example, client A updates znode z from a to a', A tells B to read z, and B reads the value of z as a, not a'. This is perfectly compatible with the guarantees that ZooKeeper makes (the condition that it does *not* promise is called "simultaneously consistent cross-client views"). To prevent this condition from happening, B should call sync on z before reading z's value. The sync operation forces the ZooKeeper server to which B is connected to "catch up" with the leader, so that when B reads z's value, it will be the one that A set (or a later value).

Slightly confusingly, the sync operation is available only as an *asynchronous* call. This is because you don't need to wait for it to return, since ZooKeeper guarantees that any subsequent operation will happen after the sync completes on the server, even if the operation is issued before the sync completes.

Sessions

A ZooKeeper client is configured with the list of servers in the ensemble. On startup, it tries to connect to one of the servers in the list. If the connection fails, it tries another server in the list, and so on, until it either successfully connects to one of them or fails because all ZooKeeper servers are unavailable.

Once a connection has been made with a ZooKeeper server, the server creates a new session for the client. A session has a timeout period that is decided on by the application that creates it. If the server hasn't received a request within the timeout period, it may expire the session. Once a session has expired, it may not be reopened, and any ephemeral nodes associated with the session will be lost. Although session expiry is a comparatively rare event, since sessions are long lived, it is important for applications to handle it (we will see how in "The Resilient ZooKeeper Application" on page 630).

Sessions are kept alive by the client sending ping requests (also known as heartbeats) whenever the session is idle for longer than a certain period. (Pings are automatically sent by the ZooKeeper client library, so your code doesn't need to worry about maintaining the session.) The period is chosen to be low enough to detect server failure (manifested by a read timeout) and reconnect to another server within the session timeout period.

Failover to another ZooKeeper server is handled automatically by the ZooKeeper client, and crucially, sessions (and associated ephemeral znodes) are still valid after another server takes over from the failed one.

During failover, the application will receive notifications of disconnections and connections to the service. Watch notifications will not be delivered while the client is disconnected, but they will be delivered when the client successfully reconnects. Also, if the application tries to perform an operation while the client is reconnecting to another server, the operation will fail. This underlines the importance of handling connection loss exceptions in real-world ZooKeeper applications (described in "The Resilient ZooKeeper Application" on page 630).

Time

There are several time parameters in ZooKeeper. The *tick time* is the fundamental period of time in ZooKeeper and is used by servers in the ensemble to define the schedule on which their interactions run. Other settings are defined in terms of tick time, or are at least constrained by it. The session timeout, for example, may not be less than 2 ticks or more than 20. If you attempt to set a session timeout outside this range, it will be modified to fall within the range.

A common tick time setting is 2 seconds (2,000 milliseconds). This translates to an allowable session timeout of between 4 and 40 seconds.

There are a few considerations in selecting a session timeout. A low session timeout leads to faster detection of machine failure. In the group membership example, the session timeout is the time it takes for a failed machine to be removed from the group. Beware of setting the session timeout too low, however, because a busy network can cause packets to be delayed and may cause inadvertent session expiry. In such an event, a machine would appear to "flap": leaving and then rejoining the group repeatedly in a short space of time.

Applications that create more complex ephemeral state should favor longer session timeouts, as the cost of reconstruction is higher. In some cases, it is possible to design the application so it can restart within the session timeout period and avoid session expiry. (This might be desirable to perform maintenance or upgrades.) Every session is given a unique identity and password by the server, and if these are passed to ZooKeeper while a connection is being made, it is possible to recover a session (as long as it hasn't expired). An application can therefore arrange a graceful shutdown, whereby it stores the session identity and password to stable storage before restarting the process, retrieving the stored session identity and password, and recovering the session.

You should view this feature as an optimization that can help avoid expired sessions. It does not remove the need to handle session expiry, which can still occur if a machine fails unexpectedly, or even if an application is shut down gracefully but does not restart before its session expires, for whatever reason.

As a general rule, the larger the ZooKeeper ensemble, the larger the session timeout should be. Connection timeouts, read timeouts, and ping periods are all defined internally as a function of the number of servers in the ensemble, so as the ensemble grows, these periods decrease. Consider increasing the timeout if you experience frequent connection loss. You can monitor ZooKeeper metrics—such as request latency statistics—using JMX.

States

The `ZooKeeper` object transitions through different states in its lifecycle (see Figure 21-3). You can query its state at any time by using the `getState()` method:

```
public States getState()
```

`States` is an enum representing the different states that a `ZooKeeper` object may be in. (Despite the enum's name, an instance of `ZooKeeper` may be in only one state at a time.) A newly constructed `ZooKeeper` instance is in the `CONNECTING` state while it tries to establish a connection with the ZooKeeper service. Once a connection is established, it goes into the `CONNECTED` state.

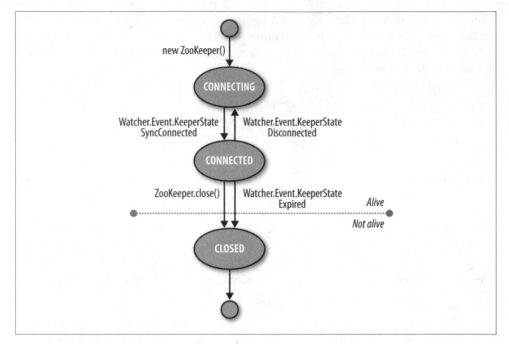

Figure 21-3. ZooKeeper state transitions

A client using the `ZooKeeper` object can receive notifications of the state transitions by registering a `Watcher` object. On entering the `CONNECTED` state, the watcher receives a `WatchedEvent` whose `KeeperState` value is `SyncConnected`.

 A ZooKeeper `Watcher` object serves double duty: it can be used to be notified of changes in the ZooKeeper state (as described in this section), and it can be used to be notified of changes in znodes (described in "Watch triggers" on page 618). The (default) watcher passed into the `ZooKeeper` object constructor is used for state changes, but znode changes may either use a dedicated instance of `Watcher` (by passing one in to the appropriate read operation) or share the default one if using the form of the read operation that takes a Boolean flag to specify whether to use a watcher.

The `ZooKeeper` instance may disconnect and reconnect to the ZooKeeper service, moving between the `CONNECTED` and `CONNECTING` states. If it disconnects, the watcher receives a `Disconnected` event. Note that these state transitions are initiated by the `ZooKeeper` instance itself, and it will automatically try to reconnect if the connection is lost.

The `ZooKeeper` instance may transition to a third state, `CLOSED`, if either the `close()` method is called or the session times out, as indicated by a `KeeperState` of type

Expired. Once in the CLOSED state, the ZooKeeper object is no longer considered to be alive (this can be tested using the isAlive() method on States) and cannot be reused. To reconnect to the ZooKeeper service, the client must construct a new ZooKeeper instance.

Building Applications with ZooKeeper

Having covered ZooKeeper in some depth, let's turn back to writing some useful applications with it.

A Configuration Service

One of the most basic services that a distributed application needs is a configuration service, so that common pieces of configuration information can be shared by machines in a cluster. At the simplest level, ZooKeeper can act as a highly available store for configuration, allowing application participants to retrieve or update configuration files. Using ZooKeeper watches, it is possible to create an active configuration service, where interested clients are notified of changes in configuration.

Let's write such a service. We make a couple of assumptions that simplify the implementation (they could be removed with a little more work). First, the only configuration values we need to store are strings, and keys are just znode paths, so we use a znode to store each key-value pair. Second, there is a single client performing updates at any one time. Among other things, this model fits with the idea of a master (such as the namenode in HDFS) that wishes to update information that its workers need to follow.

We wrap the code up in a class called ActiveKeyValueStore:

```
public class ActiveKeyValueStore extends ConnectionWatcher {

  private static final Charset CHARSET = Charset.forName("UTF-8");

  public void write(String path, String value) throws InterruptedException,
      KeeperException {
    Stat stat = zk.exists(path, false);
    if (stat == null) {
      zk.create(path, value.getBytes(CHARSET), Ids.OPEN_ACL_UNSAFE,
          CreateMode.PERSISTENT);
    } else {
      zk.setData(path, value.getBytes(CHARSET), -1);
    }
  }
}
```

The contract of the write() method is that a key with the given value is written to ZooKeeper. It hides the difference between creating a new znode and updating an existing znode with a new value by testing first for the znode using the exists operation and then performing the appropriate operation. The other detail worth mentioning is

the need to convert the string value to a byte array, for which we just use the get
Bytes() method with a UTF-8 encoding.

To illustrate the use of the ActiveKeyValueStore, consider a ConfigUpdater class that
updates a configuration property with a value. The listing appears in Example 21-6.

Example 21-6. An application that updates a property in ZooKeeper at random times

```java
public class ConfigUpdater {

  public static final String PATH = "/config";

  private ActiveKeyValueStore store;
  private Random random = new Random();

  public ConfigUpdater(String hosts) throws IOException, InterruptedException {
    store = new ActiveKeyValueStore();
    store.connect(hosts);
  }

  public void run() throws InterruptedException, KeeperException {
    while (true) {
      String value = random.nextInt(100) + "";
      store.write(PATH, value);
      System.out.printf("Set %s to %s\n", PATH, value);
      TimeUnit.SECONDS.sleep(random.nextInt(10));
    }
  }

  public static void main(String[] args) throws Exception {
    ConfigUpdater configUpdater = new ConfigUpdater(args[0]);
    configUpdater.run();
  }
}
```

The program is simple. A ConfigUpdater has an ActiveKeyValueStore that connects
to ZooKeeper in the ConfigUpdater's constructor. The run() method loops forever,
updating the */config* znode at random times with random values.

Next, let's look at how to read the */config* configuration property. First, we add a read
method to ActiveKeyValueStore:

```java
public String read(String path, Watcher watcher) throws InterruptedException,
    KeeperException {
  byte[] data = zk.getData(path, watcher, null/*stat*/);
  return new String(data, CHARSET);
}
```

The getData() method of ZooKeeper takes the path, a Watcher, and a Stat object. The
Stat object is filled in with values by getData() and is used to pass information back

to the caller. In this way, the caller can get both the data and the metadata for a znode, although in this case, we pass a null Stat because we are not interested in the metadata.

As a consumer of the service, ConfigWatcher (see Example 21-7) creates an ActiveKey ValueStore and, after starting, calls the store's read() method (in its displayCon fig() method) to pass a reference to itself as the watcher. It displays the initial value of the configuration that it reads.

Example 21-7. An application that watches for updates of a property in ZooKeeper and prints them to the console

```java
public class ConfigWatcher implements Watcher {

  private ActiveKeyValueStore store;

  public ConfigWatcher(String hosts) throws IOException, InterruptedException {
    store = new ActiveKeyValueStore();
    store.connect(hosts);
  }

  public void displayConfig() throws InterruptedException, KeeperException {
    String value = store.read(ConfigUpdater.PATH, this);
    System.out.printf("Read %s as %s\n", ConfigUpdater.PATH, value);
  }

  @Override
  public void process(WatchedEvent event) {
    if (event.getType() == EventType.NodeDataChanged) {
      try {
        displayConfig();
      } catch (InterruptedException e) {
        System.err.println("Interrupted. Exiting.");
        Thread.currentThread().interrupt();
      } catch (KeeperException e) {
        System.err.printf("KeeperException: %s. Exiting.\n", e);
      }
    }
  }

  public static void main(String[] args) throws Exception {
    ConfigWatcher configWatcher = new ConfigWatcher(args[0]);
    configWatcher.displayConfig();

    // stay alive until process is killed or thread is interrupted
    Thread.sleep(Long.MAX_VALUE);
  }
}
```

When the ConfigUpdater updates the znode, ZooKeeper causes the watcher to fire with an event type of EventType.NodeDataChanged. ConfigWatcher acts on this event in its process() method by reading and displaying the latest version of the config.

Because watches are one-time signals, we tell ZooKeeper of the new watch each time we call `read()` on `ActiveKeyValueStore`, which ensures we see future updates. We are not guaranteed to receive every update, though, because the znode may have been updated (possibly many times) during the span of time between the receipt of the watch event and the next read, and as the client has no watch registered during that period, it is not notified. For the configuration service, this is not a problem, because clients care only about the latest value of a property, as it takes precedence over previous values. However, in general you should be aware of this potential limitation.

Let's see the code in action. Launch the `ConfigUpdater` in one terminal window:

```
% java ConfigUpdater localhost
Set /config to 79
Set /config to 14
Set /config to 78
```

Then launch the `ConfigWatcher` in another window immediately afterward:

```
% java ConfigWatcher localhost
Read /config as 79
Read /config as 14
Read /config as 78
```

The Resilient ZooKeeper Application

The first of the Fallacies of Distributed Computing (*http://bit.ly/dist_computing*) states that "the network is reliable." As they stand, our programs so far have been assuming a reliable network, so when they run on a real network, they can fail in several ways. Let's examine some possible failure modes and what we can do to correct them so that our programs are resilient in the face of failure.

Every ZooKeeper operation in the Java API declares two types of exception in its `throws` clause: `InterruptedException` and `KeeperException`.

InterruptedException

An `InterruptedException` is thrown if the operation is interrupted. There is a standard Java mechanism for canceling blocking methods, which is to call `interrupt()` on the thread from which the blocking method was called. A successful cancellation will result in an `InterruptedException`. ZooKeeper adheres to this standard, so you can cancel a ZooKeeper operation in this way. Classes or libraries that use ZooKeeper usually should propagate the `InterruptedException` so that their clients can cancel their operations.[10]

---

10. For more detail, see the excellent article "Java theory and practice: Dealing with InterruptedException" (*http://www.ibm.com/developerworks/java/library/j-jtp05236.html*) by Brian Goetz (IBM, May 2006).

An `InterruptedException` does not indicate a failure, but rather that the operation has been canceled, so in the configuration application example it is appropriate to propagate the exception, causing the application to terminate.

KeeperException

A `KeeperException` is thrown if the ZooKeeper server signals an error or if there is a communication problem with the server. For different error cases, there are various subclasses of `KeeperException`. For example, `KeeperException.NoNodeException` is a subclass of `KeeperException` that is thrown if you try to perform an operation on a znode that doesn't exist.

Every subclass of `KeeperException` has a corresponding code with information about the type of error. For example, for `KeeperException.NoNodeException`, the code is `KeeperException.Code.NONODE` (an enum value).

There are two ways, then, to handle `KeeperException`: either catch `KeeperException` and test its code to determine what remedying action to take, or catch the equivalent `KeeperException` subclasses and perform the appropriate action in each catch block.

`KeeperExceptions` fall into three broad categories.

State exceptions. A state exception occurs when the operation fails because it cannot be applied to the znode tree. State exceptions usually happen because another process is mutating a znode at the same time. For example, a `setData` operation with a version number will fail with a `KeeperException.BadVersionException` if the znode is updated by another process first because the version number does not match. The programmer is usually aware that this kind of conflict is possible and will code to deal with it.

Some state exceptions indicate an error in the program, such as `KeeperException.NoChildrenForEphemeralsException`, which is thrown when trying to create a child znode of an ephemeral znode.

Recoverable exceptions. Recoverable exceptions are those from which the application can recover within the same ZooKeeper session. A recoverable exception is manifested by `KeeperException.ConnectionLossException`, which means that the connection to ZooKeeper has been lost. ZooKeeper will try to reconnect, and in most cases the reconnection will succeed and ensure that the session is intact.

However, ZooKeeper cannot tell if the operation that failed with a `KeeperException.ConnectionLossException` was applied. This is an example of partial failure (which we introduced at the beginning of the chapter). The onus is therefore on the programmer to deal with the uncertainty, and the action that should be taken depends on the application.

At this point, it is useful to make a distinction between *idempotent* and *nonidempotent* operations. An idempotent operation is one that may be applied one or more times with the same result, such as a read request or an unconditional `setData`. These can simply be retried.

A nonidempotent operation cannot be retried indiscriminately, as the effect of applying it multiple times is not the same as that of applying it once. The program needs a way of detecting whether its update was applied by encoding information in the znode's pathname or its data. We discuss how to deal with failed nonidempotent operations in "Recoverable exceptions" on page 635, when we look at the implementation of a lock service.

Unrecoverable exceptions. In some cases, the ZooKeeper session becomes invalid—perhaps because of a timeout or because the session was closed (both of these scenarios get a `KeeperException.SessionExpiredException`), or perhaps because authentication failed (`KeeperException.AuthFailedException`). In any case, all ephemeral nodes associated with the session will be lost, so the application needs to rebuild its state before reconnecting to ZooKeeper.

A reliable configuration service

Going back to the `write()` method in `ActiveKeyValueStore`, recall that it is composed of an `exists` operation followed by either a `create` or a `setData`:

```
public void write(String path, String value) throws InterruptedException,
    KeeperException {
  Stat stat = zk.exists(path, false);
  if (stat == null) {
    zk.create(path, value.getBytes(CHARSET), Ids.OPEN_ACL_UNSAFE,
        CreateMode.PERSISTENT);
  } else {
    zk.setData(path, value.getBytes(CHARSET), -1);
  }
}
```

Taken as a whole, the `write()` method is idempotent, so we can afford to unconditionally retry it. Here's a modified version of the `write()` method that retries in a loop. It is set to try a maximum number of retries (`MAX_RETRIES`) and sleeps for `RETRY_PERIOD_SECONDS` between each attempt:

```
public void write(String path, String value) throws InterruptedException,
    KeeperException {
  int retries = 0;
  while (true) {
    try {
      Stat stat = zk.exists(path, false);
      if (stat == null) {
        zk.create(path, value.getBytes(CHARSET), Ids.OPEN_ACL_UNSAFE,
            CreateMode.PERSISTENT);
```

```
            } else {
                zk.setData(path, value.getBytes(CHARSET), stat.getVersion());
            }
            return;
        } catch (KeeperException.SessionExpiredException e) {
            throw e;
        } catch (KeeperException e) {
            if (retries++ == MAX_RETRIES) {
                throw e;
            }
            // sleep then retry
            TimeUnit.SECONDS.sleep(RETRY_PERIOD_SECONDS);
        }
    }
}
```

The code is careful not to retry KeeperException.SessionExpiredException, because when a session expires, the ZooKeeper object enters the CLOSED state, from which it can never reconnect (refer to Figure 21-3). We simply rethrow the exception[11] and let the caller create a new ZooKeeper instance, so that the whole write() method can be retried. A simple way to create a new instance is to create a new ConfigUpdater (which we've actually renamed ResilientConfigUpdater) to recover from an expired session:

```
public static void main(String[] args) throws Exception {
    while (true) {
        try {
            ResilientConfigUpdater configUpdater =
                new ResilientConfigUpdater(args[0]);
            configUpdater.run();
        } catch (KeeperException.SessionExpiredException e) {
            // start a new session
        } catch (KeeperException e) {
            // already retried, so exit
            e.printStackTrace();
            break;
        }
    }
}
```

An alternative way of dealing with session expiry would be to look for a KeeperState of type Expired in the watcher (that would be the ConnectionWatcher in the example here), and create a new connection when this is detected. This way, we would just keep retrying the write() method, even if we got a KeeperException.SessionExpiredEx ception, since the connection should eventually be reestablished. Regardless of the precise mechanics of how we recover from an expired session, the important point is

---

11. Another way of writing the code would be to have a single catch block, just for KeeperException, and a test to see whether its code has the value KeeperException.Code.SESSIONEXPIRED. They both behave in the same way, so which method you use is simply a matter of style.

that it is a different kind of failure from connection loss and needs to be handled differently.

 There's actually another failure mode that we've ignored here. When the ZooKeeper object is created, it tries to connect to a ZooKeeper server. If the connection fails or times out, then it tries another server in the ensemble. If, after trying all of the servers in the ensemble, it can't connect, then it throws an IOException. The likelihood of all ZooKeeper servers being unavailable is low; nevertheless, some applications may choose to retry the operation in a loop until ZooKeeper is available.

This is just one strategy for retry handling. There are many others, such as using exponential backoff, where the period between retries is multiplied by a constant each time.

A Lock Service

A *distributed lock* is a mechanism for providing mutual exclusion between a collection of processes. At any one time, only a single process may hold the lock. Distributed locks can be used for leader election in a large distributed system, where the leader is the process that holds the lock at any point in time.

 Do not confuse ZooKeeper's own leader election with a general leader election service, which can be built using ZooKeeper primitives (and in fact, one implementation is included with ZooKeeper). Zoo-Keeper's own leader election is not exposed publicly, unlike the type of general leader election service we are describing here, which is designed to be used by distributed systems that need to agree upon a master process.

To implement a distributed lock using ZooKeeper, we use sequential znodes to impose an order on the processes vying for the lock. The idea is simple: first, designate a lock znode, typically describing the entity being locked on (say, */leader*); then, clients that want to acquire the lock create sequential ephemeral znodes as children of the lock znode. At any point in time, the client with the lowest sequence number holds the lock. For example, if two clients create the znodes at */leader/lock-1* and */leader/lock-2* around the same time, then the client that created */leader/lock-1* holds the lock, since its znode has the lowest sequence number. The ZooKeeper service is the arbiter of order because it assigns the sequence numbers.

The lock may be released simply by deleting the znode */leader/lock-1*; alternatively, if the client process dies, it will be deleted by virtue of being an ephemeral znode. The client that created */leader/lock-2* will then hold the lock because it has the next lowest sequence number. It ensures it will be notified that it has the lock by creating a watch that fires when znodes go away.

The pseudocode for lock acquisition is as follows:

1. Create an ephemeral sequential znode named *lock-* under the lock znode, and remember its actual pathname (the return value of the create operation).

2. Get the children of the lock znode and set a watch.

3. If the pathname of the znode created in step 1 has the lowest number of the children returned in step 2, then the lock has been acquired. Exit.

4. Wait for the notification from the watch set in step 2, and go to step 2.

The herd effect

Although this algorithm is correct, there are some problems with it. The first problem is that this implementation suffers from the *herd effect*. Consider hundreds or thousands of clients, all trying to acquire the lock. Each client places a watch on the lock znode for changes in its set of children. Every time the lock is released or another process starts the lock acquisition process, the watch fires, and every client receives a notification. The "herd effect" refers to a large number of clients being notified of the same event when only a small number of them can actually proceed. In this case, only one client will successfully acquire the lock, and the process of maintaining and sending watch events to all clients causes traffic spikes, which put pressure on the ZooKeeper servers.

To avoid the herd effect, the condition for notification needs to be refined. The key observation for implementing locks is that a client needs to be notified only when the child znode with the *previous* sequence number goes away, not when any child znode is deleted (or created). In our example, if clients have created the znodes */leader/lock-1*, */leader/lock-2*, and */leader/lock-3*, then the client holding */leader/lock-3* needs to be notified only when */leader/lock-2* disappears. It does not need to be notified when */leader/lock-1* disappears or when a new znode, */leader/lock-4*, is added.

Recoverable exceptions

Another problem with the lock algorithm as it stands is that it doesn't handle the case when the create operation fails due to connection loss. Recall that in this case we do not know whether the operation succeeded or failed. Creating a sequential znode is a nonidempotent operation, so we can't simply retry, because if the first create had succeeded we would have an orphaned znode that would never be deleted (until the client session ended, at least). Deadlock would be the unfortunate result.

The problem is that after reconnecting, the client can't tell whether it created any of the child znodes. By embedding an identifier in the znode name, if it suffers a connection loss, it can check to see whether any of the children of the lock node have its identifier in their names. If a child contains its identifier, it knows that the create operation succeeded, and it shouldn't create another child znode. If no child has the identifier in its name, the client can safely create a new sequential child znode.

The client's session identifier is a long integer that is unique for the ZooKeeper service and therefore ideal for the purpose of identifying a client across connection loss events. The session identifier can be obtained by calling the getSessionId() method on the ZooKeeper Java class.

The ephemeral sequential znode should be created with a name of the form *lock-<sessionId>-*, so that when the sequence number is appended by ZooKeeper, the name becomes *lock-<sessionId>-<sequenceNumber>*. The sequence numbers are unique to the parent, not to the name of the child, so this technique allows the child znodes to identify their creators as well as impose an order of creation.

Unrecoverable exceptions

If a client's ZooKeeper session expires, the ephemeral znode created by the client will be deleted, effectively relinquishing the lock (or at least forfeiting the client's turn to acquire the lock). The application using the lock should realize that it no longer holds the lock, clean up its state, and then start again by creating a new lock object and trying to acquire it. Notice that it is the application that controls this process, not the lock implementation, since it cannot second-guess how the application needs to clean up its state.

Implementation

Accounting for all of the failure modes is nontrivial, so implementing a distributed lock correctly is a delicate matter. ZooKeeper comes with a production-quality lock implementation in Java called WriteLock that is very easy for clients to use.

More Distributed Data Structures and Protocols

There are many distributed data structures and protocols that can be built with ZooKeeper, such as barriers, queues, and two-phase commit. One interesting thing to note is that these are synchronous protocols, even though we use asynchronous ZooKeeper primitives (such as notifications) to build them.

The ZooKeeper website (*http://zookeeper.apache.org/*) describes several such data structures and protocols in pseudocode. ZooKeeper comes with implementations of some of these standard recipes (including locks, leader election, and queues); they can be found in the *recipes* directory of the distribution.

The Apache Curator project (*http://curator.apache.org/*) also provides an extensive set of ZooKeeper recipes, as well as a simplified ZooKeeper client.

BookKeeper and Hedwig

BookKeeper is a highly available and reliable logging service. It can be used to provide write-ahead logging, which is a common technique for ensuring data integrity in storage systems. In a system using write-ahead logging, every write operation is written to the transaction log before it is applied. Using this procedure, we don't have to write the data to permanent storage after every write operation, because in the event of a system failure, the latest state may be recovered by replaying the transaction log for any writes that were not applied.

BookKeeper clients create logs called *ledgers*, and each record appended to a ledger is called a *ledger entry*, which is simply a byte array. Ledgers are managed by *bookies*, which are servers that replicate the ledger data. Note that ledger data is not stored in Zoo-Keeper; only metadata is.

Traditionally, the challenge has been to make systems that use write-ahead logging robust in the face of failure of the node writing the transaction log. This is usually done by replicating the transaction log in some manner. HDFS high availability, described on page 48, uses a group of journal nodes to provide a highly available edit log. Although it is similar to BookKeeper, it is a dedicated service written for HDFS, and it doesn't use ZooKeeper as the coordination engine.

Hedwig is a topic-based ipublish-subscribe system built on BookKeeper. Thanks to its ZooKeeper underpinnings, Hedwig is a highly available service and guarantees message delivery even if subscribers are offline for extended periods of time.

BookKeeper is a ZooKeeper subproject, and you can find more information on how to use it, as well as Hedwig, at *http://zookeeper.apache.org/bookkeeper/*.

ZooKeeper in Production

In production, you should run ZooKeeper in replicated mode. Here, we will cover some of the considerations for running an ensemble of ZooKeeper servers. However, this section is not exhaustive, so you should consult the ZooKeeper Administrator's Guide (*http://bit.ly/admin_guide*) for detailed, up-to-date instructions, including supported platforms, recommended hardware, maintenance procedures, dynamic reconfiguration (to change the servers in a running ensemble), and configuration properties.

Resilience and Performance

ZooKeeper machines should be located to minimize the impact of machine and network failure. In practice, this means that servers should be spread across racks, power supplies, and switches, so that the failure of any one of these does not cause the ensemble to lose a majority of its servers.

For applications that require low-latency service (on the order of a few milliseconds), it is important to run all the servers in an ensemble in a single data center. Some use cases don't require low-latency responses, however, which makes it feasible to spread servers across data centers (at least two per data center) for extra resilience. Example applications in this category are leader election and distributed coarse-grained locking, both of which have relatively infrequent state changes, so the overhead of a few tens of milliseconds incurred by inter-data-center messages is not significant relative to the overall functioning of the service.

 ZooKeeper has the concept of an *observer node*, which is like a non-voting follower. Because they do not participate in the vote for consensus during write requests, observers allow a ZooKeeper cluster to improve read performance without hurting write performance.[12] Observers can be used to good advantage to allow a ZooKeeper cluster to span data centers without impacting latency as much as regular voting followers. This is achieved by placing the voting members in one data center and observers in the other.

ZooKeeper is a highly available system, and it is critical that it can perform its functions in a timely manner. Therefore, ZooKeeper should run on machines that are dedicated to ZooKeeper alone. Having other applications contend for resources can cause ZooKeeper's performance to degrade significantly.

Configure ZooKeeper to keep its transaction log on a different disk drive from its snapshots. By default, both go in the directory specified by the dataDir property, but if you specify a location for dataLogDir, the transaction log will be written there. By having its own dedicated device (not just a partition), a ZooKeeper server can maximize the rate at which it writes log entries to disk, which it does sequentially without seeking. Because all writes go through the leader, write throughput does not scale by adding servers, so it is crucial that writes are as fast as possible.

If the process swaps to disk, performance will be adversely affected. This can be avoided by setting the Java heap size to less than the amount of unused physical memory on the machine. From its configuration directory, the ZooKeeper scripts will source a file called *java.env*, which can be used to set the JVMFLAGS environment variable to specify the heap size (and any other desired JVM arguments).

---

12. This is discussed in more detail in "Observers: Making ZooKeeper Scale Even Further" (*http://bit.ly/scal ing_zookeeper*) by Henry Robinson (Cloudera, December 2009).

Configuration

Each server in the ensemble of ZooKeeper servers has a numeric identifier that is unique within the ensemble and must fall between 1 and 255. The server number is specified in plain text in a file named *myid* in the directory specified by the dataDir property.

Setting each server number is only half of the job. We also need to give every server all the identities and network locations of the others in the ensemble. The ZooKeeper configuration file must include a line for each server, of the form:

```
server.n=hostname:port:port
```

The value of *n* is replaced by the server number. There are two port settings: the first is the port that followers use to connect to the leader, and the second is used for leader election. Here is a sample configuration for a three-machine replicated ZooKeeper ensemble:

```
tickTime=2000
dataDir=/disk1/zookeeper
dataLogDir=/disk2/zookeeper
clientPort=2181
initLimit=5
syncLimit=2
server.1=zookeeper1:2888:3888
server.2=zookeeper2:2888:3888
server.3=zookeeper3:2888:3888
```

Servers listen on three ports: 2181 for client connections; 2888 for follower connections, if they are the leader; and 3888 for other server connections during the leader election phase. When a ZooKeeper server starts up, it reads the *myid* file to determine which server it is, and then reads the configuration file to determine the ports it should listen on and to discover the network addresses of the other servers in the ensemble.

Clients connecting to this ZooKeeper ensemble should use zookeeper1:2181,zookeep er2:2181,zookeeper3:2181 as the host string in the constructor for the ZooKeeper object.

In replicated mode, there are two extra mandatory properties: initLimit and syncLimit, both measured in multiples of tickTime.

initLimit is the amount of time to allow for followers to connect to and sync with the leader. If a majority of followers fail to sync within this period, the leader renounces its leadership status and another leader election takes place. If this happens often (and you can discover if this is the case because it is logged), it is a sign that the setting is too low.

syncLimit is the amount of time to allow a follower to sync with the leader. If a follower fails to sync within this period, it will restart itself. Clients that were attached to this follower will connect to another one.

These are the minimum settings needed to get up and running with a cluster of Zoo-Keeper servers. There are, however, more configuration options, particularly for tuning performance, which are documented in the ZooKeeper Administrator's Guide (*http://bit.ly/zookeeper_admin*).

Further Reading

For more in-depth information about ZooKeeper, see *ZooKeeper* by Flavio Junqueira and Benjamin Reed (O'Reilly, 2013).

Case Studies

Composable Data at Cerner

Ryan Brush
Micah Whitacre

Healthcare information technology is often a story of automating existing processes. This is changing. Demands to improve care quality and control its costs are growing, creating a need for better systems to support those goals. Here we look at how Cerner is using the Hadoop ecosystem to make sense of healthcare and—building on that knowledge—to help solve such problems.

From CPUs to Semantic Integration

Cerner has long been focused on applying technology to healthcare, with much of our history emphasizing electronic medical records. However, new problems required a broader approach, which led us to look into Hadoop.

In 2009, we needed to create better search indexes of medical records. This led to processing needs not easily solved with other architectures. The search indexes required expensive processing of clinical documentation: extracting terms from the documentation and resolving their relationships with other terms. For instance, if a user typed "heart disease," we wanted documents discussing a myocardial infarction to be returned. This processing was quite expensive—it can take several seconds of CPU time for larger documents—and we wanted to apply it to many millions of documents. In short, we needed to throw a lot of CPUs at the problem, and be cost effective in the process.

Among other options, we considered a staged event-driven architecture (SEDA) approach to ingest documents at scale. But Hadoop stood out for one important need: we wanted to reprocess the many millions of documents frequently, in a small number of hours or faster. The logic for knowledge extraction from the clinical documents was rapidly improving, and we needed to roll improvements out to the world quickly. In Hadoop, this simply meant running a new version of a MapReduce job over data already in place. The process documents were then loaded into a cluster of Apache Solr servers to support application queries.

These early successes set the stage for more involved projects. This type of system and its data can be used as an empirical basis to help control costs and improve care across entire populations. And since healthcare data is often fragmented across systems and institutions, we needed to first bring in all of that data and make sense of it.

With dozens of data sources and formats, and even standardized data models subject to interpretation, we were facing an enormous semantic integration problem. Our biggest challenge was not the *size* of the data—we knew Hadoop could scale to our needs —but the sheer complexity of cleaning, managing, and transforming it for our needs. We needed higher-level tools to manage that complexity.

Enter Apache Crunch

Bringing together and analyzing such disparate datasets creates a lot of demands, but a few stood out:

- We needed to split many processing steps into modules that could easily be assembled into a sophisticated pipeline.
- We needed to offer a higher-level programming model than raw MapReduce.
- We needed to work with the complex structure of medical records, which have several hundred unique fields and several levels of nested substructures.

We explored a variety of options in this case, including Pig, Hive, and Cascading. Each of these worked well, and we continue to use Hive for ad hoc analysis, but they were unwieldy when applying arbitrary logic to our complex data structures. Then we heard of Crunch (see Chapter 18), a project led by Josh Wills that is similar to the FlumeJava system from Google. Crunch offers a simple Java-based programming model and static type checking of records—a perfect fit for our community of Java developers and the type of data we were working with.

Building a Complete Picture

Understanding and managing healthcare at scale requires significant amounts of clean, normalized, and relatable data. Unfortunately, such data is typically spread across a number of sources, making it difficult and error prone to consolidate. Hospitals, doctors' offices, clinics, and pharmacies each hold portions of a person's records in industry-standard formats such as CCDs (Continuity of Care Documents), HL7 (Health Level 7, a healthcare data interchange format), CSV files, or proprietary formats.

Our challenge is to take this data; transform it into a clean, integrated representation; and use it to create registries that help patients manage specific conditions, measure operational aspects of healthcare, and support a variety of analytics, as shown in Figure 22-1.

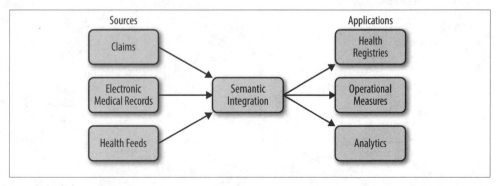

Figure 22-1. Operational data flow

An essential step is to create a clean, semantically integrated basis we can build on, which is the focus of this case study. We start by normalizing data to a common structure. Earlier versions of this system used different models, but have since migrated to Avro for storing and sharing data between processing steps. Example 22-1 shows a simplified Avro IDL to illustrate how our common structures look.

Example 22-1. Avro IDL for common data types

```
@namespace("com.cerner.example")
protocol PersonProtocol {

  record Demographics {
    string firstName;
    string lastName;
    string dob;
    ...
  }

  record LabResult {
    string personId;
    string labDate;
    int labId;
    int labTypeId;
    int value;
  }

  record Medication {
    string personId;
    string medicationId;
    string dose;
    string doseUnits;
    string frequency;
```

```
    ...
  }

  record Diagnosis {
    string personId;
    string diagnosisId;
    string date;
    ...
  }

  record Allergy {
    string personId;
    int allergyId;
    int substanceId;
    ...
  }

  /**
   * Represents a person's record from a single source.
   */
  record PersonRecord {
    string personId;
    Demographics demographics;
    array<LabResult> labResults;
    array<Allergy> allergies;
    array<Medication> medications;
    array<Diagnosis> diagnoses;
    . . .
  }
}
```

Note that a variety of data types are all nested in a common person record rather than in separate datasets. This supports the most common usage pattern for this data—looking at a complete record—without requiring downstream operations to do a number of expensive joins between datasets.

A series of Crunch pipelines are used to manipulate the data into a `PCollec tion<PersonRecord>` hiding the complexity of each source and providing a simple interface to interact with the raw, normalized record data. Behind the scenes, each `Per sonRecord` can be stored in HDFS or as a row in HBase with the individual data elements spread throughout column families and qualifiers. The result of the aggregation looks like the data in Table 22-1.

Table 22-1. Aggregated data

Source	Person ID	Person demographics	Data
Doctor's office	12345	Abraham Lincoln ...	Diabetes diagnosis, lab results
Hospital	98765	Abe Lincoln ...	Flu diagnosis
Pharmacy	98765	Abe Lincoln ...	Allergies, medications
Clinic	76543	A. Lincoln ...	Lab results

Consumers wishing to retrieve data from a collection of authorized sources call a "retriever" API that simply produces a Crunch `PCollection` of requested data:

```
Set<String> sources = ...;
PCollection<PersonRecord> personRecords =
    RecordRetriever.getData(pipeline, sources);
```

This retriever pattern allows consumers to load datasets while being insulated from how and where they are physically stored. At the time of this writing, some use of this pattern is being replaced by the emerging Kite SDK (*http://kitesdk.org/*) for managing data in Hadoop. Each entry in the retrieved `PCollection<PersonRecord>` represents a person's complete medical record within the context of a single source.

Integrating Healthcare Data

There are dozens of processing steps between raw data and answers to healthcare-related questions. Here we look at one: bringing together data for a single person from multiple sources.

Unfortunately, the lack of a common patient identifier in the United States, combined with noisy data such as variations in a person's name and demographics between systems, makes it difficult to accurately unify a person's data across sources. Information spread across multiple sources might look like Table 22-2.

Table 22-2. Data from multiple sources

Source	Person ID	First name	Last name	Address	Gender
Doctor's office	12345	Abraham	Lincoln	1600 Pennsylvania Ave.	M
Hospital	98765	Abe	Lincoln	Washington, DC	M
Hospital	45678	Mary Todd	Lincoln	1600 Pennsylvania Ave.	F
Clinic	76543	A.	Lincoln	Springfield, IL	M

This is typically resolved in healthcare by a system called an *Enterprise Master Patient Index* (EMPI). An EMPI can be fed data from multiple systems and determine which records are indeed for the same person. This is achieved in a variety of ways, ranging from humans explicitly stating relationships to sophisticated algorithms that identify commonality.

In some cases, we can load EMPI information from external systems, and in others we compute it within Hadoop. The key is that we can expose this information for use in our Crunch-based pipelines. The result is a PCollection<EMPIRecord> with the data structured as follows:

```
@namespace("com.cerner.example")
protocol EMPIProtocol {

  record PersonRecordId {
    string sourceId;
    string personId
  }

  /**
   * Represents an EMPI match.
   */
  record EMPIRecord {
    string empiId;
    array<PersonRecordId> personIds;
  }
}
```

Given EMPI information for the data in this structure, PCollection<EMPIRecord> would contain data like that shown in Table 22-3.

Table 22-3. EMPI data

EMPI identifier	PersonRecordIds (<SourceId, PersonId>)
EMPI-1	<offc-135, 12345>
	<hspt-246, 98765>
	<clnc-791, 76543>
EMPI-2	<hspt-802, 45678>

In order to group a person's medical records in a single location based upon the provided PCollection<EMPIRecord> and PCollection<PersonRecord>, the collections must be converted into a PTable, keyed by a common key. In this situation, a Pair<String, String>, where the first value is the sourceId and the second is the personId, will guarantee a unique key to use for joining.

The first step is to extract the common key from each EMPIRecord in the collection:

```
PCollection<EMPIRecord> empiRecords = ...;
PTable<Pair<String, String>, EMPIRecord> keyedEmpiRecords =
    empiRecords.parallelDo(
  new DoFn<EMPIRecord, Pair<Pair<String, String>, EMPIRecord>>() {
    @Override
    public void process(EMPIRecord input,
        Emitter<Pair<Pair<String, String>, EMPIRecord>> emitter) {
      for (PersonRecordId recordId: input.getPersonIds()) {
        emitter.emit(Pair.of(
            Pair.of(recordId.getSourceId(), recordId.getPersonId()), input));
```

```
        }
      }
    }, tableOf(pairs(strings(), strings()), records(EMPIRecord.class)
  );
```

Next, the same key needs to be extracted from each `PersonRecord`:

```
PCollection<PersonRecord> personRecords = ...;
PTable<Pair<String, String>, PersonRecord> keyedPersonRecords = personRecords.by(
    new MapFn<PersonRecord, Pair<String, String>>() {
  @Override
  public Pair<String, String> map(PersonRecord input) {
    return Pair.of(input.getSourceId(), input.getPersonId());
  }
}, pairs(strings(), strings())));
```

Joining the two `PTable` objects will return a `PTable<Pair<String, String>, Pair<EMPIRecord, PersonRecord>>`. In this situation, the keys are no longer useful, so we change the table to be keyed by the EMPI identifier:

```
PTable<String, PersonRecord> personRecordKeyedByEMPI = keyedPersonRecords
    .join(keyedEmpiRecords)
    .values()
    .by(new MapFn<Pair<PersonRecord, EMPIRecord>>() {
  @Override
  public String map(Pair<PersonRecord, EMPIRecord> input) {
    return input.second().getEmpiId();
  }
}, strings()));
```

The final step is to group the table by its key to ensure all of the data is aggregated together for processing as a complete collection:

```
PGroupedTable<String, PersonRecord> groupedPersonRecords =
    personRecordKeyedByEMPI.groupByKey();
```

The `PGroupedTable` would contain data like that in Table 22-4.

This logic to unify data sources is the first step of a larger execution flow. Other Crunch functions downstream build on these steps to meet many client needs. In a common use case, a number of problems are solved by loading the contents of the unified `PersonRecords` into a rules-based processing model to emit new clinical knowledge. For instance, we may run rules over those records to determine if a diabetic is receiving recommended care, and to indicate areas that can be improved. Similar rule sets exist for a variety of needs, ranging from general wellness to managing complicated conditions. The logic can be complicated and with a lot of variance between use cases, but it is all hosted in functions composed in a Crunch pipeline.

Table 22-4. Grouped EMPI data

EMPI identifier	Iterable<PersonRecord>
| EMPI-1 | ```
{
      "personId": "12345",
      "demographics": {
        "firstName": "Abraham", "lastName": "Lincoln", ...
      },
      "labResults": [...]
},
{
      "personId": "98765",
      "demographics": {
        "firstName": "Abe", "lastName": "Lincoln", ...
      },
      "diagnoses": [...]
},
{
      "personId": "98765",
      "demographics": {
        "firstName": "Abe", "lastName": "Lincoln", ...
      },
      "medications": [...]},
{
      "personId": "76543",
      "demographics": {
        "firstName": "A.", "lastName": "Lincoln", ...
      }
      ...
}
``` |
| EMPI-2 | ```
{
      "personId": "45678",
      "demographics": {
        "firstName": "Mary Todd", "lastName": "Lincoln", ...
      }
      ...
}
``` |

Composability over Frameworks

The patterns described here take on a particular class of problem in healthcare centered around the person. However, this data can serve as the basis for understanding operational and systemic properties of healthcare as well, creating new demands on our ability to transform and analyze it.

Libraries like Crunch help us meet emerging demands because they help make our data and processing logic composable. Rather than a single, static framework for data processing, we can modularize functions and datasets and reuse them as new needs emerge. Figure 22-2 shows how components can be wired into one another in novel ways, with each box implemented as one or more Crunch DoFns. Here we leverage person records to identify diabetics and recommend health management programs, while using those composable pieces to integrate operational data and drive analytics of the health system.

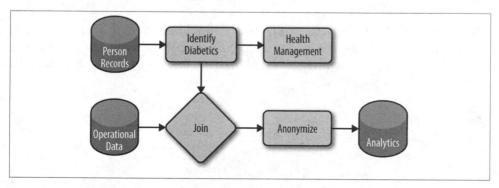

Figure 22-2. Composable datasets and functions

Composability also makes iterating through new problem spaces easier. When creating a new view of data to answer a new class of question, we can tap into existing datasets and transformations and emit our new version. As the problem becomes better understood, that view can be replaced or updated iteratively. Ultimately, these new functions and datasets can be contributed back and leveraged for new needs. The result is a growing catalog of datasets to support growing demands to understand the data.

Processing is orchestrated with Oozie. Every time new data arrives, a new dataset is created with a unique identifier in a well-defined location in HDFS. Oozie coordinators watch that location and simply launch Crunch jobs to create downstream datasets, which may subsequently be picked up by other coordinators. At the time of this writing, datasets and updates are identified by UUIDs to keep them unique. However, we are in the process of placing new data in timestamp-based partitions in order to better work with Oozie's nominal time model.

Moving Forward

We are looking to two major steps to maximize the value from this system more efficiently.

First, we want to create prescriptive practices around the Hadoop ecosystem and its supporting libraries. A number of good practices are defined in this book and elsewhere, but they often require significant expertise to implement effectively. We are using and building libraries that make such patterns explicit and accessible to a larger audience.

Crunch offers some good examples of this, with a variety of join and processing patterns built into the library.

Second, our growing catalog of datasets has created a demand for simple and prescriptive data management to complement the processing features offered by Crunch. We have been adopting the Kite SDK to meet this need in some use cases, and expect to expand its use over time.

The end goal is a secure, scalable catalog of data to support many needs in healthcare, including problems that have not yet emerged. Hadoop has shown it can scale to our data and processing needs, and higher-level libraries are now making it usable by a larger audience for many problems.

Biological Data Science: Saving Lives with Software

Matt Massie

It's hard to believe a decade has passed since the MapReduce paper (*http://research.google.com/archive/mapreduce.html*) appeared at OSDI'04. It's also hard to overstate the impact that paper had on the tech industry; the MapReduce paradigm opened distributed programming to nonexperts and enabled large-scale data processing on clusters built using commodity hardware. The open source community responded by creating open source MapReduce-based systems, like Apache Hadoop and Spark, that enabled data scientists and engineers to formulate and solve problems at a scale unimagined before.

While the tech industry was being transformed by MapReduce-based systems, biology was experiencing its own metamorphosis driven by second-generation (or "next-generation") sequencing technology; see Figure 23-1. Sequencing machines are scientific instruments that read the chemical "letters" (A, C, T, and G) that make up your genome: your complete set of genetic material. To have your genome sequenced when the MapReduce paper was published cost about $20 million and took many months to complete; today, it costs just a few thousand dollars and takes only a few days. While the first human genome took decades to create, in 2014 alone an estimated 228,000 genomes were sequenced worldwide.[1] This estimate implies around 20 petabytes (PB) of sequencing data were generated in 2014 worldwide.

---

1. See Antonio Regalado, "EmTech: Illumina Says 228,000 Human Genomes Will Be Sequenced This Year," (*http://bit.ly/genome_sequencing*) September 24, 2014.

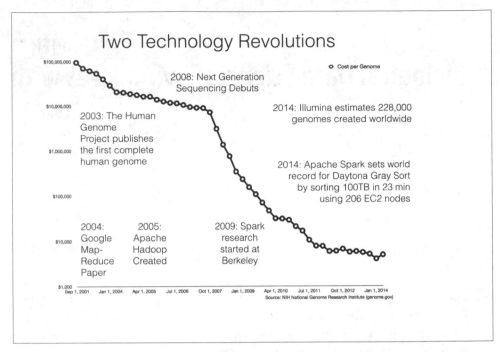

Figure 23-1. Timeline of big data technology and cost of sequencing a genome

The plummeting cost of sequencing points to superlinear growth of genomics data over the coming years. This DNA data deluge has left biological data scientists struggling to process data in a timely and scalable way using current genomics software. The AMPLab (*https://amplab.cs.berkeley.edu*) is a research lab in the Computer Science Division at UC Berkeley focused on creating novel big data systems and applications. For example, Apache Spark (see Chapter 19) is one system that grew out of the AMPLab. Spark recently broke the world record for the Daytona Gray Sort, sorting 100 TB in just 23 minutes. The team at Databricks (*http://databricks.com*) that broke the record also demonstrated they could sort 1 PB in less than 4 hours!

Consider this amazing possibility: we have technology today that could analyze every genome collected in 2014 on the order of days using a few hundred machines.

While the AMPLab identified genomics as the ideal big data application for technical reasons, there are also more important compassionate reasons: the timely processing of biological data saves lives. This short use case will focus on systems we use and have developed, with our partners and the open source community, to quickly analyze large biological datasets.

The Structure of DNA

The discovery in 1953 by Francis Crick and James D. Watson, using experimental data collected by Rosalind Franklin and Maurice Wilkins, that DNA has a double helix structure was one of the greatest scientific discoveries of the 20th century. Their *Nature* article entitled "Molecular Structure of Nucleic Acids: A Structure for Deoxyribose Nucleic Acid" contains one of the most profound and understated sentences in science:

> It has not escaped our notice that the specific pairing we have postulated immediately suggests a possible copying mechanism for the genetic material.

This "specific pairing" referred to the observation that the bases adenine (A) and thymine (T) always pair together and guanine (G) and cytosine (C) always pair together; see Figure 23-2. This deterministic pairing enables a "copying mechanism": the DNA double helix unwinds and complementary base pairs snap into place, creating two exact copies of the original DNA strand.

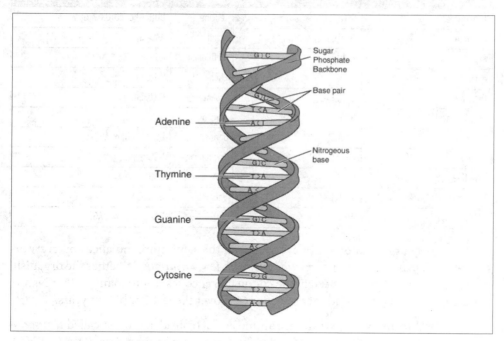

Figure 23-2. DNA double helix structure

The Genetic Code: Turning DNA Letters into Proteins

Without proteins, there is no life. DNA serves as a recipe for creating proteins. A protein is a chain of amino acids that folds into a specific 3D shape[2] to serve a particular structure or function. As there are a total of 20 amino acids[3] and only four letters in the DNA alphabet (A, C, T, G), nature groups these letters in words, called *codons*. Each codon is three bases long (since two bases would only support $4^2=16$ amino acids).

In 1968, Har Gobind Khorana, Robert W. Holley, and Marshall Nirenberg received the Nobel Prize in Physiology or Medicine for successfully mapping amino acids associated with each of the 64 codons. Each codon encodes a single amino acid, or designates the start and stop positions (see Table 23-1). Since there are 64 possible codons and only 20 amino acids, multiple codons correspond to some of the amino acids.

Table 23-1. Codon table

Amino acid	Codon(s)	Amino acid	Codon(s)
Alanine	GC{U,C,A,G}	Leucine	UU{A,G} or CU{U,C,A,G}
Arginine	CG{U,C,A,G} or AG{A,G}	Lysine	AA{A,G}
Asparagine	AA{U,C}	Methionine	AUG
Aspartic acid	GA{U,C}	Phenylalanine	UU{U,C}
Cysteine	UG{U,C}	Proline	CC{U,C,A,G}
Glutamic acid	GA{A,G}	Threonine	AC{U,C,A,G}
Glutamine	CA{A,G}	Serine	UC{U,C,A,G} or AG{U,C}
Glycine	GG{U,C,A,G}	Tryptophan	UGG
Histidine	CA{U,C}	Tyrosine	UA{U,C}
Isoleucine	AU{U,C,A}	Valine	GU{U,C,A,G}
START!	AUG	STOP!	UAA or UGA or UAG

Because every organism on Earth evolved from the same common ancestor, *every organism on Earth uses the same genetic code, with few variations.* Whether the organism is a tree, worm, fungus, or cheetah, the codon UGG encodes tryptophan. Mother Nature has been the ultimate practitioner of code reuse over the last few billion years.

DNA is not directly used to synthesize amino acids. Instead, a process called *transcription* copies the DNA sequence that codes for a protein into *messenger RNA* (mRNA). These mRNA carry information from the nuclei of your cells to the surrounding *cytoplasm* to create proteins in a process called *translation*.

---

2. This process is called *protein folding*. The Folding@home (*http://folding.stanford.edu/*) allows volunteers to donate CPU cycles to help researchers determine the mechanisms of protein folding.

3. There are also a few nonstandard amino acids not shown in the table that are encoded differently.

You probably noticed that this lookup table doesn't have the DNA letter T (for thymine) and has a new letter U (for uracil). During *transcription*, U is substituted for T:

```
$ echo "ATGGTGACTCCTACATGA" | sed 's/T/U/g' | fold -w 3
AUG
GUG
ACU
CCU
ACA
UGA
```

Looking up these codons in the codon table, we can determine that this particular DNA strand will translate into a protein with the following amino acids in a chain: methionine, valine, threonine, proline, and threonine. This is a contrived example, but it logically demonstrates how DNA instructs the creation of proteins that make you uniquely *you*. It's a marvel that science has allowed us to understand the language of DNA, including the start and stop punctuations.

Thinking of DNA as Source Code

At the cellular level, your body is a completely distributed system. Nothing is centralized. It's like a cluster of 37.2 trillion[4] cells executing the same code: your DNA.

If you think of your DNA as source code, here are some things to consider:

- The source is comprised of only four characters: A, C, T, and G.

- The source has two contributors, your mother and father, who contributed 3.2 billion letters each. In fact, the reference genome provided by the Genome Reference Consortium (GRC) is nothing more than an ASCII file with 3.2 billion characters inside.[5]

- The source is broken up into 25 separate files called *chromosomes* that each hold varying fractions of the source. The files are numbered, and tend to get smaller in size, with chromosome 1 holding ~250 million characters and chromosome 22 holding only ~50 million. There are also the X, Y, and mitochondrial chromosomes. The term *chromosome* basically means "colored thing," from a time when biologists could stain them but didn't know what they were.

- The source is executed on your biological machinery three letters (i.e., a codon) at a time, using the genetic code explained previously—not unlike a Turing machine that reads chemical letters instead of paper ribbon.

---

4. See Eva Bianconi et al., "An estimation of the number of cells in the human body," (*http://bit.ly/cell_esti mate*) *Annals of Human Biology*, November/December 2013.

5. You might expect this to be 6.4 billion letters, but the reference genome is, for better or worse, a *haploid* representation of the average of dozens of individuals.

- The source has about 20,000 functions, called *genes*, which each create a protein when executed. The location of each gene in the source is called the *locus*. You can think of a gene as a specific range of contiguous base positions on a chromosome. For example, the BRCA1 gene implicated in breast cancer can be found on chromosome 17 from positions 41,196,312 to 41,277,500. A gene is like a "pointer" or "address," whereas alleles (described momentarily) are the actual content. Everyone has the BRCA1 gene, but not everyone has alleles that put them at risk.

- A *haplotype* is similar to an object in object-oriented programming languages that holds specific functions (genes) that are typically inherited together.

- The source has two definitions for each gene, called *alleles*—one from your mother and one from your father—which are found at the same position of paired chromosomes (while the cells in your body are *diploid*—that is, they have two alleles per gene—there are organisms that are *triploid*, *tetraploid*, etc.). Both alleles are executed and the resultant proteins interact to create a specific *phenotype*. For example, proteins that make or degrade eye color pigment lead to a particular phenotype, or an observable characteristic (e.g., blue eyes). If the alleles you inherit from your parents are identical, you're *homozygous* for that allele; otherwise, you're *heterozygous*.

- A *single-nucleic polymorphism* (SNP), pronounced "snip," is a single-character change in the source code (e.g., from `ACTGACTG` to `ACTTACTG`).

- An *indel* is short for *insert-delete* and represents an insertion or deletion from the reference genome. For example, if the reference has `CCTGACTG` and your sample has four characters inserted—say, `CCTGCCTAACTG`—then it is an indel.

- Only 0.5% of the source gets translated into the proteins that sustain your life. That portion of the source is called your *exome*. A human exome requires a few gigabytes to store in compressed binary files.

- The other 99.5% of the source is commented out and serves as word padding (*introns*); it is used to regulate when genes are turned on, repeat, and so on.[6] A *whole genome* requires a few hundred gigabytes to store in compressed binary files.

- Every cell of your body has the same source,[7] but it can be selectively commented out by *epigenetic* factors like *DNA methylation* and *histone modification*, not unlike an `#ifdef` statement for each cell type (e.g., `#ifdef RETINA` or `#ifdef LIVER`).

---

6. Only about 28% of your DNA is transcribed into nascent RNA, and after RNA splicing, only about 1.5% of the RNA is left to code for proteins. Evolutionary selection occurs at the DNA level, with most of your DNA providing support to the other 0.5% or being deselected altogether (as more fitting DNA evolves). There are some cancers that appear to be caused by dormant regions of DNA being resurrected, so to speak.

7. There is actually, on average, about 1 error for each billion DNA "letters" copied. So, each cell isn't *exactly* the same.

These factors are responsible for making cells in your retina operate differently than cells in your liver.

- The process of *variant calling* is similar to running *diff* between two different DNA sources.

These analogies aren't meant to be taken too literally, but hopefully they helped familiarize you with some genomics terminology.

The Human Genome Project and Reference Genomes

In 1953, Watson and Crick discovered the structure of DNA, and in 1965 Nirenberg, with help from his NIH colleagues, cracked the genetic code, which expressed the rules for translating DNA or mRNA into proteins. Scientists knew that there were millions of human proteins but didn't have a complete survey of the human genome, which made it impossible to fully understand the genes responsible for protein synthesis. For example, if each protein was created by a single gene, that would imply millions of protein-coding genes in the human genome.

In 1990, the Human Genome Project set out to determine all the chemical base pairs that make up human DNA. This collaborative, international research program published the first human genome in April of 2003,[8] at an estimated cost of $3.8 billion. The Human Genome Project generated an estimated $796 billion in economic impact, equating to a return on investment (ROI) of 141:1.[9] The Human Genome Project found about 20,500 genes—significantly fewer than the millions you would expect with a simple 1:1 model of gene to protein, since proteins can be assembled from a combination of genes, post-translational processes during folding, and other mechanisms.

While this first human genome took over a decade to build, once created, it made "bootstrapping" the subsequent sequencing of other genomes much easier. For the first genome, scientists were operating in the dark. They had no reference to search as a roadmap for constructing the full genome. There is no technology to date that can read a whole genome from start to finish; instead, there are many techniques that vary in the speed, accuracy, and length of DNA fragments they can read. Scientists in the Human Genome Project had to sequence the genome in pieces, with different pieces being more easily sequenced by different technologies. Once you have a complete human genome, subsequent human genomes become much easier to construct; you can use the first genome as a reference for the second. The fragments from the second genome can be pattern matched to the first, similar to having the picture on a jigsaw puzzle's box to

---

8. Intentionally 50 years after Watson and Crick's discovery of the 3D structure of DNA.

9. Jonathan Max Gitlin, "Calculating the economic impact of the Human Genome Project," (*http://www.genome.gov/27544383*) June 2013.

help inform the placement of the puzzle pieces. It helps that most coding sequences are highly conserved, and *variants* only occur at 1 in 1,000 loci.

Shortly after the Human Genome Project was completed, the Genome Reference Consortium (GRC) (*http://genomereference.org*), an international collection of academic and research institutes, was formed to improve the representation of reference genomes. The GRC publishes a new human reference that serves as something like a common coordinate system or map to help analyze new genomes. The latest human reference genome, released in February 2014, was named GRCh38; it replaced GRCh37, which was released five years prior.

Sequencing and Aligning DNA

Second-generation sequencing is rapidly evolving, with numerous hardware vendors and new sequencing methods being developed about every six months; however, a common feature of all these technologies is the use of massively parallel methods, where thousands or even millions of reactions occur simultaneously. The double-stranded DNA is split down the middle, the single strands are copied many times, and the copies are randomly shredded into small fragments of different lengths called *reads*, which are placed into the sequencer. The sequencer reads the "letters" in each of these reads, in parallel for high throughput, and outputs a raw ASCII file containing each read (e.g., AGTTTCGGGATC...), as well as a quality estimate for each letter read, to be used for downstream analysis.

A piece of software called an *aligner* takes each read and works to find its position in the reference genome (see Figure 23-3).[10] A complete human genome is about 3 billion base (A, C, T, G) pairs long.[11] The reference genome (e.g., GRCh38) acts like the picture on a puzzle box, presenting the overall contours and colors of the human genome. Each short read is like a puzzle piece that needs to be fit into position as closely as possible. A common metric is "edit distance," which quantifies the number of operations necessary to transform one string to another. Identical strings have an edit distance of zero, and an indel of one letter has an edit distance of one. Since humans are 99.9% identical to one another, most of the reads will fit to the reference quite well and have a low edit distance. The challenge with building a good aligner is handling idiosyncratic reads.

10. There is also a second approach, *de novo* assembly, where reads are put into a graph data structure to create long sequences without mapping to a reference genome.

11. Each base is about 3.4 angstroms, so the DNA from a single human cell stretches over 2 meters end to end!

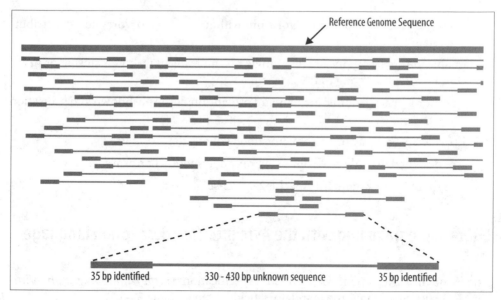

Figure 23-3. Aligning reads to a reference genome, from Wikipedia (http://bit.ly/mapping_reads)

ADAM, A Scalable Genome Analysis Platform

Aligning the reads to a reference genome is only the first of a series of steps necessary to generate reports that are useful in a clinical or research setting. The early stages of this processing pipeline look similar to any other extract-transform-load (ETL) pipelines that need data deduplication and normalization before analysis.

The sequencing process duplicates genomic DNA, so it's possible that the same DNA reads are generated multiple times; these duplicates need to be marked. The sequencer also provides a quality estimate for each DNA "letter" that it reads, which has sequencer-specific biases that need to be adjusted. Aligners often misplace reads that have indels (inserted or deleted sequences) that need to be repositioned on the reference genome. Currently, this preprocessing is done using single-purpose tools launched by shell scripts on a single machine. These tools take multiple days to finish the processing of whole genomes. The process is disk bound, with each stage writing a new file to be read into subsequent stages, and is an ideal use case for applying general-purpose big data technology. ADAM is able to handle the same preprocessing in under two hours.

ADAM is a genome analysis platform that focuses on rapidly processing petabytes of high-coverage, whole genome data. ADAM relies on Apache Avro, Parquet, and Spark. These systems provide many benefits when used together, since they:

- Allow developers to focus on algorithms without needing to worry about distributed system failures
- Enable jobs to be run locally on a single machine, on an in-house cluster, or in the cloud *without changing code*
- Compress legacy genomic formats and provide predicate pushdown and projection for performance
- Provide an agile way of customizing and evolving data formats
- Are designed to easily scale out using only commodity hardware
- Are shared with a standard Apache 2.0 license[12]

Literate programming with the Avro interface description language (IDL)

The Sequence Alignment/Map (SAM) specification (*http://samtools.github.io/hts-specs/SAMv1.pdf*) defines the mandatory fields listed in Table 23-2.

Table 23-2. Mandatory fields in the SAM format

Col	Field	Type	Regexp/Range	Brief description
1	QNAME	String	[!-?A-~]{1,255}	Query template NAME
2	FLAG	Int	[0, 2^{16}-1]	bitwise FLAG
3	RNAME	String	*|[!-()+-<>-~][!-~]*	Reference sequence NAME
4	POS	Int	[0,2^{31}-1]	1-based leftmost mapping POSition
5	MAPQ	Int	[0,2^{8}-1]	MAPping Quality
6	CIGAR	String	*|([0-9]+[MIDNSHPX=])+	CIGAR string
7	RNEXT	String	*|=|[!-()+->< -~][!-~]*	Ref. name of the mate/NEXT read
8	PNEXT	Int	[0,2^{31}-1]	Position of the mate/NEXT read
9	TLEN	Int	[-2^{31}+1,2^{31}-1]	observed Template LENgth
10	SEQ	String	*|[A-Za-z=.]+	segment SEQuence
11	QUAL	String	[!-~]	ASCII of Phred-scaled base QUALity+33

Any developers who want to implement this specification need to translate this English spec into their computer language of choice. In ADAM, we have chosen instead to use

---

12. Unfortunately, some of the more popular software in genomics has an ill-defined or custom, restrictive license. Clean open source licensing and source code are necessary for science to make it easier to reproduce and understand results.

literate programming with a spec defined in Avro IDL. For example, the mandatory fields for SAM can be easily expressed in a simple Avro record:

```
record AlignmentRecord {
    string qname;
    int flag;
    string rname;
    int pos;
    int mapq;
    string cigar;
    string rnext;
    int pnext;
    int tlen;
    string seq;
    string qual;
}
```

Avro is able to autogenerate native Java (or C++, Python, etc.) classes for reading and writing data and provides standard interfaces (e.g., Hadoop's InputFormat) to make integration with numerous systems easy. Avro is also designed to make schema evolution easier. In fact, the ADAM schemas (*http://bit.ly/bdg-formats*) we use today have evolved to be more sophisticated, expressive, and customized to express a variety of genomic models such as structural variants, genotypes, variant calling annotations, variant effects, and more.

UC Berkeley is a member of the Global Alliance for Genomics & Health (*http://genomicsandhealth.org/*), a non-governmental, public-private partnership consisting of more than 220 organizations across 30 nations, with the goal of maximizing the potential of genomics medicine through effective and responsible data sharing. The Global Alliance has embraced this literate programming approach and publishes its schemas (*https://github.com/ga4gh/schemas*) in Avro IDL as well. Using Avro has allowed researchers around the world to talk about data at the logical level, without concern for computer languages or on-disk formats.

Column-oriented access with Parquet

The SAM and BAM[13] file formats are *row-oriented*: the data for each record is stored together as a single line of text or a binary record. (See "Other File Formats and Column-Oriented Formats" on page 136 for further discussion of row- versus column-oriented formats.) A single paired-end read in a SAM file might look like this:

```
read1   99 chrom1  7 30 8M2I4M1D3M = 37  39 TTAGATAAAGGATACTG *
read1  147 chrom1 37 30 9M         = 7 -39 CAGCGGCAT         * NM:i:1
```

---

13. BAM is the compressed binary version of the SAM format.

A typical SAM/BAM file contains many millions of rows, one for each DNA read that came off the sequencer. The preceding text fragment translates loosely into the view shown in Table 23-3.

Table 23-3. Logical view of SAM fragment

Name	Reference	Position	MapQ	CIGAR	Sequence
read1	chromosome1	7	30	8M2I4M1D3M	TTAGATAAAGGATACTG
read1	chromosome1	37	30	9M	CAGCGGCAT

In this example, the read, identified as read1, was mapped to the reference genome at chromosome1, positions 7 and 37. This is called a "paired-end" read as it represents a single strand of DNA that was read from each end by the sequencer. By analogy, it's like reading an array of length 150 from 0..50 and 150..100.

The MapQ score represents the probability that the sequence is mapped to the reference correctly. MapQ scores of 20, 30, and 40 have a probability of being correct of 99%, 99.9%, and 99.99%, respectively. To calculate the probability of error from a MapQ score, use the expression $10^{(-MapQ/10)}$ (e.g., $10^{(-30/10)}$ is a probability of 0.001).

The CIGAR explains how the individual nucleotides in the DNA sequence map to the reference.[14] The Sequence is, of course, the DNA sequence that was mapped to the reference.

There is a stark mismatch between the SAM/BAM *row-oriented* on-disk format and the *column-oriented* access patterns common to genome analysis. Consider the following:

- A range query to find data for a particular gene linked to breast cancer, named BRCA1: "Find all reads that cover chromosome 17 from position 41,196,312 to 41,277,500"

- A simple filter to find poorly mapped reads: "Find all reads with a MapQ less than 10"

- A search of all reads with insertions or deletions, called *indels*: "Find all reads that contain I or D in the CIGAR string"

- Count the number of unique *k*-mers: "Read every Sequence and generate all possible substrings of length *k* in the string"

---

14. The first record's Compact Idiosyncratic Gap Alignment Report (CIGAR) string is translated as "8 matches (8M), 2 inserts (2I), 4 matches (4M), 1 delete (1D), 3 matches (3M)."

Parquet's predicate pushdown feature allows us to rapidly filter reads for analysis (e.g., finding a gene, ignoring poorly mapped reads). Projection allows for precise materialization of only the columns of interest (e.g., reading only the sequences for *k*-mer counting).

Additionally, a number of the fields have low cardinality, making them ideal for data compression techniques like run-length encoding (RLE). For example, given that humans have only 23 pairs of chromosomes, the `Reference` field will have only a few dozen unique values (e.g., `chromosome1`, `chromosome17`, etc.). We have found that storing BAM records inside Parquet files results in ~20% compression. Using the `PrintFooter` command in Parquet, we have found that quality scores can be run-length encoded and bit-packed to compress ~48%, but they still take up ~70% of the total space. We're looking forward to Parquet 2.0, so we can use delta encoding on the quality scores to compress the file size even more.

A simple example: *k*-mer counting using Spark and ADAM

Let's do "word count" for genomics: counting *k*-mers. The term *k-mers* refers to all the possible subsequences of length *k* for a read. For example, if you have a read with the sequence AGATCTGAAG, the 3-mers for that sequence would be `['AGA', 'GAT', 'ATC', 'TCT', 'CTG', 'TGA', 'GAA', 'AAG']`. While this is a trivial example, *k*-mers are useful when building structures like De Bruijn graphs for sequence assembly. In this example, we are going to generate all the possible 21-mers from our reads, count them, and then write the totals to a text file.

This example assumes that you've already created a `SparkContext` named `sc`. First, we create a Spark RDD of `AlignmentRecords` using a pushdown predicate to remove low-quality reads and a projection to only materialize the `sequence` field in each read:

```
// Load reads from 'inputPath' into an RDD for analysis
val adamRecords: RDD[AlignmentRecord] = sc.adamLoad(args.inputPath,

  // Filter out all low-quality reads that failed vendor quality checks
  predicate = Some(classOf[HighQualityReadsPredicate]),

  // Only materialize the 'sequence' from each record
  projection = Some(Projection(AlignmentRecordField.sequence)))
```

Since Parquet is a column-oriented storage format, it can rapidly materialize only the sequence column and quickly skip over the unwanted fields. Next, we walk over each sequence using a sliding window of length *k*=21, emit a count of 1L, and then `reduce ByKey` using the *k*-mer subsequence as the key to get the total counts for the input file:

```
// The length of k-mers we want to count
val kmerLength = 21

// Process the reads into an RDD of tuples with k-mers and counts
val kmers: RDD[(String, Long)] = adamRecords.flatMap(read => {
```

```
    read.getSequence
      .toString
      .sliding(kmerLength)
      .map(k => (k, 1L))
}).reduceByKey { case (a, b) => a + b}

// Print the k-mers as a text file to the 'outputPath'
kmers.map { case (kmer, count) => s"$count,$kmer"}
    .saveAsTextFile(args.outputPath)
```

When run on sample NA21144, chromosome 11 in the 1000 Genomes project,[15] this job outputs the following:

```
AAAAAAAAAAAAAAAAAAAAAAAA, 124069
TTTTTTTTTTTTTTTTTTTTTTTT, 120590
ACACACACACACACACACACACAC, 41528
GTGTGTGTGTGTGTGTGTGTGTGT, 40905
CACACACACACACACACACACACA, 40795
TGTGTGTGTGTGTGTGTGTGTGTG, 40329
TAATCCCAGCACTTTGGGAGGC, 32122
TGTAATCCCAGCACTTTGGGAG, 31206
CTGTAATCCCAGCACTTTGGGA, 30809
GCCTCCCAAAGTGCTGGGATTA, 30716
...
```

ADAM can do much more than just count *k*-mers. Aside from the preprocessing stages already mentioned—duplicate marking, base quality score recalibration, and indel realignment—it also:

- Calculates coverage read depth at each variant in a Variant Call Format (VCF) file
- Counts the *k*-mers/*q*-mers from a read dataset
- Loads gene annotations from a Gene Transfer Format (GTF) file and outputs the corresponding gene models
- Prints statistics on all the reads in a read dataset (e.g., % mapped to reference, number of duplicates, reads mapped cross-chromosome, etc.)
- Launches legacy variant callers, pipes reads into *stdin*, and saves output from *stdout*
- Comes with a basic genome browser to view reads in a web browser

However, the most important thing ADAM provides is an open, scalable platform. All artifacts are published to Maven Central (*http://search.maven.org/*) (search for group ID org.bdgenomics) to make it easy for developers to benefit from the foundation ADAM provides. ADAM data is stored in Avro and Parquet, so you can also use systems like SparkSQL, Impala, Apache Pig, Apache Hive, or others to analyze the data. ADAM

---

15. Arguably the most popular publicly available dataset, found at *http://www.1000genomes.org*.

also supports job written in Scala, Java, and Python, with more language support on the way.

At Scala.IO in Paris in 2014, Andy Petrella and Xavier Tordoir used Spark's MLlib *k*-means with ADAM for population stratification across the 1000 Genomes dataset (population stratification is the process of assigning an individual genome to an ancestral group). They found that ADAM/Spark improved performance by a factor of 150.

From Personalized Ads to Personalized Medicine

While ADAM is designed to rapidly and scalably analyze aligned reads, it does not align the reads itself; instead, ADAM relies on standard short-reads aligners. The Scalable Nucleotide Alignment Program (*http://snap.cs.berkeley.edu/*) (SNAP) is a collaborative effort including participants from Microsoft Research, UC San Francisco, and the AMPLab as well as open source developers, shared with an Apache 2.0 license. The SNAP aligner is as accurate as the current best-of-class aligners, like BWA-mem, Bowtie2, and Novalign, but runs between 3 and 20 times faster. This speed advantage is important when doctors are racing to identify a pathogen.

In 2013, a boy went to the University of Wisconsin Hospital and Clinics' Emergency Department three times in four months with symptoms of encephalitis: fevers and headaches. He was eventually hospitalized without a successful diagnosis after numerous blood tests, brain scans, and biopsies. Five weeks later, he began having seizures that required he be placed into a medically induced coma. In desperation, doctors sampled his spinal fluid and sent it to an experimental program led by Charles Chiu at UC San Francisco, where it was sequenced for analysis. The speed and accuracy of SNAP allowed UCSF to quickly filter out all human DNA and, from the remaining 0.02% of the reads, identify a rare infectious bacterium, *Leptospira santarosai*. They reported the discovery to the Wisconsin doctors *just two days after they sent the sample*. The boy was treated with antibiotics for 10 days, awoke from his coma, and was discharged from the hospital two weeks later.[16]

If you're interested in learning more about the system the Chiu lab used—called Sequence-based Ultra-Rapid Pathogen Identification (SURPI) (*http://chiulab.ucsf.edu/surpi/*)—they have generously shared their software with a permissive BSD license and provide an Amazon EC2 Machine Image (AMI) with SURPI preinstalled. SURPI collects 348,922 unique bacterial sequences and 1,193,607 unique virus sequences from numerous sources and saves them in 29 SNAP-indexed databases, each approximately 27 GB in size, for fast search.

---

16. Michael Wilson et al., "Actionable Diagnosis of Neuroleptospirosis by Next-Generation Sequencing," (*http://www.nejm.org/doi/pdf/10.1056/NEJMoa1401268*) *New England Journal of Medicine*, June 2014.

Today, more data is analyzed for personalized advertising than personalized medicine, but that will not be the case in the future. With personalized medicine, people receive customized healthcare that takes into consideration their unique DNA profiles. As the price of sequencing drops and more people have their genomes sequenced, the increase in statistical power will allow researchers to understand the genetic mechanisms underlying diseases and fold these discoveries into the personalized medical model, to improve treatment for subsequent patients. While only 25 PB of genomic data were generated worldwide this year, next year that number will likely be 100 PB.

Join In

While we're off to a great start, the ADAM project is still an experimental platform and needs further development. If you're interested in learning more about programming on ADAM or want to contribute code, take a look at *Advanced Analytics with Spark: Patterns for Learning from Data at Scale* by Sandy Ryza et al. (O'Reilly, 2014), which includes a chapter on analyzing genomics data with ADAM and Spark. You can find us at *http://bdgenomics.org*, on IRC at #adamdev, or on Twitter at @bigdatagenomics.

Cascading

Chris K. Wensel

Cascading is an open source Java library and API that provides an abstraction layer for MapReduce. It allows developers to build complex, mission-critical data processing applications that run on Hadoop clusters.

The Cascading project began in the summer of 2007. Its first public release, version 0.1, launched in January 2008. Version 1.0 was released in January 2009. Binaries, source code, and add-on modules can be downloaded from the project website (*http://www.cascading.org/*).

Map and reduce operations offer powerful primitives. However, they tend to be at the wrong level of granularity for creating sophisticated, highly composable code that can be shared among different developers. Moreover, many developers find it difficult to "think" in terms of MapReduce when faced with real-world problems.

To address the first issue, Cascading substitutes the keys and values used in MapReduce with simple field names and a data tuple model, where a tuple is simply a list of values. For the second issue, Cascading departs from map and reduce operations directly by introducing higher-level abstractions as alternatives: Functions, Filters, Aggregators, and Buffers.

Other alternatives began to emerge at about the same time as the project's initial public release, but Cascading was designed to complement them. Consider that most of these alternative frameworks impose pre- and post-conditions, or other expectations.

For example, in several other MapReduce tools, you must preformat, filter, or import your data into HDFS prior to running the application. That step of preparing the data must be performed outside of the programming abstraction. In contrast, Cascading provides the means to prepare and manage your data as integral parts of the programming abstraction.

This case study begins with an introduction to the main concepts of Cascading, then finishes with an overview of how ShareThis (*http://www.sharethis.com/*) uses Cascading in its infrastructure.

See the Cascading User Guide (*http://www.cascading.org/documentation/*) on the project website for a more in-depth presentation of the Cascading processing model.

Fields, Tuples, and Pipes

The MapReduce model uses keys and values to link input data to the map function, the map function to the reduce function, and the reduce function to the output data.

But as we know, real-world Hadoop applications usually consist of more than one MapReduce job chained together. Consider the canonical word count example implemented in MapReduce. If you needed to sort the numeric counts in descending order, which is not an unlikely requirement, it would need to be done in a second MapReduce job.

So, in the abstract, keys and values not only bind map to reduce, but reduce to the next map, and then to the next reduce, and so on (Figure 24-1). That is, key-value pairs are sourced from input files and stream through chains of map and reduce operations, and finally rest in an output file. When you implement enough of these chained MapReduce applications, you start to see a well-defined set of key-value manipulations used over and over again to modify the key-value data stream.

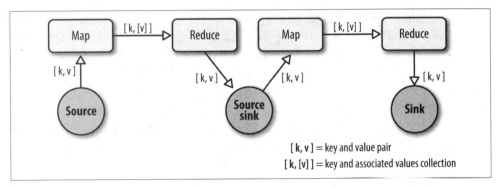

Figure 24-1. Counting and sorting in MapReduce

Cascading simplifies this by abstracting away keys and values and replacing them with tuples that have corresponding field names, similar in concept to tables and column names in a relational database. During processing, streams of these fields and tuples are then manipulated as they pass through user-defined operations linked together by pipes (Figure 24-2).

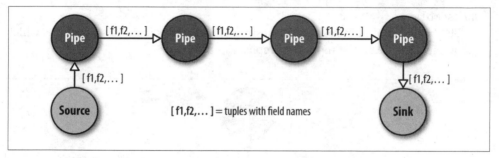

Figure 24-2. Pipes linked by fields and tuples

So, MapReduce keys and values are reduced to:

Fields

A field is a collection of either `String` names (such as "first_name"), numeric positions (such as 2 or –1, for the third and last positions, respectively), or a combination of both. So, fields are used to declare the names of values in a tuple and to select values by name from a tuple. The latter is like a SQL `select` call.

Tuples

A tuple is simply an array of `java.lang.Comparable` objects. A tuple is very much like a database row or record.

And the map and reduce operations are abstracted behind one or more pipe instances (Figure 24-3):

Each

The `Each` pipe processes a single input tuple at a time. It may apply either a `Function` or a `Filter` operation (described shortly) to the input tuple.

GroupBy

The `GroupBy` pipe groups tuples on grouping fields. It behaves just like the SQL `GROUP BY` statement. It can also merge multiple input tuple streams into a single stream if they all share the same field names.

CoGroup

The `CoGroup` pipe joins multiple tuple streams together by common field names, and it also groups the tuples by the common grouping fields. All standard join types (inner, outer, etc.) and custom joins can be used across two or more tuple streams.

Every

The `Every` pipe processes a single grouping of tuples at a time, where the group was grouped by a `GroupBy` or `CoGroup` pipe. The `Every` pipe may apply either an `Aggregator` or a `Buffer` operation to the grouping.

`SubAssembly`

The `SubAssembly` pipe allows for nesting of assemblies inside a single pipe, which can, in turn, be nested in more complex assemblies.

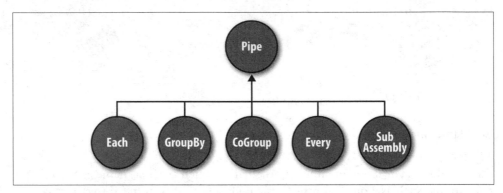

Figure 24-3. Pipe types

All these pipes are chained together by the developer into "pipe assemblies," in which each assembly can have many input tuple streams (sources) and many output tuple streams (sinks). See Figure 24-4.

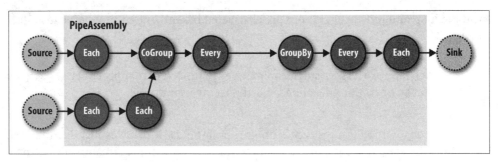

Figure 24-4. A simple PipeAssembly

On the surface, this might seem more complex than the traditional MapReduce model. And admittedly, there are more concepts here than map, reduce, key, and value. But in practice, there are many more concepts that must all work in tandem to provide different behaviors.

For example, a developer who wanted to provide a "secondary sorting" of reducer values would need to implement a map, a reduce, a "composite" key (two keys nested in a parent key), a value, a partitioner, an "output value grouping" comparator, and an "output key" comparator, all of which would be coupled to one another in varying ways, and very likely would not be reusable in subsequent applications.

In Cascading, this would be one line of code: new GroupBy(*<previous>, <grouping fields>, <secondary sorting fields>*), where *<previous>* is the pipe that came before.

Operations

As mentioned earlier, Cascading departs from MapReduce by introducing alternative operations that are applied either to individual tuples or groups of tuples (Figure 24-5):

Function

A Function operates on individual input tuples and may return zero or more output tuples for every one input. Functions are applied by the Each pipe.

Filter

A Filter is a special kind of function that returns a Boolean value indicating whether the current input tuple should be removed from the tuple stream. A Function could serve this purpose, but the Filter is optimized for this case, and many filters can be grouped by "logical" filters such as AND, OR, XOR, and NOT, rapidly creating more complex filtering operations.

Aggregator

An Aggregator performs some operation against a group of tuples, where the grouped tuples are by a common set of field values (for example, all tuples having the same "last-name" value). Common Aggregator implementations would be Sum, Count, Average, Max, and Min.

Buffer

A Buffer is similar to an Aggregator, except it is optimized to act as a "sliding window" across all the tuples in a unique grouping. This is useful when the developer needs to efficiently insert missing values in an ordered set of tuples (such as a missing date or duration) or create a running average. Usually Aggregator is the operation of choice when working with groups of tuples, since many Aggregators can be chained together very efficiently, but sometimes a Buffer is the best tool for the job.

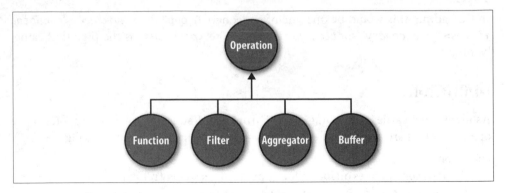

Figure 24-5. Operation types

Operations are bound to pipes when the pipe assembly is created (Figure 24-6).

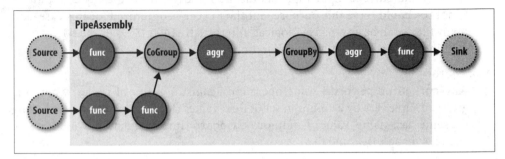

Figure 24-6. An assembly of operations

The Each and Every pipes provide a simple mechanism for selecting some or all values out of an input tuple before the values are passed to its child operation. And there is a simple mechanism for merging the operation results with the original input tuple to create the output tuple. Without going into great detail, this allows for each operation to care only about argument tuple values and fields, not the whole set of fields in the current input tuple. Subsequently, operations can be reusable across applications in the same way that Java methods can be reusable.

For example, in Java, a method declared as concatenate(String first, String second) is more abstract than concatenate(Person person). In the second case, the concatenate() function must "know" about the Person object; in the first case, it is agnostic to where the data came from. Cascading operations exhibit this same quality.

Taps, Schemes, and Flows

In many of the previous diagrams, there are references to "sources" and "sinks." In Cascading, all data is read from or written to `Tap` instances, but is converted to and from tuple instances via `Scheme` objects:

Tap

A `Tap` is responsible for the "how" and "where" parts of accessing data. For example, is the data on HDFS or the local filesystem? In Amazon S3 or over HTTP?

Scheme

A `Scheme` is responsible for reading raw data and converting it to a tuple and/or writing a tuple out into raw data, where this "raw" data can be lines of text, Hadoop binary sequence files, or some proprietary format.

Note that `Taps` are not part of a pipe assembly, and so they are not a type of `Pipe`. But they are connected with pipe assemblies when they are made cluster executable. When a pipe assembly is connected with the necessary number of source and sink `Tap` instances, we get a `Flow`. The `Taps` either emit or capture the field names the pipe assembly expects. That is, if a `Tap` emits a tuple with the field name "line" (by reading data from a file on HDFS), the head of the pipe assembly must be expecting a "line" value as well. Otherwise, the process that connects the pipe assembly with the `Taps` will immediately fail with an error.

So pipe assemblies are really data process definitions, and are not "executable" on their own. They must be connected to source and sink `Tap` instances before they can run on a cluster. This separation between `Taps` and pipe assemblies is part of what makes Cascading so powerful.

If you think of a pipe assembly like a Java class, then a `Flow` is like a Java object instance (Figure 24-7). That is, the same pipe assembly can be "instantiated" many times into new `Flows`, in the same application, without fear of any interference between them. This allows pipe assemblies to be created and shared like standard Java libraries.

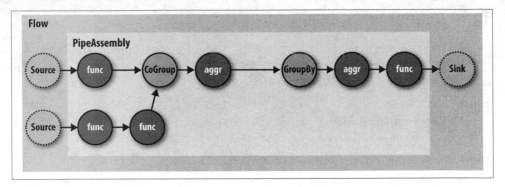

Figure 24-7. A Flow

Cascading in Practice

Now that we know what Cascading is and have a good idea of how it works, what does an application written in Cascading look like? See Example 24-1.

Example 24-1. Word count and sort

```
Scheme sourceScheme =
    new TextLine(new Fields("line")); ❶
Tap source =
    new Hfs(sourceScheme, inputPath); ❷

Scheme sinkScheme = new TextLine(); ❸
Tap sink =
    new Hfs(sinkScheme, outputPath, SinkMode.REPLACE); ❹

Pipe assembly = new Pipe("wordcount"); ❺

String regexString = "(?<!\\pL)(?=\\pL)[^ ]*(?<=\\pL)(?!\\pL)";
Function regex = new RegexGenerator(new Fields("word"), regexString);
assembly =
    new Each(assembly, new Fields("line"), regex); ❻

assembly =
    new GroupBy(assembly, new Fields("word")); ❼

Aggregator count = new Count(new Fields("count"));
assembly = new Every(assembly, count); ❽

assembly =
    new GroupBy(assembly, new Fields("count"), new Fields("word")); ❾

FlowConnector flowConnector = new FlowConnector();
Flow flow =
    flowConnector.connect("word-count", source, sink, assembly); ❿
```

```
flow.complete();⓫
```

❶ We create a new Scheme that reads simple text files and emits a new Tuple for each line in a field named "line," as declared by the Fields instance.

❸ We create a new Scheme that writes simple text files and expects a Tuple with any number of fields/values. If there is more than one value, they will be tab-delimited in the output file.

❷ ❹ We create source and sink Tap instances that reference the input file and output directory, respectively. The sink Tap will overwrite any file that may already exist.

❺ We construct the head of our pipe assembly and name it "wordcount." This name is used to bind the source and sink Taps to the assembly. Multiple heads or tails would require unique names.

❻ We construct an Each pipe with a function that will parse the "line" field into a new Tuple for each word encountered.

❼ We construct a GroupBy pipe that will create a new Tuple grouping for each unique value in the field "word."

❽ We construct an Every pipe with an Aggregator that will count the number of Tuples in every unique word group. The result is stored in a field named "count."

❾ We construct a GroupBy pipe that will create a new Tuple grouping for each unique value in the field "count" and secondary sort each value in the field "word." The result will be a list of "count" and "word" values with "count" sorted in increasing order.

❿ ⓫ We connect the pipe assembly to its sources and sinks in a Flow, and then execute the Flow on the cluster.

In the example, we count the words encountered in the input document, and we sort the counts in their natural order (ascending). If some words have the same "count" value, these words are sorted in their natural order (alphabetical).

One obvious problem with this example is that some words might have uppercase letters in some instances—for example, "the" and "The" when the word comes at the beginning of a sentence. We might consider inserting a new operation to force all the words to lowercase, but we realize that all future applications that need to parse words from documents should have the same behavior, so we'll instead create a reusable pipe called SubAssembly, just like we would by creating a subroutine in a traditional application (see Example 24-2).

Example 24-2. Creating a SubAssembly

```
public class ParseWordsAssembly extends SubAssembly ❶
  {
  public ParseWordsAssembly(Pipe previous)
```

```
    {
    String regexString = "(?<!\\pL)(?=\\pl )[^ ]*(?<=\\pL)(?!\\pL)";
    Function regex = new RegexGenerator(new Fields("word"), regexString);
    previous = new Each(previous, new Fields("line"), regex);

    String exprString = "word.toLowerCase()";
    Function expression =
        new ExpressionFunction(new Fields("word"), exprString, String.class); ❷
    previous = new Each(previous, new Fields("word"), expression);

    setTails(previous); ❸
    }
  }
```

❶   We subclass the `SubAssembly` class, which is itself a kind of `Pipe`.

❷   We create a Java expression function that will call `toLowerCase()` on the `String` value in the field named "word." We must also pass in the Java type the expression expects "word" to be—in this case, `String`. (Janino (*http://www.jani no.net/*) is used under the covers.)

❸   We tell the `SubAssembly` superclass where the tail ends of our pipe subassembly are.

First, we create a `SubAssembly` pipe to hold our "parse words" pipe assembly. Because this is a Java class, it can be reused in any other application, as long as there is an incoming field named "word" (Example 24-3). Note that there are ways to make this function even more generic, but they are covered in the Cascading User Guide (*http://www.cascad ing.org/documentation/*).

Example 24-3. Extending word count and sort with a SubAssembly

```
Scheme sourceScheme = new TextLine(new Fields("line"));
Tap source = new Hfs(sourceScheme, inputPath);

Scheme sinkScheme = new TextLine(new Fields("word", "count"));
Tap sink = new Hfs(sinkScheme, outputPath, SinkMode.REPLACE);

Pipe assembly = new Pipe("wordcount");

assembly =
    new ParseWordsAssembly(assembly); ❶

assembly = new GroupBy(assembly, new Fields("word"));

Aggregator count = new Count(new Fields("count"));
assembly = new Every(assembly, count);

assembly = new GroupBy(assembly, new Fields("count"), new Fields("word"));

FlowConnector flowConnector = new FlowConnector();
```

```
Flow flow = flowConnector.connect("word-count", source, sink, assembly);

flow.complete();
```

❶   We replace `Each` from the previous example with our `ParseWordsAssembly` pipe.

Finally, we just substitute in our new `SubAssembly` right where the previous `Every` and word parser function were used in the previous example. This nesting can continue as deep as necessary.

Flexibility

Let's take a step back and see what this new model has given us—or better yet, what it has taken away.

You see, we no longer think in terms of MapReduce jobs, or `Mapper` and `Reducer` interface implementations and how to bind or link subsequent MapReduce jobs to the ones that precede them. During runtime, the Cascading "planner" figures out the optimal way to partition the pipe assembly into MapReduce jobs and manages the linkages between them (Figure 24-8).

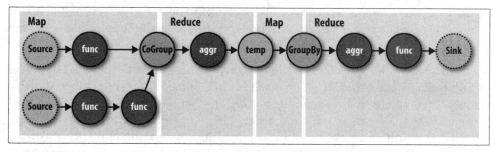

Figure 24-8. How a Flow translates to chained MapReduce jobs

Because of this, developers can build applications of arbitrary granularity. They can start with a small application that just filters a logfile, then iteratively build more features into the application as needed.

Since Cascading is an API and not a syntax like strings of SQL, it is more flexible. First off, developers can create domain-specific languages (DSLs) using their favorite languages, such as Groovy, JRuby, Jython, Scala, and others (see the project site (*http://www.cascading.org/*) for examples). Second, developers can extend various parts of Cascading, such as allowing custom Thrift or JSON objects to be read and written to and allowing them to be passed through the tuple stream.

Hadoop and Cascading at ShareThis

ShareThis (*http://www.sharethis.com*) is a sharing network that makes it simple to share any online content. With the click of a button on a web page or browser plug-in, Share-This allows users to seamlessly access their contacts and networks from anywhere online and share the content via email, IM, Facebook, Digg, mobile SMS, and similar services, without ever leaving the current page. Publishers can deploy the ShareThis button to tap into the service's universal sharing capabilities to drive traffic, stimulate viral activity, and track the sharing of online content. ShareThis also simplifies social media services by reducing clutter on web pages and providing instant distribution of content across social networks, affiliate groups, and communities.

As ShareThis users share pages and information through the online widgets, a continuous stream of events enter the ShareThis network. These events are first filtered and processed, and then handed to various backend systems, including AsterData, Hypertable, and Katta.

The volume of these events can be huge; too large to process with traditional systems. This data can also be very "dirty" thanks to "injection attacks" from rogue systems, browser bugs, or faulty widgets. For this reason, the developers at ShareThis chose to deploy Hadoop as the preprocessing and orchestration frontend to their backend systems. They also chose to use Amazon Web Services to host their servers on the Elastic Computing Cloud (EC2) and provide long-term storage on the Simple Storage Service (S3), with an eye toward leveraging Elastic MapReduce (EMR).

In this overview, we will focus on the "log processing pipeline" (Figure 24-9). This pipeline simply takes data stored in an S3 bucket, processes it (as described shortly), and stores the results back into another bucket. The Simple Queue Service (SQS) is used to coordinate the events that mark the start and completion of data processing runs. Downstream, other processes pull data to load into AsterData, pull URL lists from Hypertable to source a web crawl, or pull crawled page data to create Lucene indexes for use by Katta. Note that Hadoop is central to the ShareThis architecture. It is used to coordinate the processing and movement of data between architectural components.

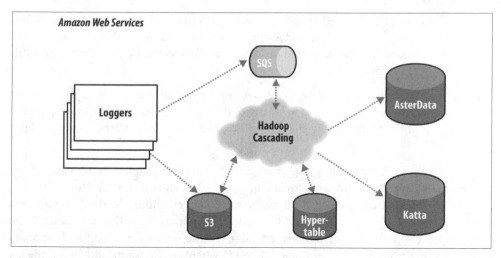

Figure 24-9. The ShareThis log processing pipeline

With Hadoop as the frontend, all the event logs can be parsed, filtered, cleaned, and organized by a set of rules before ever being loaded into the AsterData cluster or used by any other component. AsterData is a clustered data warehouse that can support large datasets and that allows for complex ad hoc queries using a standard SQL syntax. Share-This chose to clean and prepare the incoming datasets on the Hadoop cluster and then to load that data into the AsterData cluster for ad hoc analysis and reporting. Though that process would have been possible with AsterData, it made a lot of sense to use Hadoop as the first stage in the processing pipeline to offset load on the main data warehouse.

Cascading was chosen as the primary data processing API to simplify the development process, codify how data is coordinated between architectural components, and provide the developer-facing interface to those components. This represents a departure from more "traditional" Hadoop use cases, which essentially just query stored data. Cascading and Hadoop together provide a better and simpler structure for the complete solution, end to end, and thus provide more value to the users.

For the developers, Cascading made it easy to start with a simple unit test (created by subclassing `cascading.ClusterTestCase`) that did simple text parsing and then to layer in more processing rules while keeping the application logically organized for mainte-nance. Cascading aided this organization in a couple of ways. First, standalone opera-tions (`Functions`, `Filters`, etc.) could be written and tested independently. Second, the application was segmented into stages: one for parsing, one for rules, and a final stage for binning/collating the data, all via the `SubAssembly` base class described earlier.

The data coming from the ShareThis loggers looks a lot like Apache logs, with date/timestamps, share URLs, referrer URLs, and a bit of metadata. To use the data for analysis downstream, the URLs needed to be unpacked (parsing query-string data, domain names, etc.). So, a top-level SubAssembly was created to encapsulate the parsing, and child subassemblies were nested inside to handle specific fields if they were sufficiently complex to parse.

The same was done for applying rules. As every Tuple passed through the rules SubAssembly, it was marked as "bad" if any of the rules were triggered. Along with the "bad" tag, a description of why the record was bad was added to the Tuple for later review.

Finally, a splitter SubAssembly was created to do two things. First, it allowed for the tuple stream to split into two: one stream for "good" data and one for "bad" data. Second, the splitter binned the data into intervals, such as every hour. To do this, only two operations were necessary: the first to create the interval from the *timestamp* value already present in the stream, and the second to use the *interval* and *good/bad* metadata to create a directory path (for example, *05/good/*, where "05" is 5 a.m. and "good" means the Tuple passed all the rules). This path would then be used by the Cascading Templa teTap, a special Tap that can dynamically output tuple streams to different locations based on values in the Tuple. In this case, the TemplateTap used the "path" value to create the final output path.

The developers also created a fourth SubAssembly—this one to apply Cascading Asser tions during unit testing. These assertions double-checked that rules and parsing subassemblies did their job.

In the unit test in Example 24-4, we see the splitter isn't being tested, but it is added in another integration test not shown.

Example 24-4. Unit testing a Flow

```
public void testLogParsing() throws IOException
  {
  Hfs source = new Hfs(new TextLine(new Fields("line")), sampleData);
  Hfs sink =
      new Hfs(new TextLine(), outputPath + "/parser", SinkMode.REPLACE);

  Pipe pipe = new Pipe("parser");

  // split "line" on tabs
  pipe = new Each(pipe, new Fields("line"), new RegexSplitter("\t"));

  pipe = new LogParser(pipe);

  pipe = new LogRules(pipe);
  // testing only assertions
  pipe = new ParserAssertions(pipe);

  Flow flow = new FlowConnector().connect(source, sink, pipe);
```

```
flow.complete(); // run the test flow

// Verify there are 98 tuples and 2 fields, and matches the regex pattern
// For TextLine schemes the tuples are { "offset", "line" }
validateLength(flow, 98, 2, Pattern.compile("^[0-9]+(\\t[^\\t]*){19}$"));
}
```

For integration and deployment, many of the features built into Cascading allowed for easier integration with external systems and for greater process tolerance.

In production, all the subassemblies are joined and planned into a Flow, but instead of just source and sink Taps, trap Taps were planned in (Figure 24-10). Normally, when an operation throws an exception from a remote mapper or reducer task, the Flow will fail and kill all its managed MapReduce jobs. When a Flow has traps, any exceptions are caught and the data causing the exception is saved to the Tap associated with the current trap. Then the next Tuple is processed without stopping the Flow. Sometimes you want your Flows to fail on errors, but in this case, the ShareThis developers knew they could go back and look at the "failed" data and update their unit tests while the production system kept running. Losing a few hours of processing time was worse than losing a couple of bad records.

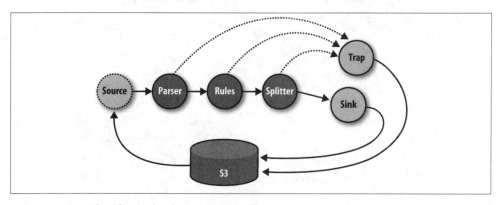

Figure 24-10. The ShareThis log processing flow

Using Cascading's event listeners, Amazon SQS could be integrated. When a Flow finishes, a message is sent to notify other systems that there is data ready to be picked up from Amazon S3. On failure, a different message is sent, alerting other processes.

The remaining downstream processes pick up where the log processing pipeline leaves off on different independent clusters. The log processing pipeline today runs once a day; there is no need to keep a 100-node cluster sitting around for the 23 hours it has nothing to do, so it is decommissioned and recommissioned 24 hours later.

In the future, it would be trivial to increase this interval on smaller clusters to every 6 hours, or 1 hour, as the business demands. Independently, other clusters are booting and shutting down at different intervals based on the needs of the business units responsible for those components. For example, the web crawler component (using Bixo, a Cascading-based web-crawler toolkit developed by EMI and ShareThis) may run continuously on a small cluster with a companion Hypertable cluster. This on-demand model works very well with Hadoop, where each cluster can be tuned for the kind of workload it is expected to handle.

Summary

Hadoop is a very powerful platform for processing and coordinating the movement of data across various architectural components. Its only drawback is that the primary computing model is MapReduce.

Cascading aims to help developers build powerful applications quickly and simply, through a well-reasoned API, without needing to think in MapReduce and while leaving the heavy lifting of data distribution, replication, distributed process management, and liveness to Hadoop.

Read more about Cascading, join the online community, and download sample applications by visiting the project website (*http://www.cascading.org/*).

Installing Apache Hadoop

It's easy to install Hadoop on a single machine to try it out. (For installation on a cluster, refer to Chapter 10.)

In this appendix, we cover how to install Hadoop Common, HDFS, MapReduce, and YARN using a binary tarball release from the Apache Software Foundation. Instructions for installing the other projects covered in this book are included at the start of the relevant chapters.

 Another option is to use a virtual machine (such as Cloudera's Quick-Start VM) that comes with all the Hadoop services preinstalled and configured.

The instructions that follow are suitable for Unix-based systems, including Mac OS X (which is not a production platform, but is fine for development).

Prerequisites

Make sure you have a suitable version of Java installed. You can check the Hadoop wiki (*http://wiki.apache.org/hadoop/HadoopJavaVersions*) to find which version you need. The following command confirms that Java was installed correctly:

```
% java -version
java version "1.7.0_25"
Java(TM) SE Runtime Environment (build 1.7.0_25-b15)
Java HotSpot(TM) 64-Bit Server VM (build 23.25-b01, mixed mode)
```

Installation

Start by deciding which user you'd like to run Hadoop as. For trying out Hadoop or developing Hadoop programs, you can run Hadoop on a single machine using your own user account.

Download a stable release, which is packaged as a gzipped tar file, from the Apache Hadoop releases page (*http://hadoop.apache.org/common/releases.html*), and unpack it somewhere on your filesystem:

```
% tar xzf hadoop-x.y.z.tar.gz
```

Before you can run Hadoop, you need to tell it where Java is located on your system. If you have the JAVA_HOME environment variable set to point to a suitable Java installation, that will be used, and you don't have to configure anything further. (It is often set in a shell startup file, such as *~/.bash_profile* or *~/.bashrc*.) Otherwise, you can set the Java installation that Hadoop uses by editing *conf/hadoop-env.sh* and specifying the JAVA_HOME variable. For example, on my Mac, I changed the line to read:

```
export JAVA_HOME=/Library/Java/JavaVirtualMachines/jdk1.7.0_25.jdk/Contents/Home
```

to point to the installed version of Java.

It's very convenient to create an environment variable that points to the Hadoop installation directory (HADOOP_HOME, by convention) and to put the Hadoop binary directories on your command-line path. For example:

```
% export HADOOP_HOME=~/sw/hadoop-x.y.z
% export PATH=$PATH:$HADOOP_HOME/bin:$HADOOP_HOME/sbin
```

Note that the *sbin* directory contains the scripts for running Hadoop daemons, so it should be included if you plan to run the daemons on your local machine.

Check that Hadoop runs by typing:

```
% hadoop version
Hadoop 2.5.1
Subversion https://git-wip-us.apache.org/repos/asf/hadoop.git -r 2e18d179e4a8065
b6a9f29cf2de9451891265cce
Compiled by jenkins on 2014-09-05T23:11Z
Compiled with protoc 2.5.0
From source with checksum 6424fcab95bfff8337780a181ad7c78
This command was run using /Users/tom/sw/hadoop-2.5.1/share/hadoop/common/hadoop
-common-2.5.1.jar
```

Configuration

Each component in Hadoop is configured using an XML file. Common properties go in *core-site.xml*, and properties pertaining to HDFS, MapReduce, and YARN go into the appropriately named file: *hdfs-site.xml*, *mapred-site.xml*, and *yarn-site.xml*. These files are all located in the *etc/hadoop* subdirectory.

 You can see the default settings for all the properties that are governed by these configuration files by looking in the *share/doc* directory hierarchy of your Hadoop installation for files called *core-default.xml*, *hdfs-default.xml*, *mapred-default.xml*, and *yarn-default.xml*.

Hadoop can be run in one of three modes:

Standalone (or local) mode
> There are no daemons running and everything runs in a single JVM. Standalone mode is suitable for running MapReduce programs during development, since it is easy to test and debug them.

Pseudodistributed mode
> The Hadoop daemons run on the local machine, thus simulating a cluster on a small scale.

Fully distributed mode
> The Hadoop daemons run on a cluster of machines. This setup is described in Chapter 10.

To run Hadoop in a particular mode, you need to do two things: set the appropriate properties, and start the Hadoop daemons. Table A-1 shows the minimal set of properties to configure each mode. In standalone mode, the local filesystem and the local MapReduce job runner are used. In the distributed modes, the HDFS and YARN daemons are started, and MapReduce is configured to use YARN.

Table A-1. Key configuration properties for different modes

Component	Property	Standalone	Pseudodistributed	Fully distributed
Common	fs.defaultFS	file:/// (default)	hdfs://localhost/	hdfs://*namenode*/
HDFS	dfs.replication	N/A	1	3 (default)
MapReduce	mapreduce.frame work.name	local (default)	yarn	yarn
YARN	yarn.resourcemanag er.hostname	N/A	localhost	*resourcemanager*
	yarn.nodemanager.aux- services	N/A	mapreduce_shuffle	mapreduce_shuffle

You can read more about configuration in "Hadoop Configuration" on page 292.

Standalone Mode

In standalone mode, there is no further action to take, since the default properties are set for standalone mode and there are no daemons to run.

Pseudodistributed Mode

In pseudodistributed mode, the configuration files should be created with the following contents and placed in the *etc/hadoop* directory. Alternatively, you can copy the *etc/hadoop* directory to another location, and then place the **-site.xml* configuration files there. The advantage of this approach is that it separates configuration settings from the installation files. If you do this, you need to set the HADOOP_CONF_DIR environment variable to the alternative location, or make sure you start the daemons with the --config option:

```
<?xml version="1.0"?>
<!-- core-site.xml -->
<configuration>
  <property>
    <name>fs.defaultFS</name>
    <value>hdfs://localhost/</value>
  </property>
</configuration>

<?xml version="1.0"?>
<!-- hdfs-site.xml -->
<configuration>
  <property>
    <name>dfs.replication</name>
    <value>1</value>
  </property>
</configuration>

<?xml version="1.0"?>
<!-- mapred-site.xml -->
<configuration>
  <property>
    <name>mapreduce.framework.name</name>
    <value>yarn</value>
  </property>
</configuration>

<?xml version="1.0"?>
<!-- yarn-site.xml -->
<configuration>
  <property>
    <name>yarn.resourcemanager.hostname</name>
    <value>localhost</value>
  </property>
  <property>
    <name>yarn.nodemanager.aux-services</name>
```

```
      <value>mapreduce_shuffle</value>
    </property>
</configuration>
```

Configuring SSH

In pseudodistributed mode, we have to start daemons, and to do that using the supplied scripts we need to have SSH installed. Hadoop doesn't actually distinguish between pseudodistributed and fully distributed modes; it merely starts daemons on the set of hosts in the cluster (defined by the *slaves* file) by SSHing to each host and starting a daemon process. Pseudodistributed mode is just a special case of fully distributed mode in which the (single) host is localhost, so we need to make sure that we can SSH to localhost and log in without having to enter a password.

First, make sure that SSH is installed and a server is running. On Ubuntu, for example, this is achieved with:

```
% sudo apt-get install ssh
```

 On Mac OS X, make sure Remote Login (under System Preferences→Sharing) is enabled for the current user (or all users).

Then, to enable passwordless login, generate a new SSH key with an empty passphrase:

```
% ssh-keygen -t rsa -P '' -f ~/.ssh/id_rsa
% cat ~/.ssh/id_rsa.pub >> ~/.ssh/authorized_keys
```

You may also need to run *ssh-add* if you are running *ssh-agent*.

Test that you can connect with:

```
% ssh localhost
```

If successful, you should not have to type in a password.

Formatting the HDFS filesystem

Before HDFS can be used for the first time, the filesystem must be formatted. This is done by running the following command:

```
% hdfs namenode -format
```

Starting and stopping the daemons

To start the HDFS, YARN, and MapReduce daemons, type:

```
% start-dfs.sh
% start-yarn.sh
% mr-jobhistory-daemon.sh start historyserver
```

 If you have placed configuration files outside the default *conf* directory, either export the HADOOP_CONF_DIR environment variable before running the scripts, or start the daemons with the --config
option, which takes an absolute path to the configuration directory:

```
% start-dfs.sh --config path-to-config-directory
% start-yarn.sh --config path-to-config-directory
% mr-jobhistory-daemon.sh --config path-to-config-directory
   start historyserver
```

The following daemons will be started on your local machine: a namenode, a secondary
namenode, a datanode (HDFS), a resource manager, a node manager (YARN), and a
history server (MapReduce). You can check whether the daemons started successfully
by looking at the logfiles in the *logs* directory (in the Hadoop installation directory) or
by looking at the web UIs, at *http://localhost:50070/* for the namenode, *http://localhost:
8088/* for the resource manager, and *http://localhost:19888/* for the history server. You
can also use Java's jps command to see whether the processes are running.

Stopping the daemons is done as follows:

```
% mr-jobhistory-daemon.sh stop historyserver
% stop-yarn.sh
% stop-dfs.sh
```

Creating a user directory

Create a home directory for yourself by running the following:

```
% hadoop fs -mkdir -p /user/$USER
```

Fully Distributed Mode

Setting up a cluster of machines brings many additional considerations, so this mode
is covered in Chapter 10.

Cloudera's Distribution Including Apache Hadoop

Cloudera's Distribution Including Apache Hadoop (hereafter *CDH*) is an integrated Apache Hadoop–based stack containing all the components needed for production, tested and packaged to work together. Cloudera makes the distribution available in a number of different formats: Linux packages, virtual machine images, tarballs, and tools for running CDH in the cloud. CDH is free, released under the Apache 2.0 license, and available at *http://www.cloudera.com/cdh*.

As of CDH 5, the following components are included, many of which are covered elsewhere in this book:

Apache Avro
A cross-language data serialization library; includes rich data structures, a fast/compact binary format, and RPC

Apache Crunch
A high-level Java API for writing data processing pipelines that can run on MapReduce or Spark

Apache DataFu (incubating)
A library of useful statistical UDFs for doing large-scale analyses

Apache Flume
Highly reliable, configurable streaming data collection

Apache Hadoop
Highly scalable data storage (HDFS), resource management (YARN), and processing (MapReduce)

Apache HBase
Column-oriented real-time database for random read/write access

Apache Hive
SQL-like queries and tables for large datasets

Hue
Web UI to make it easy to work with Hadoop data

Cloudera Impala
Interactive, low-latency SQL queries on HDFS or HBase

Kite SDK
APIs, examples, and docs for building apps on top of Hadoop

Apache Mahout
Scalable machine-learning and data-mining algorithms

Apache Oozie
Workflow scheduler for interdependent Hadoop jobs

Apache Parquet (incubating)
An efficient columnar storage format for nested data

Apache Pig
Data flow language for exploring large datasets

Cloudera Search
Free-text, Google-style search of Hadoop data

Apache Sentry (incubating)
Granular, role-based access control for Hadoop users

Apache Spark
A cluster computing framework for large-scale in-memory data processing in Scala, Java, and Python

Apache Sqoop
Efficient transfer of data between structured data stores (like relational databases) and Hadoop

Apache ZooKeeper
Highly available coordination service for distributed applications

Cloudera also provides *Cloudera Manager* for deploying and operating Hadoop clusters running CDH.

To download CDH and Cloudera Manager, visit *http://www.cloudera.com/downloads*.

Preparing the NCDC Weather Data

This appendix gives a runthrough of the steps taken to prepare the raw weather datafiles so they are in a form that is amenable to analysis using Hadoop. If you want to get a copy of the data to process using Hadoop, you can do so by following the instructions given at the website that accompanies this book (*http://www.hadoopbook.com/*). The rest of this appendix explains how the raw weather datafiles were processed.

The raw data is provided as a collection of tar files, compressed with bzip2. Each year's worth of readings comes in a separate file. Here's a partial directory listing of the files:

```
1901.tar.bz2
1902.tar.bz2
1903.tar.bz2
...
2000.tar.bz2
```

Each tar file contains a file for each weather station's readings for the year, compressed with gzip. (The fact that the files in the archive are compressed makes the bzip2 compression on the archive itself redundant.) For example:

```
% tar jxf 1901.tar.bz2
% ls 1901 | head
029070-99999-1901.gz
029500-99999-1901.gz
029600-99999-1901.gz
029720-99999-1901.gz
029810-99999-1901.gz
227070-99999-1901.gz
```

Because there are tens of thousands of weather stations, the whole dataset is made up of a large number of relatively small files. It's generally easier and more efficient to process a smaller number of relatively large files in Hadoop (see "Small files and CombineFileInputFormat" on page 226), so in this case, I concatenated the decompressed files for a whole year into a single file, named by the year. I did this using a MapReduce program, to take advantage of its parallel processing capabilities. Let's take a closer look at the program.

The program has only a map function. No reduce function is needed because the map does all the file processing in parallel with no combine stage. The processing can be done with a Unix script, so the Streaming interface to MapReduce is appropriate in this case; see Example C-1.

Example C-1. Bash script to process raw NCDC datafiles and store them in HDFS

```bash
#!/usr/bin/env bash

# NLineInputFormat gives a single line: key is offset, value is S3 URI
read offset s3file

# Retrieve file from S3 to local disk
echo "reporter:status:Retrieving $s3file" >&2
$HADOOP_HOME/bin/hadoop fs -get $s3file .

# Un-bzip and un-tar the local file
target=`basename $s3file .tar.bz2`
mkdir -p $target
echo "reporter:status:Un-tarring $s3file to $target" >&2
tar jxf `basename $s3file` -C $target

# Un-gzip each station file and concat into one file
echo "reporter:status:Un-gzipping $target" >&2
for file in $target/*/*
do
  gunzip -c $file >> $target.all
  echo "reporter:status:Processed $file" >&2
done

# Put gzipped version into HDFS
echo "reporter:status:Gzipping $target and putting in HDFS" >&2
gzip -c $target.all | $HADOOP_HOME/bin/hadoop fs -put - gz/$target.gz
```

The input is a small text file (*ncdc_files.txt*) listing all the files to be processed (the files start out on S3, so they are referenced using S3 URIs that Hadoop understands). Here is a sample:

```
s3n://hadoopbook/ncdc/raw/isd-1901.tar.bz2
s3n://hadoopbook/ncdc/raw/isd-1902.tar.bz2
...
s3n://hadoopbook/ncdc/raw/isd-2000.tar.bz2
```

Because the input format is specified to be NLineInputFormat, each mapper receives one line of input, which contains the file it has to process. The processing is explained in the script, but briefly, it unpacks the bzip2 file and then concatenates each station file into a single file for the whole year. Finally, the file is gzipped and copied into HDFS. Note the use of hadoop fs -put - to consume from standard input.

Status messages are echoed to standard error with a `reporter:status` prefix so that they get interpreted as MapReduce status updates. This tells Hadoop that the script is making progress and is not hanging.

The script to run the Streaming job is as follows:

```
% hadoop jar $HADOOP_HOME/share/hadoop/tools/lib/hadoop-streaming-*.jar \
  -D mapred.reduce.tasks=0 \
  -D mapred.map.tasks.speculative.execution=false \
  -D mapred.task.timeout=12000000 \
  -input ncdc_files.txt \
  -inputformat org.apache.hadoop.mapred.lib.NLineInputFormat \
  -output output \
  -mapper load_ncdc_map.sh \
  -file load_ncdc_map.sh
```

I set the number of reduce tasks to zero, since this is a map-only job. I also turned off speculative execution so duplicate tasks wouldn't write the same files (although the approach discussed in "Task side-effect files" on page 207 would have worked, too). The task timeout was set to a high value so that Hadoop doesn't kill tasks that are taking a long time (for example, when unarchiving files or copying to HDFS, when no progress is reported).

Finally, the files were archived on S3 by copying them from HDFS using *distcp*.

The Old and New Java MapReduce APIs

The Java MapReduce API used throughout this book is called the "new API," and it replaces the older, functionally equivalent API. Although Hadoop ships with both the old and new MapReduce APIs, they are not compatible with each other. Should you wish to use the old API, you can, since the code for all the MapReduce examples in this book is available for the old API on the book's website (in the oldapi package).

There are several notable differences between the two APIs:

- The new API is in the org.apache.hadoop.mapreduce package (and subpackages). The old API can still be found in org.apache.hadoop.mapred.

- The new API favors abstract classes over interfaces, since these are easier to evolve. This means that you can add a method (with a default implementation) to an abstract class without breaking old implementations of the class.[1] For example, the Mapper and Reducer interfaces in the old API are abstract classes in the new API.

- The new API makes extensive use of *context objects* that allow the user code to communicate with the MapReduce system. The new Context, for example, essentially unifies the role of the JobConf, the OutputCollector, and the Reporter from the old API.

- In both APIs, key-value record pairs are pushed to the mapper and reducer, but in addition, the new API allows both mappers and reducers to control the execution flow by overriding the run() method. For example, records can be processed in batches, or the execution can be terminated before all the records have been processed. In the old API, this is possible for mappers by writing a MapRunnable, but no equivalent exists for reducers.

---

1. Technically, such a change would almost certainly break implementations that already define a method with the same signature as Jim des Rivières explains in "Evolving Java-based APIs," (*http://bit.ly/adding_api_meth od*) for all practical purposes this is treated as a compatible change.

- Job control is performed through the `Job` class in the new API, rather than the old `JobClient`, which no longer exists in the new API.

- Configuration has been unified in the new API. The old API has a special `Job Conf` object for job configuration, which is an extension of Hadoop's vanilla `Configuration` object (used for configuring daemons; see "The Configuration API" on page 141). In the new API, job configuration is done through a `Configuration`, possibly via some of the helper methods on `Job`.

- Output files are named slightly differently: in the old API both map and reduce outputs are named *part-nnnnn*, whereas in the new API map outputs are named *part-m-nnnnn* and reduce outputs are named *part-r-nnnnn* (where *nnnnn* is an integer designating the part number, starting from 00000).

- User-overridable methods in the new API are declared to throw `java.lang.InterruptedException`. This means that you can write your code to be responsive to interrupts so that the framework can gracefully cancel long-running operations if it needs to.[2]

- In the new API, the `reduce()` method passes values as a `java.lang.Iterable`, rather than a `java.lang.Iterator` (as the old API does). This change makes it easier to iterate over the values using Java's `for-each` loop construct:

    ```
    for (VALUEIN value : values) { ... }
    ```

> Programs using the new API that were compiled against Hadoop 1 need to be recompiled to run against Hadoop 2. This is because some classes in the new MapReduce API changed to interfaces between the Hadoop 1 and Hadoop 2 releases. The symptom is an error at runtime like the following:
>
> ```
> java.lang.IncompatibleClassChangeError: Found interface
> org.apache.hadoop.mapreduce.TaskAttemptContext, but class was expected
> ```

Example D-1 shows the `MaxTemperature` application (from "Java MapReduce" on page 24) rewritten to use the old API. The differences are highlighted in bold.

---

2. "Java theory and practice: Dealing with InterruptedException" (*http://bit.ly/interruptedexception*) by Brian Goetz explains this technique in detail.

When converting your `Mapper` and `Reducer` classes to the new API, don't forget to change the signatures of the `map()` and `reduce()` methods to the new form. Just changing your class to extend the new `Mapper` or `Reducer` classes will *not* produce a compilation error or warning, because these classes provide identity forms of the `map()` and `reduce()` methods (respectively). Your mapper or reducer code, however, will not be invoked, which can lead to some hard-to-diagnose errors.

Annotating your `map()` and `reduce()` methods with the `@Override` annotation will allow the Java compiler to catch these errors.

Example D-1. Application to find the maximum temperature, using the old MapReduce API

```java
public class OldMaxTemperature {

  static class OldMaxTemperatureMapper extends MapReduceBase
    implements Mapper<LongWritable, Text, Text, IntWritable> {

    private static final int MISSING = 9999;

    @Override
    public void map(LongWritable key, Text value,
        OutputCollector<Text, IntWritable> output, Reporter reporter)
        throws IOException {

      String line = value.toString();
      String year = line.substring(15, 19);
      int airTemperature;
      if (line.charAt(87) == '+') { // parseInt doesn't like leading plus signs
        airTemperature = Integer.parseInt(line.substring(88, 92));
      } else {
        airTemperature = Integer.parseInt(line.substring(87, 92));
      }
      String quality = line.substring(92, 93);
      if (airTemperature != MISSING && quality.matches("[01459]")) {
        output.collect(new Text(year), new IntWritable(airTemperature));
      }
    }
  }

  static class OldMaxTemperatureReducer extends MapReduceBase
    implements Reducer<Text, IntWritable, Text, IntWritable> {

    @Override
    public void reduce(Text key, Iterator<IntWritable> values,
        OutputCollector<Text, IntWritable> output, Reporter reporter)
        throws IOException {
```

```java
      int maxValue = Integer.MIN_VALUE;
      while (values.hasNext()) {
        maxValue = Math.max(maxValue, values.next().get());
      }
      output.collect(key, new IntWritable(maxValue));
    }
  }

  public static void main(String[] args) throws IOException {
    if (args.length != 2) {
      System.err.println("Usage: OldMaxTemperature <input path> <output path>");
      System.exit(-1);
    }

    JobConf conf = new JobConf(OldMaxTemperature.class);
    conf.setJobName("Max temperature");

    FileInputFormat.addInputPath(conf, new Path(args[0]));
    FileOutputFormat.setOutputPath(conf, new Path(args[1]));

    conf.setMapperClass(OldMaxTemperatureMapper.class);
    conf.setReducerClass(OldMaxTemperatureReducer.class);

    conf.setOutputKeyClass(Text.class);
    conf.setOutputValueClass(IntWritable.class);

    JobClient.runJob(conf);
  }
}
```

Index

We'd like to hear your suggestions for improving our indexes. Send email to index@oreilly.com.

Future interface (Java), 539

G

GC_TIME_MILLIS counter, 250
GenericDatumWriter class, 350
GenericOptionsParser class, 148–152, 274
GenericRecord interface, 350, 529
GenericWritable class, 119, 120
Genome Reference Consortium (GRC), 660
Get class, 586
getACL operation (ZooKeeper), 616
getChildren operation (ZooKeeper), 616
getData operation (ZooKeeper), 616
GFS (Google), 12
globbing operation, 66
Google GFS, 12
Google Protocol Buffers, 127
graceful failover, 50
Gradle build tool, 145
Gray, Jim, 10
Gray, Jonathan, 575–602
GRC (Genome Reference Consortium), 660
Great Internet Mersenne Prime Search project, 11
grid computing, 10
Gridmix benchmark suite, 316
GROUP BY clause (Hive), 475, 510
GROUP BY operator (Pig Latin), 430
GROUP statement (Pig Latin), 432, 434, 435, 464
grouping data, 459–465
groups (ZooKeeper)
    about, 606
    creating, 607–609
    deleting, 612
    group membership, 606
    joining, 609
    listing members, 610–612
Grunt shell, 426
gzip compression, 100–101, 104
GzipCodec class, 101

H

Hadoop
    about, 7
    history of, 12–15
    installing, 685–690

hadoop command
    basic filesystem operations, 51–52
    creating HAR files, 53
    distcp program and, 76
    finding file checksum, 98
    Hadoop Streaming and, 39
    launching JVM, 29
    retrieving job results, 167
    running miniclusters from, 159
Hadoop Distributed Filesystem (see HDFS)
Hadoop Streaming
    about, 37
    MapReduce scripts and, 503
    Python example, 40
    Ruby example, 37–40
hadoop-env.sh file, 292, 332
hadoop-metrics2.properties file, 292, 332
hadoop-policy.xml file, 293, 311
hadoop.http.staticuser.user property, 148
hadoop.rpc.protection property, 314
hadoop.security.authentication property, 311
hadoop.security.authorization property, 311
hadoop.ssl.enabled property, 314
hadoop.user.group.static.mapping.overrides property, 147
HADOOP_CLASSPATH environment variable, 161, 162
HADOOP_CONF_DIR environment variable, 148, 293, 425
HADOOP_HEAPSIZE environment variable, 294
HADOOP_HOME environment variable, 425, 472, 686
HADOOP_IDENT_STRING environment variable, 295
HADOOP_LOG_DIR environment variable, 172, 295
HADOOP_NAMENODE_OPTS environment variable, 294, 332
HADOOP_OPTS environment variable, 151
HADOOP_SSH_OPTS environment variable, 296
HADOOP_USER_CLASSPATH_FIRST environment variable, 162
HADOOP_USER_NAME environment variable, 147
Hammerbacher, Jeff, 471
HAR files, 53
HarFileSystem class, 53

io.compression.codecs property, 104
io.file.buffer.size property, 307
io.native.lib.available property, 105
io.serializations property, 126
IOUtils class, 102, 230
is null operator (Hive), 443
IsEmpty function (Pig Latin), 445, 446
isro command (ZooKeeper), 605
iterative processing, 7

J
jar service (Hive), 478
Java Database Connectivity (JDBC), 408, 419
Java language
    creating directories, 63
    deleting data, 68
    environment variables, 294
    Hadoop Streaming and, 38
    HBase and, 584–587
    installing, 288
    Pig and, 426
    querying FileSystem, 63–68
    reading data from Hadoop URL, 57
    reading data using FileSystem API, 58–61
    secondary sort, 264–266
    Spark example, 554
    syslog file, 172
    user-defined counters, 251–255
    WAR files, 160
    weather dataset example, 24–30
    Writable wrappers for Java primitives, 113–121
    writing data, 61–63
Java Management Extensions (JMX), 331, 606
Java Native Interface (JNI), 56
Java Object Serialization, 126
Java virtual machine (JVM), 29, 174, 193
java.library.path property, 104
java.util.concurrent package, 539
JavaPairRDD class, 555
JavaRDD class, 555
JavaRDDLike interface, 555
JavaSerialization class, 126
JAVA_HOME environment variable, 294, 424, 686
JBOD (just a bunch of disks), 285
JDBC (Java Database Connectivity), 408, 419
JDBC drivers, 479
JMX (Java Management Extensions), 331, 606

JNI (Java Native Interface), 56
Job class
    distributed cache options, 278
    progress and status updates, 191
    setting explicit JAR files, 160
    setting input paths, 223
job counters, 248, 250
job history, 166
job history logs (MapReduce), 172
job IDs, 164, 203
job JAR files
    about, 160
    client classpath, 161
    packaging dependencies, 161
    task classpath, 161
    task classpath precedence, 162
job page (MapReduce), 166
JobBuilder class, 215
JobClient class, 185
JobConf class, 109, 160, 176
JobControl class, 179
jobs
    anatomy of MapReduce job runs, 185–192
    anatomy of Spark job runs, 565–570
    completion process, 192
    DAG construction, 566–569
    debugging, 168–171, 174
    decomposing problems into, 177–178
    default MapReduce, 214–219
    initialization process, 187
    launching, 162–164
    logging, 172–173
    packaging, 160–162
    progress and status updates, 190
    retrieving results, 167
    running as benchmarks, 316
    running locally, 157–158
    running Oozie workflow jobs, 183
    scheduling, 308, 569
    Spark support, 552
    submission process, 186, 565
    task execution, 570
    testing job drivers, 158–160
    tuning, 175–176
    viewing information about, 165–167
JobSubmitter class, 186
jobtrackers, 83
Join class, 546
JOIN clause (Hive), 505

workflow engines, 179
workflows (MapReduce)
    about, 177
    Apache Oozie system, 179–184
    decomposing problems into jobs, 177–178
    JobControl class, 178
Writable interface
    about, 110–113
    class hierarchy, 113–121
    Crunch and, 528
    implementing custom, 121–125
WritableComparable interface, 112, 258
WritableComparator class, 112
WritableSerialization class, 126
WritableUtils class, 125
write (w) permission, 52
WRITE permission (ACL), 620
WriteSupport class, 373
WRITE_OPS counter, 250
writing data
    Crunch support, 532
    using FileSystem API, 61–63
    HDFS data flow, 72–73
    Parquet and, 373–377
    SequenceFile class, 128–129

X

x (execute) permission, 52
XML documents, 235

Y

Yahoo!, 13
YARN (Yet Another Resource Negotiator)
    about, 7, 79, 96
    anatomy of application run, 80–83
    application lifespan, 82
    application master failure, 194
    building applications, 82
    cluster setup and installation, 288
    cluster sizing, 286
    daemon properties, 300–303
    distributed shell, 83
    log aggregation, 172
    MapReduce comparison, 83–85
    scaling out data, 30
    scheduling in, 85–96, 308
    Spark and, 571–574
    starting and stopping daemons, 291

YARN client mode (Spark), 571
YARN cluster mode (Spark), 573–574
yarn-env.sh file, 292
yarn-site.xml file, 292, 296
yarn.app.mapreduce.am.job.recovery.enable
    property, 195
yarn.app.mapreduce.am.job.speculator.class
    property, 205
yarn.app.mapreduce.am.job.task.estimator.class
    property, 205
yarn.log-aggregation-enable property, 172
yarn.nodemanager.address property, 306
yarn.nodemanager.aux-services property, 300,
    687
yarn.nodemanager.bind-host property, 305
yarn.nodemanager.container-executor.class
    property, 193, 304, 313
yarn.nodemanager.delete.debug-delay-sec prop-
    erty, 174
yarn.nodemanager.hostname property, 305
yarn.nodemanager.linux-container-executor
    property, 304
yarn.nodemanager.local-dirs property, 300
yarn.nodemanager.localizer.address property,
    306
yarn.nodemanager.log.retain-second property,
    173
yarn.nodemanager.resource.cpu-vcores proper-
    ty, 301, 303
yarn.nodemanager.resource.memory-mb prop-
    erty, 150, 301
yarn.nodemanager.vmem-pmem-ratio property,
    301, 303
yarn.nodemanager.webapp.address property,
    306
yarn.resourcemanager.address property
    about, 300, 305
    Hive and, 476
    Pig and, 425
yarn.resourcemanager.admin.address property,
    305
yarn.resourcemanager.am.max-attempts prop-
    erty, 194, 196
yarn.resourcemanager.bind-host property, 305
yarn.resourcemanager.hostname property, 300,
    305, 687
yarn.resourcemanager.max-completed-
    applications property, 165

About the Author

Tom White is one of the foremost experts on Hadoop. He has been an Apache Hadoop committer since February 2007, and is a member of the Apache Software Foundation. Tom is a software engineer at Cloudera, where he has worked since its foundation on the core distributions from Apache and Cloudera. Previously he was an independent Hadoop consultant, working with companies to set up, use, and extend Hadoop. He has spoken at many conferences, including ApacheCon, OSCON, and Strata. Tom has a BA in mathematics from the University of Cambridge and an MA in philosophy of science from the University of Leeds, UK. He currently lives in Wales with his family.

Colophon

The animal on the cover of *Hadoop: The Definitive Guide* is an African elephant. These members of the genus *Loxodonta* are the largest land animals on Earth (slightly larger than their cousin, the Asian elephant) and can be identified by their ears, which have been said to look somewhat like the continent of Asia. Males stand 12 feet tall at the shoulder and weigh 12,000 pounds, but they can get as big as 15,000 pounds, whereas females stand 10 feet tall and weigh 8,000–11,000 pounds. Even young elephants are very large: at birth, they already weigh approximately 200 pounds and stand about 3 feet tall.

African elephants live throughout sub-Saharan Africa. Most of the continent's elephants live on savannas and in dry woodlands. In some regions, they can be found in desert areas; in others, they are found in mountains.

The species plays an important role in the forest and savanna ecosystems in which they live. Many plant species are dependent on passing through an elephant's digestive tract before they can germinate; it is estimated that at least a third of tree species in west African forests rely on elephants in this way. Elephants grazing on vegetation also affect the structure of habitats and influence bush fire patterns. For example, under natural conditions, elephants make gaps through the rainforest, enabling the sunlight to enter, which allows the growth of various plant species. This, in turn, facilitates more abundance and more diversity of smaller animals. As a result of the influence elephants have over many plants and animals, they are often referred to as a *keystone species* because they are vital to the long-term survival of the ecosystems in which they live.

Many of the animals on O'Reilly covers are endangered; all of them are important to the world. To learn more about how you can help, go to *animals.oreilly.com*.

The cover image is from the *Dover Pictorial Archive*. The cover fonts are URW Typewriter and Guardian Sans. The text font is Adobe Minion Pro; the heading font is Adobe Myriad Condensed; and the code font is Dalton Maag's Ubuntu Mono.

Have it your way.

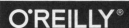

Get even more for your money.

Join the O'Reilly Community, and register the O'Reilly books you own. It's free, and you'll get:

- $4.99 ebook upgrade offer
- 40% upgrade offer on O'Reilly print books
- Membership discounts on books and events
- Free lifetime updates to ebooks and videos
- Multiple ebook formats, DRM FREE
- Participation in the O'Reilly community
- Newsletters
- Account management
- 100% Satisfaction Guarantee

Signing up is easy:

1. Go to: oreilly.com/go/register
2. Create an O'Reilly login.
3. Provide your address.
4. Register your books.

Note: English-language books only

To order books online:
oreilly.com/store

For questions about products or an order:
orders@oreilly.com

To sign up to get topic-specific email announcements and/or news about upcoming books, conferences, special offers, and new technologies:
elists@oreilly.com

For technical questions about book content:
booktech@oreilly.com

To submit new book proposals to our editors:
proposals@oreilly.com

O'Reilly books are available in multiple DRM-free ebook formats. For more information:
oreilly.com/ebooks